www.wadsworth.com

wadsworth.com is the World Wide Web site for Wadsworth Publishing Company and is your direct source to dozens of online resources.

At *wadsworth.com* you can find out about supplements, demonstration software, and student resources. You can also send e-mail to many of our authors and preview new publications and exciting new technologies.

wadsworth.com
Changing the way the world learns®

From the Wadsworth Series in Production

Albarran, Alan B., *Management of Electronic Media*

Alten, Stanley, *Audio in Media,* 5th ed.

Alten, Stanley, *Audio in Media: The Recording Studio*

Armer, Alan, *Directing TV and Film,* 2nd ed.

Armer, Alan, *Writing the Screenplay,* 2nd ed.

Azarmsa, Reza, *Multimedia: Interactive Video Production*

Butler, Jeremy G., *Television: Critical Methods and Applications*

Eastman, Susan Tyler, and Douglas A. Ferguson, *Broadcast/Cable Programming: Strategies and Practices,* 5th ed.

Gross, Lynne S., and Larry W. Ward, *Electronic Moviemaking,* 3rd ed.

Hausman, Carl, Philip B. Benoit, and Lewis B. O'Donnell, *Modern Radio Production,* 4th ed.

Hilliard, Robert L., *Writing for Television and Radio,* 6th ed.

Kurland, Daniel J., Frank Messere, and Philip J. Palombo, *Introduction to the Internet for Electronic Media: Research and Application*

Mamer, Bruce, *Film Production Technique: Creating the Accomplished Image*

Meeske, Milan D., *Copywriting for the Electronic Media,* 3rd ed.

Morley, John, *Scriptwriting for High-Impact Videos: Imaginative Approaches to Delivering Factual Information*

O'Donnell, Lewis B., Philip B. Benoit, and Carl Hausman, *Announcing: Broadcast Communicating Today,* 3rd ed.

Viera, Dave, *Lighting for Film and Electronic Cinematography*

Zettl, Herbert, *Sight Sound Motion: Applied Media Aesthetics,* 3rd ed.

Zettl, Herbert, *Television Production Handbook,* 6th ed.

Zettl, Herbert, *Television Production Workbook,* 6th ed.

Zettl, Herbert, *Video Basics 2*

Zettl, Herbert, *Video Basics 2 Workbook*

Zettl, Herbert, *Zettl's Video Lab 2.1,* CD-ROM

Audio IN Media

FIFTH EDITION

Stanley R. Alten

Syracuse University

WADSWORTH PUBLISHING COMPANY

An International Thomson Publishing Company I(T)P®

Belmont, CA • Albany, NY • Boston • Cincinnati • Johannesburg • London
Madrid • Melbourne • Mexico City • New York • Pacific Grove, CA • Scottsdale, AZ
Singapore • Tokyo • Toronto

Executive Editor: Deirdre Cavanaugh
Assistant Editor: Ryan E. Vesely
Editorial Assistant: Matthew Lamm
Marketing Manager: Mike Dew
Marketing Assistant: Shannon Ryan
Advertising Project Manager: Tami Strang
Project Editor: Cathy Linberg
Print Buyer: Barbara Britton
Permissions Editor: Yanna Walters
Designer: Gary Palmatier, Ideas to Images
Production Manager: Gary Palmatier, Ideas to Images
Copy Editor: Elizabeth von Radics
Cover Designer: Gary Palmatier
Cover Photographers: Jim Baker/studiosource (bottom) and PhotoDisc, Inc. (top)
Cover Printer: Phoenix Color, Inc.
Compositor: Ideas to Images
Printer: R.R. Donnelley & Sons, Crawfordsville

Photograph of mixing console on cover courtesy of Studio Guillaume Tell from
Prestige Studios of the World E-CD © 1996 Jim Baker/studiosource http://www.studiosource.com
Photograph of ear on cover copyright © 1997 PhotoDisc, Inc.

Printed in the United States of America.
    2   3   4   5   6   7   8   9   10

For more information contact Wadsworth Publishing Company, 10 Davis Drive, Belmont, CA 94002, or electronically at
http://www.wadsworth.com

International Thomson Publishing Europe
Berkshire House
168-173 High Holborn
London, WC1V 7AA, United Kingdom

International Thomson Editores
Seneca, 53
Colonia Polanco
11560 México D.F. México

Nelson ITP, Australia
102 Dodds Street
South Melbourne
Victoria 3205 Australia

International Thomson Publishing Asia
60 Albert Street
#15-01 Albert Complex
Singapore 189969

Nelson Canada
1120 Birchmount Road
Scarborough, Ontario
Canada M1K 5G4

International Thomson Publishing Japan
Hirakawa-cho Kyowa Building, 3F
2-2-1 Hirakawa-cho, Chiyoda-ku
Tokyo 102 Japan

International Thomson Publishing Southern Africa
Building 18, Constantia Square
138 Sixteenth Road, P.O. Box 2459
Halfway House, 1685 South Africa

Library of Congress Cataloging-in-Publication Data
Alten, Stanley R.
    Audio in media / Stanley R. Alten. — 5th ed.
        p. cm.
    Includes bibliographical references and index.
    ISBN 0-534-54801-6
    1. Sound—Recording and reproducing.   I. Title.
TK7881.4.A46   1998
    791.45'024—dc21   98–2866

To the music in my life—
my family:

Ariane,

Renee,

and "the
sweetest sound,"

Claudette.

Brief Contents

Contents

CHAPTER **13**

Field Production:
Live and Live-on-Tape   224

CHAPTER **14**

Staged Productions   261

CHAPTER **15**

Music Production   286

Preface

Since the publication of the fourth edition of *Audio in Media*, changes in audio technology and production techniques have been dramatic. The fifth edition reflects these changes while continuing to maintain its emphases on principles and process.

Like previous editions, the fifth edition takes a generic, nontechnical approach to audio production. It subsumes audio in radio, television, film, and music recording under the rubric *sound*. Content is designed for the beginner, yet the experienced practitioner will also find it beneficial. The organization facilitates using the book in total or in parts and reading chapters in or out of sequence, based on need and level of background, with no disruption in continuity.

Unlike the previous two editions, the fifth edition is streamlined to make it more manageable as a learning tool, yet it is thorough. Topics worthy of coverage, such as Musical Instrument Digital Interface (MIDI) and multimedia audio, are not included because they require more space than even an expanded book would permit. Several fine publications about MIDI are available, however, and many of the production techniques relevant to audio in media are also relevant to audio in multimedia. Please consult the Wadsworth Communications Web site for helpful links to information on MIDI:

http://www.wadsworth.com/communications

New to this edition are the chapters "Ears," "Synchronization," "Staged Productions," and "Dialogue, Sound Effects, and Music in Postproduction." There is expanded coverage of surround sound and reorganized chapters on studio and field production for live and live-on-tape productions.

STRUCTURE OF THE BOOK

The fifth edition of *Audio in Media* is divided into five parts organized to reflect process: Principles, Equipment, Sound Design, Production, and Postproduction.

In Part One, "Principles," the first chapter, "Ears," emphasizes the importance of healthy hearing and discriminating listening. Chapter 2, "Physics and Psychophysics of Sound," introduces the physical behavior of sound and its relationship to our psychophysical perception of sound stimuli. Chapter 3, "Acoustics and Psychoacoustics," develops the material in Chapter 2 as it applies to the objective behavior of received sound, its subjective effect on those who hear it, and how these factors affect studio and control room design and construction.

Part Two, "Equipment," begins with Chapter 4, "Microphones," which discusses their principles, types, characteristics, and accessories. Chapter 5, "Mixers and Consoles," covers basic signal flow and design of mixers, broadcast consoles, and production consoles—both analog and digital. Patching and console automation are also covered. Chapter 6, "Analog Recording," covers the characteristics of analog audiotape and recorders. Chapter 7, "Digital Recording," does the same thing with digital audiotape and recorders. It also covers basic digital theory and disk-based recording/ editing systems. Chapter 8, "Signal Processing," discusses the general principles of signal processors, and their effect on sound, including digital signal processing (DSP) plug-ins for disk-based systems. Chapter 9, "Loudspeakers and Monitoring," deals with the relationship between loudspeaker selection and control room monitoring of stereo and surround sound.

Part Three, "Sound Design," consists of one chapter of the same title. It sets a context for Parts Four and Five, "Production" and "Postproduction," by describing the nature and aesthetics of sound design; the basic structure of sonic communication; the cognitive and affective functions of speech, sound effects, and music; and the sound/picture relationship.

Part Four, "Production," begins with Chapter 11, "Synchronization," which is fundamental to most production and postproduction today. The rest of Part Four, Chapters 12 through 15, covers microphone and production techniques as they apply to "Studio Production: Live and Live-on-Tape," "Field Production: Live and Live-on-Tape," "Staged Productions," and "Music Production." (For readers who want full coverage of studio-based music production, the book *Audio in Media: The Recording Studio* is also available from Wadsworth.)

Part Five, "Postproduction," begins with Chapter 16, "Dialogue, Sound Effects, and Music in Postproduction," which details the techniques used in automated dialogue recording, sound-effect production, and producing music underscoring from music libraries. Chapter 17, "Editing," describes techniques of editing audio on analog and digital audiotape and hard-disk editing systems. It also addresses the aesthetic considerations that apply to editing speech, dialogue, sound effects, and music, as well as the uses of transitions. Chapter 18, "Mixing and Rerecording," covers the final stage in audio production, when sounds are combined and processed into stereo or surround sound.

FOR THE INSTRUCTOR

For instructors adopting the fifth edition of *Audio in Media,* the instructor's manual is available on Wadsworth's World Wide Web site:

http://www.wadsworth.com/communications

ACKNOWLEDGMENTS

Audio in Media has been a staple in the literature of sound production since 1981. This is due in great part to the interest, advice, and guidance of teachers and practitioners in the field who have been so forthcoming with their expertise over the years. Whatever success the fifth edition enjoys is due in no small measure to their continued good counsel.

To the following reviewers for the fifth edition, I offer my sincere gratitude for their insightful contributions: Gary Brummitt, Anderson University; Brian Cantarini, Grossmont College; Stanley Coutant, Pasadena City College; Ajit Daniel, Winona State University; Tony DeMars, University of Texas at Arlington; Mary Jane Doherty, Boston University; Kenneth J. Lopez, University of Southern California; Joseph R. McCargar, Grand Valley State University; Tom Nash, Biola University; Vaughn Obern, Los Angeles City College; Samuel J. Sauls, University of North Texas; Mark R. Turner, Southern Ohio College; and Robert Yablans, Colorado Institute of Art.

Thanks also to the following for their encouragement and suggestions in reviewing previous editions of this text: Michael H. Adams, San Jose State University; Allan Barber, Temple University; Tom Basmajian, Art Institute of Philadelphia; Dwight E. Brooks, Illinois State University; Doug Carroll, Menlo College; Paul Clatworthy, University of Southern California; John E. Craft, Arizona State University; James P. Gallagher, Art Institute of Philadelphia; John Hildebrand, San Diego City College; Vincent Ialenti, Mount Wachusett Community College; Joe Kraus, Art Institute of Philadelphia; James W. Loomis, Ithaca College; David Martin, City College of San Francisco; David R. McNutt, Wood & Cohen Advertising; William N. Monson, California State University, Fresno; Howard Pactor, University of Florida; Warren Pease, University of Arizona; Francine Podenski, City College of San Francisco; Steve Runyon, University of San Francisco; Barbara Tirre, Southern Illinois University at Edwardsville; and James W. Welke, University of Wyoming.

To the academic and industry professionals who provided their assistance, my deep appreciation:

the late John Bonner, former chief engineer, Goldwyn Sound Facility; Jerry Bruck, president, Posthorn Recordings; Benjamin Buchalter, Metric Halo Laboratories; Peter D'Antonio, president, RPG Diffusor Systems; Lee Dichter, rerecording mixer, Sound One; Martin Dombey, district manager for commercial audio, Yamaha Corporation of America; Larry Elin, professor of multimedia and multimedia producer, Syracuse University; Michael Epstein, professor of communication law, Syracuse University; Akira Fukada, NHK Broadcast Center; Rob Getty, dialogue editor, Digital Sound and Picture; David Gibson, director, California Recording Institute; Bill Hatch, postproduction consultant, Applied Technical Systems; Mike Hertlein, dialogue editor, Digital Sound and Picture; Skip Lievsay, sound editor; Jonathan Lory, postproduction mixer, ABC-TV; Dan Metivier, Metric Halo Laboratories; William Miller, engineering vice-president, ABC-TV; Walter Murch, sound designer; Shawn Murphy, scoring producer and rerecording mixer; Chris Newman, production mixer; Don Peebles, vice-president, broadcast and postproduction, Solid State Logic; Ron Remschel, senior audio consultant, Sony Corporation of America; David Robinson, Dolby Laboratories; Dave Ryan, sportscaster, ESPN; Mark Schnell, audio engineer, Syracuse University; Howard Schwartz, president, Howard Schwartz Recording; Bob Seiderman, principal mixer, Fox Sports; Frank Serafine, composer and sound designer, Serafine Productions; Mike Shane, Wheatstone Corporation; John Sherrard, audio engineer, ABC-TV; Wylie Stateman, co-founder of Soundelux; John Storyk, Walters-Storyk Design Group; Bruce Swedien, music producer/engineer; Anthony Vadala, freelance mixer for network sports; Damon Whittemore, audio producer, Awakening Productions; and Herbert Zettl, professor of broadcast communication arts, San Francisco State University.

A special salute to Gary Palmatier and his creative crew at Ideas to Images, who brought the design of the fifth edition to life and demonstrated that producing a book can be an art form.

Thanks also to Elizabeth von Radics for her precise and polished editing.

To David Rubin, dean of the Newhouse School of Public Communications, Syracuse University, my continued gratitude for his continuing support.

—Stanley Alten

Credits

ADC Telecommunications, Inc.: 5-14

AKG: 4-12, 4-27b, 4-28, 4-32a, 4-34, 4-40b,c, 4-55e

Alpha Audio: 3-11

Aphex Systems: 8-8

Atlas Sound: 4-46, 4-48

Audio Engineering Associates: 4-15

Audio Services Corporation: 14-9

Jim Baker: cover photo

beyerdynamic: 4-13, 4-27a, 4-33

Broadcast Engineering Magazine: 9-9, © Intertec Publishing Corporation. All rights reserved.

Cooper Sound Systems: 5-2

Countryman Associates: 4-25, 15-28

Crown International, Inc.: 4-30, 4-32b

dbx: 8-3

Denecke, Inc.: 11-3

Denon Electronics: 7-10

Desper Products, Inc.: 18-20

digidesign: 7-13, 17-32, 17-35, 17-40

Digital Audio Labs: 17-34

Dolby Laboratories, Inc.: 8-18, 14-15

Dan Dugan Sound Design: 13-21

Editall Products, Xedit Corporation: 17-1

Electro-Voice, Inc.: 4-6, 4-7, 4-43 (bottom left, top right), 4-52b

Gary Eskow, "Sound from the Trenches," *Mix* magazine, December 1994, p. 52: Table 13-2. All rights reserved.

Ron Estes: 15-44

Esto Photographic: 12-8

Etymotic Research: 1-5

J. L. Fisher: 4-49

Fostex: 6-10

Garner Industries: 6-8b

Bob Ghent, "Healthy Hearing," *Mix* magazine, March 1994, p. 153: 1-1

GHL: 13-15

David Gibson. *The Art of Mixing.* Mix Books, 1997: 18-4 to 18-11

Gotham Audio Corporation: 8-10

Lynne Gross and Larry Ward. *Electronic Moviemaking,* 3rd ed. Wadsworth Publishing Company, 1997: 10-1

Joseph E. Hawkins, Kresge Hearing Research Institute, University of Michigan: 1-2

HHB Communications, Ltd.: 7-4, 7-11

Ikegami: 13-5

David Immer, "Phone It In," *Mix* magazine, February 1994, p. 88: 7-14

International Tapetronics Corporation: 12-13b

M. Klemme Technology Corporation: 14-5

Lectrosonics: 4-36 to 4-39

Lexicon, Inc.: 8-9

Mackie Designs: 5-7

Magnasync/Moviola: 17-21

Bruce Mamer. *Film Production Technique*. Wadsworth Publishing Company, 1996: 14-6 to 14-8, 17-30

Marti Electronics, Inc.: 13-3

Metric Halo Laboratories: 9-14

Milab: 4-11

Nagra USA: 7-6, 7-12

Neumann USA: 4-14, 4-17, 4-31, 4-40d, 4-43 (top left, bottom right)

Rupert Neve, Inc.: 12-2

Omnimusic: 16-8, 16-10

Otari: 7-8

PSC (Professional Sound Corporation): 13-2, 13-8, 13-9, 13-20

QSound: 18-19

Record Plant, Hollywood: 3-17

Roland Corporation US: 8-11

RPG Diffusor Systems, Inc., and Peter D'Antonio: 3-10, 3-13 to 3-16

Ryder Sound Services: 16-6

Steve Sartori: 4-24, 6-9a, 11-2, 13-10, 15-1 to 15-12, 15-19, 15-21

Mark Schnell: 5-8, 5-17

Selco Products Company: 5-5, 5-6

Sennheiser Electronic Corporation: 4-4, 4-5, 4-26, 4-35

Shure Brothers, Inc: 4-47, 4-52a, 4-55a, 4-55b, 5-1, 13-1, 13-4

Bruce Siegel: 17-39

SmartSound® for Multimedia from Sonic Desktop Software: 16-9

Sony Corporation of America: 8-19

Sound Ideas: 16-3

Soundfield Research, Ltd.: 4-18 to 4-20

Steenbeck: 17-22

Steinberg North America: 8-21

William Storm: 4-40a, 4-41, 4-44, 4-45, 6-3, 6-7, 14-38, 14-41, 16-4, 16-5, 17-2, 17-3, 17-7, 17-18, 17-20, 17-23 to 17-29

Studio Technologies: 4-55c, 12-14

Summit Audio: 8-4

Switchcraft: 5-10

Taber Manufacturing and Engineering Company: 6-8a

Tascam: 6-6, 7-7

360 Systems: 12-13a

Universal City Studios, Inc.: 16-1

WAVES: 8-20, 18-23

Wheatstone Corporation: 5-3

Whirlwind: 13-19

Yamaha Corporation of America: 5-16

Herbert Zettl: 4-50, 4-51, 4-53, 4-54, 13-14

They can hear your hair growing.

> —*Frank McCourt, author of* Angela's Ashes, *describing the "ears" of the audio production team who recorded his reading of the book for audiocassette.*

The engineer has the responsibility to make the audio sound *good;* the sound designer has the responsibility to make it sound *interesting.*

> —*Anonymous*

Respect technology, but revere talent.

> —*Ham Brosious*

Principles

1

"Ears"

The eye points outward, the ear inward. Or, as the nineteenth-century philosopher and scientist Lorenz Oken observed, "The eye takes a person into the world. The ear brings the world into a human being."

We begin to hear before we are born.

> We develop in a continuous... bath of sounds: the song of our mother's voice, the swash of her breathing... the timpani of her heart. Sound rules as solitary Queen of our senses: the... world of uterine darkness makes Sight and Smell impossible, Taste monochromatic, and Touch a dim and generalized hint of what is to come. Birth brings with it the sudden and simultaneous ignition of the other four senses, and an intense competition for the throne that Sound had claimed as hers. The most notable pretender is... Sight, who dubs himself King as if the throne had been standing vacant, waiting for him. Ever discreet, Sound pulls a veil of oblivion across her reign and withdraws into the shadows, keeping a watchful eye on... Sight. If she gives up her throne, it is doubtful that she gives up her crown.*

Sight and sound are not alternatives. The senses function as a democracy, a concept that has been lost because of the dominance of the eye. Each one serves its own "constituency" and is uniquely suited to its role in the sensorial realm. The senses are also interdependent. To overlook the function of one is to miss their overall impact on a human being's

---

*Walter Murch in *Audio-Vision* by Michel Chion, edited and translated by Claudia Gorbman (New York: Columbia University Press, 1994), p. vii-viii.

relationship to, and perception of, the physical world, particularly when it comes to the contributions of audio in media.

We continue to ask, "Do you *see* what I mean?" when we converse. We admire people for their fore*sight,* in*sight,* and *vision.* Because we, of course, also possess these attributes, it is with such people that we *see eye-to-eye* and en*vision* doing so for the fore*seeable* future. On the other hand, *hear*say is something not to be believed; playing a song "by *ear*" has a pejorative connotation; children should be *seen* and not *heard;* and the term *phony* was used in the early days of the telephone, when conversants could not see one another's face to determine if what they were hearing was genuine.

We *see* a film and *watch* television, implying that the sound has little or no impact on our response. Radio and recordings are often used as background to other engrossments. Sound is taken for granted or often ignored.

Sound is a force: emotional, perceptual, physical. It can excite feeling, convey meaning, and, if it is loud enough, resonate the body. Renowned film director Akira Kurosawa has said, "The most exciting moment is the moment when I add the sound… [Then] I tremble."

Sound is omnidirectional; it is everywhere. The human eye can focus on only one view at a time. When the eye shifts, the original view is displaced. Sound can be layered—one sound can be added to another without displacement. Sound is attention-demanding. To comprehend and assimilate aural information requires active listening. Sonic communication is a dynamic activity.

What also enhances the power of sound, paradoxically, is its visual component. As one sage observed, "He who has ears to hear sees!" For decades radio drama created pictures in the "theater of the mind." Today sounds add visual dimension to radio news and documentary. Songs stir images (with no help needed from music videos). Sound in film and television, even from off-screen, often excites an image. Just hearing waves pound against a shore evokes, in the mind's eye, a turbulent sea.

Sound provides all sorts of *cognitive information*—information related to mental processes of knowledge, reasoning, memory, judgment, and perception—and *affective information*—information related to emotion, feeling, and mood. Sound is elemental.

This is all moot, however, especially for the audio professional, without "ears." In the parlance of audio, this means having healthy hearing and the ability to listen perceptively.

THE HEALTHY EAR

The human ear is divided into three parts: the *outer ear,* the *middle ear,* and the *inner ear* (see Figure 1-1). Sound waves first reach and are collected by the *pinna* (or *auricle*), the visible part of the outer ear. The sound waves are then focused through the *ear canal,* or *meatus,* to the *eardrum (tympanum)* at the beginning of the middle ear.

The tympanic membrane is attached to another membrane, called the *oval window,* by three small bones—the *malleus, incus,* and *stapes*—called *ossicles* and shaped like a hammer, anvil, and stirrup. The ossicles act as a mechanical lever, changing the small pressure of the sound wave on the eardrum into a much greater pressure. The combined action of the ossicles and the area of the tympanum allow the middle ear to help protect the inner ear from pressure changes (loud sounds) that are too great. It takes about one-tenth of a second to react and therefore provides little protection from sudden loud sounds.

The inner ear contains the *semicircular canals,* which are necessary for balance, and a snail-shaped structure called the *cochlea.* The cochlea is filled with fluid whose total capacity is a fraction of a drop. It is here that sound becomes electricity in the human head. Running through the center of the cochlea is the *basilar membrane,* resting upon which are 30,000 microscopic hair cells attached to nerve fibers composing the *organ of Corti,* the "seat of hearing." These fibers feed the auditory nerve, where the electrical impulses are passed on to the brain. Each hair cell has many hairs, or *cilia,* that bend when the basilar membrane responds to a sound. The hair cells closest to the oval window respond to high frequencies, and those closest to the other end of the spiral respond to low frequencies. High sound-pressure levels (SPLs) can

1-1 The auditory system

Outer hair cells

Inner hair cells

a

b

1-2 Severe injury to the sensory cells of the cochlea by exposure to loud sound. (a) A portion of the organ of Corti of a normal guinea pig, showing the characteristic rows of outer and inner hair cells, with their orderly patterns of stereocilia. (b) The same section after exposure to sound in the 2,000-Hz octave band at a sound-pressure level (SPL) of 120 dB. Hearing is permanently impaired, because the lost hair cells will not be replaced and the damaged hair cells, which are in disarray, may not recover.

cause the cilia to break or shear off. As the cilia become damaged, hearing impairment increases (see 1-2).

HEARING LOSS

We are a nation of the hard-of-hearing, because of the everyday, ever louder noise around us. Noise from traffic, airplanes, lawnmowers, sirens, vacuum cleaners, hair dryers, blenders, can openers, snow mobiles, even children's toys. In modern homes with wood floors, cathedral ceilings, brick or stucco walls, and many windows, sound is reflected and therefore intensified because there is little to absorb it. It is becoming increasingly rare to find quiet neighborhoods. Parks and campgrounds are being inundated with the annoying sounds of RVs, boisterous families, and blaring radios. At beaches,

the lap and wash of gentle surf has been drowned out by the roar of jet skis.

Audiologists claim that finding young people without some form of hearing degradation is difficult—with Walkmans, boom boxes, stereos, rock concerts, and parties and bars where sound levels are so loud it is necessary to shout to be heard, increasing the din even more. Too many young people have the hearing acuity of a 70 year old.

Yet hearing loss is not an inevitable consequence of aging. In societies less technologically advanced than ours, people in their eighties have normal hearing. Short of relocating to such a society, for now the only defense against hearing loss in prevention.

Usually, when hearing loss occurs, it does so gradually, typically without warning signs, and it occurs over a lifetime. When there are warning signs, they usually result from continuous, prolonged exposure to loud sound. You can tell there has been damage when it is difficult to understand a child's speech; music loses it color; quiet sounds are muffled or inaudible; it is necessary to keep raising the volume on the radio or TV; and your response to a question is usually, "What?"

Hearing damage caused by exposure to loud sound varies with the exposure time and the individual. Prolonged exposure to loud sound decreases the ear's sensitivity. Decreased sensitivity creates the false perception that sound is not as loud as it actually is. This usually necessitates an increase in levels to compensate for the hearing loss, thus making a bad situation worse.

After exposure to loud sound for a few hours, you may have experienced the sensation that your ears are stuffed with cotton. This is known as *temporary threshold shift (TTS)*—a reversible desensitization in hearing that disappears in anywhere from a few hours to several days; TTS is also called *auditory fatigue*. With TTS the ears have, in effect, shut down to protect themselves against very loud sounds.

Prolonged exposure to loud sounds can bring on *tinnitus*, a ringing, whistling, or buzzing in the ears, even though no loud sounds are present. Tinnitus is a danger signal that the ears may already have or soon will suffer *permanent threshold shift* with continued exposure to loud sound.

One audiologist's good advice is: If it's loud, turn it down. If you can't turn it down, keep your distance (or wear ear plugs.) If your ears are ringing, answer them!*

How Loud Is Loud?

This raises the question: How loud is loud? Humans have the potential to hear an extremely wide range of loudnesses. The ratio between the quietest sounds—at the **threshold of hearing**—and the loudest sounds—at the **threshold of pain**—is 1 to

10,000,000 and greater. Figure 1-3 shows the relative loudness of various sounds, many common in our everyday lives. (For a full discussion of Figure 1-3, see Chapter 2.)

Safeguards Against Hearing Loss

As gradual deterioration of the auditory nerve endings occurs through the aging process, it usually results in a gradual loss of hearing first in higher-pitched sounds and then in the lower-pitched sounds. Prolonged listening to loud sounds hastens that deterioration. To avoid premature hearing loss, the remedy is simple: Do not expose your ears to excessively loud sound levels for extended times (see Figure 1-4 and Table 1-1).

Hearing impairment is not the only detrimental effect of loud sound levels. They also produce adverse physiological effects. Sounds transmitted to the brain follow two paths. One path carries sound to the auditory center, where it is perceived and interpreted. The other goes to the brain centers that affect the nervous system. Loud sound taking the latter path can increase heart rate and blood pressure; constrict small blood vessels in the hands and feet; contract muscles; release stress-related hormones from adrenal glands; disrupt certain stomach and intestinal functions; and create dry mouth, dilated pupils, tension, anxiety, fatigue, and crankiness.

When you are in the presence of loud sound, including amplified music, wear earplugs designed to reduce loudness without seriously degrading frequency response. Some options among available earplugs are custom-fit earmolds, disposable foam plugs, reusable silicon insert plugs, and industrial headsets. The custom-fit earmold is best to use because, as the term suggests, it is made from a custom mold of your ear canal. It provides 15 to 20 *decibels*† (dB) of balanced sound-level reduction and attenuates all frequencies evenly. The disposable foam plug is intended for onetime use.

---

*Richie Moore, Ph.D., "Tips from the Doctor," *EQ,* February 1993, p. 44.

†The *decibel,* abbreviated *dB,* is a measure of relative power values and is discussed in Chapter 2.

Apparent Loudness	Ratio to dB	dB-SPL	
		220	12' in front of cannon below muzzle
		200	
Deafening		180	Rocket engines
		160	Jet engine, close up
		150	Permanent damage to hearing
	10,000,000	140	Inside a bass drum Airport runway
	3,162,000	130	Rock band—on stage; symphony orchestra, triple forte, 30' away
	1,000,000	120	Threshold of pain; loud vocals in front of mouth Thunder
Very loud	316,200	110	Electric guitar amp at maximum volume, 6" away Power tools
	100,000	100	Subway; loud vocals, 6" away
	31,620	90	Heavy truck traffic; baby crying; trombone, 16" away
	10,000	80	Acoustic guitar, 1' away
Loud	3,162	70	Busy street
	1,000	60	Average conversation
	316	50	Average office
Moderate	100	40	Subdued conversation
	32	30	Quiet office Recording studio
Faint	10	20	Furnished living room
Very faint	3	10	Insect noises at night, open field
	1	0	Threshold of hearing

1-3 Sound-pressure levels of various sound sources

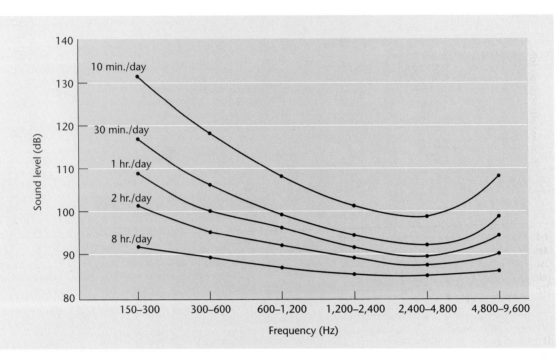

1-4 Damage risk criteria for a single-day exposure to various sound levels

Table 1-1 Hours of exposure to high sound levels permitted by the U.S. government and the British Occupational Hygiene Society

U.S. Government—Occupational Safety and Health Act (OSHA)		British Occupational Hygiene Society	
Sound Level (dB-SPL)	Daily Permissible Hours of Exposure	Sound Level (dB-SPL)	Daily Permissible Hours of Exposure
90	8	90	8
92	6	91	6
95	4	93	4
97	3	94	3
100	2	96	2
105	1	99	1
110	½	102	½
115	¼	105	¼

1-5 Attenuation effects of selected hearing protection devices. Notice that compared with a variety of commonly used hearing protectors, the Musician's and Hi-Fi plugs have relatively even attenuation across the frequency spectrum. (The ER-15 and ER-20 are products of Etymotic Research.™)

It provides noise reduction from 12 dB to 20 dB, mainly in the high frequencies. The reusable silicon insert plug is a rubberized insert cushion that covers a tiny metal filtering diaphragm. It reduces sound levels by approximately 17 dB. The silicon insert plug is often used at construction sites and firing ranges. The industrial headset has a cushioned headpad and tight-fitting earseals. It provides maximum sound-level attenuation, often up to 30 dB, and is particularly effective at low frequencies. This is the headset commonly used by personnel around airport runways and in the cabs of heavy-construction equipment (see 1-5).

The human ear is a very sophisticated electro-mechanical device. As with any device, regular maintenance is wise, especially for the audio professional. Make at least two visits a year to a qualified ENT (ear, nose, and throat) specialist to have your ears inspected and cleaned. The human ear secrets wax to protect the eardrum and cochlea from loud sound-pressure levels. Let the doctor clean out the wax. Do not use a cotton swab. You risk the chance of infection and jamming the wax against the eardrum, which obviously exacerbates the situation. If you must clean your ears between visits, ask the ENT doctor about the safest way to do it.

The implications of all this should be obvious, especially if you are working in audio. Not only is your hearing, in particular, and your physiological well-being, in general, at risk, but so is your livelihood.

THE EDUCATED EAR

For the audio professional, having healthy ears is one major requirement. Another is having educated ears—the ability to listen with careful discrimination to style, interpretation, nuance, and technical quality in evaluating the content, function, characteristics, and fidelity of a sound.

Most day-to-day aural stimuli we take for granted. We may pay attention to a particular song, to a siren, to an explosion, or to a victim's scream in a TV or film drama, but generally, sound functions as little more than background to our comings and goings. To the person in audio, however, such a lack of awareness is a liability. An audio professional must be sensitive to all sound, pleasant or unpleasant, exciting or unexciting, significant or insignificant, well performed or poorly performed.

Innate sensitivity to sound varies, and not everyone has the same perceptual acuity. You can acquire certain skills, however, through training in audio and music courses. Ear-training tapes and CDs also help (see Bibliography). Study the natural sounds of the environment. Take advantage of the vast and rich resources from the audio worlds of film sound tracks, TV, radio, and music CDs. By not listening, sound remains part of the "landscape"; it does not become part of your consciousness.

Developing an ear involves discrimination—the ability to shut out all sounds but the one you are listening to, to hear one sound among many. This is known as "putting your ear to it."

It can be argued that many sounds offer so little aesthetic satisfaction that they are not worth listening to. Many sounds even annoy, such as a loud TV from an adjacent apartment; music in an elevator; the sonic assault from sound systems in stores as you shop; hedge cutters, sirens, and blaring horns. It is all enough to desensitize aural acuity and make it difficult to enjoy worthwhile sound. Hence, it seems reasonable to conclude that listening should be selective. Such a conclusion might be appropriate for most people, but it does not apply to the audio professional.

Listening

You learn how to listen by paying attention to sound wherever and whenever it occurs: in conversation, in traffic, at sporting events, at a concert or movie, or when showering, getting dressed, dining, walking, watching television, or just lying in bed. You learn what to listen for by analyzing a sound's context and content.

In speech, words may denote meaning, but sound often defines it. On paper, the meaning of the phrase *Have a nice day* is clear. But the meaning changes when the stress on certain words changes, or when the words are spoken with a lilt, in a monotone, whine, or drawl, or by an old man, young woman, or child. Sound in speech conveys such qualities as confidence, fear, anxiety, arrogance, humor, and concern. In an interview a person may appear confident, but if there are unnatural pauses between words or phrases, or if there is a parched quality to the speech, the person's sound will belie the appearance.

In dialogue a charming, good-looking character conveys a sense of menace when his words are delivered in a harsh and guttural voice. A character whose voice rises at the end of sentences conveys a vulnerability, regardless of what is being said.

Take the sound of a dog barking. A bark is generally harsh and abrupt. But barks vary widely in pitch, loudness, rhythm, and context. For example, low-pitched barks last longer than high-pitched barks, and some barks begin with a gurgling-type sound rather than with a sharp attack. Within a bark may be a whine, yelp, growl, howl, or boom. Also some barks have regular rhythms, whereas others shift beats and produce irregular rhythms. Each of these sounds tells you something about the dog and the situation.

The sound a chick makes while hatching may seem obvious: gradual cracking of the eggshell and then peeping. But listening to a hatching reveals more: The chick peeps inside the egg before cracking it; the peeping is muffled. The shell begins cracking slowly with short, tentative splitting sounds that increase in force. With the increase in force and slightly longer cracking sounds, peeping increases in clarity, loudness, and rapidity. The final cracks of the shell sound more like crunches as the chick stumbles into the world. Once out of the shell, the peeping is unmuffled, steady, and strong, but not quite so loud as it was just before emergence.

In television, sound varies from program to program, even of the same genre. In sitcoms, laughter may come from a live audience or from a sound library. It may be more robust, or less, with a preponderance of elderly female or young male voices. In football there are different approaches to mixing the announcers' sounds with crowd sounds. Some audio operators like to keep the level of crowd sounds and the announcers' voices nearly the same to maintain excitement. Others prefer to keep the level of crowd noise relatively low so that, when the action justifies it, the level can be increased to accent the excitement.

Music presents the greatest challenge in listening. Its sonic combinations are infinite, and its aesthetic value fulfills basic human needs. Musical taste is intensely personal; two people listening to the same music may respond in two different ways, both valid.

Take two recordings of, say, Beethoven's Fifth Symphony. Keep constant as many factors as possible, such as the quality of the compact discs, the recording format (stereo, digital, analog), the audio system, and the room. You may be surprised at the differences in sound and interpretation. You may prefer the sound in one recording and the interpretation in another. That does not mean that one recording is necessarily better; it means that, based on your perceptions, one is preferable to another for certain reasons. Someone else may disagree.

Listen to music recordings for different attributes: overall production values; technical quality; the sound (or performance) of the drums, keyboard, group vocal, string section, rhythm guitar fill, and so on; a vocalist entering a bit early or late to counterpoint the lyric against the accompaniment; a vocalist rendering a lyric with meaning or just singing words; polyrhythms playing off one another to create rhythmic excitement; the sonic differences between an acoustic and an electric bass, or acoustic drums and a drum machine; the unique sound of a Zildjian™ cymbal or a Stratocaster™ electric guitar; a concert grand piano with a percussive tonality or a tonality that "sings"; the musicians' technical proficiency; the spatial distribution of instruments in a stereo or surround-sound field; the acoustics that enrich sound or dull it; stylistic differences among artists; the sonic difference between analog and digital sound or between 16-bit and 20-bit mastered CDs.

This is not to overwhelm you with detail or suggest that serious listening is clinical. Feeling the sound and sensing what works are also critical to active analysis, as is being aware of the relationship between your taste and mood and your response.

Reading reviews also provides insight into why critics think a work does or does not succeed. In fact, it is equally instructive to know why a recording or film sound track does not work as it is to know why it does, perhaps even more so.

Develop a sound vocabulary. Sound is nonverbal; it is difficult to describe. Coining words that are descriptive of the effect you are trying to achieve not only hones your own perceptions, but also provides others on the sound team with an indication of what you are going for. There are hundreds of such terms used for sound effects, such as *twung, squidge, whibble, wubba, boink, kabong, zuzz,* and so on. In music there are terms such as *honky, mellow, warm, bright, hollow, and zitsy* (also see Chapter 18).

Because response to sound is personal, standards and guidelines are difficult to establish, and so listening is the key to improving aural discrimination. The ear is capable of constant improvement in its ability to analyze sound. As your aural sensitivity improves, so will your level of auditory achievement.

MAIN POINTS

▶ The eye points outward, the ear inward.

▶ Sound is a force: emotional, perceptual, and physical.

▶ Sound is omnidirectional; it is everywhere. The human eye can focus on only one view at a time.

▶ Sound, paradoxically, has a visual component; it can create pictures in the "theater of the mind."

▶ In the parlance of audio, having "ears" means having healthy hearing and the ability to listen perceptively.

▶ The human ear is divided into three parts: the outer ear, the middle ear, and the inner ear.

▶ Temporary threshold shift, or auditory fatigue, is a reversible desensitization in hearing caused by exposure to loud sound over a few hours.

▶ Prolonged exposure to loud sounds can bring on tinnitus, a ringing whistling, or buzzing in the ears.

▶ Exposure to loud sound for extended periods of time can cause permanent threshold shift— a deterioration of the auditory nerve endings in the inner ear. In the presence of loud sound, use an ear filter designed to reduce loudness.

▶ Humans have the potential to hear an extremely wide range of loudnesses between the threshold of hearing and the threshold of pain, and beyond.

▶ Having educated ears means the ability to listen with careful discrimination to style, interpretation, nuance, and technical quality in evaluating the content, function, characteristics, and fidelity of sound.

▶ Learning how to listen begins with paying attention to sound wherever and whenever it occurs.

Physics and Psychophysics of Sound

The term *sound* can denote (1) the physical phenomenon of vibrations that set into motion longitudinal waves of compression and rarefaction propagated through molecular structures such as gas, liquids, and solids; (2) the physiological phenomenon that stimulates the sense of hearing; or (3) the psychophysical perception of sound stimuli. Chapter 1 discussed the sense of hearing; this chapter addresses the physical and psychophysical aspects of sound.

THE SOUND WAVE

Sound begins when an object vibrates and sets into motion molecules in the air closest to it. These molecules pass on their energy to adjacent molecules, starting a reaction, much like the waves that result when a stone is dropped into a body of water. The transfer of momentum from one displaced molecule to the next propagates the original vibrations longitudinally from the vibrating object to the hearer. What makes this reaction possible is air or, more precisely, a molecular medium with the property of elasticity. *Elasticity* is the phenomenon in which a displaced molecule tends to pull back to its original position after its initial momentum has caused it to displace nearby molecules.

As a vibrating object moves outward, it compresses molecules closer together, increasing pressure. *Compression* continues away from the object as the momentum of the disturbed molecules

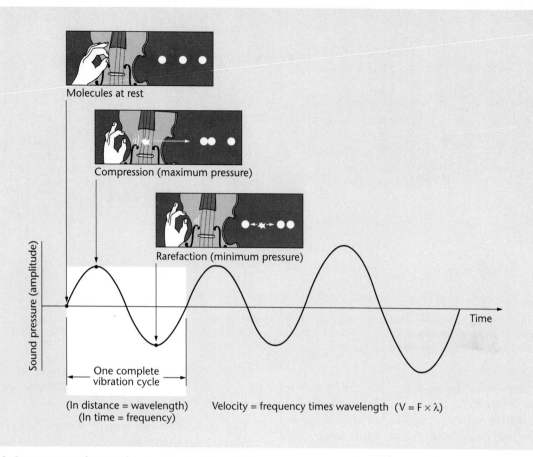

Molecules at rest

Compression (maximum pressure)

Rarefaction (minimum pressure)

Sound pressure (amplitude)

Time

One complete
vibration cycle

(In distance = wavelength)
(In time = frequency)

Velocity = frequency times wavelength $(V = F \times \lambda)$

2-1 Components of a sound wave. The vibrating object causes compression in sound waves when it moves outward (causing molecules to bump into each other). The vibrating object causes rarefaction when it moves inward (pulling the molecules away from each other).

displaces adjacent molecules and so produces a crest in the sound wave. When a vibrating object moves inward, it pulls the molecules farther apart and thins them, creating a *rarefaction*. This rarefaction also travels away from the object in a manner similar to compression, except that it decreases pressure, thereby producing a trough in the sound wave (see Figure 2-1). As the sound wave moves away from the vibrating object, the individual molecules do not advance with the wave; they vibrate at what is termed their *average resting place* until their motion stills or until they are set in motion by another vibration. Inherent in each wave motion are the components that make up a sound

wave: frequency, amplitude, velocity, wavelength, and phase (see 2-1, 2-2, and 2-7).

FREQUENCY AND PITCH

When a vibration passes through one complete up-and-down motion, from compression through rarefaction, it has completed one cycle. The number of cycles that a vibration completes in one second is expressed as its *frequency*. If a vibration completes 50 *cycles per second (cps)*, its frequency is 50 *hertz (Hz);* if it completes 10,000 cps, its frequency is 10,000 Hz, or 10 kilohertz (kHz). Every vibration has a frequency, and generally humans with

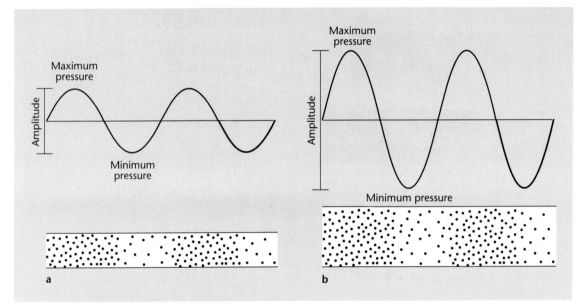

2-2 Amplitude of sound. The number of molecules displaced by a vibration creates the amplitude or loudness of a sound. Because the number of molecules in the sound wave in (b) is greater than the number in the sound wave in (a), the amplitude of the sound wave in (b) is greater.

excellent "ears" are capable of hearing frequencies from 20 Hz to 20,000 Hz. Frequencies just below the **low end** of this range, called **infrasonic,** and those just above the **high end** of this range, called **ultrasonic,** are sensed more than heard, if they are perceived at all.

Psychologically, we perceive frequency as **pitch**— the relative tonal highness or lowness of a sound. The more times per second a sound source vibrates, the higher its pitch. The G string of a guitar vibrates 196 times per second, so its fundamental frequency is 196 Hz. The A string has a frequency of 110 Hz, so the pitch of the G string is higher.

The range of audible frequencies, or the **sound frequency spectrum,** is divided into sections, each having a unique and vital quality. The usual divisions in Western music are called **octaves.** An octave is the interval between any two frequencies that have a tonal ratio of 2 to 1. The range of human hearing covers about 10 octaves. Starting with 20 Hz, the first octave is 20 Hz to 40 Hz; the second, 40 Hz to 80 Hz; the third, 80 Hz to 160 Hz; and so on (see inside back cover). Octaves are

grouped into bass, midrange, and treble, and further subdivided as follows.

■ **Low bass**—first and second octaves (20 Hz to 80 Hz). These are the frequencies associated with power, boom, and fullness. The lowest notes of the piano, organ, tuba, and bass are in this range. Sounds in these octaves need not occur often to maintain a sense of fullness. If they occur too often, or at too loud a level, the sound can become thick or muddy.

■ **Upper bass**—third and fourth octaves (80 Hz to 320 Hz). Most of the lower tones generated by rhythm and other support instruments such as drums, piano, bass, cello, and trombone are in this range. They establish a balance in musical structure. Too many frequencies from this range make it sound boomy; too few make it thin. When properly proportioned, pitches in the second, third, and fourth octaves are very satisfying to the ear, because we perceive them as giving sound an anchor, that is, fullness or bottom. Frequencies in the upper bass range serve aural structure the way the horizontal line serves visual structure—by providing a foundation.

■ *Midrange*—fifth, sixth, and seventh octaves (320 Hz to 2,560 Hz). The midrange gives sound its intensity. It contains the fundamental and the rich lower harmonics and overtones of most sound sources.* The midrange does not necessarily generate pleasant sounds, however. Too much emphasis of sixth-octave frequencies is heard as a hornlike quality; too much emphasis of seventh-octave frequencies is heard as a tinny quality. Extended listening to midrange sounds can be annoying and fatiguing.

■ *Upper midrange*—eighth octave (2,560 Hz to 5,120 Hz). We are most sensitive to frequencies in the eighth octave, a rather curious range. The lower part of the eighth octave (2,560 Hz to 3,500 Hz) contains frequencies that, if properly emphasized, improve the intelligibility of speech and lyrics. These frequencies are roughly 3,000 Hz to 3,500 Hz. If these frequencies are unduly emphasized, however, sound becomes abrasive and unpleasant; and vocals, in particular, become harsh and lispy, making some consonants difficult to understand. The upper part of the eighth octave (above 3,500 Hz), on the other hand, contains rich and satisfying pitches that give sound definition, clarity, and realism. Listeners perceive a sound source frequency in this range (and also in the lower part of the ninth octave, up to about 6,000 Hz) as being nearby, and for this reason it is also known as the *presence range*.

---

*A *fundamental*, also called the *first harmonic* or *primary frequency*, is the lowest or basic pitch of a musical instrument, its *harmonics* are exact multiples of the fundamental, and its *overtones*, also known as *inharmonic overtones*, are pitches that are not exact multiples of the fundamental. If a trumpet sounds a low G, the fundamental is 392 Hz, its harmonics are 784 Hz, 1,568 Hz, 3,136 Hz, and so on, and its overtones are the frequencies in between (see section on timbre later in this chapter). Sometimes in usage, harmonics also assume overtones. Another term for harmonics and overtones is *partials*. A harmonics-related term that is sometimes confused with inharmonic is **enharmonic**. Enharmonic notes are two different notes that sound the same. For example, C♯ and D♭, D♯ and E♭, and G♯ and A♭.

Increasing loudness at 5,000 Hz, the heart of the presence range, gives the impression that there has been an overall increase in loudness throughout the midrange. Reducing loudness at 5,000 Hz makes a sound seem farther away and transparent.

■ *Treble*—ninth and tenth octaves (5,120 Hz to 20,000 Hz). Although the ninth and tenth octaves generate only 2 percent of the total power output of the sound frequency spectrum, and most human hearing does not extend much beyond 16,000 Hz, they give sound the vital, lifelike qualities of brilliance and sparkle, particularly in the upper-ninth and lower-tenth octaves. Too much emphasis above 6,000 Hz makes sound hissy and brings out electronic noise. Too little emphasis above 6,000 Hz dulls sound.

AMPLITUDE AND LOUDNESS

We have noted that vibrations in objects stimulate molecules to move in pressure waves at certain rates of alternation (compression-rarefaction) and that rate determines frequency. Vibrations not only affect the molecules' rate of up-and-down movement but also determine the number of displaced molecules that are set in motion from equilibrium to a wave's maximum height *(crest)* and depth *(trough)*. This number depends on the intensity of a vibration; the more intense it is, the more molecules are displaced. The greater the number of molecules displaced, the greater the height and depth of the sound wave. The number of molecules in motion, and therefore the size of a sound wave, is called **amplitude** (see 2-2). Our subjective impression of amplitude is a sound's loudness or softness. Amplitude is measured in decibels.

The Decibel

The *decibel (dB)* is a dimensionless unit used to compare the ratio of two quantities usually in relation to acoustic energy, such as sound pressure, and electric energy, such as power and voltage. In mathematical terms it is 10 times the logarithm to the base 10 of the ratio between the powers of two signals: dB = 10 log (P1 / P0). P0 is usually a reference power value to which another power value, P1, is compared. It is abbreviated *dB* because it stands for one-tenth *(deci)* of a *Bel* (from Alexander Graham Bell). The Bel was the amount a signal dropped in level over a one-mile distance of telephone wire. Because the amount of level loss was too large to work with as a single unit of measurement, it was divided into tenths for more-practical application.

Sound-Pressure Level

Acoustic sound pressure is measured in terms of *sound-pressure level (dB-SPL)*, because there are periodic variations in atmospheric pressure in a sound wave. Humans have the potential to hear an extremely wide range of these periodic varia-tions, from 0 dB-SPL, the threshold of hearing, to 120 dB-SPL, the threshold of pain, and beyond (see 1-3). The range of the difference in decibels between the loudest and quietest sound a vibrating object makes is called *dynamic range*. Because this range is so wide, a logarithmic scale is used to compress loudness measurement into more-manageable figures. (On a linear scale, a unit of one adds an increment of one. On a logarithmic scale, a unit of one multiplies by a factor of 10.)

Humans have the capability to hear loudness at a ratio of 1 to 10,000,000 and greater. Sound at 60 dB-SPL is 1,000 times louder than sound at 0 dB-SPL; at 80 dB-SPL it is 10 times louder than at 60 dB-SPL. If the amplitude of two similar sounds is 100 dB-SPL each, their amplitude, when added, would be 103 dB-SPL. Nevertheless, most people do not perceive a sound level as doubled until it has increased about 10 dB.

There are other acoustic measurements of human hearing based on the interactive relationship between frequency and amplitude. These measurements are discussed in "Frequency and Loudness," later in this chapter.

Sound in Electrical Form

In order for sound (acoustic) energy to be processed through electrical equipment, it must be *transduced,* converted, into electric energy. Electric energy is measured in decibels in relation to power—dBm—

and voltage—dBu or dBv, and dBV. It is difficult to discuss these measurements here fully because they involve mathematical formulas and technical terminology that are beyond the scope of this book (see Table 2-1).

In measuring an electric circuit, a foremost concern is *impedance*—that property of a circuit, or an element, that restricts the flow of *alternating current (AC)*. Impedance is measured in *ohms (Ω),* a unit of resistance to current flow. The lower the impedance in a circuit, the better.

FREQUENCY AND LOUDNESS

Frequency and amplitude are interdependent. Varying a sound's frequency also affects perception of its loudness, and varying a sound's amplitude affects perception of its pitch.

Table 2-1 Power and voltage measurements in dB

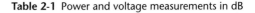

dBm is the original electrical measurement of power. It is referenced to 1 milliwatt (mW) as dissipated across a 600-ohm (Ω) load. 600Ω is the standard circuit resistance of a telephone line. (A *resistor* is a device that opposes the flow of current.) Any voltage that results in 1 milliwatt is 0 dBm, which is the same as 0.775 volt across a 600-ohm imped-ance. +30 dBm is 1 watt; +50 dBm is 100 watts.

dBu, or *dBv*, is a unit of measurement for expressing the relationship of decibels to voltage—0.775 volt to be exact.* The *u* stands for "unterminated." The figure comes from 0 dBm, which equals 0.775 volt. *dBu* is a more flexible reference than *dBm,* because it permits use of the decibel scale to obtain a relative level without regard to a standard impedance, that is, 600 ohms. It is a measurement most useful in professional audio.

dBV is also a measure of voltage but with decibels referenced to 1 volt. This measurement is used where the dBm—600 ohm/1 milliwatt—value is impractical, as it is with the measurement of micro-phone sensitivity where the zero reference is 1 volt. +10 dBV is equal to 20 volts. Otherwise, dBV is not often used in professional audio.

*Originally, the reference symbol *dBu* was designated *dBv,* but because *dBv* was often confused with *dBV,* it was changed to *dBu.* Both are still used—*dBu* mainly in the United States, and *dBv* mainly in Europe.

Equal Loudness Principle

The response of the human ear is not equally sensitive to all audible frequencies (see 2-3). Depending on loudness, we do not hear low and high frequencies as well as we hear middle frequencies. In fact, the ear is relatively insensitive to low frequencies at low levels. Oddly enough, this is called the *equal loudness principle* rather than that of unequal loudness (see 2-4).

2-3 Responses to various frequencies by the human ear. This curve shows that the response is not flat and that we hear midrange frequencies better than low and high frequencies.

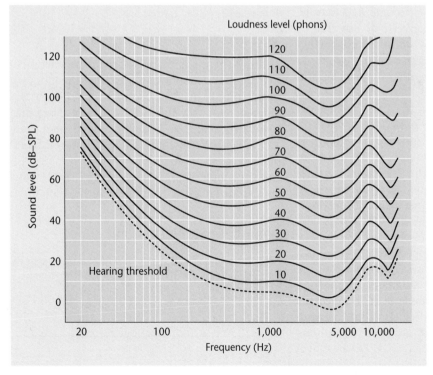

2-4 Equal loudness curves. These curves illustrate the relationships in Figure 2-3 and our relative lack of sensitivity to low and high frequencies as compared with middle frequencies. A 50-Hz sound would have to be 50 dB louder to seem as loud as a 1,000-Hz sound at 0 dB. To put it another way, at an intensity, for instance, of 40 dB, the level of a 100-Hz sound would have to be 10 times the SPL of a 1,000-Hz sound for the two sounds to be perceived as equal in loudness. Each curve is identified by the SPL at 1,000 Hz, which is known as the "phon of the curve."

(This graph represents frequencies on a logarithmic scale. The distance from 20 to 200 Hz is the same as from 200 to 2,000 Hz or from 2,000 to 20,000 Hz.) (Based on Robinson-Dadson.)

 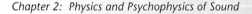

If a guitarist plucks all six strings equally hard, you do not hear each string at the same loudness level. The high E string (328 Hz) sounds louder than the low E string (82 Hz). To make the low string sound as loud, the guitarist would have to pluck it harder. This suggests that the high E string may sound louder because of its higher frequency. But if you sound three tones, say, 50 Hz, 1,000 Hz, and 15,000 Hz, at a fixed loudness level, the 1,000-Hz tone sounds louder than either the 50-Hz or the 15,000-Hz tone.

In a live concert, sound levels are usually louder than they are on a home stereo system. Live music often reaches levels of 100 dB-SPL and higher. At home, levels are as high as 70 to 75 dB-SPL and, alas, too often much higher. Sound at 70 dB-SPL requires more bass and treble boost than does sound at 100 dB-SPL to obtain equal loudness. Therefore the frequency balances you hear at 100 dB-SPL will be different when you hear the same sound at 70 dB-SPL.

In a recording or mixdown session, if the loudness level is high during recording and low during playback, both bass and treble frequencies could be considerably reduced in volume and may be virtually inaudible. The converse is also true: If sound level is low during recording and high when playing back, the bass and treble frequencies could be too loud relative to the other frequencies and may even overwhelm them.

Because sensitivity of the ear varies with frequency and loudness, meters that measure sound-pressure level are designed to correspond to these variations by incorporating one or more weighting networks. A *weighting network* is a filter used for weighting a frequency response before measurement. Generally, three weighting networks are used: A, B, and C. The A and B networks bear close resemblances to the response of the human ear at 40 and 70 phons, respectively. (A *phon* is a dimensionless unit of loudness level related to the ear's subjective impression of signal strength. For a tone of 1,000 Hz, the loudness level in phons equals the sound-pressure level in decibels.) The C network corresponds to the ear's sensitivity at 100 phons

2-5 Frequency responses of the A, B, and C weighting networks

and has an almost flat frequency response (see 2-5). Decibel values for the three networks are written as dBA, dBB, or dBC. The level may be quoted in dBm, with the notation "A weighting."

The A weighting curve is preferred for measuring lower-level sounds. The B weighting curve is usually used for measuring medium-level sounds. The C weighting, which is essentially flat, is used for very loud sounds (see Table 2-2).

Masking

Another phenomenon related to the interaction of frequency and loudness is *masking*—the hiding of some sounds by other sounds when each is a different frequency and they are presented together. Generally, loud sounds tend to mask softer ones, and lower-pitched sounds tend to mask higher-pitched ones.

For example, if a 100-Hz tone and 1,000-Hz tone are sounded together at the same level, both tones

Table 2-2 Sound level ranges of the A, B, and C weighting networks.

Weighting Network	dB
A	20–55
B	55–85
C	85–140

will be audible, but the 1,000-Hz tone will be perceived as louder. Gradually increasing the level of the 100-Hz tone and keeping the amplitude of the 1,000-Hz tone constant will make the 1,000-Hz tone more and more difficult to hear. If a 900-Hz tone is somewhat softer than a 1,000-Hz tone, the 900-Hz will be masked. If an LP (long-playing) record has scratches (high-frequency information), they will probably be masked during loud passages and audible during quiet ones. A symphony orchestra playing full blast may have all its instruments involved at once; however, flutes and clarinets will probably not be heard over trumpets and trombones, because woodwinds are generally higher in frequency and weaker in sound level than are the brass.

VELOCITY

Although frequency and amplitude are the most important physical components of a sound wave, another component—*velocity*, or the speed of a sound wave—should be mentioned. Velocity usually has little impact on pitch or loudness and is relatively constant in a controlled environment; sound travels 1,130 feet per second at sea level when the temperature is 70° Fahrenheit. The denser the molecular structure, the greater the vibrational conductivity. In water sound travels 4,800 feet per second. In solid materials such as wood and steel it travels 11,700 and 18,000 feet per second, respectively.

In air, sound velocity changes significantly in very high or very low temperatures, increasing as air warms and decreasing as it cools. For every change of 1°F, the speed of sound changes 1.1 feet per second.

WAVELENGTH

Each frequency has a *wavelength*, determined by the distance a sound wave travels to complete one cycle of compression and rarefaction; that is, the physical measurement of the length of one cycle is equal to the velocity of sound divided by the frequency of sound ($\lambda = v/f$) (see 2-1). Therefore frequency and wavelength change inversely with respect to each other. The lower a sound's frequency, the longer its wavelength; the higher a sound's frequency, the shorter its wavelength (see Table 2-3).

ACOUSTICAL PHASE

Acoustical phase refers to the time relationship between two or more sound waves at a given point in their cycles. Because sound waves are repetitive, they can be divided into regularly

Table 2-3 Selected frequencies and their wavelengths

Frequency (Hz)	Wavelength	Frequency (Hz)	Wavelength
20	56.5 feet	1,000	1.1 feet
31.5	35.8	2,000	6.7 inches
63	17.9	4,000	3.3
125	9.0	6,000	2.2
250	4.5	8,000	1.6
440	2.5	10,000	1.3
500	2.2	12,000	1.1
880	1.2	16,000	0.07

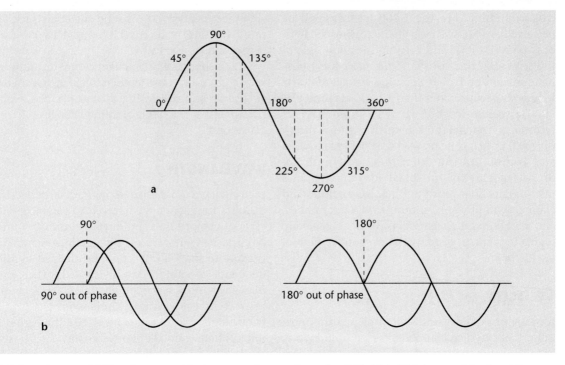

2-6 Sound waves. (a) Phase is measured in degrees, and one cycle can be divided into 360 degrees. It begins at 0 degrees with 0 amplitude, then increases to a positive maximum at 90 degrees, decreases to 0 at 180 degrees, increases to negative maximum at 270 degrees, and returns to 0 at 360 degrees. (b) Selected phase relationships of sound waves.

occurring intervals. These intervals are measured in degrees (see 2-6).

If two identical waves begin their excursions at the same time, their degree intervals will coincide and the waves will be *in phase*. If two identical waves begin their excursions at different times, their degree intervals will not coincide and the waves will be *out of phase*.

Waves that are in phase reinforce each other, increasing amplitude. Conversely, waves that are out of phase weaken each other, decreasing amplitude. When two sound waves are exactly in phase (0-degree phase difference) and have the same frequency, shape, and peak amplitude, the resulting waveform will be twice the original peak amplitude (see 2-7a). Two waves that are exactly out of phase (180-degree phase difference) and have the same frequency, shape, and peak amplitude cancel each other (see 2-7b). These two conditions rarely occur in the studio, however.

It is more likely that sound waves will begin their excursions at different times. If the waves are partially out of phase, there would be **constructive interference**, increasing amplitude, where compression and rarefaction occur at the same time, and **destructive interference**, decreasing amplitude, where compression and rarefaction occur at different times (see 2 8).

TIMBRE

For the purpose of illustration, sound is often depicted as a single, wavy line (see 2-1). Actually, a wave that generates such a sound (known as a **sine wave**) is a **pure tone**—a single frequency devoid of harmonics and overtones.

Most sound, however, consists of several different frequencies that produce a complex **waveform**—a graphical representation of a sound's characteristic shape, which can be seen, for

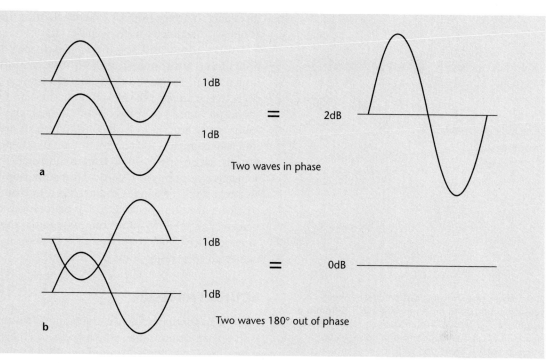

2-7 Sound waves in and out of phase. (a) In phase: Their amplitude is additive. Here the sound waves are exactly in phase—a condition that rarely occurs. It should be noted that decibels do not add linearly. These values have been assigned only to make a point. The actual additive amplitude here would be 6 dB. (b) Out of phase: Their amplitude is subtractive. Sound waves of equal amplitude 180 degrees out of phase cancel each other. This situation also rarely occurs.

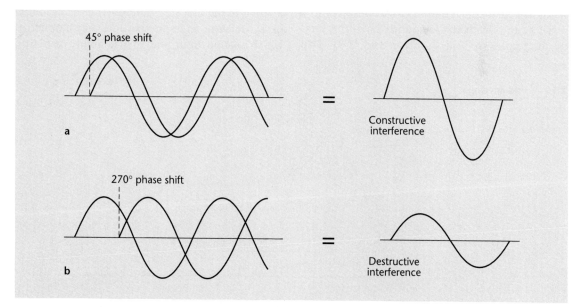

2-8 Waves partially out of phase (a) increase amplitude at some points and (b) decrease it at others

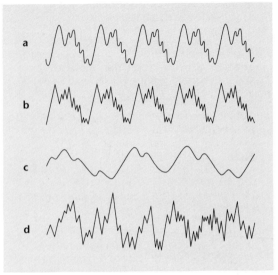

2-9 Waveforms showing differences between musical sounds and noise. (a) The pitch C from a piano. (b) The pitch C from a clarinet. (c) The waveform of an oboe. (d) The waveform of a noise. Notice its irregular pattern compared with the regular pattern of musical sounds.

example, on test equipment and on hard-disk editing systems (see Figures 9-14 and 17-35). Each sound has a unique tonal mix of fundamental and harmonic frequencies that distinguishes it from all other sound, even if the sounds have the same pitch, loudness, and duration (see 2-9). This difference between sounds is what defines their *timbre*—tone quality or tone color.

Unlike pitch and loudness, which may be considered unidimensional, timbre is multi-dimensional. The sound frequency spectrum is an objective scale of relative pitches; the table of sound-pressure levels is an objective scale of relative loudnesses. But there is no objective scale that orders or compares the relative timbres of different sounds. The best we can do is try to articulate our subjective response to a particular distribution of sonic energy. For example, sound consisting mainly of lower frequencies played by cellos may be perceived as mellow, mournful, or quieting; these same lower frequencies played by a bassoon may be perceived as raspy, honky, or comical.

SOUND ENVELOPE

Another factor that influences the timbre of a sound is its shape, or envelope, which refers to changes in loudness over time. A *sound envelope* has four stages: attack, initial decay, sustain, and release (ADSR). *Attack* is how a sound starts after a sound source has been vibrated. *Initial decay* is the point at which the attack begins to lose amplitude. *Sustain* is the period during which the sound's relative dynamics are maintained after its initial decay. *Release* refers to the time and manner in which a sound diminishes to inaudibility (see 2-10).

2-10 Sound envelope

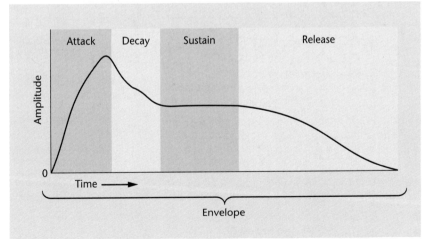

Two notes with the same frequency and loudness can produce different sounds within different envelopes. A bowed violin string, for example, has a more dynamic sound overall than does a plucked violin string. If you take a piano recording and edit out the attacks of the notes, the piano will start to sound like an organ. Do the same with a French horn and it sounds similar to a saxophone. Edit out the attacks of a trumpet and it creates an oboelike sound.

In this chapter we have examined the components of a sound wave and how they are heard without taking into consideration that we hear most sound in built-up or enclosed spaces. Behavior of sound waves in such spaces, and our perception of them, is the province of acoustics and psycho-acoustics, which is the subject of Chapter 3.

MAIN POINTS

▶ A sound wave is a vibrational disturbance that involves mechanical motion of molecules transmitting energy from one place to another.

▶ A sound wave is caused when a body vibrates and sets into motion the molecules nearest to it; the initial motion starts a chain reaction. This chain reaction creates pressure waves through the air, which are perceived as sound when they reach the ear and brain.

▶ The pressure wave compresses molecules as it moves outward, increasing pressure, and pulls the molecules farther apart as it moves inward, creating a rarefaction by decreasing pressure.

▶ The components that make up a sound wave are frequency, amplitude, velocity, wavelength, and phase.

▶ Sound acts according to physical principles, but it also has a psychological effect on humans.

▶ The number of times a sound wave vibrates determines its frequency or pitch. Humans can hear frequencies between, roughly, 20 Hz and 20,000 Hz—a range of 10 octaves. Each octave has a unique sound in the frequency spectrum.

▶ The size of a sound wave determines its amplitude or loudness. Loudness is measured in decibels.

▶ The decibel (dB) is a dimensional unit used to compare the ratio of two quantities usually in relation to acoustic energy, such as sound-pressure level (SPL), and electric energy, such as power—dBm—and voltage, such as dBu (or dBv), and dBV.

▶ Impedance is that property of a circuit, or an element, which restricts the flow of alternating current (AC). Impedance is measured in ohms, a unit of resistance to current flow.

▶ Humans can hear from 0 dB-SPL, the threshold of hearing, to 120 dB-SPL, the threshold of pain, and beyond. The scale is logarithmic, which means that adding two sounds each with a loudness of 100 dB-SPL would bring it to 103 dB-SPL. The range of difference in decibels between the loudest and quietest sound a vibrating object makes is called dynamic range.

▶ The ear does not perceive all frequencies at the same loudness even if their amplitudes are the same. This is the principle of equal loudness. Humans do not hear lower- and higher-pitched sounds as well as they hear midrange sounds.

▶ Masking—covering a weaker sound with a stronger sound when each is a different frequency and both vibrate simultaneously—is another perceptual response dependent on the relationship between frequency and loudness.

▶ Velocity, the speed of a sound wave, is 1,130 feet per second at sea level and 70°F. Sound increases or decreases in velocity by 1.1 feet per second for each change of 1°F.

▶ Each frequency has a wavelength, determined by the distance a sound wave travels to complete one cycle of compression and rarefaction. The length of one cycle is equal to the velocity of sound divided by the frequency of sound. The lower a sound's frequency, the longer its wavelength; the higher a sound's frequency, the shorter its wavelength.

▶ Acoustical phase refers to the time relationship between two or more sound waves at a given point in their cycles. If two waves begin their excursions at the same time, their degree intervals will coincide and the waves will be in phase, reinforcing each other and increasing amplitude. If two waves begin their excursions at different times, their degree intervals will not coincide and the waves will be out of phase, weakening each other and decreasing amplitude.

▶ Timbre is the tone quality or color of a sound.

▶ A sound's envelope has four stages: attack, initial decay, sustain, release (ADSR).

Acoustics and Psychoacoustics

In the broad sense, *acoustics* is the study of auditory sensation in the ear and the sound waves that cause that sensation, and *psychoacoustics* deals with the perception of that sensation. *Acoustics* is also used to describe the physical behavior of sound waves in a room. In that context, psychoacoustics is concerned with the relationship of our subjective response to such sound waves.

DIRECT, EARLY, AND REVERBERANT SOUND

When a sound is emitted in a room, its acoustic "life cycle" can be divided into three phases: direct sound, early sound, and reverberant sound (see Figure 3-1).

    Direct sound reaches the listener first, before it interacts with any other surface. Depending on the distance from the sound source to the listener, the time, T_0, is 20 to 200 *milliseconds (ms)*. Direct waves provide information about a sound's origin, size, and tonal quality.

    The same sound reaching the listener a short time later, after it reflects from various surfaces, is *indirect sound*. Indirect sound is divided into *early sound*, also known as *early reflections*, and reverberant sound (see 3-2). The difference between the two is that early reflections reach the listener within about 40 to 50 milliseconds of the direct sound. *Reverberant sound*, or *reverberation* (*reverb*, for short), is the result of the early reflections becoming smaller and smaller and the time between them decreasing until they combine, making the reflections indistinguishable.

Early sound adds loudness and fullness to the initial sound and helps create our subjective impression of the room's size. Reverb fills out the loudness and body of a sound and contains much of a sound's total energy. Also depending on the *decay time*, or *reverberation time* (the time it takes a sound to decrease 60 dB-SPL after its steady-state sound level has stopped), reverb provides information about the absorption and reflectivity of a room's surfaces, as well as about a listener's distance from the sound source. The longer it takes a sound to decay, the larger and more hard-surfaced the room is perceived to be, and the farther from the sound source the listener is or senses him- or herself to be.

Reverberation and Echo

Reverberation and *echo* are often used synonymously—but incorrectly so. Reverberation is densely spaced reflections created by random, multiple, blended repetitions of a sound. The time between reflections is imperceptible. If a sound is

3-1 Anatomy of reverberation in an enclosed space. At time$_0$ (T_0) the direct sound is heard. Between T_0 and T_1 is the initial time delay gap—the time between the arrival of the direct sound and the first reflection. At T_2 and T_3 more early reflections of the direct sound arrive as they reflect from nearby surfaces. These early reflections are sensed rather than distinctly heard. At T_4 repetitions of the direct sound spread through the room reflecting from several surfaces and arriving at the listener so close together that their repetitions are indistinguishable.

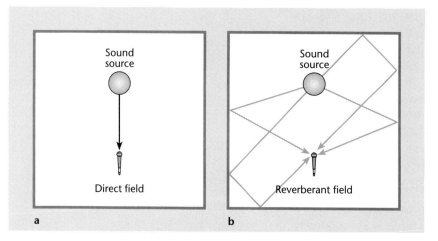

3-2 Acoustical behavior of sound in an enclosed room. (a) The direct sound field is all the sound reaching the listener (or microphone) directly from the sound source without having been reflected off any of the room's surfaces. (b) The indirect sound is all sound reaching the listener (or microphone) after being reflected off any of the room's surfaces.

delayed by 35 ms or more, the listener perceives *echo,* a distinct repeat of the direct sound.

In large rooms discrete echoes are sometimes perceived. In small rooms these repetitions, called *flutter echoes,* are short and come in rapid succession. They usually result from reflections between two parallel surfaces that are highly reflective. Because echoes usually inhibit sonic clarity, studios and concert halls are designed to eliminate them.

Precedence Effect

When a sound is emitted in a sound-reflectant space, direct sound reaches our ears first, before it interacts with any other surface. Indirect sound or *reflected sound,* on the other hand, reaches our ears only after bouncing off of one or more surfaces. If similar sounds reach the ear within about 20 ms of one another, the reflected sounds and the direct sound are usually perceived as coming from the same direction, even if the immediate repetitions coming from another direction are louder. This is known as the *precedence effect,* or *Haas effect.* As the time between the direct and indirect sounds reaching the ears increases beyond 20 ms, localization becomes increasingly difficult.

Another aspect of the precedence effect is that direct and reflected sounds reaching the ear approximately 10 to 20 milliseconds after the original waves are perceived as a single sound; the ear does not distinguish among them. This is called *temporal fusion.* This effect gradually disappears as the time interval between direct and reflected sounds increases from roughly 30 to 50 milliseconds.

MATCHING ACOUSTICS TO PROGRAM MATERIAL

Although the science of acoustics is highly developed, there is no such thing as a sound room with perfect acoustics. The sonic requirements, for example, of rock-and-roll and classical music are different; as they are for a radio studio and a studio used for dialogue rerecording in film and television.

A reverberant studio might be suitable for a symphony orchestra, because the reflections add needed richness to the music, as they do in a concert hall. The extremely loud music a rock group generates would swim amid too many sound reflections, becoming virtually unintelligible. At the same time, a studio with relatively few reflections, and therefore suitable for rock-and-roll, would render the sound of a symphony orchestra lifeless.

A radio studio is relatively quiet, but does have some room tone so the sound is not too closed down or closetlike. In radio it is important to maintain the intimate sonic rapport between announcer and listener that is essential to the personal nature of the medium. Rerecording dialogue in postproduction for a film or TV drama requires a studio virtually devoid of room tone to prevent acoustics from coloring the dialogue and so room tone appropriate to a scene's setting can be added later.

Rooms with reverberation times of one second or more are considered to be "live." Rooms with reverberation times of one-half second or less are considered to be "dry" or "dead" (see 3-3). Live

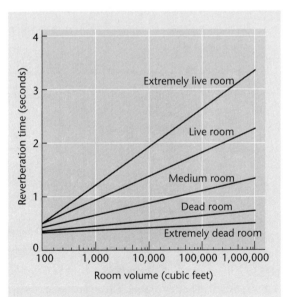

3-3 Room liveness in relation to reverberation time and room size

rooms reinforce sound, making it relatively louder and more powerful, especially, although not always, in the lower frequencies. They also tend to diffuse detail, smoothing inconsistencies in pitch, tonal quality, and performance.

In dry rooms sound is reinforced little or not at all, causing it to be concentrated and lifeless. Inconsistencies in pitch, tonal quality, and other aspects of undesirable performance are readily apparent. In instances where dry rooms are required for recording, signal processing is used to provide appropriate reverberation (see 3-4 and Chapter 8). Liveness can be added by increasing the frequencies between, roughly, 500 and 2,000 Hz and adding reverberation in the range of one to two seconds.

Intimacy and warmth are two other considerations in the acoustics of a room or recording. *Intimacy* relates to the closeness of the listener to the sound source and the ability to hear sonic detail. Intimacy results from early reflections that follow the direct sound by no more than 15 to 20 ms.

Warmth is a sonic quality usually associated with the lower frequencies and increased reverberation time—specifically, the frequencies between, roughly, 125 and 250 Hz and a high reverb time relative to the midrange frequencies.

Acousticians have calculated optimum reverb times for various types of sonic material that have proved suitable for emulation in the production room (see 3-5). That said, preference for the amount of reverberation and reverb time is a matter of individual taste, as all judgments in sound should be.

STUDIO DESIGN

The behavior of sound waves in an acoustic environment and how that behavior affects aural perception leads logically to a consideration of the factors that influence this behavior: (1) the isolating of sound outside and inside a room, (2) the dimensions of the room, (3) the shape of the room,

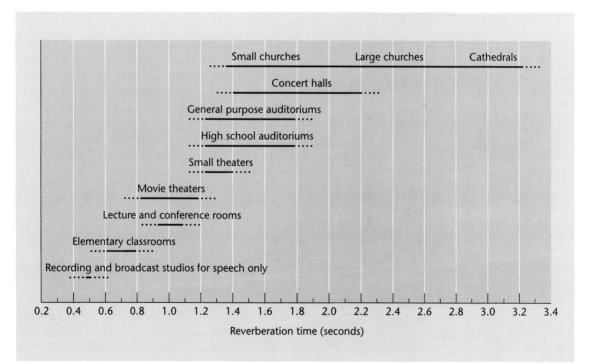

3-4 Typical reverberation times for various performance spaces

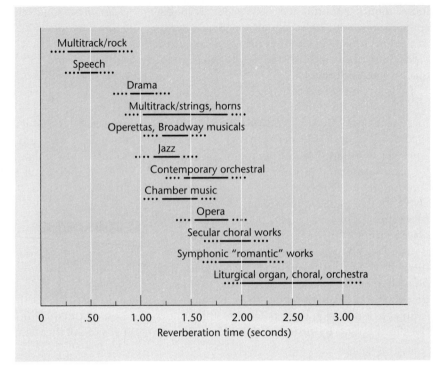

3-5 Optimum reverberation times for various types of music and speech produced indoors

Multitrack/rock

Speech

Drama

Multitrack/strings, horns

Operettas, Broadway musicals

Jazz

Contemporary orchestral

Chamber music

Opera

Secular choral works

Symphonic "romantic" works

Liturgical organ, choral, orchestra

0   .50   1.00   1.50   2.00   2.50   3.00

Reverberation time (seconds)

(4) absorption, reflection, diffraction, and diffusion in the room, and (5) the acoustical features of the room. These five factors are directly related to one overriding concern: noise.

Noise

Noise—unwanted sound—is enemy number one in audio production. As noted in Chapter 1, noise is everywhere. Outside a room it comes from traffic, airplanes, jackhammers, thunder, rain, and so on. Inside a room noise is generated by fluorescent lights, ventilation and heating systems, air conditioning, and appliances. And these are only the more obvious examples. A few not so obvious examples include the "noise" made by the random motion of molecules, by our nervous and circulatory systems, and by our ears. In short, noise is part of our existence and can never be completely eliminated. (Audio equipment also generates *system noise,* and recording tape generates tape noise.)

Even though unwanted sound is always present, in producing audio it must be brought within tolerable levels so that it does not interfere with the desired sound. Among other things, noise can mask sounds, make speech unintelligible, create distraction, and cause annoyance.

To this end, acousticians have developed *noise criteria (NC)* that identify, by means of a rating system, background noise—also called *ambient noise*—levels (see 3-6). From this rating system, NC levels for various types of rooms are derived (see Table 3-1). This raises the question: Once NC levels for a particular sound room are known, how is noise control accomplished?

Sound Isolation

Sound studios must be isolated to prevent outside noise from leaking into the room and to keep loud sound levels generated inside the room from disturbing neighbors. This is accomplished in two ways. The first is by determining the loudest outside

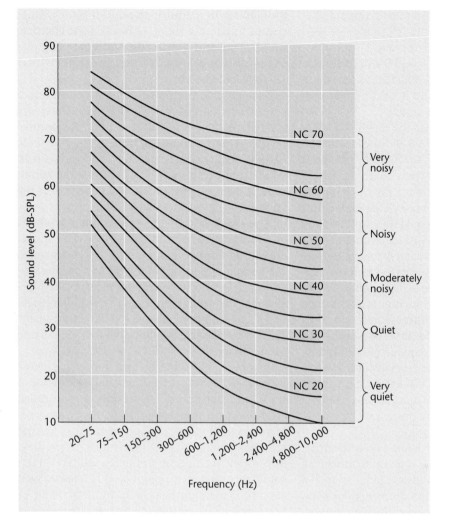

3-6 Noise criteria (NC) curves

Table 3-1 Recommended noise criteria levels for selected rooms

Type of Room	Recommended NC Curve	dB
Broadcast and recording studios	NC 15–25	25–35
Concert halls	NC 20	30
Drama theaters	NC 20–25	30–35
Motion picture theaters	NC 30	40
Sports coliseums	NC 50	60

sound level against the minimum acceptable NC level inside the studio. This is usually between NC 15 and NC 25 (approximately 25–35 dBA), depending on what type of sound the studio is used for. It is also done by determining the loudest sound level inside the studio against a maximum acceptable noise floor outside the studio.

For example, assume that the maximum measured noise outside a studio is 90 dB-SPL and the maximum acceptable noise level inside a studio is 30 dB-SPL, at, say, 500 Hz. (These values are always frequency-dependent but are usually based on 500 Hz.) That means the construction of the studio must reduce the loudness of the outside sound level by 60 dB. If the loudest sound inside a studio is 110 dB-SPL and the maximum acceptable noise outside the studio is 45 dB-SPL, the studio's construction must reduce the loudness level by 65 dB.

The amount of sound reduction provided by a barrier—wall, floor, or ceiling—is referred to as *transmission loss (TL)*. Because TL works both ways, determining barrier requirements is equally applicable to sound traveling from inside to outside the studio, and vice versa. Therefore the barriers constructed to isolate the studio in this example would have to reduce the loudness level by at least 65 dB (500 Hz).

Just as it is convenient to define a noise spectrum by a single NC number, so it is useful to measure a barrier on the basis of its transmission loss; such a measurement is called *sound transmission class (STC)*. Sound transmission class varies with the type and mass of materials in a barrier. A 4-inch concrete block has an STC of 48, indicating that sound passing through it will be attenuated by 48 dB. An 8-inch concrete block has an STC of 52, which means it attenuates 4 dB more sound than the 4-inch block.

Room Dimensions

Sometimes a room's dimensions accentuate noise by reinforcing certain frequencies, thereby altering, or "coloring," the natural sound. This may also increase reverb time. Such coloration affects perception of tonal balance, clarity, and imaging as well. Audio mixed in a control room with these

problems will sound markedly different when played in another room. Other factors related to the shape of and construction materials used in a studio (discussed in the following two sections) may also affect coloration.

Rooms have particular resonances at which sound will be naturally sustained. These are related to the room's dimensions. *Resonance* results when a vibrating body with the same natural frequencies as another body causes it to vibrate sympathetically and increases the amplitude of both of them at those frequencies if the vibrations are in acoustical phase.

The story is told of soldiers on horseback galloping across a wooden bridge. The sound created by the hoofbeats on the wood generated the resonant frequency of the bridge, causing it to collapse. In another incident wind excited the resonant frequency of a modern steel-and-concrete bridge, increasing amplitude until it was torn apart.* These are interesting examples, but they are extreme for our purpose.

In a room, resonances occur at frequencies whose wavelengths are the same as or a multiple of one of the room's dimensions. These resonances are called *eigentones* or, more commonly, *room modes*—increases in loudness at resonant frequencies that are a function of a room's dimensions. When these dimensions are the same or multiples of a common value, the resonance amplitude is increased. Such a room's dimensions may be 10 by 20 by 30, or 15 by 30 by 45. This creates unequal representation of the frequencies generated by a sound source. In other words, certain frequencies will be reinforced while others will not be. To avoid additive resonances, room dimensions should not be the same, nor be integer multiples of one another. Dimensions of, say, 10 by 11.4 by 13.9, or 15 by 27 by 31.5, would be satisfactory.

Resonance is not always bad, however. The tubing in wind and brass instruments, the pipes in an organ, and the human mouth, nose, chest, and throat are resonators. Air columns passing through

---

*Tacoma Narrows Suspension Bridge at Puget Sound, Washington, in 1940.

them excite resonant frequencies, creating sound. Without resonators such as the "box" of a guitar or violin, weak sound sources would generate little sound. Some studios use this principle to construct resonators that help amplify certain frequencies to enhance the type of sound being produced. As we shall see in the section headed "Absorption, Reflection, Diffraction, and Diffusion," resonators are also used to absorb sound.

Room Shape

Acoustics is a science of interacting relationships. Although studio walls, floors, and windows may have been properly constructed and their dimensions conform to a set of preferred standards, the room's shape is also important to good noise reduction and sound dispersion.

Except for bass frequencies, sound behaves like light; its angle of incidence is equal to its angle of reflectance (see 3-7). If a studio has reflective parallel walls, sound waves reinforce themselves as they continuously bounce between opposing surfaces (see 3-8a). If there are concave surfaces, they serve as collecting points, generating unwanted concentrations of sound (see 3-8b). A studio should be designed to break up the paths of sound waves (see 3-8c).

Typical studio designs have adjacent walls at angles other than 90 degrees (see 3-9) and different-shaped wall surfaces, such as spherical, cylindrical, and serrated, to help disperse the sound waves. Even the glass between the studio and the control room is angled toward the floor for sound dispersal (and also to avoid light reflections), but it is not enough to break up the paths of sound waves; they must be controlled once they hit a surface.

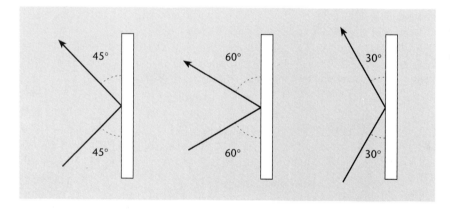

3-7 Angle of incidence and angle of reflectance. In sound, as in light, these angles are equal.

3-8 Shape of a room's surface affecting direction of sound reflections. (a) Two parallel surfaces opposite each other generate standing waves by reinforcing sound. (b) Concave surfaces concentrate sound waves by converging them. (c) Convex surfaces are more suitable in studios because they disperse sound waves.

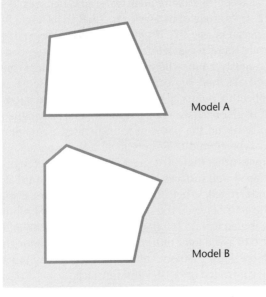

Model A

Model B

3-9 Examples of studio shapes with nonparallel plane surfaces

ABSORPTION, REFLECTION, DIFFRACTION, AND DIFFUSION

When sound hits a surface, one or a combination of five things happens, depending on the surface's material, mass, and design. Sound is absorbed, reflected, partially absorbed and reflected, diffracted, or diffused.

Absorption and Reflection

When sound hits a surface and is absorbed, it is soaked up. There is little or no reflection; hence, the sonic result is lifeless or dead. When sound hits a surface and is reflected, it bounces off the surface and is perceived as reverberation or echo, depending on its interaction with other live surfaces in the vicinity. Conditions under which sound is completely absorbed or reflected are rare. Most materials absorb and reflect sound to some degree (see 3-10).

3-10 Absorption and reflection in relation to temporal and spatial response

The amount of indirect sound energy absorbed is given an acoustical rating called a ***sound absorption coefficient,*** also known as a *noise reduction coefficient (NRC).* Theoretically, on a scale from 1.0 to 0.0, material with a sound absorption coefficient of 1.0 completely absorbs sound, whereas material with a sound absorption coefficient of 0.0 is completely sound reflectant. Soft, porous materials absorb more sound than do hard, nonporous materials. Drapes, for example, have a higher absorption coefficient than does glass. Sound absorption ratings for the same material vary with frequency, however (see Table 3-2).

Three classifications of acoustic absorbers are porous absorbers, diaphragmatic absorbers, and Helmholtz absorbers. Examples of ***porous absorbers*** are acoustical tiles, carpet, fiberglass, and urethane foams (see 3-11). Porous absorbers are most effective with high frequencies. Because the wavelengths of high frequencies are short, they tend to get trapped in the tiny air spaces of the porous materials. The range and degree of high-frequency absorption depends on the density and thickness of the porous materials.

Diaphragmatic absorbers are generally flexible panels of wood or pressed wood mounted over an air space (see 3-12). When a sound wave hits the panel, it resonates at a frequency (or frequencies) determined by the stiffness of the panel and the size of the air space. Other sound waves of the same frequency (or frequencies) approaching the panel, therefore, are dampened. Diaphragmatic absorbers are used mainly to absorb low frequencies; for this reason they are also called *bass traps.* This principle can also be applied to absorbing high frequencies. Because it is difficult to completely dissipate standing waves, especially in small rooms and even with optimal acoustics, bass traps are usually designed to introduce significant absorption for frequencies between 30 and 100 Hz.

A ***Helmholtz absorber,*** also called a *Hemholtz resonator,* is a tuned absorber designed to remove sound at specific frequencies or within specific frequency ranges, usually the lower-middle frequencies. It functions, in principle, not unlike the action created when blowing into the mouth of a soda bottle. The tone created at the frequency of the

3-11 Polyurethane-foam sound absorber

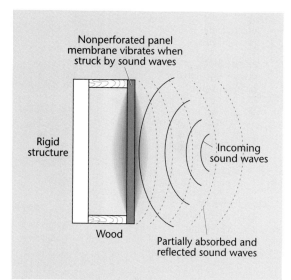

3-12 Diaphragmatic absorber. The approaching sound wave strikes the cover panel or diaphragm, setting it into motion and canceling resonant frequencies and reflecting nonresonant frequencies.

bottle's resonance is related to the air mass in the bottle. By filling the bottle with water, the air mass is reduced, so the pitch of the tone gets higher.

Diffraction

When sound reaches a surface, in addition to being partially absorbed and reflected, it diffracts—spreads or bends around the surface. The amount of ***diffraction*** depends on the relation between wavelength and the distances involved. You will recall that each frequency has a wavelength;

Table 3-2 Sound absorption coefficients of commonly used materials (figures for people—adult, youth, and child—are determined by adding their absorption units to other absorbers in a room)

Materials	125 Hz	250 Hz	500 Hz	1,000 Hz	2,000 Hz	4,000 Hz
¾-inch mineral fiber acoustical tile						
hard backing	0.03	0.27	0.83	0.99	0.82	0.71
suspended	0.68	0.67	0.65	0.84	0.87	0.74
1-inch fiberglass tile						
hard backing	0.06	0.25	0.68	0.97	0.99	0.91
suspended	0.69	0.95	0.74	0.98	0.99	0.99
Brick						
unglazed	0.03	0.03	0.03	0.04	0.05	0.07
painted	0.01	0.01	0.02	0.02	0.02	0.03
Carpet, heavy						
on concrete	0.02	0.06	0.14	0.37	0.60	0.65
on foam pad	0.08	0.24	0.57	0.69	0.71	0.73
Concrete block						
coarse, unpainted	0.36	0.44	0.31	0.29	0.39	0.25
painted, sealed	0.10	0.05	0.06	0.07	0.09	0.08
Fabric						
10-oz. medium velour hung flat to wall	0.03	0.04	0.11	0.17	0.24	0.35
14-oz. medium velour draped to half area	0.07	0.31	0.49	0.75	0.70	0.60
18-oz. heavy velour draped to half area	0.14	0.35	0.55	0.72	0.70	0.65
Floor materials						
concrete or terrazzo	0.01	0.01	0.01	0.02	0.02	0.02
tile on concrete	0.02	0.03	0.03	0.03	0.03	0.02
wood parquet on concrete	0.04	0.04	0.07	0.06	0.06	0.07
wood on wood joinsts	0.15	0.11	0.10	0.07	0.06	0.07
Glass						
standard window glass	0.35	0.25	0.18	0.12	0.07	0.04
heavy plate glass	0.18	0.16	0.14	0.03	0.02	0.02
Gypsum wallboard						
nailed to 2 × 4 studs	0.29	0.10	0.05	0.04	0.07	0.09
Plaster						
smooth, on brick	0.01	0.02	0.02	0.03	0.04	0.05
rough, on lath	0.14	0.10	0.06	0.05	0.04	0.03
¾-inch plywood paneling	0.28	0.22	0.17	0.09	0.10	0.11
Water surface, as in a swimming pool	0.008	0.008	0.013	0.015	0.020	0.025
Audience, seated in upholstered seats	0.60	0.74	0.88	0.96	0.93	0.85
unoccupied cloth-covered seats	0.49	0.66	0.80	0.88	0.82	0.70
unoccupied leather-covered seats	0.44	0.54	0.60	0.62	0.58	0.50
Chairs, metal or wood, unoccupied	0.15	0.19	0.22	0.39	0.38	0.30
People						
adult				4.2		
youth				3.8		
child				2.8		

bass waves are longer, treble waves shorter. Hence, the diffraction of bass waves are more difficult to control acoustically than the diffraction of treble waves.

Diffusion

The overriding challenge for the acoustician is controlling the physical behavior of sound waves in a studio. The goal is the uniform distribution of sound energy in a room so that its intensity throughout the room is approximately equal (see 3-13). This is called *diffusion*. No matter how weak or strong the sound and regardless of its wavelength, the diffused energy is reduced in amplitude and spread out in time, falling off more or less exponentially. Figures 3-14 through 3-16 display various forms of diffusors to meet specific needs.

3-13 Diffusion in relation to temporal and spatial response

3-14 Abffusor.™ Provides reflection control by simultaneously using absorption and diffusion down to 100 Hz for all angles of incidence.

3-15 Omniffusor.™ Sound diffusor that scatters sound into a hemisphere; useful when omnidirectional coverage and high sound attenuation are desired.

3-16 B.A.S.S. Trap.™ Bass-absorbing soffit system to control low-frequency reverberation in small rooms.

VARIABLE ACOUSTICS

Basic principles of acoustics apply to any room in which sound is generated. As noted earlier, however, a room's purpose has a great deal to do with how those principles are applied. If a studio is used for rock music and speech, the acoustics must absorb more individual sound than they diffuse so that there is minimal interference from other sounds or from reverberation, or from both. On the other hand, studios used for classical music and some types of jazz should diffuse more sound than they absorb to maintain a balanced, blended, open sound imaging.

Theoretically, this means that a studio designed to fulfill one sonic purpose is inappropriate for another. In fact, to be more functional, many studios are designed with variable acoustics. They have adjustable panels, louvers, or partitions and portable baffles, or *gobos*, to alter diffusion, absorption, and reverb time (see 3-17 through 3-19).

3-17 Example of acoustic treatment along walls.
(a) Scoring stage with alternating doors and slats that can be opened or closed to vary acoustics.
(b) Detail of doors and slats shown in (a).

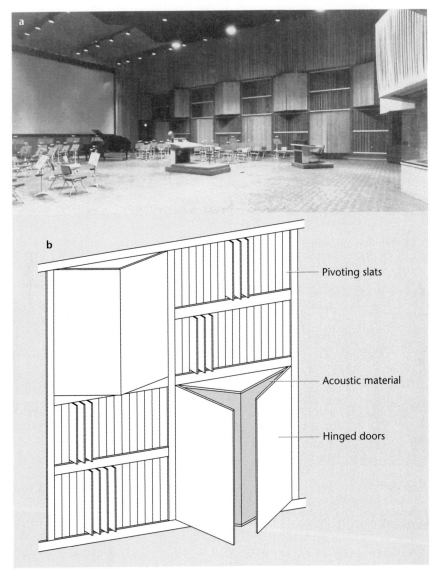

Pivoting slats

Acoustic material

Hinged doors

Reflective surface

Absorbent surface

3-18 Sketch of a variable, adjustable, acoustic partition used in one recording studio.
This partition is connected to the ceiling and can be raised or lowered to vary studio
reverberation time between two and four seconds. Reverb times can be further refined
by turning the bottom panels to their reflective or absorbent surfaces. For example, in
recording an orchestra, the panels over the strings and woodwinds could be turned to
their reflective side to enhance these weaker-sounding instruments, and the panels over
the brass and timpany could be turned to their absorptive side to help control these
stronger-sounding instruments.

3-19 Movable baffles or gobos showing absorbent and reflective surfaces

CONTROL ROOM DESIGN

Purpose also affects design differences between studios and control rooms. Studios are designed for sound that is appropriate for microphone pickup, whereas control rooms are designed for listening to loudspeakers. Therefore, to accurately assess the reproduced sound in a control room, the main challenge is to reduce the number of unwanted reflections at the monitoring location(s) so it is a relatively reflection-free zone (see 3-20 and Chapter 9).

ERGONOMICS

Sound control is obviously the most important factor in studio and control room design, but human needs should not be ignored. Production is

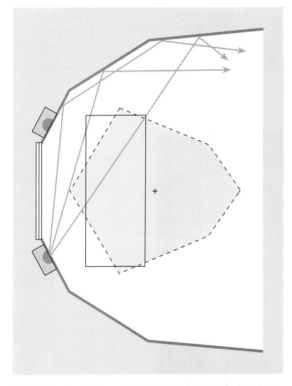

3-20 The shaded area in this control room design is a reflection-free zone

stressful enough without personnel having to endure poor lighting, hard-to-reach equipment, uncomfortable chairs, and so on. Designing an engineering system with the human element in mind is called *ergonomics*. A few of the more important ergonomic considerations are as follows.

■ **Lighting** Studio and control room atmosphere are important in a production session, and lighting—adjustable lighting in particular—goes a long way in enhancing the environment. One audio operator may like a lot of light in the control room, whereas another audio operator may prefer it dim. Talent, particularly musicians, may like low-key lighting, assorted colored lights, or flashing lights, depending on the emotional bolstering they may need.

■ **Size** Ample room for personnel and equipment should prevent a cramped, claustrophobic feeling.

■ **Position of equipment** Equipment and remote controls should be situated within arm's reach, and easy access should be provided to equipment that cannot be so positioned. The operator should be located at the point where hearing and seeing are optimal.

■ **Furniture** Furniture should be functional, rather than just decorative, and reflect as little sound as possible. Chairs should be comfortable and move around easily on wheels without squeaking. A chair should be adjustable, have a five-star base so it does not tip, and flexibility when sliding or leaning. Most people prefer armrests and even flexible headrests. A chair should provide back support, particularly in the lower back, and not cut off blood circulation in the legs. Cushions should be firm and shaped to support the body. If different contoured chairs are needed to accommodate the regular control room personnel, it is worth the investment.

■ **Floor covering** Rugs should be static-free and permit anything on wheels to move about easily.

Production is very demanding, mentally and physically. *Make it as easy on yourself as possible.*

▶ Acoustics is the study of auditory sensation in the ear and the sound waves that cause that sensation. The term is also used to describe the physical behavior of sound waves in a room. Psychoacoustics deals with the perception of auditory sensations in the ear and our subjective response to the behavior of sound waves in a room.

▶ The acoustic "life cycle" of a sound emitted in a room can be divided into three phases: direct sound, early sound, and reverberant sound.

▶ Direct sound reaches the listener first, before it interacts with any other surface. The same sound reaching the listener a short time later, after it reflects from various surfaces, is indirect sound.

▶ Indirect sound is divided into early reflections (early sound) and reverberant sound (reverb).

▶ Early reflections reach the listener within about 40 to 50 milliseconds of the direct sound.

▶ If sound is delayed by 35 ms or more, the listener perceives echo, a distinct repeat of the direct sound.

▶ Reverberant sound is the result of the early reflections becoming smaller and smaller and the time between them decreasing until they combine, making the reflections indistinguishable.

▶ Reverberation is densely spaced reflections created by random, multiple, blended reflections of a sound.

▶ Reverberation time, or decay time, is the time it takes a sound to decrease 60 dB-SPL, after its steady-state sound level has stopped, usually from average loudness—85 dB-SPL—to, generally, inaudible—25 dB-SPL.

▶ Direct sound provides information about a sound's origin, its size, and its tonal quality. Early reflections add loudness and fullness to the initial sound and help create our subjective impression of room size. Reverberation fills out the loudness and body of a sound and contains most of its tonal energy.

▶ If similar sounds reach the ear within roughly 20 milliseconds of one another, the reflected sounds and the direct sound are usually perceived as coming from the same direction, even if the immediate repetitions coming from another direction are louder. This is known as the precedence, or Haas, effect.

▶ No one sound room is acoustically suitable for all types of sound. Therefore it is important to match studio acoustics to sonic material.

▶ Rooms with reverberation times of one second or more are considered to be "live." Rooms with reverberation times of one-half second or less are considered to be "dry" or "dead."

▶ Five factors influence how sound behaves in an acoustic environment: (1) isolation of sound outside and inside the room, (2) dimensions of the room, (3) shape of the room, (4) absorption, reflection, diffraction, and diffusion in the room, and (5) acoustical features of the room.

▶ Noise is any unwanted sound (except distortion) in the audio system, the studio, the environment, and so on.

▶ The noise criteria (NC) system rates the level of ambient, or background, noise.

▶ Sound isolation in a room is measured in two ways: by determining the loudest outside sound level against the minimum acceptable NC level inside the room, and by determining the loudest sound level inside the studio against a maximum acceptable noise floor outside the room.

▶ Transmission loss (TL) is the amount of sound reduction provided by a barrier—a wall, floor, or ceiling. This value is given a measurement called sound transmission class (STC).

▶ The dimensions of a sound room—height, width, and length—should not equal or be exact multiples of one another or else certain frequencies will be reinforced, thereby coloring the sound.

▶ Resonance, another important factor in studio design, results when a vibrating body with the same natural frequencies as another body causes that body to vibrate sympathetically, thereby increasing the amplitude of both of them at those frequencies if the variables are in acoustical phase.

▶ The shape of a studio is significant for good noise reduction and sound dispersion.

- When sound hits a surface, one or a combination of reactions occur: It is absorbed, reflected, partially absorbed and reflected, diffracted, or diffused.

- The amount of indirect sound energy absorbed is given an acoustical rating called a sound absorption coefficient, also known as a noise reduction coefficient (NRC).

- Three classifications of acoustic absorbers are porous absorbers, diaphragmatic absorbers, and Helmholtz absorbers or resonators.

- When sound reaches a surface, in addition to being partially absorbed and reflected, it diffracts—spreads or bends around the surface.

- Diffusion is the uniform distribution of sound energy in a room so that its intensity throughout the room is approximately equal.

- To be more acoustically functional, many studios are designed with variable acoustics—movable panels, louvers, walls, and gobos to alter reverberation time.

- Studios are designed for sound that is appropriate for microphone pickup. Control rooms are designed for listening through loudspeakers.

- To accurately assess the reproduced sound in a control room, the main challenge is to reduce the number of unwanted reflections at the monitoring location(s) so it is a relatively reflection-free zone.

- Ergonomics addresses the design of an engineering system with human comfort and convenience in mind.

PART Two

Equipment

4

Microphones

The analogy can be made that microphones are to audio production what colors are to painting. The more colors and hues available to a painter, the greater the possibilities for coloration in a visual canvas. In recording sound, the more models of microphones there are, the greater variety of tones in the sonic "palette" and, hence, the greater the possibilities for coloration in designing an aural canvas.

When choosing a ***microphone,*** or *mic,* there are three basic features to consider: operating principles, directional characteristic(s), and sound response. Appearance may be a fourth feature to consider if the mic is on-camera.

OPERATING PRINCIPLES

The microphone is a ***transducer***—it converts one form of energy into another. The mic converts acoustic energy into electric energy. (Another example of a transducer is the loudspeaker, which converts electric energy into acoustic energy.) The electric energy flows through a circuit as voltage. You will recall that resistance to the flow of voltage is called *impedance.*

Impedance

Low-impedance microphones have two advantages over high-impedance mics: (1) They are much less susceptible to hum and electrical noise, such as static from motors and fluorescent lights, and (2) they can be connected to long cables without increasing the noise. For these reasons professionals use low-impedance mics (and equipment). Professional mics usually range in impedance from 150 to 600 ohms.

Transducing Elements

The device that does the transducing in a microphone is mounted in the mic head and is called the *element*. Each type of microphone get its name from the element it uses. The elements in professional microphones operate on one of two physical principles: *magnetic induction* and *variable capacitance*.

Magnetic Induction

Magnetic induction uses a fixed magnet and a movable diaphragm to which a small, lightweight coil is attached. The coil is placed in the magnetic field and moves when sound hits the diaphragm. When the coil moves, voltage is generated. Such mics are called ***moving-coil microphones*** (see Figure 4-1).

Another type of mic employing magnetic induction is the ***ribbon microphone*** (see 4-2). Instead of a moving coil, it uses a metal ribbon attached to a fixed magnet. As the ribbon vibrates from the pressure of the sound waves, voltage is generated.

Microphones using the magnetic induction principle are commonly known as ***dynamic microphones***.

Variable Capacitance

Microphones operating on the variable capacitance principle transduce energy using voltage (electrostatic) variations, instead of magnetic (electromagnetic) variations, and are called ***capacitor microphones***. They are also referred to, incorrectly, as *condenser microphones,* which is a holdover from the past.

The element consists of two parallel plates separated by a small space (see 4-3). The front plate is a thin metalized plastic diaphragm, the only moving part in the mic head, and the back plate is fixed. Together these plates or electrodes form a *capacitor*—a device that is capable of holding an electric charge. As acoustic energy moves the diaphragm back and forth in relation to the fixed back plate, the capacitance change causes a voltage change, varying the signal. The signal output, however, is delicate and has a very high impedance

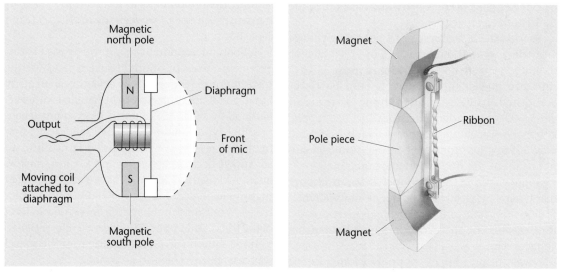

4-1 The element of a moving-coil microphone   **4-2** The element of a ribbon microphone

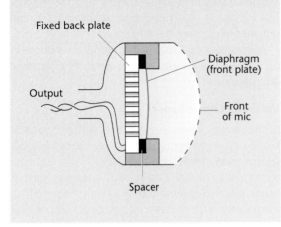

4-3 Cross-section of the element of a capacitor microphone

requiring a preamplifier (mounted near the mic capsule) to bring it to useable proportions.

Most preamps in capacitor microphones use a transistor circuit which, generally, produces a clean sound. Over the past several years, a growing number of capacitor mics using a tube circuit in the preamp have become available. The popularity of these *tube microphones* is due to the particular sonic characteristic they give to sound, which many perceive as being more present and livelier than the transistorized capacitors.

Because the capacitor requires polarizing voltage and the preamplifier requires power voltage to operate, capacitor microphones must have a separate power supply either from batteries contained inside the microphone or from an external, or so-called phantom, power supply. External power eliminates the need for batteries and may be supplied from the console, studio microphone input circuits, or portable units.

Some capacitor microphones have an electret diaphragm. An electret is a material (high-polymer plastic film) that can hold a charge permanently, thus eliminating the need for external polarizing voltage. Because a small battery is all that is required to power the preamp, *electret microphones* can be made more compact, which facilitated the design of lavalier and mini-mics.

GENERAL TRANSDUCER PERFORMANCE CHARACTERISTICS

Each type of microphone is unique. It is not a matter of one microphone being better than another, but that one microphone may be more suitable for a particular application than another.

Moving-coil microphones are well suited for high sound-pressure-level applications. They are quite rugged, generate low self-noise, and tend to be less susceptible to humidity and wide temperature variations. They are usually less expensive than the other professional types and come in a wide variety of makes and models.

Generally (there are a number of exceptions), the frequency response of moving-coil mics is transparent; they tend not to color sound. They are slower to respond to *transients*—sounds that begin with a quick attack, such as a drum hit or breaking glass, and then quickly decay.

The more mass to the parts inside a microphone that must be moved by sound pressure, the less accurate the reproduction, especially in relation to transients. The element in a moving-coil mic has considerably more mass than the element in a capacitor microphone, which has the lowest mass of the three types of professional mics. This makes the capacitor mic best suited to handle transient sounds. The ribbon mic has relatively low mass; its transient response is between the moving-coil and capacitor mics.

Ribbon microphones are not widely used today, except in music recording, concerts, and for the speaking voice. They are more expensive than many moving-coil mics and have to be handled with care, particularly when it comes to loud sound levels.

Older-type ribbon mics have mediocre high-frequency response, which can be turned into an advantage because it gives sound a warm, mellow quality. Modern ribbon mics have a more extended high-frequency response. Generally, ribbon mics have low self-noise but have the lowest output level of the three major types. This means a poorer signal-to-noise ratio if the mic is too far from the sound source or if the cable run is too long.

Capacitor microphones are high-performance instruments. They reproduce clear, detailed sound and are the choice among professional-quality microphones when it is necessary to record sounds rich in harmonics and overtones. Capacitor mics have high sensitivity, which makes them the preferred microphone for distant miking. They also have the highest output level, which gives them a wide signal-to-noise ratio. These advantages come at a cost, for capacitors are generally the most expensive type of microphone.

DIRECTIONAL CHARACTERISTICS

A fundamental rule of good microphone technique is that a sound source should be **on-mic**—at an optimal distance from the microphone and directly in its pickup pattern. **Pickup pattern**, also known as **polar response pattern**, refers to the direction(s) from which a mic hears sound. Depending on the design, a microphone is sensitive to sound from (1) all around—**omnidirectional**, (2) its front and rear—**bidirectional**, or (3) its front only—**unidirectional** (see 4-4). Omnidirectional mics are also called **nondirectional**, and unidirectional mics are also called **directional**. **Cardioid** is still another commonly used name for a unidirectional microphone, because its pickup pattern is heart-shaped. Five unidirectional patterns are in common use: *subcardioid* (also referred to as *wide-angle cardioid*), *cardioid, supercardioid, hypercardioid,* and *ultracardioid* (see 4-5).

Figures 4-4 and 4-5 show basic microphone directionalities. The precise pattern varies from mic

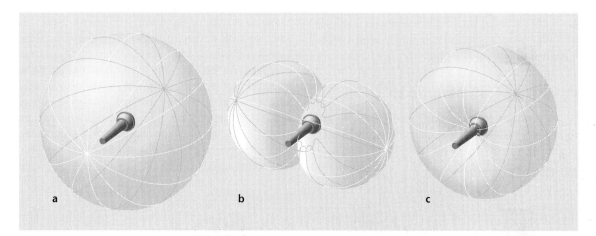

4-4 Pickup patterns: (a) Omnidirectional, (b) bidirectional, and (c) unidirectional or cardioid.

4-5 Pickup patterns: (a) Supercardioid and (b) hypercardioid.

to mic. To get a better idea of a microphone's pickup pattern, study its polar response diagram (see the following section).

A microphone's unidirectionality is facilitated by ports at the side and/or rear of the mic that cancel sound coming from unwanted directions. (For this reason you should not cover the ports with a hand or with tape.) In relation to the ports, directional mics are referred to as *single-entry-port micro-phones*, or *single-D™*—having ports in the capsule; or *multiple-entry-port microphones*, also called *variable-D™*—having ports in the capsule and along the handle. In a single-entry directional mic, the rear-entrance ports handle all frequencies (see 4-6). A multiple-entry directional mic has several ports, each tuned to a different band of frequencies (see 4-7). The ports closer to the diaphragm process the higher frequencies; the ports farther from the diaphragm process the lower frequencies. Ports also influence a microphone's proximity effect, which is discussed later in this chapter.

Polar Response Diagrams

A microphone's directional sensitivity, or polar response pattern, can be displayed on a graph. The graph consists of concentric circles, usually divided into segments of 30 degrees, to depict directionality. Reading inward, each circle represents a decrease in sound level of 5 dB.

The omnidirectional polar pattern shows that sound is picked up almost uniformly from all directions (see 4-8). The bidirectional polar pattern indicates maximum sensitivity to sound coming from the front and rear, from 0 and 180 degrees (see 4-8). Sensitivity decreases when moving toward the sides. Sound that reaches the mic at roughly 45, 135, 225, and 315 degrees is reduced by 5 dB; for sound at 90 and 270 degrees, there is minimal response.

The cardioid polar pattern illustrates response from, in effect, one direction with least sensitivity at 180 degrees off-axis (see 4-8). The subcardioid has a less directional pickup pattern than does the cardioid. Supercardioid and hypercardioid polar patterns are more directional than the cardioid, with least off-axis sensitivity at the sides (see 4-8). Between the two, the hypercardioid mic has a far narrower on-axis pickup than the supercardioid mic and it is least sensitive about 120 degrees off-axis, whereas the supercardioid is least sensitive about 150 degrees off-axis. Although the hyper-cardioid mic is more directional and has better side rejection than the supercardioid mic, its rear

4-6 Microphone with single-entry ports.
Note: This figure and Figure 4-7 indicate the position of the ports on these microphones. The actual ports are concealed by the mic grille.

4-7 Microphone with multiple-entry ports

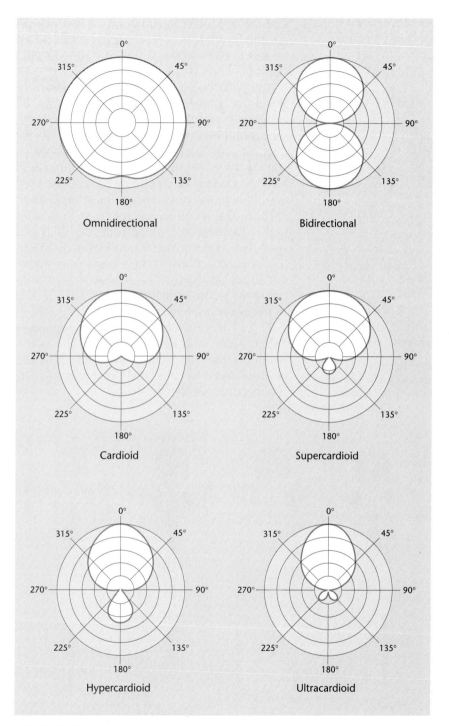

4-8 Principal microphone polar patterns

4-9 Polar pattern indicating differences in directionality at certain frequencies. Notice that the lower the frequency, the less directional the pickup.

rejection is poorer. The ultracardioid microphone has the most focused on-axis pickup and widest off-axis sound rejection of the conventional mics (see 4-8).

The polar diagrams shown here are ideals. In actual use, a microphone's directional sensitivity varies with frequency. Because treble waves are shorter and bass waves are longer, the higher the frequency, the more directional a mic becomes, and the lower the frequency, the less directional a mic becomes, regardless of pickup pattern. Even omnidirectional microphones positioned at an angle to the sound source tend not to pick up higher frequencies coming from the sides and rear, thus making the nondirectional pattern somewhat directional at these frequencies. Figure 4-9 shows an example of a polar pattern indicating the relationship of on- and off-axis pickup to frequency response.

Pickup pattern also affects a microphone's "reach"—the working distance from the microphone that the sound source can be and still remain on mic—and its relative effectiveness in rejecting reverberation (see 4-10).

4-10 Differences in relative working distances among omnidirectional, cardioid, supercardioid, and hypercardioid microphones and their relative effectiveness in rejecting reverberation

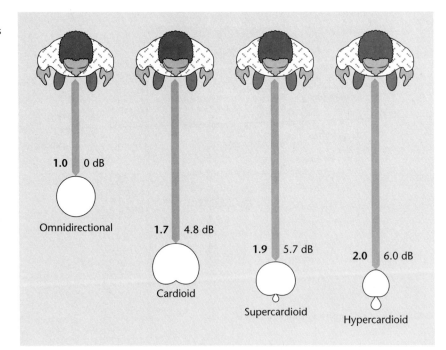

Variable Directional Microphones

Microphones with a single directional response have one fixed diaphragm (or ribbon). By using more than one diaphragm, and a switch to select or proportion between them, a microphone can be made *multidirectional* (or *polydirectional*), providing two or more pickup patterns (see 4-11).

System Microphones

One multidirectional mic of sorts is the *system microphone*, which uses interchangeable heads or capsules, each with a particular pickup pattern, that can be mounted onto a common base (see 4-12). Because these systems are capacitors, the power supply and preamplifier are in the base, and the mic capsule simply screws into the base. Any number of directional capsules—omnidirectional and bidirectional, cardioid, supercardioid, and hypercardioid—can be interchanged on a single base.

Stereophonic Microphones

Stereophonic microphones are actually microphone capsules with electronically separate systems housed in a single case (see 4-13). The stereo mic has two distinct elements. The lower element is

Pickup patterns

Roll-off

Pad

Bidirectional capsule

Hypercardioid capsule

Omnidirectional capsule

Cardioid capsule

Shotgun capsule

Powering module with preamplifier and bass roll-off

4-11 Multidirectional microphone with five pickup patterns: Omnidirectional, wide-angle cardioid, cardioid, hypercardioid, and bidirectional. This microphone also has a three-position bass roll-off (flat, 200 Hz, and 500 Hz) and a three-position pad (0, –10 dB, and –20 dB). See "Overload" and "Proximity Effect" later in this chapter.

4-12 Example of a system microphone

usually stationary, and the upper one rotates 180 to 360 degrees, depending on the mic, to facilitate several different stereo pickup patterns. Some stereo mics can be remote-controlled.

Middle-Side Microphones

Most *middle-side (M-S) microphones* consist of two mic capsules housed in a single casing. One capsule is designated as the midposition microphone aimed at the sound source to pick up mostly direct sound; it is usually cardioid. The other capsule is designated as the side-position microphone. It is usually bidirectional with each lobe oriented 90 degrees laterally to the sides of the sound source to pick up mostly ambient sound. The outputs of the cardioid and bidirectional capsules are combined into a sum-and-difference matrix through a controller (see 4-14 through 4-16).

4-13 Stereo microphone with two separate capsules. The upper capsule in this model can be turned 360 degrees, in 10-degree increments. The pattern selectors on the microphone body can be set to *R* for remote control of the capsule configurations.

4-14 Middle-side microphone and matrix controller

4-15 Another matrix controller, front and rear views

$$M + S = L$$
$$M - S = R$$

(M + S) = L and (M – S) = R
In summed mono [L + R], the S component disappears
(M + S) + (M – S) = 2M

4-16 M-S pickup pattern and capsule configuration

The systems in Figures 4-14 and 4-15 make it possible to remote-control the ratio of mid-to-side information to adjust the stereo width of the direct-to-ambient sound. It is also possible to adjust for only left-to-right stereo imaging (also called *XY stereo*). In addition to its advantage in recording stereo sound, the M-S microphone's matrixed stereo signal is completely *mono-compatible*, that is, the stereo signal can be played in mono with no distortion of sonic imaging.

Microphones for Three-Dimensional Imaging

Another concept in variable directional microphony is picking up sound from three, instead of two, dimensions. The addition of vertical or height information to the sonic depth and breadth reproduced by conventional stereo and M-S mics make sound quite spacious and localization very realistic. Two of the most familiar microphones used for recording three-dimensional sound are the binaural microphone head and the SoundField microphone system.

Binaural Microphone Head   The *binaural microphone head* (also known as *artificial head* or *dummy head* [Kunstkopf] *stereo*) consists of an artificial head with an omnidirectional capacitor microphone or microphone capsule placed in each ear canal (see 4-17). Some binaural microphone systems go so far as to construct the head and upper torso based on statistical averaging and variations

4-17 Binaural microphone head. Two omnidirectional capacitor microphones mounted in "ear" cavities reproduce binaural sound. To hear the binaural effect, it is necessary to listen with headphones.

in real humans. Some even feature felt hair and shoulder padding to simulate the characteristics of hair and clothing.

Binaural hearing   To better understand the interest in binaural recording, it may be useful to say a word about *binaural hearing*. There are three essential differences between the way a stereo microphone "hears" sound and the way humans hear it. (1) With stereo there is no solid object, like the head, between the microphones. When sound comes from the left, particularly midrange and high frequencies, it reaches the left ear sooner and with greater intensity than it does the right ear. The sound reaching the right ear is delayed, creating a sound shadow. The converse is also true: Sound coming from the right is louder in the right ear and casts a sound shadow in the left ear. The listener's shoulders and torso also reflect sound. (2) With the low frequencies, this shadow is largely neutralized

because the longer wavelengths diffract around the head. Therefore, we depend upon their time of arrival—relative phases—for perceptual clues. (3) The human ear itself also modifies sound. The folds in the outer ear (pinna) resonate and reflect sounds into the ear canal, causing phase cancellations at certain frequencies. Combined, these *head-related transfer functions (HRTF)* are the theoretical bases for binaural head construction and recording.

Binaural sound is an extraordinary listening experience; the sound is enveloping. It has not been commercially viable, however, because it is possible to get its full effect only through stereo headphones; loudspeakers will not do.

SoundField Microphone System The *SoundField microphone system* is a method of recording an entire soundfield as defined by absolute sound pressure and three pressure gradients of the left/right, front/rear, and up/down directions. The microphone contains four mic capsules mounted as a tetrahedron. The outputs of these elements are fed into a matrix network that can be controlled to reproduce a number of different pickups (see 4-18 to 4-20).

The four outputs, known as the A-format, feed the high left-front-right-rear and the low right-front-left-rear information into the matrix network. After the signals are mixed, they are

4-18 SoundField microphone (a) and controller with its functions (b)

a

b

1 **Gain switch** 0 to +30 dB microphone input gain in 10 dB steps.

2 **Gain Trim** Fine gain adjustment –10 dB to +10 dB.

3 **Capsule Solo** Each of the four microphone capsules may be soloed as required. This facility is useful for checking the continuity of connection cables.

4 **Test Osc** This button controls the test oscillator, which is used to calibrate the console input gain to match the output of the SoundField system. It provides a continuous 0 dBm 1 kHz signal at the B-format W output, while X, Y, and Z have differing pulse rates to assist in track identification.

5 **End** Switches the SoundField MKV for endfire use.

6 **Invert** Reverses left/right to allow for the microphone being suspended in an inverted position.

7 **Dub** Allows B-format replay to include the gain trim for remixing purposes.

8 **Tape** Allows the B-format replay signal to be monitored.

9 **SoundField In** Routes the signal through the SoundField control section.

10 **B-format** Connects the SoundField controls into the B-format signal path.

11 **SoundField Azimuth** Allows a simulated pair of microphones to be electronically rotated through a full 360 degrees.

12 **SoundField Elevation** This control simulates tilting the stereo microphone system up or down by ±45 degrees.

13 **SoundField Dominance** This control provides an effect similar to moving the microphone forward or backward.

14 **LCD Bargraph Display** Shows B-format signals X, Y, Z, and W or stereo L/R and M/S, depending on the stereo monitor switch

15 **Stereo Monitor** Switches bargraph display from B-format to stereo (left/right, M/S)

16 **Polar Patterns** Continuous adjustment from omnidirectional through subcardioid, cardioid, hypercardioid to figure of eight.

17 **Angle** Continuous adjustment of the angle between left and right in a stereo pair from 0 degrees to 180 degrees.

18 **Headphones** Controls signal level to the stereo output headphone socket.

19 **High Pass Filter** Used to remove rumble and wind noise from the stereo output signals.

20 **M/S** Switches the microphone outputs into M and S mode. Left = middle. Right = side.

4-19 Four rotating capsules of the SoundField microphone

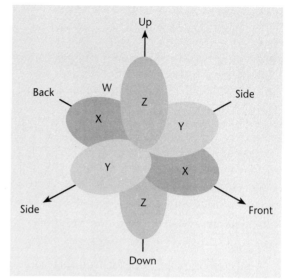

4-20 Pickup arrays of the SoundField microphone system

W = omnidirectional pattern:
left front + right rear + right front + left rear

X = bidirectional pattern:
(front-to-back) LF + RF – (LR + RR)

Y = bidirectional pattern:
(side-to-side) LF + LR – (RF + RR)

Z = bidirectional pattern:
(up and down) LF + RR – (RF + LR)

converted into the so-called B-format, from which they can be manipulated to produce a variety of pickups. The operation is complex but worth the trouble. The resulting three-dimensional sound is quite spacious, and localization is realistic, although it does not provide quite the enveloping sonic experience of binaural sound. But, then, SoundField recordings do not require headphones for listening. They do, however, require four loudspeakers, two in front of the listener and two to the rear. SoundField has given this surround-sound experience the name *ambisonic*.

AGM MR-1 Another relatively recent entry into the three-dimension microphone field is the AGM MR-1, developed by Digital Arts. The AGM MR-1 is a complete recording chain that can deliver 20-bit digital, discrete four-channel sound. It consists of the four-capsule microphone, analog-to-digital conversion, matrix processing of the four microphone channel signals, stereo reduction-encoding, and a variety of two-channel formats at the output.

SOUND RESPONSE

Clearly, a microphone's operating principal and directional characteristics affect its sound response. The particular sonic features that are important to consider when selecting a microphone include its frequency response, overload limit, maximum sound-pressure level, sensitivity, self-noise, signal-to-noise ratio, proximity effect, and humbucking.

Frequency Response

A microphone's *frequency response* is the range of frequencies that it reproduces at an equal level, within a margin of ±3 dB. That is, at a given level, a frequency will not be more or less than 3 dB off.

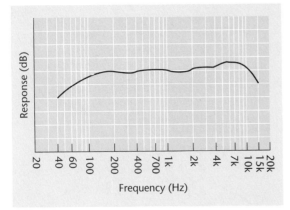

4-21 Response curve of the Electro-Voice 635A mic

A microphone's *response curve* is displayed in a graph with the vertical line indicating amplitude (dB) and the horizontal line indicating frequency (Hz) (see 4-21). It shows the tonal balance of the microphone pickup at a designated distance from a sound source, usually 2 or 3 feet.

When the curve is reasonably straight or *flat*, response has little coloration—all frequencies are reproduced at the same level. But flat is not necessarily desirable. In looking at a response curve, it is important to know for what purpose the microphone was developed and what your sonic requirements are. In Figure 4-21, for example, the bass begins "rolling off" at 150 Hz, there is a boost in the high frequencies between 4,000 and 10,000 Hz, and the high end rolls off beyond 10,000 Hz. Clearly, this particular microphone would be unsuitable for instruments such as the bass drum, organ, and cello, because it is not very sensitive to the lower frequencies from these instruments. It is also unsuitable for high-frequency sound sources, such as the female singing voice, cymbals, and the piccolo, because it is not that sensitive to their higher frequencies or harmonics. The microphone was not designed for these purposes, however; it was designed for the speaking voice. And for this purpose, it is excellent. Reproduction of frequencies through the critical upper bass and midrange is flat, the slight boost in the upper midrange adds presence, and the roll-offs in the bass and treble are beyond the ranges of most speaking voices.

Overload Limit

All microphones will distort if sound levels are too high—a condition identified as *overload*—but some mics handle it better than others. Moving-coil and capacitor microphones are not as vulnerable as ribbon mics to distortion caused by excessive loudness. Moving-coil mics can take high levels of loudness without internal damage. Using a ribbon mic when there may be overload risks damaging the element.

In the capacitor system, although loud sound-pressure levels may not create distortion at the diaphragm, the output signal may be great enough to overload the electronics in the mic. To prevent this, many capacitors contain a built-in pad. Switching the pad into the mic system eliminates overload distortion of the mic's preamp, thereby reducing the output signal several decibels (see 4-11).

Maximum Sound-Pressure Level

Maximum sound-pressure level is the level at which a microphone's output signal begins to distort, that is, produces a 3 percent *total harmonic distortion (THD)*. **Harmonic distortion** occurs when an audio system introduces harmonics into the output signal that were not present originally. If a microphone has a maximum sound-pressure level of 120 dB-SPL, it means that the mic will audibly distort when the level of a sound source reaches 120 dB-SPL. A maximum SPL of 120 dB is good, 135 dB is very good, and 150 dB is excellent.

Sensitivity

Sensitivity measures the voltage that a microphone produces (dBV), which indicates a microphone's efficiency. Sensitivity does not affect a mic's sound quality, but it can affect a recording's overall sound quality. The lower the output voltage, the less sensitive the microphone. The less sensitive the microphone, the closer it has to be to a sound source to maintain a decent signal-to-noise ratio, or the more level gain the signal needs at the console, or both. Increased level often means increased noise. Ribbon and small moving-coil mics have low sensitivity (–85 dBV); larger moving-coil mics have medium sensitivity (–75 dBV); capacitor mics have high sensitivity (–65 dBV).

Self-noise

Self-noise is the electrical noise, or hiss, a microphone (or any electronic device) produces. Self-noise measurement is in dB-SPL, A-weighted. A fair self-noise rating is around 40 dB-SPL; a good rating is around 30 dB-SPL; an excellent rating is 20 dB-SPL or less.

Signal-to-Noise Ratio

Signal-to-noise ratio (S/N) is the difference between the signal and the noise levels in an electronic component and is measured in decibels.* In relation to microphones, S/N is the difference between sound-pressure level and self-noise. For example, if the microphone's maximum SPL is 94 dB and the self-noise is 30 dB-SPL, the signal-to-noise ratio is 64 dB. The higher the S/N, the more noise-free the signal. An S/N of 64 dB is fair, 74 dB is good, and 84 dB and higher is excellent.

Proximity Effect

When most bidirectional and unidirectional microphones are placed close to a sound source, bass frequencies increase in level relative to midrange and treble frequencies. This response is known as *proximity effect* or *bass tip-up* (see 4-22).

---

*Signal-to-noise (S/N) is the ratio of audio signal compared with the level of noise measured at some point in an audio system. In audio equipment S/N is expressed as the ratio of the weighted noise floor compared with a standard reference level. For example, an analog tape recorder's signal-to-noise ratio may be given as the ratio of noise present when compared with a reference level of a 1-kHz tone recorded at the tape's optimum recording level.

Signal-to-noise ratios for various audio components give an indication of their ability to reproduce a sound cleanly and are expressed in negative numbers. Professional-quality analog tape recorders may have an S/N ratio of about –65 dB. Digital audio recorders have an S/N ratio of about –95 dB and better. Hence, the S/N of a digital audio recorder is considerably better than that of an analog tape recorder.

4-22 Proximity effect. (a) A typical cardioid moving-coil mic and (b) a cardioid capacitor mic.

Proximity effect is most pronounced in pressure-gradient (ribbon) microphones—mics in which both sides of the diaphragm are exposed to incident sound. Response is generated by the pressure differential, or gradient, between the sound that reaches the front of the diaphragm relative to the sound that reaches the rear of the diaphragm. As mic-to-source distance decreases, acoustic pressure on the diaphragm increases. Because pressure is greater at lower frequencies and the path between the front and rear of the diaphragm is short, bass response rises.

Response of directional microphones is, in part, pressure-gradient and, therefore, also susceptible to proximity effect, but not to the extent of ribbon mics. Omnidirectional microphones are not subject to proximity effect.

Proximity effect can be a blessing or a curse, depending on the situation. For example, in close-miking a bass drum, cello, or thin-sounding voice, proximity effect can add power or solidity to the

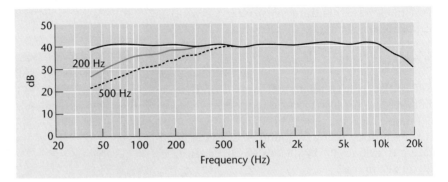

sound source. Where a singer with a deep bass voice works close to the mic, proximity effect can increase boominess, masking middle and high frequencies.

To neutralize unwanted proximity effect (rumble, or 60-cycle hum), most microphones susceptible to the effect include the feature, called *bass roll-off*, of a limited in-mic equalizer (see 4-11). When turned on, the roll-off attenuates bass frequencies several decibels from a certain point and below, depending on the microphone, thereby canceling or reducing any proximity effect (see 4-23).

Because bass roll-off has so many advantages, it has become a common feature even on microphones that have little or no proximity effect. In some models bass roll-off has been extended to include several different frequency settings at which attenuation can occur, or different levels of attenuation at the same roll-off frequency (see 4-24).

Another way to reduce proximity effect is to use a directional microphone with multiple-entry ports, because these mics have some distance between the rear-entry low-frequency ports and the sound source. At close mic-to-source distances, however, most multiple-entry-port microphones have some proximity effect.

To avoid proximity effect at close working distances down to a few inches, directional microphones have been designed that are frequency

Brilliance control

a

b

4-24 (a) Five-position roll-off control and (b) its effect on bass response. S = speech, M (not shown) = music. This particular microphone also has a brilliance control. The response curve (b) shows the curve when the high-frequency boost is switched into the pickup.

independent. Such mics use two transducers, one to process high frequencies, the other to process low frequencies. This *two-way system* design also produces a more linear response at the sides of the microphone.

Humbucking

Humbucking is not so much a response characteristic as it is a feature built into many microphones. Hum is an ever-present concern in audio, in general, and in microphone pickup, in particular. To minimize this problem, microphones are designed with a **humbuck circuit**—a circuit that reduces hum by several decibels. It is built into the microphone system and requires no special operation to activate it. The amount of hum reduction varies with the microphone.

SPECIAL-PURPOSE MICROPHONES

In addition to a microphone's operating principle, directional characteristic(s), and sound, certain mics have also been designed to meet specific production needs.

a

4-25 (a) Lavalier microphone
(b) Directional lavalier. Hypercardioid mic with windscreen, clip, and battery power module.

Lavalier Microphones

The first TV microphone created primarily for looks was the small and unobtrusive **lavalier microphone** (see 4-25a), although, by today's standards it was not so small and unobtrusive. The microphone was hung around the neck, hence the name (*lavaliere* is French for pendant). Today these mics are, indeed, quite small and are also known as *miniature microphones,* or **mini-mics.** They are attached to a tie or the front of a dress in the sternum area, or to a lapel.

Lavaliers designed for use under the chin have two things in common: (1) Most are omnidirectional, although directional lavaliers are available and used under certain conditions (see 4-25b and Chapter 13), and (2) most have a built-in high-frequency boost. The omnidirectional pickup is necessary because, with the mic being mounted under the chin, a speaker does not talk directly into the mic but across it. A directional response would not pick up much room presence and would sound too dead. In addition, as a speaker talks, high frequencies, which are directional, travel straight ahead. The chin cuts off many of the less directional high frequencies with longer wavelengths that otherwise would reach the mic. The built-in high-frequency boost compensates for this loss. If you hold in front of your mouth a lavalier that was designed for use under the chin, its response will be overly bright and hissy. Their sensitivity to breathing and popping sounds also makes lavaliers unsuitable for use in front of the mouth; they have no pop filter, although windscreens come with many models (see "Windscreens and Pop Filters" later in this chapter).

Lavaliers are either moving-coil or electret capacitors, which are the most common by far. Sonically, lavaliers are either *proximity oriented*—they add presence to close speech while reducing background sound—or *transparent*—their sound blends more naturally with the overall sound, which means that they pick up more ambience.

Shotgun Microphones

Television created the need for a good-looking on-camera microphone, but the need for an off-camera mic first became apparent in sound motion pictures. The problem was to record performers' voices without a microphone being visible. Directors had many ingenious ways to hide a mic on the set; they used flowerpots, vases, lamps, clothing, and virtually anything else that could conceal a microphone. These attempts only made more obvious the need for a microphone capable of picking up sound from a distance.

The solution was the **shotgun microphone** (see 4-43, right). The basic principle of all shotgun mics is that they attenuate sound from all directions except a narrow angle at the front. This creates the perception that they have greater reach. Actually, most microphones have extended reach. Omnidirectional, bidirectional, and cardioid mics, however, pick up a diffused sound that includes the target sound and the acoustics interacting with it. Because the shotgun mic is supercardioid, hypercardioid, or ultracardioid, it can discriminate against unwanted ambience and lock in on the main sound source to varying degrees.

Compared with an omnidirectional microphone, mic-to-source distances can be 1.7 times greater with a cardioid, 1.9 times greater with a supercardioid, and 2.0 times greater with a hypercardioid and not affect on-mic presence (see 4-10). Some shotguns are better than others, so be careful when you choose one, especially for use in mediocre acoustic environments. The main consideration should be how well it discriminates sound, front-to-back, in a given situation. Also consider that many models of shotgun mics sacrifice quality for greater reach. The shotgun becomes less directional at lower frequencies, as do all directional mics, because of the inability to deal well with wavelengths that are longer than the length of its tube, called the *interference tube*. Interference tubes come in various lengths from 6 inches to 3 feet and longer. The longer the interference tube, the more highly directional the microphone. If the tube of a shotgun mic is 3 feet long, it will maintain directionality for frequencies of 300 Hz and higher—that is, wavelengths of approximately 3 feet and less. For 300 Hz and lower, the mic becomes less and less directional, canceling fewer and fewer of the lower frequencies. Many shotgun mics do have bass roll-off, however.

Parabolic Microphone System

Another microphone that is used for long-distance pickup, mainly outdoors at sporting events, film and video shoots, and in gathering naturalistic recordings of animals in the wild, is the **parabolic microphone system**. It consists of either an omni- or a unidirectional microphone facing inward and attached to a parabolic reflector (see 4-26). More than canceling unwanted sound, the parabolic dish,

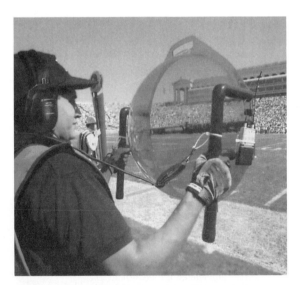

4-26 Parabolic microphone system. This particular system is using a wireless lavalier microphone with the transmitter attached to the parabolic reflector.

a

b

4-27 (a) **Headset microphone system with omnidirectional mic.** (b) Small headset microphone system with cardioid mic for vocalists, singing instrumentalists, and radio talk-show hosts. Headset microphone systems can be wired or wireless.

which is concave, concentrates the sound waves from the sound source and directs them to the microphone. As with the shotgun mic, the parabolic mic is most effective within the middle- and high-frequency ranges; its sound quality is not suitable for critical recording.

Headset Microphones

Sports broadcasting has led to the development of the *headset microphone*—a mic mounted on headphones. The microphone is usually a moving coil, with built-in pop filter, because of its ability to handle the loud sound-pressure levels that sports announcers project (see 4-27). It may be unidirectional to keep background sound to a minimum or omnidirectional for added event ambience.

The headphones can carry two separate signals; the program feeds through one headphone and the director's cues through the other. The headset system frees the announcer's hands and frontal working space. Another benefit is that the announcer's distance from the mic does not change once the headset is in place.

Contact Microphones

Not to quibble about semantics, but some lavaliers can be classified as *contact microphones* and vice versa. Essentially, the difference between the two is that a contact mic has been specially designed to attach to a vibrating surface (see 4-28). Exact positioning of a contact mic is important if the sound is to be free of standing-wave resonance from the vibrating surface, especially if it is a musical instrument.

4-28 Contact microphone, also called *acoustic pickup mic.* This particular contact mic is designed for attachment to string instruments. Its size is 1 by .50 by .03 inch.

Contact mics come in various impedances, so it is important to select low-impedance models for professional recording. They also come in different designs. One electret capacitor version is enclosed in a strip and is flexible enough to adhere to almost any surface, flat or curved.

Boundary Microphones

When a conventional microphone is placed on or near a surface, such as a wall, floor, or ceiling, reflections from that surface can create a *comb-filter effect*—additive and subtractive phase shifts that give sound an unnatural, hollow coloration (see 4-29). But it has been determined that if the mic is less than .04 inch from the surface, comb filtering will not start below 20 kHz, out of the range of most human hearing. The *boundary microphone* does just that, by positioning its mic capsule very close to a primary reflecting surface (see 4-30).

Most boundary microphones are mounted on rectangular, square, or circular plates. If the mic is positioned centrally in a symmetrical plate, acoustical phasing from the edges of the plate may interfere with pickup and cause irregularities in response. Therefore, most boundary mics are positioned off-center (see 4-31).

Boundary microphones have an electret transducer. Their pickup pattern is hemispheric, directional, or stereophonic (see 4-32). Their response is open and, in suitable acoustics, spacious.

4-30 Boundary microphone

4-31 Triangular-shaped plate with boundary microphone inset off-center to reduce linear distortion

a

b

4-32 Boundary mics with (a) hypercardioid pickup and (b) stereo pickup. The stereo boundary mic is a PZM™ (pressure zone microphone) called SASS™, for Stereo Ambient Sampling System. It uses two boundary-mounted mics, with a foam barrier between them, to make each mic directional.

Level (dB)

20   50 100 200   500 1k   2k   5k 10k 20k
Frequency (Hz)

4-29 Comb-filter effect. Delayed reflected sound combined with direct sound can create this effect.

Noise-Canceling Microphones

A *noise-canceling microphone* is designed for use close to the mouth and has excellent rejection of ambient sound (see 4-33). Due to its noise-canceling design, the mic must be used close to the sound source. If it is held even a short distance away, the performer's words may be clipped, and the pickup may be off-mic entirely.

Wireless Microphone System

The *wireless microphone system*, also called a *radio mic, FM mic, transmitter mic,* or *cordless mic,* consists of three components (four, if you count the mic): transmitter, antenna, and receiver. A standard mic is used with the system in one of two ways: lavalier and handheld. The lavalier system uses a standard

lavalier microphone connected to a battery-powered bodypack transmitter. The handheld wireless mic operates with the transmitter and microphone in a single housing (see 4-34 and 4-35). An alternative to the single-housed handheld mic is the plug-on transmitter, a wireless transmitter with an XLR connector that plugs into the end of the microphone (the XLR connector is discussed later in this chapter) (see 4-36; see also 14-9).

4-33 Noise-canceling microphone. This particular mic is hypercardioid and designed to be handheld in venues with very loud background noise. It is equipped with a built-in pop filter, shock mount, and convenient on/off switch. Handling noise is insignificant.

4-34 Wireless microphone system. (a) Bodypack transmitter. (b) Handheld transmitter with microphone. (c) Diversity receiver. This particular system is UHF and operates in the 766 to 805 megahertz (MHz) range.

4-35 Multichannel wireless microphone system with (a) tuneable multichannel bodypack transmitter and (b) multichannel receiver system

4-36 Plug-on wireless microphone transmitter

The microphone's signal is sent to the transmitter, which relays the signal to a receiver anywhere from several feet to many yards away, depending on the system's power. Wireless microphone systems operate in the VHF (very high frequency) and UHF (ultrahigh frequency) bands. Each system has its own FCC-approved* frequency, because its transmissions may be subject to interference from other transmitting devices in a given vicinity.

Before using a wireless microphone system, there are a few operational and performance criteria to consider: frequency assignment, diversity reception, companding, transmission range, antenna, sound quality, and power supply.

■ **Frequency assignment and usage** Wireless microphone systems transmit on frequencies in or near the VHF and UHF television bands. In the VHF band, the frequencies are between 169 and 216 *megahertz (MHz)*; in the UHF band, they are between 470 and 806 MHz.

The differences between VHF and UHF wireless mic systems relate to bandwidth, flexibility, power, multipath reception, and cost. Because the VHF

bandwidth is far narrower than UHF, there is much less room for available frequencies. This limits both its use in large metropolitan areas, where the spectrum is crowded with VHF TV stations, and its flexibility in operating a number of wireless systems simultaneously. Although maximum operating power for UHF wireless systems is greater than for VHF wireless systems, the shorter UHF wavelengths can exhibit more instances of multipath reception. *Multipath* is a physical phenomenon in which more than one *radio frequency (RF)* signal from the same source arrives at the receiver's front end, creating phase mismatching (see 4-37). The area affected by each null in UHF systems is small, compared with larger, albeit fewer, nulls in VHF wireless microphone reception. As for cost, VHF wireless systems are usually far less expensive.

■ **Diversity reception** A wireless microphone system transmits radio waves from a transmitter, through the air, to a receiver. Because VHF and UHF waves are transmitted "line-of-sight," there is the danger that the radio waves will encounter obstructions on the way to the receiver, resulting in a *dropout* or null in the transmission. The technique used to deal with dropout is known as *diversity reception* (see 4-38).

---

*FCC stands for Federal Communications Commission.

4-37 Multipath dropout

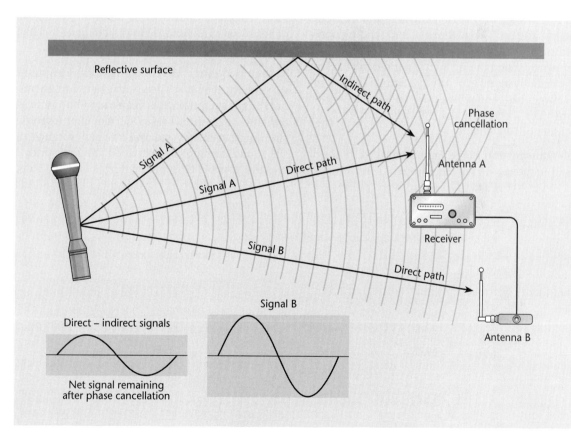

4-38 Diversity reception

When a wireless system is used in a controlled environment where dropout is not a problem, a **nondiversity receiver** can be used. Nondiversity systems have a single antenna mounted on the receiver. They are, generally, less expensive than diversity systems.

To check if a wireless system is operating correctly, walk the signal path from the transmitter to the receiver, speaking into the microphone as you go. If you hear dropout, buzzing, or any other sonic anomaly, note the location(s). Check the system to make sure it is working properly. If it is, change microphone, transmitter, or receiver placement if you can and retest the signal transmission.

■ **Companding** To increase dynamic range and reduce noise inherent in the transmission system, wireless mics use *companding*—a contraction of the terms *compressing* and *expanding*. The audio signal is compressed during transmission and expanded at the receiver. Even though companding sometimes creates noise, coloration, and the audible pumping sound caused by compander mistracking, particularly in less expensive systems, a wireless mic is always better off with a compander than without one (see 4-39; see also "Double-Ended Noise Reduction" in Chapter 8).

■ **Transmission range** Because the FCC limits the output power of wireless systems, transmission range for high-quality systems is virtually the same: about 250 feet effective in mediocre conditions up to 1,500 feet effective in optimum conditions. In most controlled studio environments, 150 feet is sufficient operating distance.

Inexpensive wireless systems are 100-feet effective. In optimum conditions their range can increase up to 250 feet.

■ **Antenna** The antenna should be fully extended and several feet away from any obstruction, including the floor. Avoid taping "whip" antennas (and bodypacks) to the skin as perspiration inhibits signal transmission.

Both the transmitter and receiver antennas should be oriented either vertically or horizontally. If they are not, it hinders reception. Because performers usually stand, the most common antenna position is vertical. Some antennas are more effective than others. To improve system performance, a dipole antenna could increase signal pickup by 3 dB or more.

■ **Sound quality** Wireless microphone systems vary widely in quality. Clearly, in professional audio only a system with wide frequency response and dynamic range should be used. Frequency response should be well beyond the frequency range of the sound being recorded. Good wireless systems are now capable of dynamic ranges up to 115 dB.

4-39 Compander action

A system with poorer dynamic range needs more compression at the transmitter and more expansion at the receiver, creating an annoying squeezed sound that results from companding loud levels.

■ **Power supply** Battery lifetime varies widely. The better systems operate up to eight continuous hours on a new 9-volt alkaline battery, even longer with a lithium battery. Some newer systems use AA batteries. Regardless of the voltage a system requires, install only the highest-quality batteries, preferably lithium for added lifetime. To reduce power-supply problems, batteries should be replaced before they have a chance to run down. It simply is not worth holding up a production session to save a few cents, trying to squeeze maximum life out of a battery.

Other Types of Special-Purpose Microphones

Two other types of special-purpose microphones warrant mention: the *ice zone mic* and the *underwater mic* or *hydrophone*. The ice zone mic is designed for implantation in an ice rink to pick up the skating sounds. The underwater mic is designed for recording sound underwater. Incidentally, if the need arises to record underwater sound, in the absence of the specially designed underwater mic, wrapping a small, conventional mic in a thin,

airtight plastic cover will work. Of course, the connector cannot be submerged.

MICROPHONE ACCESSORIES

Microphones come with various accessories. The most common are windscreens and pop filters, shock mounts, cables, connectors, and stands and special-purpose mounts.

Windscreens and Pop Filters

Windscreens and *pop filters* are designed to deal with distortion that results from blowing sounds caused by breathing and wind, the sudden attack of transients, the hiss of sibilant consonants like *s* and *ch,* and the popping plosives of consonants like *p* and *b.* (In practice, the terms *windscreen* and *pop filter* are used interchangeably, but for clarity of discussion here, they have been given slightly different applications.)

Windscreens are mounted externally and reduce the distortion from blowing and popping but rarely eliminate it from particularly strong sounds (see 4-40). A pop filter is built-in and is most effective against blowing sounds and popping (see 4-41). It allows very close microphone placement to a sound source with little fear of this type of distortion.

4-40 Windscreens. (a) Various windscreens for conventional microphones. (b) So-called zeppelin windscreen enclosure for shotgun microphones. (c) Stocking (fabric) windscreen designed for use between the sound source and the microphone. This particular model has two layers of mesh material attached to a lightweight wooden ring. (d) Windscreen cover or windjammer to cover zeppelin-type windscreens.

d

Pop filter

4-41 Built-in pop filter

4-42 The effect on frequency response of various windscreens

Foam windscreen

Zeppelin windscreen

Zeppelin plus windjammer windscreens

Frequency (Hz)

Windscreens also slightly affect response, somewhat reducing the crispness of high frequencies (see 4-42). Many directional microphones with pop filters are designed with a high-frequency boost to compensate for reduced treble response.

Pop filters are mainly found in moving-coil, newer ribbon, and some capacitor microphones, particularly directional models, because they are more susceptible than omnidirectional mics to breath and popping noise, due to their partial pressure-gradient response. (They are also more likely to be used closer to a sound source than are other microphone types.) An omnidirectional mic is about 15 dB less sensitive to wind noise and popping than a unidirectional microphone of similar size.

Another way to minimize distortion from sibilance, transients, blowing sounds, and popping is through microphone placement. (These techniques are discussed throughout Part Four, "Production.")

Shock Mounts

Because solid objects are excellent sound conductors, the danger always exists that unwanted vibrations will travel through the mic stand to the microphone. To reduce noises induced by vibration, place the microphone in a *shock mount*—a device that suspends and mechanically isolates the mic from the stand (see 4-43). Some microphones are designed with a shock absorber built-in.

Cables

A microphone cable is either a *balanced line*—consisting of two conductors and a shield—or an *unbalanced line*—consisting of one conductor with the shield serving as the second conductor. A quad mic cable uses a special four-conductor design for added noise control. As with all professional equipment, the balanced line is preferred because it is less susceptible to electrical noise.

4-43 Various types of shock mounts. See also 4-11 and 4-18 (a).

When winding mic cable, do not wind it around your arm, and be careful not to make the angle of the wrap too severe or it can damage the internal wires. It is also a good idea to secure the cable with a clasp specially made for this purpose to prevent it from getting tangled (see 4-44).

Connectors

Most professional mics and mic cables use a three-pin plug that terminates the two conductors and shield of the balanced line. These plugs are generally called *XLR connectors* (*X* is the ground or shield, *L* is the lead wire, and *R* is the return wire). Usually, the female plug on the microphone cable connects to the mic, and the three-prong male plug connects to the console (see 4-45).

It is always important to make sure that the three pins in all microphones being used in a session are connected in exactly the same way. If pin 1 is ground, pin 2 is positive, and pin 3 is negative, all mics must be wired in the same configuration,

4-44 Microphone cable. To keep cable intact and avoid damage to internal wires and connections, wind and secure cable when not in use.

Safety lock

Female wall receptacle microphone input to console

Safety lock

Male microphone connector

Female microphone connector on cable

Male microphone connector on cable

4-45 Microphone connectors. The female cable connector plugs into the male microphone connector; the male cable connector plugs into the female wall receptacle, which is connected to the microphone input on the console.

4-46 Gooseneck stand

otherwise the mismatched microphones will be electrically out of polarity and reduce or null the audio level.

Microphone Mounts

Just as there are many types of microphones to meet a variety of needs, many types of microphone mounts are available for just about every possible application. Commonly used microphone mounts are displayed in Figures 4-46 to 4-55.

4-47 Desk stands

4-48 Floor stands

Mic tilt and turn grip

Crank to adjust
boom length

Pan-and-tilt lock screws

Operator's
seat

Control to raise or
lower platform

Steering
control

Platform for
mounting TV
monitor

Brake and
gear change

4-49 Parambulator (mobile) boom. On most booms
used in TV and film, the boom arm extends and retracts,
and moves up and down and side to side. Some booms
rotate 180 degrees; others rotate 300 degrees. This
particular boom rotates 360 degrees.

Microphone to
be attached here

Counterweight

Handle for moving
boom assembly

Microphone
rotation control

4-50 Tripod or "giraffe" mobile boom

4-51 Handheld "fishpole" boom

4-52 Handheld microphones. (a) Microphone with thin tube. It is easily handheld and is also shock resistant and has a pop filter. All are essential in a handheld microphone. (b) Handheld mic with a long handle for added control in broadcast applications.

a   b

Hanging shotgun mics
for hosts and guests

PZM hanging mic with
reflector for audience pickup

4-53 Hanging microphones

Lavalier mic taped to
rear view mirror

4-54 Hidden microphone

a

b

c

d

e

4-55 Special microphone mounts. (a) Redundant mono microphone
mount, (b) stereo microphone mount, (c) remote panner boom mount
and control module, (d) hypercardioid microphone and mount for
attachment to drums (e) hypercardioid microphone and mount for
attachment to brass and woodwind instruments.

MICROPHONE CARE

Poor care of audio equipment adversely affects sound quality—this cannot be stressed enough. Moisture from high humidity or breath can greatly shorten a microphone's life. When moisture is a problem, a windscreen will help protect the microphone element.

Dirt, oil from hands, cigarette smoke, and jarring also reduce microphone efficiency. Microphones should be cleaned and serviced regularly and kept in carrying cases when not in use. Microphones left on stands between sessions should be covered with a cloth or plastic bag but not so tightly as to create a condensation problem. The working environment should be temperature- and humidity-controlled, kept clean, and vacuumed regularly.

MAIN POINTS

▶ Microphones are transducers that convert acoustic energy into electric energy. The device that does the transducing is called the element.

▶ The elements in professional microphones operate on one of two physical principles: magnetic induction and variable capacitance.

▶ The two types of professional microphones that use magnetic induction are the moving-coil and the ribbon mics. The type of professional microphone using variable capacitance is the capacitor mic.

▶ Capacitor microphones require a power supply in order to operate.

▶ Each type of microphone is unique. One type is not so much better than another as it is more suitable for a particular application.

▶ Microphones pick up sound from essentially three directions: all around—omnidirectional; front and rear—bidirectional; and front—unidirectional.

▶ The unidirectional, or cardioid, design has even narrower pickup patterns. They are supercardioid, hypercardioid, and ultracardioid.

▶ A microphone's directional sensitivity, or polar response pattern, can be displayed graphically.

▶ A microphone's unidirectionality is facilitated by ports at the side and/or rear of the mic that cancel sound coming from unwanted directions.

▶ The sensitivity of a unidirectional microphone varies with frequency: The higher the frequency, the more directional the pickup; the lower the frequency, the less directional the pickup.

▶ Multidirectional microphones have more than one pickup pattern.

▶ Other types of microphones with variable pickup patterns are the system, stereo, and middle-side (M-S) mics.

▶ Among the microphones used for three-dimensional sound imaging are the binaural microphone head and the SoundField microphone system.

▶ A microphone's frequency response is the range of frequencies that it produces at an equal level, within a margin of ±3 dB, and can be displayed in a response curve graph.

▶ All microphones will distort if sound levels are too high—a condition identified as overload.

▶ Maximum sound-pressure level is the level at which a microphone's output signal begins to distort.

▶ To help protect against loudness distortion, many capacitor microphones are equipped with a pad to reduce overloading the mic's electronics.

▶ Sensitivity measures the voltage that a microphone produces (dBV), which is an indication of a microphone's efficiency.

▶ Self-noise is the electrical noise, or hiss, a microphone (or any electronic device) produces.

- Signal-to-noise ratio (S/N) is the difference between the signal and the noise levels in an electronic component; it is measured in decibels.

- Bidirectional and most unidirectional microphones are susceptible to proximity effect—an increase in the level of bass frequencies relative to midrange and treble frequencies—when they are placed close to a sound source. To neutralize proximity effect, most of these microphones are equipped with bass roll-off.

- To minimize the problem of hum, some microphones are designed with a humbuck circuit.

- Microphones have been developed for special purposes: the lavalier and other mini-mics to be unobtrusive; the shotgun and parabolic mics for long-distance pickup; the headset mic to keep background sound to a minimum by maintaining a close mic-to-source distance; the contact mic to be attached to a vibrating surface; the boundary mic for use on a boundary (a hard, reflective surface) so that the reflected sounds arrive at the microphone in phase; the noise-canceling mic for use close to the mouth with excellent rejection of ambient sound; the wireless mic for greater mobility and flexibility in plotting sound pickup, regardless of camera-to-source distance; the ice zone mic to pick up ice-skating sounds; and the underwater mic, or hydrophone, to record underwater sounds.

- When using a wireless microphone system, consider: frequency assignment and usage; transmission dropout; companding; transmission range; sound quality; and the power supply.

- Windscreens and pop filters are used to reduce distortion caused by wind and transients. An external shock mount, or a built-in shock absorber, is used to prevent unwanted vibrations from reaching the microphone element.

- Standard accessories used for professional microphones include the following: twin conductor cables called balanced lines, XLR connectors, and various types of stands and clips for microphone mounting.

Mixers and Consoles

Mixers and *consoles* take input signals and amplify, balance, process, combine, and route them to broadcast or recording. The difference between them is that a mixer is small, quite portable, and performs limited processing functions. The console (or *board*) is larger, substantially so in many models, and performs numerous processing functions. In many systems these functions are computer-assisted. Their purposes and differences notwithstanding, mixers and consoles, from the most basic to the most elaborate, have at least three basic control sections: input, output, and monitor.

Signals from a sound source, such as the microphone, feed to the *input section,* which routes them to the output section. The *output section* routes the signals to a recorder or broadcast, or both. The *monitor section* enables the signals to be heard. Consoles designed for multichannel recording usually have a master section as well. In those consoles the output section routes signals to a multitrack recorder, and the *master section* routes the final mix to its recording destination.

MIXERS

The mixer is used when audio need not be or cannot be complex, as is often the case with news, local sports broadcasts, and disc-jockey programs done on location (see Chapter 13). The most basic type of mixer is the *microphone mixer,* which, as the name suggests, handles only mics. The format can be

Slate pushbotton inserts 1-second low-frequency tone

On/off switch

Power-on LED

VU meter

Low-cut filter

Battery check pushbutton

Channel 1 gain control pulls out to activiate 1kHz tone oscillator for level setting

VU lamp push-button to illuminate VU meter

Peak LED flashes at onset of limiting

Headphones jack

Headphones volume control

a

Slate microphone pushbutton

Master gain control

Output limiter

XLR connector

DC external power jack

Mic/line switch with phantom power provided in mic position

b

5-1 Microphone mixer. (a) Front, (b) side.

mono or stereo, and operation can be manual or automatic (see Figures 5-1 and 13-21a). Signal flow is straightforward: Microphones are plugged into the mixer's input channels, where their signals are preamplified and their loudness levels are controlled by *faders*—usually rotary. A fader is also known as an *attenuator, gain* or *volume control,* or *pot* (short for *potentiometer,* a device that regulates the level coming from a preamp). The signals are then routed to the output channel, where they are combined, and a *master fader* controls their overall loudness level before they are sent on to broadcast or recording. In the field, monitoring is usually done through headphones. In the studio, it is done through loudspeakers.

Mic mixers may have other features, such as pan control, high-pass filter, oscillator, and slate microphone. These features are discussed in "Production Consoles" later in this chapter.

Somewhat more elaborate portable mixers are designed to accommodate a limited number of additional inputs, such as recorders and CD players. They may include a few functions found in larger consoles as well, such as equalization, sends and returns, and patching (see 5-2). These functions are also covered in the "Production Consoles" section.

5-2 Portable mixer designed for recording or broadcasting in the field and its functions

Input channels

Channel power

Input gain control

Microphone phantom power (12-48 v)

Phase

High-pass filter 1: 100 Hz

Pads: –20, –40

High-pass filter 2: 70 Hz

Equalizers: high-frequency and low-frequency shelving at 10 kHz and 100 Hz; mid-frequency selectable from 500 to 5 kHz

Auxiliary (pre/post selectable)

Mix bus

Pre-fade listen (PFL)

Pan pot

Peak-level detector

Limiter

Channel fader

Output module

Meters

Power on/off

Master phantom (PH) on

Light on

Battery test

Communications: on/off for talkback to headphones

Mute for oscillator and slate

Meter section

Headphones section

Monitors section

PB: playback (tape return)

Private line: slate microphone

Oscillator frequency select: 100 Hz/1kHz/10 kHz

Slate on

Remote roll to control recorder

ANALOG CONSOLES

The basic differences between analog and digital consoles are in the way signals are processed and routed. These differences are more easily explained once the operational features of analog consoles are understood.

Analog consoles come in a variety of designs to meet particular needs. Basically, they fall into two categories: on-air broadcast consoles and production consoles.

On-Air Broadcast Consoles

Operationally, on-air consoles are simple compared with production consoles. They are mainly used to handle, in addition to the announcer(s), program materials that have already been produced, such as commercials, news reports, and music CDs.

In on-air broadcast consoles, the input, output, and monitor sections are separate (see 5-3). Consoles with separate input, output, and monitor functions are called **split-section consoles**. This is not the case with most production consoles today, in which the input and output, and some monitor, functions are located in a single module and are known as **in-line consoles** (see "The In-line Production Console" later in this chapter).

The input section takes an incoming signal from a microphone, CD player, recorder, or phone-in caller. Each input channel is configured for either low-level sound sources, such as microphones, or high-level sound sources, such as CD players and recorders. The loudness level of each channel is regulated by a fader (sliding or rotary). A delegation switch on each channel can either turn off the signal flow or route it to one of three destinations: *program,* which sends it to the console's output; *monitor,* so it can be heard; or to a second monitor system, called *audition* or *cue*. The audition or cue system makes it possible to listen to program material while preparing it for broadcast, without it being heard on the air.

At the output section, there is a master fader to adjust the level of the combined signals feeding to

Mic/line inputs with A/B dual sourcing

Program/audition/telephone assign switches

Cue

Microphone on/off switches

Telephone bus for mix-minus feed to telephone caller

VU meters for program

VU meters for audition

Output section (under meter bridge)

Tape remote controls

Stereo preselector

Built-in cue speaker

Talkback

Cue speaker level control

Studio speaker level control

Headphone level control

Control room speaker level control (with automatic mute when control room mic is on)

Machine start/stop

Timer (with start/stop, reset, and hold buttons)

Source select (selects PGM, AUD, or TEL feed to control room)

Headphone jack

5-3 Example of an on-air radio broadcast console

it from the input channels. This is the last stop at the console before the output signal is sent on its way to transmission.

For stereo, faders usually carry a tandem left/right stereo signal. Some on-air consoles may use stereo pairs, with the left fader carrying the left signal and the right fader carrying the right signal.

Input and output signals are heard as sound through monitor loudspeakers. As they pass through the console, however, they are in the form of voltage. Therefore meters are necessary to measure the voltages in the input and output sections, respectively. By using the fader, these voltages can be kept within acceptable limits. The meter most commonly used with on-air broadcast consoles in the United States is the **volume unit (VU) meter** (see 5-5). The **peak program meter** is generally preferred in Europe, although it is found on production consoles here and abroad. Both meters are discussed in the following section.

Production Consoles

Production consoles are used to produce a variety of demanding and complex audio applications for commercials, film and television sound tracks, sports, news, and music recordings. They therefore require a greater number of inputs, outputs, and signal-processing functions than on-air consoles. They are also designed to meet specific needs.

For example, production is so complex these days that consoles with computer-assisted automation are a necessity, allowing operational data from production sessions to be stored on and retrieved from disk. In film and television, automated panning facilitates the matching of movement to picture. A production console for music recording often requires a number of *submixers* to *premix* groups of similar voicings, such as strings, backup vocals, and the components of a drum set. Network TV news is essentially a one-mic show, yet with recorded music intros, reports from the field, and interviews, it can easily occupy a 36-input production console. Specialized, compact consoles, with integrated machine interface systems, are required

to handle the unique requirements of automated dialogue replacement and Foley recording (see 16-1). Consoles used for the final postproduction mix in film and television must have the output capabilities to handle surround sound.

Input/Output Specifications

Two indications of a console's layout and capabilities are provided by the number of input sources it can accommodate at the same time and the number of discrete output signals it can send to its master bus. A *bus* is a common junction of several different signal paths. Consoles are often specified by their number of inputs and master outputs. For example, an 8 × 2 (or 8-in, 2-out), has 8 inputs and 2 master (stereo) outputs; a 32 × 4 (or 32-in, 4-out) has 32 inputs and 4 master outputs. Clearly, an 8 × 2 console is limited to a few sound sources, but as an on-air console for a stereo radio station, it may be adequate. By contrast, a 32 × 4 console is designed for large-scale recording assignments that require many inputs and stereo and surround-sound output capability. Indeed, consoles are available with an even greater number of inputs—several dozen and counting, in fact. Production consoles may have a three-number specification, such as 36 × 8 × 2, which indicates 36 inputs, 8 submasters (for submixes, in which selected channels are combined before they reach the master outputs, where all signals are combined), and 2 master outputs.

The In-line Production Console

Most analog production consoles today are *in-line consoles*. The in-line console locates in each channel an **input/output (I/O) module**. The I/O module houses the input, output, and some monitor controls, bringing these functions vertically "in a line."

This makes it possible to route a signal from, say, the input of channel 4 either directly to track 4 of the multitrack recorder or to the master output(s). The signal is then routed back into channel 4's input section, passing through the equalizer (and/or other effects modules) for delegation either to the monitor section or the master section. Such signal routing is possible during both recording and **mixdown**.

There are two parallel signal paths, *channel* and *monitor*. In the I/O section, equalization (EQ) and other signal processing can be delegated to the monitor system for auditioning without affecting the signal being sent to the multitrack recorder, or the signal can be sent to the multitrack recorder, or both.

Although features of the in-line console differ from model to model, the basic design includes four main sections—input/output, master, monitor, and communications. As noted, in the I/O design each section may include some functions belonging to another section.

In most in-line consoles, the following are typical functions of each section. Some consoles may have fewer or more features and, depending on the design and manufacturer, the sequence of functions, signal flow, and terminology may differ.

Input/Output Section During recording, the input/output section processes and delegates incoming signals and sends them out to the multitrack recorder. During mixdown, the I/O section processes signals from the multitrack recorder and routes them to the master section, where they are combined into one (mono), two (stereo), or more channels and sent to the master recorder.

▓ **Microphone-line input selector** You will recall that two types of signal sources feed to input modules: low-level, such as microphones, and high-level, such as recorders. The *microphone-line input selector* controls which signal source enters the input section.

▓ **Microphone preamplifier** A microphone signal entering the console is weak. It requires a *mic preamplifier* to increase its voltage to a usable level.

A word about mic preamps in consoles: Whether the audio is analog or digital, each component in the signal flow must be as noise-free as possible. Given the low-noise, high-sensitivity, and high-SPL specifications of many of today's microphones, it is important that the mic preamp be capable of handling a mic's output without strain. If the console's preamp is inadequate to meet this

requirement, it is necessary to use an outboard mic preamp.

Inboard or outboard, a good-quality mic preamp must deliver high gain, low circuit noise (hiss), high *common-mode rejection ratio* (CMRR)—the ratio between signal gain and interference rejection—freedom from radio frequency (RF) interference, and freedom from ground-induced buzz or hum.

Console preamps may be located many feet from a microphone. The more circuitry a signal navigates, the greater the chance for increased noise. By placing a mic preamp in close proximity to a microphone and amplifying mic signals to the required levels before they travel very far, noise can be dramatically reduced. A mic preamp should be stable at very low and/or very high gain settings. The CMRR values should be at least 80 to 90 dB at crucial frequencies, such as 50 to 60 Hz and above 10 kHz—not just at 1 kHz, the only frequency at which many mic preamps are measured.

▓ **Phantom power** Just ahead of the microphone preamplifier is the *phantom power* supply (48 volts DC). When activated it provides voltage for capacitor mics, thus eliminating the need to bother with batteries.

▓ **Trim** The *trim* is a gain control that changes the input sensitivities to accommodate the nominal input levels of various input sources. Trim boosts the lower-level sources to usable proportions or prevents overload distortion in higher-level sources.

▓ **Overload indicator** The *overload indicator* is a light-emitting diode (LED) that flashes when the input signal is approaching or has reached overload and is clipping. In some consoles the LED flashes green when the input signal is peaking in the safe range and red either to indicate clipping or to warn of impending clipping.

▓ **Pad** A *pad* reduces the power of a signal. On a console it is placed ahead of the mic input transformer to prevent overload distortion of the transformer and mic preamplifier. It is used when the trim, by itself, cannot prevent overload in the mic signal. The pad should not be used otherwise, because it reduces signal-to-noise ratio.

■ **Channel assignment switches** This is a group of switches on each I/O channel used to direct the signal from that channel to one or more outputs; or several input signals can be combined and sent to one output. For example, assume that three different microphone signals are routed separately to channels 1, 3, and 11 and the recordist wishes to direct them all to channel 18. By pressing assignment switch 18 on channels 1, 3, and 11, the signals are fed to channel 18's active combining network and then on to recorder track 18.

An *active combining network (ACN)* is an *amplifier* at which the outputs of two or more signal paths are mixed together to feed a single track of a recorder. To save space the assignment switches are sometimes paired, either alternately—1 and 3, 2 and 4, and so on—or adjacently—1 and 2, 3 and 4, et cetera. Usually, odd numbers are left channels and even numbers are right channels.

■ **Direct switch** The *direct switch* connects the channel signal to the channel output, directing the signal to its own track on the recorder, bypassing the channel ACN and thus reducing noise. For example, using the direct switch routes the signal on, say, channel 1 to recorder track 1, the signal on channel 2 to recorder track 2, and so on.

■ **Equalizer and filter** An *equalizer* is an electronic device that alters a signal's frequency response by boosting or attenuating the level of selected portions of the audio spectrum. A *filter* alters frequency response by attenuating frequencies above, below, or at a preset point. Most production consoles have separate equalizer controls for selected frequencies grouped in the low, middle, and high ranges. Filters are usually high-pass and low-pass. (Equalizers and filters are discussed in Chapter 8.)

■ **Channel/monitor control** The *channel/monitor control* switches the equalizer, and usually selected *send* functions (see below), into either the channel signal path to the recorder, or the monitor signal path to the monitor section.

■ **Polarity reversal** *Polarity* (sometimes referred to as *phase*) *reversal* is a control that inverts the polarity of an input signal 180 degrees. It is used to reverse the polarity of miswired equipment, usually microphones, whose signal is out of phase with the signal from a piece of similar equipment correctly wired. Sometimes, intentional polarity reversal is helpful in canceling leakage from adjacent microphones or in creating *electroacoustic* special effects by mixing together out-of-phase signals from mics picking up the same sound source.

■ **Pan pot** A *pan pot* (short for *panoramic potentiometer*) is a control that can shift the proportion of sound to any point from left to right between two output buses and, hence, between the two loudspeakers necessary for reproducing a stereo image (see 5-4). To hear a signal louder in one bus than in the other, the pan pot varies the relative levels being fed to each of the two output buses. This facilitates the positioning of a sound source at a particular place in the stereo field between two loudspeakers.

■ **Cue send (pre- or postfader)** *Cue send* is a monitor function that routes a signal from an input channel to the headphone, or foldback, system. *Foldback* is a monitor system that feeds signals from the console to the headphones. The cue send level control adjusts the loudness of the headphone

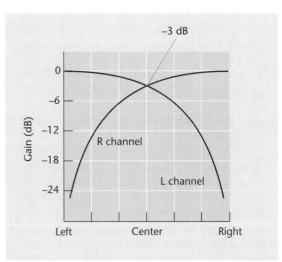

5-4 Effect of a typical pan pot

signal before it is sent to the master cue sends in the monitor module.

At the input channel, the cue send can be assigned before or after the channel fader. Before, or *prefader cue,* means that the level control at cue send is the only one affecting the loudness of the channel's cue send. After, or *postfader cue,* means that the main channel fader also affects the cue send level. In the postfader mode, the level control at cue send is still operational but the main channel fader overrides it.

Pre- and postfader controls add flexibility in providing a suitable headphone mix to performers. In music recording, for example, if the musicians were satisfied with their headphone mix and did not want to hear channel fader adjustments being made during recording, cue send would be switched to the prefader mode. On the other hand, if the musicians did want to hear changes in level at the channel fader, cue send would be switched to the postfader mode.

▧ **Reverb (or echo) send (effects send, aux send) (pre- or postfader)** The *reverb send* control feeds the input signal to an external (outboard) reverberation system or other signal processor (see Chapter 8). Some consoles call this feature "echo send." But *echo* is a misnomer, because reverberation, not echo, is the effect usually being achieved (see Chapter 3).

After the "dry" reverb send signal reaches the reverberation system, reverb is added and it returns "wet" to the reverb return in the master section for mixing with the main output. The wet signal may also feed to a monitor return system.

Reverb send may be called *effects send* or *aux* (for auxiliary) *send* to indicate that this function can be used to send a signal to any external signal processor so long as it is wired to the console's patch bay (see "Patching" later in this chapter).

The send function also has pre- and postfader controls whereby any signal can be sent from before or after the channel fader.

▧ **Solo and prefader listen** Feeding different sounds through several channels at once can create an inconvenience if it becomes necessary to hear one of them to check something. Instead of shutting off or turning down all the channels but the one you wish to hear, you can activate the *solo* control, located in each input module, automatically cutting off all other channels feeding the monitor system; it has no effect on the output system. More than one solo can be pushed to audition several channels at once and still cut off the unwanted channels.

The solo function is usually prefader. On some consoles, therefore, it is called *prefader listen (PFL)*. In consoles with both solo and prefader listen functions, PFL is prefader and solo is postfader.

▧ **Mute (channel on/off)** The *mute* function, also called *channel on/off,* turns off the signals from the I/O channel. During mixdown when no sound is feeding through an input channel for the moment, it shuts it down or mutes it. This prevents unwanted channel noise from reaching the outputs.

▧ **Channel and monitor faders** The *channel and monitor faders* control the channel level of the signal being recorded and its monitor level, respectively. During recording, channel levels to the multitrack recorder are set for optimal signal-to-noise ratio. That is, levels are set to reach or slightly exceed 0 VU (see "Meters," next section). Level balances are made during mixdown. To enable the recordist to get a sense of what the balanced levels will sound like, the monitor faders are adjusted to taste, with no effect on the signal being recorded.

Meters

It is a paradox in sound production that the only way to determine levels in mixers and consoles (and recorders) is visually—by watching a meter that measures the electric energy passing through an input or output. Audio heard through a monitor system is acoustic. It passes through the console as voltage, however, which cannot be heard and, therefore, must be referenced in another way. Two types of meters are in general use today: the volume unit (VU) meter and the peak program meter (ppm).

VU Meter In most multichannel production consoles, there is a VU meter for each input and master channel and usually for the monitor system as well. The VU meter is a voltage meter originally designed to indicate level as it relates to the human ear's perception of loudness. Two calibrated scales are on the face of the VU meter: a percentage of modulation scale and a volume unit scale (see 5-5). A needle, the volume indicator, moves back and forth across the scales, pointing out the levels. The needle responds to the electric energy passing through the VU meter. If the energy level is excessively high, the volume indicator will *pin*—slam against the meter's extreme right-hand side. Pinning can damage the VU meter's mechanism, rendering the volume indicator's reading unreliable.

Percentage of modulation is the percentage of an applied signal in relation to the maximum signal a sound system can handle. It is a linear scale defined such that 100 percent of modulation is equal to 0 VU on the volume unit scale. Therefore 30 percent of modulation is equal to slightly less than –10 VU, 80 percent of modulation is equal to –2 VU, and so on.

Any sound below 20 percent of modulation is too quiet, or *in the mud,* and levels above 100 percent of modulation are too loud, or *in the red.* (The scale to the right of 100 percent is red.) As a guideline, the loudness should "kick" between about –5 and +1, although the dynamics of sound make such evenness difficult to accomplish, if not aesthetically undesirable. Usually, the best that can be done is to *ride the gain*—adjust the faders from time to time so that, on average, the level stays out of the mud or the red.

The operator should ride the gain with a light, fluid hand and not jerk the faders up and down or make adjustments at the slightest fall or rise in loudness. Changes in level should be smooth and imperceptible, because abrupt changes are disconcerting to the listener, unless an abrupt change is called for in, say, a transition from one shot to another.

When the VU meter is in the red, it is a warning to be cautious of loudness distortion. All modern consoles are designed with headroom so that a signal peaking a few decibels above 0 VU will not

5-5 Volume unit (VU) meter

distort. **Headroom** is the amount of level the equipment can take, above working level, before overload occurs. The problem is that although the console may have sufficient headroom, other equipment in the sound chain, such as the recorder, may not be able to handle the additional level. In digital recording there is no such thing as headroom; when you have run out of room, there is nothing left (see Chapter 7).

Because a VU meter is designed to reflect a signal's perceived loudness, it does a poor job of indicating transient peaks. To help remedy the problem, modern production consoles build in a headroom of +4 dB or more; although the signal is in the red, there is still leeway before *clipping*—distortion—occurs.

Peak Program Meter   The peak program meter (ppm) was specifically designed to indicate transient peaks (see 5- 6). As signal levels increase, there is a warning of impending overload distortion. The level indicator makes this easier to notice, because its rise time is rapid and its fallback is slow.

The ppm's scale is linear and in decibels, not volume units. The scale's divisions are 4-dB intervals, except at the extremes of the range, and zero level is 4, in the middle of the scale. Advocates of the ppm think that it gives a more accurate indication of a signal's actual level of loudness than does the VU meter. The argument is that although humans may not hear momentary peaks in loudness, the electronics do. The ppm is therefore

−12 dB −8 dB −4 dB −0 dB +4 dB +8 dB

5-6 Peak program meter with equivalent dB values. Dual-movement ppms with two indicators are for two-channel stereo applications.

better insurance against signal distortion, particularly in digital audio. Consoles are available with both the VU and peak program meters.

Bargraph Meters Whereas VU and peak program meters are mechanical, *bargraph meters* are electronic. Their rise time is quite fast because there is no mechanical inertia to overcome. This can create problems riding gain. Two popular types of bargraph meters are LED and plasma displays.

LED meters *LEDs* (light emitting diodes) are small light sources. The meters are arranged horizontally or vertically. Usually, green LEDs indicate safe levels and red ones register in the overload region. On professional equipment the LEDs are about 2 dB apart, so resolution is fair. The advantages of LED meters are that they take up little space and are easy to see. Their disadvantage is that they are not as accurate as the VU and peak program meters.

Plasma displays *Plasma displays* are columns of light that display safe levels in one color, usually green, and overload levels in red. They are more complex than LED meters and have good resolution, with an accuracy of 1 dB. Some consoles use plasma displays that are switchable to a VU or ppm response.

Master Section The master section contains the master controls for the mixing-bus outputs, reverb send and reverb return, master fader, and other functions.

■ **Buses** After a signal leaves an input/output module, it travels to its assigned *bus(es)*. In many consoles these signals may be grouped for pre-mixing at submaster buses before being finally combined at the master bus(es).

There may be any number of submaster buses, but usually there are only a few master buses, because most final output signals are mixed down to two-channel stereo or four-, five-, or six-channel surround-sound.

■ **Master fader** The *master fader* controls the signal level from the master bus to the master recorder. It is configured either as a single fader carrying a tandem left/right stereo signal or as a stereo output pair with the left fader carrying the left signal and the right fader carrying the right signal. A console may have two or four such faders or sets of faders and a mono master fader as well.

■ **Reverb (or echo) send (effects send, aux send)** The *reverb sends* from the I/O channels are first routed to the master reverb sends before output to the reverb unit or other signal processor.

■ **Reverb (or echo) return (effects return, aux return)** Signals routed to the reverb unit, or other signal processor, from the master sends are returned at the master returns and mixed with the main program signal.

■ **Level, mute, PFL, solo, and pan pot** Each master reverb send and return usually has a level control and mute switch. The master returns also usually have PFL, solo, and pan controls.

■ **Meters** Most in-line recording consoles have a VU meter (and/or peak program meter) for each master fader; a mono meter to indicate the level of a summed stereo signal; a phase meter to show the phase relationship between the left and right stereo signals; and metering to display master send and/or return levels. Some consoles also have meters for the control room monitor outputs.

Monitor Section Monitor functions, such as setting monitor level and panning for each channel, are performed by the I/O module. The monitor module, among other things, allows monitoring of the line or recorder input, selects various inputs to the control room and studio monitors, and controls their levels.

■ **Line-in/line-out switch** This switch selects all the I/O channels for either line input monitoring from the multitrack recorder or line out monitoring from console channel out. Each I/O channel has a line-in/line-out control for individual channel switching, but the monitor line-in/line-out overrides the channel control.

■ **Recorder select switches** These switches select a recorder (other than multitrack) for direct feed to the monitor system, bypassing the I/O controls. There may also be *auxiliary (aux) in* switches for direct feeds to the monitor system from other sound sources such as a CD player or cassette recorder.

■ **Send switches** These route signals from the sends to the input of the control room or studio monitors, or both.

■ **Mix switches** These select the mix input (i.e., stereo or surround-sound) for the monitor system.

■ **Speaker select switches** These select the control room or studio loudspeakers for monitoring. There is a level control for each set of loudspeakers. Some monitor sections also have a *dim* switch for the control room monitors. Instead of having to turn the monitor level down and up during control room conversation, the dim function reduces monitor level by 15 dB or more at the touch of a button.

■ **Mono switch** Directs a left + right mono signal to the control room monitors.

A monitor section may also have a pan pot, mutes for the left and right channel signals to the control room, and a phase coherence switch. The *phase coherence switch* inverts the left channel signal before it combines with the right channel signal. If the stereo signals are in phase, sound quality should suffer and, in particular, the sonic images in the center (between the two loudspeakers) should be

severely attenuated. If the phase coherence check improves the mono signal, there is a problem with the stereo signal's mono compatibility.

Communications Section As the name suggests, the communications section facilitates communication between the control room and the studio. It also contains the modules used for cueing and equipment calibration.

■ **Talkback** The *talkback* permits the recordist in the control room to speak into a console microphone to the studio performers or music conductor, or both. The talkback may be directed through the studio monitor, headphones, or slate system.

■ **Slate/talkback** Multichannel consoles also have a *slate* feature that automatically feeds to the recorder anything said through the talkback. It is a convenient way to transcribe information about the name of the recording, the artist, the number of the *take,* and so on.

■ **Oscillator** An *oscillator* is a signal generator that produces pure tones or sine waves (sound waves with no harmonics or overtones) at selected frequencies. On a console it is used to (1) calibrate the console with the recorder so that their meters indicate the same levels and (2) put reference tone levels on recordings.

■ **Patch bay** The inputs and outputs of console components are wired to jacks in the *patch bay*—a central routing terminal—to facilitate the routing of sound through pathways not provided in the normal console design (see 5-7 and "Patching" later in this chapter).

As noted earlier, in-line consoles differ in their array of features, complexity, and signal flow. Figure 5-7 should give you an idea of how their basic modules function and interrelate. The purpose of Figure 5-8 is to correlate the functions of selected modules in Figure 5-7 to the way they are symbolized in a flowchart. Learning how to read a flowchart helps you to master console operation more quickly. It also helps you track down operational problems when they occur. Having said this, flowcharts vary in technical complexity. The

Trim: sets input gain of signal source

Aux: sends paths to effects processors

EQ: 12-kHz high-frequency shelving; midrange boost/cut; midrange sweep 100 Hz to 8kHz; 80-Hz low-frequency shelving

Pan: positions signal in stereo field

Solo: sends assigned signal to monitors

Bus assign: sends assigned signal to assigned tape track

Faders: control individual signal levels

Aux: return paths of effects processors

Monitor section: control room monitor, headphones; solo/VU meters allow isolated monitoring of individual signal sources

Headphone jack

Master bus faders: control master output levels

a

b

Studio mic jack #1

Mic pre-amp input

Mic pre-amp output

EQ input

EQ output

Fader input

c

Normaled connection

1 Power cord connection and fuse
2 Power switch
3 Phantom power switch
4 Main left/right outputs (balanced/unbalanced)
5 Mono output gain control
6 Mono output (balanced/unbalanced)
7 Main left/right channel inserts: break normal sign paths
8 RCA tape inputs (unbalanced)
9 RCA tape outputs (unbalanced)

10 Control room outputs (balanced/unbalanced)
11 Submaster outputs 1–4 (balanced/unbalanced)
12 Stereo aux returns 1–4 (balanced/unbalanced): return path from external effects processors
13 Aux sends 1–6 (balanced/unbalanced): feed signals to external effects processors
14 Direct outs, channels 1–8 (balanced/unbalanced)
15 Channel inserts (unbalanced): break normal signal paths
16 Channel line inputs (balanced/unbalanced): inputs for line-level signals
17 Channel mic preamp inputs (balanced): inputs for mic-level signals

5-7 Basic in-line console. (a) Front view, (b) rear view with patch bay, (c) patch bay signal flow. Patch bays in large production consoles are far more extensive than the one shown here, but the principles are the same.

5-8 Flow chart of the console in Figure 5-7

diagrams a technician requires to install a console are quite different from those a nontechnical person needs to understand signal flow.

PATCHING

Regardless of how elaborate the console or the studio, signal flow—the paths a signal takes from its source to its destination—is restricted by how active components are wired. When components are wired directly to one another (for example, a microphone to a recorder, or the output of a microphone, CD player, and recorder to the input of another recorder), they are considered **hardwired**. The signal can travel only one route (see 5-9). In a small production control room with little equipment, hardwiring may not present a problem.

Multichannel production consoles, however, require flexibility in routing signals to various components within the console and to and from outboard signal processors, such as limiter-compressors, noise gates, reverb units, and so on. In these circumstances the multiple routes a signal may have to take make hardwiring impractical.

Active components are therefore not wired directly to one another but to the console or studio patch bays, or both. Each hole in the bay (or panel), called a **jack**, becomes the connecting point to the input or output of each electronic component in the sound studio (see 5-10). *Patching* is the interconnecting of these inputs and outputs using a **patch cord** (see 5- 11; also see 5-14). In this context a patch bay is more like an old-fashioned telephone switchboard.

5-9 Hardwiring can limit signal flow. In (a) signal flow can go only one way, so hardwiring makes no difference. In (b), however, the microphone could feed to tape recorder 1, tape recorder 2 could feed to tape recorder 1, and so on. If these sound sources are hardwired as shown, such flexibility is not possible.

5-10 Patch bay with a row of jacks

5-11 Use of patch bay. Any sound source wired to the patch panel can be connected to any other one with a patch cord plugged into the appropriate jacks.

But such flexibility is not without potential problems. In a well-equipped and active facility, the patch bay could become a confusing jungle of patch cords. In all studios, regardless of size and activity, a signal travels some paths more often than others. For example, it is more likely that a signal in a console will travel from mic (or line) input to pan pot to equalizer to delegation control to fader, rather than directly from mic (or line) input to output bus. It is also more likely that a signal will travel from mic to console to recorder than directly from one recorder to another.

As a way of both reducing the clutter of patch cords at the patch bay and simplifying production, terminals wired to certain equipment can also be wired, or *normaled,* to one another. A *normal* connection is one that permits a signal to flow freely among components without any patching. To route a signal through components that have terminals not normaled or wired to one another, patch cords are put in the appropriate jacks to *break normal*— that is, interrupt the normal signal flow—thus rerouting the signal (see 5-12).

The ability to reroute a signal is also advantageous when equipment fails. Suppose a microphone is plugged into studio mic input 1, which connects directly to console channel 1, and channel 1 becomes defective. With all inputs and outputs connected at the patch bay, the defective console channel 1 can be bypassed by patching the output from studio mic input 1 to any other working console channel.

Some other features of patch bays include the following.

■ **Input/output** Most patch bays are wired so that a row of input jacks is directly below a row of output jacks. By reading a patch bay downward, it is possible to get a good idea of the console's (or studio's) signal flow.

■ **Full-normal and half-normal** Input jacks are wired so that a patch cord always interrupts the normal connection. These connections are called *full-normal.* Output jacks may be wired as either full-

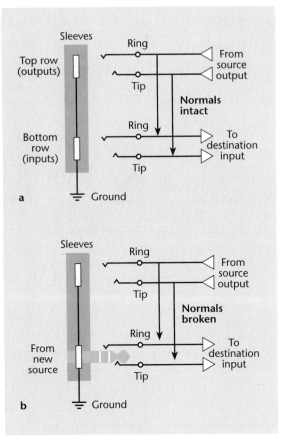

5-12 Normaling. (a) With no patch cords inserted, output of source equipment is automatically normaled to the input of another piece of equipment (tip = high, ring = low, sleeve = grounded shield). (b) When a patch cord is inserted in the bottom-row (input) jack, the normals are interrupted, breaking the original signal routing. The new source signal will now feed the destination.

normal or *half-normal*—connections that continue rather than interrupt signal flow. Hence, a half-normal connection becomes a junction rather than a switch (see 5-13).

■ **Multiple** Most patch bays include jacks called *multiples* (or "mults") that are wired to one another instead of to any electronic component. Multiples provide the flexibility to feed the same signal to several different sources at once.

5-13 (a) Full-normal and (b) half-normal patch configurations

■ **Tie line** When the only patch bay in a control room is located in the console, the other control room equipment, such as recorders, CD players, and signal processors, have to be wired to it in order to maintain flexibility in signal routing. *Tie lines* in the patch bay facilitate the interconnecting of outboard devices in the control room. When a control room has two patch bays, one in the console and one for the other control room equipment, tie lines can interconnect each patch bay. The tie line is also used to interconnect separate studios, control rooms, or any devices in different locations.

General Guidelines for Patching

☑ Do not patch microphone-level signals into line-level jacks and vice versa. The signal will be barely audible in the first instance and will distort in the latter one.

☑ Do not patch input to input or output to output.

☑ Unless jacks are half-normaled, do not patch the output of a component back into its input, or feedback will occur.

☑ When patching microphones, make sure the fader controls are turned down. Otherwise, the loud popping sound that occurs when patch cords are inserted into jacks with the faders turned up could damage the microphone or loudspeaker element.

Plugs

While we are on the subject of patching, something more should be said about the plugs on the end of the patch cords. The plugs most commonly used in professional facilities are the *¼-inch phone plug* and the *bantam* (also called *mini* and *tiny telephone*) *phone plug*. The bantam plug, and the smaller patch panel with which it is used, is replacing the larger ¼-inch phone plug and its patch panel (see 5-14).

5-14 Patch cords with (a) ¼-inch phone plugs and (b) bantam (mini) phone plugs

5-15 (a) Mono unbalanced phone plug; (b) stereo balanced phone plug

These plugs are either unbalanced—tip and sleeve—or balanced—tip, ring, and sleeve (see 5-15). An unbalanced audio cable has two conductors: a center wire and a braided shield surrounding it. A balanced audio cable has three conductors: two center wires and a braided shield. The balanced line is preferred for professional use, because it is not as subject to electrical interference and can be used in long cable runs without undue loss in signal-to-noise ratio.

CONSOLE AUTOMATION

Console automation greatly facilitates the operation and recordkeeping involved in mixing many tracks down to a few.

Types of Automation Systems

Four types of console automation systems are in use today. They are voltage-controlled automation, moving-fader automation, software-controlled automation, and MIDI-based automation. Given today's complex production consoles, automation has become indispensable.

Voltage-Controlled Automation

In voltage-controlled automation, fader levels (and other functions) are regulated by *voltage-controlled amplifiers (VCAs)* or by *digitally controlled amplifiers (DCAs)*. The VCA is a special type of amplifier that is used to decrease level, unlike conventional amplifiers that become unstable if operated with loss. It is regulated by DC voltage. In a typical VCA-equipped console, faders vary the DC control voltage that changes the VCA's gain in relation to the fader movement. This control voltage is digitized and stored for later retrieval. In addition to fader levels, it is possible to automate channel and group mutes, solo functions, and in-board signal processors, such as the equalizer. DCA is an amplifier whose gain is remotely controlled by a digital control signal.

Moving-Fader Automation

With moving-fader, also called *flying fader,* automation, instead of using DC voltage to control a VCA, it drives a small servo-motor that is attached to the fader. As the control voltages are regenerated, it activates the motor, which moves the fader automatically; no hand-operated assistance is necessary. It is possible to control automatically one fader or groups of faders at the same time.

Software-Controlled Automation

Software-controlled automation uses specially designed computer programs for console automation. It is usually employed in hard-disk recording and editing systems (see Chapter 7).

Adjustments are made through *virtual faders* displayed on a video monitor. A *virtual* control is simulated on a computer monitor and adjusted at the computer keyboard or with a mouse. More-complex programs, in addition to automated level control, also allow automated control of all in-board signal processing, such as equalization, panning, compression, and effects.

MIDI-Based Automation

MIDI is a communications protocol. It is short for *Musical Instrument Digital Interface.* The *Digital* refers to a set of instructions in the form of digital (binary) data, like a computer program, that must be interpreted by an electronic sound-generating or -modifying device, such as a synthesizer, that can respond to the instructions. *Interface* refers to the hardware connection that permits the control signals generated by one device to be transmitted to another. A specified system of digital commands and hardware interface allow musical instruments and other devices to communicate with one another.

In the same way that MIDI can automate musical instruments, it can also be used to automate console operations, such as fader levels, send and return levels, EQ, and pans. MIDI-automated consoles may physically resemble consoles with conventional automation or may be "black boxes" with input and output jacks. These boxes may either use a virtual console computer graphic interface or dedicated controllers with slides and knobs that control the box through MIDI commands.

Two methods are used to translate slider and knob changes to MIDI: snapshot control and continuous control. With *snapshot control,* the automation system takes an instant reading of the console settings for recall from storage. With *continuous control,* each console setting is assigned to a specific MIDI continuous controller. Any movement of these controls transmits corresponding MIDI continuous controller messages.

MIDI console automation has limitations in handling the large amounts of data that other types of automation do not have. But because many conventional console automation systems are so complex, recordists are turning to MIDI-based automation systems as a simpler alternative.

Operating Modes

Console automation systems have at least three basic operating modes: write, read, and update. All functions may be used independently on any or all channels.

■ **Write mode** The *write mode* is used to create an automated mix. In the write mode, the automation system monitors and stores data from the faders. Only current fader movements are stored in the write mode.

■ **Read mode** The *read mode* plays back or recalls the stored automation data. In the read mode, the console's faders are inoperative. They take their control voltage information only from the stored data on the disk to reproduce the "recorded" fader movements in real time.

■ **Update mode** The *update mode* allows the operator to read the stored information at any time and make changes by simply moving the appropriate fader. A new data track is generated from the original data track with the changes that have been made.

Advantages of Console Automation

Mixing various sounds, once they are recorded, can be exacting and tedious. It requires dozens, maybe hundreds, of replays and myriad adjustments to get the right equalization, reverberation, blend, spatial balance, timing of inserts, and so on. Comparing one mix with another is difficult unless settings are written down (which is time-consuming) so that controls can be returned to previous positions if necessary. It is not uncommon to discard a mix because someone forgot to adjust one control or decided after a few days to change a few settings without noting the original positions. Then the controls have to be set up all over again. Mixing one song can take many hours or even days; a production can take months.

Console automation has greatly facilitated the recordkeeping and accuracy of mixing; it has made the engineer's arms "longer." Many productions are so involved that they would be virtually undoable without automation. But it has its disadvantages.

Disadvantages of Console Automation

Automation systems tend to be confusing, even to experienced operators. Some systems are so complex that it is easy to lose track of the many operations necessary to perform a mix, which defeats the purpose of console automation. Some systems may not play back exactly what the operator wrote. If the mix is complex, a difference of a few decibels, overall, may not be perceptible. That would not be the case, however, in more-subtle mixes.

Automation systems, like all computer systems, are vulnerable to crashing. Getting the system operational again, even assuming that you had the forethought to make a backup copy of the mix before completion, often involves a frustrating loss of production time and continuity, to say nothing of the financial cost.

An aesthetic concern with automation is "sameness." Unless an automated mix is done with skill, its dynamics can sound the same from beginning to end.

DIGITAL CONSOLES

Aside from their differences in technologies, the main innovation in digital consoles, compared with analog consoles, is the divorcing of circuitry from panel controls. The control surface is still made up of the familiar controls—faders, EQ, sends, returns, and so on—but there is no physical connection between the controls on the console surface and the audio circuit elements, nor are specific controls necessarily dedicated to particular channels.

The digital console consists of *actuators*. Although they look like the familiar controls, when activated they send out digital commands that operate the faders, EQ, sends, returns, and other switches. These commands are stored for instant recall at any time and they are assignable.

The *assignable* concept was first developed in analog production consoles as a way to reduce their ever increasing size and improve manageability. Assignable consoles use two basic approaches. In one configuration, instead of each input module carrying its own set of functions, only one control module is used. This system works in combination with a group of controls, each one corresponding to an input channel. This means that instead of routing a signal through an existing input channel and making individual adjustments—such as EQ, cue and reverb send, and

bus assignment at that channel—the various controls of an input channel are grouped into separate, centralized panels. From these panels a signal is assigned to a channel, processed, and routed. Routing assignments are entered into a central control panel and stored on disk.

A second configuration uses as many modules as there are input channels. But each module has only one control fader that works in conjunction with a group of function buttons. All required effects are distributed among the function buttons. In this system you choose a module and assign one or more functions to the control fader of that particular module. In both assignable approaches, a given control set may be used to perform either the same set of functions for a variety of channels or different functions for a single channel.

The assignable console design has several advantages over large, conventional production consoles: (1) It makes many more operations possible in a more compact chassis; (2) an operator can remain in the central listening location without having to move back and forth to adjust controls; (3) signals can be handled more quickly and easily because functions are grouped and, with fewer controls, there are fewer operations to perform; and (4) the reduced number of controls lessens the chance of error and makes console layout easier on the eye.

Digital consoles are available in three configurations. One configuration is actually an analog console that is digitally controlled. The signal path is distributed and processed in analog form, but the console's control parameters are maintained digitally.

The all-digital console uses two approaches. The analog input signal is first encoded into a digital signal or it is directly accepted as digital information. In either case, the data are distributed and processed digitally. The output might be either decoded back into analog or remain in digital form, depending on its destination (see 5-16 and 5-17).

A third type of digital mixer is actually a virtual console. As the term suggests, a virtual console is not a console per se, but an integrated system that

Data display

Meter bridge

Trim

TB level

Display controls

Studio/phones levels

DSP controls

Aux controls

Selected channels controls

Tape monitor levels

Select/channels on/off

Panning controls

Faders

Scene memory

Data adjust controls

a

Stereo inputs

Master fader

Monitor outputs

Stereo out (analog)

Signal inputs (analog): mic and line levels

b

Time code input

Stereo out (digital)

MIDI

Modular digital multitrack recorder I/O (DA88/A-DAT)

5-16 Example of a digital console and its functions. (a) Front view, (b) rear view.

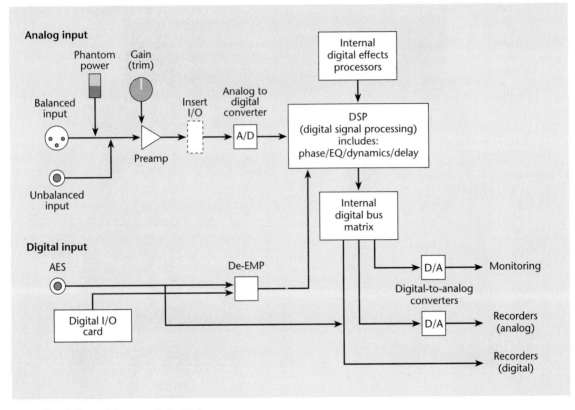

5-17 Signal flow of the console in 5-16

combines a hard-disk computer and specialized software to record and process audio direct to disk. Instead of feeding a sound source to a conventional console, it is fed directly to the computer. On the computer monitor are displayed the console controls—faders, EQ, panning, and so on—which are maneuvered by a mouse or keyboard, or both (see Chapter 7).

The digital console has several advantages over its all-analog counterpart: (1) It is virtually distortion- and noise-free; (2) every control move, manual or preprogrammed, is stored and retrieved accurately; (3) operating one control can direct several pre-programmed functions to occur simultaneously; and (4) in-board patch bays are unnecessary.

MAIN POINTS

▶ Mixers and consoles take input signals and amplify, balance, process, combine, and route them to broadcast or recording.

▶ The difference between a mixer and a console is that a mixer is small, highly portable, and performs limited processing functions, whereas a console is larger and performs numerous processing functions. In many consoles, these functions are computer-assisted.

▶ Mixers and consoles have at least the three basic control sections: input, output, and monitor. Many consoles have an additional master control section.

▶ The input section takes incoming signals and routes them to the output section.

- The output section routes signals to broadcast or recording.

- The master section contains, among other things, the master output bus(es) that route the final mix to the master recorder.

- The monitor section enables signals to be heard.

- On-air broadcast consoles, particularly for radio, are not as elaborate as production consoles, because most of the audio they handle has been produced already.

- Split-section consoles have separate input, output, master, and monitor sections. In-line consoles bring the input and output functions vertically in line, enabling any signal processing to be routed to the monitor or master system.

- The main sections of an in-line console are: input/output, master, monitor, and communications.

- The input/output section includes: microphone-line input selector, microphone preamplifier, phantom power, trim, overload indicator, pad, channel assignment switches, direct switch, equalizer and filter, channel/monitor control, polarity reversal control, pan pot, cue send, reverb (or effects) send, solo and prefader listen (PFL), mute, channel and monitor faders, and VU (or ppm) meters.

- The volume unit (VU) meter is a voltage meter that measures the amount of electric energy flowing through the console. The meter has two scales: percentage of modulation and volume units. Percentage of modulation is the percentage of an applied signal in relation to the maximum signal a sound system can handle.

- The VU meter responds to average sound intensity, unlike another popular meter, the peak program meter (ppm), which is designed to indicate transient peaks.

- The master section includes: master buses, master fader, reverb (or effects) send, reverb (or effects) return, and meters.

- The monitor section includes: the line-in/line-out control, recorder select, send, mix, loudspeaker select, and mono switches. It may also have a pan pot and phase coherence switch.

- The communications section includes: talkback, slate/talkback, and oscillator.

- Most modern production consoles include a patch bay, a central routing terminal to which are wired the inputs and outputs of the console or the equipment in a studio, or both. The patch bay makes multiple signal paths possible. Patch cords plugged into jacks connect the routing circuits.

- The signal paths that are used most often are wired together at the terminals of the patch bay. This normals these routes and makes it unnecessary to use patch cords to connect them. It is possible to break normal and create other signal paths by patching.

- Plugs at the end of patch cords are either unbalanced, comprising a tip and a sleeve, or balanced, comprising a tip, ring, and sleeve.

- Console automation makes it possible to automate fader functions, decoding positional information as adjustments in level are made. The data is stored on and retrieved from a computer disk.

- There are four types of console automation systems in use: voltage-controlled automation, moving-fader automation, software-controlled automation, and MIDI-based automation.

- Most console automation systems have at least the three basic operating modes: write, read, and update.

- Digital consoles use the assignable concept in three configurations: in an analog console that is digitally controlled, in an all-digital console, and in a virtual console which is not a console per se, but an integrated system that combines a hard-disk computer and specialized software to record and process audio direct to disc.

- With digital consoles, instead of individual controls for channel-to-track routing on each channel strip, these functions have been centralized into single sets so they can be assigned to any channel. Once assigned, the commands are stored in the console's computer, so different functions can be assigned to other channels. There is no physical connection between the controls on the console surface and the audio circuit elements.

6

Analog Recording

The wonderful thing about audio is that, in the final analysis, it's all a matter of taste. "Ears" are uniquely individual, which leaves ample room for varied opinion. Nowhere has this been more apparent than in the debate over analog versus digital sound.

In audiotape recording, electrical signals are transduced into magnetic signals at the recording stage and encoded onto tape. At the playback stage, these taped magnetic signals are reconverted into electrical signals. This process is accomplished in two different ways: using the analog method or the digital method.

On one hand, advocates of analog recording claim that it produces a warmer sound and that it is a more forgiving production format—technical problems are not as apparent as they are with digital. On the other hand, proponents of digital recording praise its virtually noise-free, crystal clear sound and its technology, which greatly increases production flexibility.

So far, predictions of analog's demise have been premature. Analog recording remains robust; equipment and tape sales are holding their own and are expected to continue for the foreseeable future.

Implicit in the analog versus digital debate is that one format is not so much superior to the other, but simply different. Each has positive and negative attributes. Clearly, the world of audio is headed toward the digital domain but, for a while at least, coexistence of both formats ensures expansive sonic prospects.

ANALOG AUDIOTAPE RECORDING

In *analog recording*, the waveform of the signal being processed resembles the waveform of the original sound; they are analogous. Or to put it another way, the frequency and amplitude of an electrical signal changes continuously in direct relationship to the original acoustic sound waves; it is always "on." If these continuous changes were examined, they would reveal an infinite number of variations, each instant different from any adjacent instant. During processing, noise—electrical, electronic, or tape—may be added to the signal. Hence the processed signal is analogous to the original sound plus any additional noise (see Figure 6-1). Although the digital tape recording process is entirely different (see Chapter 7), the tape and tape recorders used in analog and digital recording have a number of features in common.

Physical Characteristics of Audiotape

We tend to take tape for granted, perhaps because it is so familiar and easy to obtain. Consider, however, that tape stores the record of your creative output. Therefore, to avoid using inferior, defective, or inappropriate tape, you should be aware of the properties and composition of your storage medium.

Composition

Audiotape is a thin plastic ribbon consisting of (1) hard, needlelike magnetic particles composed of iron (ferric) oxide, chromium dioxide, cobalt-doped iron oxide, or pure metal particles; (2) a plastic base material that supports the oxide; (3) a binder of synthetic varnish that holds the magnetic particles and adheres them to the base; and (4) a back coating to reduce slippage and buildup of magnetic charges (see 6-2).

The plastic material used for a tape's backing is strong, supple, and resistant to temperature extremes as well as humidity. Its one significant drawback is that it stretches when placed under too much tension or when used too often. Once a tape is stretched, so is the recording.

To reduce the possibility of stretching, use only the highest-quality tape, make sure that tape recorders have the proper tension when spooling, and use new tape for each project.

6-2 The four layers that make up audiotape and the random distribution of magnetic domains on the microscopic magnetic particles

Dimensions

The two physical dimensions of magnetic audiotape worth noting are thickness and width.

Thickness Professionally used open-reel audiotape comes in two thicknesses, measured in *mils* (thousandths of an inch): 1 and 1½ mil. (Measurement is taken from the plastic base; actually the plastic base plus the magnetic coating is slightly thicker.) A tape's thickness determines how much can be spooled onto a given size of reel and how long the playing time. The most common professionally used open-reel sizes are 7, 10½, and 14 inches (see Table 6-1).

In analog recording 1½ mil is used for two reasons: (1) It is the thickest and most durable tape available and is therefore the least likely to crease, snap, stretch, or shrink; and (2) *print-through* is considerably lessened. Print-through usually occurs in storage, when a signal from one layer of tape "prints" a low-level replica of itself on an adjacent layer. When the tape is played back, you can hear both signals, one strongly and one faintly. The thicker the tape, the less chance of sound "spilling" from layer to layer. Other factors that affect print-through are discussed later in this

6-3 Open-reel audiotape in ¼-, ½-, 1-, and 2-inch widths

chapter. (In digital open-reel recording, 1-mil tape is used; see Chapter 7.)

Width Open-reel audiotape is available in four widths: ¼, ½, 1, and 2 inches (see 6-3). Analog cassette tape is roughly .15 inch wide.

Magnetic Properties of Audiotape

Tape used in professional audio is designed to provide particular response characteristics to meet certain needs. For example, the type normally used to record popular music is *high-output tape* capable of handling higher levels than is standard tape. The louder recording levels make print-through more noticeable, however. *Low-output tape* is used to preserve program material for long periods of time with reduced print-through.

Certain measures are used to determine how suitable a tape is for a particular recording. Three ways to determine a tape's ability to retain magnetic information are to check (1) how strong a force field must be to change the magnetic charge of a given particle, (2) how well the tape retains magnetization once the force field is removed, and (3) how great an output level the

Table 6-1 Recording times for open-reel analog tape.
Times are not exact because extra tape is provided to spool around the takeup and feed reels.

Reel Size (inches)	Tape Thickness (mils)	Tape Length (feet)	Playing Time (minutes)			
			30 ips*	15 ips	7½ ips	3¾ ips
7	1.5	1,200	7.5	15	30	60
7	1	1,800	11.25	22.5	45	90
10.5	1.5	2,500	16.6	33.3	66.6	133.2
14	1.5	5,000	33.3	66.6	133.3	266.4

*Inches per second

tape can reproduce. The terms used to describe these measures are coercivity, retentivity, and sensitivity.

Coercivity

Coercivity indicates the magnetic force (current) necessary to erase a tape fully. It is measured in *oersteds*—units of magnetic intensity. Professionally used analog open-reel tapes usually have oersted measurements between 360 and 380. The oersted measurements of digital open-reel tapes are in the 700s. Digital audio cassette tape is 1,500 oersteds (see Chapter 7).

The higher the coercivity, the more difficult it is to erase the tape. A tape recorder should be able to completely erase the tape being used. If it does not, some part of a previously recorded signal may be heard with a newly recorded signal.

Retentivity

Retentivity is a measure of the tape's magnetic field strength remaining after an external magnetic force has been removed. Retentivity is measured in *gauss*—a unit of magnetic density. A higher gauss rating means greater retentivity, which, in turn, indicates that a tape has a greater potential output level. Greater is not necessarily better; what is better depends on what you are recording and why. Gauss ratings between 1,200 and 1,700 are typical in professionally used open-reel tapes, analog and digital. Digital audio cassette tape has gauss ratings between 2,300 and 2,500.

Sensitivity

Sensitivity is similar to retentivity in that it indicates the highest output level a tape can deliver; sensitivity is measured in decibels, however, and the test must be made against a reference tape. If the maximum output level of a reference tape is 0 dB and the output of the tape you are testing is +3dB, your tape is capable of handling 3 dB more loudness before it *saturates*—becomes fully magnetized.

Tape Defects

Most tape defects are the product of inferior manufacturing, and it is false economy to try to save money by purchasing such tape. To make the point emphatically: *Do not use cheap tape!*

Following are several consequences of using cheap tape (see 6-4):

▪ *Dropout*—sudden, irregular drops in sound level caused by poor distribution or flaking of the magnetic coating

▪ *Cinching*—slippage between the tape layers due to loose packing (also known as *windowing*)

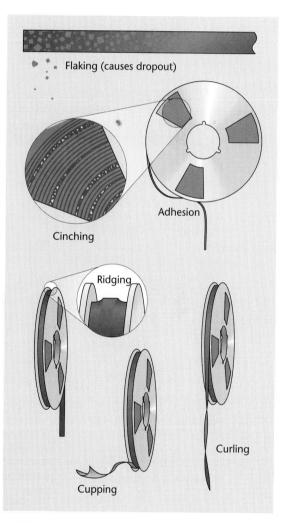

6-4 Common problems of poorly made tape

■ *Ridging*—a bulge or depression, seen after winding, caused by deformed layer(s) of tape

■ *Adhesion*—one tape layer sticking to another

■ *Cupping*—deformation of the backing due to expansion of the magnetic coating and base (usually occurs only with cheap tape)

■ *Curling*—twisting of tape when it hangs due to a problem in the binding between the plastic and magnetic coating

Each of these defects adversely affects the sound quality, to say nothing of accelerated tape head and machine wear.

Care of Tape

Because the entire tape-recording process ultimately depends on the tape, it is important to exercise proper care when handling and storing magnetic tape.

Handling

☑ Never handle the tape surface—front or back. The oil from a fingerprint can catch dust and grime that can damage the tape surfaces. If touching the tape cannot be avoided, use lint-free gloves. This is especially important when using digital tape.

☑ Do not smoke or eat in the tape area. Smoke and food particles can contaminate the tape and also cause damage.

☑ Carry the tape reel by the hub.

☑ Trim damaged tape ends to avoid depositing debris on the tape transport and record heads.

☑ Always store tape in a dust-proof container when it is not in use.

☑ Do not stack tapes on top of one another. Store tapes vertically so they will be supported by the hub.

☑ Keep tape away from heat-generating equipment and magnetic fields when not in use.

Storage

If you intend to keep a recording for any length of time, take the following precautions against alteration of the magnetically encoded signal.

☑ Use low-print-through tape 1½ mils thick.

☑ Store the tape in a controlled environment, between 60 and 75°F and 40 and 60 percent humidity.

☑ Play, as opposed to fast-forward, the tape *tails out*—with the end of the recording on the outside of the reel. If print-through does occur, the weaker signal or sound decay will be post-echo (transferred into the stronger signal), thus masking the print-through, instead of pre-echo (before the signal), thus being audible.

☑ Beware of exposed edges that result from *scattered wind* or *stepping* of tape due to uneven winding (see 6-5).

☑ If the tape is in long-term storage, try to play it at least once a year as an added precaution. Even if print-through has occurred, rewinding reduces it somewhat.

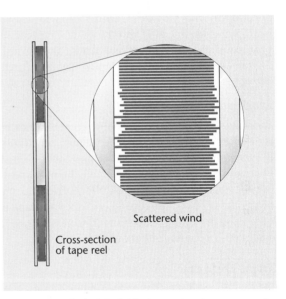

Scattered wind

Cross-section of tape reel

6-5 Scattered wind. Individual tape strands are exposed and vulnerable to damage.

Feed reel

Head assembly

Tape guide

Individual VU meters for each channel

±12% pitch control

Tape-speed control

Takeup reel

Pinch roller

Tape guide

Capstan

Hour/minute/ second LED tape position counter

Channel-independent input and output dials calibrate sound levels with the entire production suite

Syncs internally, externally, or manually

Edit button lets unwanted tape section "spill" rather than be taken up by the reel for easier splicing

Three auto-location points and return-to-zero controls for editing

6-6 Example of an open-reel analog audiotape recorder and its functions

OPEN-REEL AUDIOTAPE RECORDERS

Open-reel audiotape recorders, and audiotape recorders (ATRs) in general, have three essential elements: (1) the tape transport system, (2) magnetic heads, and (3) record and playback electronics. You may consider the recording tape as a fourth element (see 6-6). Of interest here are the tape transport system and magnetic heads.

Tape Transport System

Tape transports are designed to pull the tape across the magnetic heads at a constant speed and tension without causing fluctuations in the tape movement. In a typical *tape transport system*, a tape is prepared for record or play by placing it on the *feed (supply) reel*, threading it past the *tape guide*, across the *head assembly*, and between the *capstan* and *pinch roller,* through another tape guide to the takeup reel. The tape guides correctly position the tape on the heads during spooling.

The **capstan** is a precision drive shaft that regulates the tape speed. When you put the machine in play mode, the tape is forced against the motor-driven shaft by the **pinch roller**. The pinch roller is usually rubber, and as the spinning capstan comes into contact with it, the capstan drives the roller and the two together pull the tape at a constant rate of speed.

Wow and Flutter

Constant tape movement and tension are critical to acceptable recording. If a problem results from any change in the constant transport speed during recording or playback, the sound may take on audible changes in frequency called wow or flutter. Slow changes are called **wow;** faster changes are called **flutter**.

Wow and flutter are usually not a problem with regularly maintained professional equipment. If either or both are present in a recording, however, it may be not audible on the original tape. But as analog tape is **dubbed**—copied—from one generation to another, noise builds up and the wow or flutter becomes audible. (There is also noise buildup.)

Most professional open-reel ATRs come with **scrape flutter filters** to reduce flutter. Scrape flutter filters are installed between the heads to reduce the amount of unsupported tape, thereby restricting the degree of tape movement as it passes across the heads (see 6-7).

Scrape flutter filter

Erase head   Record head   Playback head

6-7 Audiotape recorder with three magnetic heads.
These are half-track heads (see Figure 6-9).

The lower the wow and flutter specification, the better. Although it is beyond the scope of this book to explain the following wow and flutter measurements, 0.05% WRMS (weighted root mean square) is very good; 0.04% WRMS is excellent.

■ **Tension (reel-size) control** Electric current to the feed and takeup motors keeps the torque on the reels constant, but it does not control differences in tension created when tape winds from one reel to a different-sized reel. Modern professional ATRs use a microprocessor for reel-tension control. Older models that are designed to take different-sized reels have a *tension* or *reel-size* switch so that the tape wind from reel to reel is constant regardless of tape distribution and reel sizes.

■ **Safety control** The *safety control* or *idler arm* (the term may vary with the tape recorder manufacturer) stops the transport when it senses the absence of tape along the guide path because the tape ran out or broke. The control may be a light beam interrupted by the presence of tape in its path, or the control may be incorporated in the tape-tension sensor. Because the safety control stops the transport without turning off the entire recorder, it cuts down on machine wear and tear.

■ **Tape speeds** Five speeds generally are used in analog audiotape recording: 1⅞, 3¾, 7½, 15, and 30 *inches per second (ips)*. In analog recording, the faster the speed, the better the frequency response and signal-to-noise ratio. Many ATRs operate at two, three, or four speeds.

Professionals generally use 7½ ips as a common speed when distributing or airing tape recordings, but they often work at 15 or 30 ips for improved sound quality and ease of editing. In any case, it is not wise to use speeds lower than 7½ ips. To give you an insight into the relationship between speed and sound quality, one top-quality professional tape recorder has a frequency response to 20,000 Hz at 15 ips; at 7½ ips response reaches 15,000 Hz, and at 3¾ ips it goes only as high as 10,000 Hz. A record/play frequency response of 40 Hz to 18 kHz is considered excellent for an open-reel analog ATR.

Faster speeds also make it easier to edit tape (see Chapter 17). The more tape that passes across the heads per second, the more spread out the sound is on the tape. (A speed of $1\frac{7}{8}$ ips is standard for analog audio cassette recorders. Digital ACRs run at $\frac{1}{4}$ ips.)

Tape Transport Controls

Several different controls operate the tape transport system (see 6-6).

▓ **On/off switch** This control turns the electric power to the tape recorder on or off.

▓ **Speed control** Most professional recorders operate at more than one speed. This control selects the speed.

▓ **Variable-speed control** Modern multispeed audiotape recorders have a control that adjusts tape speed to a rate that is ±5 to 50 percent of the machine's set speeds. This *variable-speed control* comes in handy when you want to change the pitch of a sound for special effect or to correct slight anomalies in pitch resulting from AC voltage changes or batteries that gradually lose power during recording. The variable-speed control also permits a shortening or lengthening of material that may be desirable and acceptable if the change in frequency and rate is unimportant.

▓ **Play** This control activates the tape transport in the play mode.

▓ **Record** This control activates the erase and record electronics. To avoid accidental erasure, it usually will not work unless the *play* button is also pressed.

▓ **Fast-forward and rewind** These controls disengage the capstan/pinch roller and wind or rewind the tape at high speed. In either mode tape lifters hold the tape away from the heads to avoid the increased friction that would rapidly wear both tape and heads and to mute the annoying high-pitched squeal that comes when running the tape at high speed. If that high-pitched squeal is loud enough, by the way, it can damage the tweeter(s) in a loudspeaker (see Chapter 9).

▓ **Stop** This control stops the feed and takeup reels and disengages the pinch roller from the capstan.

▓ **Edit control** This control disengages the takeup reel while allowing the rest of the tape transport to continue functioning. This permits the spooling off of unwanted tape without the takeup reel turning.

Magnetic Heads

Professional open-reel analog tape recorders have at least three heads: erase, record, and playback (see 6-7). A good way to identify them is to remember that the erase head is always closest to the feed reel, the record head is in the middle, and the playback head is closest to the takeup reel. Machines with four heads use the fourth as a synchronization head for time code (see Chapter 11).

Bias

Before examining the function of each magnetic head, it is necessary to discuss *bias*. The response of magnetic particles on recording tape (and magnetic film) is nonlinear—their magnetic energy is not a perfect analog of the signal from the record head. A method is needed to force the magnetic properties of the particles as the audio current directs.

That force is a high-frequency current several times that of the highest recorded frequency and, therefore, far above the frequency limits of human hearing (100,000 Hz and higher). This high-frequency current, referred to as *bias current*, is added to the audio signal during recording. It affects the magnetic tape particles so that they respond and conform to the audio signal. During playback the bias frequency is not reproduced, because the playback head is unable to read such high frequencies.

In addition to making magnetic recording linear, the strength of the bias current also affects frequency response, distortion, and signal-to-noise ratio. A particular amount of bias current will work best with a particular type of recording tape. It is critical, therefore, that the tape recorder you use has been *biased* for the specific tape that you are using. Otherwise, a bias current set too high results in loss of high frequencies, and one set too low results in increased distortion and background noise. Always check with a technician to be sure.

Types of Heads

Erase Head The *erase head* is activated during recording. Its function is to neutralize the polarities of the magnetic particles—to remove sound from the tape with a high-frequency current before the tape passes across the record head.

Bulk Erasers Another way to erase tape is with a *bulk eraser* (also known as a *degausser*)—a large magnet that can erase an entire reel at once (see 6-8). It is fast and easy to use but generally gives a poorer signal-to-noise ratio than does the erase head. When using a bulk eraser with no conveyor belt, take the following precautions.

☑ Keep the tape (and your watch) away from the demagnetizer when it is switched on or off, because the tape could get a surge of magnetism that may be difficult to remove with an erase head.

☑ Before (and after) degaussing, slowly move the tape into (and away from) the bulk eraser's field.

☑ Rotate the tape over the degausser slowly at a rate not more than 2 inches per second. Faster rates will leave residual magnetism on the tape. Do not scrape the tape too hard or jerk it across the surface of the bulk eraser or it will reduce signal-to-noise ratio and increase tape noise in the form of periodic noise surges—known as *spoking*—as the tape plays. Be sure to erase *both* sides of the entire reel.

☑ Know the use time of the demagnetizer; older models tend to heat up quickly and will burn out if left on too long.

Record Head The *record head* transduces electric energy into the magnetic force that magnetizes the tape. It carries two signals: the record bias current and the audio current—the signal fed to the recorder from the original sound.

Playback Head The *playback head* transduces the magnetic field from the tape back into electric energy.

Head Sizes and Track Formats

The amount of surface area on a magnetic head (or *headstack*, as it is called on multitrack heads) varies

a   b

6-8 High-quality bulk erasers. (a) This model erases open-reel tapes from 150-mil to 2-inch widths, as well as cartridges, cassettes, and magnetic film. The erase field electronically diminishes at the end of each 20-second cycle. A fan blower protects the eraser from overheating. (b) High-energy bulk eraser for high-coercivity tapes.

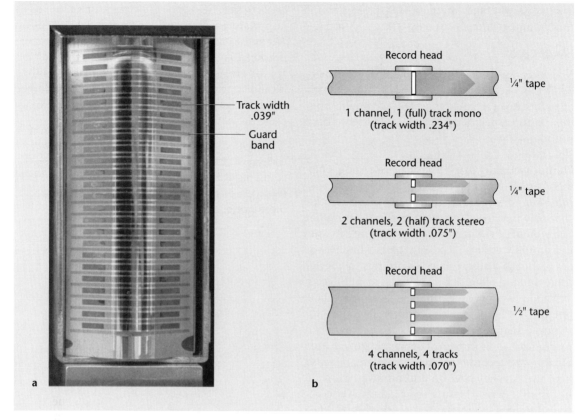

Track width
.039"

Guard
band

Record head

¼" tape

1 channel, 1 (full) track mono
(track width .234")

Record head

¼" tape

2 channels, 2 (half) track stereo
(track width .075")

Record head

½" tape

4 channels, 4 tracks
(track width .070")

a   b

6-9 (a) 24-track headstack used with 2-inch tape. (b) Channel and track formats of selected standard-gauge open-reel analog recorders.

with the width of the head and whether the head is standard-gauge or narrow-gauge.

Standard-Gauge Heads Standard-gauge heads on open-reel analog tape recorders are manufactured today in ¼-inch and 2-inch widths. The ¼-inch head actually houses two separate heads and is used for stereo recording. Each head records or plays back a separate tape track. Two-inch headstacks house 16 or 24 separate heads and can record or play back 16 or 24 tape tracks. Each head is separated by a *guard band* that considerably reduces the chance of *crosstalk*— leakage of a signal from one track into an adjacent track (see 6-9).

Do not confuse channel with track; these terms are not synonyms. A *channel* is a conduit through

which signal flows. The path the signal makes on the tape is the *track*.

Narrow-Gauge Heads Analog tape recorders are also available with a narrow-gauge headstack, which make it possible to record more tracks on a given track width. They are available in ¼-, ½-, and 1-inch sizes with as many as 8 tracks on a ¼-inch head, 8 or 16 tracks on a ½-inch head, and 16 or 24 tracks on a 1-inch head.

Narrow-gauge formats were developed for industrial-grade and nonprofessional audio production. The main advantage of these formats is greater multitrack capability at a lower cost, because narrow-gauge ATRs are considerably less expensive than standard-gauge analog recorders.

Their disadvantages are generally poorer sound quality and greater risk of crosstalk.

Head Care

Magnetic heads require very careful treatment. Scratches, wear, magnetic buildup, the slightest change in their alignment, or any accumulation of dust, dirt, or magnetic particles adversely affects sound quality.

Demagnetizing the Heads Before using a tape recorder (and once or twice during long sessions), make sure the heads are free of any magnetization that may have been left from previous use. When heads build up enough permanent magnetism, they can partially erase a recording; higher frequencies are particularly susceptible. Recordings so affected sound muddy, often lacking presence and brilliance.

Various types of head demagnetizers are available (see 6-10). Choose one that does not produce too strong a magnetic field, or it can permanently magnetize a head instead of demagnetizing it. Turn off the tape recorder before demagnetizing. Also, turn the demagnetizer on and off away from the heads; otherwise, the surge or cut in power could leave remnant magnetization on the heads. Make sure, too, that the demagnetizer does not touch or scrape the heads, or they could be scratched and permanently damaged. An etched head acts like sandpaper in scraping magnetic particles off of tape.

Aligning the Heads Whether or not you align the heads, you should be aware of the five adjustments that are made and some problems that can result when the heads are out of alignment (see 6-11).

6-10 Head demagnetizer

■ ***Zenith*** The vertical angle of the heads is important in maintaining uniform tape tension across the entire width of the tape-to-head contact. If a head is tilted and the top or bottom portion applies greater pressure to the tape than the other, it causes the tape to *skew*—ride up or down on the head. In less severe cases, the lack of pressure can cause degraded performance.

■ ***Height*** The heads must present themselves to the tape at exactly the right height. Otherwise, the result could be signals that are only partially recorded or reproduced, crosstalk between tracks, more noise, or poor erasure.

6-11 Five alignment adjustments to a magnetic head

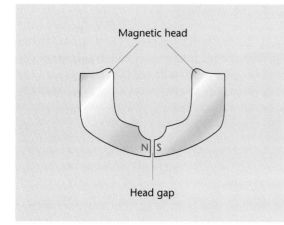

6-12 The poles and head gap of a magnetic head

▓ *Tangency* The head-to-tape contact at the head gap must be at the right pressure. The *head gap* is the space between the poles of a magnetic head (see 6-12). The farther forward the head, the greater the pressure. Too little or too much pressure noticeably degrades a signal by reducing high-frequency response and causing dropout.

▓ *Wrap* The angle at which the tape curves around the head must ensure proper contact at the gap. Without firm tape-to-head contact, as with poor tangency, there is sound dropout and high-frequency loss.

▓ *Azimuth* Adjustment of the gap must be exactly perpendicular to the length of the tape. Heads that are not in azimuth alignment record and reproduce out-of-phase stereo signals.

It is difficult to visually spot heads that are out of alignment, but you can hear many of the problems caused by misaligned heads. Most studios have a routine schedule of preventive maintenance that includes head alignment. If you are getting poor sound from a tape recorder, have a technician check the heads.

Electronic Alignment Another important procedure in a tape recorder's preventive maintenance is *electronic alignment* (or *calibration*). Because specifications such as bias requirements, frequency response, and sensitivity vary from one tape formulation to another, audiotape recorders have various electronic adjustments so that they all operate at a given standard. Without such a standard, tapes recorded on one ATR may not have the identical response as a recording made on another ATR.

The National Association of Broadcasters (NAB) has established standards for 3¾ ips, 7½ ips, and 15 ips that are in use throughout the United States and much of the world. Europe conforms to the DIN standard set by Deutsche Institute Norme. The Audio Engineering Society (AES) has established the standard for 30 ips.

To perform a physical alignment, you need to use the appropriate alignment tape and follow playback and record alignment procedures. These procedures are available in a number of technical audio books and from the NAB and the AES.

Cleaning the Heads Dust, dirt, and magnetic particles collect on the heads and tape guides even in the cleanest studios. Some of these particles are abrasive; when the tape picks them up and drags them across the heads, they can scratch both the heads and the tape's magnetic coating. If the particle buildup is substantial, sound quality suffers noticeably. For example, if oxide particle buildup is ¹⁄₁₀₀₀ of an inch on the playback head, a recording running at 15 ips will have a loss of 55 dB at 15 kHz.

The best preventive maintenance is to clean the heads and tape guides each time you use a tape recorder. Dense-packed cotton swabs and an approved head cleaner or easy-to-obtain and inexpensive denatured alcohol will do. Try not to use isopropyl alcohol or rubbing alcohol, because they can leave a film on the head and they contain water.

Use one cotton swab for each head and guide (two if the cotton turns brown) and swab the head gently. Commercial head cleaner is available, but it may be too potent for some heads and dissolve part of the plastic. Check with a technician if you are in doubt. For pinch rollers, a rubber cleaner is better, because alcohol could swell and crack the rubber.

Features of Audiotape Recorders

Audiotape recorders have various features that increase their flexibility in production.

Selective Synchronization (Sel Sync)

Multitrack recorders were developed to permit greater control of the sound sources during recording and playback by making it possible to assign each one to its own track. Multitrack recorders also make it possible to record various sound sources at different times by *overdubbing*— recording new material on open tracks and synchronizing it with material on tracks already recorded. The technology that facilitates this production technique, called by the trademarked term **Sel Sync** (short for *selective synchronization*), was developed by Ampex; the innovator was guitarist Les Paul.

Under normal conditions, if you first recorded, say, only the instrumental accompaniment to a vocal, the vocalist would have to listen to the recording (through headphones) to synchronize the words to the music. A distance of a few inches separates the record and playback heads, however, which creates a delay between the music and the lyrics when they are played back together (see 6-13). To eliminate this delay, Sel Sync uses the record head as a playback head for the previously recorded tracks and plays them in sync with the new material being recorded (see 6-14).

Tape Timing

Professional tape recorders are equipped with a *tape timer* that reads out actual tape time in hours, minutes, and seconds and/or with *time code* that reads out in hours, minutes, seconds, and frames. With time code each "frame" of audiotape is coded with a different number. Tape timers provide an easy and, in most cases, indispensable way not only to locate recorded material but also to synchronize it (see Chapter 11).

6-13 Overdubbing Without Sel Sync. This method creates an offset between the sound being played back and the sound being recorded.

Auto-Locator

Even with a tape timer and time-coded tape, locating specific cue points can be time-consuming. An accessory that is part of most professional analog ATRs makes it possible to program cues and store them in memory. At the touch of a few buttons, the tape transport automatically spools to a precise location on the tape. The controller used for this function is generically known as an *auto-locator* (see 6-6).

With an auto-locator, specific cue points on a tape are coded and entered into memory using a keypad. The code is a number in tape time or in time code and is usually interchangeable between the two. To recall the cue point from memory, the coded number is reentered via the key pad. By pressing a *search* button, the auto-locator shuttles the tape to the desired position. At that point, the transport either stops, places itself into *play,* or cycles. *Cycling* loops the tape between two cue points in a play-relocate-play sequence.

CARTRIDGE AND CASSETTE TAPE RECORDERS

The analog cartridge and cassette tape recorders revolutionized audio production techniques and have been a mainstay in audio since their appearance in 1958 and 1963, respectively. But since the development of the digital cartridge and cassette recorder, their analog counterparts are being phased out. Cartridge and cassette recorders are therefore covered in their digital incarnations in Chapter 7.

AUDIO ON ANALOG VIDEOTAPE

The digital revolution has made analog *videotape recorders (VTRs)* obsolescent, but given the heavy investment many TV stations and production houses have in analog VTRs and the cost of changeover to digital VTRs, conversion will be gradual for many. A few analog VTR formats remain in widespread-enough use to merit some discussion here.

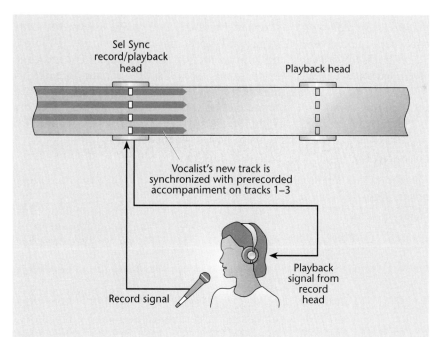

6-14 Overdubbing with Sel Sync. Playback and record are synchronized.

Analog Videotape Formats

Analog VTRs encode analog video and audio that may be analog, frequency modulated, or digital. The three analog formats still in comparatively wide use are Betacam SP, S-VHS, and Hi8.

Betacam SP

The *Betacam SP* (SP stands for superior performance) is a ½-inch format VCR developed for use in TV news and field production. It has two fixed audio heads for conventional longitudinal analog recording. The two tracks can be used separately for monaural recording or for stereo. Although there is Dolby C noise reduction, sound quality is mediocre (see discussion of noise reduction in Chapter 8).

The Betacam SP also has two additional *AFM (audio frequency modulation)* tracks that deliver high-fidelity sound. AFM tracks are recorded by audio heads on the spinning video head drum in the larger video portion of the tape, without interfering with the video signal (see 6-15). The higher tape-to-head speed and the larger recording area help improve audio quality; noise reduction and the use of metal particle tape (coercivity: 1,500 oersteds) also help. The trade-off is that audio and video cannot be recorded separately on AFM tracks.

Betacam SP uses 30-minute cassettes. It can also accommodate large cassettes that provide up to 90 minutes of recording time.

S-VHS

S-VHS is the high-grade version of the well-known VHS consumer system. It is used in news, corporate video, and schools that teach video production. The format is ½-inch, with two longitudinal analog audio channels and two AFM channels with noise reduction.

Even with AFM audio, S-VHS sound quality is not up to Betacam SP standards. One reason is that it uses cobalt-doped iron oxide tape with lower coercivity than metal particle tape. Cassette record time can be up to 120 minutes.

Hi8

Hi8 gets its name from the 8-millimeter width of the cassette tape it uses. It is used in news, industrial production, and production classes in schools.

It has one AFM channel, stereo is optional, and, unlike the Betacam SP and S-VHS VCRs, it has optional two-channel digital sound (see 6-16). A Hi8 cassette cartridge can record up to 120 minutes.

The problem with Hi8, in relation to sound and picture, is that with multiple dubs the audio lags behind the video. The digital audio tracks are recorded by the video heads in spurts. This "segmented" audio has to be reconstructed into a continuous analog audio signal. The process, which takes up to 1/30 of a second, creates an increasingly more noticeable delay of audio behind picture with each dub. Hi8 must therefore be dubbed up to a higher-quality format for extensive postproduction editing.

6-15 Betacam format

6-16 Hi8 format

AUDIO ON FILM

There are three basic types of film—silent, sound, and magnetic—and they come in two gauges: 35mm and 16mm (see 6-17). *Silent film* carries no sound information; it consists of the picture area and two columns of sprocket holes, one on each edge of the film. It is used during shooting when picture and sound are recorded separately—picture with a camera, and sound with an audio recorder (see "Synchronizing Sound and Picture on Film"

6-17 Various film stock formats

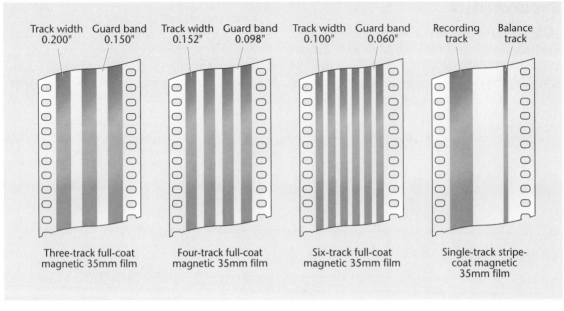

Track width 0.200" Guard band 0.150" Track width 0.152" Guard band 0.098" Track width 0.100" Guard band 0.060" Recording track Balance track

Three-track full-coat magnetic 35mm film   Four-track full-coat magnetic 35mm film   Six-track full-coat magnetic 35mm film   Single-track stripe-coat magnetic 35mm film

6-18 Types of 35mm magnetic film

in Chapter 11). *Sound film* carries both picture and optical sound. The optical process is used for release prints and done photographically in a laboratory. In 16mm optical film, the optical audio track replaces the sprocket holes on one edge of the film.

Magnetic film is similar to audiotape in that it contains all sound and no picture, and it has similar magnetic characteristics, but it is the same size as regular film stock and contains sprocket holes. Magnetic film is available either full coat or stripe coat, and records analog sound.

With *full coat* the oxide coating covers most or all of the film width (see 6-18). The 16mm variety is usually full width for single-track monaural audio; 35mm full coat has three, four, or six magnetic stripes, with clear base between, for three-, four-, or six-channel recording.

In 35mm *stripe coat*, there are two stripes of oxide: a wide stripe for recording single-track mono and a narrow balance stripe to ensure that the film wind on reels is smooth. In 16mm the oxide stripe coat is either down the edge of the film *(edge track)* or down the center of the film *(center track)*.

Sound quality—dynamic range, signal-to-noise ratio, and frequency response—in 16mm magnetic film is mediocre; in 35mm it is a little better. But Dolby processing and other sonic improvements have greatly increased 35mm sound quality.

MAIN POINTS

▶ In audiotape recording, electrical signals are transduced into magnetic signals during the recording phase. During playback the magnetic signals are transduced back into electrical signals.

▶ In analog recording, signals are oriented on the tape in patterns analogous to the waveform of the original signal. The signal is continuous—it is always "on."

▶ Most recording tape is composed of a thin, plastic ribbon of polyester, microscopic needlelike magnetic particles, a binder of synthetic varnish so the particles adhere to the polyester, and a back coating to reduce slippage.

▶ Analog audiotape comes in two thicknesses: 1 and 1½ mil. Professionals prefer the 1½-mil analog tape because it is least likely to crease,

- snap, or stretch and it reduces the chance of print-through.

- Audiotape comes in five widths—$\frac{1}{4}$, $\frac{1}{2}$, 1, and 2 inches (and .15 inch, for analog cassette tape)— to accommodate the various formats used in recording today.

- There are several measures of a tape's ability to reproduce sound: coercivity, the magnetic force it takes to erase a tape fully; retentivity, a measure of the tape's magnetic field strength remaining after an external magnetic force has been removed; and sensitivity, the output level a tape can reproduce.

- Some tape is made for special purposes. Low-print-through tape has lower retentivity and sensitivity so it can handle lower energy levels, thus reducing the chance of magnetic information transferring from one tape layer to another. High-output tape has higher coercivity and sensitivity and, therefore, is capable of reproducing higher output levels.

- Cheap tape can have several defects, which may cause dropout, cinching, ridging, adhesion, cupping, and curling. All adversely affect sound quality.

- Tape should be handled carefully. The tape surface can be sullied by fingerprints, smoke, and dust, and the tape reels can be damaged by being stacked one upon the other. Tape should be stored tails out in a controlled environment of 60 to 75°F and 40 to 60 percent humidity.

- The three essential sections of a tape recorder are the tape transport system, the magnetic heads, and the record and playback electronics.

- A number of controls operate the transport: the power switch, selectable and variable-speed control, play, record, stop, fast-forward, rewind, and the tape edit control.

- An important function of the transport system is to maintain the tape movement at a precise, constant speed. A change in the transport speed could result in audible changes in a recording's frequency. Slow changes are called wow; faster changes are called flutter.

- Analog tape recorders run at various speeds: $1\frac{7}{8}$, $3\frac{3}{4}$, $7\frac{1}{2}$, 15, and 30 inches per second (ips). Generally, the faster the speed, the better the sound quality.

- Most professional analog tape recorders have at least three heads: erase, record, and playback. Many models also have a fourth head for time code.

- Because the magnetic particles on tape respond to magnetization nonlinearly (they cannot make sense of the information carried by the input signal), the record head has a high-frequency bias current that linearizes the magnetic information so it can be encoded on the tape.

- The position of the heads is critical, and any change in their physical alignment—zenith, height, tangency, wrap, or azimuth—adversely affects sound quality. Heads must also be electronically aligned regularly.

- Heads should be demagnetized and cleaned before each session and during long sessions.

- A standard-gauge $\frac{1}{4}$-inch head houses two separate heads and is used for stereo recording. A standard-gauge 2-inch headstack houses 16 or 24 separate heads and can record or play back 16 or 24 tape tracks. Narrow-gauge headstacks are available in $\frac{1}{4}$-, $\frac{1}{2}$-, and 1-inch sizes with as many as 8 tracks on a $\frac{1}{4}$-inch head, 8 or 16 tracks on a $\frac{1}{2}$-inch head, and 16 or 24 tracks on a 1-inch head.

- Multitrack tape recorders have a variety of features including Sel Sync, which temporarily changes selected tracks on the record head into the playback mode. This permits various elements in a recording to be taped synchronously at different times.

- Analog videotape recorders encode analog video and audio that may be analog, frequency modulated, or digital.

- Basically, analog videotape recording encodes a video track, usually two audio tracks, a control or cue track, and an address or time code track.

- There are three types of film: silent, sound, and magnetic.

- Silent film carries no sound information. Sound film carries both picture and optical sound. Magnetic film contains all sound and no picture.

- Magnetic film comes in either full coat or stripe coat.

- Sound quality in 16mm magnetic film is mediocre; in 35mm, without Dolby processing, it is a little better. With Dolby and other processing, 35mm sound quality is greatly improved.

7

Digital Recording

Compared with analog recording, digital recording virtually eliminates noise, distortion, crosstalk, wow and flutter, print-through, and degeneration of sound quality in dubbing. Dynamic range is at least 96 dB and often better. Although the popularity of analog remains stable, and its sonic characteristics are unique, audio is headed toward a digital future—and the future is upon us.

DIGITAL AUDIO

Instead of an analogous relationship between the acoustic sound and the electronically processed signal, *digital recording* uses a numerical representation of the audio signal's actual frequency and amplitude. In analog, *frequency* is the time component and *amplitude* is the level component. In digital, *sampling* is the time component and *quantization* is the level component.

Sampling

Sampling takes periodic samples (voltages) of the original analog signal at fixed intervals and converts them into digital data. The rate at which the fixed intervals sample the original signal each second is called the *sampling frequency*. For example, a sampling frequency of 48 kHz means that samples are taken 48,000 times per second, or each sample period is $\frac{1}{48,000}$ of a second. Because sampling and the component of time are directly related, a system's sampling rate determines its upper frequency limits.

7-1 Sampling. (a) A signal sampled frequently enough contains sufficient information for proper decoding. (b) Too low a sampling rate loses too much information for proper decoding.

Theoretically, the higher the sampling rate, the greater a system's frequency range.

It was determined several years ago that if the highest frequency in a signal were to be digitally encoded successfully, it would have to be sampled at a rate at least twice its frequency.* In other words, if high-frequency response in digital recording is to reach 20 kHz, the sampling frequency must be at least 40 kHz. Too low a sampling rate would cause loss of too much information (see Figure 7-1).

Think of a movie camera that takes 24 still pictures per second. A sampling rate of ¹⁄₂₄ second seems adequate to record most visual activities. Although the camera shutter closes after each ¹⁄₂₄

---

*This concept was developed by a Bell Laboratories researcher named Harry Nyquist. To honor this discovery, the sampling frequency has been named the Nyquist frequency.

second and nothing is recorded, not enough information is lost to impair perception of the event. A person running, for example, does not run far enough in the split second the shutter is closed to alter the naturalness of the movement. If the sampling rates were slowed to 1 frame per second, the running movement would be quick and abrupt; if it were slowed to 1 frame per minute, the running would be difficult to follow.

Digital audio today uses five sampling rates: 32, 44.056, 44.1, 48, and 96 kHz. The international sampling rate, 32 kHz, is used for broadcast digital audio. Because the maximum bandwidth in broadcast transmission is 15 kHz, the 32 kHz sampling rate is sufficient. For laser disc, compact disc, and digital tape recording, however, 44.056, 44.1, and 48 kHz, respectively, are used. For the *digital versatile disc (DVD)*, 48 and 96 kHz are the standards.

Quantization

As samples of the waveform are taken, these voltages are converted into discrete quantities and assigned values, a process known as **quantization**. The assigned value is in the form of *b*inary dig*its* (bits). Most of us learned math using the decimal, or base 10, system which consists of 10 numerals—0 through 9. The binary, or base 2, system uses two numbers—0 and 1. In converting the analog signal to digital, when the voltage is off, the assigned value is 0; when the voltage is on, the assigned value is 1.

A quantity expressed as a binary number is called a *digital word:* 10 is a two-bit word, 101 is a three-bit word, 11010 is a five-bit word, et cetera. Each *n*-bit binary word produces 2^n discrete levels. Therefore, a one-bit word produces two discrete levels—0,1; a two-bit word produces four discrete levels—00, 01, 10, and 11; a three-bit word produces eight discrete levels—111, 110, 101, 100, 011, 010, 001, and 000; and so on. So the more quantizing levels there are, the longer the digital word must be. The longer the digital word, the better the sonic resolution. For example, the number of discrete voltage steps possible in an 8-bit word is 256; in a 16-bit word, it is 65,536; and in a 20-bit word it is 1,048,576. The greater the number of these quantizing levels, the more accurate the representation of the analog signal and the wider the signal-to-noise ratio (see 7-2).*

This raises a question: How can a representation of the original signal be better than the original signal itself? Assume that the original analog signal is an ounce of water with an infinite number of values (molecules). The amount and "character" of the water changes with the number of molecules; it has one "value" with 500 molecules, another with 501, still another with 2,975, and so forth. But all together the values are infinite. Moreover, changes in the original quantity of water are inevitable: Some of it may evaporate, some may be lost if poured, and some may be contaminated or absorbed by dust or dirt.

But what if the water molecules are sampled and then converted to a stronger, more durable form? In so doing, a representation of the water would be obtained in a facsimile from which nothing would be lost. But sufficient samples would have to be obtained to ensure that the character of the original water is maintained.

For example, suppose the molecule samples were converted to ball bearings and a quantity of 1 million ball bearings was a sufficient sample. In this form the original water is not vulnerable to evaporation or contamination from dust and dirt. Even if a ball bearing is lost, they are all the same; therefore, losing one ball bearing does not affect the content or quality of the others.

THE DIGITAL RECORDING/ REPRODUCTION PROCESS

The digital recording/reproduction process essentially involves two complementary procedures in the encoding and decoding of a signal.

The Recording Process

Converting analog signals into a digital format for recording occurs in five basic steps: anti-aliasing, sample and hold, analog-to-digital conversion, signal coding, and data storage (see 7-3).

To keep unwanted high frequencies from *aliasing*—becoming audible when the analog signal begins its passage through the digital sampling system—they are rolled off using a low-pass filter. The process is called *anti-aliasing*.

After anti-aliasing, a *sample-and-hold* circuit temporarily holds the analog voltage level for the duration of a single sample period. This allows

---

*In quantizing the analog signal into discrete binary numbers (voltages), noise, known as *quantizing noise,* is generated. The signal-to-noise ratio in an analog-to-digital conversion system is 6 dB for each bit. A 16-bit system is sufficient to deal with quantizing noise. This gives digital sound a signal-to-noise ratio of 96 dB (6 dB × 16-bit system), which is pretty good by analog standards. But by digital standards, 20-bit systems are dramatically better, which gives you an idea of the extraordinary fidelity produced by the 24-bit systems now on the market.

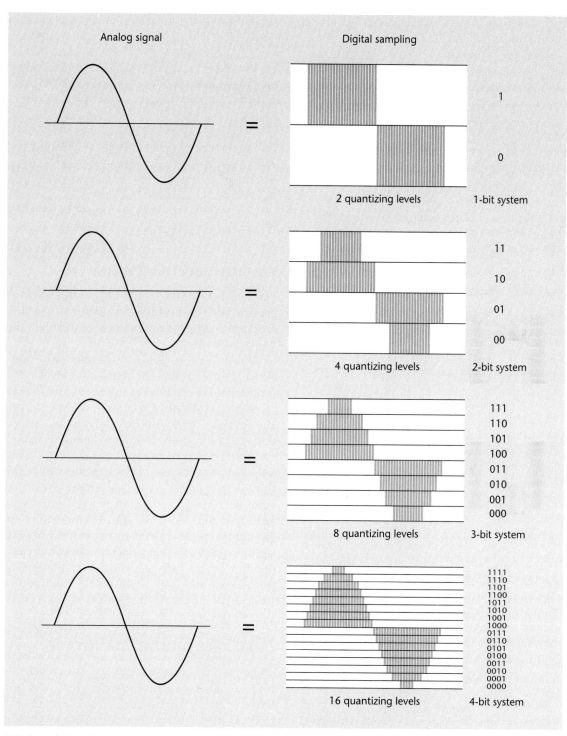

Analog signal

Digital sampling

2 quantizing levels — 1-bit system

1
0

4 quantizing levels — 2-bit system

11
10
01
00

8 quantizing levels — 3-bit system

111
110
101
100
011
010
001
000

16 quantizing levels — 4-bit system

1111
1110
1101
1100
1011
1010
1001
1000
0111
0110
0101
0100
0011
0010
0001
0000

7-2 Quantizing. As the number of quantizing levels increases, the digital sampling of the analog signal becomes more accurate. In 16-bit systems, the audio spectrum is divided into 65,536 values in a single sample. A 20-bit system captures 1,048,576 values in a single sample.

7-3 Basic steps in analog-to-digital conversion

enough time for the analog-to-digital converter to generate a digital word that corresponds to the sampled voltage.

During analog-to-digital conversion, the signal is sampled and quantized in a remarkable operation. For example, in a 16-bit system at a sampling rate of 48 kHz, as the signal is sampled and held, 16 successive approximations are performed within $\frac{1}{48,000}$ of a second.

Once the signal has been converted into digital form, it is coded. This process involves data coding, error correction, and record (or data) modulation. *Data coding* prevents ambiguity by making it easier to identify the beginning of each digital word in the bit stream. Data coding serves much the same purpose as spaces between words in a sentence. *Error correction* is necessary to minimize the effect of storage defects. Because digital data is packed at very high density, storage defects are inevitable. These defects would degrade the quality of digital audio, especially with digital audiotape recorders and compact disc formats. Data error rate for hard disks and optical disks is very low. Error correction minimizes the number of errors during the storage process. *Record (or data) modulation* is the final processing of digital data before storage. Although the data is in the form of 1s and 0s, binary code is not an efficient way to store data. Therefore, it is modulated and stored as pulses of magnetic energy. Data may be stored onto any recording medium such as tape, compact disc, or computer disk.

The Reproduction Process

The five basic steps in the digital reproduction process are: demodulation, error correction, digital-to-analog conversion, sample and hold, and low-pass filtering.

Demodulation performs three important functions. (1) It amplifies the signals, which are at a very low level; (2) it takes the waveforms, which are inevitably distorted by the conversion process, and reshapes them into their original modulated states; and (3) it returns the modulated signals to their original binary form of 1s and 0s. *Error correction* compensates for errors introduced during storage. In *digital-to-analog* conversion, the digital word is converted to an analog voltage that is analogous to the original signal before sampling. The output *sample-and-hold* circuit removes irregular signals, called *switching glitches,* from the reproduction chain. *Low-pass filtering* at the output smoothes in the final waveform any nonlinearity that was introduced by the digital sampling process.

OPEN-REEL DIGITAL AUDIOTAPE

There are three essential differences between the type of audiotape used for analog recording and that used for digital. First, digital tape does not have to be as thick as tape used for analog recording, the magnetic coating in particular. In the analog system, varying signal strengths recorded on the tape correspond to the different levels from the input signal. To a great extent, the thickness of the oxide coating determines the tape's signal-to-noise ratio. Moreover, saturating the tape with too much signal must be avoided.

In digital recording, the sampling frequency is constant, and at each sample the tape is saturated with a series of pulses. There is no resultant distortion, because the digital system has to deal only with the presence (1) or absence (0) of a pulse. Therefore, tape thickness is not a factor in the tape's ability to reproduce dynamic range. The total thickness of open-reel digital tape (base, back, and magnetic coating) is about 1 mil.

Second, the coercivity of nonmetal tape used for digital recording is about twice that of analog tape. Greater coercivity is needed to retain the very short wavelengths of the higher frequencies and the densely packed digital information, which is about 10 times that stored in analog recording.

Third, any tape requires care in handling, but digital tape requires more care than analog does. It is essential that the working area be as free of dust and dirt as possible. Moderate temperature and low humidity should be kept within ranges of ±10 percent. Oils from the hands can cause quality degradation of both the magnetic and back coatings. If tape is soiled, it should be wiped gently with a soft cloth. Cleaning liquids used on tape recorder heads must be completely dry before digital tape is used.

DIGITAL AUDIOTAPE RECORDERS

Digital audiotape recorders come with either stationary or rotary heads. The stationary-head machines professionals use are open reel. Professional- and consumer-grade rotary head recorders are cassettes.

Stationary-Head Digital Audio Recording

The *stationary-head digital audiotape (S-DAT) recorder* is similar in looks and operation to the open-reel analog machine. Its recording format and head configuration, though, are different.

DASH Format

To standardize the S-DAT design, companies agreed to manufacturer their recorders in either of two formats: *DASH (Digital Audio Stationary Head)* or *Pro Digi* (Professional Digital, or PD). The DASH format is used with most stationary head machines. Pro Digi recorders are still in use, but the format is no longer marketed.

The **DASH format** specifies sampling frequency, tape format, track geometry, packing density, and error correction for 24- and 48-channel digital tape recorders. DASH also specifies protocols for two-channel, open-reel DTRs, although these machines are no longer being actively marketed in the United States.

Tape width for both the 24- and 48-track machines is ½ inch; tape speed is 30 ips; and sampling rates are 44.1, 44.056, and 48 kHz. Playing time for a 10½-inch reel is 30 minutes; a 12½-inch reel is 45 minutes; and a 14-inch reel is 60 minutes.

DASH machines have either two or three heads. On two-head machines, the heads are record and playback. The three-head machines, in addition to the Record and Playback heads, also have a *sync record* head for insert or Sel Sync recording. Both configurations also include an analog erase head.

Rotary-Head Digital Audio Recording

Storing video information on tape requires a different recording system than the one used to record sound in stationary-head recorders. Due to the considerable bandwidth it takes to store video, very high tape speeds are necessary. In a stationary-head format, the tape speed would have to be many times faster than the 30 ips of today's fastest ATRs and it would take thousands of feet of tape to make a video recording. Therefore, instead of increasing longitudinal tape speed in video recording, the videotape head rotates at very high speed (2,000 revolutions per minute in stereo R-DATs, and more than 14,000 rpm in modular digital multitrack recorders). This creates the tape-to-head velocity essential for the wide bandwidth to store the video information without requiring faster longitudinal tape speeds. This technique is called **helical scanning**, due to the somewhat spiral shape of the tape when it is threaded around the head assembly (the Greek word for spiral is *helix*). Helical videotape recording has made it possible not only to record picture on tape, but also to produce digital sound on audio- and videocassette as well.

Rotary-Head Digital Audiotape Recorders

The **rotary-head digital audiotape (R-DAT) recorder** (see 7-4) has the wide dynamic range, low distortion, and immeasurable wow and flutter common to digital audio. Although the R-DAT uses cassette tape, it equals or exceeds many standard digital specifications.

At the very least, professional R-DATs operate at two sampling frequencies: 44.1 kHz and 48 kHz. Many models also include 32 kHz. Recording and playback can be done at all three sampling rates. Longitudinal tape speed is about ⅓ ips, one-sixth the speed of analog cassette recorders. The very slow speed does not affect sound quality, however, due to the high speed of the head drum and digital processing of the audio signal. The recording format is two-channel stereo.

R-DAT has other advantages. For example, the encoding of nonaudio data permits automatic cueing to a particular selection, skipping over selections, and numbering selections. A high-speed search function facilitates quick search-to-cue spooling. Some R-DATs have time code. R-DAT machines are available in portable, lightweight

Additional switches under lid for: analog/digital input selector, sampling frequency selector (32, 44.1, or 48 kHz), digital I/O format selector (AES/EBU or SPDIF), cassette eject, and clock/calendar set

Switches for end search, consecutive renumbering of start IDs, actual/recorded time and date display, end ID write, ID erase, and auto/manual ID indexing

Internal monitor speaker

DC power input (12V DC)

Headphone matrix: selects stereo, mono left, mono right, mono sum, and M/S (mid-side) stereo headphone monitoring modes

Remote-control socket

Headphone jack

Switches for power on/off, key hold (locks transport controls), and cassette compartment window

Selector switches for L/R line; flat response or high-pass filtered mic inputs; L/R mic input attenuation (0dB or −20 dB); 48V phantom power on/off; and mic/line limiter on/off

Transport controls for ID search (back and forward), rewind/review, play (with LED indicator), fast-forward/cue, and stop

Front panel controls for record and pause (with LED indicators), independently lockable L/R record level, ID write, time display format, counter/margin indicator reset, display illumination on/off, and tape/source monitoring

Display for clock and counter, battery status, peak-level metering, margin indicator, source/tape monitor, transport status, and sample rate

Monitor level control for headphone and internal speaker

7-4 R-DAT. This particular model is portable. Its head configuration allows both the monitoring of source material and monitoring directly from tape; most R-DATs permit only monitoring of the source material. This machine comes with a separate time code unit; most time code R-DATs have the time code generator built-in.

cassette-size units, as well as in rack-mountable studio models.

R-DAT Audiocassette Tape

Digital audiotape (DAT) is about ⅟₇-inch wide, slightly wider than the standard analog audio-cassette; tape thickness is about ¼ mil. The cartridge itself is half the size of an analog cassette, and the length of tape in a cartridge is one-fourth that of an analog cassette. Cassettes are available in different lengths up to two hours at 48 and 44.1 kHz and four hours at 32 kHz. As it is in analog recording: The slower the speed, the poorer the sound quality, the digital format notwithstanding. Most digital audiocassette tape is metal particle, not lower than 1,500 oersteds.

Although the tape is enclosed in a plastic cartridge, its thinness and the density of the encoded information (114 million bits per square inch) make the tape and data extremely susceptible to damage from dirt, dust, and mishandling, especially because the track width of the encoded data is about one-tenth the thickness of a human hair (see 7-5).

7-5 Tape pattern of an R-DAT recorder. Actual digital audio data are recorded on the center portion of the tape. The width of each data bit is 13.591 microns, about one-tenth the thickness of a human hair. The ATF (automatic track finding) pilot signal is used for servo track alignment. Subcode data enable rapid program access.

Bulk erasing cannot totally eliminate the recorded signal on the high-density DAT surface. A recorded signal can be completely removed only by rerecording.

Many R-DATs have a moisture prevention cutoff to help protect the tape. Any moisture entering the unit from the tape stops the recorder, which then heats up to evaporate the moisture. When the unit is dry, it begins to function again.

Problems with DAT

It is natural to assume that because the digital recording process converts analog signals into a more durable format, the sonic results are relatively invariable, regardless of the digital cassette tape used. Such is not the case. Qualitative differences exist among the various brands of DAT, just as they do among the various brands of analog tape.

▪ **Wear** The R-DAT's rotary head spins at 2,000 rpm which, over time, can create a molecular break-down that could lead to tape shedding and head clogging. Interference with tape-to-head contact is of much greater consequence in digital recording than it is in analog recording, due to the densely packed digital information, among other things.

▪ **Error concealment** In R-DAT errors result from tape noise, tape defects, head-to-tape contact problems, and sullied or creased tape. To the extent it can, the system tries to conceal them. But if there are more errors than it can handle, they become audible. Certain makes of DAT are better able to deal with concealment than others.

▪ **Cassette shells** Like cassette tape, the plastic cassette tape shell is also subject to wear. A worn tape shell could create audible error rate variations caused by problems with tape rotation, accelerated tape wear, debris that could roughen the running of the tape, timing errors, and tape vibration.

▪ **Erasure** Some DATs have a higher remnance. *Remnance* is residual magnetization from a previous recording after erasure. In rerecording, this could create a significant error rate.

■ Aging Because an increasing number of recordings are being mastered onto DAT, tape aging has become a concern. When DAT is in good condition, digital copies can be made with no sonic degradation. But if a DAT has deteriorated, the inevitable increased error rate creates a loss in sound quality that would be quite audible.

Storage in a scrupulously controlled cool-temperature and low-humidity environment is necessary. Warm temperatures and high humidity accelerate tape deterioration. Indeed, high humidity can lead to water penetration into the gaps of wound tape after long storage periods, causing tape layers to stick or the magnetic particles to rust, or both. Rusting is particularly notable because R-DATs are subject to buildup of condensation and, unless the tape's magnetic particles are protected in some way, rusting could be accelerated.

Care of R-DATs

Concerns about potential problems with DAT lead logically to the consideration of R-DAT care.

Aligning an R-DAT

Proper alignment is critical to the operation of all tape recorders, particularly the R-DAT. The mechanisms are quite delicate and require extremely fine tuning.

R-DATs are designed to correct errors due to noise, slight mistracking, and dropout. But if there is significant mistracking, error correction cannot handle it, and the audio mutes.

Of particular importance are the tape guides. If they are not properly adjusted, the tape will not track correctly as it passes around the head drum's scanner. A reference tape is used for alignment of the guides.

Proper tape tension is also important to alignment, because it affects track angle and, therefore, must be checked before making adjustments to the drum. Usually, a specially designed cassette with a tension gauge built into each hub is used. The amount of tension is read off a scale in the body of the cassette. Tension is adjusted for normal play, reverse, and shuttle.

Proper track spacing in record mode is determined by checking the frequency-generating wheel on the capstan shaft to make sure the frequency is correct. This is done with a scratch tape.

Tracks recorded at the proper angle and spacing and with correct timing will play back accurately on another R-DAT. If timing is off, however, the recorder will be able to play its own tapes, but those tapes may not play back accurately on another machine. Recording begins when a sensor generates a pulse once each revolution of the scanner. A timing reference tape is used to adjust the relative timing between the event on the reference tape and the sensor pulse.

Cleaning an R-DAT

The importance of having a regular equipment maintenance schedule cannot be overemphasized. With R-DATs, that is almost as easily done as said, using cleaning tapes especially made for them. These tapes are nonabrasive, gentle to the heads, and good at removing small, loose particles in the tape path. It is wise to clean an R-DAT after about 20 hours of use. It takes five to 10 seconds to run a cleaning tape.

Cleaning tapes usually will not remove grime and debris that get into the nooks and crannies of the small working parts. To do this, you have to get inside the R-DAT and clean the tape path and heads, if you are technically able. For this operation use a lint-free lens-cleaning cloth, a chamois, foam-tipped cleaner dipped in an approved VCR cleaning solvent, or a small, round wooden stick soaked in VCR cleaning solvent. The wood should be strong enough to dislodge the debris but soft enough to not scratch the drum surface. Do not use anything that could clog the tape path and heads, such as cotton swabs, tissue, or cotton cloth.

Rotary-Head Open-Reel Digital Audiotape Recorders

The rotary-head format is used in the open-reel design by Nagra. The Nagra-D is a 24-bit, two- or four-channel, ¼-inch tape recorder designed for use in the field (see 7-6). The four-channel recording system consists of pairs of tracks. Data

Lockout for either pair of channels can be selected during recording

Hermetically sealed, transparent cover

When not using a PC, the small built-in display gives access to and information about time code, counters, in/out configuration, and drop-out files

Selection of the signal to the headphone outputs can be made via the phones switches

Audio levels are shown on microprocessor-driven level indicators

The main function keys are easily accessible and can be operated while wearing gloves

a

Level adjustment is via two concentric potentiometers for each channel: the outer ring for input sensitivity, the inner ring for fade control (recording the control on the tape gives a nondestructive fade-out)

Three-position, low-cut filters are available on each channel

Each channel is equipped with an individual direct amplifier, permitting phase switching

Sockets for synchronization with video (PAL, SECAM, NTSC), EXT (32, 44.1, or 48 kHz), AES, or time code (SMPTE/EBU)

The RS 422 serial communication port can be used to connect a PC for external control or editing

The four analog audio channel inputs on XLR connectors are individually switchable: line, T12 V, Ph+12V, and Ph+48 V

b

There is one AES input/output for each pair of channels, allowing 24 bits per sample to be recorded

Four-channel analog audio outputs provide connection to external analog equipment

c

The internal battery pack can be connected to an external current control charger

Continuous selectable monitoring of all four channels or the cue track is possible via a monitoring amplifier fed to two ¼" headphone jacks

7-6 Rotary-head open-reel digital audiotape recorder. (a) Front view; (b) left side view; (c) right side view.

for channels 1 and 2 are on one track; data for channels 3 and 4 are on the other track. This configuration allows simple lockout of either pair. There are also three longitudinal tracks for cue, control, and time code. Sampling frequencies are 32, 44.1, and 48 kHz; tape speeds are about 1.9 ips for two channels and about 3.9 ips for four channels; signal-to-noise ratio is 98 dB.

Modular Digital Multitrack Recorders

The *modular digital multitrack (MDM) recorder* also uses rotating heads to record audio. But instead of using an R-DAT transport with digital audiocassette tape, the MDM uses a videocassette transport with videocassette tape. It can record up to eight channels and be linked to multiple units, thereby expanding track capability in eight-channel increments (see 7-7). As many as 16 MDMs (of the same format) can be stacked with

a cable loop-through, and run synchronously, to provide a total of 128 tracks. This capability is what the *modular* refers to.

The two formats of MDMs are distinguished by the tape and transport used. One format, the *digital tape recording system (DTRS)* uses Hi8 video-cassette tape. The other format, *ADAT* (the *A* stands for Alesis, its developer), uses S-VHS. Although standard Hi8 and S-VHS tape can be used, versions of these tapes optimized for MDM are available. Currently, Sony and Tascam support DTRS; Alesis, Fostex, and Panasonic support ADAT.

A major operational difference between the two formats is the maximum recording time. The tape speed of DTRS is just slightly faster than standard-play speed, which yields 108 minutes per tape. ADAT runs at about three times normal speed for a recording time of 60 minutes per tape.

There are a number of features of MDMs that facilitate production, although they vary with make

Hours, minutes, seconds, frames LED counter

Variable-speed shuttle dial for pinpoint section location and cueing

15-segment record-level LEDs mimic those of many mixing consoles for matching recording levels

Familiar tape deck controls

Dual locate and memo points to save time during punch-in rehearsing and overdubbing

7-7 Modular digital multitrack tape recorder. This model has eight tracks and can record 108 minutes on a standard 120-minute Hi8 videotape. A single cable can lock up and synchronize two machines for 16-track recording. This modular approach allows up to 16 of these MDMs to be interlocked, providing 128 tracks (in eight-track increments) of recording capability. In addition to the usual transport functions such as *play, record,* and so on, there are controls for tape shuttle, sample rate selection, locator points, rehearse and auto-punch, clock source selection, time code generate/record, and soft keys that are used in conjunction with a display button that allows the setting of preroll and crossfade times.

and model. Features such as location memories, auto-loop/rehearse in both record and playback, digital crossfade times, time code, and variable-pitch change.

MDMs have several advantages:

■ They provide an inexpensive way for a studio to have digital multitrack capability that is expandable in eight-channel increments, and at relatively low cost.

■ Sound quality is not sacrificed with multiple tracks, because the widest portion of the tape, the video portion, is used to encode the audio.

■ Dubbing can be done between recorders, in sync if necessary.

■ Operational data such as locate points, time code, frame rate, and other information can be stored and retrieved.

■ Some MDMs can be converted from the standard eight-channel, 16-bit recorder to a four-channel, 20-bit recorder.

■ MDMs take up comparatively little space, even when several units are stacked.

DIGITAL AUDIO ON DIGITAL VIDEOCASSETTE TAPE

It is somewhat ironic that it became possible to digitize an audio signal on videotape before it was possible to digitize a video signal. In the late 1980s, the first *digital videotape recorder (DVTR)* was introduced. At last writing, five systems were in use. Today there are double that number—and counting.

The major differences among these systems have more to do with the way in which video is processed than with the audio. There are also differences in compatibility among systems, tape width, and cassette recording time.

Sound in DVTRs is digital quality. The differences in audio among the various systems come down to bit rate and number of audio channels.

Due to the number of DVTR systems available and that their principal advantages and disadvantages have more to do with video than audio, a discussion of these systems is better left to the television production books. Table 7-1, however, gives you an idea of the similarities and differences among their audio formats.

Table 7-1 Digital videotape formats

Type	Tape Width	Number of Digital Audio Channels	Sound Channel Coding*
D-1	About ¾ inch	4	16–20-bit @ 48 kHz
D-2	About ¾ inch	4	16-bit @ 48 kHz
D-3	½ inch	4	20-bit @ 48 kHz
D-5[†]	½ inch	4	20-bit @ 48 kHz
D-6	About ¾ inch	10	20-bit @ 48 kHz
Digital Betacam	½ inch	4	20-bit @ 48 kHz
Betacam SX	½ inch	4	16-bit @ 48 kHz
Digital S	½ inch	4	16-bit @ 48 kHz
DVCPRO	¼ inch	2	16-bit @ 48 kHz
DVCAM	¼ inch	2 4	16-bit @ 48 kHz 12-bit @ 32 kHz

*In the 20-bit machines, the coding tape can handle this quantization but some may not be equipped with 20-bit converters. 18-bit converters are more common.

[†]There is no D-4 because in Japanese culture the number *4* has a negative stigma attached.

DISK-BASED AUDIO SYSTEMS

Until the computer revolution, tape was *the* medium for recording audio. Today audio (and video) information is also produced and stored on disk. Disk-based systems have several advantages over tape-based systems: All data are digital; recording, playback, and signal processing are possible in a self-contained unit; information retrieval is nonlinear and virtually instantaneous; encoded data can be nondestructive; synchronization options are extensive; and storage capacity is substantial. Not to be overlooked are the greatly increased creative and technical possibilities disk-based systems have afforded.

Disk-based systems can be divided into two groups: record/playback and delivery. Record/playback systems are used in production and postproduction. Delivery systems are what the final production is transferred to for distribution. Examples of delivery systems are the music CD, CD-ROM, and *digital versatile disk (DVD)*.* Because this book deals with the audio production process, only disk-based record/playback systems are addressed.

Disk-Based Record/Playback Systems

Record/playback production systems include the magneto-optical disc, mini disc, digital cartridge

---

*The DVD is the same diameter and thickness as the compact disc, but its difference in makeup provides for a data capacity of about eight times that of the CD. To further add to the DVD's storage capabilities, discs can be either dual-layer, dual-sided, or both.

Although the DVD is essentially a delivery system, at this writing, it is also being developed as a record/playback system. The DVD's various formats, or "books," for application to various uses are labeled A through E and aligned as follows:

    A: DVD-ROM
    B: DVD Video
    C: DVD Audio
    D: DVD Recordable
    E: DVD-RAM

The DVD-ROM and Video standards were the first completed, followed by the DVD-RAM and Recordable formats. The Audio format is the last to be ratified.

disk, recordable compact disc, rewritable compact disc, solid-state recorder, and hard disk.

Magneto-Optical Recording

Magneto-optical (MO) recording, like magnetic digital tape recording, uses tiny magnetic particles to encode digital information. But unlike magnetic tape recording, (1) the MO recording medium is disc-based, (2) instead of magnetic heads to orient the particles, a laser beam is used, and (3) to orient the magnetic particles, they must be heated to extremely high temperatures.

The MO disc's main advantages are: (1) unlike recordable CDs, it is erasable and can be used like tape; (2) it is two-sided to increase playing time; and (3) perhaps most significant of all, it uses an optical instead of a mechanical process, which makes it less susceptible to wear. Its main disadvantages are that it is not interchangeable with ordinary CD players and that, even with two-sided recording, playing time is limited (see 7-8).

Mini Disc

The *mini disc™ (MD™)*, originally intended for the consumer market, has become a popular, inexpensive alternative to higher-priced disk-based systems, particularly in radio and project studios. The mini disc is a 2½-inch-wide magneto-optical disc with a recording time of 74 minutes in stereo and about 148 minutes in mono (see 7-9). Audio is digital quality with low distortion, low noise, and a dynamic range of 105 dB.

The MD system uses two types of media: audio discs and data discs. *Audio discs* are two-channel CD-type media for prerecorded material. *Data discs* are blank, recordable magneto-optical media. The MD offers instantaneous random locate capability, easy portability, and, depending on the system, two or four tracks. Its data compression scheme limits its use for critical recording, however.

Digital Cartridge Disk System

The *digital cartridge disk system* is the successor to the analog tape cartridge system. Like the tape cart, the disk cart can be a recorder/player unit or a player-only unit. Unlike the tape cart, which used only audiotape, the disk cart's record/play medium

7-8 Magneto-optical disk recorder/player. MO discs provide stereo recording times of approximately 12, 20, 50, or 60 minutes using 128, 230, 540, or 640 MB disks at a sampling rate of 44.1 kHz. This model also permits editing and adopts the PC-standard (.WAV) file format for interchange of audio between Mac- and PC-based digital audio workstations.

7-9 Comparison between mini disc and compact disc

CD

MD

4.7 inch (120mm)

2.5 inch (64mm)

can be a compact disc, magneto-optical disc, mini disc, floppy disk, or hard disk. The cartridge is the plastic container that holds the disk.

The cartridge disk is used for short program materials, such as songs, spot announcements, station IDs, program "intros" and "outros," jingles, and bumpers (music lead-ins or lead-outs that immediately precede or follow a program segment). It facilitates tight and reliable production with its instant start, automatic recueing, and a variety of other features that include back cueing, track selection, automatic fade-in, and an information display (see 7-10). Digital cart systems can be interfaced with a computer for editing and to assemble a playlist, for automatic cueing, and for starting the various audio segments. A playlist is made up of any combination of audio program materials, including their length and time of broadcast.

Recordable Compact Discs

In one sense, the *recordable compact disc (CD-R)* is not a production tool because, once encoded, the information cannot be manipulated—edited, equalized, remixed, and so on. In another sense, it is a record/playback medium and as such has become a valuable production tool that has made in-studio CD premastering possible and affordable (see 7-11).

The CD-R makes the compact disc somewhat similar to recording tape in that it has unlimited playback, but until recently it could be recorded on only once and could not be erased. Even false starts are there for good. Hence, many users assembled their audio on DAT or hard disk and then transferred it to CD-R.

The recordable compact disc conforms to the standards document known as *Orange Book*. According to this standard, data encoded on a CD-R

7-10 Digital cartridge mini disc recorder and player. The recorder is also capable of editing data on a disc as well as reading and writing text information such as disc and track names. The cart player includes rotary-knob track selection, instant start, and automatic cue to audio.

7–11 Compact-disc recorder. This model CD-R accepts any frequency from 32 kHz to 48 kHz and converts to CD-standard 44.1 kHz. IDs for DAT, MD, and CD can be copied, enabling one-touch cloning, and skip-ID settings can be recorded to CD.

does not have to be recorded all at once but can be added to whenever the user wishes, making it more convenient to produce sequential audio material. But CD-Rs conforming to the Orange Book standard are not compatible with standard CD players. To be playable on any standard CD player, the CD-R must conform to the *Red Book* standard, which requires that a table of contents (TOC) file be encoded onto the disc.* A TOC file is written at the start of the disc and includes information related to subcode and copy prohibition data, index

*In addition to the Orange and Red Book standards, there are Yellow, Green, White, and Blue Book standards. The *Yellow Book* format describes the basic specifications for computer-based CD-ROM (compact disc–read-only memory). The *Green Book* format describes the basic specifications for CD-I (compact disc–interactive), also designated CD-ROM XA (the *XA* is short for extended *a*rchitecture). It is aimed at multimedia applications that combine audio, graphic images, animation, and full-motion video. The *White Book* describes basic specifications for full-motion, compressed videodiscs. The *Blue Book* format provides specifications for a high-density compact-disc (HDCD) format.

numbering, and timing information. The TOC, which is written onto the disc after audio assembly, tells the CD player where each cut starts and ends. Once it is encoded, any audio added to the disc will not be playable on standard CD players due to the write-once limitation of CD-R. It is therefore important to know the types of "color book" standards with which a CD recorder is compatible.

One answer to this problem is to use preformatted TOC tracks of different lengths, depending on the amount of TOC data to be encoded. Audio program data can be written on the first available track and continue to be written uninterrupted across track boundaries until the recorder is stopped. The disadvantage to this approach, however, is that preformatting reduces disc time for program material.

Compact-disc recorders are available in different recording speeds. For example, single- (1×), double- (2×), quad- (4×), and 6× speed. Single-speed machines record in real time, that is, at the CD's playback speed, 2× machines records at twice the playback speed, reducing by half the time it takes to create a CD, and so on.

CD-R technology has revolutionized pre-mastering, particularly in music recording, by making it convenient and relatively inexpensive to produce a finished, customized music CD at the end of a recording session—in the studio.

Rewritable Compact Disc

As revolutionary as the CD-R technology has been, it will be short-lived. Its successor—the rewritable compact disc—is on the market. *CD-rewritable (CD-RW)* is like audiotape in that it can be recorded on, erased, and used again for another recording. If the driver program supports it, erase can even be random. Like the CD recorders, CD-RW drives operate at different speeds to shorten recording time, but they include the added abilities to play CD-ROMs and to record and play CD-R discs. However, CD-RWs must be read in either CD-RW drives or new CD-ROM drives that support MultiRead, a specification set by the Optical Storage Technology Association (OSTA) and agreed to by the major manufacturers of CD-R, CD-RW, CD-ROM, and DVD-ROM discs and drives.

Solid-State Digital Audio Recorder/Editor

The solid-state digital audio recorder/editor is a 16-bit recorder/player with built-in virtual editing that uses *PCMCIA (Personal Computer Memory Card International Association)* cards as the storage medium (see 7-12). The machine shown in

7-12 Solid-state digital audio recorder/editor. This machine uses PCMCIA cards as the recording medium, uses D-size batteries, weighs about 6 pounds (with the pack), and provides up to five hours of recording time with a four-cell pack and up to 15 hours of continuous operation with an eight-cell pack.

Figure 7-12 is designed for use in broadcast news reporting from the field. Recording capacity is 40 minutes (mono) on one PCMCIA card; there is a double card holder for continuous, extended recording time. The recording method is digital compression. Sampling rates are 16, 24, 32, and 48 kHz.

Hard-Disk Recording

What once took various types of equipment—console, tape recorder(s), and signal processors, to name the most obvious—located in different areas of the control room to do a production, now can be done at a central location with a single hard-disk recorder.

Hard-disk recording resembles tape recording in that it encodes, stores, and reproduces a signal on a few or several different tracks. But there the resemblance ends. Unlike tape recording, hard-disk recording has a different, more versatile channel-track configuration; information access is random and quick; storage capacity is far greater; data is nondestructive; editing is nonlinear (see Chapter 17); and it is possible to do signal processing, such as equalization, reverberation, and delay (see Chapter 8).

On a professional analog open-reel tape recorder, one input, one output, and one channel are dedicated to each track. Once a track has been magnetically encoded, that information is tied to that track; it cannot be moved to another track or slipped out of time without being rerecorded.

With hard-disk recording, the relationships of channels to inputs, outputs, and tracks are not directly linked. Once the computer-based audio data is recorded and stored, it can be assigned to any output(s) and moved in time. For example, a hard-disk recorder may have four inputs, eight outputs, 16 channels, and 256 virtual tracks. This means that up to four inputs can be used to record up to four channels at one time; up to eight

channels at one time can be used for internal mixing or routing; up to 16 channels (real tracks) are simultaneously available during playback; and up to 256 separate **soundfiles*** can be maintained and assigned to a virtual track. **Virtual tracks** provide all the functionality of an actual track, but cannot be played back simultaneously. For example, in a 16-channel system with 256 virtual tracks, only 16 tracks can play back at once. Think of 16 stacks of index cards totaling 256 cards. Assume that each stack is a channel. A card can be moved from anywhere in a stack to the top of the same stack or to the top of another stack. There are 256 cards, but only 16 of them can be on top at once. In other words, any virtual track can be assigned to any channel(s) and slipped along that channel or across channels.

There are two basic types of hard-disk recorders: modular (stand-alone) and computer-based. Both types also usually have editing capability (see Chapter 17).

It is difficult to discuss recording operations generically, because terms, configurations, and visual displays differ from system to system, but Figure 7-13 should give you a sense of the procedures.

Digital Audio Workstations

Hard-disk recorder/editors are also known as **digital audio workstations (DAW)**, although some purists make a distinction between the two. A DAW combines a host computer with specialized hardware and software and can be upgraded and expanded. Modular units do not require a desktop computer as host, and the choice of supported peripherals for expansion is limited.

---

*Audio that is encoded onto the disk takes the form of a *soundfile*. The soundfile contains information about the sound such as amplitude and duration. When the soundfile is opened, most systems display that information on a monitor.

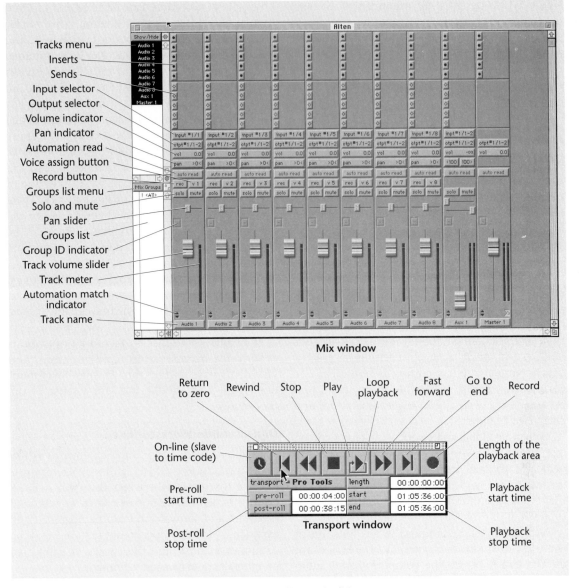

Tracks menu
Inserts
Sends
Input selector
Output selector
Volume indicator
Pan indicator
Automation read
Voice assign button
Record button
Groups list menu
Solo and mute
Pan slider
Groups list
Group ID indicator
Track volume slider
Track meter
Automation match indicator
Track name

Mix window

Return to zero
Rewind
Stop
Play
Loop playback
Fast forward
Go to end
Record

On-line (slave to time code)
Pre-roll start time
Post-roll stop time

Length of the playback area
Playback start time
Playback stop time

transport = **Pro Tools**		length	00:00:00:00
pre-roll	00:00:04:00	start	01:05:36:00
post-roll	00:00:38:15	end	01:05:36:00

Transport window

7-13 Mix and transport windows of one hard-disk recording and editing system

A DAW can be integrated with and networked to a collection of devices, such as other audio, video, and MIDI sources, within or among facilities in the same or different locations. A DAW's systemwide communication with other external devices is facilitated through the distribution of standard digital interfaces such as *AES/EBU*, *SPDIF*, and *SCSI* (see Table 7-2).

DIGITAL AUDIO NETWORKING

Recording has come a long way since the days when overdubbing provided a way to manipulate time and space. Signal processing added to that capability with effects such as delay, reverberation, time compression, and pitch shifting. Digital technology provided the means to access data randomly and nonlinearly. Workstations facilitated speedy interstudio interchange of encoded, digital-quality audio. Now, through telephone lines, a recording can be produced in real time between studios across town or across the country with little or no loss in audio quality and at relatively low cost.

Integrated Services Digital Network (ISDN) is a public telephone service that allows cheap use of a flexible, wide-area, all-digital network (see 7-14). With ISDN it is possible to have a vocalist in New York, wearing headphones for the foldback feed, singing into a microphone whose signal is routed to a studio in Los Angeles. In L.A. the singer's audio is fed through a console, along with the accompaniment from, say, the L.A. studio (it could be from elsewhere), and recorded. When necessary, the singer in New York, the accompanying musicians (from wherever), and the recordist in L.A. can communicate with each other through a talkback system. Commercials are now being done with the announcer in a studio in one city, and the recordist adding the effects in another city. And unlike much of today's advanced technology, ISDN is a relatively uncomplicated service to use.

Table 7- 2 Standard digital interfaces

The *AES/EBU* interface is a professional digital audio connection standard specified jointly by the Audio Engineering Society and the European Broadcast Union. Its standard calls for two audio channels to be encoded in a serial data stream and transmitted through a balanced line using XLR connectors.

SPDIF (Sony/Philips Digital Interface) is the consumer version of the AES/EBU standard. It calls for an unbalanced line using phono connectors. SPDIF is implemented on consumer digital audio equipment such as CD players.

SCSI (Small Computer Systems Interface). Pronounced "scuzzy," SCSI is the standard for hardware and software command language. It allows two-way communication between, primarily, hard-disk and CD-ROM drives to exchange digital data at fast speeds. SCSI can also be used with other components, such as scanners.

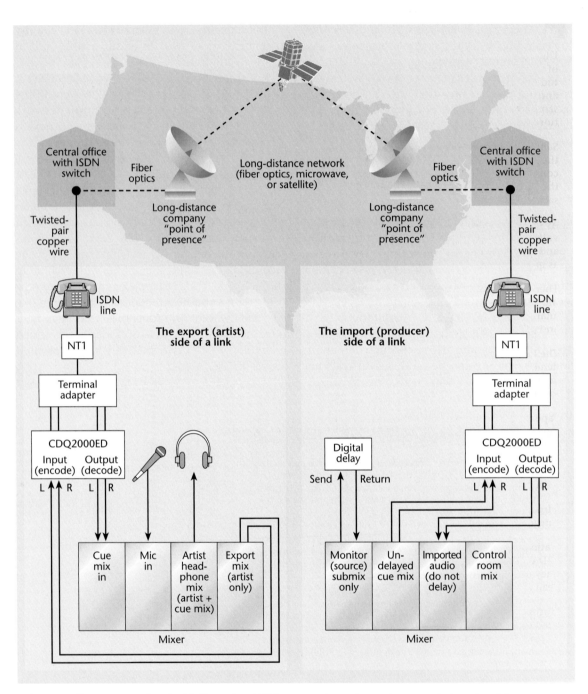

7-14 Long-distance recording. In this illustration, NT1 is a network terminator that protects the network from electrical malfunctions. CDQ2000ED code enables you to send a cue mix to an artist in another location, delay the mix sent to your monitors, not delay the received artist's solo signal, mix the two, give direction, and make production judgments in real time.

▶ Digital audio uses a numerical representation of the sound signal's actual frequency and amplitude. In analog, frequency is the time component, and amplitude is the level component. In digital, sampling is the time component, and quantization is the level component.

▶ Sampling takes periodic samples (voltages) of the original analog signal at fixed intervals and converts them into digital data. The rate at which the fixed intervals sample the original signal each second is call the sampling frequency.

▶ As samples of the waveform are taken, these voltages are converted into discrete quantities and assigned values. This process is known as quantization.

▶ There are five basic steps in the digital recording process: anti-aliasing, sample and hold, analog-to-digital conversion, signal coding, and data storage.

▶ The basic steps in digital reproduction are: demodulation, error correction, digital-to-analog conversion, sample and hold, and low-pass filtering.

▶ Tape used for digital recording is different from tape used for analog recording. It is thinner, has about twice the coercivity, must be used in an environment whose temperature and humidity are more closely controlled, and must be handled with greater care.

▶ Digital audiotape recorders fall into two categories: stationary head and rotary head.

▶ Stationary-head digital audiotape recorders (S-DATs) are similar in operation to analog ATRs. They differ, however, in recording format and head configuration.

▶ Most manufacturers conform their stationary-head digital audiotape recorders to the DASH format. Recorders using the Pro Digi format are still in use, but are no longer marketed.

▶ The rotary-head digital audiotape recorder (R-DAT) uses the principle of the videotape recorder's spinning heads to encode audio onto tape.

▶ Most R-DATs operate at three sampling speeds: 32 kHz, 44.1 kHz, and 48 kHz. Longitudinal tape speed is $\frac{1}{3}$ ips, one-sixth the speed of analog cassette recorders.

▶ Audiocassette tape for R-DAT is about $\frac{1}{7}$-inch wide and similar in thickness to a 90-minute analog cassette (about $\frac{1}{4}$ mil). The cartridge is half the size of an analog cassette, and the tape length is one-fourth that of an analog cassette.

▶ When selecting and using digital cassette tape, be wary of problems with wear, error concealment, the cassette shell, erasure, and aging.

▶ Even though the digital format is robust, R-DATs and digital cassette tape require regular maintenance and cleaning to ensure proper tape tracking, tape tension, and track spacing and to prevent the buildup of grime and debris that could wreak havoc on encoding and error correction.

▶ Modular digital multitrack (MDM) tape recorders use a videocassette transport with videotape, instead of an R-DAT transport, to record up to eight channels of audio per unit. Units can be linked, expanding track capability in eight-channel increments.

▶ MDMs come in two formats: the digital tape recording system (DTRS), which uses Hi8 videocassette tape; and ADAT, which uses S-VHS videocassette tape.

▶ Digital videotape recorders (DVTRs) come in a variety of formats, which differ more in the way they process video than the way they process audio. The differences in audio among the various systems come down to bit rate and number of audio channels. All sound in DVTRs is digital quality.

▶ Disk-based audio record/playback systems include the magneto-optical disc, mini disc, digital cartridge disk, recordable compact disc, solid-state recorder, and hard disk.

▶ Magneto-optical (MO) recording, like magnetic digital tape recording, uses tiny magnetic particles to encode digital information. But unlike magnetic tape recording, MO recording is a disc-based optical process; a laser beam orients the magnetic particles, and the magnetic particles are heated to extremely high temperatures.

▶ The mini disc (MD) is a $2\frac{1}{2}$-inch-wide compact disc. The MD system uses MO media for recordable blank discs and CD-type optical media for prerecorded software.

▶ The digital cartridge disk system is the successor to the analog tape cartridge system. The disk cart can be a recorder/player unit or a player-only unit. The disk cart's medium can be a compact disc, magneto-optical disc, mini disc, floppy disk, or hard disk.

▶ The recordable compact disc (CD-R) is somewhat similar to recording tape in that it has unlimited playback. Until recently, it could not be erased. Now rewritable CDs (CD-RWs) are available.

▶ The solid-state digital audio recorder/editor is designed for use in broadcast news reporting from the field. Its recording medium is the PCMCIA card.

▶ Hard-disk recording encodes, stores, and reproduces a signal on a multitrack hard-disk recorder. The channel-track configuration is versatile; information access is nonlinear, random, and quick; and storage capacity is far greater than with tape.

▶ The digital audio workstation (DAW) is an expandable recording, mixing, signal-processing, and editing system that is integrated with and networked to a collection of devices, such as other audio, video, and MIDI sources, within or among facilities.

▶ Digital audio networking makes it possible to produce a recording in real time between studios across town or across the country with little or no loss in audio quality and at relatively low cost.

Signal Processing

Signal processors are devices used to alter some characteristic of a sound. Generally, signal processors can be grouped into four categories: spectrum processors, time processors, amplitude processors, and noise processors. A ***spectrum processor***, such as the equalizer, affects the spectral balances in a signal. A ***time processor***, such as a reverberation or delay device, affects the time interval between a signal and its repetition(s). An ***amplitude processor***, such as the compressor-limiter, affects a signal's dynamic range. A ***noise processor***, such as the Dolby system, does not alter a signal so much as it makes the signal clearer by reducing noise.

Some signal processors can belong to more than one category. For example, the equalizer also alters a signal's amplitude and, therefore, can be classified as an amplitude processor as well. The flanger, which affects the time of a signal, also affects its frequency response. A de-esser alters amplitude and frequency. Moreover, several signal processing functions may be combined in a single unit, which can be delegated to, say, time-compress, delay, pitch-shift, and/or flange a signal. The signal processors discussed in this chapter have been categorized according to their primary functions.

SPECTRUM SIGNAL PROCESSORS

Spectrum signal processors include equalizers, filters, and psychoacoustic processors.

Equalizers

The best-known and most often used signal processor is the **equalizer**—an electronic device that alters frequency response by increasing or decreasing the level of a signal at a specific portion of the spectrum. This alteration can be done in two ways: by boost or cut (also known as *peak* or *dip*) or by **shelving**.

Boost/cut increases or decreases the level of a band of frequencies around a **center frequency**, the frequency at which maximum boost or cut occurs. This type of equalization is often referred to as *bell curve* or *haystack,* due to the shape of the response curve (see Figure 8-1).

Shelving also increases or decreases amplitude but gradually flattens out or shelves at the maximum selected level when the chosen (turnover) frequency is reached. Level then remains constant at all frequencies beyond that point (see 8-2).

The number of frequencies on equalizers varies. Generally, the frequencies are in full-, half-, and third-octave intervals. If the lowest frequency on a full-octave equalizer is, say, 50 Hz, the other frequencies ascend in octaves: 100 Hz, 200 Hz, 400 Hz, 800 Hz, and so on, usually to 12,800 Hz. A half-octave equalizer ascends in half octaves. If the lowest frequency is 50 Hz, the intervals are at or near 75 Hz, 100 Hz, 150 Hz, 200 Hz, 300 Hz, 400 Hz, 600 Hz, and so on. A third-octave equalizer would have intervals at or near 50 Hz, 60 Hz, 80 Hz, 100 Hz, 120 Hz, 160 Hz, 200 Hz, 240 Hz, 320 Hz, 400 Hz, 480 Hz, 640 Hz, and so on. Obviously, the more settings, the better the sound control—but at some cost. The more settings there are on an equalizer (or any device, for that matter), the more difficult it is to use correctly, because problems such as added noise and phasing may be introduced.

Two types of equalizers are in general use: fixed-frequency and parametric.

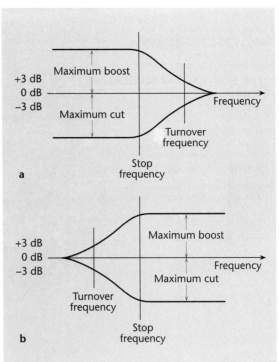

8-2 (a) **Low-frequency shelving equalization and** (b) **high-frequency shelving equalization.** The turnover frequency is that frequency where the gain is 3 dB above (or below) the shelving level—in other words, the frequency where the equalizer begins to flatten out. The stop frequency is the point where the gain stops increasing or decreasing.

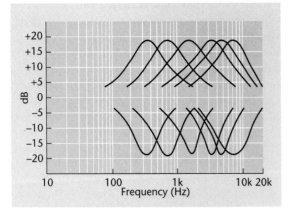

8-1 Bell or haystack curves showing 18-dB boost or cut at 350, 700, 1,600, 3,200, 4,800, and 7,200 Hz

Fixed-Frequency Equalizer

The *fixed-frequency equalizer* is so called because it operates at fixed frequencies usually selected from two (high and low) or three (high, middle, and low) ranges of the frequency spectrum. Each group of frequencies is located at a separate control, but only one center frequency at a time per control may be selected. At or near each frequency selector is a level control that boosts or cuts the selected center and band frequencies. On consoles where these controls are concentric to save space, the outer ring chooses the frequency, and the inner ring increases or decreases level.

A fixed-frequency equalizer has a preset *bandwidth*—a range of frequencies on either side of the center frequency selected for equalizing that is also affected. The degrees of amplitude to which these frequencies are modified forms the *bandwidth curve*. If you boost, say, 350 Hz a total of 18 dB, the bandwidth of frequencies also affected may go to as low as 80 Hz on one side and up to 2,000 Hz on the other. The peak of the curve is 350 Hz—the frequency that is boosted the full 18 dB (see 8-1). The adjacent frequencies are boosted also,

but to a lesser extent, depending on the bandwidth. Because each fixed-frequency equalizer can have a different fixed bandwidth and bandwidth curve, it is a good idea to study the manufacturer's specifications before you use one.

Usually, the high and low fixed-frequency equalizers on consoles are shelving equalizers. The midrange equalizers are center-frequency boost/cut equalizers.

Graphic Equalizer

The *graphic equalizer* is a type of fixed-frequency equalizer. It consists of sliding, instead of rotating, controls that boost or attenuate selected frequencies. It is called "graphic" because the positioning of these controls gives a graphic display of the frequency curve set. (The display does not include the bandwidth of each frequency, however.) Because each frequency on a graphic equalizer has a separate sliding control, it is possible to use as many as you wish simultaneously (see 8-3).

Parametric Equalizer

The main difference between a *parametric equalizer* (see 8-4) and a fixed-frequency equalizer

8-3 Graphic equalizer. This model is a dual 15-band graphic equalizer with two-thirds octaves frequency centers ranging from 25 Hz to 16 Hz. Boost and cut ranges are switchable from ±6 dB to ±15 dB. Also included are a high-pass/low-cut filter, limiting, and dbx Type III™ noise reduction, providing up to 20 dB of broadband noise reduction.

8-4 Parametric equalizer. This model uses both tube and solid technologies. There are four bands of seven switch-selectable frequencies, plus high- and low-pass filters with three frequencies each.

8-5 Selectable bandwidths of a parametric equalizer. In this example the boost curves are broad and the cut curves are tight. Other parametric equalizers use the same range of adjustment for the boost and cut curves.

8-6 Example of low-pass filter curves

is that the parametric has continuously variable frequencies and bandwidths. Because the parametric equalizer's frequencies and bandwidths are continuously variable, it is possible to change a bandwidth curve by making it wider or narrower, thereby altering the affected frequencies and their levels (see 8-5). This provides greater flexibility and more precision in controlling equalization.

Paragraphic Equalizer

A *paragraphic equalizer* combines the sliding controls of a graphic equalizer with the flexibility of parametric equalization (see 8-20).

Filters

A *filter* is a device that attenuates certain bands of frequencies. A filter is a component of an equalizer. There are differences between attenuating with an equalizer and attenuating with a filter, however. First, with an equalizer attenuation affects only the selected frequency and the frequencies on either side of it, whereas with a filter all frequencies above or below the selected frequency are affected. Second, an equalizer allows you to vary the amount of the drop in loudness; with a filter the drop is usually preset and relatively steep.

Among the most commonly used filters are high-pass, low-pass, bandpass, and notch filters.

High- and Low-Pass Filters

A *high-pass (low-cut) filter* attenuates all frequencies below a preset point; a *low-pass (high-cut) filter* attenuates all frequencies above a preset point (see 8-6).

Suppose, in a recording, that there is a bothersome rumble between 35 and 50 Hz. By setting a high-pass filter at 50 Hz, all frequencies below that point are cut and the band of frequencies above it continues to pass—hence the name "high-pass (low-cut)" filter.

The low-pass (high-cut) filter works on the same principle but affects the higher frequencies. If there is tape hiss in a recording, you can get rid of it by setting a low-pass filter at, say, 10,000 Hz. This cuts the frequencies above that point and allows the band of frequencies below 10,000 Hz to pass through. But you should keep in mind that *all* sound above 10 kHz—the program material, if there is any, along with the tape hiss—will be filtered.

Band-Pass Filter

A *band-pass filter* is a device that sets high- and low-frequency cutoff points and permits the band of frequencies between to pass (see 8-7). Band-pass filters are used more for corrective rather than creative purposes.

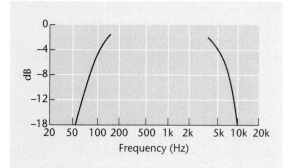

8-7 Band-pass filtering. The frequencies below 120 Hz and above 5,000 Hz are sharply attenuated, thereby allowing the frequencies in the band between to pass.

Notch Filter

A *notch filter* is also used mainly for corrective purposes. It can cut out an extremely narrow band, allowing the frequencies on each side of the notch to pass. For example, a constant problem in audio is AC (alternating current) hum, which has a frequency of 60 Hz. A notch filter can remove it without appreciably affecting adjacent frequencies.

Psychoacoustic Processors

A *psychoacoustic processor* is designed to add clarity, definition, overall presence, and life or "sizzle" to program material. Some units add tone-generated odd and even harmonics* to the audio; others are fixed or program-adaptive high-frequency equalizers. A psychoacoustic processor might also achieve its effect by adding comb filtering and by introducing narrow-band phase shifts between stereo channels. One well-known psychoacoustic processor is the Aural Exciter™ (see 8-8).

---

*Each harmonic or set of harmonics adds a characteristic tonal color to sound, although they have less effect on changes in timbre as they rise in pitch above the fundamental. In general, even-number harmonics—second, fourth, and sixth—create an open, warm, filled-out sound. Odd-number harmonics—third and fifth—produce a closed, harsh, stopped-down sound. The second harmonic, an octave above the fundamental, can be barely audible, yet it adds fullness to sound. The third harmonic (called musical twelfth or quint) softens sound. Harmonics above the seventh harmonic give sound edge, bite, and definition.

The *overhang drive* control sets the optimum level required for Big Bottom to work effectively, indicated by the green LED at the right of the control.

This switch selects the amount of *harmonics* being generated by the Aural Exciter circuit—normal and high.

The *process in/out* switch turns both of the enhanced sidechain signals on and off when the *in* posion is selected. Selecting *off* sends only the unmodified signal to the outputs, actively bypassing the circuitry.

The *girth mix* control adjusts the amount of enhancement being added to the original signal. The lower the setting, the subtler the effect. The higher the setting, the more dramatic the effect.

The *tune* control adjusts the corner frequency of the high-pass filter, setting a range of frequencies from 800 Hz to 6 kHz.

The *mix* control varies the amount of enhancement mixed back into the original signal, from the sidechain.

8-8 One type of Aural Exciter™ and its functions

TIME SIGNAL PROCESSORS

Time signal processors are devices that affect the time relationships of signals. These effects include reverberation, delay, and pitch shifting.

Reverberation

Reverberation, you will recall, is created by random, multiple, blended repetitions of a sound or signal. As these repetitions decrease in intensity, they increase in number. Reverberation increases average signal level and adds depth, spatial dimension, and additional excitement to the listening experience.

A common principle is basic to reverberation and, hence, reverb systems. Think of what it takes to produce an echo: A sound has to be sent, hit a reflective object, and then bounce back. In the parlance of audio, the sound sent is *dry*—without reverb—and the sound returned is *wet*—with reverb.

Actually, as defined, remember that there is a difference between echo and reverb. Echo is one or, at most, a few discrete, discernable repetitions of a sound (or signal); reverb consists of many blended repetitions (see Chapter 3). To produce either, the dry sound must be sent, "reflected," and returned wet. Three reverb systems in current use are digital, plate, and chamber reverberation.

Digital Reverberation

Digital reverberation is the most commonly used today. The *digital reverberation (reverb) unit* is a device that artificially reproduces the sound of different acoustic environments. The reverb is accomplished electronically. The analog signal, when fed into the circuitry and digitized, is delayed for several milliseconds. The delayed signal is then recycled to produce the reverb effect. The process is repeated many times a second, with amplitude reduced to achieve decay. After processing, the signal is reconverted into analog. High-quality digital reverb units are capable of an extremely wide range of effects, produce high-quality sound, and take up very little room.

Some digital reverb systems can simulate a variety of acoustical and mechanical reverberant sounds, such as small and large concert halls, bright- and dark-sounding halls, small and large rooms, and small and large reverb plates (see "Plate Reverberation" in the next section). With each effect it is also possible to control individually the attack; decay; diffusion (density); high-, middle-, and low-frequency decay times; and other sonic colorings.

Programmable digital reverb systems are also available. They come with preprogrammed effects but also permit newly created effects, not previously in the memory, to be programmed and stored for reuse. This provides an extensive variety of reverberant effects (see 8-9).

Plate Reverberation

The *reverberation plate* is a mechanical-electronic device consisting of a thin, steel plate suspended under tension in an enclosed frame (see 8-10). It is large and heavy and requires isolation in a separate room. A moving-coil driver, acting like a small speaker, vibrates the plate, thus transducing the electrical signals from the console into mechanical energy. A contact microphone (two for stereo) picks up the plate's vibrations, transduces them back into electric energy, and returns them to the console. The multiple reflections from the vibrating plate create the reverb effect.

A characteristic of plates is long reverb times (more than two seconds) at high frequencies that produce a crisp, bright decay. Plates are susceptible to overload, however. With louder levels, low frequencies tend to increase disproportionately in reverb time compared with the other frequencies, thus muddying sound. Rolling off the unwanted frequencies will help, but too much roll-off reduces a sound's warmth.

Acoustic Chamber Reverberation

The *acoustic reverberation chamber* is the most natural and realistic type of simulated reverb, because it works on acoustic sound in an acoustic environment. It is a room with hard, highly sound-reflective surfaces and nonparallel walls to avoid *flutter echo*—multiple echoes at a rapid, even rate—and *standing waves*—apparently stationary waveforms created by multiple reflections between

Bank	Program Name									b
Bank 1 480 Halls	**1.1** Large Hall	**1.2** Large + Stage	**1.3** Medium Hall	**1.4** Medium + Stage	**1.5** Small Hall	**1.6** Small + Stage	**1.7** Large Church	**1.8** Small Church	**1.9** Jazz Hall	**1.0** Auto Park
Bank 2 480 Rooms	**2.1** Music Club	**2.2** Large Room	**2.3** Medium Room	**2.4** Small Room	**2.5** Very Small Room	**2.6** Large Wood Rm	**2.7** Small Wood Rm	**2.8** Large Chamber	**2.9** Small Chamber	**2.0** Small & Bright
Bank 3 Wild Spaces	**3.1** Brick Wall	**3.2** Buckram	**3.3** Big Bottom	**3.4** 10W-40	**3.5** 20W-50	**3.6** Metallica	**3.7** Silica Beads	**3.8** Inside Out	**3.9** Ricochet	**3.0** Varoom
Bank 4 Plates	**4.1** A Plate	**4.2** Snare Plate	**4.3** Small Plate	**4.4** Thin Plate	**4.5** Fat Plate					
Bank 5 Effects	**5.1** Illusion	**5.2** Surfin'	**5.3** Vocal Whispers	**5.4** Doubler	**5.5** Back Slap	**5.6** Rebound	**5.7** Git It Wet	**5.8** Sudden Stop	**5.9** In the Past	**5.0** Tremolo L & R
Bank 6 Twin Delays	**6.1** 4-Voice Double	**6.2** Double Delay	**6.3** 4-Bounce De}ay	**6.4** Pitter Patter	**6.5** X-Pan Double	**6.6** Delay Cave	**6.7** Circles	**6.8** There & Back	**6.9** Soft Roller	**6.0** On and On
Bank 7 Samplers*	**7.1** Stereo 3 Sec.	**7.2** Mono 6 Sec.	**7.3** Mono 3 Sec.	**7.4** Dual Rate Change	**7.5** Mono Fwd & Rev	**7.6** Stereo 3S Drum	**7.7** Dual Rate Chg Drum	**7.8** Mono Fwd Rev Drum	**7.9** Stereo 10S Rate Chg	**7.0** Mono 20S Rate Chg
Bank 8 Pitch/ Doppler	**8.1** Pitch Change	**8.2** Pitch Chorus	**8.3** I~b Up I~o Down	**8.4** Barber Pole	**8.5** Half Steps	**8.6** Stair Case	**8.7** XPres Subway	**8.8** Indy Corner	**8.9** Airport Land	**8.0** Airport Tkof
Bank 9 Mastering	**9.1** The In-Out	**9.2** Stereo Adjust	**9.3** PONS Adjust	**9.4** M/S Decode	**9.5** Invert L-R	**9.6** Channel Swap	**9.7** Stereo Param EQ	**9.8** Stereo 60Hz Ntch	**9.9** Mono Param EQ	**9.0** Panorama
Bank 10 Compressor	**10.1** 2:1 Comp	**10.2** 6.24:1 Comp	**10.3** 18.28:1 Comp	**10.4** Transfer	**10.5** Vox Easy	**10.6** FM	**10.7** Nailed	**10.8** Noise Gate	**10.9** 2-Slp- Mach A	**10.0** 2-Slp Mach B
Bank 11 Random Hall	**11.1** Large R Hall	**11.2** Large R + Stage	**11.3** Medium R Hall	**11.4** Medium R + Stage	**11.5** Small R Hall	**11.6** Small R + Stage	**11.7** Large R Church	**11.8** Small R Church	**11.9** Jazz R Hall	**11.0** Auto Park R
Bank 12 Random Spaces	**12.1** Music Club R	**12.2** Large Room R	**12.3** Medium Room R	**12.4** Small Room R	**12.5** Very Small R	**12.6** Large Chamber R	**12.7** Small Chamber R	**12.8** Small & Bright R	**12.9** Chorus Room	**12.0** Wet & Tacky
Bank 13 Ambience	**13.1** Very Large Ambience	**13.2** Large Ambience	**13.3** Medium Ambience	**13.4** Small Ambience	**13.5** Strong Ambience	**13.6** Heavy Ambience	**13.7** Ambient Hall	**13.8** Announcer	**13.9** Closet	**13.0** Gated Ambience

8-9 Digital reverberation and effects system. (a) This system's control console is known as LARC (Lexicon Alphanumeric Remote Console); (b) an example of its programs.

8-10 Reverberation plate

A good test to check for muddy sound is to listen to a singer. If the reverb system makes the lyrics more difficult to understand, it is not clear or transparent enough. To check for density and randomness of the early reflections, try a transient sound such as a sharp drumbeat or handclap. Poorer reverb systems will produce a sound like an acoustic flutter. To check for randomness of the later reflections, listen to a strong male voice completely wet—with no dry feed from the reverb send on the console. If the lyrics are clear, the combined wet and dry signals will probably be muddy.

opposite, usually parallel, room surfaces. It usually contains two directional microphones (for stereo), placed off room center, and a loudspeaker, usually near a corner at angles to or back-to-back to the mic(s) to minimize the amount of direct sound picked up by the mic(s). The dry sound feeds from the console through the loudspeaker, reflects around the chamber, is picked up by the mic(s), and is fed back wet into the console for further processing and routing.

Reverb times differ from chamber to chamber. Generally, however, reverb time should be about 3.5 seconds at 500 Hz, and about 1.25 seconds at 10,000 Hz. Reverb times can be varied by using movable acoustic baffles.

Although an acoustic chamber creates very realistic reverberation, it is the most expensive of the reverb systems. It must be at least 2,000 cubic feet in size (too small a room is poor for bass response) with specially treated surfaces; and it must be isolated. Even with a chamber, studios use other reverb devices to provide additional sonic alternatives.

Choosing a Reverberation System

In choosing a reverberation system, personal taste notwithstanding, the system should sound natural. The high end should be bright and lifelike, and the low end should not thicken or muddy the sound. Good diffusion is essential; repeats should be numerous and random. There should be an absence of flutter, twang, "boing," and tinniness.

Delay

Delay is the time interval between a sound or signal and its repetition. By manipulating delay times, it is possible to create a number of sonic effects (see the following section on uses of delay). Today this is most commonly done with an electronic digital delay.

Digital Delay

A *digital delay* converts an analog signal to digital information at the input and reconverts it back into analog at the output. After conversion at the input, the signal is fed to a memory that stores it. After the selected amount of delay time, it is read out, converted back to analog, and sent to the output. The amount and number of delay times vary with the unit (see 8-11).

The better digital delays have excellent signal-to-noise ratio, low distortion, good high-frequency response with longer delay times, and an extensive array of effects. They are also excellent for pre-reverb delay (see section on delay with reverberation). Lower-grade units are not as clean-sounding and high-frequency response is noisier with longer delay times.

Uses of Delay

Delay has a number of creative applications. Among the effects most frequently used in-studio, are doubling, chorusing, slap back echo, and pre-reverb delay.

8-11 Digital delay. This particular unit can produce a delay of up to 4.5 seconds set in 0.1 steps from 0 to 10 ms and in 1-ms steps for periods over 10 ms. Eight different programmable memories can store the settings of delay time, feedback level, output level, modulation rate, modulation, and feedback phase. Frequency response is 10 Hz to 17 kHz for delay times up to 1,500 ms, and 10 Hz to 8 kHz for delay times up to 4,500 ms.

■ **Doubling** One popular use of delay is to fatten sound. The effect gives an instrument or voice a fuller, stronger sound and is called *doubling*. It is created by setting the delay to around 15 to 35 ms. These short delays are like early sound reflections and lend a sense of openness or ambience to dead-sounding instruments or voices.

Doubling can also be done live by recording one track and then overdubbing the same part on a separate track in synchronization with the first. Because it is not possible to repeat a performance exactly, variations in pitch, timing, and room sounds add fullness or openness to sound. By continuing this process, it is possible to create a chorusing effect.

■ **Chorus** The *chorus effect* is achieved by recirculating the doubling effect. The delay time is about the same as in doubling—15 to 35 ms—but is repeated. This effect can make a single voice sound like many and add spaciousness to a sound. Two voices singing in a relatively dead studio can be made to sound like a choir singing in a hall by chorusing the original sound.

■ **Slap back echo** A *slap back echo* is a delayed sound that is perceived as a distinct echo, much like the discrete Ping-Pong sound emitted by sonar devices when a contact is made. Slap back echo can be created with delay times of around 35 ms or more.

■ **Prereverb delay** In an acoustic situation, there is a definite time lag between the arrival of direct

waves from a sound source and the arrival of reflected sound. In some reverb systems, there is no delay between the dry and wet signals. Therefore by delaying the input signal before it gets to the reverb unit, it is possible to improve the quality of reverberation, making it sound more natural. Many reverb systems have a delay line of their own.

Flanging

Flanging is a time-delay effect that gets its name from the way in which it was first produced. The same signal was fed to two different tape recorders and recorded simultaneously. The playback from both was fed to a single output, but one playback was delayed, usually by applying some pressure to the flange of the supply reel to slow it down. The sonic result is a kind of swishing sound that has many uses in creating special effects for music recording and sound effects for TV and film.

Today these effects are produced electronically. The delay time is automatically varied from 0 to 20 ms. Ordinarily, the ear cannot perceive time differences between direct and delayed sounds that are this short. But due to phase cancellations when the direct and delayed signals are combined, the result is a series of peaks and dips in the frequency response (called the *comb filter effect*), which creates a filtered tone quality that can sound swishy, hollow, or spacey, depending on the settings of the flanger controls.

Flanging can be "positive," meaning that the direct and delayed signals have the same polarity.

Or it can be "negative," meaning that these two signals are opposite in polarity. Negative flanging can create strong, sucking effects like a sound being turned inside out. Flanging can also be resonant; that is, by feeding some of the output back into the input, the peaks and dips are reinforced creating a science fiction–type effect.

Phasing

Phasing and flanging are similar in the way they are created, except that phasing uses a phase shifter instead of a time-delay circuit. The peaks and dips are more irregular and farther apart than in flanging. Sonically, this results in something like pulsating, wavering vibrato or the undulating sound produced by playing an instrument underwater. Phasing is produced electronically.

Pitch Shifting

A *pitch shifter* is a device that changes the pitch (frequency) of a signal. It is used to correct minor off-pitch problems, create special effects, or change the length of a program without changing its pitch. The latter function is called *time compression*. Some pitch shifters can change

frequencies over a couple of octaves without changing duration, allowing you to harmonize an input signal. For example, if a singer delivers a note slightly flat or sharp, it is possible to raise or lower the pitch so that it is in tune. To create harmony, the input signal can be mixed with the harmonized signal at selected pitch ratios.

As a time compressor, a pitch shifter can shorten recorded audio material with no editing, no deletion of content, and no alteration in pitch (see 8-12).

Morphing

Morphing is the continuous, seamless transformation of one effect (aural or visual) into another. For example, in Michael Jackson's video *Black and White,* a Chinese woman is transformed into an African American man, who is transformed into an Irishman, who is transformed into a Hispanic woman, and so on. In *Terminator II* the silver terminator could melt, slither through cracks, and transform into various objects. These effects are more than sophisticated dissolves (the sonic counterpart of dissolve is crossfade). Morphing is a complete restructuring of two completely different

8-12 Example of time compression of an event sequence

and independent effects. Because most audio morphing effects are delay-based, audio morphing devices can be classified as time signal processors.

A few examples of audio morphing are: spinning vowel-like sounds, varying their rate and depth, and then freezing them until they fade away; flanging cascades of sound across stereo space, adding echo, and varying the envelope control of rates; adding echoing rhythms to a multivoice chorus which become more dense as they repeat, with the effect growing stronger as the notes fade away; and taking a musical instrument and adding pitch sweeps that dive into a pool of swirling echoes that bounce from to side to side or wind up being sucked up.

AMPLITUDE SIGNAL PROCESSORS

Amplitude signal processors are devices that affect dynamic range. These effects include compressing, limiting, and expanding a signal.

Compressors

The *compressor* is a processor whose output level increases at a slower rate as its input level increases (see 8-13). Compressors usually have four controls—for compression ratio, compression threshold, attack time, and release time, each one of which can affect the others.

The *compression ratio* establishes the proportion of change between the input and output levels. The ratios are usually variable, and, depending on the compressor, there are several selectable points between 1.1 to 1, and 20 to 1. If you set the compression ratio for, say, 2 to 1, it means that for every 2-dB increase of the input signal, the output will increase by 1 dB; at 5 to 1, a 5-dB increase of the input signal increases the output by 1 dB. This is how sound with a dynamic range greater than a tape can handle is brought to usable proportions.

The *compression threshold* is the level at which the compression ratio takes effect. You set it based

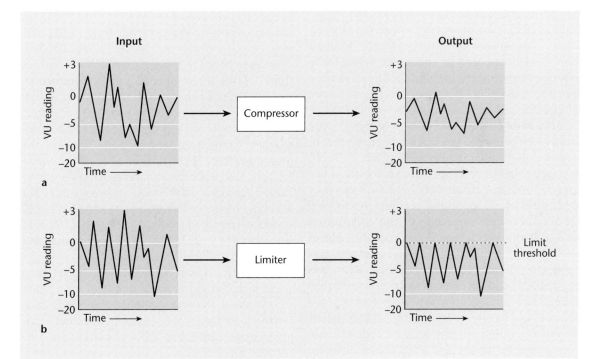

8-13 Effect of (a) compression and (b) limiting

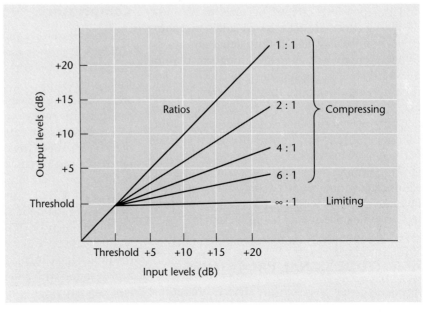

8-14 A representation of the relationship of various compression ratios to a fixed threshold point. The graph also displays the difference between effects of limiting and compressing.

on your judgment of where compression should begin. (For an idea of the relationship between compression ratio and threshold, see 8-14.) There is no way to predetermine what settings will work best for a given sound at a certain level; it is a matter of listening and experimenting.

Attack time is the length of time it takes the compressor to react to the signal being compressed. Attack times, which usually range from .25 to 10 ms, can enhance or detract from a sound. If the attack time is long, it can help to bring out percussive attacks, but if it is too long, it can miss or overshoot the beginning of the compressed sound. If the attack time is too short, it reduces punch by attenuating the attacks, sometimes producing popping or clicking sounds. When it is controlled, a short attack time can heighten transients and add a crisp accent to sound. Generally, attack time should be set so that signals exceed the threshold level long enough to cause an increase in the average level. Otherwise, gain

reduction will decrease overall level. Again, set attack time by using your ear.

Release time (or *recovery time*) is the length of time it takes a compressed signal to return to normal. Release times vary from 50 ms to several seconds. It is perhaps the most critical variable in compression, because it controls the moment-to-moment changes in the level and, therefore, the overall loudness. One purpose of the release-time function is to make the variations in loudness level caused by the compression imperceptible. For example, longer release times are usually applied to music that is slower and more legato (that is, smoother and more tightly connected), and shorter release times to music that is fast.

Generally, release times should be set long enough that if signal levels repeatedly rise above the threshold, they cause gain reduction only once. If the release time is too long, a loud section of the audio could cause gain reduction that continues through a soft section.

These suggestions are not to imply rules—they are only guidelines. In fact, various release times produce various effects. Some enhance sound, others degrade it, as the following list of potential effects suggests:

■ A fast release time combined with a low compression ratio makes a signal seem louder than it actually is.

■ Too short a release time with too high a ratio causes the compressor to pump or breathe. You actually hear it working when a signal rapidly returns to normal after it has been compressed and quickly released.

■ A longer release time smoothes a fluctuating signal.

■ A longer release time combined with a short attack time gives the signal some of the characteristics of a sound going backward. This effect is particularly noticeable with transients.

■ A release time longer than about half a second for bass instruments prevents harmonic distortion.

■ Too long a release time creates a muddy sound and can cause the gain reduction triggered by a loud signal to continue through a soft one that follows.

Limiters

The *limiter* is a compressor whose output level stays at or below a preset point regardless of its input level. It has a compression ratio between 10 to 1 and infinity; it puts a ceiling on the loudness of a sound at a preset level (see 8-13). Regardless of how loud the input signal is, the output will not go above this ceiling. This makes the limiter useful in situations where high sound levels are frequent or where a performer or console operator cannot prevent loud sounds from going into the red.

The limiter has a preset compression ratio but a variable threshold; the threshold sets the point where limiting begins. Attack and release times, if they are not preset, should be relatively short,

especially the attack time. A short attack time is usually essential to a clean-sounding limit.

Unlike compression, which can have little effect on the frequency response, limiting can reduce high-frequency response. Also, if limiting is severe, the signal-to-noise ratio drops dramatically.

Some compressors are equipped with a filter to help control stronger, more annoying high-frequency sounds such as *s, z, ch,* and *sh.* The filter, called a *de-esser,* is frequency selective and handles the highly sibilant signals without affecting the rest of the sound.

Uses of Compressors and Limiters

Compressors and limiters have many applications, several of which are listed here.

■ Compression minimizes the wide changes in levels of loudness caused when a performer fails to maintain a consistent mic-to-source distance.

■ Compression smoothes the variations in attack and loudness of instruments with wide ranges or wide sound-pressure levels, such as the guitar, bass, trumpet, French horn, and drums. It can also smooth percussive sound effects such as jangling keys, breaking glass, and crashes.

■ Compression can improve the intelligibility of speech in an analog tape recording that has been rerecorded, or dubbed, several times.

■ Compression reduces apparent noise if the compression ratios are low. Higher ratios add more noise.

■ Limiting prevents high sound levels, either constant or momentary, from saturating the tape.

■ The combination of compression and limiting can add more power or apparent loudness to sound.

■ The combination of compression and limiting is often used by AM radio stations to prevent distortion from loud music and to bring out the bass sounds. This adds more power to the sound, thus making the station more obvious to someone sweeping the dial.

■ Compression in commercials is used to raise average output level and thus sonically capture audience attention.

Expanders

An *expander*, like a compressor, affects dynamic range (see 8-15). But whereas a compressor reduces it, an expander increases it. Like a compressor, an expander has variable ratios and is triggered when sound reaches a set threshold level. The ratios on an expander, however, are the inverse of those on a compressor: 1 to 2, 1 to 3, and so on. At 1 to 2, each 1 dB of input expands to 2 dB of output; at 1 to 3, each 1 dB of input expands to 3 dB of output. Because an expander is triggered when a signal falls below a set threshold, it can be used as a *noise gate* to reduce or eliminate unwanted low-level noise

from amplifiers, ambience, rumble, tape hiss, and leakage from one microphone to another.

Assume, for example, that you have two microphones, one for a singer and one for an accompanying piano. When the singer and pianist are performing, the sound level will probably be loud enough to mask unwanted low-level noises. But if the pianist is playing quietly and the vocalist is not singing, or vice versa, the open, unused microphone may pick up these noises.

An obvious solution to this problem is to turn down the fader when a microphone is not being used, cutting it off acoustically and electronically. But this could become hectic for a console operator if there are several sound sources to coordinate. Another solution is to set the expander's threshold level at a point just above the quietest sound level that the vocalist (or piano) emits. When the vocalist

8-15 Effect of (a) expansion and (b) noise gating. Without noise gating, ambient noise is masked during singing and audible when singing is not present. Noise gating eliminates the ambient noise when there is no singing.

stops singing, the loudness of the sound entering the microphone falls below the threshold point of the expander, which shuts down, or *gates,* the mic.

The key to successful noise gating is in the coordination of the threshold and ratio settings. Because there is often little difference between the low level of a sound's decay and the low level of noise, you have to be wary that in cutting off noise, you do not cut off program material also. Always be careful when you use a noise gate; unless it is set precisely, it can adversely affect response.

Noise gates are also used to create effects. Shortening decay time of the drums can produce a very tight drum sound. Taking a 60-Hz tone and feeding it so that it is keyed or triggered by an electric bass can produce not only a simulated bass drum sound but also one that is synchronized with the bass guitar.

NOISE SIGNAL PROCESSORS

Of the many links in the sound chain, analog tape is a major cause of noise. *Noise signal processors* are designed to reduce that noise.

You will recall that the dynamic range of human hearing is 120 dB-SPL and beyond. The best analog recording produces a dynamic range of 80 to 90 dB. Much analog recording is in the 65 to 70 dB range, half as much as humans are capable of hearing and far less than the dynamic range of digital recording (see 8-16). Recording at high levels improves dynamic range but could also increase distortion. And there is the problem of tape noise.

The inherent unevenness of a tape's magnetic coating, even in the highest-quality tapes, always leaves a slight polarization of the magnetic particles in the coating after erasure, regardless of how

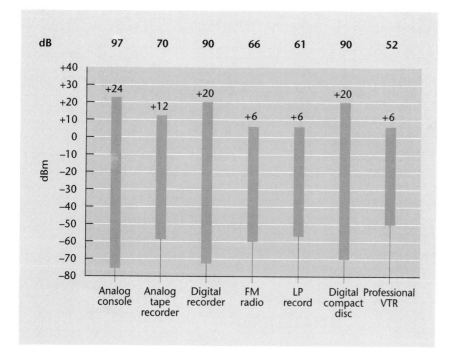

8-16 Dynamic ranges of various audio devices in dBm (an electrical measurement of power) and in dB

complete the erasure is. Each time a tape is used, some of the magnetic coating is worn away, thus decreasing the signal-to-noise ratio. Poor dispersion of the magnetic particles creates sound dropout and noise. Residual magnetization after erasure due either to an improper erase current or to a poor bulk-erasing technique increases tape noise. A problem with the record current will result in a recording that is not uniformly magnetized. A tape recording made at a level that is too quiet will underpolarize the magnetic particles, thereby creating hiss. Multitrack tape brings an associated increase in tape noise.

To improve dynamic range and reduce noise, the signal must be processed before it is encoded on tape and after it is decoded from tape. Such a process is called *double-ended noise reduction*. Noise reduction that occurs either just before recording or just after playback is called *single-ended noise reduction*.

Double-Ended Noise Reduction

A compressor can process noise "before the fact"—during recording—and the expander can process noise "after the fact"—during playback. During recording, the input signal is compressed; that is, dynamic range is reduced. Where quiet passages occur in the sound, they are recorded at a higher-than-normal level. During playback the signal is expanded—returned to its original dynamic range—but with one difference: The level is reduced, and so is the noise, in all of the places where it was increased during recording (see 8-17).

Using the compressor and expander for noise reduction is an exacting and time-consuming job. It is also expensive. It involves setting the appropriate thresholds and ratios on each unit for each tape track being produced; a 24-track recording would require 24 compressors and 24 expanders to

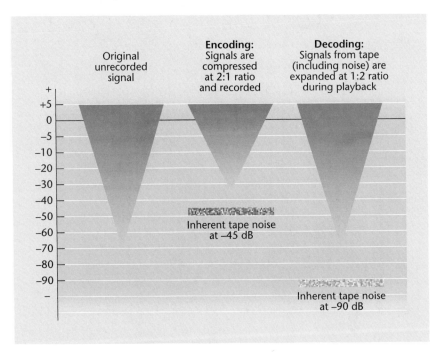

8-17 Companding dynamic range. Compression treats dynamic range before recording, so the program material is above the noise floor. During playback, expansion restores the original dynamic range with reduced tape noise.

reduce overall tape noise. Therefore the double-ended process of noise reduction has been incorporated into a single unit called a **compander** (from its functions, *com*pression and ex*pan*sion). The compander is more popularly known as a *noise reducer.*

In double-ended noise reduction, a tape encoded with noise reduction must be decoded during playback. If it is not, the increased signal and noise level that was encoded during recording will be annoyingly perceptible. The most commonly used double-ended noise reduction systems are Dolby and dbx. These systems are not compatible, so tapes made with one are not interchangeable with the other.

The Dolby System

The Dolby company has a number of systems currently in use. The one most prevalent in professional recording is *SR (spectral recording).*

Spectral recording uses the principle of least treatment to the audio signal (see 8-18). At the lowest levels or when no signal is present, SR applies a fixed gain/frequency characteristic that reduces

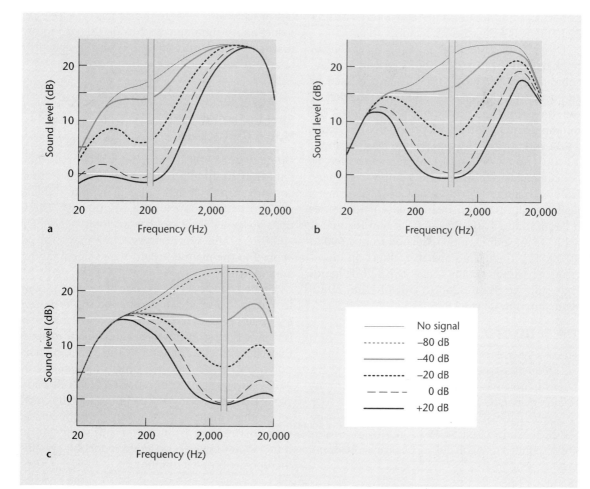

8-18 Examples of Dolby SR noise reduction at (a) 200 Hz, (b) 800 Hz, and (c) 3,000 Hz

noise and other low-frequency disturbances. Noise reduction is applied to those regions that contain low- and medium-level signal components. Similar to the response of the human hearing system, SR responds to changing amplitudes in various regions of the frequency spectrum, rather than to instantaneous variations in the signal's overall waveform. To put it another way, SR changes the gain only by the amount required and only at frequencies where the change is needed, thereby achieving as nearly optimal a level as possible at all frequencies. Spectral recording increases dynamic range as much as 24 dB at high frequencies and 10 dB at low frequencies, increasing headroom to the point where the risk of underrecording analog tape and overrecording digital tape is reduced considerably.

Other Dolby systems are the S, B, and C. *Dolby S* noise reduction is based on the SR process. It is less complex and less costly than SR and is used in audiocassettes and semipro multitrack recorders. It uses three fixed and two sliding bands to lower the midrange and high-frequency noise floor by about 24 dB and the low-frequency noise floor by about 10 dB. The *Dolby B* and *C* systems are used in consumer cassette decks and semipro recorders. Dolby C is also used with some videotape formats. Dolby B reduces high-frequency noise 10 dB. It uses a single sliding band that starts at 500 Hz, and it achieves maximum noise reduction from 1,500 to 20,000 Hz. There is no operating effect on lower-frequency noises. Dolby C uses two sliding bands that start at about 125 Hz and provide 20-dB reduction upward from 375 Hz.

The dbx System

The dbx system reduces noise 30 dB across a single, full-frequency-range band from 20 to 20,000 Hz. There is no division of noise reduction among frequency bands. The compression ratio is 2 to 1, so sonic material with a dynamic range of, say, 90 dB is compressed to 45 dB during recording and expanded to 90 dB during playback; dbx is not level-dependent.

The original dbx noise reduction system, designated Type I, was developed for use in professional recording studios. Broadcast cartridges and telephone transmission lines do not offer the excellent frequency response available in professional tape recorders, however; the low end and high end fall off considerably. To meet the needs of broadcasters, the dbx Type II noise reduction system was developed. The Type I and Type II systems are incompatible; a tape encoded with one system cannot be decoded by the other.

There is also a dbx Type III noise reduction system. When any equalizer is in the signal chain, movement of controls—fader, send, EQ, and so on—usually adds noise to the signal. Type III noise reduction is a simultaneous encode/decode process that is built into dbx equalizers and designed to neutralize such noise (see 8-3).

Single-Ended Noise Reduction

Double-ended noise reduction systems do not remove noise from a signal, they prevent it from entering. Single-ended noise reduction systems work to reduce source noise in one pass. These units are generally applied to microphones, guitar amplifiers, and synthesizers. They may also be applied to the main left/right stereo signal during a mixdown.

Single-ended systems use one of two techniques to reduce noise: *dynamic filtering* or *downward expansion*. With dynamic filtering, a variable filter is applied during quiet passages and usually to noise that changes with the level of the signal, such as noisy synthesizer patches. Downward expansion works like an expander by reducing the level of any signal that drops below a preset threshold. It is used for ambient noise and relatively constant noise, such as the buzz from guitar amps and 60-Hz hum. Some single-ended noise reduction systems incorporate both techniques.

a

Reverberation (6 types)
Hall reverb
Room reverb
Plate reverb
Gated reverb
Ducking reverb
Spacious ambience

Delay (11 types)
Stereo delay
Double delay
Multitap delay
Tempo delay
Long delay
Mono delay
Modulation delay
Ping Pong delay
Hold delay
Panpot tap delay
Dimension delay

Dynamics (4 types)
Limiter
Compressor
DAL-1000 limiter
Driver

Filter (7 types)
Multiple PEQ
Dynamic exciter
Wah
Dynamic filter
Amp simulator
Subharmonic generator
Bottom ambiencer

Gate (2 types)
Gate
Slow attacker

Chorus (4 types)
Stereo chorus
Band chorus
Deca chorus
Stereo ensemble

Flanger (4 types)
Stereo flanger
Band flanger
Step flanger
Triggered flanger

Phaser (2 types)
Stereo phaser
Triggered phaser

Panning (3 types)
Stereo panning
Haas panning
Triggered panning

Pitch (4 types)
Stereo pitch shifter
Multipitch shifter
Intelligent pitch shifter
Reverse shifter

Sound Effect (5 types)
Doppler
Ring modulator
Vocoder
Pitch breaker
Pitch roller

Others (4 types)
Rotary speaker
Vocal canceler
Freeze
Vibrate and tremolo

Combination (5 types)
Delay + reverb
Chorus + delay
Chorus + reverb
Pitch + delay
Pitch + chorus

b

8-19 (a) Multieffects signal processor and (b) a sampling of its effects

MULTIEFFECTS SIGNAL PROCESSORS

A *multieffects signal processor* combines several of the functions of individual signal processors in a single unit, and some units do it digitally (see "Digital Signal Processing" in the next section). The number of signal-processing functions varies with the unit. Figure 8-19 displays one example of a multieffects processor.

DIGITAL SIGNAL PROCESSING

Much of the signal processing available in consoles and out-board equipment is also available with *digital signal processing (DSP)* in hard disk recorder/editors as part of the software program. And what is not included can be added as a plug-in. In a sense, DSP is like a multieffects processor, particularly those with DSP architecture, but more so. In computers, the EQ, limiting, compression, expansion, pitch shifting, delay, noise reduction, and so on can more easily accommodate additional functions, applications are more flexible, and storage is far greater (see 8-20).

Digital signal processing does not come without some disadvantages, however. Unless you are careful, DSP can eat up considerable memory, and effects can begin to have similar sonic characteristics.

Paragraphic equalizer

Reverb system

8-20 Examples of DSP menus

Part Two: Equipment

Compressor

Compressor/expander/noise gate

8-20 Examples of DSP menus (continued)

Noise Reduction with Digital Signal Processing

A considerable advantage of DSP is its potency in noise reduction, particularly when converting analog recordings to digital (see 8-21). Virtually any unwanted sound can be eliminated.

In addition to the conventional noise reduction associated with Dolby, for example, digital noise reduction can act on other noises as well. One system uses three main tools: manual de-clicking for removal of clicks, pops, thumps, electrostatic ticks, and other impulse noises; production de-clicking and de-crackling for automatic click and scratch detection and removal; and broadband de-noising to eliminate hiss, surface noise, and unwanted background noise.

The system is particularly effective at removing constant, steady noises. For example, in a vocal track with high-level background noise from lights, ventilating fans, and studio acoustics, 85 percent of the noise can be removed without affecting voice quality.

In digital noise reduction, there are parameters to control and balance. You have to consider the amount of noise being removed from the signal, the amount of signal being removed from the program material, and the amount of new sonic colorations being added to the signal. Failure to coordinate these factors can be sonically detrimental to the program material, if not exacerbate the original noise problem.

8-21 Example of DSP noise reducer. This plug-in, designed for a hard disk recording/editing system, removes unwanted clicks from a recording without altering the undamaged sound immediately before and after a click.

▶ Signal processors are devices used to alter some characteristic of a sound. They can be grouped into four categories: (1) spectrum, (2) time, (3) amplitude, and (4) noise.

▶ The equalizer and filter are examples of spectrum processors, because they alter the spectral balance of a signal. The equalizer increases or decreases the level of a signal at a selected frequency by boost or cut (also known as peak and dip), or by shelving. The filter attenuates certain frequencies above, below, between, or at a preset point(s).

▶ Two types of equalizers in common use are the fixed-frequency and the parametric.

▶ The most commonly used filters are high-pass (low-cut), low-pass (high-cut), band-pass, and notch.

▶ Psychoacoustic processors add clarity, definition, and overall presence to sound.

▶ Time signal processors affect the time relationships of signals. Reverberation, delay, and pitch shifting are three such effects.

▶ The three most common types of reverberation systems used today are (1) digital, (2) plate, and (3) acoustic chamber.

▶ Delay is the time interval between a sound or signal and its repetition.

▶ Most delay effects today, such as doubling, chorusing, and slap back echo, are produced electronically using a digital delay device.

▶ Flanging and phasing split a signal and slightly delay one part to create controlled phase cancellations that generate a pulsating sound. Flanging uses a time delay; phasing uses a phase shifter. A pitch shifter can change the pitch of a sound or running time of a program without altering pitch.

▶ Amplitude signal processors affect a sound's dynamic range. These effects include compressing, limiting, and expanding a signal.

▶ With compression, as the input level increases, the output level also increases but at a slower rate, reducing dynamic range. With limiting, the output level stays at or below a preset point regardless of its input level. With expansion, as the input level increases, the output level also increases but at a greater rate, increasing dynamic range.

▶ Noise processors are designed to reduce tape noise in recording. They are either double-ended or single-ended. In double-ended noise reduction, noise is prevented from entering a signal. In single-ended noise reduction, existing noise in the signal is reduced.

▶ Multieffects signal processors combine several of the functions of individual signal processors in a single unit.

▶ Using software programs for digital signal processing (DSP), it is possible to perform almost any signal-processing function in a hard disk recorder/editor, such as EQ, compression, expansion, pitch shifting, delay, noise reduction, and so on.

9

Loudspeakers and Monitoring

Each component in the *sound chain*—microphone, console, signal processor, and recorder—is important. But no matter how good these components are, when you listen to their product, *the quality of every sound you evaluate—analog or digital—is based on what you hear from the loudspeaker,* the last link in the chain. The tendency is to underestimate the importance of the loudspeaker. Perhaps there may be a subconscious correlation between last and least.

The point seems straightforward: Always use the best loudspeaker. But which is best? Is it the most expensive? The largest? The loudest? The one with the widest, flattest frequency response? The one suitable for symphonic music or hard rock? Although a loudspeaker is critical to every audio operation, choosing the one best for your needs, unfortunately, is not so straightforward. It involves several decisions; each influences later decisions, and most are mainly subjective.

In deciding which loudspeaker is "best," you should look at several factors: frequency response, linearity, amplifier power, distortion, output-level capability, sensitivity, polar response, arrival time, and phase. Placement also affects the sound. These factors are discussed later in this chapter.

Like the microphone, the loudspeaker is a transducer, but it works in the opposite direction: Instead of changing acoustic energy into electric energy, it changes electric energy back into acoustic energy. But unlike microphone usage, only one type of loudspeaker is in common use—the *moving-coil loudspeaker*.

LOUDSPEAKER SYSTEMS

The function of a loudspeaker is to convert the electric energy that drives it into mechanical energy and in turn into acoustic energy. Theoretically, a loudspeaker should be able to reproduce all frequencies linearly—that is, having an output that varies proportionately with the input. In reality, this does not happen. A loudspeaker that is large enough to generate low-frequency sound waves most likely will not be able to reproduce the high frequencies efficiently. Conversely, a speaker capable of reproducing the shorter waves may be incapable of reproducing the longer wavelengths.

To illustrate the problem, many radio and television receivers contain a single speaker; even many stereo radios and tape recorders contain only one loudspeaker in each of the two loudspeaker enclosures. Because a single speaker has difficulty coping with the entire range of audible frequencies, a compromise is made: The long and the short wavelengths are sacrificed for the medium wavelengths that a single, midsized loudspeaker can reproduce more efficiently. Therefore, regardless of a recording's sound quality, a receiver with just one loudspeaker cannot reproduce it with full-frequency response.

Crossover Network and Drivers

To widen the loudspeaker's frequency response and make reproduction of the bass and treble more efficient, the *crossover network* was created. Also, individual speaker elements, called *drivers*, were developed to handle the different physical requirements necessary to emit the long, powerful bass frequencies and the short, more directional treble frequencies.

The crossover network divides the frequency spectrum between the low and high frequencies. The actual point, or frequency, where the bass and treble divide is called the *crossover frequency*. A driver large enough to handle the low frequencies is dedicated to the bass, and a driver small enough to handle the high frequencies is dedicated to the treble. Informally, these drivers, or loudspeakers, are called the *woofer* and the *tweeter*. Low- and high-frequency range drivers are contained in a single cabinet. The size of the drivers is related to the power output of the loudspeaker system.

If a loudspeaker system divides the frequency spectrum once, it is called a *two-way system loudspeaker*. The crossover frequency in a two-way system is in the neighborhood of 1,500 to 2,000 Hz. The frequencies below the crossover point are assigned to the woofer, and the frequencies above the crossover are assigned to the tweeter. A loudspeaker may have more than one driver for each frequency range.

A loudspeaker system that uses two crossover frequencies is called a *three-way system loudspeaker*, and one that has three crossover frequencies is called a *four-way system loudspeaker*. Three-way systems divide the frequency spectrum at roughly 400 to 500 Hz and 3,500 to 5,000 Hz. Four-way systems divide it at anywhere between 400 to 500 Hz, 1,500 to 2,000 Hz, and 4,500 to 6,000 Hz.

SELECTING A MONITOR LOUDSPEAKER

Loudspeakers are like musical instruments in that they produce sound. They are not like purely electronic components such as consoles, which can be objectively tested and rationally evaluated. No two loudspeakers ever sound quite the same. Comparing the same make and model loudspeakers in one room tells you only what they sound like in that acoustic environment; in another room they may sound altogether different. Furthermore, a loudspeaker that satisfies your taste might be unappealing to someone else.

A loudspeaker's specifications can be used only as a reference. No matter how good a speaker looks on paper, keep in mind that the measurements are based on tests made in an *anechoic chamber*—a room with no reflections of any kind. Clearly, that will not be the case in actual use.

Thus it is extremely difficult to suggest guidelines for selecting a studio monitor. Nevertheless, all loudspeakers used for professional purposes should meet certain requirements.

Frequency Response

Evaluating *frequency response* in a loudspeaker involves two considerations: (1) how wide it is and (2) how flat, or linear, it is. Frequency response ideally should be as wide as possible, from at least 40 to 20,000 Hz. But the relationship between the sound produced in the studio and the sound reproduced through the audience's receiver/loudspeaker becomes a factor when selecting a monitor loudspeaker (see Figures 9-1 and 9-2).

For example, TV audio can carry the entire range of audible frequencies. You may have noticed during a televised music program, however, that you see certain high- and low-pitched instruments being played but you hear them only faintly or not at all. Overhead cymbals are one example. Generally, their frequency range is between 300 and 12,000 Hz (including overtones), but they usually begin to gain good definition between 4,500 and 8,000 Hz, which is well within the frequency range of television transmission. The highest response of many home TV receivers is about 6,000 Hz, however, which is below a good part of the cymbals' range.

Assume that you wish to boost the cymbal frequencies that the home TV receiver can barely reproduce. Unless you listen to the sound over a monitor comparable in output level and response to the average TV speaker, you cannot get a sense of what effect the boost is having. But that monitor will not give you a sense of what viewers with upgraded TV sound systems, such as stereo and surround sound, are hearing.

Due to the differences between the potential sound response of a medium and its actual response after processing, transmission, and reception, most professional studios use at least two types of studio monitors: one to provide both wide response and sufficient power to reproduce a broad range of

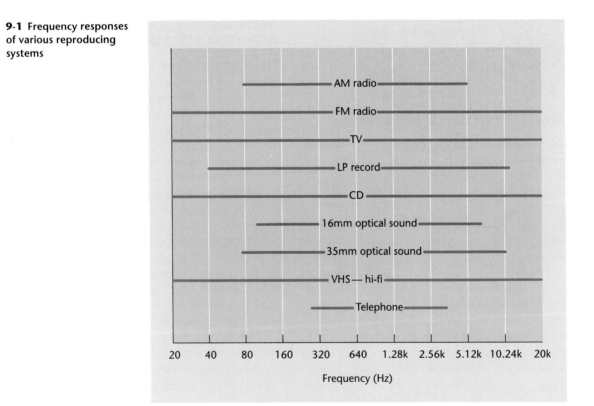

9-1 Frequency responses of various reproducing systems

sound levels, and the other with response and power that reflect what the average listener hears. Many studios use three sets of monitors to check sound: (1) low-quality loudspeakers with only midrange response and limited power output, such as those in portable and car radios, portable and desktop TVs, and cheap tape decks; (2) average-quality loudspeakers with added high and low response, such as moderately priced component systems; and (3) high-quality loudspeakers with a very wide response and high output capability.

Linearity

The second consideration in evaluating frequency response in a loudspeaker is how linear it is. *Linearity* means that frequencies being fed to a loudspeaker at a particular loudness are reproduced at the same loudness. If they are not, it is very difficult to predetermine what listeners will hear.

If the level of a 100-Hz sound is 80 dB going in and 55 dB coming out, some—if not most—of the information may be lost. If the level of an 8,000-Hz sound is 80 dB going in and 100 dB coming out, the information may be overbearing.

Loudspeaker specifications include a value that indicates how much a monitor deviates from a flat frequency response, either by increasing or decreasing level. This variance should be no greater than ±3 dB.

Amplifier Power

To generate adequately loud sound levels without causing distortion, the loudspeaker amplifier must provide sufficient power. At least 30 watts for tweeters and 100 watts for woofers is generally necessary. Regardless of how good the rest of a loudspeaker's components are, if the amplifier does not have enough power, efficiency suffers

9-2 Frequency responses of various receiver/loudspeaker systems

considerably. There is a commonly held, seemingly plausible notion that increasing amplifier power means a proportional increase in loudness; for example, that a 100-watt amplifier can play twice as loud as a 50-watt amplifier. In fact, if a 100-watt and a 50-watt amp are playing at top volume, the 100-watt amp will sound only slightly louder. What the added wattage gives is clearer and less distorted reproduction in loud sonic peaks.

Distortion

Discussion of amplifier power leads naturally to consideration of *distortion*—appearance of a signal in the reproduced sound that was not in the original sound. Any component in the sound chain can generate distortion. Because distortion is heard at the reproduction (loudspeaker) phase of the sound chain, regardless of where in the system it was generated, and because loudspeakers are the most distortion-prone component in most audio systems, it is appropriate to discuss briefly the various forms of distortion: intermodulation, harmonic, transient, and loudness.

Intermodulation Distortion

The loudspeaker is perhaps most vulnerable to *intermodulation distortion (IM)*, which results when two or more frequencies occur at the same time and interact to create combination tones and dissonances that are unrelated to the original sounds. Audio systems can be most vulnerable to intermodulation distortion when frequencies are far apart, as when a piccolo and a baritone saxophone are playing at the same time. Intermodulation distortion usually occurs in the high frequencies, because they are weaker and more delicate than the low frequencies.

Wideness and flatness of frequency response are affected when IM is present. In addition to its obvious effect on perception, even subtle distortion can cause listening fatigue.

Unfortunately, not all specification sheets include percentage of IM, and those that do often list it only for selected frequencies. Nevertheless, knowing the percentage of IM for all frequencies is important to loudspeaker selection. A rating of .5 percent IM or less is considered good for a loudspeaker.

Harmonic Distortion

You will recall that **harmonic distortion** occurs when the audio system introduces harmonics into a recording that were not present originally. Harmonic and IM distortion usually happen when the input and output of a sound system are **nonlinear**—that is, when they do not change in direct proportion to each other. A loudspeaker's inability to handle amplitude is a common cause of harmonic distortion. This added harmonic content is expressed as a percentage of the total signal or as a component's *total harmonic distortion (THD)*.

Transient Distortion

Transient distortion relates to the inability of an audio component to respond quickly to a rapidly changing signal, such as that produced by percussive sounds. Sometimes, transient distortion produces a ringing sound.

Loudness Distortion

Loudness distortion, also called *overload distortion,* occurs when a signal is recorded or played back at a level of loudness that is greater than the sound system can handle. The clipping that results from loudness distortion creates a fuzzy, gritty sound.

Output-Level Capability

Overly loud signals give a false impression of program quality and balance; nevertheless, a loudspeaker should be capable of reproducing loud sound levels without distorting, blowing fuses, or damaging its components. An output capability of 110 dB-SPL is desirable for studio work. Even if studio work does not often call for very loud levels, the monitor should be capable of reproducing them, because it is sometimes necessary to listen at a loud level to hear subtlety and quiet detail.

Sensitivity

Sensitivity is the on-axis sound-pressure level a loudspeaker produces at a given distance when driven at a certain power (about 3.3 feet with 1 watt of power). A monitor's sensitivity rating gives you an idea of the system's overall efficiency. Typical ratings range from 84 dB to more than 100 dB.

In real terms, however, a sensitivity rating of, say, 90 dB indicates that the loudspeaker could provide 100 dB from a 10-watt input and 110 dB from a 100-watt input, depending on the type of driver. The point is that it is the combination of sensitivity rating and power rating that tells you whether a monitor loudspeaker will be loud enough to suit your production needs. Generally, a sensitivity rating of 93 dB or louder is required for professional applications.

Polar Response

Polar response indicates how a loudspeaker focuses sound at the monitoring position(s). Because it is important to hear only the sound coming from the studio or the tape, without interacting reflections from the control room walls (vertical surfaces) and ceiling or floor (horizontal surfaces), dispersion must be controlled (see Chapter 3).

Bass waves are difficult to direct because of their long wavelengths. Therefore bass traps and other low-frequency absorbers are included in control room design in order to handle those bass waves not focused at the listening position.

Frequencies from the tweeter(s), on the other hand, are shorter and easier to focus. The problem with high frequencies is that as the wavelength shortens, the pattern can narrow. Therefore the *coverage angle*, defined as the off-axis angle or point at which loudspeaker level is down 6 dB compared with the on-axis output, may not be wide enough to include the entire listening area.

To help in selecting a loudspeaker with adequate polar response, specifications usually list a monitor's horizontal and vertical coverage angles. These angles should be high and wide enough to cover

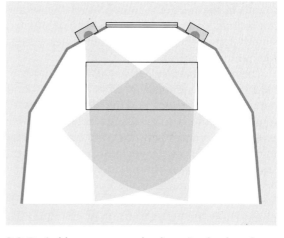

9-3 Desirable coverage angle of monitor loudspeakers

the listening position and still allow the operator or audience some lateral movement without seriously affecting sonic balance (see 9-3).

Arrival Time

Even if coverage angles are optimal, unless all reproduced sounds reach the listening position(s) at relatively the same time they were produced, aural perception will be impaired. When you consider the differences in size and power requirements among drivers and the wavelengths they emit, you can see that this is easier said than done.

In two-, three-, and four-way system loudspeakers, the physical separation of each of the speakers in the system causes the sounds to reach the listener's ears at different times. Arrival times different by more than 1 ms are not acceptable in professional applications.

Phase

Sometimes, although dispersal and arrival time are adequate, sound reaching a listener may not be as loud as it should be or the elements within it may be poorly placed. For example, a rock band may be generating loud levels in the studio, but the sounds in the control room are, in relative terms, not so loud; or an actor is supposed to be situated slightly left in the aural frame, but is heard from the right loudspeaker.

These problems may be the result of out-of-phase loudspeakers: One loudspeaker is pushing sound outward (compression), and the other loudspeaker is pulling sound inward (rarefaction). *Phase* problems can occur between woofer and tweeter in the same loudspeaker enclosure or between two separate loudspeakers. In the latter case, it is usually because the connections are not wired properly (see 9-4 and 9-5). If you think that sound is out of phase, check the VU meters. If they show a similar level and the audio still sounds skewed, the speakers are out of phase; if they show different levels, the phase problem is probably elsewhere.

MONITOR PLACEMENT

Where you place monitor loudspeakers also affects sound quality, dispersal, and arrival time. Loudspeakers are often designed for a particular room location and are generally positioned in one of four places: (1) well toward the middle of a room, (2) against or flush with a wall, (3) at the intersection of two walls, or (4) in a corner at the ceiling or on the floor. Each position affects the sound's loudness and dispersion differently.

A loudspeaker hanging in the middle of a room radiates sound into what is called a *full sphere* (or *full space*), where, theoretically, the sound level at any point within a given distance is the same (see 9-6). If a loudspeaker is placed against a wall, the wall concentrates the radiations into a *half sphere,* thereby theoretically increasing the sound

9-4 Properly wired loudspeakers. These loudspeakers will reproduce in phase.

9-5 Improperly wired loudspeakers. These loudspeakers will reproduce out of phase.

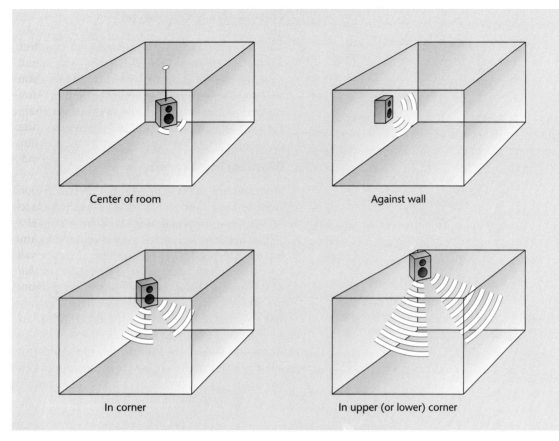

9-6 Four typical loudspeaker locations in a room and the effects of placement on overall loudness levels

level by 3 dB. With loudspeakers mounted at the intersection of two walls, the dispersion is concentrated still more into a *one-quarter sphere,* thus increasing the sound level another 3 dB. Loudspeakers placed in corners at the ceiling or on the floor radiate in a *one-eighth sphere,* generating the most concentrated sound levels in a four-walled room. A significant part of each increase in the overall sound level is due to the loudness increase in the bass (see 9-7).

For informal listening, one of these monitor positions is not necessarily better than another; placement may depend on a room's layout, furniture placement, personal taste, and so on. In professional situations it is preferable to flush-mount loudspeakers in a wall or soffit. The most

9-7 An example of the effects of loudspeaker placement on bass response

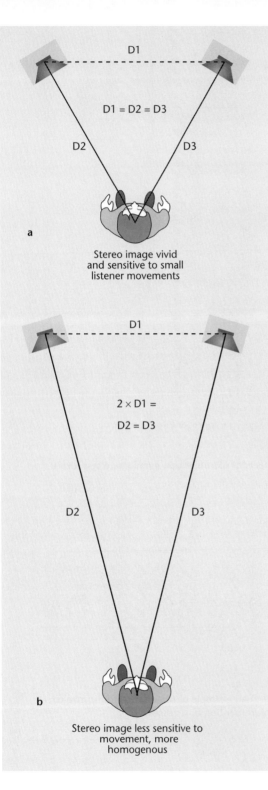

a

Stereo image vivid
and sensitive to small
listener movements

$D1 = D2 = D3$

$2 \times D1 =$

$D2 = D3$

b

Stereo image less sensitive to
movement, more
homogenous

important thing in monitor placement is to avoid any appreciable space between the loudspeaker and the wall and any protrusion of the loudspeaker's cabinet edges. Otherwise, the wall or cabinet edges, or both, will act as secondary radiators, degrading frequency response. Flush-mounting also improves low-frequency response through avoiding back-wall reflections.

Monitoring Stereo

Stereo sound is two-dimensional. It has depth—front-to-back—and width—side-to-side. It therefore requires two discrete loudspeakers for monitoring. In placing these loudspeakers, it is critical that they be positioned to reproduce an accurate and balanced stereo image (see 9-8). That is, the location of the front-to-back and side-to-side sound sources are where they should be. If the original material has the vocal in the center (in relation to the two loudspeakers), the first violins on the left, the bass drum and bass at the rear center, the snare drum slightly left or right, and so on, these should be in the same spatial positions when the material is played through the monitor system.

Near-Field Monitoring

Even in the best of monitor–control room acoustic environments, the distance between wall-mounted

9-8 To help create an optimal travel path for sound from the loudspeakers to the listening position, carefully measure the loudspeaker separation and the distance between the loudspeakers and the listening position. (a) The distance between the acoustic center (between the loudspeakers) and the listening position is equal. In this arrangement head movement is restricted somewhat, and the stereo image will be emphasized or spread out, heightening the sense of where elements in the recording are located. Shortening D2 and D3 will produce a large shift in the stereo image. (b) The distance between the acoustic center and the listening position is about twice as long. With this configuration the movement of the head is less restricted, and the stereo image is reduced in width although it is more homogeneous. The more D2 and D3 are lengthened, the more monaural the stereo image becomes (except for hard-left and hard-right panning).

loudspeakers and the listening position is often wide enough to generate sonic discontinuities from unwanted control room reflections. To reduce these unwanted reflections, another set of monitors is placed on or near the console's meter bridge (see 9-9).

Near-field monitoring reduces the audibility of control room acoustics by placing loudspeakers close to the listening position. Moreover, near-field monitoring improves source localization, because most of the sound reaching the listening position is direct; the early reflections that hinder good source localization are reduced to the point where they are of little consequence. At least, that is the theory. In practice, problems with near-field monitoring still remain (see 9-10).

9-9 Near-field monitors on console's meter bridge

9-10 Near-field monitoring. (a) If a meter bridge is too low, early reflections will bounce off the console, degrading the overall monitor sound reaching the operator's ears. (b) One way to minimize this problem is to place the near-field monitors a few inches or so in back of the console.

Among the requirements for near-field monitors are: loudspeakers that are small enough to put on or near the console's meter bridge without the sound "blowing you away"; a uniform frequency response from about 70 to 16,000 Hz, especially smooth response through the midrange; a sensitivity range from 87 to 92 dB; sufficient amplifier power; and good vertical dispersion for more-stable stereo imaging.

Monitoring Surround Sound

Surround sound differs from stereo by deepening the dimension of depth, thereby placing the listener more in the center of the aural image than in front of it. To accomplish this requires additional audio channels routed to additional loudspeakers. To augment the left and right stereo channels and loudspeakers, a center channel and loudspeaker and an additional channel for the surround loudspeakers are required. Therefore to monitor surround sound, the frontal loudspeaker array should be positioned left, center, and right, and the surround loudspeakers should be placed behind the console operator (see 9-11). It is all to the better if additional loudspeakers are positioned to the sides in the monitoring environment to enhance the surround-sound imaging. A recent development in surround sound, the 5.1 channel system, adds a subwoofer to the frontal loudspeaker array for low-frequency effects and two surround-sound stereo channels (see 9-12 and 9-13). Also see Chapter 18 for a full discussion of surround sound.

ADJUSTING MONITOR SOUND TO ROOM SOUND

As important as the "ear" and personal taste are to monitor selection and evaluation, it is critical to obtain an objective measure of the correlation between monitor sound and room sound. This is

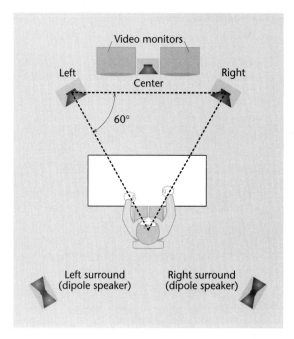

9-11 Example of a control room plan for surround-sound monitoring

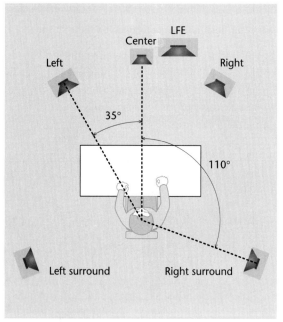

9-12 Loudspeaker placement in a typical 5.1 surround-sound listening field. LFE = low-frequency effects.

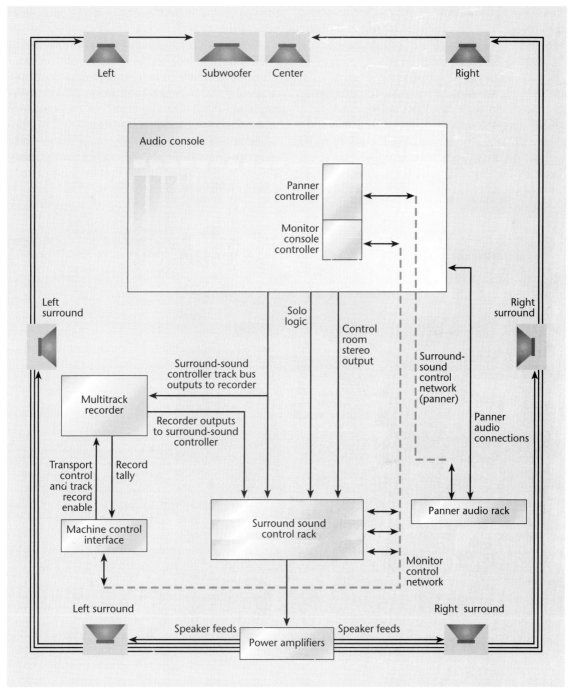

9-13 Example of the monitor placement and signal flow for surround-sound recording done using a *real-time analyzer*—a device that displays response curves on an instantaneous basis (see 9-14). Real-time analysis should be taken at different amplitudes.

When problems with frequency response show up, particularly serious ones, avoid the temptation to offset them with equalization. For example, if control room acoustics boost loudspeaker sound 6 dB at 250 Hz, try not to equalize the monitors by, in this case, attenuating their response 6 dB at 250 Hz. Aside from adding noise by running the signal through another electronic device, an equalizer can change the phase relationships of the audio that passes through it.

To deal with discontinuities in monitor–control room interface, look to the source of the problem and correct it there. It may be necessary to change or modify the monitor, monitor position, power amplifier, sound diffusing materials, or impedance mismatch between sections of the monitor system. Whatever it takes, "natural" provides a truer sonic reference than "artificial," especially if the recording has to be evaluated or further processed in a different control room.

9-14 Audio analysis and monitoring system. This system provides a range of measurement and visualization tools, such as real-time oscilloscopes, real-time spectrum analysis, peak, RMS (root mean square), envelope history, time code clock, and phase analysis.

EVALUATING THE MONITOR LOUDSPEAKER

The final test of any monitor loudspeaker is how it sounds. Although the basis for much of the evaluation is subjective, there are guidelines for determining loudspeaker performance:

☑ Begin with rested ears. Fatigue alters aural perception.

☑ Sit at the designated listening position—the optimal distance away from and between the loudspeakers. This position, known as the *sweet spot,* should allow some front-to-back and side-to-side movement without altering perception of loudness, frequency response, or spatial perspective. It is important to know the boundaries of the listening position(s) so that all sound can be monitored on-axis within this area (see 9-3).

☑ Use material with which you are intimately familiar for the evaluation, preferably on a CD or DAT. Otherwise, if some aspect of the sound is unsatisfactory, you will not know whether the problem is with the original material or with the loudspeaker.

☑ Listen at a comfortable loudness level; 85 dB-SPL is often recommended.

☑ Listen for sounds you may not have heard before, such as hiss, hum, or buzz. Good monitors may reveal what inferior monitors cover up, or it could indicate that the monitors you are listening to have problems. In either case, you have learned something.

☑ In listening for spatial balance, make sure that the various sounds are positioned in the same places relative to the original material. As an additional test, put the monitor system into mono and check to make sure that the sound appears to be coming from between the two loudspeakers. Move toward the left and right boundaries of the sweet spot. If the sound moves with you before you get near the boundaries, reposition the monitors. Then recheck their dispersion in both stereo and mono until you can move within the boundaries of the listening position without the sound following you or

skewing the placement of the sound sources. If monitor repositioning is necessary to correct problems with side-to-side sound placement, be sure it does not adversely affect front-to-back sound dispersion to the listening position.

☑ In evaluating treble response, listen to the cymbal, triangle, flute, piccolo, and other high-frequency instruments. Are they too bright, crisp, shrill, or dull? Do you hear their upper harmonics?

☑ In testing bass response, include instruments such as the tuba and bass, as well as the low end of the organ, piano, bassoon, and cello. Sound should not be thin, boomy, muddy, or grainy.

☑ Assess the transient response, which is also important in a loudspeaker. For this, drums, bells, and triangle provide excellent tests, assuming they are properly recorded. Good transient response reproduces a crisp attack with no distortion or breakup.

☑ If you are evaluating a number of different loudspeakers, compare only a few at a time and take notes. Trying to remember, for example, how different speakers color the presence range, their differences in low-end warmth, or their degree of darkness or brightness is unreliable. Our ability to retain precise auditory information is limited, particularly over time and when comparison testing.

☑ In evaluating monitor loudspeakers for surround sound, consider the following: Is the imaging of the sound sources cohesive or disjointed? Does the sound emanate from the appropriate loudspeaker location or does it seem detached from it? In moving around the listening environment, how much of the positional information, or sonic illusion, remains intact? How robust does that illusion remain in another listening environment? If there are motion changes—sound moving left-to-right, right side–to–right front, and so on—are they smooth? Does any element call unwanted attention to itself?

Other important elements to evaluate, such as intermodulation, harmonic, and loudness distortion, were touched upon earlier in this chapter.

Monitoring in an Unfamiliar Control Room

When you do a session in a facility you have not worked in before, it is essential to become thoroughly familiar with the interaction between its monitor sound and its room sound. A relatively quick and reliable way to get an objective idea of that interaction is to do a real-time analysis. It is also crucial to put the real-time analysis into perspective with reference CDs and your ears.

Reference CDs (or DATs) can be commercial recordings with which you are entirely familiar, or discs specially designed to help assess a listening environment, or both. Knowing how a recording sounds in a control room whose monitors and acoustics you are intimately familiar with makes a good test CD in determining the sonic characteristics of, and among, the monitors and acoustics in a strange environment. For example, if you know that a recording has clear high-end response in your own control room but the high end sounds thinner in another control room, it could indicate, among other things, that the other studio's monitors have inadequate treble response; the presence of harmonic distortion; a phase problem; the room's mediocre sound diffusion; or any combination of these factors.

Compact discs specially produced for referencing are also available. They are variously designed to test monitor and/or room response to a particular instrument, such as the drums; individual or groups of instruments, such as the voice and clarinet, or strings, brass, and woodwinds; various sizes and types of ensembles, such as orchestras, jazz bands, and rock groups; room acoustics; spatial positioning; and spectral balances (see Bibliography).

HEADPHONES

Headphones (also referred to as "cans") are a too-often-overlooked but important part of monitoring, especially in field recording (see Chapter 13). Four considerations are basic when using headphones for professional purposes: (1) frequency response should be wide, flat, and uncolored; (2) you must be thoroughly familiar with their sonic characteristics; (3) they should be *circumaural* (around-the-ear)—as airtight as possible against the head for acoustical isolation—and comfortable; and (4) the fit should stay snug even when you are moving.

Headphones are usually indispensable in field recording, because monitor loudspeakers are often unavailable or impractical. In studio control rooms, however, there are pros and cons to using headphones. The pros are that (1) sound quality will be consistent in different studios; (2) it is easier to hear subtle changes in the recording and the mix; and (3) there is no aural smearing due to room reflections. The cons are that (1) the sound quality will not be the same as with the monitor loudspeakers; (2) the aural image is inside the head rather than out in front; (3) there is no interaction between the program material and the acoustics, so the tendency may be to mix in more artificial reverberation than necessary; (4) if open-air, or *supra-aural,* headphones are used, bass response will not be as efficient as with circumaural headphones, and outside noise might interfere with listening; and (5) in panning signals for stereo, the distance between monitor loudspeakers is greater than the distance between your ears.

MAIN POINTS

▶ Loudspeakers are transducers that convert electric energy into sound energy.

▶ The moving-coil loudspeaker is the type most often used.

▶ A single, midsized speaker cannot reproduce high and low frequencies very well; it is essentially a midrange instrument.

▶ For improved response, loudspeakers have drivers large enough to handle the bass frequencies, and drivers small enough to handle the treble frequencies. These drivers are called, informally, woofers and tweeters, respectively.

- A crossover network separates the bass and treble frequencies at the crossover point and directs them to their particular drivers.

- Two-way system loudspeakers have one crossover network, three-way system loudspeakers have two crossovers, and four-way system loudspeakers have three crossovers.

- Each medium that records or transmits sound, such as a CD or TV, and each loudspeaker that reproduces sound, such as a studio monitor or home receiver, has certain spectral and amplitude capabilities. For optimal results, audio should be produced with an idea of how the system through which it will be reproduced works.

- In evaluating a monitor loudspeaker, frequency response, linearity, amplifier power, distortion, output-level capability, sensitivity, polar response, arrival time, and phase should also be considered.

- Linearity means that frequencies being fed to a loudspeaker at a particular loudness are reproduced at the same loudness.

- Amplifier power must be sufficient to drive the loudspeaker system or else distortion, among other things, will result.

- Distortion is the appearance of a signal in the reproduced sound that was not in the original sound. Various forms of distortion include inter-modulation, harmonic, transient, and loudness.

- Intermodulation distortion (IM) results when two or more frequencies occur at the same time and interact to create combination tones and dissonances that are unrelated to the original sounds.

- Harmonic distortion occurs when the audio system introduces harmonics into a recording that were not present originally.

- Transient distortion relates to the inability of an audio component to respond quickly to a rapidly changing signal, such as that produced by percussive sounds.

- Loudness distortion, or overload distortion, results when a signal is recorded or played back at an amplitude greater than the sound system can handle.

- The main studio monitors should have an output-level capability of 110 dB-SPL.

- Sensitivity is the on-axis sound-pressure level a loudspeaker produces at a given distance when driven at a certain power. A monitor's sensitivity rating provides a good overall indication of its efficiency.

- Polar response indicates how a loudspeaker focuses sound at the monitoring position(s).

- A sound's arrival time at the monitoring position(s) should be no more than 1 ms; otherwise, aural perception is impaired.

- Where a loudspeaker is positioned affects sound dispersion and loudness. A loudspeaker in the middle of a room generates the least concentrated sound; a loudspeaker at the intersection of a ceiling or floor generates the most.

- Stereo sound is two-dimensional; it has depth and breadth. In placing loudspeakers for monitoring stereo, it is critical that they be positioned to reproduce an accurate and balanced front-to-back and side-to-side sonic image.

- Near-field monitoring enables the sound engineer to reduce the audibility of control room acoustics by placing loudspeakers close to the monitoring position.

- Surround sound differs from stereo by deepening the depth dimension, thereby placing the listener more in the center of the aural image than in front of it. Therefore, monitoring surround sound requires frontal loudspeakers positioned left, center, and right, and surround loudspeakers placed behind the console operator. Additional surround loud-speakers positioned to the sides of the operator further enhance surround-sound imaging.

- Headphones are an important part of monitoring, particularly on location. Four considerations are vital in using headphones: (1) frequency response should be wide, flat, and uncolored; (2) you must be thoroughly familiar with the headphones' sonic characteristics before you use them; (3) the headphones should be airtight against the head for acoustical isolation; and (4) the fit should stay snug even when you are moving.

Three

Sound Design

CHAPTER 10   Sound Design

Sound
Design

Sound design is the process of creating the overall sonic character of a production (usually in relation to picture). Its development begins in pre-production and is ongoing throughout the production process, because so much of the audio is produced after shooting. Responsibility for the sound design falls to a designated sound designer who advises the audio production team and, ordinarily, has a hands-on role during one or more stages of production.

THE SOUND DESIGNER

Like the cinematographer, who is responsible for the overall look of a film or video, the ***sound designer*** is responsible for its overall sonic complexion. The term was first used as a professional craft designation in theatrical film in 1979 when an academy award for sound design was given to Walter Murch for *Apocalypse Now.* Over the years, the term has been diluted to include just about anyone on the audio production team, particularly creators of sound effects and sound-effect editors, who has a hand in producing the audio. The preferred meaning, though, denotes the one person responsible for creative control of the audio—and the one member of the audio team who has the director's ear.

Whether or not there is a designated sound designer, all members of the audio team contribute creatively to the sound in a production.

Hence, the material in this chapter applies to sound design in general and the various components of audio in particular, rather than to a specific role carried out by a particular member of the audio production team.

COMPONENTS OF SOUND STRUCTURE AND THEIR EFFECTS ON PERCEPTION

All sound—speech, sound effects, and music—are made up of the same basic components: pitch, loudness, timbre, tempo, rhythm, attack, duration, and decay. During audio production everyone involved, consciously or subconsciously, is dealing with these components and assessing their effects on perception. Because each element contains certain characteristics that affect our response to sound, understanding those effects are fundamental to sound design.

Pitch refers to the highness or lowness of a sound. High-pitched sound often suggests something delicate, bright, or elevated; low-pitched sound may indicate something sinister, strong, or peaceful.

Loudness describes sound in terms of how loud or soft it is. Loud sound can suggest closeness, strength, or importance; soft sound may convey distance, weakness, or tranquility.

Timbre is the characteristic tonal quality of a sound. It not only identifies a sound source— reedy, brassy, tympanic—but also sonic qualities such as rich, thin, edgy, or metallic. Reedy tonal qualities produced by a clarinet or oboe, for example, can suggest something wistful, lonely, or sweet. A brassy sound can imply something cold, harsh, fierce, bitter, forceful, martial, or big. A tympanic or percussive sound can convey drama, significance, or power.

Tempo refers to the speed of a sound. Fast tempos agitate, excite, or accelerate; slow tempos may suggest monotony, dignity, or control.

Rhythm relates to a sonic time pattern. It may be simple, constant, complex, or changing. A simple rhythm can convey deliberateness, regularity, or lack of complication. A constant rhythm can imply dullness, depression, or uniformity. Rhythmic complexity suggests complication or elaborateness.

Changing rhythms can create a sense of uncertainty, vigor, or the erratic.

Attack—the way a sound begins—can be hard, soft, crisp, or gradual. Hard or crisp attacks can suggest sharpness, excitement, or danger. Soft or gradual attacks can imply something gentle, muted, or blasé.

Duration refers to how long a sound lasts. Sound short in duration can convey restlessness, nervousness, or excitation; more-sustained sounds can create a sense of peace, persistence, or tiredness.

Decay—how fast a sound fades from a certain loudness—can be quick, gradual, or slow. Quick decays can create a sense of confinement, closeness, or definiteness; slow decays can convey distance, smoothness, or uncertainty.

Other aspects of sound, such as changing pitch, changing loudness, and acoustic interactions, also affect response. Of course, these elements are not heard individually but in combination.

Someone speaking in a loud, high-pitched voice at a rapid rate conveys excitement, whatever meaning the words may have. Lowering pitch, reducing loudness, and slowing tempo may also convey excitement, but this combination of sounds suggests something more profound and deeply felt. Words spoken at a deliberate tempo in a reverberant—that is, acoustically live—room may suggest a weightier content than those same words spoken in an acoustically drier environment.

These same factors can be applied to music and sounds. A trumpet or violin played loudly and rapidly at a high pitch could also suggest excitement, agitation, or gaiety—perhaps agitation in drier acoustics and gaiety in livelier acoustics.

Striking a wooden door or metal barrel loudly and rapidly can also suggest agitation or gaiety. And again, lowering pitch, reducing loudness, and slowing tempo changes the response to something more serious, whether the sound source is a trumpet, violin, wooden door, or metal barrel.

That these characteristics are elemental in sonic structure is not to suggest that sound design is prescriptive or developed by applying formulas; the basic components of sound structure do not occur separately, but together in myriad forms. Rather, it is to introduce and define the building blocks of sound from which the sound designer shapes aural structure and meaning.

FUNCTIONS OF SOUND

There are three domains to work with in creating a sound design: speech, sound effects, and music. This may not seem to be an impressive arsenal, especially when compared with the number of elements available in pictorial design—light, color, picture composition, scenery, costumes, depth of field, camera angle, camera movement, and so on. Sound is a formidable agent in communicating cognitive and affective information, however.

Picture requires continual redirection of attention. Sound washes over us. Even more, sound influences how we look at a picture. Two different sound tracks for the same film or video produce two different messages. Try watching a film or television, first with the sound off, and then with the sound on but without the picture. Usually, you will find that more information comes from the sound than from the picture.

Sound design in relation to picture is not a contest of superiority, however. The sound/picture relationship is symbiotic; they are two different "organisms" that are mutually beneficial.

Speech

Speech interpretation is the responsibility of the director and performer, not the sound designer. Nevertheless, it is important for those involved in audio production to know the various ways in which speech—verbal and nonverbal—affects meaning. Speech has basically two functions, narration and dialogue, and conveys meaning primarily through emphasis, inflection, and aural mood.

Narration

Narration is usually descriptive and voiced-over; that is, a narrator describes events from outside the action, not as a participant but as an observer.

Three types of narration are direct, indirect, and contrapuntal.

Direct narration describes what is being seen or heard. If we see or hear an automobile coming to a stop, a car door opening and closing, footsteps on concrete and then on stairs, and a wooden door opening and closing, and are told as much, the narration is direct. If, on the other hand, the narrator tells us that the person emerging from the car and going into the building is an ambassador on an urgent mission and is meeting with his counterparts from other countries who are waiting in the building, this is *indirect narration*. What you are being told is not evident in what is being shown. Indirect narration adds more information to the picture. *Contrapuntal narration*, as the term suggests, counterpoints narration and action to make a composite statement not explicitly carried, or suggested, in either element. For example, the action may contain people happily but wastefully consuming a more-than-ample meal, while the narration comments on the number of starving people in the world. The conflict between the two pieces of information makes a separate comment.

These examples may suggest that indirect and contrapuntal narration are better than direct narration because they supplement and broaden information and, therefore, provide more content. Indirect and contrapuntal narration are preferable if the action is somewhat obvious. But direct narration is useful in radio when sounds may not convey the necessary meaning. It is also helpful in educational or instructional programs, when information requires reinforcement to be remembered and understood.

Narration provides nonverbal information as well. If the style of the delivery is formal and unemotional, the content comes across as impersonal and objective. If the sound is heavily inflected and personalized, the content takes on a more emotional and subjective quality.

Although the particular narrational approach depends on the script, understanding the influences of narration on content in general results in a better-conceived sound design.

Dialogue

Dialogue is a conversation between two or more people. Obviously, the verbal content of the conversation is essential to meaning, but nonverbal sound in dialogue also shapes meaning. Some examples follow.

Accent An accent can tell you if a character is cultured or crude, an American from the Deep South or someone from England, France, or India. It can also color an entire drama. Suppose a drama set in Russia and depicting events that led to the 1917 Bolshevik Revolution has an all-British cast. Although acting and dialogue may be superb, the refined, rounded, mellifluous British sound may not be so effective as the more guttural Slavic sound and may not give the necessary edge to people and events. Shakespeare played by actors who are not British seems to sound unnatural. Films rerecorded from one language to another rarely sound believable.

Pace The pace of dialogue can convey nonverbal information about the passion, urgency, or boredom of a situation. For example:

She: Go away.
He: No.
She: Please.
He: Can't.
She: You must.
He: Uh-uh.

Certainly, there is not much verbal content here apart from the obvious. But by pacing the dialogue in different ways, meaning can be not only defined but also changed. Think of the scene played deliberately, with each line and the pauses between them measured, as opposed to a rapid-fire delivery and no pauses between lines. The deliberately paced sound design can convey more stress or, perhaps, more inner anguish than the faster-paced version. On the other hand, the faster pace can suggest nervousness and urgency.

Patterns Dialogue patterns are important to natural-sounding speech and believable characteri-

zation. Although dialogue patterns are inherent in the script, a writer must be equally aware of how words should sound. If a character is supposed to be highly educated, the vocabulary, sentence structure, and speech rhythms should reflect erudition. If a character is being formal, vocabulary and sentence structure should be precise, and speech rhythms should sound even and business-like. Informality would sound looser, more relaxed, and more personal. An actor playing a nineteenth-century character should speak with a vocabulary and syntax that evokes that period to modern ears. That is, unless the character has a modern outlook and temperament, which would make the sound of contemporary vocabulary and sentence structure appropriate.

Emphasis Emphasis—stressing a syllable or word—is important to all speech—narration and dialogue. It often conveys the meaning of what is being said. On paper the words "How are you?" suggest concern for someone's welfare. But often the words are used as another way of saying "Hello," or making a perfunctory recognition with no expression of concern. Emphasis is what tells you so. Moreover, it is possible to emphasize the *how,* the *are,* or the *you* and communicate three different meanings. The words remain the same; the aural emphasis alters the message.

Take the line, "He'd kill us if he got the chance." If it was delivered with the emphasis on *us*—"He'd kill *us* if he got the chance"—the meaning conveyed would be defensive, that is, unless we kill him first. If the emphasis was on *kill*—"He'd *kill* us if he got the chance"—it suggests that the "us" did something to him first or that the "us" did something that would provoke him if he found it out.

Inflection Inflection—altering the pitch or tone of the voice—can also influence verbal meaning. By raising the pitch of the voice at the end of a sentence, a declarative statement becomes a question. Put stress on it, and it becomes an exclamation. Take the sentence "And the bombing continued." As a declarative statement, it is a fact.

As a question, it introduces skepticism or perhaps even anguish. As an exclamation it becomes a statement of devastation or pride.

"So help me God" is usually said at the end of an oath, as a declarative statement with almost equal emphasis on "help me God." But if the inflection rose at the end of the sentence, it would become a plea, perhaps underscoring the weight of responsibility now borne by the new office holder.

Mood   Sound affects the mood or feeling of words and sentences. Aside from meaning, the sound of *dine* is more refined than the sound of *eat*. If the idea is to convey an edge to the action, *eat* is the better choice. *Lounge* has a softer, more gradual sound than *bar*. *Bestial* conveys more of a sense of the word's meaning than *barbaric*, because of its harder sounds and shorter, more staccato attacks at the beginning of its two syllables.

In the line "lurid, rapid, garish, grouped," by poet Robert Lowell, the sounds in each word not only contribute to the overall meaning but are contained in the other words to enhance further the mood of the line.

In the sentence "He plodded homeward, weary and forlorn," the sound of the vowels and consonants is subdued and dark. Changing the sentence to "He walked home tired and depressed" makes the sound snappier and dilutes, sonically and semantically, the overall meaning of the words.

Sound Effects

Sound effects can be classified as anything sonic that is not speech or music. They are essential to storytelling, helping amplify the reality created in a production. Generally, sound effects perform two functions—contextual and narrative—although these functions are not mutually exclusive.

Contextual Sound

Contextual sound emanates from and duplicates a sound source as it is. It is also referred to as *diegetic sound*—coming from within the story space. (*Nondiegetic sound* comes from outside the story space. Music underscoring is an example of nondiegetic sound.) If a rocket fires, a horse gallops, or paper rustles, that is what you hear; the sound is natural or normal in structure and perspective. In other words, contextual sound is like direct narration.

Narrative Sound

Narrative sound adds more to a scene than what is apparent and so performs an informational function. It can be descriptive or commentative.

Descriptive sound, as the term suggests, describes sonic aspects of a scene, usually those not directly connected with the main action. A conversation in a hot room with a ceiling fan slowly turning is contextual sound. Descriptive sound would be the buzzing about of insects, oxcarts lumbering by outside, and an indistinguishable hubbub of human activity. A child leaves the house on the way to school and you hear descriptive sounds of the neighborhood: birds chirping, one neighbor calling to another, a car turning down the street, and the grinding sound of the school bus growing louder.

Commentative sound also describes, but it makes an additional statement, one that usually has something to do with the story line. For example: A longtime athlete is released from the team. As he walks across the playing field for the last time, the wind comes up. Infused in the wind sound is the faint sound of cheering, giving the scene a wistful quality as the athlete reflects on the crowds that will be rooting for him no longer. Or behind the scene of a verdant, halcyon countryside is heard machinery and building to comment on the inevitable encroachment of industrialization.

Functions of Sound Effects

Sound effects also have specific functions within the general contextual and narrative categories. They focus attention, define space, establish locale, create environment, emphasize and intensify action, depict identity, set pace, provide counterpoint, create humor, symbolize meaning, and unify transition.

Focusing Attention   In shots other than close-ups, in which a number of elements are seen at the same time, how do you know where to focus attention? Of course, directors compose shots to direct the eye, but the eye can wander. Sound, however, draws attention and provides the viewer with a focus. In a shot of a large room filled with people, the eye takes it all in, but if a person shouts or begins choking, the sound directs the eye to that individual.

Defining Space Sound defines space by establishing distance, direction of movement, position, openness, and dimension. Distance—how close to or far from you a sound seems to be—is created mainly by relative loudness. The louder a sound, the closer to the listener-viewer it is. A person speaking from several feet away will not sound as loud as someone speaking right next to you. Thunder at a low sound level tells you that a storm is some distance away; as the storm moves closer, the thunder grows louder.

By varying sound level, it is possible to indicate direction of movement. As a person leaves a room, sound will gradually change from loud to soft; conversely, as a sound source gets closer, level changes from soft to loud. In stereo these gradual changes in loudness can also occur laterally.

With moving objects, frequency also helps establish distance and direction of movement. As a moving object such as a train, car, or siren approaches, its pitch gets higher; as it moves away or recedes, its pitch gets lower. This phenomenon is known as the *Doppler effect* (named for its discoverer, C. J. Doppler, an early-nineteenth-century Austrian physicist).

Sound defines relative position—the location of two or more sound sources in relation to one another, whether close, distant, or (in stereo) side to side. Relative position is established mainly through relative loudness. If two people are speaking and a car horn sounds, the loudness of the three sound sources tells you their proximity to one another. If person A is louder than person B, and person B is louder than the car horn, (assuming monaural sound) person A will sound closest, person B farther away, and the car horn farthest away. If the car horn is louder than person B, it will be perceived as being between persons A

and B. If the aural image is in stereo, relative position will be influenced by how far left or right the sounds are. Here, too, imaging is mainly due to loudness, as lateral perspective is changed by panning. Once the lateral perspective is established, a further change in loudness moves the sound closer or farther away.

Openness of outdoor space can be established in a number of ways—for example, thunder that rumbles for a longer than normal period of time and then rolls to quiet; wind that sounds thin; echo that has a longer than normal time between repeats; background sound that is extremely quiet—all these effects tend to enhance the size of outdoor space.

Dimension of indoor space is usually established by means of reverberation (see Chapter 3). The more reverb, the larger the space is perceived to be. For example, Grand Central Station or the main hall of a castle would have a great deal of reverb, whereas a closet or an automobile would have little reverb.

Establishing Locale Sounds can establish locale. A cawing seagull places you at the ocean; the almost derisive, mocking cackle of a bird of paradise places you in the jungle; honking car horns and screeching brakes place you in city traffic; the whir and clank of machinery places you in a factory; the crack of a bat hitting a ball and the roar of a crowd place you at a baseball game.

Creating Environment Establishing locale begins to create an environment, but more brush strokes are often needed to complete the picture. Cowboy music may establish the Old West, but sounds of a blacksmith hammering, horses whinnying, wagon wheels rolling, and six-guns firing create environment. A prison locale can be established in several ways, but add the sounds of loudspeakers blaring orders, picks and shovels hacking and digging, grunts of effort, dogs barking, and whips cracking and you have created a brutal prison environment. To convey a sense of alienation and dehumanization in a high-tech office, the scene can be orchestrated using the sounds of ringing telephones with futuristic tonalities, whisper-jet spurts of laser printers, the buzz of fluorescent lights, machines humming in monotonous tempos, and synthesized Muzak in the background.

Emphasizing Action   Sounds can emphasize or highlight action. A person falling down a flight of stairs tumbles all the harder if each bump is accented. A car crash becomes a shattering collision by emphasizing the impact and sonic aftermath—including silence. Creaking floorboards underscore someone slowly and methodically sneaking up to an objective. A saw grinding harshly through wood, rather than cutting smoothly, emphasizes the effort involved and the bite of the teeth.

Intensifying Action   Whereas emphasizing action highlights or calls attention to something important, intensifying action increases or heightens dramatic impact. As a wave builds and then crashes, the roar of the build and loudness of the crash intensifies the wave's size and power. The slow, measured sound of an airplane engine becoming increasingly raspy and sputtery heightens the anticipation of its stalling and then crashing. In cartoons, sound (and music) intensify the extent of a character's running, falling, crashing, skidding, chomping, and chasing.

Depicting Identity   Depicting identity is, perhaps, one of the most obvious uses of sound. Barking identifies a dog, slurred speech identifies a drunk, and so on. But on a more informational level, sound can also give a character or object its own distinctive sound signature: the rattle sound of a rattlesnake to identify a slippery villain with a venomous intent; thin, clear, hard sounds to convey a cold character devoid of compassion; labored, asthmatic breathing to identify a character's constant struggle in dealing with life; the sound of a dinosaur infused into the sound of a mechanical crane to give the crane an organic character.

Setting Pace   Sounds, or the lack of sounds, help to set pace. The incessant, even rhythm of a machine creates a steady pace to underscore

monotony. The controlled professionalism of two detectives discussing crucial evidence becomes more vital if the activity around them includes such sonic elements as footsteps moving quickly, telephones ringing, papers being shuffled, and a general hubbub of voices. Car-chase scenes get most of their pace from the sounds of screeching tires, gunned engines, and shifting gears. Sounds can also be orchestrated to produce a rhythmic effect to enhance a scene. In a gun battle, bursts can vary from *ratta tat tat* to *ratta tat,* then a few pauses, followed by *budadadada*. Additionally, sounds of the bullets hitting or ricocheting off different objects can add to not only the scene's rhythm but also its sonic variety.

Providing Counterpoint   Sounds provide counterpoint when they are different from what is expected, thereby making an additional comment on the action. A judge bangs a gavel to the accompanying sound of dollar bills being peeled off, counterpointing the ideal of justice and the reality of corruption; or a smiling leader is cheered by a crowd, but instead of cheers, tortured screams are heard, belying the crowd scene.

Creating Humor   Sounds can be funny. Think of *boings, boinks,* and *plops;* the swooping of a penny whistle; and the *chuga-chuga-burp-cough-chuga* of a steam engine trying to get started. Comic sounds are indispensable in cartoons in highlighting the shenanigans of their characters.

Symbolizing Meaning   Sound can be used symbolically. The sound of a faucet dripping is heard when the body of a murder victim killed in a dispute over water rights is found. An elegantly decorated, but excessively reverberant, living room symbolizes the remoteness or coldness of the occupants. An inept ball team nicknamed "the Bulls" gathers in a parking lot for a road game. As the bus revs its engine, the sound is infused with the sorry bellow of an dispirited bull, comedically symbolizing the team's incompetence. A condemned prisoner walks through a steel gate that squeaks when it slams shut. Instead of just any squeak, the sound is mixed with an agonized human groan to convey his anguish.

Unifying Transition Sounds provide transitions and continuity between scenes, linking them by overlapping, leading-in, or segued effects. *Overlapping* occurs when the sound used at the end of one scene continues, without pause, into the next scene. A speech being delivered by a candidate's spokesperson ends one scene with the words "a candidate who stands for..."; the next scene begins with the candidate at another location, saying "equal rights for all under law." Or the sound of a cheering crowd responding to a score in an athletic contest at the end of one scene overlaps into the next scene as the captain of the victorious team accepts the championship trophy.

A *lead-in* occurs when the audio that introduces a scene is heard before the scene actually begins. As a character thinks about a forthcoming gala event, the sounds of the gala are heard before the scene changes to the event itself. While a character gazes at a peaceful countryside, an unseen jet fighter plane is heard in action, anticipating and leading into the following scene, in which the same character is a pilot in an aerial dogfight.

A *segue*—cutting from one effect (or recording) to another with nothing in between—links scenes by abruptly changing from a sound that ends one scene to a similar sound that begins the next scene. As a character screams at the discovery of a dead body, the scream segues to the shriek of a train whistle; a wave crashing on a beach segues to an explosion; the sound of ripping cloth segues to the sound of a jet roar at takeoff.

Music

As we have already indicated, music has the same basic structural elements common to all sound: pitch, loudness, tempo, tone color, and envelope. But it also contains other characteristics that broaden its perceptual and aesthetic meaning, such as melody and tonality; harmony and its qualities

of consonance, dissonance, and texture; dynamic range that is quite wide compared with speech and sounds; and style in limitless variety.

A production may have three types of music: production source, source, and underscore. *Production source music* emanates from an on-screen singer or ensemble and is produced live during shooting or in postproduction, or *post. Source music* is background music from a stereo, radio, jukebox, and so on, and is added during post. *Underscore music* is original or library music added to enhance the informational or emotional content of a scene. Underscore music is the focus of the following discussion.

Underscoring serves picture in a number of ways. Broadly speaking, composer Aaron Copland observed that it creates a more convincing atmosphere of time and place; it underlines psychological refinements—the unspoken thoughts of a character or situation; it serves to fill pauses between conversation; it builds a sense of continuity; it underpins dramatic buildup and gives finality to a scene.[*]

Functions of Music

Music performs many of the same functions in audio design that speech and sound effects perform, plus a few others. These similarities notwithstanding, it is music's unique and universal language and vast vocabulary that make it so widely applicable in aural communication.

Establishing Locale Many musical styles and themes are indigenous to particular regions. By recalling these styles and themes or by simulating a reasonable sonic facsimile, music can establish a locale such as Asia, the American West, old Vienna, Russia, Hawaii, the city, the country, the sea, outer space, and other environments.

Emphasizing Action Music emphasizes action by defining or underscoring an event. The crash of

---

[*]Aaron Copland. *Our New Music* (New York: McGraw-Hill, 1941).

a chord defines the impact of a fall or collision. A dramatic chord underscores shock or a moment of decision. A romantic theme highlights that flash of attraction between lovers when their eyes first meet. Tempo increasing from slow to fast emphasizes coming danger.

Intensifying Action Music intensifies action, usually with crescendo or repetition. The scariness of sinister music builds to a climax behind a scene of sheer terror and crashes in a final, frightening chord. The repetition of a short melody, phrase, or rhythm intensifies boredom, the threat of danger, or an imminent action.

Depicting Identity Music can identify characters, events, and programs. A dark, brooding theme characterizes the "bad guy." Tender music indicates a gentle, sympathetic personality. Strong, evenly rhythmic music suggests the relentless character out to right wrongs. A particular theme played during an event identifies the event each time it is heard. Themes also have long served to identify radio and television programs, films, and personalities.

Setting Pace Music sets pace mainly through tempo and rhythm. Slow tempo suggests dignity, importance, or dullness, whereas fast tempo suggests gaiety, agility, or triviality. Changing tempo from slow to fast accelerates pace and escalates action; changing from fast to slow decelerates pace and winds down or concludes action. Regular rhythm suggests stability, monotony, or simplicity, whereas irregular (syncopated) rhythm suggests complexity, excitement, or instability.

Providing Counterpoint Music that provides counterpoint adds an idea or feeling that would not otherwise be obvious. Revelers flitting from party to party are counterpointed with music that is monotonous and empty to belie their apparent good cheer. Football players shown blocking, passing, and running are counterpointed with ballet music to underscore their grace and coordination. A man proposing to a woman is accompanied by skittish music to counterpoint the seriousness of the occasion with the insincerity of the man's intent.

Creating Humor A sliding trombone, clanking percussion, a galumping bassoon, or a cackling heckelphone can define a comic highlight or underscore its humor. For example, a bumbling jungle explorer is made all the more ridiculous by the mocking caw of a bird of paradise, or a fight is made silly, instead of violent, by adding the sounds of boings, bonks, and splats.

Unifying Transition Music is used to provide transitions between scenes for the same reasons that sounds are used: to overlap, lead in, and segue. *Overlapping* music provides continuity from one scene to the next. *Leading-in* music establishes the mood, atmosphere, locale, pace, and so on, of the next scene before it actually occurs. *Segued* music changes the mood, atmosphere, pace, subject, and so on, from one scene to the next. By gradually lowering and raising levels, music can also be used to fade out and fade in scenes. Usually, this type of transition makes a definite break in continuity; hence, the music used at the fade-in would be different from the music used at the fade-out.

Fixing Time Among the many uses for musical style is fixing time. Depending on the harmonic structure, the voicings in the playing ensemble, or both, it is possible to suggest the Roman era, Elizabethan England, the roaring twenties, the World War II years, the future, morning, noon, night, and so on.

Recalling or Foretelling Events If music can be used to fix a period of time, it can also be used to recall a past event or foretell a future occurrence. A theme used to underscore a tragic crash is repeated at dramatically appropriate times to recall the incident. A character begins to tell or think about the first time she saw her future husband at a party as the music that was playing during that moment is heard. A soldier kisses his girl good-bye as he goes off to war, but the background music indicates he will not return. A youth who aspires to be a composer looks wistfully at a secondhand piano through a pawnshop window as the strains of his most famous composition, yet to be written, are heard.

Evoking Atmosphere, Feeling, or Mood Perhaps no other form of human communication is as effective as music in providing atmosphere, feeling, or mood. There is a musical analogue for virtually every condition and emotion. Music can evoke atmospheres that are thick, unsavory, cold, sultry, and ethereal. It can evoke feelings that are obvious and easy to suggest, such as love, hate, and awe, and also subtle feelings such as friendship, estrangement, pity, and kindness. As for moods, music can convey the obvious and the subtle: ecstasy, depression, melancholy, and amiability.

Music in Spot Announcements

Because of music's effects on memory and emotion, it is a staple in spot announcements—commercials, public service announcements (PSAs), promotional announcements (promos), and jingles. The majority of spot announcements incorporate music in some way. But too often, due to lack of imagination, time, or understanding of its potency, music for spots is chosen or composed carelessly, to the detriment of the message. For example, a producer using a music bed will simply grab a CD, start it playing at the beginning of the copy, and fade it out when the copy ends. Such short-sightedness is a particular handicap in a medium like radio, which has only one sensory channel to exploit.

Well-selected music can enhance the effectiveness of a spot announcement in a number of ways:

■ Music creates mood and feeling. The purpose of most spots is to have emotional appeal. Nothing reaches the emotions as quickly or as comprehensively as music.

■ Music is memorable. Music in spots should have a simple, short, melodic line or lyric, or both—something that sticks in the mind and can be easily, even involuntarily, recalled.

■ Music gets the audience's attention. A musical spot should grab attention at the start with a compelling musical figure. It can be a catchy rhythm or phrase, percussive accents, an electronic effect, a sonic surprise, or a lyrical statement that impels an audience to listen to its resolution.

■ Music is visual—it provokes visual images. It can set scenes in the country, at the seashore, on shipboard, on the ski slopes, and so on. By so doing, music saves precious copy time spent evoking such scenes verbally.

■ Music can be directed to the taste of a specific audience. The type of music in a spot announcement can be suitable both to the audience to which the message is aimed and, if appropriate, to the radio station's musical format. This makes the sound of the spot at once comfortable and familiar.

■ Music style can be matched with the product. Music for an airline can be open, spacious, and establish a floaty feeling; for a car commercial, it can evoke the feeling of power, speed, or luxury; for a perfume it can be romantic, sensuous, or elegant.

■ Music unifies. In a series of spots emphasizing different copy points about a single product or message, the same music can be used as a thematic identifier to unify the overall campaign. Music also bonds the various elements in spots with, say, multiple copy points and two or more voices.

All that said, music in spot announcements is not always recommended, however, for a few reasons: (1) More copy points can be covered in a spoken announcement than in one that is sung; (2) a spot with music usually has to be aired several times before the music is remembered; and (3) music can place an announcement in a less serious light than can the spoken word.

Silence

A producer was once asked why he chose to show the explosion of the first atomic bomb test with no sound. He replied, "Silence was the most awesome sound that I could find." Silence is not generally thought of as sound; it seems like a contradiction in terms. But it is the pauses or silences between words, sounds, and musical notes that help create rhythm, contrast, and power—elements important to sonic communication.

In situations where we anticipate sound, silence is a particularly powerful element. Thieves break into and rob a bank with barely a sound. As the burglary progresses, silence heightens suspense to an oppressive level as we anticipate an alarm going off, a tool clattering to the floor, or a guard suddenly shouting "Freeze!" A horrifying sight compels a scream—but with the mouth wide open there is only silence, suggesting a horror that is unspeakable. Birds collect on telephone wires, rooftops, and TV aerials and wait silently; absence of sound makes the scene eerie and unnatural.

The silence preceding sound is equally effective. Out of perfect quiet comes a wrenching scream. In the silence before dawn, there is the anticipation of the new day's sounds to come.

Silence is also effective following sound. An explosion that will destroy the enemy is set to go off. The ticking of the bomb reaches detonation time. Then, silence. Or the heightening sounds of passion build to resolution. Then, silence.

FUNCTIONS OF SOUND IN RELATION TO PICTURE

A good bit of the foregoing discussion is applicable to any audio or audiovisual medium. For the most part, it assumed neither the presence nor the absence of picture. When picture is present, however, the sound/picture relationship creates certain dynamics that affect overall meaning. Generally, there are five relationships: (1) Sound parallels picture, (2) sound defines picture, (3) picture defines sound, (4) sound and picture define effect, and (5) sound counterpoints picture.

Sound Parallels Picture

When sound parallels picture, neither the aural nor the visual element is dominant. This function of audio in relation to picture may be the best known

because it is often misunderstood to be sound's only function. In other words, what you see is what you hear. A character knocks on a door and you hear it. An orchestra plays and you hear the music. On-screen is a raging typhoon, with mountainous waves crashing on a shore and trees bent almost double by fierce winds, and in the sound track are the sounds of the storm.

This sound/picture relationship should not be dismissed as unworthy just because it is so common; not all shots require special sonic treatment.

Sound Defines Picture

When sound defines picture, audio is not only dominant, but it also determines the point of view—the subjective meaning of the image(s). Take a scene in which prison guards are standing battle-ready in front of a cell block. A sound track consisting of crashing, breaking, yelling sounds suggests a prison riot and casts the guards as "good guys," as protectors of law and order. If the same scene were accompanied by the song, "Freedom," the music then casts the prisoners sympathetically and the guards as their oppressors. The same scene augmented by a dissonant, distorted rendering of "The Star-Spangled Banner" not only conveys the idea of the guards as oppressors but also adds an element of irony.

Consider a picture showing a man apologizing to a woman for his many wrongs. Her look is stern and unforgiving. The music underscoring the scene is gentle and sympathetic, indicating her true feelings. In the same scene, if the music were light and farcical, both his past wrongs and his pleading would be defined as not very serious. Change the music to sound dissonant and derisive, and the woman's stern, unforgiving look becomes nasty and gloating.

Picture Defines Sound

Picture helps define sound by calling attention to particular actions or images. In a scene where a person walks down a city street, with traffic sounds in the background, cutting to close-ups of the traffic increases the impact of the sounds. The sound of metal wheels on a horse-drawn wagon clattering down a cobblestone street is intensified all the more when the picture changes from a medium shot of the carriage to a close-up of one of the wheels.

Sound and Picture Define Effect

When sound and picture define effect, the aural and visual elements are different yet complementary. Together they create an impact that neither could alone. Take the obvious example of a wave building and then breaking on a beach, accompanied by the swelling and crashing sounds. Separately, neither sound nor picture conveys the overall impact of the effect. Together they do. Neither sound nor picture is dominant, and although they are parallel, they are reinforcing each other to produce a cumulative effect. Another example would be an elderly man sitting on a park bench watching a mother playing with her child, lovers walking hand-in-hand, and teenagers playing touch football, accompanied by a music track that evokes a feeling first of pleasure, then of loneliness, and finally of futility. Sound and picture are complementary, with both contributing equally to an effect that would not be possible if one element were dominant or absent.

Sound Counterpoints Picture

When sound counterpoints picture, both elements contain unrelated information that creates an effect or meaning not suggested by either element alone. For example, the audio conveys the sounds of different groups of happy, laughing people, while the picture shows various shots of pollution. The audio/video counterpoint suggests an insensitive, self-indulgent society. Or consider the shot of an empty hospital bed, with the music evoking a sense of unexpected triumph. The audio-video counterpoint creates the idea that whoever had been in the bed is now, by some miracle, recovered. Change the music to sound spiritual and ascending, and the person who had been in the bed will have died and "gone to heaven."

STRATEGIES IN DESIGNING SOUND

There is no set procedure for designing sound. At the outset the most important thing to do is study the script, determine its overall sonic concept, if there is to be one, and analyze its auditory requirements line-by-line. When there is a director, of course it is necessary to consult. There is no right or wrong method in this type of creative decision making. For the director or sound designer, or both, decisions are often made on the intuitive basis of what "feels" best, of what "works." This is not to suggest that sound design is simply "touchy-feely." Reasoned bases should underlie determinations.

Script Analysis

Script analysis involves two things: (1) determining the overall sound design to various scenes or to an entire work and (2) *spotting*—deciding on the placement of sound effects and music.

In deciding on a sound design, the overriding questions are: How is the audience to think or feel about a particular story, character, action, or environment? And from what point of view? Moreover, is the sound design to be carried out mainly in the sound effects, the music, or both?

Some examples:

▨ In a story about a reclusive, paranoid, unsuccessful writer, his environment, where there should be various sounds of life and living things, there are few sounds, and those are spare, disjointed, reverberant, and mechanical.

▨ In a story about a musician whose life and music were one, the music is constantly intertwined throughout the scenes of the musician's story.

▨ In a story about the Amish, who are forbidden to use man-made synthetic products, backgrounds and ambiences are devoid of any sounds that would be generated by those products.

▨ In a story about a completely self-involved person, not hearing any background sounds wherever he is, regardless of the locale, would underscore his psychic isolation.

In a story that takes place in the 1930s, using audio equipment from that time to produce authentic effects and music tracks would sonically frame the story in that period.

In a story about the fourteenth century, using musical instruments and styles from that period in the underscoring would add to the story's authenticity.

In a scene showing a raging fire, designing the sonic effect of a fire on a building, such as the sound of metal warping, pipes creaking, small, puffy explosive *whomps,* and the roaring crackle of the fire itself would intensify the scene.

In a scene taking place on a neighborhood street on the hottest day of the year, the ambience is dense and the sounds of sparse traffic, people strolling, and children playing halfheartedly are muted and slowed slightly.

In a scene about building a car, tying the rhythm of the machines to the rhythm of the music underscoring creates a unifying gestalt.

The following radio commercial and dramatic excerpt provide specific examples of how one might go about designing sound.

Radio Commercial Example

The following radio commercial is for the Opulent 3QX, an expensive, full-size luxury sedan. The target audience is affluent, suburban, college-educated, in their late thirties to early sixties. The Modest AV is a mid-priced, midsize, family-type sedan. The target audience is in the socio-economic middle class, urban-suburban, with at least a high school education, in their mid-twenties to late thirties.

MUSIC: UP AND UNDER

ANNOUNCER:

Today is a big day at your [Opulent, Modest] dealer. Next year's exciting new [Opulent 3QX, Modest AV] is on display. And as a way of saying "Come on down," your [Opulent, Modest] dealer will give you an eight-year, 80,000-mile full power-train warranty free if you purchase a new [Opulent 3QX, Modest AV] before October first. Even if you decide not to

buy, there's a special free gift for you just for coming down to say hello. That's at your [Opulent 3QX, Modest AV] dealer now.

MUSIC: UP TO FINISH

The commercial is straightforward, indeed routine. Yet sound can not only bring it to life, but change its impact to suit the two different audiences, even though the copy is the same.

The spot calls for an announcer and music. But what type of announcer? What kind of music? First let's discuss the announcer.

It is not enough for an announcer to have a "good" voice. The announcer's voice quality and delivery have to be compatible with the content of the message. If the message is "having a good time," the announcer should sound that way, delivering the copy with a smile in the voice and buoyancy in the intonation. If the message is lighthearted or comedic, the announcer's sound should be playful, whimsical, or offbeat. A serious message is better served with a composed, perhaps cultured, delivery from a performer who sounds that way. Good announcers (and narrators) are also actors.

In selecting the announcers for the Opulent and Modest commercials, the sound designer must first consider the products themselves. The Opulent is an expensive luxury automobile usually affordable to upper-middle- and upper-class professionals with a college education and social position. The Modest, on the other hand, is generally a lower-middle- to middle-class automobile affordable to a broad group of people including blue- and white-collar workers, some with a high school education and some college educated, some with and some without social position. These two groups of consumers call for two different announcing approaches.

The announcer delivering the commercial for the Opulent may have a cultured sound: rounded-sounding vowels, deliberate pacing, stable rhythm, somewhat aloof but friendly. Among the important words to be emphasized are *special, gift,* and, of course, the product's name.

The sound for the Modest commercial would be brisker and more excited. The announcer might sound younger than the announcer for the Opulent and more like the person next door—warm, familiar, and friendly. Pacing might be quicker and rhythms syncopated. The important words to emphasize are, at least, *big, exciting, new, free, come on down,* and the product's name.

No doubt there are other equally valid approaches to the commercial. The point is that, through sound design, the same words take on different meanings and address different audiences just by changing the announcer and the announcer's delivery.

Music can emphasize the differences even more. For the Opulent, perhaps an orchestra playing a bright but melodic, sophisticated theme in moderate tempo, or a small jazz ensemble playing in a light, laid-back, "cool" style would be appropriate. This would not only complement the product's image but also provide compatible counterpoint to the announcer's sound and delivery. What would not be appropriate is a rock or a large jazz band. For the Modest, however, these alternatives might make more sense. Again, we have the same commercial, but with two different sound designs and two different messages.

Film or Television Script Example

In the following scene, Mike and Paula, a couple in their midtwenties, in the third day of a camping trip, are emerging from dense woods into a wide clearing.

FADE IN

1 EXTERIOR, WOODS—LATE AFTERNOON ON A SUMMER DAY. MIKE AND PAULA HAVE BEEN BACKPACKING AND ARE EMERGING FROM DENSE UNDERBRUSH INTO A CLEARING.

2 MIKE STOPS AT THE EDGE OF THE CLEARING TO LOOK AROUND.

MIKE: Wow! This looks like a perfect place to camp for the night.

3 PAULA, FOLLOWING FROM UNDERBRUSH, STANDS NEXT TO MIKE.

PAULA: Sure is. [beat] Seems kind of unusual though, doesn't it?

MIKE: What?

PAULA: To have such a large clearing with no trees or plants in the middle of such dense woods. We've been hiking for almost two days and have barely seen a trail. And now, all of a sudden, this. I mean, look at how well manicured it is. Almost as if someone's been caring for it.

4 MIKE TURNS TO PAULA AND SMILES—WALKS FARTHER INTO CLEARING, REMOVES HIS BACKPACK, AND DROPS IT TO THE GROUND.

MIKE: Are you complaining? For the first time in two days we can pitch the tent and not have to sleep in the woods on dead leaves and soggy ground. To say nothing of the cozier advantages.

5 PAULA WALKS TO MIKE AND THEY KISS—SUDDENLY, A HOWL SOUNDS IN THE DISTANCE.

MIKE: What was that?

PAULA: Don't know! Never heard anything like it before.

6 THEY LOOK AROUND SLOWLY, STARING INTO THE WOODS.

PAULA: *Brrr.* [beat] It must be getting chilly or I'm scared!

MIKE: It's the wind—starting to blow up a bit. [laughs nervously] That's all we need, wind, then thunder and lightning. The only thing missing is the dark castle on the hill.

7 AS MIKE SAYS LAST LINE, THUNDER SOUNDS IN THE DISTANCE.

This scene is brief and uncomplicated, yet its many sound cues can be handled in a number of ways. Moreover, most of the scene's impact depends on the audio. Let's explore a few possible approaches to the sound design in order to convey some idea of the creative possibilities here.

The scene opens in woods with dense underbrush, in the late afternoon of a summer day. Among the elements to consider here are the sounds coming from the woods and the sounds of walking through woods and on underbrush—whether these sounds will be natural and benign, or unnatural and foreboding.

One function that sound performs is creation of an unseen environment. Woods exude a close atmosphere, a thickness of air that should be present in the sound. Woods are filled with sounds in summer: birds twittering, insects buzzing, perhaps frogs croaking, and, at night, an owl hooting or crickets chirping. By adding such sounds to the audio track, it is possible to "picture" the woods and provide a sense of density without actually showing it.

In this case, walking through woods and underbrush requires a few different sounds: clothes scraping against branches, the crunch and crackle caused by stepping on twigs or dry leaves, two pairs of footsteps—one lighter than the other—and, perhaps, increased rates of breathing or panting. The weight, rhythm, and sharpness of the sounds can detail the amount of underbrush and the characters' level of fatigue.

If the purpose of these effects is to provide a contextual sonic complement to the picture, they should sound natural. If they are to suggest the frightening experience to come, they should be unnatural in some way, taking on a narrative function.

Any number of narrative approaches might work. The animal sounds could be edged, harsh, or screechy. Their rhythms could be chattering and nervous. The buzzing could increase or decrease in loudness, as opposed to a more natural steady drone, to reflect a sense of impending attack. The animal sounds could take on a nonorganic, otherworldly quality. Or there could be no sound—perhaps the most unnatural and ominous sound effect of all.

A main difference between nonorganic and organic sounds is that nonorganic sounds are less realistic and tend to make a sound track less emotional. Conversely, organic sounds are more realistic and tend to make a sound track more emotional.

The footsteps could sound larger-than-life, setting the stage for the theme of Man, the intruder; or they could sound smaller to establish the characters' vulnerability. The snap of the branches could sound more like a whip, the crackle and crunch of the dry leaves underfoot like bones breaking or squooshy like the crushing of an insect—sonic foretelling of events to come.

Emergence from the underbrush requires a change in ambience, footsteps, and animal sounds (assuming they were present during the previous scene). The change from the closed-in woods to the large clearing would be accompanied by a more open-sounding ambience. The sound of the footsteps would have to reflect the difference between the dry leaves and the firmer but cushioned meadow grass. The animal sounds may be less intense, underscoring the difference between being in the woods and in the clearing. They may also sound more distant, to emphasize the change even more.

When Mike removes his backpack, it calls for the scrape of the straps on his shirt, maybe a grunt of relief, sigh of satisfaction, or slight *"ahh"* of anticipated pleasure. There are a few possibilities for the sound of the backpack hitting the ground: a bigger-than-life thud to emphasize its weight; a metallic thud to give a sense of what is inside; a jangly crash to sharply punctuate the quieter, open ambience, to provide a sense of what is in the backpack, and perhaps to foretell the jarring events to come.

Sonically, the kiss could be used to set the stage for the first howl. Before the kiss, background sound could diminish to silence, then subtly become more intense, climaxing with the howl; or the background sound could change, again subtly, from natural to unnatural.

The howl suggests a number of possibilities not only as a sound but also as a narrative expression. Of course, any determination about it has to be made within the context of the story line. Let's assume that the howl is from a creature—half man, half beast—who is looking for revenge after being severely wounded by hunters. The howl should convey these facts. It should sound like a wail to establish the pain but be guttural enough to project the idea of a dangerous animal. The wail could embody human characteristics by being within the frequency range of the human voice and by vacillating expressively to convey both a sense of pain and a cry for help. The guttural edge would also provide a counterpoint to the wail by sounding angry and menacing.

A nonorganic approach could be taken by using electronically generated sounds. This approach creates an alien creature, perhaps changing the half-man part to something more fantastic. In any case, not only the condition but also the personality of the creature would be conveyed by the sound.

The wind sound could be designed to convey a number of moods and conditions: mysterious, gloomy, empty, gentle, stormy, cold, and so on. As its frequency increases, wind becomes more active and turbulent.

In this scenario, Paula says *"Brrr... ,"* so the wind should be pitched high enough to convey chill; because it has just come up, it should have some low-end sound as well to convey mystery or danger. A gradually increasing shrillness or whistle would suggest the impending storm.

Thunder has several sonic characteristics: ripping attack; sharp, deep-throated crack; rolling, continuous rumble; and gradually increasing and decreasing loudness as it moves closer and then farther away. In this case, because the thunder sounds in the distance, the sound design calls for a low-throated, continuous rumble. As it comes closer with the storm, its other sonic characteristics would be added.

The wind and thunder also could be generated electronically. This would give the environment an alien quality, particularly if the animal sounds in the woods were also synthesized to suggest the presence of some unworldly beast.

These are only a few possible approaches to the sound design of this brief scene. Music provides even more alternatives to the informational and emotional content. The possibilities, however, are too numerous for discussion here. On the other hand, an absence of music could enhance the sense of isolation and threat.

Another important factor in the sound design of this scene is how the cues are mixed. Mixing layers the sonic elements and establishes their balance and perspective, aspects of sound that are discussed at length in Chapter 18.

Spotting

Spotting takes place at different times in the production process, because sound effects can be produced during and after shooting, whereas music is usually spotted after the picture is edited. Regardless, its purpose is the same: to decide on the placement of sound effects and music in a production.

Spotting Sound Effects

Spotting sound effects involves going through the script or edited work print and specifically noting on a spotting sheet each effect that is called for. A *spotting sheet* not only indicates the sound effect, but also whether the effect is synchronous or nonsynchronous, its in- and out-times, and its description. If the sounds have been recorded, notes about their dynamics, ambience, the way they begin and end, and any problems that require attention are also noted (see Figure 10-1).

Spotting also has to take into consideration how the effects should be "played." If there are surf sounds in a beach scene, how active and dense-sounding are the waves? In a love scene, how much clothes rustle is to be heard? At a dance, is the background *walla* to be murmured, lively, or punctuated with shouts? In a dinner scene, do the sounds of plates, glasses, and cutlery continue through the scene and the various shot changes from long, to medium, to close up? And, if not, to what extent do they change?

Spotting Music

In deciding when and where to spot music, there are several questions to consider:

▨ How much music is there in the production?

▨ Where is it used? How is silence used?

▨ Where does the music enter?

▨ What is the dramatic motivation for each cue?

▨ Is the music used to play scenes that have important dramatic or psychological text or subtext, or is it used as filler to keep scenes from seeming too empty?

▨ How does it enter—does it sneak in softly or enter loudly?

▨ How does it end? What is the dramatic motivation for ending the music?*

---

*From Fred Karlin, *Listening to Movies* (New York: Schirmer Books, 1994).

SPOTTING SHEET

Project Title _____ *The Event* _____   Page Number __*4 of 6*__

Spotter _____ *A.M.* _____   Date Prepared __*10/21*__

Item	Syn/Nonsync	In-time	Out-time	Description
1	NS	01:42:15:10	01:43:12:09	Airplanes taking off
2	NS	01:45:26:29	01:46:15:12	Muddled voices
3	S	01:49:52:12		Door slam
4	NS	01:49:52:12	01:53:05:05	Traffic noises
5	NS	01:54:03:27	01:56:22:17	Restaurant noises
6	S	01:56:13:25		Gunshot
7	NS	02:03:14:23	02:04:03:10	Phone ringing
8	NS	02:10:52:12	02:11:01:24	Glass breaking
9	NS	02:11:27:03	02:12:04:19	Dog barking
10	S	02:12:46:18		Glass breaking
11	NS	02:15:33:16		Thunder
12	NS	02:16:12:15	02:19:22:04	Rain, wind, and thunder
13	S	02:21:45:23		Car backfire
14	NS	02:21:50:20	02:23:47:04	Children playing
15	NS	02:23:47:04	02:26:33:12	Ocean waves
16	NS	02:24:55:23		Thunder
17	NS	02:26:10:10		Thunder
18	S	02:30:12:14		Hit glass
19	NS	02:33:05:06	02:34:55:07	Dogs barking
20	NS	02:35:12:14		Door slam
21	S	02:36:36:11		Door slam

10-1 Example of a spotting sheet listing the sound effects required for a production

Part Three: Sound Design

In the process of spotting music in a production, decisions are made about the music design overall, and in various segments and scenes. Overall, is the music to complement, supplement, or counterpoint the production? In action and romantic films, music generally plays a major role in underscoring events. In fact, in action stories there is often more reliance on music (and sound effects) than there is on dialogue to generate the impact. In a love story, is the music to be emotionally "hot" and aggressive or "cool" and restrained? By what type of an ensemble—orchestral, jazz, chamber—is it to be played and therefore colored?

Decisions related to segments include the main title and pivotal scenes throughout a production. Main title music usually provides clues about what type of story it is going to be or what type of characters are in the story. Lively, quirky main title music tells you to expect a comedy. If it is a horror story, spooky-sounding music is appropriate. Perhaps the main title theme is neutral so as not to tip off the audience about the psychological thriller to come. Maybe there is no main title music, or little music throughout a drama, in order to allow the audience to develop their own opinions about where the events are taking them.

In spotting individual scenes, decisions are made about whether music should enter before or after a character says a line; whether it should carry through the scene or punctuate its most dramatic aspects; whether it should be melancholy, stirring, romantic, threatening, heroic, and so on.

When and Where to Place Music Deciding where music cues should start, fade under, and stop is perhaps the most challenging decision of all. If there are no rules, but only guidelines, in underscoring music, decisions about when and where to incorporate it are as varied as the productions that use music and the creativity of spotting teams. With that caveat, in the most general way, spotters have made certain observations about when and where to place music:

■ It is better to bridge into a scene from a previous line of dialogue, or come into the scene a bit later under a line of dialogue or under an action from a character, than it is to start music on a scene change.

■ If music starts within a scene, it should not be fragmented; it should play through the scene.

■ It is less obvious, less intrusive, and more effective to start music at the moment when emphasis shifts, such as a scene change, a camera movement, or a reaction shot.

■ In covering the entrance of a music cue so that it is unobtrusive, it can be sneaked in or distracted from by some visual action.

■ In action scenes with music and considerable sound effects, either the sound effects should play over the music or vice versa to avoid sonic muddle and confusing the action's emphasis and point of view.

■ Perhaps music is easiest to spot when it covers scenes without dialogue. Simplified, this means: music up when they kiss and down when they talk.

■ Trust your instincts. Look at the piece many times, until you have some kind of response—cerebral or emotional. If after many viewings nothing occurs to you, maybe instinct is suggesting that the scene does not need music.

When spotting music it is always best to do it with the composer, music editor, and director present. Whether the score is original or taken from a music library, underscoring is so much a matter of intuition, taste, and biases that final decisions are better made in consultation than individually. Even when one person has the final say, the ideas, reactions, and perspectives from the other spotters provide a far more wide-ranging basis for decision making.

- Sound design is the process of creating the overall sonic character of a production (usually in relation to picture).

- The sound designer is responsible for the overall sonic complexion of a film or video, although all members of the audio team contribute creatively to the sound in a production.

- Sound can be grouped into three categories: (1) speech, (2) sound effects, and (3) music. All sound is made up of the same basic components: pitch, loudness, timbre, tempo, rhythm, attack, duration, and decay.

- Meaning in speech can be communicated verbally and nonverbally.

- Speech has two basic functions: narration—direct, indirect, contrapuntal—and dialogue.

- Nonverbal meaning in speech can be communicated through accent, pace, dialogue patterns, emphasis, inflection, and aural mood.

- Sound effects perform two general functions: contextual and narrative. Contextual sound is also known as diegetic sound. Narrative sounds can be descriptive or commentative.

- Sounds and music can focus attention, define space, establish locale, create environment, emphasize and intensify action, depict identity, set pace, provide counterpoint, create humor, symbolize meaning, unify transition, and evoke atmosphere, feeling, or mood.

- A production may have three types of music: production source, source, and underscore.

- Production source music emanates from a primary on-screen source. Source music is background music from an on-screen source. Underscore music is original or library music added to enhance a scene's content.

- Well-selected music in spot announcements can enhance the effectiveness of the message in a number of ways. There are instances, however, when music in spot announcements can distract from the message.

- Silence can be used to enhance sonic effect, particularly in situations where sound is expected or anticipated.

- Sound has several functions in relation to picture. Sound can parallel picture; sound can define picture; picture can define sound; sound and picture can define effect; and sound can counterpoint picture.

- There is no set procedure for designing sound, but thorough script analysis goes a long way in facilitating decision making.

- Script analysis involves determining the overall sound design to various scenes or to an entire work, and spotting—deciding on the placement of sound effects and music in a production.

- Determining a sound design involves consideration of how the audience is to think or feel about a particular story, scene, character, or action, and from what point of view, and whether that is to be carried out mainly in the sound effects or music, or both.

PART Four

Production

11

Synchronization

These days little in production and postproduction can be accomplished without *synchronization*—the ability to lock two or more devices that have microprocessor intelligence so that they operate at precisely the same rate. That includes almost any combination of audio and video equipment from a simple audio-to-audio or audio-to-video recorder interface—analog or digital, tape or disk—to a complete studio system that interfaces a digital audio workstation, console, synthesizer, sequencer,* effects processors, and recorders (see Figure 11-1).

Accurate synchronization requires both a system to code the recording media, and a *synchronizer* to read the codes, compare them, and adjust the positions and speeds of machine transports so that they run at exactly the same rate.

TIME CODES

Time code is changed into different forms depending on the application, but each adheres to the same basic rules of counting time. Consequently, the forms are compatible with one another for synchronization so long as the proper translation device is used. There are three basic time codes: ***longitudinal time code (LTC)*** and vertical interval

---

*A *sequencer* is a device that can record performance data for synthesizers and other electronic instruments and, during playback, pass on that data to the instruments so that they play what has been recorded.

Video master

SYNC ref

Control

Loop thru

SMPTE/EBU

Dedicated audio

Control

SMPTE/EBU

SMPTE/EBU

Cart

Events-trigger 1

Reverb/effects

Events-trigger 2

Beat trigger

Master keyboard controller

| Master code in | Video In | Time code out | Dedicated code in | Computer interface |

Computer

AUX out

AUX in

Remote

MIDI in   MIDI out   MIDI thru/out

Remote controller

Sequencer

Drum machine

Sound modules

11-1 Example of a synchronization system flowchart

time code (VITC), both of which are forms of SMPTE time code; MIDI time code (MTC); and the IEC (International Electrotechnical Commission) standard.

SMPTE Time Code

SMPTE time code (pronounced "semp-ty") is a high-frequency electronic digital signal consisting of a stream of pulses produced by a time code generator. It is recorded along the length of a tape track in the same way a conventional audio track is recorded.

Time code was originally developed to make videotape editing more efficient; hence, its identifying code numbers are broken down into hours, minutes, seconds, and frames. The code number 01:22:48:15 is read as 1 hour, 22 minutes, 48 seconds, and 15 frames. (Videotape has 30 frames to the second, or 29.97, to be exact.) Each $\frac{1}{30}$ of a second of audiotape or each frame of videotape is tagged with a unique identifying code number called a *time code address*. By decoding the time code address with a time code reader, an operator can select the appropriate code numbers that instruct recorders to locate a certain point and begin playing in sync from there. SMPTE LTC time code is a digital signal converted to audio frequencies so it can be recorded on an audio track.

Many recorders have a built-in time code generator and reader as well as a time code head (see Chapters 6 and 7). SMPTE code may be recorded during or after production.

Vertical Interval Time Code

Vertical interval time code (VITC) (pronounced "vit-see") carries the same information as SMPTE code but it is used with videotape and encodes its information vertically within the video signal, outside the visible picture area. Because VITC is part of the video signal, it can be read at slow speeds and in still-frame, with the time code displayed through a *window burn* or *window dub* (see 11-2). Two other advantages are that it does not require a dedicated audio track and it can be converted to SMPTE code for equipment that requires it.

There are also some disadvantages to VITC. Many VCR systems cannot read the code at all shuttle speeds and, unlike SMPTE, which can be recorded at any time, VITC must be recorded simultaneously with the video image.

Of the two time code systems, SMPTE is more popular, but both are usually employed in complex video production.

MIDI Time Code

MIDI time code (MTC) was developed as a way to translate SMPTE time code into MIDI messages. An absolute timing reference, SMPTE time code remains constant throughout a program. In MIDI recording, timing references are relative and vary with both tempo and tempo changes. Because most studios use SMPTE time code addresses (as opposed to beats in a musical bar) as references, trying to convert between the two timing systems to cue or trigger an event would be tedious and time-consuming. MIDI time code allows MIDI-based devices to operate on the SMPTE timing reference independent of tempo. In MIDI devices that do not recognize MTC, integrating an MTC sequencer is necessary. Converting SMPTE to MIDI time code is straightforward: SMPTE comes in and MIDI goes out.

11-2 Window dub with SMPTE time code "burned in"

With SMPTE to MIDI time code conversion, the recorder "sets the pace"; the sequencer follow the recorder. But it would be desirable in some situations for the recorder to follow the sequencer. The problem is that devices such as synthesizers, drum machines, signal processors, and consoles are electronic, and tape recorders use mechanical transports. Moreover, MIDI timing references are relative, based on tempo; but for automation, tape decks require an absolute reference, such as SMPTE. To deal with this problem, the *MIDI Machine Control* protocol was developed. It includes provisions for virtually any recorder command, including *start, stop, record, shuttle, chase,* and *locate.*

The IEC Standard

The *IEC standard*, established by the International Electrotechnical Commission, is the most recent addition to time codes. As the term suggests, it is an attempt to standardize time coding. The IEC standard code is the time code system used in digital audiocassette recorders as agreed to by all manufacturers of R-DATs, thus ensuring compatibility among all R-DAT equipment.

The main difference between the IEC R-DAT code and other time codes is that the IEC code provides more flexibility in adjusting frame rates during playback. IEC time code R-DATs extract time code information and put it on tape without it being contained in the frame rate. This makes it possible to set the playback machine's output to whatever frame rate you want. If a playback machine is equipped with an auto-detect mode, it will automatically output the recorded time information at the same frame rate that the code came in.

Using Time Code

When encoding SMPTE time code, set the generator to the preferred starting time. Although time code readout is in hours, minutes, seconds, and frames, it is easy to confuse them if any numbers are duplicated on the same tape or on other tapes belonging to the same production. To avoid this confusion, time code is used employing either the zero-start or the time-of-day logging method.

Zero start indicates the lapsed time of a recording. The first tape begins at zero, and each successive reel begins at 01:00:00:00, then 02:00:00:00, 03:00:00:00, et cetera. For example, if the first tape segment starts at zero and ends at 00:00:02:46, the second segment could start at 00:00:02:47. It would be wiser to spool the tape ahead several frames, however, to make the segments easier to access and also to avoid accidental erasure.

Time-of-day numbering is synchronized with clock time. This is a handy way to keep track of when material is recorded, but tapes used day to day must be clearly marked with the date to avoid any confusion about inevitable duplication of coding times.

Recording SMPTE Time Code on Audio- and Videotape

On audiotape, record time code on the highest-number edge track: on an 8-track tape, that would be track 8; on a 16-track tape that would be track 16, and so on. Record level is usually –5 VU to –10 VU. To prevent crosstalk between the time code signal and program material, leave the track adjacent to the time code blank: on an 8-track tape, that would be track 7; on a 16-track tape, that would be track 15. Do not record the time code signal at a lower level; otherwise synchronization is adversely affected.

In fact, recording time code onto analog tape can be difficult, even at recommended levels, because it tends to distort. The problem becomes particularly acute when dubbing tapes. By the second or third generation, distortion can be so great that the code becomes unreadable. Most time code generators have features designed to reduce or alleviate problems in reading time code. The two most commonly used are called jam sync and freewheel.

Jam sync produces new time code during dubbing, either to match the original time code or to regenerate new address data, thereby replacing defective sections of code. *Freewheel* mode allows the bypassing of defective code without altering the speed of the synchronized tape transports.

Frame rate is usually set next (see "Frame Rates" later in this chapter). For audio-only productions, use 30 frames per second, nondrop frame rate. Start recording time code 20 to 30 seconds before the program material begins, to allow sufficient time for the tape machines to interlock. Once recording commences, it must be continuous—without pause. Tapes should be coded simultaneously. If that is not possible, a time code editor will be needed to correct offsets in the synchronization.

Newer-format videocassette recorders include a dedicated cue/time code track. As for time code levels, because of the differences between analog and digital audio and the number of different VCR formats, it is best to consult the recorder and tape specifications and then run tests to determine the optimum time code level.

If a tape recorder has an *automatic gain control (AGC)* it should *not* be used for recording time code, or the time code signal will distort; gain should be set manually. In video, time code must be synchronized to the picture material, and, as with audiotape, encoding should begin before the program material starts.

Time Formats with Hard-Disk Recorder/Editors

Hard-disk recorder/editors have SMPTE time code, at least. Many systems also include other time formats, such as real time, music time, and film time. These format names differ among programs, but their functions are essentially comparable.

Real time displays the time scale in actual minutes and seconds. Many systems are able to refine real time to tenths, hundredths, and thousandths of a second.

Music time is in bars and beats and usually requires tempo data to base it on. It can be adjusted to preserve relative timing to a variety of values, such as ¼ note, ¼ triplet, ⅛ note, ⅛ triplet, and so on.

Film time displays the time scale in feet and frames.

FRAME RATES

Four frame rate standards are used within SMPTE time code: 30, 29.97, 25, and 24 frames per second (fps). *Frame rate* refers to the number of frames that pass in one second of real time—*fps* (frames per second).

Drop Frame and Nondrop Frame

In the days before color television, the frame rate of American black-and-white TV was 30 fps. With color TV the rate was reduced to 29.97 fps to allow easier color syncing of new programs and reproduction of black-and-white programs. Today American television and videotape recorders run at 29.97 fps.

The problem is that 30-fps time code running at 29.97 fps comes up 108 frames short every hour. To correct this problem, a time code format called *drop frame* was developed. Drop frame skips the first two frame counts in each minute, except for each tenth minute (00, 10, 20, etc.), to force the time code to match the clock time.

Solving one problem, however, created another. A frame rate of 29.97 fps for, say, a one-minute commercial will show as exactly one minute on a clock but will read 00:00:59:28 on a SMPTE display.

One hour of real time will read out as 00:59:56:12. In editing, not working with whole numbers can be bothersome, to say nothing of trying to get an exact program time in broadcasting. To resolve this problem, the 30-fps and 29.97-fps frame rates can be adjusted between drop frame and *nondrop frame*.

Drop frame is necessary when precise timing is critical and when synchronizing audio to video. But in most other production—audio and video—nondrop frame is used because it is easier to work with. It is worth remembering that tapes used in any given production must employ one mode or the other; the two modes cannot be interchanged.

As for the 25-fps and 24-fps frame rates, European video and film shot for television use 25 fps; 24 fps is the frame rate used for pure film applications in the United States, although 24 fps is little used once a film is shot. After production, material is usually transferred to tape or disk for postproduction.

SYNCHRONIZING SOUND AND PICTURE ON FILM

The problem in recording sound and picture synchronously in film production is that audiotape does not have sprocket holes like film does. Moreover, audiotape recorders and film cameras run at different speeds. Solution to the problem is the technique known as *double-system recording*. In double-system recording, sound and picture are recorded separately and in sync; the camera records the picture, and an audio recorder handles the sound.

Single-system recording records both sound and picture on the same medium, which, today, is usually videotape. It is particularly convenient and efficient in TV news, where time is of the essence (see Chapter 13). But if extensive postproduction is necessary and sound quality is important, double-system recording is used.

In film the two methods of synchronizing sound and picture in double system are with a crystal synchronizing oscillator in both camera and recorder or with time code.

Crystal Synchronization

Crystal synchronization regulates the camera and tape recorder motors to run at the same speed so they stay in sync. The oscillator in the tape recorder regulates tape speed to camera speed and also puts the synchronizing tone onto the tape.

Sync Tones

Sync tones or pulses that help synchronize sound and picture are recorded in various ways, depending on the system employed. Nagra analog tape recorders that use sync tones employ the *neopilottone* system. It records a 60-Hz signal with its sync head on two narrow center tape tracks superimposed over the main audio signal. During playback the sync head reads the sync signal, but at the playback head the tones are 180 degrees out of phase, so they cancel each other and do not interfere with the sound on the main track. *Synchrotone* is used for stereo recording. It has a separate third track for pulse tone recorded down the center of the tape. This type of recording, however, has just about been supplanted by time code synchronization using digital recorders (see Chapter 7 and "Time Code Synchronization" later in this chapter).

Slating

An important but often underestimated synchronizing procedure in double-system film recording is *slating*. Although picture and sound are shot in sync, to match them properly the editor has to know the precise point at which recording began. For this purpose a *clapslate* (clapstick attached to a slate) is used (see 11-3). The clapslate is filmed just before each take, after the camera and the tape recorder have begun rolling. It serves two purposes: First, it displays the names of the production, director, and cameraperson; the number of the scene and take; the number of the sound take; the date; and whether the shot is interior or exterior. Second, on top of the slate is a clapstick, which can be opened and then closed quickly to produce a loud snapping sound. This sound is the sync mark

11-3 Time code clapslate

that tells the editor at exactly what point to begin synchronizing sound with picture.

Once sound has been recorded on tape, it is transferred to magnetic film, multitrack tape, or a hard-disk system, a process called *resolving*.

Resolving

Although the double-system method records the sound and picture in synchronization, there is no way to align the audiotape and film for postproduction because of their physical differences. In resolving, as the audio is transferred to magnetic film or hard disk, the sync signal is interpreted so that each "frame" of sound is exactly the same length as each frame of picture so they can be aligned frame-to-frame. During transfer the sync pulse on the audiotape controls the speed of the transfer machine so that it matches the speed of the camera motor.

Time Code Synchronization

In time code synchronization for film, a SMPTE clapslate is used. It includes a time code generator

that runs parallel to a time code generator in the audio recorder. If the recorder is multitrack, the generator is external. The clapslate displays a running time code (see 11-3). At the moment the clapstick closes, the time code showing at that instant freezes; that is the start point. Audio that is time code synchronized can be transferred directly to videotape for postproduction.

SYNCHRONIZERS

Although time code permits the accurate interlocking of recorders, anytime two or more transports must run together simultaneously, frame-for-frame, a device called a **synchronizer** is necessary. It controls the position and speed of the "slave" transport(s) to lock to the "master" machine's transport using time code as its reference. Synchronization systems using time code vary widely in sophistication, from those that synchronize one master machine to one slave, to those that synchronize several transports at once and perform a variety of other computer-assisted functions as well (see 11-1).

Most synchronizers have available two types of locking modes: *frame lock* and *phase lock*. *Frame lock* locks the master and the slave units using time code so that any variations in the master reference are passed on to the slave. *Phase lock* (also referred to as *sync lock*) prevents sudden speed variations in the master, such as wow and flutter, from being passed to the slave.

Other synchronizer features include automatic switching from play mode to cue mode that allows the slave transport to "chase" the master whenever it is rewound, and resync to it when it is again put into play. Offsets can be set between machines, allowing a tape to be "slipped" out of sync, by less than one frame if necessary. Synchronizers control transport record/edit functions, enabling in- and out-points to be repeated accurately to as little as $\frac{1}{100}$ of a frame in some units. To isolate themselves from speed changes during time code dropouts, synchronizers can *freewheel*, passing over time code loss at a constant speed.

A note of caution: When time code is recorded during production, it is continuous. When the material is dubbed to an edit master for editing, any discontinuity in time code will confuse the synchronizer. Therefore, a continuous time code should be recorded onto the edit master(s). This, however, creates two sets of time code numbers, one for the production and one for the edited material. Good recordkeeping is essential to avoid mixups.

MAIN POINTS

▶ Synchronization is the ability to lock two or more devices that have microprocessor intelligence so that they operate at precisely the same rate.

▶ Accurate synchronization requires both a system to code the recording media, and a synchronizer to read the codes, compare them, and adjust the positions and speeds of machine transports so that they run at exactly the same rate.

▶ There are three basic time codes: longitudinal time code (LTC) and vertical interval time code (VITC), both of which are forms of SMPTE time code; MIDI time code (MTC); and the IEC (International Electrotechnical Commission) standard.

▶ SMPTE time code is a high-frequency electronic digital signal consisting of a stream of pulses produced by a time code generator. Its identifying code numbers are broken down into hours, minutes, seconds, and frames.

▶ Vertical interval time code carries the same information as SMPTE code but it is used with videotape and encodes the information vertically within the video signal, outside the visible picture area.

► MIDI time code translates SMPTE time code into MIDI messages.

► The IEC standard is the time code system used in digital audiocassette recorders to ensure compatibility among all R-DAT equipment.

► Because all time code readouts are in the same form, it is easy to confuse them if any numbers are duplicated on the same tape or other tapes in a production. Two ways to avoid this confusion are to use the zero-start or time-of-day logging method.

► In recording SMPTE time code, be careful to record it at the recommended level. If the signal is recorded at too low a level, synchronization is adversely affected. If is recorded at too high a level, the time code signal will distort.

► Four frame rate standards are used within SMPTE time code: 30, 29.97, 25, and 24 frames per second (fps).

► Frame rates for television are in either drop frame or nondrop frame formats.

► In double-system recording, sound and picture are recorded separately and in sync; the camera records the picture, and an audio recorder handles the sound.

► In single-system recording, both sound and picture are recorded on the same medium.

► Two methods used to synchronize the camera and audio recorder in double-system recording are crystal synchronization and time code synchronization.

► In double-system recording, a clapslate is used to make a visible and audible sync mark on the film and audiotape, respectively. This helps in identifying and synchronizing scenes during their transfer from audiotape to magnetic film and in editing.

► Time code permits the accurate interlocking of two or more recorders, but a synchronizer is necessary to ensure that their transports run together simultaneously.

Studio Production: Live and Live-on-Tape

The production chain generally begins with the performer—announcer, disc jockey, newscaster, actor, interviewer/interviewee, and so on—and therefore involves considerations that relate to producing speech. How that speech is handled depends on four factors: (1) the type of program or production—disc jockey, news, commercial, drama, and so on; (2) whether it is produced on radio or, as in the case of film and television, using the single- or multicamera technique; (3) whether it is done in the studio or in the field; and (4) whether it is live, live-on-tape—recorded but run as though it was a live show—or produced for later release. The principal difference between live and live-on-tape programs and material produced for later release, aside from the broadcast or distribution date, is postproduction. Live programs are processed, "edited," and mixed during broadcast or taping. Audio is similarly handled during live-on-tape production, but with some leeway for postproduction, although postproduction time is limited due to an imminent or relatively imminent broadcast deadline. Material for later release is produced with postproduction in mind.

This chapter focuses on live and live-on-tape studio production for radio and multicamera television. Chapter 13 covers live and live-on-tape field production for radio, single-camera, and multicamera television. Chapter 14 deals with multi- and single-camera staged productions for TV and film, which are usually produced for later release.

SOUND AND THE SPEAKING VOICE

The frequency range of the human speaking voice, compared with that of some musical instruments, is not wide (see the diagram on the inside front cover). Fundamental voicing frequencies produced by the adult male are from roughly 80 to 240 Hz; for the adult female they are from roughly 140 to 500 Hz. Harmonics and overtones carry these ranges somewhat higher. (Ranges for the singing voice are significantly wider—see Chapter 15.)

Despite these relatively narrow ranges, its harmonic richness makes the human voice a highly complex instrument. Frequency content varies with the amount of vocal effort used. Changes in loudness and intensity change pitch. Loud speech boosts the midrange frequencies and reduces the bass frequencies, thus raising overall pitch. Quiet speech reduces the midrange frequencies, lowering overall pitch.

In relation to the recording/playback process, if speech is played back at a level louder than originally recorded, as is possible in radio and film, the bass frequencies will be disproportionately louder. If speech is played back at a quieter level than originally recorded, as is possible in radio and TV, the bass frequencies will be disproportionately quieter.

Regardless of the dynamic range in voicing sounds, speech must be intelligible while maintaining natural voice quality. Moreover, in audio production speech must also be relatively noise-free. Although background noise does not affect speech intelligibility when the noise level is 25 dB below the speech level, such a signal-to-noise (S/N) ratio is still professionally unacceptable. Even when the S/N ratio is acceptable, other factors, such as distance between speaker and listener, the listener's hearing acuity, and other sounds can adversely affect speech intelligibility. These factors as they relate to aural perception in general are discussed elsewhere in this book. Two other influences on speech intelligibility—sound level and distribution of spectral content—are explored in the following sections.

Sound Level

Speech intelligibility is at a maximum when levels are about 70 to 90 dB-SPL. At higher levels intelligibility declines slightly. It also declines below 70 dB-SPL and falls off rapidly under about 40 dB-SPL. Distance between speaker and listener also affects intelligibility: As distance increases, intelligibility decreases (see Figure 13-6 and the discussion of the inverse square law in Chapter 13).

Distribution of Spectral Content

Each octave in the audible frequency spectrum contributes a particular sonic attribute to a sound's overall quality (see Chapter 2 and the diagram on the inside back cover). In speech certain frequencies are more critical to intelligibility than others. For example, an absence of frequencies above 600 Hz adversely affects the intelligibility of consonants; an absence of frequencies below 600 Hz adversely affects the intelligibility of vowels.

Various procedures have been developed to evaluate and predict speech intelligibility. One such procedure is based on the relative contribution to intelligibility by various frequencies across one-third and full-octave ranges (see Table 12-1).

Table 12-1 Percentage of contribution to speech intelligibility by various frequency ranges

Band Center Frequency (Hz)	Percentage of Contribution	
	One-third Octave	Full Octave
200 and below	1.2	
250	3.0	7.2
315	3.0	
400	4.2	
500	4.2	14.4
680	6.0	
800	6.0	
1,000	7.2	22.2
1,250	9.0	
1,600	11.2	
2,000	11.4	32.8
2,500	10.2	
3,150	10.2	
4,000	7.2	23.4
5,000 and above	6.0	

Source: From the American National Standards Institute (ANSI).

BASIC CONSIDERATIONS IN MIKING SPEECH

One of the most important and generally subjective influences on sound shaping is microphone selection and placement. Microphones directly affect the quality of recorded or transmitted sound. But because no two audio people achieve their results in exactly the same way, there can be no hard-and-fast rules about selecting and positioning microphones. The purpose of discussing microphone technique in this and in subsequent chapters is to suggest *guidelines,* using as examples the types of situations you are most likely to encounter.

Phase and Polarity

Before moving on, it is necessary to say a word about phase and polarity. In acoustics **phase** is the time relationship between two or more sound waves at a given point in their cycles (see Chapter 2). In electricity *polarity* is the relative position of two signal leads—the high (+) and the low (−)—in the same circuit.

Phase

Phase is an important acoustic consideration in microphone placement. If sound sources are not properly placed in relation to microphones, sound waves can reach the mics at different times and be out of phase. For example, sound waves from a source (performer or musical instrument) that is slightly off center between two spaced microphones will reach one mic a short time before or after they reach the other mic, causing some cancellation of sound. Perceiving sounds that are considerably out of phase is relatively easy: When you should hear sound, you hear little or none. Perceiving sounds that are only a little out of phase is not so easy.

By changing relative time relationships between given points in the cycles of two waves, a *phase shift* occurs. Phase shift is referred to as *delay* when it is equal in time at all frequencies. Delay produces a variety of out-of-phase effects that are useful to the recordist (see Chapter 8). To detect unwanted phase shift, however, listen for: unequal levels in frequency response, particularly in the bass and midrange; slightly unstable, wishy-washy sound; or a sound source that is slightly out of position in relation to where it should be in the aural frame.

One way to avoid phase problems with microphones is to follow the ***three-to-one rule***—place no two microphones closer together than three times the distance between one of them and its sound source. If one mic is 2 inches from a sound source, for example, the nearest other mic should be no closer to the first mic than 6 inches; if one mic is 3 feet from a sound source, the nearest other mic should be no closer than 9 feet to the first; and so on (see Figure 12-1).

If a sound source emits loud levels, it might be necessary to increase the ratio between microphones to 4 to 1 or even 5 to 1. Quiet levels may facilitate microphone placement closer than that prescribed by a ratio of 3 to 1.

Phasing problems can also be caused by reflections from surfaces close to a microphone bouncing back into the mic's pickup. This condi-

12-1 The three-to-one rule. Most phasing problems generated by improper microphone placement can be avoided by placing no two microphones closer together than three times the distance between one of them and its sound source.

tion is discussed in "Miking Speech in Radio" later in this chapter.

Polarity

Signals in a microphone circuit that are electrically out of polarity, depending on degree, considerably reduce sound quality or cancel the sound altogether. A cause of mics being out of polarity is incorrect wiring of the microphone plugs. Male and female XLR connectors used for most mics have three pins: a ground, a positive pin for high output, and a negative pin for low output. (XLR five-pin connectors are used for stereo microphones.) Mic cables house three coded wires. All mics in the same facility must have the same-number pin connected to the same-color wire. If they do not and are used simultaneously, they will be electrically out of polarity.

To check the polarity of two mics, first make sure that both are delegated to the same output channel. Adjust the level for a normal reading as someone speaks into a mic. Turn down the fader and repeat the procedure with another mic. Then open both mics to the normal settings. If the VU or ppm meter reading decreases when the levels of both mics are turned up, there is a polarity problem.

The obvious way to correct this condition is to rewire the equipment, assuming the problem is not in the mic itself. If there is no time for that, most multichannel consoles have a polarity reversal control that reverse polarity by 180 degrees (see 5-2).

Moving-Coil Versus Capacitor Microphones

In deciding what type of microphone to use, the choice, usually, will be between a moving-coil and a capacitor mic. Often circumstances make the decision for you. For example, if it is necessary to record a relatively uncolored sound, the moving-coil mic would likely be the mic of choice; if transient sounds are important, the likely choice is the capacitor mic. If there is an option between choosing either type of mic, remember that each has particular attributes (see "General Transducer Performance Characteristics" in Chapter 4).

Omnidirectional Versus Unidirectional Microphones

Another common decision in microphone selection is deciding what directional pattern to choose. Usually, the choice is between an omnidirectional or a unidirectional mic. Again, circumstances sometimes make the decision for you. In a noisy environment, a unidirectional microphone discriminates against unwanted sound better than does an omnidirectional mic; to achieve a more open sound, the omnidirectional microphone is the better choice. If there is an option of choosing either pickup pattern, each has certain advantages and disadvantages, depending on the demands of a given situation (see Tables 12-2 and 12-3).

Table 12-2 The omnidirectional microphone

Advantages	Disadvantages
Does not have to be held directly in front of the mouth to provide adequate pickup	Does not discriminate against unwanted sound
Does not reflect slight changes in the mic-to-source distance	Is difficult to use in noisy environments
Gives a sense of the environment	Presents greater danger of feedback in reverberant location
Is less susceptible to wind, popping, and handling noises	
Is not subject to the proximity effect	
Is natural sounding in rooms with good acoustics	

Table 12-3 The unidirectional microphone

Advantages	Disadvantages
Discriminates against unwanted sound	Must be angled correctly to the mouth, or the performer will be off-mic
Gives little or no sense of the environment (which could also be a disadvantage)	May be subject to the proximity effect
Significantly reduces the danger of feedback in reverberant locations	Is susceptible to wind and popping, unless there is a pop filter
	Is more susceptible to handling noises
	Requires care not to cover the ports, if handheld
	Is less natural sounding in rooms with good acoustics

Based on the differences detailed in Tables 12-2 and 12-3, the omnidirectional pickup pattern seems to be the more useful of the two. In fact, unidirectional mics are far more widely used, which does not necessarily suggest that they are better. As it is with the choice between moving-coil and capacitor mics, so it is with deciding between an omni- and a unidirectional mic: A microphone's suitability depends on the sonic needs of the production.

MIKING SPEECH IN RADIO

Radio performers are for the most part stationary. Whether they are seated or standing, microphone positioning during a broadcast changes relatively little. When performers do change it, it is usually to adjust for a small shift in their position. Under these apparently straightforward circumstances, however, there are a number of miking techniques to consider.

12-2 Microphone mounted on a flexible swivel stand

Single Speaker

In radio, positioning a microphone in front of a seated or standing performer—disc jockey, newscaster, talk-show host, guest—is the most common miking placement. The mic usually is mounted on a flexible swivel stand suspended in front of the performer (see Figure 12-2); sometimes it is on a table stand (see Figure 12-3).

In selecting and positioning the mic, it is important to keep excessive sound that is reflected from room surfaces, furniture, and equipment from reaching the mic. This can result in comb filtering, creating a hollow sound quality.

To minimize sound reflections reaching the microphone, a performer should work at a relatively close mic-to-source distance and use a directional microphone. How directional depends on how much front-to-rear sound rejection is needed. Keep in mind that the more directional the mic, the more restricted the side-to-side movement. Because radio

12-3 Performer speaking into a microphone mounted on a desk stand

12-4 Directional microphone positioned so that performer speaks across the mic face. This placement may reduce popping and sibilance, but it also reduces the frequency response. Sound reaches the microphone from off-axis.

studies are acoustically quiet, there is little need for highly directional mics, unless more than a few speakers are using microphones in close proximity. Therefore, the cardioid pattern is most commonly used. It allows relatively wide side-to-side movement, yet its directional pickup produces the intimate sound essential to creating radio's lip-to-ear rapport with the listener.

It is difficult to suggest an optimal mic-to-source working distance because voice projection and timbre vary from person to person. Here are a few guidelines:

☑ Always stay within the microphone's pickup pattern.

☑ Maintain voice level between 60 and 100 percent of modulation; some stations like it between 80 and 100.

☑ Working too close to a mic may create sound that is devoid of ambience and is oppressive and unnatural.

☑ Working too close to a mic emphasizes tongue movement, lip smacking, and teeth clicks. It could also create proximity effect.

☑ Working too far from a mic diffuses the sound quality, creating spatial distance between performer and listener.

Sometimes a microphone is positioned to the side of or under a performer's mouth, with the performer speaking across the mic face (see 12-4). Usually this is done to reduce the popping and sibilance that often occur when the performer talks directly into a mic.

Speaking across a directional microphone can reduce these unwanted sounds. Unless the mouth-to-mic angle is within the microphone's pickup pattern, however, talking across the mic degrades the response. To eliminate popping and reduce sibilance without overly degrading the response, (1) use a windscreen, (2) use a microphone with a built-in pop filter, or (3) point the mic at about a 45-degree angle above, below, or to the side of the performer's mouth, depending on the mic's pickup pattern (see 12-5).

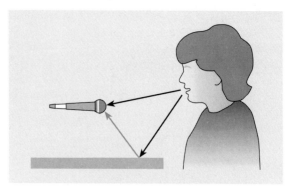

12-6 Incorrect placement of microphone. Indirect sound waves reflecting back into a mic cause phase cancellations that degrade the response. To avoid this, a microphone should not be placed parallel to or more than a few inches from a reflective surface.

12-7 Correct placement of microphone. Placing a microphone at an angle to a reflective surface reduces indirect sound bouncing back into the mic.

12-5 Speaking at a 45-degree angle into a directional mic. This reduces popping and sibilance.

In positioning a mic, make sure that its head is not parallel to or facing the tabletop. Remember that the angle of a sound's incidence is equal to its angle of reflectance in midrange and treble frequencies (see 3-7). Therefore sound waves bouncing from the table will reflect back into the mic's pickup pattern, creating the comb-filter effect. Any hard surface that is close to a mic, like a copy stand or a window, should be angled so that the sound waves do not reflect directly into

the mic (see 12-6 and 12-7). If changing the microphone's angle presents a problem, cover the hard surface with a soft material to absorb most of the unwanted reflections.

Space and Perspective: Monaural and Stereo Sound

AM and FM radio are broadcast in stereo, yet talent is still miked monaurally. In monaural sound, aural space is one-dimensional—that is, perceived in terms of depth—so perspective is near-to-far. Reverberation notwithstanding, the closer a microphone is placed to a sound source, the closer to the audience the sound source is perceived to be; the farther a microphone is placed from a sound source, the farther from the audience the sound source is perceived to be. If the microphone is omnidirectional, both the closer and more distant sounds are perceived as more open than if the mic is directional; a directional microphone reproduces a closer, tighter sound.

In stereo sound, aural space is two-dimensional—that is, perceived in terms of depth and breadth—so perspectives are near-to-far and side-to-side. Moreover, stereo space includes more ambience than does monaural space. Stereo miking involves using either two microphones or a stereo mic (see "Stereo Microphone Technique" in Chapter 14 and "Off-Miking" in Chapter 15).

Stereo radio transmission and reception have little effect on single-speaker miking; talent is still miked with one microphone. If the performer is not sonically "stage-center," localization is disconcerting to the listener. Stereo sound in stereo radio is in the music and often in the spot announcements as well, but not in the spatial positioning of the talent.

Interview and Panel

When there is more than one speaker, as in interview and panel programs, it is customary today to mike each participant with a separate microphone for better sonic control. Directional microphones, usually cardioid or supercardioid, are preferred. If the participants are sitting opposite each other, the cardioid is sufficient because it is least sensitive at 180 degrees off-axis. If the participants are sitting side-by-side, facing the host, the supercardioid could be a better choice. Its on-axis response allows sufficient side-to-side head movement and it is less sensitive at the sides than the cardioid. The hypercardioid mic would also work in the latter situation, but there are the potential problems of restricted head movement, due to its quite narrow on-axis pickup, and of reduced sound quality, because of its poorer rejection at 180 degrees. In any case, microphones are commonly fixed to flexible mic mounts to free

12-8 Radio talk/interview studio

frontal working space and to make minor positioning adjustments easier (see 12-8).

When more than one microphone is used, they must have the same directional pattern. Mics with different polar patterns, say, a cardioid mic used with a supercardioid mic, will have perceptible sonic differences. With the cardioid and supercardioid mics, for example, the cardioid will produce a more open sound than the supercardioid; or, to put it another way, the supercardioid will sound tighter than the cardioid.

In miking a radio program with two or more participants, usually the host and guest(s) are in the studio and an operator is in the control room, or the host operates the control panel in the studio at the table where the guest(s) is sitting. The studio control panel can usually handle telephone feeds for listener call-in, as well. Some radio stations even put a simple control console at the guest station(s). In both situations, host and guest(s) have their own directional microphones or, as is often the case with telephone call-in programs, headset mics. A headset mic facilitates the feeding and balancing of all program information to each participant, reduces problems of microphone placement, allows host and guest(s) more freedom of movement, and clears frontal desk space for scripts and note taking. Because it is radio, appearance is of no concern except that the participants must be comfortably and sensibly arranged for optimal interaction.

MIKING SPEECH FOR MULTICAMERA TELEVISION

Television productions aired live or live-on-tape generally use the multicamera approach. By employing two or more cameras and feeding the signals to a switching console, a shot from one camera can be broadcast (or taped) while other cameras prepare the next shots—in essence, "editing as you go." Sound is similarly handled during live or live-on-tape production. Post-production time is limited due to an imminent or relatively imminent broadcast deadline. Programs such as news, sports, interview, panel, talk, and game shows, awards shows, and parades are carried live or live-on-tape and use the multicamera production technique.

Productions that do not have an imminent release deadline, such as theatrical TV dramas, films made for television, magazine programs, and commercials, frequently use the single-camera production method. Scenes are shot one at a time—first from a general perspective and then from various individual perspectives. These different views are edited during postproduction into a meaningful sequence of events to build the structure and create the pace. It is also in postproduction that dialogue and sound effects are recorded or rerecorded, if necessary, and music is added (see Chapter 16).

This categorizing is not to imply hard-and-fast production conventions; they are simply generalizations. For example, episodes of soap operas are shot well in advance of their broadcast dates yet use the multicamera camera approach. Commercials shot in studios, as opposed to on location, often use the multicamera technique.

News and Interview Programs

In news and interview programs, the participants are usually seated at a desk or in an open set. The mic almost universally used in these situations is the omnidirectional lavalier. It is unobtrusive and easy to mount; its sound quality with speech is satisfactory (using a moving-coil mic) to excellent (using a capacitor); and the omnidirectional pickup pattern ensures that ambience is natural and that a performer will stay on-mic regardless of head movement. If background sound is troublesome, which is unlikely in a broadcast studio, the directional lavalier is a suitable alternative. Generally, for optimal sound pickup, the recommended placement for a lavalier is in the area of the wearer's sternum—hooked to a tie, shirt, or dress—6 to 8 inches from the chin. Sometimes the mic is attached to the collar, but beware of getting it too close to the mouth; otherwise the sound will lack openness.

Although the lavalier is unobtrusive (many are smaller than a dime), directors prefer to make it even more low profile by hiding the mic cord underneath the performer's clothing (see 12-9). This is usually done with a specially designed belt clip to keep the microphone in position, isolate it from the rest of its cord, and reduce the sound of clothes rustling, which the cord often picks up through mechanical conductance (see 12-10). Some directors are unconcerned about the mic cord showing, believing that the audience accepts it as a natural part of the picture.

Sometimes the mic itself is hidden underneath clothing. Unless it is important that the mic not be seen, as in drama, this is usually not a good idea. Clothing inhibits higher frequencies (shorter wavelengths) from reaching the mic and, thereby, can degrade the sound quality. Also, some lavalier models are even more sensitive to the sound of clothes rustling than is the cord. (See also "Using Wireless Body Microphones" in Chapter 14.) These problems can be avoided if performers wear the proper clothing. Cotton clothing does not make much rustling sound; polyester, rayon, and dacron do. Test different clothing samples to determine

12-9 Hidden microphone cord. Directors concerned with making a lavalier unobtrusive often hide the cord underneath clothing. Some directors think this is unnecessary, because microphones in a shot have become an accepted part of many types of programs.

Belt clip

12-10 Mic cord secured by belt clip. This technique prevents the cord from rubbing against clothing or distracting the viewer.

which generate the least rustling noise. It is also important to keep a lavalier from knocking against jewelry, such as tie clips or necklaces, that performers may wear.

Because the lavalier and its mic cord can pick up rubbing sounds from movements, be careful when miking a performer, such as a weathercaster, who moves about within a small set. The performer should use a belt clip, leave enough play in the mic cord so it drags across the floor as little as possible, and avoid sudden, wrenching motions. If the mic cord is put underneath a pant leg or dress to keep it out of sight, it is a good idea to tape it to the leg to reduce rustling sounds.

Why, then, do some newscasters wear two lavaliers, when the general goal is to keep mics unobtrusive? In these instances the microphones are capacitors, and one is simply for backup in case the on-air mic fails.

Having said all this, directors avoid most of the problems associated with wired lavaliers—belt clips, visible mic cords, constrained movement, and so on—by using wireless microphone systems on the set, if not for seated talent, then certainly for the moving performers, such as the weathercaster. The wireless mic system is cordless, it can be easily used with a lavalier, and, in a controlled studio environment, it is normally free from interference problems (see Chapter 4).

In interview programs, the host sometimes sits behind a mic mounted on a desk stand. In many instances, the mic is not live. It is being used as a set piece to create a closer psychological rapport between the host and the television audience or to fill the open table space in front of the host, or both. Otherwise, with a few exceptions, desk mics are seldom used.

If you do use a live desk mic, select one that does not block the face and is good-looking so it does not call attention to itself; use one with a built-in shock mount to isolate the mic from desk noises; and make sure the sound is on-axis.

Panel and Talk Programs

Television panel and talk programs employ a few basic set arrangements. When the host or moderator is seated, guests sit in a line either diagonal to and facing the host, or, if an audience is participating in the show, the guests sit in a horizontal line facing the audience and the host moves between them and the audience. Sometimes the set design is in the shape of an inverted U. The moderator sits at one desk centered between interviewers to the moderator's right and the guest at a third desk to the moderator's left, across from the interviewers. Or panel participants might sit in a semicircle with the moderator opposite them at the center of the semicircle. In some instances, equipped with a wireless mic, the moderator moves inside the semicircle to query the panelists.

Choosing a Microphone

In most circumstances, for host and guest alike, the lavalier's multiple advantages make it the microphone of choice:

■ It is unobtrusive and tends to disappear on-camera.

■ It is easy to mount.

■ It is easily adaptable to use with a wireless system.

■ It keeps the mic-to-source distance constant.

■ It reduces the need for frequent loudness adjustments once the levels have been set.

■ It requires no special lighting or additional audio operator.

■ It makes it possible to place participants comfortably in a set without concern for keeping the mic, such as a boom mic, out of the picture.

The lavalier's main disadvantage is that it's a single-purpose microphone. It rarely sounds good used away from the body, particularly when handheld (see Chapter 4).

There are situations in panel and talk programs in which microphone mounts, other than the lavalier, are preferred. For a host moving about a set among guests or going into the audience for questions, the handheld mic is the popular choice. In situations where the studio is very large and the audience is seated amphitheater-style, except for overall coverage mics of the audience sound, handheld mics are the only choice for host, guest(s), and audience participants.

The handheld microphone has these advantages:

■ It allows the host to control the audience questioning.

■ It allows the host to control mic-to-source distances.

■ Like the desk mic, it helps the host generate a closer psychological rapport with the television audience.

A handheld microphone should have a built-in pop filter to minimize sibilance and popping and an internal shock mount to eliminate handling noise. Optimal position is about 6 to 12 inches from the mouth, pointing upward at about a 45-degree angle (see 12-11).

A disadvantage of the handheld mic is that it ties up one of the host's hands. This is not a problem with the boom mic, and for some situations that is the mic of choice.

When guests are coming and going during the course of a show, for example, the boom mic is often used once they are seated. It is less awkward

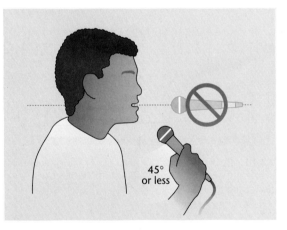

12-11 Handheld microphone positioning. Ideally, a handheld microphone should be positioned 6 to 12 inches from the user's mouth, at an angle of 45 degrees or less. Positioning the microphone at an angle of about 90 degrees may result in popping sounds when consonants like *p* and *t* are pronounced.

than having a guest put on and take off a lavalier on camera. Usually no more than a few guests are seated on the set at any one time, which allows one boom to cover the group adequately. In this type of situation, generally, the host uses a live desk mic for several reasons: (1) to set the host apart from the guests, (2) to enhance, psychologically, the rapport with the television audience, and (3) to avoid the lighting and logistical problems that result from having two booms on a set in close proximity.

If the relationship between a host and guest is intended to be perceived as more informal, such as in an entertainment-oriented interview program, they may sit on living-room-type chairs or a half sofa, proximate enough for one boom mic to cover. In such an environment, even the low-profile lavalier mic could intrude on the intimate setting. But with the extremely small mini-mics available, this is not the concern it once was.

Whenever one boom covers two or more people in conversation, the boom operator has to make sure that none of the program's content is inaudible or off-mic. A good boom operator must therefore quickly learn the speech rhythms and inflections of the people talking, listen to their conversations, anticipate the nonverbal vocal cues that signal a change in speaker, and when the change occurs, move the mic from one speaker to another, quickly and silently.

If performers are seated, there is little need to do anything but rotate the mic itself. If performers are mobile, moving the boom arm and extending and retracting it are also important aspects of good boom operation (see Chapter 14).

Controlling Multiple Sound Sources

Individually miking several program participants can be a challenge for the console operator trying to control various levels simultaneously, especially when other sound sources such as the announcer, bumper (intro and outro) music, and recorded spot announcements are also part of the operator's program responsibilities. It is best to use as few mics as possible in a given situation to reduce system noise, phasing, and coordination problems. But with the multichannel console and sophisticated signal processing, separate control of each sound source is preferable to more-conservative miking techniques. To help reduce the problems associated with controlling multiple, simultaneous microphone voice feeds, the console operator has a number of options.

One option is to put a moderate limit or some compression on each mic, once levels are set. With the lavalier and handheld mics, the proximity of the mic to the speaker's mouth is close enough to be a potential problem with loud sound surges and, hence, overloading. Limiting keeps such surges under control, thereby helping maintain more uniform levels. Also because mic-to-source distance with a lavalier is close, there is little problem with voice levels being too quiet. Such may not be the case with the boom. With the boom, compression helps keep both quieter voices above the noise floor and louder voices from overloading.

When omnidirectional lavaliers are used closer than the recommended three-to-one ratio, phasing problems can create the hollow, "tin can" sound that results from comb filtering. Compression is definitely needed to reduce the dynamic range of each mic. If that is not sufficient, it might be necessary to put adjacent microphones out of phase with each other. When adjacent microphones are out of phase, a null is created between them, which keeps the same sound from reaching an adjacent mic at slightly different times by canceling the delayed sound. This technique works only if the participants are not mobile and do not lean into the null.

A way to avoid the problems created by omnidirectional lavaliers being too close to each other is to use directional lavaliers. But keep in mind that directional lavaliers, and directional mics in general, produce a drier, more closed sound than omnis, which directors tend not to like for speaking voices in panel and talk programs.

Using a noise gate is yet another way to control these phasing problems, although it can be a solution that is more trouble than it is worth. Setting precise thresholds takes time, and the gating effect may be audible as microphones are open and closed.

Another way to control multiple sound sources is to use an automatic microphone mixer. For a discussion of the automatic mic mixer, see "Multiple Pickups" in Chapter 13.

Miking the Audience

When a talk show (or almost any entertainment program) takes place before an audience, their response becomes integral to the program's presentation. Applause, laughter, and other reactions contribute to the show's spontaneity and excitement. The presence of an audience creates two challenges for the sound designer: (1) the people at home must be able to hear them; and (2) the audience must be able to hear the participants, wherever they are in the studio.

For the home viewer, the studio audience should sound relatively close and uniform so that the viewer feels a part of the action. No single voice or cadence or group of similar-sounding voices (that is, high-pitched cackle, halting laugh, children, elderly women, and so forth) should predominate, unless that is the intention. (Some game shows, for example, whose viewers make up the majority of a particular demographic group like to have that group sonically evident in its audience reaction.)

Typically, the way to achieve these ends is to mount directional shotgun microphones—usually cardioid or supercardioid—several feet above the audience and distribute them in equal quadrants throughout the audience area for uniform pickup (see 12-12; see also 4-53). Sometimes, depending on the studio acoustics and the size of the audience, omnidirectional mics or boundary mics with hemispheric pickup patterns are also used to help blend the overall audience sound.

To free the operator's hands for other audio control operations, audience microphones are sometimes controlled by a foot pedal under the console. The pedal is used to open and close the mics.

In order for the audience to hear the program participants, loudspeakers must be mounted in the

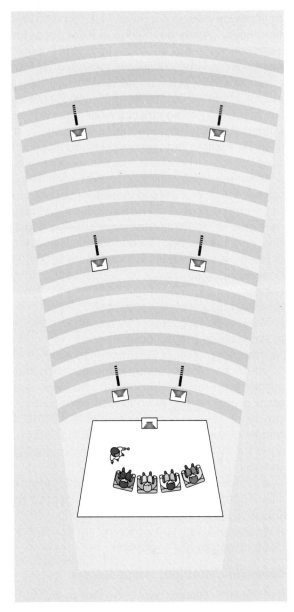

12-12 Talk-show studio with audience area. Shotgun microphones are placed above the audience in quadrants for uniform and controlled directional pickup. Above and behind the mics are small directional loudspeakers situated to avoid feeding back into the mics and to cover specific audience areas. A small loudspeaker above the stage feeds audience sound to the guests during questioning. Depending on the layout and studio size, this loudspeaker may be phased so that it covers a narrow stage area or to avoid interference with the studio loudspeakers, or both.

audience area of the studio. This places microphones and loudspeakers close together, creating the potential for *feedback*—that high-pitched squeal from a signal feeding from a mic to a loudspeaker, around and around. To avoid feedback, the loudspeakers are placed so that their sound is off-axis to the microphone's pickup pattern (see 12-12).

If the loudspeaker is too loud, however, feedback will occur anyway. To minimize this risk, smaller, more directional loudspeakers are used and their levels are kept moderate. If the danger of feedback still exists, still smaller loudspeakers may be used or their sound may be compressed, or both.

A small loudspeaker above the stage feeds audience sound to the guests during questioning. Depending on the layout and studio size, this loudspeaker may be phased so that it covers a narrow stage area or to avoid interference with the studio loudspeakers, or both.

"Producing" Audience Response

Audiences usually react in two ways: by laughing and by applauding. Raising the levels of these sounds when they occur adds to their uplift and to the program's overall fun and excitement. This is known as *milking the audience*. But such level adjustments have to be accomplished gracefully; they cannot be abrupt. Skillfully done, increasing the level of laughter can add to its infectiousness, thus reinforcing the impact of a funny line or joke, or, in the case of applause, it can heighten its intensity, perhaps even its enthusiasm.

The audience sound may be controlled by a limiter. When the audience microphones reach the limit level, the limiter kicks in to increase apparent loudness but not the actual peak level.

Audiences do not always react as expected, however. When a funny line or a climactic moment is not greeted with the anticipated intensity of laughter or applause, recorded applause and laugh tracks are sometimes used to reinforce or "sweeten" audience reactions. Cartridge tapes or disks with different types and degrees of audience reactions are run continuously, but are *deadpotted*—played with the faders off. Or they can be played on a digital program repeater, which performs the same looping function as cart machines and can record and store effects as well (see 12-13).

Laughter and applause sometimes occur relatively close together. When this happens, because applause is louder than laughter, the general

12-13 Devices than can be used to provide or reinforce various types of audience reactions. (a) This hard-disk cartridge machine includes an internal hard disk offering up to 49 hours of storage and the capability to also use removable 100 MB Zip disks for recording. (b) Digital program repeater used to record and reproduce repetitively occurring program material. In this model *track* and *start* buttons control program reproduction, and an LED readout selectively indicates track selection, reproduction time of that selection, or the amount of memory utilized or available.

guideline is to decrease the loudness level of the recorded applause and increase the level of the recorded laughter.

RECORDING SPEECH

Recording a good speech sound begins with good acoustics. This statement may seem obvious, but in fact favorable acoustics are more important to speech than to singing. For one thing, the spectral density and energy generated by the singing voice can somewhat overcome mediocre acoustics. For another, in multitrack recording, other tracks recorded with better acoustics can mask a vocal track that is less than acoustically acceptable, to say nothing of the "distraction" of a good lyric or performance, or both.

But mediocre acoustics make speech sound boxy, oppressive, lifeless, ringy, hollow, or honky— qualities difficult to mask because a speaking voice, unlike a singing voice, is usually not accompanied by other sonic elements during recording. Even when other sound sources do accompany speech, their acoustics are often different.

For example, when an announcer reads a commercial accompanied by recorded music or sounds, the music and sounds usually have ambient qualities different from each other as well as from the announcer. A narration for a documentary is often accompanied by a variety of voices, sounds, music, or all three, each, perhaps, with a different background sound. Not only are good acoustics important to recording speech, but the acoustics must be neutral as well; that is, free from perceptible ambience and not suggestive of any environment or locale, unless the performer is supposed to be on location. Furthermore, keeping ambience on the announce track to a minimum helps reduce the building of background noise when mixing with other audio tracks of sonic information.

Narration

Keeping the acoustics neutral does not mean that speech should be recorded devoid of ambience. Even under optimal conditions, room presence is part and parcel of the recording. In fact, adding just a bit of high-quality artificial reverberation to narration increases apparent loudness and energy without distracting from the speech. This is especially effective in dramatic narration. Slightly compressing narration tightens sound, giving it more punch and attack. Used properly, compression can also help reduce noise. Compression and limiting can help prevent distortion and peaking in the red.

As for the procedure in recording narration, typically it is recorded, edited, and then added to the other program elements. Usually, a script does not call for a narrator to speak continuously, but to take pauses to allow for other types of aural and visual information.

In recording narration (or drama), take time to record the ambience separately; after the narrator finishes recording, *overroll* the tape or disk—keep it running for a while. This makes it possible in the mix to maintain a consistent background sound by editing in the recorded ambience during the pauses in the narration, and in so doing, avoiding ambience "drop outs" in the narrator's track. Such changes are often subtle, but they are perceptible as differences in the openness and closeness of the aural space. Even if the narrator is recorded in a quiet studio, the changes could be noticeable.

Dialogue

Dialogue is recorded in two ways: It is either taped during production and processed from the original recording in postproduction, or it is rerecorded after production in a facility known as a *dialogue rerecording studio*. Recording dialogue during production is discussed in Chapter 14; dialogue rerecording in postproduction is covered in Chapter 16.

STUDIO INTERCOMMUNICATION SYSTEMS

Vital to coordinating the functions of the production team during broadcast or recording is the director's ability to talk to them and their ability to talk to each other without the sound going to air or tape. This is done through an audio intercommunication (intercom) system. Three types of studio intercom systems are in general use: the PL (private line or phone line), SA (studio-address), and IFB (interruptible foldback) systems.

The PL System

The *PL (private line) system,* also known as the *phone line system,* connects production and technical personnel. It consists of a headset with an earpiece and a small microphone. The headsets may be wireless or wired and connected to wall or camera outlets. In instances where it is necessary to hear both the director's cues and the program feed, as is often the case for the boom operator, a double headset with two earpieces is used. If surroundings are noisy or there is a loud sound source such as a rock band, circumaural PL headsets are available.

PL systems can also provide for separate communication lines. For example, audio personnel can confer on one channel while the director talks to, say, the camera operators on another.

The SA System

The *SA (studio-address) system,* also called a *talkback,* is used like a public-address system to communicate with people in the studio not connected to a PL, such as the performers, and for general instructions to all studio personnel. It consists of a small microphone at or in a console close to the director, a spring-loaded switch to activate it, and a small studio-address loudspeaker.

The IFB System

The *IFB (interruptible foldback) system* connects the director, producer, and other control room personnel with the performer(s), through an earpiece, to convey directions before and during a broadcast. The earpiece is small enough to be inserted into the ear canal and carries program sound, the performer's voice included. When the director, or anyone else connected to the system, has an instruction for the performer, the program feed to the performer's earpiece is interrupted for the instruction (see 12-14).

12-14 IFB controller (front and rear views). This model contains two independent IFB channels, each with a complete set of controls. Each IFB output (program and interrupt audio) is sent to four places: the talent amplifier output, a line output, a telephone interface, and a monitor amplifier.

For example, a newscaster delivering a story is about to introduce a field reporter with more details from the scene. If the field reporter is not standing by because of some delay, that information is conveyed to the newscaster via IFB to prevent a premature cue. Then, of course, it is up to the newscaster to "fill" until the director indicates that the field reporter is ready.

Clearly, using IFB effectively requires performers who are able to bifurcate their concentration by thinking about what they are saying while listening to what the director is telling them—and to do both without making it obvious to the audience.

As with all audio equipment, intercom systems vary in quality. It is essential, however, particularly with PL and IFB systems, that they be as noise-free as possible and that the talk be distinct and easily heard not only at normal speaking levels, but at quiet ones too. Wireless IFB systems are also available.

MAIN POINTS

▶ The production chain (in non-music production) generally begins with the talking performer and therefore involves considerations that relate to producing speech.

▶ How speech is produced depends on the type of program or production, the method of production, where the production is done, and the production's release time or date.

▶ The frequency range of the human voice is not wide compared with that of other instruments. The adult male's fundamental voicing frequencies are from roughly 80 to 240 Hz; for the adult female, they are from roughly 140 to 500 Hz. Harmonics and overtones carry these ranges somewhat higher. (Ranges for the singing voice are significantly wider.)

▶ Speech intelligibility is at a maximum when levels are about 70 to 90 dB-SPL. Certain frequencies are also more critical to speech intelligibility than others.

▶ Acoustical phase refers to the time relationship between two (or more) sound waves at a given point in their cycles. Electrical phase refers to the relative electrical polarity of two signals in the same circuit. When these waves or polarities are in phase—roughly coincident in time—their amplitudes are additive. When these waves or polarities are out of phase—not coincident in time—their amplitudes are reduced.

▶ The closer a microphone is placed to a sound source, the closer to the audience the sound source is perceived to be, and the warmer, denser, bassier, drier, more intimate, and more detailed is the perceived sound.

▶ The farther a microphone is placed from a sound source, the farther from the audience the sound source is perceived to be, and the more distant, diffused, open, spacious, reverberant, and detached, and the less detailed, is the perceived sound.

- In selecting and positioning a mic, keep excessive sound that is reflected from room surfaces, furniture, and equipment from reaching the mic or comb filtering can result.

- In monaural sound, aural space is one-dimensional—measured in terms of depth—so perspective is near-to-far.

- In stereo sound, aural space is two-dimensional—measured in terms of depth and breadth—so perspectives are near-to-far and side-to-side.

- In stereo miking, the angle or distance between the two microphones (or microphone capsules) determines side-to-side perspective. The smaller the angle or distance between the mics, the narrower the left-to-right stereo image; the larger the angle or distance, the wider the left-to-right image.

- In disc jockey, interview, or panel programs, the participants should sound as though they are coming from the front and center of the aural space. With more than one participant, using individual microphones, the loudness levels for the participants must be similar if the sound is to be perceived as coming from the front and center of the aural space.

- The techniques used to mike speech for picture in television and film (and to produce sound, in general) depend on whether the production is broadcast live, or live-on-tape, or is taped/filmed for showing at a later date.

- In radio a microphone can be placed anywhere without regard for appearance. In television, if a mic is in the picture, it must be good-looking and positioned so that it does not obscure the performer's face. If it is not in the picture, it must be positioned close enough to the performer so that the sound is on-mic.

- Generally, for optimal sound pickup the recommended placement for a lavalier is in the area of the performer's sternum, about 6 to 8 inches below the chin.

- Hiding a lavalier under clothing requires that the mic and mic cable are or can be made insensitive to rustling sounds and that the clothing be made of material that is less likely to make those sounds.

- In television a desk mic is used mainly as a prop. If the desk mic is live, make sure it does not block the performer's face, interfere with the performer's frontal working space, or pick up studio noises.

- The handheld mic allows the host to control audience questioning and mic-to-source distance and, like the desk mic, helps to generate closer psychological rapport with the audience.

- A boom, like the lavalier hidden under clothing, is used when mics must be out of the picture. Often one boom mic covers more than one performer. To provide adequate sound pickup, the boom operator must anticipate when one performer is about to stop talking and another starts in order to move the boom at the right time to the right place.

- Different techniques are used in controlling levels, leakage, and feedback of mic feeds from multiple sound sources. They are: following the three-to-one rule, moderate limiting or compression, noise gating, or using an automatic microphone mixer.

- If an audience is present, it must be miked to achieve an overall sound blend and prevent one voice or group of voices from predominating.

- Increasing audience laughter or applause, or both, by using recorded laughter or applause tracks adds to a program's spontaneity and excitement.

- Recording speech begins with good acoustics. Mediocre acoustics can make speech sound boxy, oppressive, lifeless, ringy, or hollow.

- Studio intercommunication systems are vital in coordinating the functions of the production team. Three types of studio intercom systems are the private line or phone line—PL; studio address—SA; and interruptible foldback—IFB.

Field Production: Live and Live-on-Tape

13

Production is a challenge no matter where it takes place. But in the field, away from a controlled studio environment, it presents its own particular problems, especially given the immediate and relatively immediate demands of live and live-on-tape broadcasting. Yet field production is almost as commonplace as studio production. Producers go on location, or on a *remote,* as broadcasters often refer to field production, to cover news and sports, to do a disc jockey program promoting a sponsor, to heighten realism in a drama, to add authenticity to a setting, or to provide surroundings that are difficult or impossible to reproduce in a studio.

Live and live-on-tape field production for radio and television can be grouped into two basic categories: electronic news production and electronic field production. ENG uses highly portable equipment to cover news for immediate or imminent broadcast. EFP involves more-complex productions, such as sports, parades, and awards programs.

ELECTRONIC NEWS GATHERING

Electronic news gathering (ENG) refers to radio or TV news gathered in the field and, when necessary, transmitted to the studio for live broadcast or recording. ENG covers broadcast news as it is happening.

Radio ENG

Radio ENG (often abbreviated *RENG*) is relatively uncomplicated to produce and can be broadcast on the spot with comparative logistical ease. It usually involves a reporter with portable recording and, if necessary, transmitting equipment. At its most basic, all the radio reporter needs to record a story is a microphone, headphones, and a recorder. To transmit the story to the radio station's newsroom, add a telephone. Even when somewhat more elaborate production is called for, a microphone mixer, a more sophisticated transmitting device, and a mobile unit will usually handle it.

Microphone

Because RENG usually involves one reporter delivering a story or doing an interview, or both, the handheld, omnidirectional, moving-coil microphone with pop filter is generally the microphone of choice. A handheld mic requires no special mounting and takes no time at all to set up. Field reporting is often done outdoors, and a pop filter is better at reducing unwanted wind sound than a windscreen; nevertheless, it does not hurt to use a pop filter *and* a windscreen just to be safe. If wind, or traffic rumble, is severe, a high-pass filter can be plugged into the mic line to diminish bassy noise (see Figure 13-1). But conditions should justify using the high-pass filter, because it may also attenuate desired low frequencies. When hum and electrical noise from motors, fluorescent lights, and the like are the problems, a quad mic cable, a four-conductor design available from a number of

13-1 High-pass filter. This device can be plugged into a microphone line to reduce unwanted low-frequency sounds. A similar-looking low-pass filter is also available to reduce unwanted high-frequency sounds.

manufacturers, can greatly reduce these sonic nuisances. Field productions that require more-critical noise reduction, and have the time to set up the appropriate equipment, may use a background noise suppressor (see "Noise Reduction" in Chapter 14).

An omnidirectional mic maintains a sense of environment. The body blocks sounds coming from behind the reporter, reducing the overall level of background sound. Mic-to-source distance can be adjusted by moving the microphone closer to or farther from the mouth to compensate for noisy environments. If a locale is too noisy, try a directional microphone. But be aware that directional mics are more prone to wind noise than omnidirectional mics. Also, their on-axis response is drier and more concentrated than omnis, so working too close to the mic can create a denser, even distorted, sound.

Recorder

Both analog and digital cassette recorders are used in RENG, although the digital format is supplanting analog. At the studio, analog cassette reports have to be dubbed to cartridge, open-reel ATRs or to hard-disk systems for ease of editing and handling and to improve playback sound quality with signal processing when necessary.

In news, although getting and airing the story take precedence over production values, R-DATs are replacing analog cassette recorders. They provide features not found in analog cassettes, not the least of which is time code to speed any postproduction that may be necessary, as well as faster and more precise cueing (see 7-4). And though digital sound quality is not essential to news, it is not detrimental either.

Progress being what it is, as portable R-DATs are replacing analog cassettes in broadcast news, the portable hard-disk recorder may soon be the replacement for the R-DAT. In addition to providing sonic and operational features similar to R-DATs, the portable hard-disk recorder uses a removable hard disk capable of storing four hours of mono recording, provides the ability to edit in the field, and can transmit via standard telephone lines or by using ISDN (see 7-12).

Microphone Mixer

When one microphone is used for field reporting, it is a simple matter to plug it directly into the recorder. If two mics are needed, a recorder with two mic inputs suffices. (Assuming in both cases that the recorder uses balanced [XLR] connectors.) When there are more microphones than recorder inputs, or if the recorder takes an unbalanced mini- or phono plug, you need a microphone mixer. Remember that mic mixers are available in mono and stereo and have features such as low-cut filters, pan pots, phantom power, tone oscillator, and slate tone (see 5-1). Clearly, a console would also meet the need for multiple microphone inputs. But a console, even a highly portable, suitcase-sized model (see 5-2), is more than most radio reporters require; it is also neither as lightweight nor as compact as a mic mixer.

Transmission

In the world of news, where stories must be filed fast and first, field reporters often do not have the luxury of bringing their stories back to the newsroom. They may have to transmit them to the station from the field for broadcast or recording. Various transmitting systems are used, the most common of which are the mobile telephone, cellular telephone, and remote transmitter.

The *mobile telephone* is a radio unit connected to telephone equipment that sends the signal to phone wires for transmission to the station. With mobile telephones it is possible to call anyone, anywhere. Sound quality is mediocre but can be improved with a telephone line interface (see 13-2). Mobile telephones are vulnerable to *radio frequency (RF)* and electrical interference from high-voltage lines, transformers, and motors. This is another reason to use an interface, because the better interfaces have a balanced line which helps protect against interference. An unbalanced line is more vulnerable to RF and electrical noise. As an additional safeguard against interference, insulate cables by wrapping them in electrician's tape.

13-2 Telephone line interface. This device enables broadcasters from the field to feed balanced or unbalanced line or microphone level signals into a standard phone line.

The *cellular telephone* is similar to a mobile telephone, but instead of sending signals over wires, it sends them over radio waves through a computer-controlled network of ground stations. Areas in a locale are divided into cells, and as a mobile unit passes from one cell to another, calls are automatically transferred from one ground station to another. Among the advantages of cellular telephones are improved sound quality and greater flexibility in feeding material to the station. Handheld cellular phones are available that require no link to a mobile unit.

The *remote transmitter,* more commonly called a *remote pickup, RPU,* or *Marti,* after a leading RPU manufacturer, is a transmitter that allows a reporter freedom of movement. It may be used for direct broadcast from the remote unit, or it can be removed from a news mobile unit and operated on AC current. It also has better sound quality than the other types of mobile transmission; in some units frequency response extends from 20 to 15,000 Hz. Remote transmitters have inputs for at least one microphone and one line source, such as a recorder. Many also include a basic mixer, which, in effect, converts a mobile unit into a ministudio on wheels. The disadvantages of RPUs include their vulnerability to RF and electrical interference; their inability to entirely cover large metropolitan areas, which means they must be supplemented with a cellular telephone; and their sound quality, which makes it seem as though reports were done in the studio.

a

XLR mic input

b

13-3 **(a) Hand-carried transmitter and (b) mobile relay receiver.** The transmitter sends the signal to the receiver. This unit weighs 7 pounds and includes 2.5 watts of continuous output, dual frequency provision, internal battery charger and AC supply, compressor-limiter, and one microphone and one line level input with individual mixing controls. The receiver relays a broadcast to the base station, usually in the newsroom. This unit weighs 5½ pounds and has dual frequency capability, monitor speaker, noise reduction, and terminals for feeding telephone lines.

(Some news directors feel that location-quality sound in field reports adds authenticity and the sense of "being there.") Fully portable RPUs are also available (see 13-3). In fact, an RPU can be used for local sports broadcasting, thereby saving on transmission line charges.

Mobile Unit

In radio a *mobile unit* used for news can be anything from a small car to a van. Because even modest radio news operations are using more field equipment these days, production flexibility in mobile units is important. In addition to meeting a reporter's typical recording and transmission needs, mobile units are designed to facilitate the producing, packaging, and broadcasting of stories in the field. A two-way mixer with some or all of the following features helps to make this possible.

☑ A microphone preamplifier with wide dynamic range and sensitivity

☑ At least one input for a recorder

☑ The ability to listen to recorder audio for previewing, editing, and cueing

☑ Push-to-talk capability at the mic input

☑ Immunity from radio frequency (RF) interference

☑ A cue audio input from the car radio or RPU channel

☑ VU metering, not only to monitor levels but also to aid visibility—LEDs are difficult to see in sunlight

☑ An external limiter

Headphones

Headphones are an important but often overlooked piece of equipment in field production (see Chapter 9). Regardless of the medium—radio, TV, film, or music recording—the purpose of the production, or its scale, headphones are as important on location as loudspeakers are in the studio. Unless there is another way to monitor audio, headphones are the only reference you have to sound quality and balance. Use the best headphones available, study their frequency response, and get to know their sonic characteristics. First-rate headphones are expensive—but worth it. They have a wide, flat response; they are sensitive; they have superb channel separation (for stereo); and their cushioned earpieces keep outside sound from leaking through. All these characteristics are essential in producing audio on location, when loudspeakers are unavailable.

It is also to your advantage to have a headphone amplifier handy (see 13-4). It provides the ability to monitor a mix at a convenient level without affecting the original signal sources. This is particularly useful when the loudness of background sound makes it difficult to hear program audio. By plugging headphones into a headphone amplifier and plugging the amplifier into the mic mixer (or console) headphone output, you can drive the headphones to the desired loudness level.

Television ENG

The obvious differences between radio and television ENG are the addition of the camera and equipment necessary to transmit picture as well as sound and the added production considerations that go along with the video. That said, using the

Rear view   Front view

13-4 Stereo headphone amplifier

single-system recording technique greatly simplifies field coverage of TV news, where time is of the essence.

In *single-system recording*, both sound and picture are recorded on the same medium; in the case of ENG, the medium is videotape. The recording device is called a camcorder—a portable TV camera with a video recorder.

Camcorder

The *camcorder* is a combination camera and recorder that is portable, lightweight, battery-powered, and is operated handheld or shoulder-borne. The recorder can be an analog or digital, ½-inch or Hi8 videocassette (see Chapters 6 and 7), that is built into the camera unit or dockable to it; or it can be a dockable small hard-disk drive.

One hard-disk camcorder on the market provides four digital-quality audio tracks, time code, 2.5 gigabytes of video, and cut-and-paste in-camera editing (see 13-5). The *CamCutter*, as it has been dubbed, has a disk capacity of only 20 minutes, which is relatively short considering its high cost. Undoubtedly, storage capacity and cost will improve with time. With videocassette camcorders, depending on the format, field recording times run from 20 minutes per cartridge up to two hours.

Built-in
microphone
mount

13-5 Camcutter. This DNG (digital news gathering) camera has a small hard drive attached to it. The hard drive can store up to 20 minutes of digital video and audio material. It is called a CamCutter because it allows "cutting" (editing) in the field.

Obviously, sound (and picture) quality is considerably better in digital camcorders than in analog units, and with the advent of the hard-disk field recorder, the era of ENG is becoming the era of *DNG (digital news gathering)*.

Microphone

As in RENG, the handheld, omnidirectional, moving-coil microphone with pop filter is still the microphone of choice for TV ENG, because the omni pickup pattern provides a sense of sonic environment and the reporter can control mic-to-source distance. If the environment is too noisy, a directional mic may be more suitable. The mic may be wired or, as is more likely today, wireless. The reporter carries the transmitter, and the receiver is usually mounted on the camera.

With wireless mics be sure to check on RF interference beforehand. This is easy to do using a handheld scanner set to the wireless mic's frequencies. If wireless reception is a problem, putting the beltpack receiver on the front of the reporter, instead of on the side or back (out of sight, of course), should improve signal pickup. When camera-to-source distance is wide, placing the receiver closer to the reporter, if possible, minimizes dropout and multipath reflections. In rainy and snowy conditions, mounting the beltpack just above the ankle and placing the receiver as close to the ground as possible can minimize poor reception because of absorption.

Although audiences are accustomed to seeing a microphone in the picture, particularly in news, care still has to be taken to keep the microphone from being too obtrusive. In typical stand-up reports and on-the-scene interviews, this usually is not a problem. But if an interview is lengthy, it may be preferable to take the time to body-mount two lavaliers. It could be annoying to the audience (and the person being interviewed) to see one handheld mic moved back and forth between reporter and interviewee for several minutes. On the other hand, if there is nothing to occupy the reporter's hands, using body mics may be more of a distraction. Moreover, unless the camera operator directs the viewer where to look with the video, the viewer may find it distracting without a handheld mic in the picture to help focus attention.

Camcorders also come with a built-in microphone mount (see 13-5). Its advantages are: it allows one person to operate audio and video simultaneously; the mic of choice is super- or hypercardioid to pick up sound several feet away; when used in addition to the reporter's mic, it provides another sound pickup; and, when it is the only mic used, it frees the reporter's hands.

The disadvantages of using a microphone fixed to the camera are: the mic may pick up sound from a zoom lens motor or a hum from the monitor; if it is highly directional, which it usually is, it has to be pointed straight at the sound source to reduce unwanted sound; and it cannot adequately handle shots that change from one focal length to another. Unless the camera moves, it is difficult to adjust the sound for a change from, say, a medium shot to a close-up or a long shot. Finally, there is the *inverse square law:* Outdoors, when mic-to-source distance is doubled, the sound-pressure level drops approximately 6 dB, thus reducing loudness to one-fourth. Conversely, cutting the mic-to-source distance in half increases loudness approximately 6 dB (see 13-6). The precise effect of this law depends on the openness of the area and how directional the microphone is.

Camcorder Audio Inputs, Outputs, and Controls

Professional-quality camcorders have at least two XLR microphone inputs to record two separate audio tracks on the videotape. There are also line level inputs to receive audio from another VCR, audio recorder, or other line level sound sources. An *audio input selector* tells the VCR whether the signal is coming from the camera or from a microphone or line source.

Camcorders may have an input feature called an *automatic gain control (AGC)*. Avoid using it. AGC automatically boosts sound level when loudness falls below a preset (built-in) level. During recording, when there is no foreground sound for the mic to pick up, the AGC brings up the background sound as it seeks volume. If a reporter makes slight pauses when delivering a story, it may be possible to hear the increases in background sound level as the AGC automatically increases volume. AGC should not be confused with a built-in limiter, which can be useful.

The outputs on a camcorder are for feeding sound to another recorder—audio or video—and for monitoring through headphones. Some camcorders have an RF output that mixes audio and video together and makes it possible to see and hear the recording on a conventional TV set. On VCRs

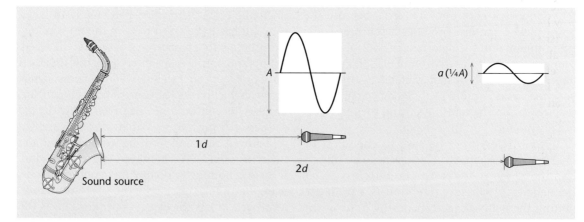

13-6 Illustration of the inverse square law. As the distance *(d)* from a sound source doubles, loudness *(A)* decreases in proportion to the square of that distance.

with two audio channels, an *audio monitor control* selects which one is heard in the headphones; in the *mix* position both channels are heard together. Camcorders also have an intercom jack.

In addition to the usual recorder controls—*play, record, stop,* and so on—an *audio dub* function allows the recording of new audio onto a pre-recorded tape without erasing the video. Record level controls adjust the loudness of the input, output, and monitor audio. Camcorders also have VU meters. There is an *audio mode selector,* which is similar to the bias control on analog audio-cassette recorders that adjusts to the type of low-bias or high-bias tape being used, such iron oxide or metal particle. On camcorders the audio mode selector controls the output of VCRs that are capable of recording "normal" analog audio and "high-fidelity" digital sound.

Despite the convenience and handiness of the audio level controls on camcorders, be aware that they are not as finely "tuned" as similar controls on audio recorders and microphone mixers. The primary function of camcorders, after all, is recording picture. Therefore, whenever it is possible, feed sound to the camcorder through a mic mixer or use a separate audio recorder. And always monitor the sound through high-quality headphones.

Mobile Unit

ENG mobile units, even at their most basic, require more technical support than RENG vehicles not only because of the video component but because transmission to the studio requires microwave capability. ENG vans require more space and, therefore, may provide additional audio support that includes a small console, signal processors, recorders, and shelf-type loudspeakers (see 13-7).

It is worth noting, however, that what often influences the equipment brought into the field is not production need but how many people are in the production crew.

ENG Production

The main purpose of ENG is to facilitate fast access to the news scene, quick setup time, uncomplicated

13-7 ENG van. The port in the roof is for an extendable microwave transmission antenna.

production, immediate distribution, if necessary, and simple postproduction, when time permits and production circumstances require. In news the immediacy is more important than the aesthetics, but this is not to say that news producers ignore production values. They simply do the best they can under the circumstances.

Preproduction

Preproduction planning in ENG is obviously difficult because news can occur anywhere, anytime. The best you can do is always be prepared. In audio, preparation means making sure that the following items are available and ready:

☑ AC extension cords

☑ Alligator clips and leads

☑ A backup recorder

☑ Clamp-on mic stands for a podium

☑ Distribution amplifiers for multiple feeds (see 13-8)

☑ Duct and masking tape

☑ Extra and fresh battery supplies for capacitor mics, recorders, mic mixers, and wireless microphone systems—lithium batteries provide extended operating time

13-8 Distribution amplifier. This is used when additional outputs are required, for example, for video assist, remotes, and split feeds to recorders. This model features three isolated and electronically balanced unity gain outputs with individual volume controls for each.

13-9 Phone tap. This device is used as an interface for recording audio from a standard telephone line.

☑ Extra microphone cables, belt clips for body mics, and windscreens

☑ Head cleaner and cotton swabs

☑ High-pass filters to insert into the mic line to cut low-frequency noise

☑ High-quality headphones

☑ Line-to-mic adapters to match impedance from auditorium amplifiers

☑ Log sheet or laptop computer for recordkeeping, such as time, location, and content of recorded information; problems with audio quality; and suggestions that anticipate editing

☑ Nondirectional and directional handheld and lavalier microphones

☑ Pads (40 dB) if line-to-mic adapters are insufficient to reduce level

☑ Phone taps (see 13-9)

☑ Plenty of recording tape and/or disks

☑ Portable microphone mixer

☑ Rechargeable battery supply

☑ Tool kit

☑ XLR, phone, phono, and mini plugs and adapters (see 13-10)

13-10 Commonly used connectors for audio. (Left to right) ¼-inch phone plug (stereo), Bantam phone plug (stereo), mini plug (stereo), mini plug (mono), RCA or phono plug. (See 4-45 for XLR connectors, not shown here.)

Production

Field production often presents the problem of background sound interfering with the intelligibility of the on-mic/on-camera reporters. In news, however, sense of locale is important to reports from the field, particularly in radio. In fact, as noted earlier, some news producers do not want the sound quality of actualities—reports from the field—upgraded to studio quality precisely in order to preserve location presence.

Miking the Stand-up News Report The omnidirectional, moving-coil, handheld microphone is used most often in stand-up news reports from the field. It picks up enough background sound to provide a sense of environment in normal conditions without overwhelming the reporter's sound. It is possible to control the balance of background-to-reporter sound by moving the microphone closer to or farther from the speaker. The closer the mic-to-source distance, the more the reduction in background sound (see 13-11).

Another advantage of the omnidirectional microphone is that it can be held comfortably below the mouth and in a relatively unobtrusive position on-camera. For interviews, the mic can be situated between reporter and interviewee without necessarily having to move it back and forth for questions and answers (see 13-12).

In noisy environments an omnidirectional microphone may not discriminate enough against unwanted sound even at a close mic-to-source distance. In such a situation, a directional micro-

13-12 Using an omnidirectional microphone for on-location interviews. It can be positioned between the principals, usually with little need for repositioning, at least in quiet surroundings.

13-11 Reducing background sound. (a) Holding an omnidirectional microphone at chest level usually creates an optimal mic-to-source distance. (b) If background noise is high, its level can be reduced by decreasing the mic-to-source distance.

phone may be suitable. The sound balance between reporter and background can still be maintained by moving the mic closer to or farther from the reporter's mouth. But remember, directional mics must be held at an appropriate angle to be on-axis to the mouth (see 13-13). Moreover, during interviews the microphone must be moved back and forth between interviewer and interviewee if the sound is to be on-mic. In television the microphone should not obstruct the mouth.

13-13 Miking when on-location background noise is too loud. Use a directional microphone (a) either several inches from the mouth or (b) close to it, depending on the performer's voice projection. Because the microphone is directional, it must be held at the proper angle if the performer is to be on-mic.

Split-Track Recording Another way to control the audio balances between reporter and background sounds or in an interview is by using split-track recording. *Split-track recording* employs a recorder with two separate audio tracks, such as a stereo recorder or a camcorder. Using two microphones, it is possible to feed the output of each to a separate channel. It is like doing a mini-multitrack, rather than a stereo, recording to better control the audio quality and mix of two sound sources.

In a stand-up report, for example, the speaker can hold the microphone close to the mouth to reduce background sound to a minimum. The other microphone is used just to record background sound. With each element separately recorded, they can be balanced properly in the mix under controlled conditions.

In an interview, either the two principals can be miked separately, or one mic can be used between them, with the second mic used to pick up background sound. In either case, the two microphone feeds facilitate more control over the sound balance. If one voice is dominating the other in an interview, using two mics makes it is possible to employ a polarity reverse cable on the dominant voice to partially cancel it.

Split-track recording may not be possible or necessary on an everyday basis, but the improvement in audio quality and control is worth the time, if you have it. Not only is this technique useful in ENG, but it can also be applied in any type of field recording.

Recording Background Whether you record using the split-track method or put all the audio on one track, make sure you record enough background sound (indoor or outdoor) by itself by running the recorder in *record* for a while either before or after recording, the technique known as *overrolling*. Background sound is useful in postproduction editing to bridge transitions or cover awkward edits (see Chapter 17).

Camcorders used in ENG have at least two audio channels. Recording background may be a problem in TV, however, if it means wasting the picture portion of the videotape unless a number of *cutaways*—shots other than the main action—are taken. It is a good idea, therefore, to bring another audio recorder with a microphone to record additional background sound separately.

Transmission and Mix-Minus

When the distance between the reporter and the station is thousands of miles or if the signal is being sent via satellite, there will be a slight delay between the time the reporter's words are spoken and the time they reach the station. When the reporter's words are fed back through the IFB earpiece, the reporter and the crew will hear the reporter's words after they have been spoken. This is analogous to the disorientation a public-address announcer hears in a stadium when the spoken words are heard a split second after they are delivered. To avoid disorientation, the station sends the incoming report back to the field, *mix-minus;* that is, all the audio in returned minus the reporter's words.

Mix-minus can be used in any situation in which sound is being returned via a foldback or IFB system. Another example is in a music recording when, say, the conductor wishes to hear only the orchestra in the headphones, minus the vocalist, or vice versa.

Some consoles include a mix-minus module, which is particularly useful for call-in programs. It facilitates a variety of mix-minus feeds to studio guests and listeners calling in.

ELECTRONIC FIELD PRODUCTION

Electronic field production (EFP) refers to video production done on location, involving program materials that take some time to produce. The major differences between ENG and electronic field production (EFP) are scale, time, and purpose; in principle they are the same. They both make it possible to produce program material in the field. But whereas ENG is designed to cover news events quickly, EFP is used to produce, more deliberately, material such as entertainment programs, drama, sports, documentaries, and commercials. Therefore EFP generally takes more time in planning, production, and postproduction, and results in a technically and aesthetically superior product.

Small-Scale EFP

EFP can be divided into small-scale and large-scale productions. The main difference between them is in the complexity of the production and, therefore, in the amount of equipment and personnel required. Commercials, documentaries, disc jockey programs, and local sports can be produced with a minimum of hardware and people, whereas a

nationally telecast football game, parade, or the Academy Awards show cannot.

Radio

Electronic field production in radio is usually limited to personality programs such as disc jockey and talk shows, as well as sports. Sometimes it may involve a live concert.

The absence of the visual component drastically cuts down on production needs in radio, compared with TV and film, and on the time needed for preproduction planning. In sports, for example, a few microphones, a mixer or portable mixing console, and a remote pickup or transmission line are sufficient. A disc jockey program can be mounted with a self-contained remote unit consisting of a microphone, CD and cartridge players, and a small console.

Vans are also used in radio remotes. They may be ENG units equipped with CD players and recorders, or EFP units with removable side panels so the personalities can be seen.

Transmission

Remote radio broadcasts carried by a local station use wired telephone services if they must be transmitted across distances too far for RPU transmission, or if they would be difficult to carry by microwave because of the hundreds of relay stations needed to get the signal from one area to another. Using a satellite to beam signals for long-range transmission also solves this problem, although the solution does not come cheap. Generally, satellites are used for global and continental transmission by networks and syndicated programmers.

There are several wired telephone services, analog and digital. They range from an inexpensive and relatively poor-quality dial-up voice line for radio remotes, to more expensive, higher-quality voice lines, to digital transmission with very high quality and greater data capacity. The number of services and their technical parameters are the domain of the engineer and beyond the purview of this book.

There is one useful bit of information to pass on about telephone lines for remote broadcasting:

13-14 Control centers in a remote truck

Labels (diagram):

Big cab with sleeping quarters

Cab

Monitors
Switcher
Technical director (TD)
Director
Monitors
Intercom
Producer
Effects monitors
Preview monitor (PV)
Audio console
Telephones
Monitors
Camera control units (CCUs)
Monitors above VTRs 1–5

PV   Line
Line
Production assistant
C.G. operator
Line   Window
Audio patch bay
Video patch bay

Instant-replay controls
1
2
3
4
5
Power

Monitors
Intercom
TD and director
Asst. director
Line

Stairs
Outside audio patch bay
Stairs
Outside video patch bay
Stairs
Storage

Program control
Character generator (C.G.)
Audio control
Video control
Videotape recording and playback

When a line is installed, one terminus will be at the broadcast station. The other terminus—called the *telco drop*—will be at the remote site. Make sure you know where the phone company has left that terminal block, otherwise valuable and frantic time could be spent searching for it.

Television

Small-scale EFP for television is closer to ENG; large-scale EFP is more like a major studio production. Because ENG is covered earlier in this chapter, let's move on to large-scale EFP.

Large-Scale EFP

Large-scale electronic field production involves recording or broadcasting an event, such as a football or baseball game, a parade, or an awards program, on the spot. As major productions, these events require the same technical support on location that large-scale productions require in the studio. A huge trailer (sometimes more than one), literally a studio-type technical facility on wheels, and the dozens of engineering and production personnel to go with it provide that support (see 13-14). The trailer contains all the equipment necessary to process and route signals from the many cameras and microphones that cover the event outside the truck and from the video and studio sources, such as instant replay, slow motion, and sound carts, inside the truck.

Increasing attention to the production of high-quality sound and the ever-growing audio technology have led to the development of sophisticated audio-only mobile units. These contain the types of equipment found in recording-studio control rooms—multichannel console, multitrack and stereo tape recorders, hard-disk recorders, and signal processors (see 13-15). Audio mobile units are used for on-location concert production and in TV and film shoots to support the video EFP or film unit.

MULTICAMERA EFP

Events produced in the field are either covered or staged. A covered event occurs regardless of media, and production conforms to the event (at least in theory). Sports, parades, and concerts are examples of covered events. Staged events, such as drama, variety, and awards programs, are produced especially for the media and are more tightly controlled. The production approach to an event depends on the type of event it is.

Covered events usually require the multicamera TV approach. Several cameras feed a switcher,

13-15 Audio mobile unit

several microphones feed a mixer, and all signals feed to tape or broadcast, or both. Shots are selected as the event progresses, and there is little or no postproduction. Staged events can be produced using the multicamera TV or single-camera film approach. The event is constructed in postproduction.

The following sections cover multicamera EFP of speeches and news conferences and sporting events. Chapter 14 focuses on the single-camera approach to recording staged productions.

Remote Survey

Except for news, field production takes careful planning. The more complex the production, the more detailed the planning has to be. To address the logistics of, among other things, what equipment will be needed and where it will be positioned, a remote, or site, survey is essential. A *remote survey* consists of an inspection of a production location by key production and engineering personnel, and the written plan they draft based on that inspection. The plan helps coordinate the ordering and setting up of production equipment, and the communication hookup between the key production people during shooting or broadcast. A remote survey can take whatever form suits a particular need. Figure 13-16 displays one example.

In surveying a field location, clearing access to the site and acquiring police permits and written permissions from property owners are also necessary. Diagrams and photographs of the various shooting areas at the production site are often required and are always helpful. At a glance, camera and microphone positions, cable and power runs, signal feeds, and other equipment locations can be easily determined.

REMOTE SURVEY FORM

SURVEY DATE _____   PROGRAM _____
LOCATION SITE _____   AIR DATE & TIME _____
LOCATION SITE ADDRESS _____   PRODUCER _____
_____   DIRECTOR _____
SET UP DATE(S) _____   TD _____

CAMERAS

NUMBER	LOCATION	TYPE	LENS	CABLE RUN

VIDEOTAPE

VTR DESIGNATION	TYPE	FUNCTION	VID FEED	AUD FEED

MICROPHONES

TYPE/MODEL	LOCATION	CABLE RUN/WIRELESS

REMOTE SURVEY FORM (cont.)

PROGRAM _____

LIGHTING

TYPE	LOCATION	AVAILABLE LIGHT IN FC

IFB DELEGATION

DESIGNATION	CHANNEL	LOCATION	FEEDS

POWER

LOCATION ELECTRICIAN CONTACT _____
POWER REQUIREMENTS _____

AC OUTLETS (VOLTAGE/CONNECTOR TYPE/LOCATION)

LOCATION CONTACTS

NAME	TITLE/JOB	NUMBER

SPECIAL INSTRUCTIONS _____

13-16 Example of a remote survey form for television

Production meetings are also essential, particularly after the remote survey has been completed. If something is to go wrong, and it usually does, it is more likely to occur in the field than in a studio. In production meetings key personnel coordinate their responsibilities, explain their needs, discuss audio and video, and resolve problems. The remote production schedule, including setup and rehearsal times, is also planned. Scheduling production meetings seems like common sense, but you would be surprised how many field productions proceed without them. As you might expect, these particular productions are apt to be more nerve-racking, to run over schedule, to cost more, and to be aesthetically inferior. In this business of communications, communication is sometimes the element that is overlooked.

How to determine audio needs in a remote survey is, perhaps, better understood in the context of the actual production situation and is therefore explained in the sections on production of speeches and news conferences and of sports programs later in this chapter.

Field Intercom Systems

Intercommunication among personnel is always vital during production. This is particularly so in the field, where crew and facilities are more widely dispersed than they are in the studio.

Among the intercom systems employed in the field are interruptible foldback (IFB), program sound receiver, paging, intercom, cellular telephone, and walkie-talkie. The IFB system is covered in Chapter 12.

The *program sound receiver,* which looks like a pager, lets you hear the sound portion of the telecast to monitor director's cues.

Paging systems are wireless and similar to the small, belt-clipped receivers used by people who have to be contacted when they are not near a telephone.

Field *intercom systems* are wireless and similar to those used in the studio. They make it possible for two-way communication between the remote truck and the field crew.

The *cellular telephone* can be used to feed a performer program sound and IFB information, particularly when a performer is beyond a station's transmitting range.

The *walkie-talkie* is a handheld, two-way communications device with adequate reach if the field site is not too widespread. It can also be interfaced with other intercom devices.

Production of Speeches and News Conferences

Recording someone speaking from a podium at an event such as a press conference, dinner, awards ceremony, and the like is almost an everyday assignment in broadcasting. In preparing for such an assignment, it is important to know whether you will be taking the sound from your own microphone(s), from the house public-address (PA) system, or from a common output feed, other than the PA system, called a *multiple* (also known as a *press bridge*).

Setting Up Your Own Microphones

The directional microphone is usually the best one to use for a speaker at a podium. Its on-axis response focuses the sound from the speaker, and its off-axis cancellation reduces unwanted room and audience noises (see 13-17).

Cardioid microphones are most frequently used at a podium due to their wider on-axis response and—because the audience faces the back of the mic—their sound rejection at 180 degrees off-axis. Supercardioids may be better, however. Their acceptance angle is at least 120 degrees, wide enough to permit normal side-to-side head movement with little adverse effect on response. Moreover, their off-axis rejection is wider than a cardioid mic's and, therefore, reduces unwanted audience sound coming not only from the rear of the microphone but from the sides as well.

The advantages of setting up and using your own microphones are that you have control of the sound quality and exclusive use of the content. Nevertheless, there are situations in which you have little or

(Not recommended)

13-17 Commonly used techniques when miking a podium speaker with two directional microphones.
(a) This mic placement provides a wide, smooth response and allows comfortable side-to-side head movement, but is often unnecessary. (b) This array is not recommended because it requires the speaker to remain between the mics to ensure smooth response. (c) In many situations a single cardioid or supercardioid is sufficient. Two parallel microphones, one above the other (see 4-55a) or three triangularly arrayed mics are often used in podium setups for redundancy.

no say in these matters and have to take your sound from a common source.

Public-Address Pickups

Talks delivered in many types of rooms and halls require a public-address system so that the audience can hear the speaker. The miking for the PA system is at the podium. On occasion, adding your mics to those already at the podium could create a clutter that may be visually distracting and also obscure the speaker from some of the audience. In such instances you may have to take the audio feed from the PA system.

This entails patching into an output jack in the PA amplifier or PA control panel and feeding the signal to your mixer. It should not interfere with the loudspeaker sound, because the PA feed from the podium mics is usually split into, at least, two separate routing systems. Because many PA loudspeaker systems are not noted for their sound quality, this arrangement gives you some control over the audio. If the house technicians control the sound feed, however, which is often the case, it is necessary to coordinate your needs with them in advance.

Splitting Microphones

An alternative to public-address pickups is splitting the microphone feed. This is manageable if your station or company is the only one, or one of only a few, covering an event. Otherwise, microphone and cable clutter could result.

Microphone splitting is accomplished in two ways: using a Y-adapter (see 13-18) or a transformer-isolated microphone splitter (see 13-19). The Y-adapter splits the microphone signal to the PA system and your microphone mixer. This arrange-

XLR male connector
to PA mixer

XLR female connector
to mic cable

XLR male connector
to recording mixer

13-18 Y-adapter

Male XLR connectors

Ground switches

Female XLR connector

13-19 Transformer-isolated microphone splitter

13-20 **Press bridge.** This "mult" device has three inputs, two microphone and one line level, and 12 outputs providing transformer-isolated, microphone level audio feeds.

ment sometimes causes hum unless both the PA and mic mixer are plugged into the same AC outlet or strip. A better alternative is the microphone splitter, because it isolates the two microphone feeds, reducing the possibility of hum.

Multiple Pickups

Several stations or networks often cover the same event. If they all set up microphones at the podium, not only would the clutter be unsightly, but also a good sound pickup might depend on how lucky the producer was in getting a mic close enough to the speaker. Although this often happens at news conferences, sometimes because the speaker believes a clutter of mics makes the event appear important, it is not ideal or preferred. If the facilities exist, it is better to take the sound from a *multiple,* or *"mult"* for short. A multiple (not to be confused with the *multiple* that interconnects jacks on a patch bay) is a distribution amplifier—an amplifier with several individual line and mic level outputs. Each station then obtains a separate, good-quality sound feed without struggle by patching into one of the amplifier's output connectors. This type of feed is usually agreed upon in advance by those involved and set up either cooperatively by them or by the sound people who operate the in-house audio system. This type of multiple is also known as a

presidential patch or **press bridge** (see 13-20). Microphones used for questions from the audience are connected to the multiple as well. Thus all networks and stations get the same high-quality feed from the few mics used.

A challenge periodically encountered on remotes is the need to mike several speakers at a conference, symposium, press parley, and the like. The obvious way to produce such a program is to use a multichannel console and control the mic levels of each participant manually. But, depending on the number of participants, this could become unwieldy, especially if the operator has to handle other sound sources such as announcer and cart players. Then, too, with the possibility of a number of mics being open at the same time, comb filtering, ambient noise, reverberation buildup, and, if there is a PA system operating, feedback could occur.

For several years automatic microphone mixers have been available. Operating like a noise gate, they automatically open and close mics when sound level rises above or below a preset threshold. The problem with using them for broadcast has been the perceptible action of the gating as the mics were opened and closed. Also, it was difficult for some automatic mixers to discriminate between background noise and low-level speech reaching an adjacent mic.

Automatic microphone mixers have been developed, however, in which the gating action is relatively seamless and noise-adaptive threshold settings activate a microphone for speech and not background sound (see 13-21). (These automatic mic mixers can also be used in recording music on location.) But an automatic mic mixer can do only so much. Table 13-1 lists a few tips to reduce the most common problems associated with having multiple open microphones.

a

Channel Controls

System speech/music When in the *speech* mode, the constant equivalent gain of one open channel is distributed over the group of channels according to the pattern of the channels' levels. In the *music* mode, each channel's gain is expanded with a two-to-one ratio below the threshold. The threshold varies, following the signal level from the music system threshold input.

Auto mix gain All lights are on at normal full gain.

On, auto, and off keys These control the automatic mixing. In *on,* the VCA is at unity gain. In *auto,* the channel performs music or speech automatic mixing. In *off,* the channel is fully muted.

Bypass This controls a relay bypassing all circuitry. All channels are bypassed when power is off. The amber LED calls attention to a bypassed channel.

NOM (normally on) When off, this allows the channel to be exempted from the *Number of Open Microphones* gain limiting system.

Auto mix threshold In the speech mode, this changes the relative weighting of the channel in the automatic mix without changing its level. Usually left on "0" in this mode. The threshold may be lowered to give less weight to a mic in a noisy location, without changing the gain of the mic when someone is speaking into it. In the music mode, the *threshold* control sets the muting threshold for each channel.

Override This programs the channel's response when the momentary *override* key is pressed in the master section or by remote contact.

Preset This programs the channel's condition on power-up, after the *preset* key in the master section is pressed, or by remote contact.

b

13-21 (a) Automatic microphone mixer with (b) its channel and master control functions and (c) its effects on speech and music mixing

b *(contintued)*

Gain limit threshold This sets the number of active mics at which master gain limiting begins. Gain limiting has nothing to do with the signal levels, loud or soft. It relates only to how many mics are in use.

NOM master This shows the master attenuation applied to all *auto* mode channels.

Override (momentary) When activated, this makes channels with *override* assign switches *on* come to normal gain, and all other channels to mute. The LED shows the actuation of the key or remote contacts.

Preset This sets the *on/auto/off* modes of all channels to the condition of their *preset* switches.

Master Controls

Last hold This keeps the last channel to come to full gain at full until superseded by another. Used with the *music* system if constant rather than suppressed ambience is desired.

Music system threshold input This controls the gain of the music system threshold input, a line input, typically fed from a preamplified room ambience mic. This signal is used only by the *music* system, to make the adaptive muting threshold. The pot is a master for the channel *auto mix threshold* controls.

Auto mix depth master This sets how far down auto-mixed channels will go. Less attenuation may be used if more subtle muting is desired.

Mute (momentary) This switch mutes all channels. The red LED shows actuation of the button or remote contacts.

How It Works—The Speech System

Ambient noise—all mics attenuated to equal the gain of one normal mic

One talker—that mic at normal gain; all others attenuated

Another talker—gain shifts instantly to talker

Two talkers—each attenuated 3 dB

How It Works—The Music System

Sound level at ambient sensing mic A determines position of 2:1 expansion window B

Ambient noise—all mics attenuated

One singer—that mic at normal gain; all others attenuated

Four singers— attenuated 6 dB

c

Table 13-1 Suggested solutions for multiple-open-microphone problems

Problem	Indicators	Tips
Comb filtering	Thin, hollow sound	Reduce number of mics Observe three-to-one rule
Excessive ambient noise reverberation	Distant, washed-out sound Loss of clarity and intelligibility	Reduce number of mics Reduce mic-to-source distances
Feedback	Feedback before the system is loud enough for the audience to hear it	Reduce number of mics Reduce mic-to-source distances Increase mic-to-loudspeaker distances

Production of Sports Programs

Sound in sports broadcasts is essential to the excitement of the event, and producing it is a sophisticated, complex endeavor. Sports audio provides three elements: (1) the sound of the announcers, (2) the sound of the crowd, and (3) the sound of the game action.

The Announcers

In sports broadcasting, the announcers have to be heard clearly, whether they project their voices over the constant din of a large, vocal crowd or speak quietly during a golf or tennis match. No microphone is better suited to meet both these demands than the headset mic (see 4-27a). Its design allows the mic to be positioned close to the announcer's mouth for optimal pickup of normal and quieter-than-normal speech. Its moving-coil element and built-in pop filter can withstand loud speech levels without overloading the mic, although limiting or compressing are usually necessary. The unidirectional pickup pattern reduces sound leakages from outside sources, and the omnidirectional pattern adds more background color to the sound. Each earpiece can carry separate information—the director's cues on one and the program audio on the other—and the space in front of the announcer can be kept clear for papers, TV monitors, and other paraphernalia.

It is also critical that the announcers can hear themselves in the headphone mix and have a means of communicating with the director through the IFB. To this end, headphone and talkback controls are often placed within an announcer's reach, as is a "cough button" to kill the announcer's mic when the throat has to be cleared.

The Crowd

Crowd sound is vital to the excitement of most sporting events. The cheers, boos, and general hubbub punctuate the action, adding vitality to the event and making the audience at home feel a part of things.

Depending on the venue, crowd sound is picked up either by dedicated crowd microphones or the mics that are used to pick up the action sounds, or a combination of both. Dedicated crowd mics are generally employed in outdoor stadiums, because sound is more diffuse in an open space than it is indoors. The microphones, usually an X-Y pair of shotgun mics, a stereo mic, or a middle-side (M-S) microphone, are positioned facing the crowd and mounted either low in the stands, aimed toward the crowd; high in the stands at press box level aimed straight ahead; on the field; or a combination of the three.

As with any sound source, proper microphone placement directly influences the quality of the pickup. This makes a location survey mandatory, because each stadium and arena has its own acoustics and seating patterns. For example, some outdoor stadiums are more live than others; the proximity of the crowd to the field may be closer in one stadium than in another; an indoor arena may have a concave roof relatively close to, or farther away from, the playing surface—all of which have a direct effect on the density and loudness of crowd sound.

One famous example of the need for location surveys and testing is a professional football game broadcast by NBC several years ago, without the announcers. It was an experiment to determine how well crowd and action sounds could sustain the game's excitement. (The experiment was also in response to the criticism that sports announcers talk too much.) The game was at season's end and meaningless but the experiment failed because it was a sonically dull broadcast. It turns out that the stadium was built on sand, which absorbed much of the action and crowd sounds.

In addition to the typical needs considered in a location survey, such as type of microphones, designation, length of cable required, and so on, there are a number of steps to take in making decisions related to crowd pickup.

☑ Identify points where sound is more intense or live, or both. Sound-collecting points, usually at the concavities of stadiums and arenas, are good places to begin.

☑ Remember that sound is more concentrated and louder in enclosed venues than in open ones. In domed stadiums sound collects at and bounces from the concave roof to the crown of the playing surface. If microphones near the playing surface are not properly positioned, their sound quality will be degraded.

☑ Avoid dead spots where crowd sound will be hollow, thin, and unexciting.

☑ If attendance is likely to be less than capacity, know which seats will be filled and place the crowd mic(s) in that area(s).

☑ Be aware that home-team fans are likely to far outnumber those of a visiting team. To help maintain excitement no matter which team generates it, position a mic(s) in front of or nearby the section where the visiting fans are seated, particularly if the game is important or involves a heated rivalry, or both.

The Action

The sound of the action itself adds impact to a sporting event—the whoosh of the ball crossing the plate on its way to the whomp of it hitting the catcher's mitt or the crack of the bat on the ball in baseball, the signal calling of the quarterback and the crunch of hitting linemen in football, the skating sounds and slamming of bodies against the boards in hockey, the bouncing ball, squeaking sneakers, and swish of the ball through the basket in basketball, and so on. In fact, many sports producers consider the action sounds as important as—or more important than—the crowd sound.

To capture these sounds, separate microphones, other than the crowd mic(s), are used. The mics are mounted close to the area of play and pointed toward the action. A synthesis of the various approaches to microphone placement for picking up action and crowd sounds used by the major networks in the various sports are displayed in Figures 13-22 through 13-32.

Mixing the Elements

Philosophies vary about how crowd, action, and announcers' sounds should be mixed in the overall sound design of a sporting event. In any approach, however, the play-by-play and color commentary must always be clear and intelligible. Although mixing is covered in Chapter 18, a few of the more commonly used approaches are listed below.

☑ Keeping crowd level lower during periods of inaction and increasing crowd sound during exciting plays to add to the drama of an event's natural pace.

☑ Keeping crowd level constant throughout the broadcast to maintain interest.

☑ Burying the announcers' voices in the crowd sound to make the announcers part of the event and to unify overall intensity.

☑ Keeping the announcers' voices out in front of the crowd sound to avoid masking the play-by-play and color commentary and to reduce listener fatigue engendered by too much sonic intensity

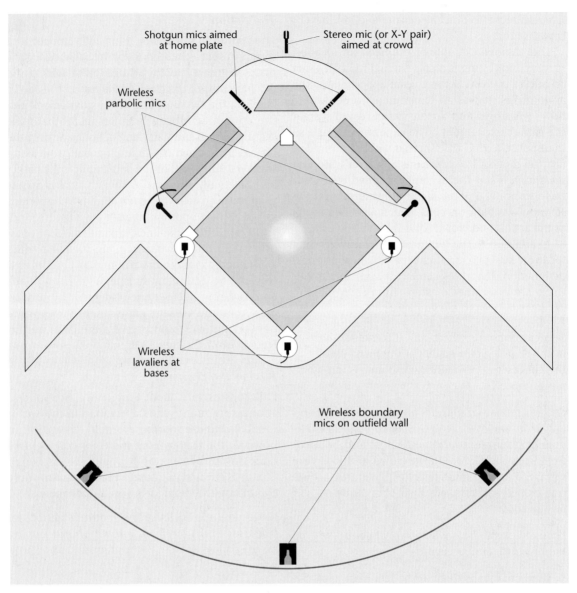

13-22 Miking baseball. Although most baseball sound is broadcast in mono-compatible stereo, only the crowd sound is miked for and reproduced in stereo. The main crowd mic, either a stereo mic or an X-Y pair of shotguns, is usually situated behind home plate, facing the crowd. For additional crowd sound reinforcement, and to help pick up the sound of an outfielder crashing against the wall, wireless boundary mics are mounted on the outfield wall in left, center, and right fields. These mics are panned to enhance the stereo imaging of the crowd sound. Shotgun microphones aimed at the plate pick up action sounds of the ball whooshing across the plate, the umpire's call, and the crack of the bat on the ball. The left shotgun mic (looking in toward home plate) is used when a right-hand batter is at the plate; the right shotgun is used when a left-hand batter is up. Only one shotgun at a time is live. For the whooshing sound of the ball crossing the plate, the level of the working shotgun mic is boosted for that split second of time. Other action sounds from the field are picked up by omnidirectional parabolic mics at the camera locations at first and third bases and wireless lavaliers at the bases. Omnidirectional mics are employed because they reproduce a wider image than unidirectional microphones. Because all sound sources are mono, except the crowd, too narrow an image of the action sounds would be disconcerting when switching back and forth between them and crowd reaction.

13-23 Miking football. Crowd sound is picked up through a stereo pair of shotgun microphones, or a middle-side (M-S) mic, placed in the stands usually at press box level and pointed straight across the stadium. Crowd sound is also picked up by shotgun mics mounted on the sideline cameras (not shown) and/or shotguns mounted on high poles, depending on how well or poorly the crowd sound carries. The crowd microphones are mixed for stereo. Wireless parabolic mics pick up the sounds of field action such as the quarterback signals and colliding linemen. Four parabolic mics are usually employed, two on either side of the field, each assigned to cover from the 50-yard line to the end zone. Before the game it is important to make sure that the wireless mics transmit unobstructed sound, with no dropout, over their entire coverage area. Also at field level is a wireless handheld mic for the on-field color/interview announcer.

Miking is not all that the sound crew has to deal with. In the remote truck, the sound sources have to be assigned and mixed. Table 13-2 shows one approach to the audio on a network-level football broadcast.

Table 13-2 Example of sound source assignments in mixing audio for a network professional football game using a 48-channel console

Channel	Source Assignment
1–6	Returns from limiters and effects devices
7–8	Two wireless interview mics on the field
9–14	Left and right of three routers for video playback
15	Wireless field mic for sideline reporter (if not the same person doing interviews)
16–17	Two handheld microphones in the announcer's booth for the game announcers on-camera open
18–20	Three headset mics for the game announcers and any guest who comes by
21	Open
22	Feed from the house public-address system
23	Referee mic, feed from stadium
24–27	Shotgun mics on the sideline handheld cameras
28	Umpire's mic (to pick up sound from the break of the huddle to the snap of the ball, including the linebackers calling out defensive signals)
29	Feed from the submix of the sideline parabolic mics
30–31	Left and right crowd mix from X-Y shotguns set up high at the 50-yard line
32	Surround channel crowd mics located high in the stadium
33–36	Submasters for the left, center, right, and surround sends to the Dolby encoder
37	Announce submaster
38	Send to the stereo synthesizer
39–44	Music playback devices, such as cart machines, CD players, and cassettes
45–46	Feeds from incoming remotes of other football games
47–48	Return loops for cueing and updating announcers

13-24 Surround-sound miking for football. For overall crowd sound, four shotgun mics are positioned on the far side of the field—across from the press box—spaced in pairs on the 20- and 40-yard lines for the main left and right pickups. The near-side shotgun mics are for more-immediate left and right crowd sound and, along with the directional mic at press box level, are fed into the surround channel. The wireless parabolic mics are used to capture field sounds.

13-25 Miking basketball. Lavalier microphones are mounted to the foam rubber padding at the bottom of each backboard to pick up the sounds of the ball hitting the basket and swishing through the net. Shotguns mics aimed at the key pick up the ball-bouncing and sneaker sounds, grunts and groans from the players, and calls from the referees. Shotgun mics on handheld cameras also pick up court sounds, as well as talk from the bench and the cheerleading. As the action moves up and down the court, the microphones at either end are opened and closed to avoid undue concentration of crowd sound and the pickup of out-of-shot sounds. A shotgun mic at midcourt, either camera-mounted or handheld, helps fill the transitions as the endcourt mics are opened and closed. The midcourt shotgun is kept open throughout the up- and down-court action. There is no dedicated crowd mic, because the array of microphones around courtside are usually adequate to pick up more-than-sufficient crowd sound due to the highly reflective acoustics in most indoor arenas. There may be an additional shotgun mic behind the backboard (not shown) to pick up the band. But due to the possible copyright infringement of music rights, music licensing agencies such as ASCAP (American Society of Composers, Authors, and Publishers) and BMI (Broadcast Music, Inc.) require a fee from the performing organization or its sponsor to broadcast the music. Therefore miking for such a music pickup should be cleared in advance. The same is true for similar situations in other sports.

13-26 Miking ice hockey. For the main action and crowd mics, one approach uses eight supercardioid boundary mics on transparent plastic plates mounted on the inside of the glass that surrounds the rink. The mics are positioned on either end of the blue lines and at the end of the rink in the corners, on either side, to pick up the skating and impact sounds. They also pick up sufficient crowd sound due to the concentrated acoustics in enclosed arenas. There may be additional audio pickup from handheld shotgun mics or from the shotguns on handheld cameras. A handheld shotgun may also be assigned to the penalty box. In the American Hockey League, permission is often given to put wireless mics on the goalies, players, and/or coaches. These microphones and the penalty box mic are used for replay in case something interesting happens and to screen foul language.

In mixing hockey audio, the board operator must be adept at following the play-by-play on the monitor and riding levels accordingly, because hockey is so unpredictable. When an action is anticipated, such as a body slam against the boards or a goal, the operator will boost the level to enhance the sound of the play action or crowd reaction.

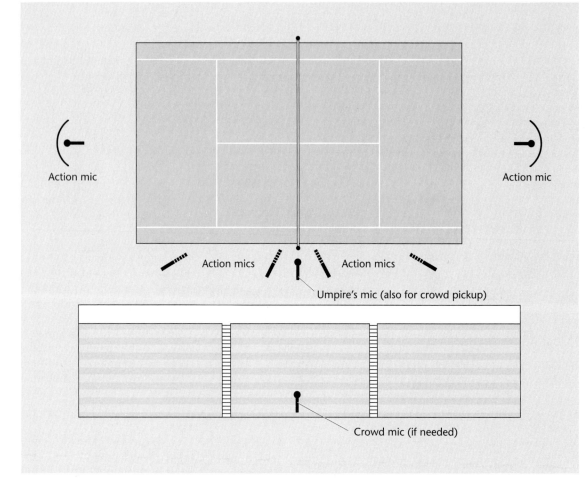

13-27 Miking tennis. In tennis, sound is critical because the announcers do not talk when the ball is in play, and the crowd must be quiet. Microphones must, therefore, be strategically placed to pick up the court action. An omnidirectional microphone is set up next to the umpire to hear his calls, the players talking to him, and the crowd sound. Two directional mics are positioned on either side of the net, pointing at the court, to pick up the sounds of the ball when it hits the net on a service, the ball hitting the strings of the tennis racket, and players' comments near midcourt. Directional mics are aimed at the service lines to pick up the *whopping* sound when the player connects with the ball. Parabolic mics placed behind each baseline pick up the string sound on the racket when the ball is hit deep and the players' grunts and groans when they hit the ball. If the crowd mic at the umpire's location does not pick up enough crowd sound, another crowd mic is mounted from an overhang in the stands.

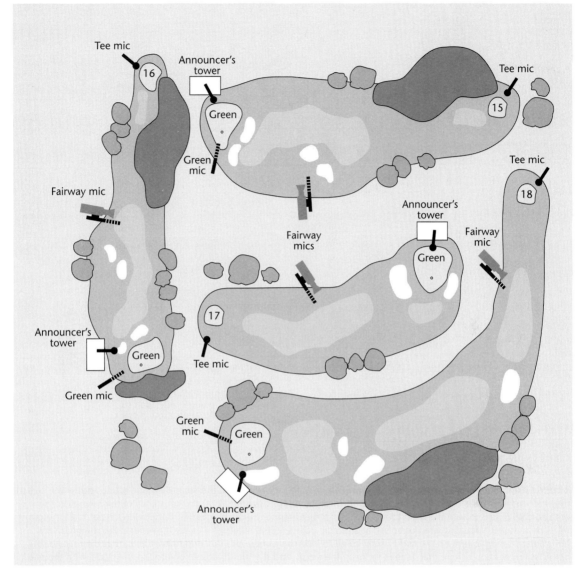

13-28 Miking golf. Omnidirectional or directional microphones are placed near the tees to pick up the sound of the drive and the crowd sound. In the fairways directional mics, either handheld or mounted on minicams, pick up fairway shots and conversation among golfers. At the greens directional mics pick up the sound of the putt and the crowd sound. Wireless mics are placed in the cup, with the transmitter aerial wrapped around the outside, to pick up the sound of the ball falling into the cup. At each hole are announcers' towers with omnidirectional microphones outside the towers to pick up crowd sound and general ambience, or the crowd sound pickup is through the mics already arrayed at the hole. Other wireless operators cover shots where balls are in difficult positions.

Recording and mixing golf presents a unique challenge in that while play at one hole is on the air, play at other holes is being taped. This requires separate audio effects mixes for the play at each hole.

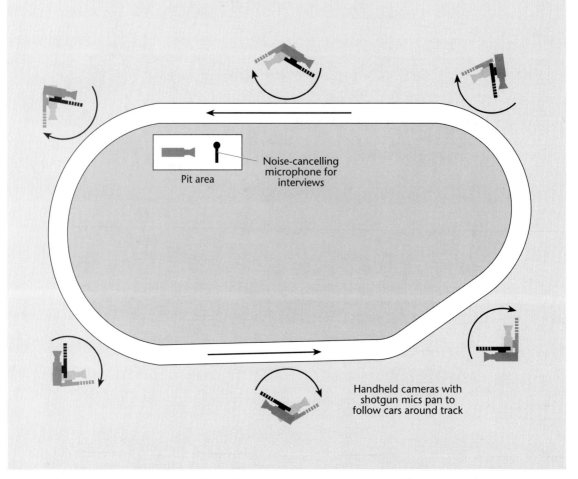

Pit area

Noise-cancelling
microphone for
interviews

Handheld cameras with
shotgun mics pan to
follow cars around track

13-29 Miking auto racing. The main audio problem in auto racing is that it is essentially a one-sound sport—the cars as they careen around the track. Announcers' commentary and interviews break up the constancy of the racing car sounds, but the challenge is to vary the racing sounds to make them as interesting as possible. Handheld cameras with shotgun mics, or handheld shotguns, are positioned at strategic points on the racetrack—at the curves and the straightaways. The camera and mics pick up the cars as they come toward the camera position and follow the cars as they race to the next camera position, where that camera picks up the action and the sound, and so on around the track. With the mics in these locations, the Doppler effect of the pitch changes as the cars come toward the camera and move away from it; the shifting gears; the slowing down and speeding up of the engines; the screeching brakes; and, unfortunately, the crashes—all vary the audio and help create sonic perspective. Crowd sound is not the factor in auto racing that it is in other sports. Even when a microphone is placed in the stands, crowd reaction may not be audible above the engine roar. Due to the high levels of track noise, a noise-canceling microphone is usually employed for interviews in the pit area.

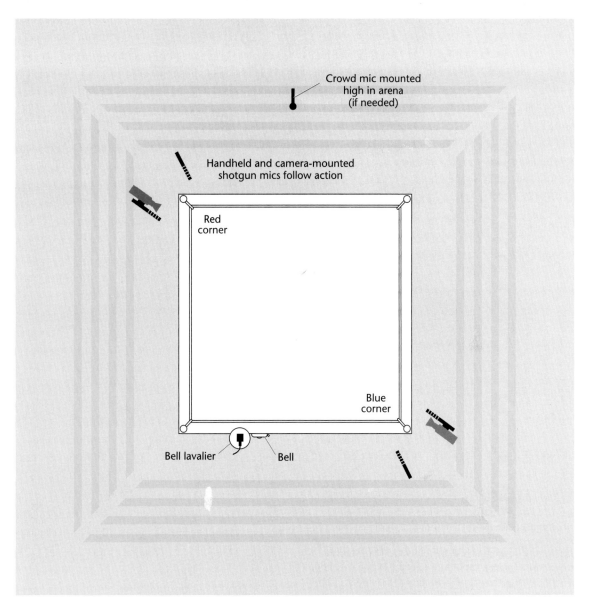

Crowd mic mounted
high in arena
(if needed)

Handheld and camera-mounted
shotgun mics follow action

Red
corner

Blue
corner

Bell lavalier   Bell

13-30 Miking boxing. Two shotgun microphones, one at the red corner, the other at the blue corner, are aimed into the ring to pick up the fight sounds. As the fighters move around the ring, the shotguns follow the action and are opened and closed (although not fully closed) as the fighters move closer to and farther from the mics. Shotgun mics on hand-held cameras in the red and blue corners are used between rounds to pick up the exchanges between the fighters and their handlers. Because fights usually take place indoors and the crowd is close to the ring, the shotgun mics are usually adequate to pick up crowd sound as well. If not, a crowd mic, shotgun or omnidirectional, depending on how much reinforcement is needed for the crowd sound, is mounted high in the arena. A lavalier picks up the sound of the bell. The ringside announcers almost always use headset microphones for their commentary and a handheld mic for interviews.

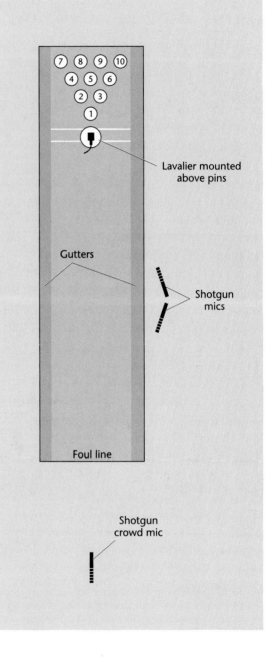

13-31 Miking bowling. Due to the usually high ambient levels in bowling alleys, directional mics are the microphones of choice. Either two shotguns or directional boundary mics are positioned at the side of the lane, one facing toward the foul line, the other facing toward the pins. This technique captures the sounds of the ball drop, the roll down the alley, and the pin strike. A lavalier may be mounted above the pin pit to reinforce the pin strike and pin fall, and, if wanted, the initial action of the pin setup mechanism. If the action mics are insufficient to deal with crowd sound, an additional mic, usually directional, is aimed toward the crowd from in front and above.

13-32 Miking track and field and gymnastics. Because the action takes place in various locations in the same venue and each event requires a different apparatus, producing audio for track and field and gymnastics requires inventiveness in miking and coordination in mixing. To pick up the action sounds, place a mic anywhere you can put one. When action is moving from one point to another, as in the hurdles, mics should be spaced evenly on side stands between the start and finish lines to pick up the sound oncoming and passing. With continuous events, such as hurdles and other types of racing, mics should be opened and closed as the action dictates, otherwise the sonic density will mask the audio due not only to the action sounds but to the pickup of crowd sound. Music to accompany gymnastic routines is usually picked up by the action mics. Examples of selected track and field and gymnastic events are shown below and on the next page.

(a) High jump and (b) pole vault. Wireless lavaliers placed at the approach and landing area pick up the sounds of the pole vault or jump, the landing, and any sounds the athlete makes. The mics are opened only for the action they cover. The approach mic opens for the approach and closes after the leap, and the landing mic, which is closed for the approach, opens after the leap. Of course, the mixer must coordinate the levels for a smooth transition.

Lavaliers
mounted on
uprights

c

Lavaliers
mounted on
frame

d

13-32 *(continued)* **(c) Pommel horse.** Wireless lavaliers mounted near the top of either one or both uprights are usually sufficient to pick up the gymnast's sounds. Two mics are used to ensure that hits on the left and right sides of the horse are heard, or to reinforce the action sounds, or both. Mics mounted directly on the underside of the horse could produce a muffled sound because of the padding in the pommel horse.

(d) Rings. Wireless lavaliers mounted on one or both sides of the frame not only pick up the action sounds of the gymnast, but any squeaking or metallic creaking sounds as well. Placing the mics between the middle and top of the frame helps in picking up the sounds of ring attachments. It is wise to place thin padding between the lavalier and the metal frame to prevent the mic from slipping or from being audibly jarred by the frame's movement.

over a long period. Sometimes this is done by compressing crowd sound.

☑ Compressing the sounds of the announcers, crowd, and action to control their dynamic ranges and give each element more punch.

☑ Compressing one or more sonic elements also creates a layering effect.

Stereo Sound

As with stereo TV in general, producing stereo sports involves providing sonic spaciousness or depth while dealing with localization and stereo-to-mono compatibility (see Chapter 18). Of the three audio components involved—announcers, crowd, and action—the crowd is often the principal or only stereo element.

Announcers present the least problem. Because they are the primary source of information and are stationary during an event, it is natural that they be positioned in the center of the stereo image, although their voices may be fed through a stereo synthesizer so that they sound more a part of the overall sonic setting instead of separate from it.

The crowd is miked and mixed in stereo. Primary crowd pickup comes from a main microphone array and assigned full left and right. The fan at home must feel that he or she is "sitting in one seat" and close to the action—not moving around with the shot. If additional crowd mics are used, they should be for fill, not for emphasis to coincide with a shot.

Action sounds are handled in two ways: either straight down the middle or somewhat localized. Sound panned to the center gives an up-front feeling to coincide with the generally tighter shot it accompanies. Localized sounds are picked up by one mic and panned slightly to the left or right to coincide with their relative position in the playing area. This means that the action mics must be very directional and precisely aimed to make stereo imaging easier for the mixer. But even in ideal circumstances, trying to localize sound, especially moving sound, with shot changes is difficult. The mixer must constantly anticipate a director's shot change. Even if synchronization is achieved, camera angles may cut across the 180-degree axis, creating "reverse angle" audio.

Surround sound has also become a part of the sound in TV sports. See Figure 13-24 and Chapter 18, for examples of surround-sound production.

MAIN POINTS

▶ Producers go on location to cover news and sports, to do a disc jockey program, to heighten realism in a drama, to add authenticity to a setting, or to provide surroundings that are difficult or impossible to reproduce in a studio.

▶ Live and live-on-tape field production for radio and television can be grouped into two basic categories: electronic news gathering (ENG) and electronic field production (EFP). The main difference between ENG and EFP is that ENG covers news events, whereas EFP is employed with the types of productions that take more time to plan and produce.

▶ Thanks to small, lightweight equipment—such as portable microphone mixers, consoles, handheld cameras, audio- and videotape recorders, editors, high-quality headphones, mobile and cellular telephones, remote pickup, and microwave transmission from a mobile unit—it is possible to transmit from the field to the radio or TV station for recording or direct broadcast.

▶ Field production often presents the problem of background sound interfering with the intelligibility of the on-mic/on-camera reporters. But in news, most producers believe that some sonic sense of locale is important in reports from the field.

▶ Recording background sound on a separate track is useful in postproduction to bridge transitions or cover awkward edits.

▶ When it is possible, preproduction planning is essential for most on-location broadcasting or recording. Preparation involves drafting a remote (site) survey, making sure where the power will come from; deciding who will take care of the equipment, program, and administration details; planning the IFB system; and bringing to the production site the essential tools and backup supplies.

▶ As they are in studio production, intercommunication systems are vital in the field, particularly because crew and facilities are usually more widely dispersed. Among the intercom systems used in the field are interruptible foldback (IFB), program sound receiver, paging system, intercom system, cellular telephone, and walkie-talkie.

▶ Three ways to record someone speaking from a podium are to (1) set up and use your own microphones, (2) patch into the public-address (PA) system, or (3) patch into a multiple pickup.

▶ When several speakers have to be miked, an automatic microphone mixer may be more convenient to use than having one operator try to control all of the mic levels.

▶ Miking sporting events requires sound pickup from the announcers, the crowd, and the action.

▶ In miking and mixing sporting events in stereo, the announcers are centered, action sounds are either centered or somewhat localized, and crowd sound is assigned full left and right.

▶ Philosophies vary about how crowd, action, and announcers' sounds should be mixed in the overall sound design of a sporting event. In any approach, however, the announcers' play-by-play and commentary must always be intelligible.

14

Staged Productions

Staged material—such as commercials, sitcoms, and drama—for radio, television, or film is almost always produced for later release; hence, it is recorded with postproduction in mind. This allows more flexibility during production. Scenes are done in several takes to provide different dramatic perspectives and to give the editor choices in establishing continuity, pace, point of view, and so on.

In audio the principal challenge during production is dialogue recording. Sound effects are usually handled in postproduction; music always is. Regardless of the venue, studio or location, recording dialogue that is clear, intelligible, and as noise-free as possible is the production recordist's goal. Even when dialogue is to be ultimately recorded or rerecorded in postproduction, it is important to preserve an actor's performance on the set, if for no other reasons than for timing and interpretation. (Also see "Automated Dialogue Replacement" in Chapter 16.)

RADIO DRAMATIZATIONS

Dramatizations produced in radio today are played out in commercials and other types of spot announcements. Although the days of bona fide radio drama have long since passed, many of the microphone and production techniques that were used are still with us; some have been updated.

Dramatizations on radio entail creating a "theater of the mind," using sound to compel the listener to "see" mental images. The stimuli that trigger the imagination are words, sound effects, and music, as well as the methods used to produce these elements. Generating illusions of perspective and movement is accomplished, for the most part, through miking.

Single-Microphone Technique

Using one microphone in radio dramatization involves positioning performers at the mic and having them play to it as if it were the ear of the audience. To make the illusion effective, a sense of perspective and, if necessary, movement must be created. In addition, appropriate microphones must be selected and properly mounted.

Creating Perspective

To create perspective acoustically, performers are positioned at appropriate distances relative to the mic and to each other, as the dramatic action dictates. If an actor is close to the mic, the audience perceives the sound as near or the space as small, or both, particularly with a directional microphone. If a performer is farther from the mic, the sense of distance increases and the space becomes larger. If a man and woman are on-mic playing opposite each other in a scenario that calls for them to be equally enthusiastic, position the man farther from the microphone than the woman to compensate for the (usually) more powerful male voice. If they are equidistant from the mic, the man will sound closer than the woman (see 14-1). The audience's perspective will be from the performer in the closer position. This assumes a relatively quiet, acoustically controlled studio. In a more open ambience, moving an actor too far from the mic to compensate for a stronger voice would also increase the level of his room tone, therefore placing the actor in an aural frame that is different from that of the more softspoken actor.

Maintaining perspective does not always mean keeping voice levels balanced. If a scene requires one character to call to another from a distance, perspective is created by placing on-mic the actor who is supposed to be closer, and off-mic the one who is supposed to be farther.

Creating Movement

If movement is involved, such as someone leaving or entering a room, there are three ways to create the effect: (1) by moving from the live to the dead side of a directional microphone, or vice versa; (2) by turning in place toward or away from the mic; or (3) by walking toward or away from the mic.

Moving the fader up or down—also known as *board fade*—will also create the effect of coming or going, but not so well as having the performers do it. The difference between the two techniques is that using the fader influences not only the actor's voice level but also the room's acoustics. When a person enters or leaves a room, the space does not change; only the person's position within it changes.

Once the proper aural balances are determined, it is a good idea to mark or tape the studio floor so the performers will know exactly where to stand and how far to move. Marking the studio floor also assists in traffic control around a microphone when several performers are in a scene and have to yield and take on-mic position.

Microphone Selection and Mounting

The best microphone to use for the single-mic technique is a multidirectional capacitor. Capacitors not only provide extremely wide and flat response, they also give the human voice a rich, realistic timbre. Ribbon microphones are good for voice, but older models lack the high-frequency response that gives sound its lifelike quality, assuming the medium reproduces those frequencies.

As for moving-coil microphones, several models have excellent voice response, but almost all are either omnidirectional or unidirectional. If the number of performers changes within a dramatization or if a studio is delegated for such productions, it is easier to set up one multidirectional microphone than to change mics every time the situation requires. When a narrator with a large part is involved and all performers are recorded in the same run, using one directional and one multidirectional mic is a convenient alternative.

The preferred microphone mount for radio dramatizations is the boom. It gives easy access to the mic, there is no floor stand to get in the way,

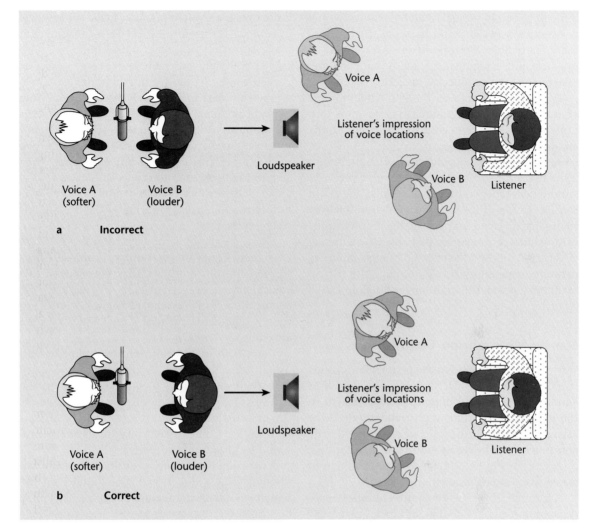

14-1 Balancing two voices with different loudnesses. Positioning the stronger voice farther from the microphone keeps the voices in proper aural perspective relative to the listener. But do not position the stronger voice too far from the mic, or it could take on an ambient quality noticeably different from that of the softer voice.

and, with shock mounting, there is less chance of sound conductance from movement across the studio floor.

Another advantage of the boom is that performers deliver their lines standing, which is better for breathing. It also allows some freedom of movement for performers who like to swing an arm to help their delivery, or both arms if one hand is not holding the script.

Multimicrophone Technique

With multichannel/multitrack recording, producing a dramatization can take advantage of all the flexibility that it affords. Performers can be miked separately to allow greater sound control during recording. Then the various tracks can be processed, edited, and mixed in postproduction. Although added sound control is an advantage of this technique, there are also disadvantages. It is more difficult to obtain natural spatial relationships and perspective between performers and the environment; it reduces the opportunity for talent to interact; and it requires the additional time and expense of a postproduction session.

Deciding whether to use the single-microphone or multimicrophone technique in radio dramatizations should depend on your aesthetic philosophy and the complexity of the script. All in all, however, single-microphone production, although old-fashioned, has two major advantages: (1) It produces a more believable performance because the talent can interact, and (2) it produces a more realistic sound shape. Having said that, for the sound shaping of individual performances, particularly when using effects, and for the added flexibility in production, including the ability to postproduce the performances in stereo, the multimicrophone approach is the technique of choice.

Stereo Microphone Technique

When stereo placement of the performers is called for, and the multimicrophone technique is employed during recording, spatial placement in the stereo frame is done in postproduction. If the "single" microphone approach is used, the performers must be stereo-miked during recording, otherwise it is quite difficult to position them in stereo space in postproduction.

A number of the production techniques applicable to monaural radio dramatizations also apply to stereo. But stereo does bring its own set of problems, not the least of which is *mono compatibility*. Although stereo has been around for many years, and AM and FM radio transmit in stereo, much of the audience still listens in mono, particularly to AM radio. This means that material recorded in stereo must be capable of also being reproduced in mono.

Stereo requires two discrete signals, A (left) and B (right). To reproduce these signals in mono, they are summed—A + B. Discrete stereo is also referred to as sum-and-difference stereo because one channel is summed (A + B), and the other channel is subtracted (A − B). If the stereo signals are in phase when they are added, level can increase 3 to 6 dB;

if the signals are out of phase in stereo, they cancel in mono. It is therefore critical during recording to make sure that problems with stereo-to-mono compatibility are anticipated.

Stereo miking uses two microphones (or microphone capsules) to feed each discrete signal to a separate channel. Sound reaches the microphones with intensity and time differences. The difference in arrival time between the signals reaching the two microphones creates phase problems later when combining the signals to mono. The narrower the angle or space between the mics, the less the difference in arrival time between the signals reaching the mics.

There are a number of ways to mike for stereo. One technique—coincident miking—ensures stereo-to-mono compatibility; another—near-coincident miking—can be mono-compatible if the angle or space between the microphones is not too wide. Coincident and near-coincident arrays are also called *X-Y miking*.

Coincident miking positions two microphones, usually directional, in virtually the same space with their diaphragms located vertically on the same axis (see 15-34). This arrangement minimizes the arrival time difference between the signals reaching each mic. Stereo imaging is sharp, and sound localization is accurate.

Near-coincident miking positions two microphones, usually directional, horizontally on the same plane, angled a few inches apart. They may be spaced or crossed (see 15-35). The wider angle or space between the mics adds more depth and warmth to the sound, but stereo imaging is not as sharp as it is with the coincident array. As a guideline in radio dramatizations, keep the angle or space between the mics to 90 degrees or less. At more than 90 degrees, not only could mono compatibility be a problem, but the stereo image would be more diffuse.

In stereo miking, the lateral imaging of the stereo field is also important. If the angle between the microphones is too narrow, sound will be concentrated toward the center (between two loudspeakers). If the angle between the microphones is too wide, sound will be concentrated to the left and right with little sound coming from the center, a condition referred to as "hole in the middle." The angle between the microphones is contingent on the width of the sound source: the wider the source, the wider the angle; the narrower the source, the narrower the angle. (If a sound source is too wide for the coincident and near-coincident arrays, as may be the case with orchestral ensembles in concert halls, spaced mics are employed—see 15-12.)

In stereo radio dramatizations, performers are usually not widely spaced at a single microphone. The center of the stereo space is where the main action is likely to take place. Too much "ping-ponging" of sound left and right can create dislocation of the sound sources, confusing the listener. If action is played left or right of center, it is usually not too wide afield.

Assuming that there are no acute acoustic problems, the inclusive angle between the micro-phones should be between 60 and 90 degrees. At the least, that is a good starting point; further positioning depends on the number of people in a scene and the size of the aural "set."

Using the multimicrophone approach, on-mic spacing is not a factor. Stereo imaging is handled in postproduction.

Perspective

In positioning performers, take care to ensure that they are in the same positions and perspectives as the associated voices. If a script calls for conversation among performers in various parts of a room, they cannot be grouped around the mics—some closer, some farther—in stereo as they would be in mono. To maintain the stereo perspective, each actor should be in about the same position, relative to the others, as he or she would be if the situation were real (see 14-2).

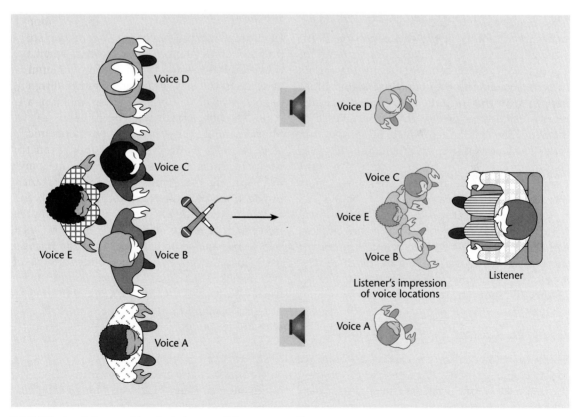

14-2 Effects of stereo miking technique on listener perception

More studio space is required for stereo radio dramatizations than for mono, because the dead sides of the mics cannot be used for approaches to and recedes from the mics. To produce the illusion of someone walking from left to right, a performer cannot simply walk in a straight line across the stereo pickup pattern. If that happened, the sound at the center would be disproportionately louder than the sound at the left and right, and the changes in level would be too abrupt. To create a more realistic effect, a performer has to pass the microphones in a semicircle, always staying the same distance from the mics. Also, the studio must have a short reverb time, because acoustics are much more apparent with stereo than they are with mono.

PRODUCTION RECORDING IN MULTI- AND SINGLE-CAMERA PRODUCTION

Recording dialogue that is clear, intelligible, and as noise-free as possible, in the studio or in the field, is the responsibility of the production recordist. Production recording preserves the sonic record of a production, regardless of whether the dialogue is to be rerecorded in postproduction. Many things happen in life that are difficult to remember, much less re-create—the precise rhythmic nuance of dialogue, the unplanned cough or sputter that furnished a perfect dramatic highlight, the train that happened to go by at exactly the right moment. The live situation is more real and more delicate than the re-created one.

Capturing dialogue on the set in multicamera or single-camera production usually means employing a boom, body-mounted wireless, or plant microphone, or a combination of the three. The type of mic generally preferred is the capacitor—lavalier and shotgun.

Using the Boom

The important decisions in using a boom are logistical and aesthetic. They involve (1) plotting the best microphone positions and angles for each scene in a production to ensure optimal aural balance; (2) keeping the boom out of the lighting pattern so that its shadow does not fall across the set; (3) making sure that the boom does not get in the way of the performers; (4) making sure that the boom can move freely; (5) trying to keep cameras and boom out of the audience's sight line as much as possible; and (6) positioning the boom at mic-to-source distances that are relative to the fields of view of the shots to help maintain acoustic perspective between sound and picture.

It is worth noting that because of the logistical and operational concerns associated with using the boom, many directors use the wireless body mic instead, regardless of whatever sonic advantages the boom may have in a given situation (see "Using Wireless Body Microphones" later in this chapter). Their thinking is that easier is better and more economical; any aesthetic shortcomings can be offset in postproduction. Reality notwithstanding, always try to take the best aesthetic approach.

Blocking

In drama, miking decisions are made in the preproduction planning stages when you **block** the production—work out the movements of performers, cameras, and sound boom(s). Blocking begins with a *floor plan*—a diagram, drawn to scale, showing where scenery, cameras, microphones, and performers will be positioned.

If there is limited physical movement by the performers and the set is small, one boom microphone can usually handle the action, provided the performers are not more than 6 to 9 feet from the mic when they speak. If physical movement is active or the set is large, or both, two booms and sometimes wireless body mics are used. In multicamera staged productions, using two booms is standard. With two booms, one is usually positioned to cover the front and front left of a set (looking into the set); the other covers the rear and rear right.

Perambulator Boom

In studios it is also necessary to think about the boom mount when blocking. The *perambulator boom,* for instance, is large, bulky, and difficult to move quickly over extended distances, especially when cameras, cables, and set furniture are in the way (see 4-49). It is easier to leave the boom mount in place and swing, extend, or retract the boom arm to cover the action. If the boom has to be moved, use boom movers, because it is time-consuming and inconvenient to have the operator come down from the boom seat each time the boom has to be repositioned.

An obvious but vital concern is making sure the boom mic is positioned so that it does not get into the shot. A boom mic positioned out of the picture in a close-up could show up in a longer shot (see 14-3). Also, the boom should be out of an audience's line of sight as much as possible. Although TV studios have TV monitors for the audience, it is to the program's advantage to make the audience feel like part of the event, especially with comedy.

If the boom stays just above (or below) the frame line, the acoustic mic-to-source distance should be proportionate to the size of the shot, matching the aural and visual space, which is one of the boom's main aesthetic advantages. Here are a few guidelines to using the boom:

☑ Position the boom above and in front of the performer's mouth. Remember: Sound comes from the mouth, not from the top of the head.

☑ Establish mic-to-source operating distance by having the performer raise an arm at a 45-degree angle toward the tip of the microphone and extending a finger; the finger should just touch the mic. Appropriate working distances can be planned from there. For example, if the mic-to-source distance in a close-up is 3 feet, in a

14-3 Microphone positioning. (a) Mic-to-source distance adjusted so the boom does not show in the picture. (b) Shot changed to a wider angle and the mic-to-source distance not increased; the microphone shows up in the picture.

medium shot it could be about 6 feet, and in a long shot up to 9 feet.

☑ Directional shotgun microphones compress distance between background and foreground. Aim the microphone directly at the performer(s) so as not to increase background sound.

☑ Hypercardioid shotgun microphones have considerable rear sensitivity, so avoid pointing the back end toward a source of unwanted noise such as ventilators, parabolic lights, and so on.

☑ Capacitor shotguns are high-output, high-sensitivity instruments and, therefore, can be used at somewhat longer mic-to-source distances than moving-coil mics without degrading sound quality.

☑ To facilitate learning the shot changes in multicamera production, provide each boom operator with cue sheets and a TV monitor placed on the boom (assuming a perambulator boom) or near it, as well as headphones that feed the program sound to one ear and the director's cues to the other ear. Boom dolly movers should also have access to cue sheets. Rehearse each shot so that the exact mic-to-source distances are established.

☑ Rehearse all boom operations. Even the slightest movements such as turning the head while talking or bending down can require complicated boom movements. For example, as a head turns while talking, the boom has to be panned and the mic rotated at the same time.

☑ Learn about lighting. A boom operator has to know what side of a set to work from so that the boom does not throw a shadow. Outside it is necessary to be opposite the sun side so that the shadow falls away from the performers.

☑ Anticipate the performer's movements so that the boom leads, rather than follows, the talent.

☑ Position the boom's base toward the front of the set, not to the side. From the side it is difficult to judge the microphone's height in relation to the cameras, because cameras are usually placed in an arc around the front of the set.

Due to the size of perambulator booms, they may be unwieldy in small sets or difficult to maneuver when relatively frequent repositioning is called for, especially if there is no boom mover. Two alternatives are the tripod (giraffe) boom and the fishpole boom.

Tripod (Giraffe) Boom

The *tripod*, or *giraffe*, *boom* is smaller and easier to operate than a perambulator boom, but it has disadvantages (see 4-50). First, because it is lightweight, it is subject to shock and vibration likely to be picked up by the microphone. It therefore requires a lighter mic and a very good shock mount. Second, it has a limited boom arm reach. Third, once the boom arm has been extended to a particular length, it cannot be extended farther or retracted without interrupting shooting to do so. To change mic-to-source distance during shooting, the entire tripod has to be rolled in or rolled out, and this movement could be audible. Fourth, the height extension is quite limited, presenting the dangers of the boom shadow.

Fishpole Boom

The *fishpole boom* is used in-studio when larger booms cannot negotiate small spaces and is preferred for field production because it is more mobile, easier to manage, takes up less space, and requires fewer crew than wheeled booms. A fishpole is handheld and, therefore, can be moved about in a set with relative ease (see 14-4).

Fishpole booms come in various lengths, and most of them have a telescoping tube that can be extended or retracted (see 14-5). Shorter fishpoles can extend from 16 inches out to more than 6 feet and weigh as little as 11 ounces; medium-sized fishpoles can extend from 23 inches out to 8 feet and weigh about 14 ounces; longer fishpoles can extend from a little less than 3 feet out to more than 16 feet and weigh a little over a pound.

The fishpole boom does present a few problems. It gets heavy if it has to be carried about the set or held for any length of time, particularly if the mic it carries is a heavy one. It can be difficult to control

14-4 Using a fishpole with a directional microphone pointed at the performer's mouth from (a) above or (b) below. The mic's position depends on the focal length and angle of the shot. Better sound is usually obtained by positioning the mic above the performer, because sound rises and the bounce from the floor or ground can brighten the pickup.

Two sets of slots accommodate most types of mic cables

Captive collet

Collar with directional dimples

Telescoping sections

Low handling-noise finish

Attach accessories to bottom coupling

Mushroom pole base

14-5 Fishpole boom and its features

precisely, particularly in wider shots when it has to be held high. Furthermore, handling noises can be heard if the fishpole operator is not careful.

The following are some operational tips when using the fishpole boom, particularly in field production (see also 14-6, 14-7, and 14-8):

☑ Always use a windscreen, especially with directional capacitors, which are particularly sensitive to even minute air movement; barrier, mesh-style windscreens are quite effective (see 4-40b), especially with a windjammer (see 4-40d).

☑ Always use a shock mount. High-quality microphones, particularly capacitors with high sensitivity, are apt to pick up sound conductance through the metal tube. It is a good idea to tape foam rubber around the tube a few inches above the handgrip and below the microphone mount to inhibit sound conductance.

14-6 Boom leading subject. Subject movement requires the boom to lead the subject through a space.

14-7 Moving the boom for broad movements. For broad movements, such as characters moving in front of a dollying camera, the boom operator has to walk backward or sideways when leading.

Lav mic

Dolly

14-8 Miking complicated movement. In cases of complicated movement, a subject may need multiple mic setups.

☑ Use high-quality headphones when operating a fishpole boom mic. Except for the recordist, who may be some distance away, there is no other way to tell what sounds are being picked up or how they are balanced, particularly in relation to the foreground and background sounds.

☑ If the fishpole operator must move with the performer(s), make sure that there is enough cable and cleared space on the floor. To avoid the cable problem altogether, boom-mount a wireless mic (see 14-9).

☑ Have the fishpole operator remove all jewelry before recording and wear gloves to help dampen handling noise.

☑ If the fishpole has to be held for any length of time, secure a flag holder around the operator's waist and sit the pole end in its pocket. Some longer fishpoles come with a handle grip on the pole to help support it against the body.

The advantage of the boom-mounted microphone on location, as in the studio, is that by varying its distance to the sound source you can make it reflect the focal length of shots. This advantage applies especially in the field, where there is more likely to be background sound whose relationship to the principal sound source often helps establish overall sonic environment. This technique is called *perspective miking*, because it establishes audio viewpoint. Moreover, it helps convey the mood and style of a production.

14-9 Wireless boom with mounted transmitter

If a scene takes place in a seedy hotel room, for example, aiming the microphone at a slight angle to the performer's mouth so that it also picks up more room sound will "cheapen" the sound, thereby better articulating the visual atmosphere. If a scene is to convey an anticipatory atmosphere, widening mic-to-source distance, even in a tight shot, creates an open sound that encompasses background sounds such as a clock ticking, board creaking, drink pouring, owl hooting, siren screaming, and so on.

Fishpole booms also permit microphone changes to alter perspective. In handling a strong voice against a weak one, the mic can be aimed so that it favors the weak voice on-axis and picks up the strong voice slightly off-axis. In addition to perspective and flexibility, overhead miking in general tends to provide a crisp, natural sound compared with body mics, which are often sterile in texture.

Perspective

The challenge in operating any boom is to maintain aural perspective while simultaneously keeping the boom mic out of the picture and the performers in the mic's pickup pattern. To create a realistic setting, sound and picture must work together; the aural and visual perspectives should match. If you see two performers talking in the same plane, you should hear them at relatively the same loudness; if you see one performer close up engaged in dialogue with another actor farther away, the performer who is closer should sound louder.

Performers in the Same Plane   The easiest way to pick up performers talking in the same plane and to maintain their aural relationship is to position the microphone equidistant between them and close enough so that they are on-mic (see 14-10). If one performer walks a short distance away, blocking will have determined either how far the boom can follow, keeping the performer on-mic yet remaining close enough to get back in time to cover the other performer, or whether a second boom should be used (see 14-11 and 14-12).

14-10 Two performers on the same plane. The easiest way to boom-mic them is to place the microphone equidistant between them and swivel it back and forth.

14-11 Two performers on the same plane but with some movement. One boom mic can be used when there is some movement between performers on the same plane and the distances between them are not wide.

14-12 Two performers on the same plane but with significant movement. Two boom mics may be needed when blocking calls for more-dynamic movement, as it often does.

Performers in Different Planes During a scene it is typical for shots to change from, say, a medium shot of a group with performer A talking, to a close-up of performer A, to a close-up of performer B responding, to another medium shot of the group, to a close-up of performer C talking, and so on. To keep visual and aural perspective consistent, the sound in the medium shot should not be quite so loud as the sound in the close-up.

In a medium shot compared with a close-up, for example, the boom has to be higher and therefore farther from the actors. In a long shot compared with a medium shot, the mic has to be higher and farther still. The aural difference in the mic-to-source distance, reflected by the acoustic change in the loudness level and the proportion of direct to indirect waves, should match the visual difference in the audience-to-source distance.

Regardless of the visual perspective, however, the audience must hear the performers clearly. Someone close up should sound more present than someone farther away, but only to a certain extent. A performer in a close-up shot should not sound "on top of the audience," and the audience should not have to strain to hear a performer in a long shot. The mic also has to be close enough to a performer so that it does not pick up too much ambience. You have to cheat a bit with mic placement to reduce the unwanted reflections so that the difference in loudness levels is obvious but not disconcerting.

Suppose a scene calls for two performers to talk several feet apart. First, the distance between them has to be within the microphone's range. Second, the mic should be between them but closer to the performer in the foreground (see 14-13). Third, if further changes in the loudness level are necessary, the range of the boom arm should be increased to get the mic closer or the performers' positions should be changed. If the performers are too far apart to cover with one boom, use two (see 14-14). Remember, within the same scene and locale,

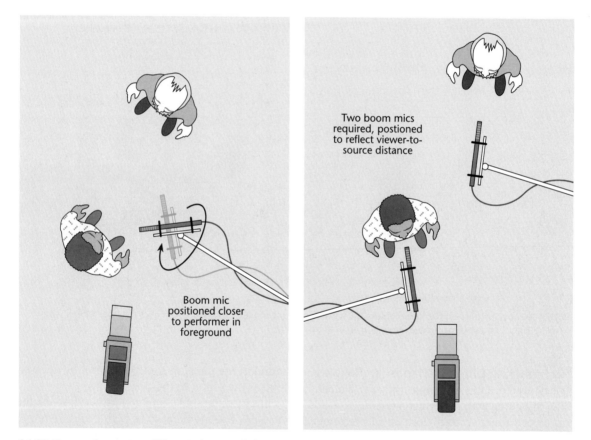

14-13 Two performers on different planes and close enough to be covered by one boom. The microphone should be placed between the performers, but mic-to-source distance should reflect viewer-to-source distance. In other words, the person who looks closer should be louder.

Boom mic positioned closer to performer in foreground

14-14 Two performers on different planes and too far apart to be covered by one boom. Two booms should be used. To some extent, mic-to-source distance should complement camera-to-source distance.

Two boom mics required, postioned to reflect viewer-to-source distance differences in levels of loudness should be apparent but not marked. Do not worry about the slight discrepancies between the visual and aural perspectives. If the audio sounds realistic enough, the psychological effect of the picture's perspective should make up for the difference between the two.

Adjusting Microphone Levels at the Console

Another way to change the aural perspective is to use the fader; increasing loudness brings sound closer, and decreasing it moves sound farther away. Unless loudness changes are minor, this technique is not recommended. Using the fader to make level adjustments that are obvious not only affects loudness but changes ambient relationships as well. Remember: the relationship of actors on a set may change, but the space itself does not.

Using Wireless Body Microphones

The wireless mic has liberated the performer from being tethered to a microphone cord. This has been a particular blessing in staged productions where actors are mobile. The advantages of the body mic are that dialogue is clear, intelligible, and present, with a minimum of background sound. The disadvantages are that sonic perspective, regardless of a shot's focal length, is the same and the sound tends to be sterile.

It is possible to compensate for these drawbacks to some extent. There are two basic types of lavaliers used for body miking: proximity-prone and transparent. *Proximity-prone lavaliers* tend to add presence to close dialogue and reject background sound. *Transparent lavaliers* have a more open and natural sound; they pick up more ambience. Their advantage is that sound can be blended more naturally with boom and plant mics. The disadvantage of transparent lavaliers is that they pass more ambience.

Body mics are usually omnidirectional; directional lavaliers have not proved practical. They have to be pointed precisely in the direction of the sound, which, in body-miking actors or in using plant mics, is often not effective. Also remember that sound-canceling ports are what make a mic directional. Clothes or mounting tape could block some of the ports, thereby degrading pickup.

When using a wireless body mic, you must consider all of the following: aural perspective, microphone placement, number of mics in use at the same time, and sound levels.

Perspective

The main sonic difference between a body-mounted wireless mic and a boom mic is in creating aural perspective. Remember, with a boom, mic-to-source distance must be adjusted with the shot, thereby automatically matching aural/visual perspective (at least in theory). When a wireless mic is attached to the body, mic-to-source distance is close and never varies, regardless of the shot's focal length, which means that aural perspective must be adjusted in postproduction.

Placement

When a wireless microphone is body-mounted for drama, it must be hidden, so the type of fabric and clothing become important factors in deciding what mic to use and where to place it. For this reason a sound designer should make it a point before miking to consult with the person responsible for wardrobe. Remember that cotton does not make as much rustling sound as do synthetic fabrics such as polyester, rayon, nylon, and dacron. Synthetic fabrics are also more likely to build static electricity, which creates interference, than are wool, suede, cotton, and leather. Leather does, however, make noise.

The design of performers' clothing is also important. A microphone can be hidden inside a tie, in the seam of a shirt or blouse, in a pocket, in the collar of a jacket or turtleneck sweater, behind a scarf, under a bodice, and so on. Certain mics are less susceptible to interference from rustling, jostling, static electricity, and so on than are others; you have to test to determine which are which. Obviously, a microphone with a windscreen and shock absorbency is better than a mic without one or both. Tying a knot in the microphone cable underneath the head of the mic can sometimes, but not always, reduce or eliminate clothing noise. If the proximity of the microphone to the mouth creates problems with sibilance, popping, and *nose blast,* invert the mic (so long as it is omnidirectional).

Clothing style also has something to do with where a mic can be hidden—costumes from different periods and cultures pose different challenges. Hiding a mic on a performer playing an eighteenth-century Austrian prince clothed from neck to ankle in tight-fitting raiment presents one type of problem; hiding a mic on a woman in a low-cut, strapless dress presents another. Here, again, the person handling wardrobe can help. Maybe a pocket for the microphone can be sewn underneath the prince's vest; the bodice of the dress can be tubed and the mic placed inside. It is, of course, easier to hide a microphone in loose-fitting clothes than in tight-fitting ones. Loose-fitting garments also reduce the chance of picking up rustling sounds.

If it can be done, the best thing is to get the microphone in the open as much as possible. Try to mount it in the shadow area of a coat lapel, or sew it to the material, or stick it through material to look like a button, tie clasp, or decorator pin. Use lavaliers that are available in black, which is easier to conceal than gray or shiny metal.

An externally mounted lavalier can be made inconspicuous by camouflaging it to match wardrobe. Marking pens can be used to color small strips of tape or foam windscreens, or both, which are then attached to the mic and clasp, thereby subduing their appearance. An alternative is to use small patches of felt or cloth to cover the mic.

Two types of clothes noise often encountered are contact and acoustic. Contact clothing noise is caused by a garment flapping into or rubbing across the mic capsule. The solution is to carefully immobilize all clothing that may create this problem by taping down everything on either side of the mic. Try sandwiching the mic between two sticky triangles of tape (formed by folding a strip of tape like a flag, sticky side out). Because contact noise can also be caused when clothing rubs against the mic cable, form a loop near the mic for strain relief, and then apply a few lengths of tape along the cable. Try double-faced tape or sticky triangles to immobilize clothing and keep it from rubbing.

Clothing rubbing against itself generates noise; treating the clothing with static guard generally solves the problem. A light spray of water can soften starched fabrics. Because synthetic fabrics are much noisier than naturals, they should be avoided whenever possible.

It is important never to allow the mic line and the antenna to cross when rigging a wireless body mic, and also to keep the antenna rigid and not looped over itself. A good way to keep the antenna rigid is to affix a rubber band to the tip and then safety-pin the rubber band to the clothing. If the antenna has to run in a direction other than straight up and down or to the side, invert the transmitter pack and let the mic cable, rather than the antenna, loop. Check the performer regularly to make sure that the mic and cable are secure—tape tends to loosen from moisture, and costumes tend to shift from movement.

All of this is well and good, but what can you do when the costume, such as a man's bathing suit or chain mail on a knight, makes it difficult to use a body mic? In the case of the bathing suit, cooperation may be needed from the hairdresser: With skill, a wireless microphone can be hidden in the hair; sound does rise and the body does resonate. The chain mail, on the other hand, may be too noisy for any successful body miking, in which case either take a more conventional miking approach or rerecord the dialogue in postproduction.

Still another reason for working with wardrobe is to arrange with the costumer when to mount the body mic on the performer. The best time is usually when the performer is dressing at the start of the production day, even if the microphone will not be needed right away. By mounting the mic before production starts, the performer has more time to get used to it, and shooting does not have to be interrupted to put it in place when it is needed.

Moreover, a performer has a great deal to think about, and disrupting concentration to body-mount a microphone is not a good idea.

Using Two or More Wireless Microphones

Using two or more wireless microphone systems in the same immediate area requires that they be on different and, preferably, widely separated frequencies to avoid interference. The wireless systems and microphones should be of similar make and model to ensure sonic uniformity. If this is not possible and only different systems and mics are available, each performer should be given the same make and model to use throughout production so at least the individual's sound is consistent.

An ever-present problem with body mics is noise, not only from fabric but from props in a pocket that may jingle or rustle, such as coins, keys, or paper. For example, suppose two (or more) actors using wireless mics are exchanging dialogue at relatively close proximity. Actor A is nervously jangling coins, and the sound is interfering with the pickup of his dialogue. Assuming the pocket containing the coins is closer to the body mic than it is to the mouth, actor A's dialogue probably is also being picked up by actor B's mic, but with the sound of the coins not as loud. Therefore, in postproduction the recording from actor B's microphone can be used in place of the recording from actor A's mic. This enables continued use of the wireless systems, which may be desirable for logistical or other reasons. This technique also helps solve problems of unwanted or unintelligible overlapping dialogue.

Controlling Levels

A frequent problem in recording dialogue is trying to maintain suitable levels when performers are speaking at different and varying loudnesses. If sound is too loud, level is "in the red"; if sound is too quiet, level is "in the mud." Controlling levels both to avoid distortion, particularly with digital sound, and to keep sound above the noise floor, yet still preserve the relative dynamics of the performers, is handled in different ways, depending on the miking.

Suppose that in a scene a distraught man is alternately sobbing and shouting at a woman, who is responding in a quiet, controlled voice, trying to calm him. In such a scene, the level changes would be wide and acute and difficult to ride. Putting a limiter on the sound is not always preferred or recommended, because it can reduce sound quality. Nor may it be possible through blocking to place the microphones properly to compensate for the widely fluctuating levels. And it is imprudent to depend completely upon postproduction to fix problems that occur in sound recording during production. By then, the sound may be beyond repair, because either it is distorted or the signal-to-noise ratio is unacceptable, or both. Thus, to handle the widely varying sound levels, either boom or body mics may be employed.

When using the boom, recordists in a situation like this may set the level on the loudest sound emitted, in this case on the man's shouts. If the shouts are set at, say, zero level (100 percent of modulation), it ensures that, at worst, the peaks will only momentarily get into the red. This makes riding levels less critical in situations where the dynamic range is wide and changes quickly, and it keeps both dialogue and ambience in perspective. Because there is no headroom with digital sound, it may be necessary to set an appropriate limit on the audio level.

In terms of perspective, by setting a maximum loudness level, the woman's level will be quite a bit lower than the man's, because she has a less powerful voice and is speaking quietly. But increasing her loudness level during the quiet passages will also increase her ambience disproportionately to the man's. This creates different background noise levels between the two performers and different spatial relationships as well. If quieter levels are at or below the noise floor, slight adjustments in microphone selection or placement, performer placement, or voice projection can be made, or compression can be used. (Another alternative to using the boom is to shoot and mike the scene entirely from the woman's perspective.)

With the body mic, handling the scene is somewhat easier. Because each performer is individually miked, it is possible to set and control levels separately. If in the scene the woman also has to shout at the man, perhaps to admonish him to stop feeling sorry for himself, another option is to put two wireless mics on each performer. Levels for one pair of mics would be set for the louder dialogue, and levels for the other pair set for the quieter dialogue. The production mixer then has four faders to worry about, but overall sound quality probably will be better, and the editor has more to work with in postproduction.

Here are some other tips to keep in mind when considering or using wireless body mics:

☑ When complex movement is called for, do not automatically choose a wireless body mic before considering whether good boom work can meet the challenge. Remember that a boom-mounted microphone produces a more realistic sound.

☑ Because wireless microphones are subject to interference from noise, avoid using them in heavy traffic areas, such as downtown streets, parking lots, major highways, airports, or in areas where there are frequent RF transmissions.

☑ Place the receiver properly—in line of sight with the transmitter and as close as possible to the set.

☑ Check transmission frequencies to make sure that no one else in the area is using your band(s).

☑ Do a sound check by walking around the same area(s) the performers will be using.

☑ Adjust the transmitter's gain control for the individual performer.

☑ Always power down; that is, do not turn off the transmitter without turning off the receiver. Otherwise, the receiver will keep looking for a signal and could lock into most unpleasant VHF white noise. (**White noise** is a wideband noise that contains equal energy at each frequency, as opposed to **pink noise**, which is wideband noise that maintains constant energy per octave. Both types of noise are generally used for testing electronic audio equipment.)

☑ Bring backup wireless systems and plenty of fresh batteries, preferably longer-lasting lithium batteries.

Plant Microphones

Plant microphones, also called *fixed mics*, are positioned around a set to cover action that cannot easily be picked up with a boom or a body mic or to provide fill sound. A plant mic can be either a conventional-size or, preferably, a miniature capacitor. Plant mics can be hidden practically anywhere—in flowers, on a desktop nameplate, in a doorway, on the edge of a windowsill, on an automobile visor, or in a plant, which is where the name comes from.

Because a plant mic is almost always used along with the main boom or body mic, beware of phasing from overlapping sound. Also, if possible, try to match the perspective sound quality of the main and plant mics; that will probably be easier to do with a boom mic than with a body mic.

Multiple Miking with Different Microphone Mounts

As pointed out earlier, miking dialogue for staged productions might involve using a combination of boom, body, and plant microphones.

For example, in single-camera production a master shot and then various perspectives of the shot are recorded in separate takes. A master shot is a single shot of an entire scene from a far-enough distance to cover all the action. Suppose the scene is a party in a large living room, where host and hostess are mingling with guests and exchanging pleasantries. The master shot would be a wide shot of the room and party, taking in all the action. Other takes might consist of a group shot with host, hostess, and a few guests, and three-, two-, and one-shots of the host and hostess in a selected exchange with one person in the group.

To take advantage of all the sonic possibilities, sound can be recorded during each take. By audio-recording as many takes as possible, the various sonic qualities and perspectives provide the editor with more options in cutting sound and picture. For example, the master shot could be miked from overhead, using boundary mics with hemispheric pickup to capture the overall hubbub. Directional overhead mics could be added for more selective, but still open, pickup of particular interactions among host and hostess and certain guests or groups of guests. Wireless mics attached to host and hostess would record their dialogue for close-ups to be shot later. In the group shot, a boom with an omnidirectional or wide-angle pattern could be used for the overall pickup to provide a more open sonic perspective than that provided by the directional overhead mics. For the tighter three-, two-, and one-shots, body-mounted wireless mics provide the sonic complement to these closer cutaways. Also, if a multitrack tape recorder is available, there is no reason not to continue using the overhead mics for each take to provide additional recordings of the ambient party sounds.

The point is that in single-camera production, shooting each scene several times to record as many different visual perspectives as possible is part and parcel of the technique. Each shot often requires time to reposition the camera, change the lighting, refluff the performers' clothes, recomb hair, and retouch makeup. If such pains are taken for the picture, similar time and attention should be given to the sound so that the audio recorded also has as many different perspectives as possible. Enlightened directors do this; the problem is that, even today, too many directors still give sound short shrift, to the detriment of the finished product.

By the standards of most multicamera production for television, the length of each continuous shot recorded in single-camera production is often relatively short. Long takes are uncommon, because when performer and camera movement change appreciably, it is often also necessary to reposition performers, crew, and equipment. But long takes over relatively far-flung distances are done from time to time.

A key to such takes, in addition to having mics strategically mounted and located, is placement of recorders. Clearly more than one recorder is necessary to handle a long take over some distance. Where the recorders are placed is dictated by the length of mic cable runs or the transmission range of a wireless mic system, or both, and, if necessary, where recorders and operators can be hidden.

FIELD PRODUCTION

In production always be prepared. Time is money, to say nothing of the physical and psychological angst caused by unnecessary delay. This applies even more so to field production, where away from the security of the studio, if something can go wrong, it will. Moreover, it is useful to keep in mind that directors tend to be more understanding when time has to be taken to set up for picture than they are when time has to be taken for the sound.

Preproduction Planning

Before actual production gets under way, decisions are made about the production site, the equipment, and any special needs. Some of these decisions may be out of the sound person's control. But even as a consultant, the sound person can facilitate the preparation and production of audio by anticipating problems and needs and being ready to provide knowledgeable advice when asked. The importance of proper preparation for on-location production cannot be overemphasized. Consider the loss of time and money, to say nothing of the inconvenience to all the people involved, if you have to hold up production because someone brought the wrong microphone, forgot the batteries for the tape recorder, neglected to pack the tool kit, planned to mount a heavy camera crane on soil too soft to hold it, chose a shooting site several days in advance of production without realizing that a building nearby was slated for demolition on the day of recording, scouted the shooting site at noon although the script called for the scene to take place at dusk, or selected a shooting site filled with ragweed without checking whether any of the key people were allergic to pollen. Planning to shoot on location is a careful, meticulous procedure involving more than just decisions about production.

Selecting a Location

In selecting a site, sound designers prefer one with suitable acoustics indoors and no distracting sounds outdoors, although these qualities are rarely found away from the controlled environment of the studio. The first thing to understand about a production site is that directors are interested in what it looks like, not what it sounds like. The second thing to understand is: Be prepared to deal with unwanted sound. If possible, try to reduce the difficulties by suggesting to the director those sites with the fewest sound problems. But keep in mind that where you shoot is determined by the demands of the picture, not by the demands of the sound.

The main challenge in doing a production on location is to record the principal sound source with little or no sonic leakage from either the acoustics or other sound sources. Therefore, judge the recording site on what is possible to achieve in neutralizing unwanted sound.

Dealing with Unwanted Sound

Unwanted sound is generated by many sources. Some are obvious, and some not so obvious: the low-frequency rumble from traffic that becomes midrange hiss on a wet day, blowing sound from wind, clatter from a nearby office, buzz from fluorescent lights, excessive reverb from rooms that are too live, jet roar from planes that fly over the production area, noise from construction, church bells that ring every hour on the hour, a far-off foghorn, clanking pipes, creaking floorboards, whine from an air conditioner, chirping from birds, barking from dogs, and so on.

Being aware of the problems is not enough: You have to know what, if anything, to do about them. For example, you can usually roll off low-frequency rumble from traffic, but the midrange hiss from wet tires on a wet surface is difficult to equalize out. Gentle wind presents little problem for a mic equipped with a pop filter and windscreen. With capacitor mics these filters will not completely offset the effect of noise from strong winds, although the mesh-style zeppelin windscreen and windjammer are quite effective, especially when they are used together. If a room is reverberant, you can make it less so by placing a lot of sound-absorbent material in the area and using tight, highly directional miking; but these techniques may not work in large, extremely reverberant spaces. If the director insists

on a site where sound problems cannot be neutralized, plan to record the audio in the studio during postproduction.

Two other considerations in choosing a production site with audio in mind are (1) the available space—make sure the boom or fishpole operator has enough room to move with the action and still keep the microphone out of the picture; and (2) the power supply—if the production site does not have enough power outlets or wattage, or if the circuits are noisy, plan to bring the main and backup power supplies.

Prerecorded Material

Any prerecorded announcements, sound effects, or music used during production must be included in preproduction planning. Also plan for the equipment to be used to play them: disc player, open-reel tape recorder, cartridge player, and so on.

Other Equipment and Materials

Anticipating the need for less obvious, but nevertheless important, equipment and materials is also part of preproduction planning. The following are among the important items to have handy (also see Chapter 13):

- ☑ AC power checker
- ☑ Adjustable wrench
- ☑ Backup microphones and mic accessories, such as cables and connectors
- ☑ Batteries for every piece of equipment using them
- ☑ C-clamp and pony clips
- ☑ Clip leads
- ☑ Cotton swabs
- ☑ Demagnetizer
- ☑ Drill and drill bits
- ☑ Editing materials
- ☑ Flashlight or lantern light
- ☑ Fuses
- ☑ Head cleaner

- ☑ Headphones and headphone amp

- ☑ Knee bench

- ☑ Log sheets or a laptop computer to record time, location, and content of production information

- ☑ Lubes and glues

- ☑ Multimeter

- ☑ Nut drivers

- ☑ Oscillator

- ☑ Oscilloscope

- ☑ Pens and paper

- ☑ Pocket knife

- ☑ Recording tape

- ☑ Rope

- ☑ Scripts and rundown sheets

- ☑ Soldering pencil

- ☑ Stopwatch

- ☑ Time code generator and reader

- ☑ Tape—both duct and masking

- ☑ Tape measure

- ☑ Tool kit with ruler, needle-nose and regular pliers, wire cutters, Phillips-head and conventional screwdrivers, hammer, awl, file/saw

- ☑ Vise grip

Production Recording

Production recording was discussed earlier in this chapter, and many of the same considerations that apply to studio recording also apply to field recording, including the challenge of getting the sound right with little leeway to experiment with it, refine it, or, should something go wrong, fix it. Perhaps one difference between studio and field production recording is the additional pressure that comes from being away from the security of the studio, particularly when a director insists that

there will be no rerecording of dialogue in postproduction—that the original sound will be used in the final mix. Being flexible and imaginative in solving problems are essential to good production recording.

Suppose a director wants to shoot a scene with constrained action in a very large stone-and-marble room using a boom, but does not want to rerecord the dialogue in postproduction. The reverberation is so dense, however, that the actors cannot pick up cues from one another. Clearly, the walls and ceiling cannot be acoustically treated; the room is far too large. What the production recordist did in this actual situation was to devise a canopy secured to four extendable legs and position it over the action. In addition, a rolling, absorbent baffle 20 feet high was used to reduce the length of the room and therefore the reverberant space. It should be noted that this type of solution would not have worked had the scene required a lot of movement. In that case, the director might have had to use body mics.

A director wants an actor to sing while revving a racecar engine on a racetrack. Clearly, the engine sound will drown out the singing. But with a noise-canceling mic on the actor, the singing can be recorded loud and clear. Because of the inverse square law, if the sound-pressure level of a sound source is high enough, it is possible to close-mike the source and reduce leakage.

It should also be noted that signal processing is rarely used during production recording except for bass roll-off and a slight midrange boost to help punch dialogue. Anything else is usually done in postproduction. Productions shot with a single camera are done out of sequence and with different takes of most scenes; prematurely processing sound on the set could cause a myriad of matching problems, particularly with stereo and surround sound. Spatial imaging should be left to postproduction. To attempt it during production recording makes little sense, because there is no way to know how a scene ultimately will be edited.

The only "processing" that should be done in production recording is riding mic levels with smooth and imperceptible changes and balancing the loudness extremes of each actor with a top-quality mixer whose controls are easy to see and get at. Slight gain adjustments on mixers of mediocre quality are too often apparent on the track.

Automated dialogue replacement is tedious. It often involves recording one actor at a time, affording little opportunity to interact with another actor(s) who may be in the same scene. Because ADR studios are acoustically dry, when an actor has to project, the tendency is to overcompensate. Concentrating on synchronizing dialogue to the lip movements on-screen can distract from concentrating on the performance.

Split-Track Recording

By split-track recording, it is possible to use the fishpole boom, the body mic, and the plant mic to their advantages. By miking a performer with a body mic and a boom and recording each signal on a separate track, the tighter sound of the close shots and the more open sound of the longer shots are covered as each shot is taken. This saves time without reducing flexibility in postproduction editing and mixing. This also comes in handy when dialogue and sound effects, particularly loud effects, have to be recorded at the same time. Close-miking the performer(s) and the effects and feeding them to two separate tracks keeps the sounds from interfering with or even drowning out the dialogue. When in doubt, however, remember that the first priority of production recording is to record usable dialogue.

Multitrack Recording

As the section on split-track recording implies, additional microphones and available tape tracks on a set provide considerable flexibility in production recording. With the audio mobile unit, the multitrack recorder, and time code, such flexibility is possible. Whether multiple cameras are feeding picture through a video switcher to tape (or filming) or to separate video recorders, sound can be routed either directly to the VCR(s) or to one or more ATRs, including multitrack. If one camera is being used, the picture can be routed directly to tape (or film), but the sound can be routed to either the VCR or ATR, or both. Such versatility facilitates various miking arrangements and therefore allows better control of dialogue, background, and sound-effects recording. It also takes more time to plan and set up, but the sound control in editing and mixing makes it worthwhile.

Take a simple outdoor scene where a couple is walking in the countryside and focal lengths vary from wide shots to close-ups. Instead of worrying about how to cover the scene with a fishpole, you could use two body mics for the couple and a separate microphone—omnidirectional or boundary mic—to pick up background sound. Recording the three tracks separately not only allows control of each sonic element during production and postproduction but also reduces the need for the extra step of dialogue rerecording.

In staged productions, because scenes are often shot a few times from different perspectives, the preceding example may be shot as a master scene of the couple, then as close-ups from the man's and woman's perspectives. This allows an editor to cut from shots of the couple to individual shots of their interaction.

As for miking, because the master scene would be shot wider than the one-shot close-ups, clip-on boundary mics could be used as the wireless body microphones. The audio would be more open and would include more background sound than would that of the typical omnidirectional lavalier, thus better reflecting the wider focal lengths of the shot. During the one-shots the boundary mic could be changed to an omnidirectional or directional lavalier to sonically articulate the closer focal lengths and reduce background sound. A separate microphone to record background sound could still be employed for added flexibility in mixing. The microphone's pickup pattern may be omnidirectional, directional, or hemispheric, depending on the quality of the background sound required. Indeed, all three pickups may be recorded on separate tracks to further increase flexibility in the mix, but be careful of additive ambience in combining the tracks.

Monitoring several inputs at once in multitrack production recording is, of course, difficult. The approach a number of recordists take is to adjust and sample all input levels before a shot and then watch the meters during recording, laying down the tracks at 100 percent of modulation.

Blocking and Rehearsing

Despite the considerable flexibility that modern technology provides in producing staged material, scenes are still shot one at a time, out of sequence, and often in segments. Each shot is blocked and lit, and camera movements are rehearsed. Just as the visual elements must be painstakingly planned and practiced, so too should the audio. For each shot, microphone positions are blocked, movements are rehearsed, and sound balances are determined.

The responsibilities of the sound people, in some ways, are perhaps greater than those of the crew responsible for producing the picture. The sound crew is often left on its own, not because the director does not care (although this sometimes is the case) but because audio is usually the one major production component of film and TV that a director is likely to know least about. As a result, blocking and rehearsing become all the more important for the audio people. The director may proceed with shooting when the pictorial elements are in place and assume that, or not bother to check if, sound is ready. It had better be! Too many directors who would understand a delay if a light had to be repositioned would have little patience if a similar delay were due to an audio problem.

Noise Reduction

The value of noise reduction throughout the production process cannot be overemphasized, especially in relation to dialogue and field recording. Noise is an ever-present annoyance. Fortunately, there are a number of ways to deal with it.

One method involves using highly directional microphones with good off-axis rejection. Many capacitor mics have high output, so it may be unnecessary to increase their levels appreciably during quiet passages, thereby avoiding a boost in background noise. The output of moving-coil microphones is sometimes too low to pick up quiet levels without noise. Moreover, capacitor mics do not have to be brought as close to a sound source, and so you avoid the dangers of popping and sibilance and avoid getting the microphone in the picture.

Equalization also helps. By rolling off the low frequencies, air-conditioning noise and rumbling sounds are reduced. (Some directors have the air-conditioning turned off during shooting.) Cutting the high frequencies reduces hiss. With dialogue it is possible to use a relatively narrow frequency range, because the frequency spectrum of the speaking voice is not wide.

Putting gentle compression on a voice raises the quieter levels above the noise floor. Using a noise gate can also reduce ambient noise level, but be careful that its action is not perceptible. A de-esser reduces sibilance, but be careful of too much signal processing during recording because (1) once it is part of a recording, it is very difficult to remove, and (2) the more electronic devices in the signal chain, the worse the signal-to-noise ratio. Having said that, use whatever miking technique or signal processing is necessary to reduce rumble, AC hum, buzz, and hiss—they are unacceptable in a recording. Better to deal with these problems during production recording than to leave them to postproduction.

Whatever other means you employ to increase sonic fidelity, the importance of using noise reduction with any analog recording cannot be overemphasized. A noise reducer should be part of the audio signal chain during each stage of production and postproduction.

A main source of acoustic noise is the sets. Art directors can eliminate many potential noise problems by following a few principles of acoustic design, such as constructing sets whose walls are not parallel, using absorptive materials (including sound-absorbing paint), and building flooring so that it does not squeak—unless the director wants this effect.

Directors can also help reduce ambient noise by not blocking action near a flat surface or, worse, a corner. Regardless of how good the microphone and how effective the sound-absorbing materials, it is difficult to avoid signal degradation when sound bounces from walls and corners into a mic at close range. Too much sound absorption is not good either. Heavy carpeting on a set, for example, could make sound lifeless.

In field recording, most venues, no matter how carefully chosen with sound in mind, have background noise problems from wind, traffic, ventilating units, and so on. Bringing a background noise suppressor on location to reduce broad-band noise is a good idea (see 14-15). Although the point has been made before, it bears repeating: Most background noise, once it becomes part of a recording, is difficult if not impossible to remove without altering the sound quality of the program material.

Processor and power supply/control units

Remote control

14-15 Background noise suppressor. In this modular system, low- and high-frequency faders adjust the amount of noise suppression above and below dominant midfrequency signals such as dialogue. A control also permits varying the preset operating level for recording at unusually high or low levels, although overall gain of the unit remains fixed. A remote-controlled module can be operated up to 50 feet from the control unit.

- Staged productions, such as commercials, sitcoms, and drama, are usually produced with postproduction in mind.

- The principal challenge during production is recording dialogue that is clear, intelligible, and as noise-free as possible. Sound effects are often handled during postproduction; music always is.

- Dramatizations on radio involve creating a "theater of the mind," using sound to impel the listener to "see" the action.

- To create perspective using one microphone in radio dramatization, performers are positioned at appropriate distances relative to the mic and to each other, as the dramatic action dictates.

- Using the multimicrophone technique in radio dramatization, perspective is created in the postproduction mix.

- Using the "single" microphone approach for stereo radio dramatizations, the coincident or near-coincident microphone arrays are employed. Coincident miking positions two microphones, usually directional (or a stereo mic), in virtually the same space, with their diaphragms located vertically on the same axis. Near-coincident miking positions two microphones, usually directional, horizontally on the same plane, angled a few inches apart.

- Recording dialogue on the set in multi- or single-camera production usually means employing a boom, body-mounted wireless, or plant microphone, or a combination of the three. The microphones of choice are usually the lavalier and shotgun capacitor mics.

- The main sonic difference between the boom and body-mounted microphones is perspective. The boom better reproduces the mic-to-source distances that are relative to the fields of view

of the shots. This helps maintain acoustic perspective between sound and picture. On the other hand, the body-mounted mic always picks up dialogue that is clear and present with a minimum of background sound, but sonic perspective remains the same regardless of a shot's focal length.

- Miking decisions are made in preproduction planning, during blocking, when the movements of performers and cameras are worked out.

- The challenge in operating a boom is to maintain aural perspective while simultaneously keeping the boom mic out of the picture and the performers in the mic's pickup pattern.

- Care must be taken when using a body mic to ensure that it is inconspicuous and that it does not pick up the sound of clothes rustle. Cotton does not make as much rustling sound as do synthetic fabrics.

- Plant, or fixed, microphones are positioned around a set to cover action that cannot easily be picked up with a boom or a body mic.

- Preproduction planning is essential in any production, but it is especially so when working in the field, away from the security and resources of the studio. Preproduction planning involves selecting a location; determining how to deal with unwanted sound; preparing, in advance, prerecorded material; and anticipating all the main and backup equipment needs.

- In production, taping the most intelligible, clearest, noise-free dialogue is the primary challenge of the production recordist, regardless of a director's intention to use it or redo it in postproduction.

- The value of noise reduction throughout the production process cannot be overemphasized, especially in relation to dialogue and field recording.

Music Production

The focus of this chapter is studio music production using the close-miking recording technique. There are two basic ways to record musical instruments: distant miking and close miking. ***Distant miking*** uses two or a few microphones to record an entire ensemble. ***Close miking*** places a microphone relatively close to each sound source or group of sound sources in an ensemble. Generally, distant miking is employed when all sounds or voicings are recorded at the same time and it is important to preserve the ensemble sound. Orchestral and choral music and certain types of jazz are examples of music that use distant miking. Distant miking attempts to reproduce the aural experience that audiences receive in live concerts and, therefore, is mostly employed outside the studio at concert sites.

The underlying concept of distant miking is often used in-studio, however, along with the close-miking technique, to enhance a recording with a more acoustically natural, open sound. But because the mic-to-source distances are less considerable, the technique is referred to as ***off-miking***. Off-miking is covered later in this chapter.

CLOSE MIKING

In studio recording, close miking is the technique of choice for a number of reasons: greater control in recording the nuances of each musical element; the sound from each instrument, and sonic leakage from other instruments, is better contained; in popular music, the difference in loudness between electric and acoustic instruments can be very difficult to balance with distant miking; much of pop music is played loudly, and close-miking helps prevent the music from being awash in reverberation. Reverberation, spatial positioning, and blend are added in the postproduction mixdown.

Most of the discussion that follows assumes the use of directional microphones. Remember that among the reasons for close miking are better sonic control of each instrument and reduced leakage. If acoustics and recording logistics permit, there are three good reasons why omnidirectional mics should not be overlooked: (1) The better omni capacitors have extraordinarily wide, flat response, particularly in the lower frequencies, and little or no off-axis coloration. (2) Omnis are not as subject to proximity effect, sibilance, plosives, and breathing sounds as are directional mics. (3) Because of the inverse square law, it is possible to close-mike with an omni and still reduce leakage if the instrument's sound-pressure level is high enough.

Before getting into specific applications of close miking, it will be helpful to keep in mind four principles:

■ The closer a microphone is to a sound source, the more detailed, intimate, drier, and, if proximity effect is a factor, bassier the sound; the farther a microphone is from a sound source, the more diffused, open, and ambient the sound.

■ The higher the frequency, the more directional the sound wave and, therefore, the mic pickup; the lower the frequency, the more omnidirectional the sound wave and mic pickup, regardless of the mic's directional pattern.

■ Although close miking may employ a number of mics, more may not always be better. Each additional microphone adds a little more noise to the system and means dealing with another input at the console.

■ Generally, large-diaphragm microphones are more suitable in reproducing low-frequency instruments, and small-diaphragm mics are more suitable in reproducing high-frequency instruments.

DRUMS

Perhaps no other instrument provides as many possibilities for microphone combinations, and therefore as much of a challenge, as the drums. Several different components make up a drum set— at least a bass drum, floor (low-pitched) tom-tom, medium and high (-pitched) tom-toms, snare drum, hi-hat cymbal, and two overhead cymbals (see Figure 15-1).

Characteristics

Drums consist of at least one membrane (drumhead) stretched over a cylinder and, usually, a second membrane that resonates with the struck head. Drums produce loud sound levels and steep transients. They are not considered pitched instruments, although drumheads can be tuned to a musical pitch, and the pitch relationships of the floor, medium, and high tom-toms must be maintained. Also, various sonic effects can be achieved by tuning the top and bottom heads to different tensions relative to each other.

It is important that tension be uniform across the head to produce a single pitch. When several pitches are produced simultaneously, the sonic result is dissonance.

Drums radiate sound perpendicular from the heads, particularly the top head. High-frequency transients are most pronounced on-axis, perpendicular to the point where the stick hits the drumhead. This is the sound responsible for most of the drum's "kick." Harmonics and overtones are produced from the tension rings, the shell, and the bottom head.

Bass (Kick) Drum   The bass drum is the lowest pitched of the drums. Its fundamental frequencies range from 30 to 147 Hz, with harmonics extending from 1 to 6 kHz. It is commonly called the *kick drum* because it is struck with a beater controlled by the drummer's foot. The drum stands on its side with the "top," or beater, head facing the drummer. The "bottom" head is usually removed or has a hole cut into it because of the low-frequency resonances and very steep

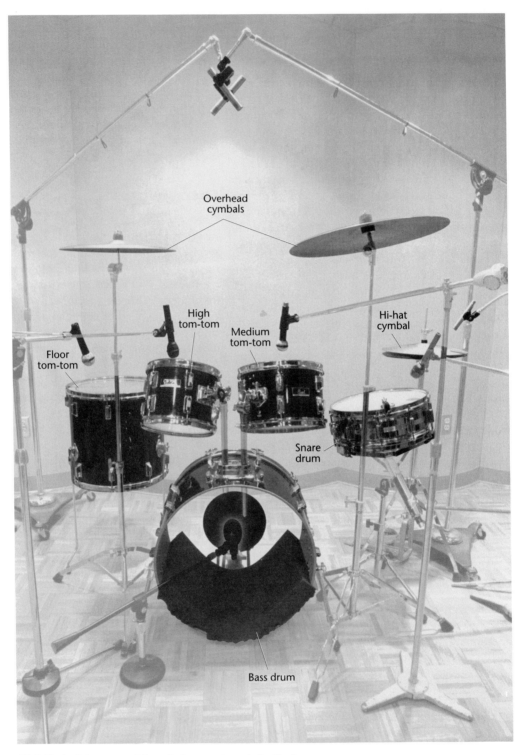

15-1 Typical drum set with each drum and cymbal miked

transients that the drum can generate. Most of the drum's low frequencies are emitted omnidirectionally, though vibrations from the shell and heads resonate throughout the instrument.

Tom-toms

Tom-toms come in a variety of sizes and pitches and usually have two heads. They produce the steep transients and radiating characteristics common to most drums. Lower-pitched toms generate more-omnidirectional waves; higher-pitched toms generate more-directional waves. Because tom-toms are often used to accent a piece, they are tuned to have more sustain than the kick and snare drums.

Snare Drum

The snare can be characterized as a tom-tom tuned to a higher pitch and with less sustain. Fundamental frequencies range from 100 to 200 Hz, with harmonics that extend from 1 to 15 kHz. The major difference between a tom-tom and a snare drum are the chainlike *snares,* stretched across the bottom head of the instrument, that give the drum its name, characteristic crispness, and high-frequency cutting power.

Cymbals

Cymbals are usually round, metal plates shaped like a flattened bell. They may be struck with a hard, wooden drumstick, a soft mallet, or brushes. The type of striker used is largely responsible for the sound produced. Unlike drums, cymbals have a long decay. The harder the striker, the more high frequencies of the transients are produced. A cymbal tends to radiate sound perpendicular to its surface, with a ringing resonance near its edge.

A cymbal's pitch is determined by, among other things, size and thickness. Cymbals are also designed to produce different textures, the ring of the ride cymbal or the splash of the crash cymbal to name two common examples.

Generally, their fundamentals range from 300 to 587 Hz. Harmonics extend from 1 to 15 kHz.

Hi-hat Cymbal

The hi-hat cymbal is actually two cymbals with the open end of the bells facing each other. A foot pedal, controlled by the drummer, raises and lowers the top cymbal to strike the bottom cymbal, or the top cymbal is struck with a drumstick, or both. Different timbres are generated by varying the pressure and distance between the two cymbals. The hi-hat is integral to the drum sound both for its high frequencies that "cut through" a recording and as a timekeeper. For these reasons the high-frequency transients perpendicular to the contact point and the shimmer from the edges are important.

Tuning the Drums

A good drum sound begins with the musicianship of the drummer and the quality and tuning of the drum set. No miking technique will save the drum sound of an incompetent drummer or a low-quality drum set.

Therefore, before drums are miked, they must be tuned. Tuning the drum set is important to the sound of individual drums and also to the overall drum sound. Many studios have their own in-house drum set always tuned and ready to go, not only to ensure the desired drum sound but also to avoid having this necessary and time-consuming procedure cut into recording time.

As you might expect, there are many ways to tune a drum set: in fifths and octaves; in thirds; by tapping on the sides of the drum, finding its fundamental pitch, and then tuning the head to it; or by pitching the bass drum low enough to leave room in the upper bass and midrange for the tom-toms and snare drum. If the bass drum is pitched too high, it pushes too close to the toms, which in turn get pushed too close to the snare drum, making the drum sound smaller. Moreover, by not separating the individual drum sounds, little room is left for such instruments as the bass and guitar.

One problem with even the best of drum sets is ringing. Damping the drums helps to reduce ringing, and undesirable overtones as well. To damp a bass drum, place a pillow, blanket, foam rubber cushion, or the like inside the drum (see 15-2). To damp a tom-tom and snare, tape a cotton or gauze pad near the edge of the drumhead so it is not in the way of the drumstick. Specially made drum silencers are also available (see 15-6). Because many drummers do not care to have things taped to their drums, another effective way to damp them is with O-rings placed inside the drumhead.

Make sure the damping does not muffle the drum sound. It helps to leave one edge of the damping material untaped so it is free to vibrate. To reduce cymbal ringing, apply masking tape from the underside of the bell to the rim in narrow radial strips or use specially made cymbal silencers.

Where the drum set is placed in a studio also affects its sound. Isolated in a drum booth (to reduce leakage into other instruments' microphones), the overall sound takes on the acoustic properties of the booth: If the booth is live, the drums will sound live; if it is absorptive, the drums will sound tight or dull. On a hard floor, the drums sound live and bright; on a carpet they sound tighter and drier. In a corner they sound boomier, because the dominant lower frequencies are more concentrated. Often drums are put on a riser that can resonate to reduce low-end leakage.

Miking

Although the drum set consists of several different-sounding instruments, it must be miked so that they sound good individually and blend as a unit. Having said this, drums are miked in many ways. The approach you take depends on both how much sound control you want and what type of music you are recording. Explaining how to deal with sound control is relatively easy: The more components you want to regulate, the more mics you use (although this can have its drawbacks—possible phasing, for one). Achieving a particular drum sound for a certain type of music involves many variables and is more difficult to explain.

Generally, in rock-and-roll and contemporary music, producers like a tight drum sound for added punch and attack. Because this usually requires complete control of the drum sound, they tend to use several microphones for the drums. In jazz many styles are loose and open; hence, producers are more likely to use fewer drum mics to achieve an airier sound.

Bass (Kick) Drum The bass (kick) drum is the foundation of the drum set, because it provides the bottom sound that, along with the bass guitar,

supports the other musical elements. Because the bass drum also produces high levels of sound pressure and steep transients, large-diaphragm moving-coil microphones usually work best. That said, there are a few large-diaphragm capacitor mics that also work well, particularly by adding some midrange coloration.

As for mic placement, the common technique is to use the hole often cut in the front drumhead or remove it entirely and place the mic inside. This usually gives the sound of the bass drum more punch. Pointing the mic perpendicular to the back drumhead produces a fuller sound (see 15-2), and pointing it toward the side of the drum picks up more of the drum's overtones (see 15-3). Placing

15-2 A directional microphone pointed at the drumhead produces a fuller sound. Foam rubber padding is placed in the drum to reduce vibration.

15-3 A microphone pointed to the side of the drum produces more of the drum's overtones

Part Four: Production

the mic close to the beater picks up the hard beater sound and, if you are not careful, the action of the beater pedal as well.

Drum mics are usually directional to increase sound separation and reduce leakage from the rest of the drum set, though an omnidirectional mic can be effective in a bass drum. Placing the mic in close proximity to a loud sound source usually prevents leakage from the other drums (remember the inverse square law). To separate the bass drum even more, use a low-pass filter, shelving, or parametric equalizer to cut off or reduce frequencies above its upper range. Be careful, though—the perceived punch of the bass drum goes into the midrange frequencies. In fact, boosting from 1,600 to 5,000 Hz adds a brighter, sharper snap to the bass drum sound. The dull, thuddy, cardboard sound the bass drum tends to produce can be alleviated by attenuating between 300 and 600 Hz.

A word about equalizing during recording: First, equalization should not be used as a substitute for good microphone technique or to correct poor mic technique. Second, if you must equalize, make sure you know exactly what you are doing. Even if mistakes in equalizing during recording can be undone in the mixdown, the additional noise and possibly distortion created in passing a signal through an electronic device cannot.

Tom-toms Tom-toms come in a variety of sizes and pitches. Typical drum sets have three toms: the low-pitched, fuller-sounding floor tom; the middle-pitched medium tom, and the higher-pitched, sharper-sounding high tom.

Although toms produce loud transients (all drums do), they are not as strong as those the bass drum produces; you can therefore mike them with moving-coil, capacitor, or the more rugged ribbon mics. Placement, as always, depends on the sound you want. Generally, the mic is placed from 1 to 10 inches above the tom and is aimed at the center of the skin. It is usually mounted just over the edge of the rim to avoid interfering with the drummer's sticks (see 15-4 and 15-5).

The mic-to-source distance depends on the low-frequency content desired from the drum sound itself. If it has little low-frequency content, place

15-4 Miking a floor tom

15-5 Miking the high tom (left) and medium tom (right)

a directional mic with proximity effect close to the drum skin to boost the lower frequencies. Placing a mic inside the drum gives the best isolation, but it also produces a closed, dull sound. Whatever technique you use, remember that the sonic relationships of the toms must be maintained; using the same make and model of microphone on each tom helps.

Snare Drum   Of all the components in a drum set, the snare usually presents the biggest problem in miking. Most producers prefer a crisp snare drum sound. Miking the snare drum too close tends to produce a lifeless sound, whereas miking it too far away tends to pick up annoying overtones, ringing, and leakage from the other drums.

Another problem is that the snare drum sometimes sounds dull and thuddy. In this instance the problem is most likely the drum itself. Two ways to add crispness to the sound are to use a mic with a high-frequency boost or to equalize it at the console. Boosting at around 4,000 to 5,000 Hz adds crispness and attack. The better alternatives are to retune the drum set and, if that does not work, to replace the drumhead(s).

Moving-coil or capacitor microphones work well on the snare drum; the moving-coil mic tends to give it a harder edge, and the capacitor mic tends to make it sound richer or crisper. To find the optimal mic position, begin at a point 6 to 10 inches from the drumhead and aim the mic so that its pickup pattern is split between the head and the side of the drum (see 15-6). This picks up the sounds of the snares and the stick hitting the head. To get the snares' buzz and the slight delay of the snares' snap, use two mics: one over and one under the drum (see 15-7).

15-6 Miking a snare drum. The pad on the skin of the drum reduces vibrations.

15-7 Miking a snare drum over and under

15-8 Miking the hi-hat cymbal and the snare drum

15-9 Miking over the hi-hat cymbal

Hi-hat Cymbal The hi-hat cymbal produces two sounds: a clap and a shimmer. Depending on how important these accents are to the music, the hi-hat can either share the snare drum's mic or have a microphone of its own. If it shares, place the mic between the hi-hat and the snare and adjust the sound balance through placement of the mic (see 15-8).

If the hi-hat has a separate mic, the two most common positions for it are 4 to 6 inches above the center stem with the mic pointing straight down (see 15-9), and off the edge (see 15-10). Sound is brightest over the edge of the cymbal. Miking too close off the center produces ringing, and miking off the edge may pick up the rush of air produced each time the two cymbals clap together (see 15-11). Equalize by rolling off the bass to reduce low-frequency leakage, but only if the hi-hat is miked separately. If the mic is shared with the snare drum, rolling off the bass adversely affects the low-end sound of the snare.

Overhead Cymbals Two types of overhead cymbals are the ride, which produces ring and shimmer, and the crash, which has a splashy sound. In miking either cymbal, the definition of the characteristic sounds must be preserved. To this end, capacitors usually work best; and for stereo pickup, the coincident, near-coincident (see 15-1), or spaced pair can be used (see 15-12 ; see also

15-10 Miking at the edge of the hi-hat cymbal

15-11 A mic aimed at the point where the cymbals clap may pick up the rush of air as they come together

15-12 A spaced pair of directional microphones to pick up the sound of the overhead cymbals and add spaciousness to the overall sound of the drum set

"Off-Miking" later in this chapter). When using the spaced pair, remember to observe the three-to-one rule to avoid phasing problems.

Because the overhead microphones usually blend the sounds of the entire drum set, they must be at least a few feet above the cymbals. If they are too close to the cymbals, the drum blend will be poor and the mics will pick up annoying overtones that sound like ringing or gonging, depending on the narrowness of the mic's pickup pattern. If blending the drum sound is being left until the mixdown, and it is important to isolate the cymbals—roll off the low frequencies reaching the cymbal microphones from the other drums.

ACOUSTIC STRING INSTRUMENTS

Acoustic string instruments derive their sound from stretched strings, held taught in a frame, that are set into vibratory motion by being bowed, plucked, or struck. As strings do not produce much loudness, the frame, which also vibrates with the strings, serves to amplify and radiate sound. Three variables help determine the pitch of a vibrating string: length, tension, and mass, or thickness.

Plucked String Instruments

Plucked string instruments include the guitar, banjo, and mandolin.

Characteristics

Because the six-string guitar is clearly the most popular of the plucked string instruments, it is considered here. The guitar's six strings are stretched across a hollow body with a flat top and sound hole that resonates the fundamental frequencies and harmonics of the vibrating strings. Fundamental frequencies range from 82 to 988 Hz, with harmonics extending from 1 to 15 kHz.

The guitar has a fingerboard with raised metal frets that divide the effective length of the strings into exact intervals as the strings are pressed down onto the frets. Where the guitar string is plucked affects sound quality because of the relationship between the distance from the point of contact to the ends of the strings. For example, a string plucked close to the bridge contains more high-frequency energy due to the relatively short distance between the point of contact and the bridge. A string plucked farther from the bridge produces a warmer sound due to the presence of longer wavelengths and, therefore, lower frequencies.

Overall, most high frequencies are near the bridge. The joint between the neck and body produces more lower frequencies; and the most lower frequencies are resonated by the back of the guitar and are generated from the sound hole.

What the strings are made of and what is used to pluck them also affect a guitar's sound quality. For example, metal strings tend to sound brighter than nylon, and a string plucked with a pick will be brighter than one plucked with the finger.

Miking

Because most of a guitar's sound radiates from the front of the instrument, centering a microphone off the middle of the sound hole should, theoretically, provide balanced sound. But if a mic is too close to the hole, sound is bassy or boomy. If it is moved closer to the bridge, detail is lost. If it is moved closer to the neck, presence is reduced; if it is moved farther away, intimacy is affected. On the other hand, if a guitar lacks bottom, mike closer to the sound hole; if it lacks highs, mike closer to the bridge; to increase midrange, aim a mic at the neck.

Plucking creates quick attacks. Using a dynamic mic, which has slower transient response than a capacitor microphone, can slow the attacks and diminish detail, particularly in the guitar's bass

frequencies. But if a capacitor mic brings out too much crispness, a good moving-coil microphone can reduce it. Dozens, perhaps hundreds, of methods have been used to mike the guitar. A few general techniques are discussed here, but keep in mind that many factors affect a guitar's sound, as just noted.

One way to achieve a natural, balanced sound is to position the microphone about 1 to 3 feet from the sound hole. To set a more high- or low-frequency accent, angle the mic either down toward the high strings or up toward the low strings. To brighten the natural sound, place the microphone above the bridge and even with the front of the guitar, because most high-frequency energy is radiated from a narrow lobe at right angles to the top plate (see 15-13 and 15-14). Miking off the twelfth fret, across the strings, produces a sound rich in harmonics.

Another way to achieve natural sound is to place a microphone about 8 to 12 inches above the guitar, 1 to 2 feet away, aimed between the hole and the

15-13 Miking an acoustic guitar. Aiming a microphone at the center of the guitar hole 2 to 3 feet away produces a sound with balanced highs, middles, and lows.

15-14 Miking an acoustic guitar. A microphone placed about 6 inches above the bridge and even with the front of the guitar brightens the natural sound of the instrument.

bridge. A good-quality capacitor mic reduces excess bottom and warms the sound.

A microphone perpendicular to the sound hole about 8 inches away reduces leakage from other instruments but adds bassiness. Rolling off the bass creates a more natural sound. If isolation is critical, move the microphone closer to the sound hole. In this position bassiness increases and sound becomes boomy or muddy; bass roll-off definitely would be needed.

A microphone about 4 to 8 inches from the front of the bridge creates a warm, mellow sound, but the sound lacks detail; this lack is beneficial if pickup and string noises are problematic.

For a classical guitar, which requires acoustic interaction, place the microphone more than 3 feet from the sound hole. Make sure mic-to-source distance is not too great, or the subtleties of the instrument will be diminished.

Clipping a microphone to the tip of the sound hole facing in toward the center or placing the microphone inside the guitar gives good isolation and added resonance. A mic attached inside the sound hole also reproduces more bass and less string noise.

A natural part of the sound of most plucked string instruments is the screechy, rubbing noises called *fret* sounds caused by the musician's fingering. Fret noises, which are a natural part of the instrument's sound, usually bring to a head the issue of whether they should be part of the recording. Personal taste is the determining factor. If you do not care for the fret sounds, mike farther from the instrument or use a supercardioid or hypercardioid mic placed at a slight angle to the neck of the instrument. This puts the mic's dead side facing the frets. Make sure the mic's angle is not too severe, or the sound from the instrument will be off-mic. There are also strings specially designed to reduce finger noises and sprays to reduce friction.

Bowed String Instruments

The well-known bowed string instruments are the violin, viola, cello, and bass.

Characteristics

Bowed string instruments are similar to plucked string instruments in that their strings are stretched across a fingerboard and hollow body, which resonates the vibrating strings. But bowed instruments have only four strings and no metal frets on the fingerboard; intervals are determined by the placement of the musician's fingers on the fingerboard. Another difference is that the strings are vibrated using a bow drawn across the strings, thereby generating a smoother attack than that of a plucked string. The bridge in a bowed instrument is connected to a top plate through a sound post to the back plate. It is important to the overall sound, as are the *f*-holes in the top plate that allow the air inside the body to resonate. The dynamic range of bowed string instruments is not as wide as that of most other orchestral instruments, nor is their projection as strong (see 15-15).

Violin   The four violin strings are tuned to perfect fifths and have a fundamental frequency range of 196 to 3,136 Hz, with harmonics that extend from 4 to 15 kHz. The violin radiates lower frequencies in a roughly spherical pattern. As frequencies get higher, the violin radiates frequencies about evenly in the front and back, as both the top plate and the back plate are designed to resonate with the strings. The highest frequencies are radiated upward from the top plate.

Viola   The viola is essentially a larger, lower-pitched version of the violin. The strings are tuned a fifth lower than the violin; their fundamental frequency range is 131 to 1,175 Hz, with harmonics that extend from 2 to 8.5 kHz. The radiating pattern is similar to that of the violin, but is less directional due to its lower frequency range.

Cello   The cello's strings are tuned a full octave below the viola, with a fundamental frequency range of 65 to 698 Hz and harmonics that extend from 1 to 6.5 kHz. The cello's radiating pattern is more omnidirectional than directional, but it is affected by the playing position. The cello rests on

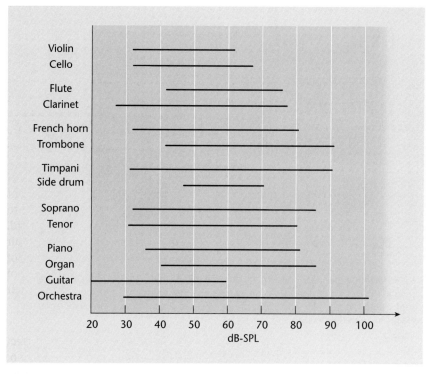

15-15 Dynamic range of selected musical sound sources

a rubber- or plastic-tipped spike that is set on the floor. Hence, vibrations are transmitted to the floor, which reflects and absorbs the sound waves to some degree, depending on the sound absorption coefficient of the floor's material.

Bass The bass strings are tuned in fourths rather than fifths and have a fundamental range from 41 to 294 Hz, with harmonics extending from 1 to 5 kHz. It radiates sound omnidirectionally and, because it is positioned like the cello, the sound is affected by the floor's material.

Miking

Because the dynamic range of bowed string instruments is not wide, sound has to be reinforced by using several instruments or multiple miking, or both, depending on the size of the sound required. Overdubbing is another method used to reinforce string sound. The need for reinforcement is compounded by the dearth of competent string players in many communities, to say nothing of the cost of hiring very many of them where they do exist in sufficient numbers.

Individually, miking a violin or viola a few feet above the instrument, aiming the mic at the front face, produces an open, natural sound, assuming fairly live acoustics (see 15-16). Although sound radiation is uniform up to 500 Hz, depending on the microphone, a single mic may not hear sufficient low end and therefore not reproduce a robust sound. Miking "over and under" ensures that the highs, which are concentrated above 500 Hz and radiate perpendicularly to the sound board, are picked up from above the instrument and the lows are picked up from both above and below. This technique also tends to make one instrument sound like a few and a few sound like several (see 15-17). Overdubbing will accomplish this with greater effectiveness, however.

15-16 Miking a violin or viola. (a) Placing the mic several feet above the instrument, aimed at the front face, tends to produce an open, natural sound. (b) To produce a country fiddle sound, place the microphone closer to the bridge but not close enough to interfere with the bowing.

15-17 Enlarging the sound of a violin or viola. Place one microphone several feet above the instrument(s) and one microphone below the instrument(s). This tends to make one instrument sound like a few and a few sound like several.

Miking a few inches from the side or above the strings of a violin produces a country fiddle sound; the closer a microphone is to the strings, the coarser or scratchier the sound. But take care not to interfere with the musician's bowing when close-miking over bowed instruments.

Generally, for either the cello or the acoustic bass, miking off the bridge 2 to 3 feet produces a brighter sound, and miking off the *f*-hole produces a fuller sound. The right contact mic placed behind the bridge produces a tight, robust sound (see 15-18). The wrong contact mic can produce a closed, dull sound.

With a plucked bass, used in jazz, some producers like to clip a mic to the bridge or *f*-hole for a more robust sound. A danger with this technique is getting a thin, midrange-heavy sound instead. Close-miking a plucked bass picks up the attack. If close-miking also produces too boomy a sound,

compress the bass slightly or roll off some of the low end, but beware of altering the characteristic low-frequency sound of the instrument.

Capacitor and ribbon microphones work particularly well with bowed string instruments. Capacitor mics enrich the string sound and enhance detail. Ribbon mics produce a resonant, warm quality, although there may be some loss of high-end detail. As for plucked strings, capacitors are preferred because of their excellent transient response.

Clip-on and contact microphones are other alternatives in miking bowed string instruments. Assuming the musician does not mind having a mic attached to the instrument, clip-on and contact mics tend to produce a harsher sound when placed near the bridge and a resonant, but closed, sound when attached to the body of the instrument. A better approach to this type of miking is the so-called *symphonic microphone system,* a noninvasive

15-18 Three ways to mike a cello or bass. (a) Off the bridge produces a brighter sound. (b) Off the *f*-hole produces a fuller sound. (c) A contact mic behind the strings, near or at the bridge, taped to the body of the instrument, produces a more resonant sound, which could also be dull and devoid of harmonics.

system designed to put a mic inside string instruments, connected through the end pin. The air motion inside the instrument creates a more natural sound than does a clip-on or contact mic vibrating against the instrument.

Struck String Instruments: Piano

The best known example of a struck string instrument is the piano.

Characteristics

The piano's strings are stretched across a bridge attached to a soundboard that resonates in sympathy with the vibrating strings after they are struck. The strings are struck by hammers controlled by the keys on the keyboard. The strings continue to vibrate until the key is released and a damper stops the vibration of the string. The piano's fundamental frequency and dynamic ranges are quite wide (see inside front cover and Figure 15-15).

Radiation is generally perpendicular to the soundboard, primarily upward in a grand piano. The lower-frequency strings are more omnidirectional; the higher-frequency strings are located closer to an axis perpendicular to the sound board. The lid is also a factor in a piano's sound radiation, but directionality depends on the angle at which the lid is open.

Because of the percussive nature of the key striking the strings, timbre is affected by how hard the string is struck. Higher harmonics are more present in strings that are struck hard. Strings struck more gently produce a warmer sound.

Miking

The piano offers almost unlimited possibilities for sound shaping. Perhaps more than with many other instruments, the character of the piano sound is dependent on the quality of the piano itself. Smaller grand pianos may have dull, wooden low-end response. Old or abused pianos may sound dull or ring or thump. Steinways, generally, are built to produce a lyrical sound. Yamahas produce crisp sound with more attack. The Bosendorfer aims for additional sonority by adding semitones in the bass range. Mic technique and signal processing cannot change a piano's voicing from dull to bright, from thin to rich, or from sharp to smooth, but they can alter a piano's existing sound.

Another factor in piano miking is the music. Classical music and jazz generally require a more open sound and, therefore, mic placement and pickup should capture the full sonic radiation of the instrument. Popular music, such as rock and country, requires a more closed sound, so mic placement and pickup are generally closer and tighter.

There are several common miking techniques for the grand piano (see 15-19) and the upright piano (see 15-20). The techniques displayed in Figure 15-19 are among the common ones used in miking a grand piano and address the fact that you have to be some distance from the piano to get its full sound—close distances yield only partial sound—because its dynamic range can be so wide. In studio recording, however, there is the additional problem of leakage in the piano mics from other instruments, thus necessitating closer mic-to-source distances. Because there is more piano sound across the bridge–rail axis than horizontally along the keyboard, by miking along the piano instead of across it reproduces a more spacious, full-bodied sound (see 15-21). But a clear low-end/high-end stereo image is sacrificed because the sound is more blended.

WOODWINDS

Just as the vibrating string is the acoustical foundation of string instruments, a vibrating column of air is the foundation of woodwind (and brass) instruments. All wind instruments have in common a tube, or cone, through which air is blown, generating a standing wave of vibrating air within. In woodwinds the vibrations are produced in the clarinet and saxophone using one reed, in

15-19 Miking the grand piano. (a) A middle-side (MS) microphone high over the sound board, with the lid off, and aimed toward the midrange strings picks up the piano's direct and indirect radiations in a balanced, and relatively spacious, low-end to high-end stereo image (assuming proper acoustics). (b) For a more spacious stereo image, an X-Y pair of near-coincident mics can be employed. One popular coincident microphone technique is the ORTF (Office de Radiodiffusion-Television Française, the French broadcasting system) array. It spaces the X-Y pair just under 7 inches apart at a 110-degree angle, 55 degrees to the left and right of center. Whatever the distance between the mics, the imaging from the low to midrange to high frequencies must be balanced. (c) When the piano lid remains attached, in addition to the main microphone array, off-miking can be used to pick up more of the indirect reflections from the bounce off the lid. The off-mics can either be spaced, which reproduces a more spacious stereo image than the near-coincident array, or they can be arrayed in an X-Y pattern. (d) If acoustics permit, the off-mics placed several feet from the piano can serve as the main pair. A problem with using spaced microphones is that the wider the spacing, the less mono-compatible the sound. In all of these arrays, a few insurance mics placed on the floor under the piano's sound board can help ensure that the full range of the instrument's radiations is captured.

15-20 Miking an upright piano. (a) For mono, position a mic over an open top for a natural sound, or behind the sound board for a fuller, tubby sound. (b) For stereo, position two microphones, one for low-end pickup and the other for high-end pickup, over an open top or behind the sound board. Mics also can be placed inside the piano to pick up the hammer sound. When spacing the mics, remember the three-to-one rule.

15-21 Miking across the bridge–rail axis. This produces a spacious, full-bodied sound, but at the expense of low-end/high-end stereo imaging.

the oboe and bassoon using a double reed, and in the flute and piccolo by blowing across the air hole.

Characteristics

The sounds of woodwinds are determined by the length of the tube, whether the tube is open at one end (clarinet) or at both ends (flute), and by the opening and closing of the holes in the tube. A tube open at one end has odd-number harmonics: third, fifth, seventh, and so on. A tube open at both ends, and flared or conical tubes (oboe and bassoon), has the normal harmonics: second, third, fourth, fifth, and so on. The vibrating reed and sound holes generate their own overtones. In general, higher frequencies radiate from the bell, and lower frequencies radiate from the holes.

Flute   The flute is a tube that is held horizontally. The musician blows air across a sound hole and controls pitch and timbre by varying the blowing force. Pitch is also determined by opening and closing the holes in the side of the instrument. Sound radiates from the sound hole, the side holes, and the end of the flute. Fundamental frequencies range from 261 to 2,349 Hz, and harmonics extend from 3 to 8 kHz. Its dynamic range is limited.

Clarinet   The clarinet is a single-reed tube played almost vertically, with the bell pointed toward the floor. Its fundamental frequency range is 165 to 1,568 Hz, with harmonics extending from 2 to 10 kHz. Sound is generated from the mouthpiece and reed, the side holes, and the bell. Reflections from the floor also may affect the clarinet's sound.

Oboe and Bassoon   The fundamental frequencies of the oboe and bassoon are 261 to 1,568 and 62 to 587 Hz, with harmonics extending from 2 to 12 kHz and 1 to 7 kHz, respectively. Both instruments, despite their relatively narrow frequency response and limited dynamic range, are comparatively rich in harmonics and overtones. The oboe's sound emanates from the mouthpiece and reed, sound holes, and bell. Like the clarinet, it is played aimed at the floor and

may also be affected by sound that is absorbed by and/or reflected from the floor. The bassoon curves upward at its bottom, pointing toward the ceiling. If the ceiling is high enough, the bassoon's overall sound is usually not affected.

Saxophone   The family of saxophones includes the soprano, alto, tenor, and baritone. Saxophones have a conical shape with a bell that curves upward (except for the soprano saxophone, which may be straight). The saxophone's sound radiates mostly from the bell, but the sound holes also generate significant detail. Fundamental frequency ranges are roughly as follows: soprano—200 to 1,100 Hz; alto—138 to 820 Hz; tenor—100 to 600 Hz; and baritone—80 to 400 Hz.

Miking

Woodwind instruments, such as the flute, clarinet, and oboe, are among the weaker-sounding instruments and have a limited dynamic range. Alto, tenor, and baritone saxophones are stronger sounding. But the higher-pitched woodwinds—flute, clarinet, and soprano saxophone—can cut through the sound of more-powerful instruments if miking and blending are not properly attended to (or if the sound designer intends it).

Because most woodwinds are not powerful instruments, the tendency is to close-mike them, but, due to their sound radiation, this results in an uneven pickup. They should be miked far enough away so that the pickup sounds blended and natural.

Because the flute and piccolo (a smaller, higher-pitched version of the flute) radiate sound in shifting patterns sideways and from the instruments' end hole, close miking, or, worse, contact miking, tends to miss certain frequencies and emphasize others. Moreover, dry, less reverberant sound can distort some tonalities.

For the flute, mic-to-source distance depends on the music. For classical music it should be about 3 to 8 feet; for pop music, about 6 to 24 inches. Microphone positioning should start slightly above the player, between the mouthpiece and the bell. To add the breathy quality of the blowing sound, mike toward the mouthpiece—how close depends on how much breath sound you want. If breath noise is a problem regardless of where the mic is placed, and you want to eliminate it, try placing the microphone behind the player's head, aiming it at the finger holes (see 15-22). This technique also reduces high-frequency content. A windscreen or pop filter reduces unwanted breath noise, too. In miking a flute or any woodwind, be careful not to pick up the sound of the key action.

Microphone positioning for the clarinet and oboe must take into account the narrowing of high frequencies radiating in the vertical plane in front of the player, as well as floor reflections from the bell being aimed downward. Close miking tends to emphasize these disparities. If close miking is unavoidable, position the mic to the side of the bell rather than straight at it. This should smooth most of the sonic anomalies. Miking off the bell also tends to reduce leakage and makes the sound brighter and harder. Another possibility is to mike toward the bottom third of the instrument and far enough away to blend the pickup from the finger holes and bell (see 15-23).

15-22 Miking flute and piccolo. (a) Placing a microphone over the finger holes nearer the end of the instrument picks up most of the sounds these instruments emit and does not pick up the breathy sounds that miking the mouthpiece produces. (b) Some producers feel that these sounds are part of the instruments' overall aural character, however, and mike the mouthpiece to produce a thinner-textured sound. (c) If unwanted breath sounds persist, place the microphone behind the musician's head and aimed at the finger holes.

15-23 Miking clarinet and oboe. Place a microphone over the finger holes toward the bottom third, because most of the sounds come from this part of the instrument. In miking the keys of any instrument, avoid close mic-to-source distances; otherwise, the sound of the moving keys will be heard.

15-24 Miking a saxophone. Aiming a microphone at the holes from above the bell produces a natural, blended sax sound. Miking too close to the instrument may pick up blowing, spit, or key sounds.

Saxophones radiate more sound from the bell and some sound from the holes. But the proportion of sound radiating from holes and bell constantly changes as the keys open and close. Miking saxophones off the bell produces a bright, thin, hard sound. Miking too close to the bell further accentuates the high frequencies, making the sound piercing or screechy. Miking off the finger holes adds fullness, presence, and warmth. Aiming a microphone at the holes from above the bell produces a natural, more blended sound (see 15-24).

BRASS

Brass instruments—trumpet, trombone, baritone, tuba, and French horn—generally are conical and have a cup-shaped mouthpiece that acts as a vibrating "reed" when the musician blows into it.

They are the loudest acoustic musical instruments with the widest dynamic range (see 15-15).

Characteristics

Trumpet The fundamental frequency range of the trumpet is 165 to 988 Hz, with harmonics extending from 1 to 7.5 kHz. In addition to the sound control by lip pressure and tension at the mouthpiece, a series of three valves is used to vary the tube length and, hence, the pitches. Most of the sound radiates from the bell, with higher frequencies located on an axis closer to the center of the bell.

Trombone The trombone is the orchestra's most powerful instrument. Its distinctive feature is a slide that is moved in and out to vary the length of the tube and change pitches. (Some trombone models use valves instead of a slide.) The fundamental frequency range is 73 to 587 Hz, with harmonics and a radiation pattern similar to that of the trumpet.

Tuba The tuba is lowest-pitched of the brass instruments, with a fundamental frequency range of 49 to 587 Hz and harmonics extending from 1 to 4 kHz. It uses valves to vary its effective length and emits sounds upward from a wide, curved bell. Higher-frequency harmonics are present at the axis of the bell although, to a live audience, they are not a recognizable component of the tuba's sound because they are generated upward. Most of a tuba's distinctive bass sound is radiated omnidirectionally.

French Horn The French horn is a curved, cone-shaped tube with a wide bell and valves that is played with the bell pointed to the side, or behind, the musician, often with the musician's hand inside the bell for muting. The instrument's sound is therefore not closely related to what the live audience hears. Its fundamental range is relatively narrow—87 to 880 Hz, with harmonics extending from 1 to 6 kHz—but the French horn's sound can cut through the sound of louder instruments with wider frequency response.

Miking

Brass instruments require care in microphone placement and careful attention in adjusting levels at the console, because of their loudness and dynamic range. They also emit the most directional sound; high-frequency harmonics radiate directly out of the bell. But the most distinctive frequencies of the trumpet and trombone are around 1,200 Hz and 700 Hz, respectively, which are radiated from the sides of the bell. Below 500 Hz, radiation tends to become omnidirectional. Therefore, close-miking brass instruments with a directional microphone does not quite produce their full frequency response. A directional mic close to and in front of the bell produces a bright, biting quality. Miking at an angle to the bell or on-axis to the side of the bell produces a more natural, mellower, more hornlike sound (see 15-25).

About 1 to 5 feet is a good working mic-to-source distance. Closer placement gives a tighter sound, although miking too close to a brass instrument could pick up spit and valve sounds. More-distant placement makes the sound fuller and more emphatic.

For the French horn, a mic-to-source distance of at least 5 feet is recommended. It is not the most powerful brass instrument but, as noted above, it can cut through and overwhelm louder instruments, and its levels fluctuate considerably. To increase control and minimize French horn leakage, move the instrument away from the ensemble (see 15-26).

In miking brass sections, trumpets and trombones should be blended as a chorus. One microphone for each pair of instruments produces a natural, balanced sound and provides flexibility in the mixdown. If you try to pick up more than two trumpets or trombones with a single mic, it has to be far enough from the instruments to blend them, and the acoustics have to support the technique. Of course, leakage will occur. Mike baritones and tubas individually from above (see 15-27).

15-25 Miking off the bell. Mike trumpets, trombones, baritones, and tubas at an angle to the bell for a natural, mellower sound, being careful to avoid close mic-to-source distances so that air flow and spit sounds are not heard. Miking in front of the bell produces a brighter sound.

15-26 Miking the French horn. (a) To control leakage, place the musician away from the ensemble and the microphone near a soft baffle pointing at the bell. (b) If this arrangement creates a blending problem due to the French horn's lack of presence, placing a hard baffle a few feet from the bell should carry the sound to the mic in sufficient proportions.

15-27 Miking the baritone and tuba from above the bell

The type of microphone you use also helps shape the sound of brass. The moving coil can smooth transient response; the ribbon can add a fuller, warmer tonality; and the capacitor can produce accurate transient response.

ELECTRIC INSTRUMENTS

Electric instruments—bass, guitar, keyboards— generate their sound through an electric pickup that can be sent to an amplifier or directly to the console.

Three techniques are generally used to record an electric instrument: (1) plugging the instrument into an amplifier and placing a mic in front of the amp's loudspeaker, (2) *direct insertion (D.I.),* or plugging the instrument directly into the mic input of the console through a direct box, or (3) both miking the amp and using direct insertion.

Electric instruments are usually high impedance, whereas professional-quality audio equipment is low impedance. Not surprisingly, high- and low-impedance equipment are incompatible and produce sonic horrors if connected. The direct box is a device that matches impedances, thus making the output of the instrument compatible with the console's input (see 15-28).

Although this chapter deals with the close-miking technique, it is important to know the differences between miking an amp and going direct. Deciding which method to use is a matter of taste, practicality, and convenience (see Tables 15-1 and 15-2).

15-28 Direct box. A direct box has an isolated transformer that is less vulnerable to damage, distortion, grounding problems, volume loss, and changes in tone quality. This particular direct box can be battery- or phantom-powered. To improve sound quality further, many direct boxes are transformerless.

Table 15-1 Advantages and disadvantages of miking an amplifier loudspeaker

Advantages	Disadvantages
Adds interaction of room acoustics to sound	Could leak into other mics
Captures more midbass for added punch	Could be noisy due to electrical problems with amp
Creates potential for different sound textures	Level of amp can make it difficult for musicians to hear less powerful instruments
Gives musician greater control over an instrument's sound output	Distortion
Permits other instrumentalists more chance to hear what the electric instruments are playing so that the acoustic players can interact better with the electric instruments	

Table 15-2 Advantages and disadvantages of direct insertion

Advantages	Disadvantages
Has a cleaner sound	Has a drier sound—no room ambience
Captures more high and low frequencies	May use a transformer, which adds another electronic device to the sound chain
Allows more sound control at the console	Too present
Eliminates leakage	
Does not require an amp	

When miking an amp loudspeaker, the moving-coil mic is most often used because it can handle loud levels without overloading. With the bass guitar, the directional moving coil is less susceptible to vibration and conductance, especially with a shock mount, caused when the instrument's long, powerful wavelengths are amplified. Due to its powerful low end, the bass is usually recorded direct to obtain a cleaner sound. The fundamental frequency range of the electric bass is 41 to 300 Hz, with harmonics extending from 1 to 7 kHz.

Recording electric bass presents a particular challenge. If there is too much bass, the mix will sound muddy. This could mask the fundamentals of other instruments and result in a thickening and weighing down of the overall sound. Among the ways to improve clarity are to have the bassist increase treble and reduce bass on the guitar or to equalize in the control room by attenuating around 250 Hz and boosting around 1,500 Hz.

Compression is commonly used in recording the electric bass. It helps reduce noise, smooth variations in attack and loudness, and tighten the sound. Be careful in setting the compressor's release time.

If it is too fast in relation to the decay rate of the bass, the sound will be organlike. A slower release time maintains the natural sound of the instrument; too slow a release time muddies the sound.

With an electric guitar, a directional moving coil adds body to the sound. But if it is necessary to reproduce a subtler, warmer, more detailed sound, a capacitor or one of the more rugged ribbon mics may be used. The fundamental frequency range of the electric guitar is 82 to 1,319 Hz. When amplified the harmonics extend from 1 to 3.5 kHz; going direct the harmonics range from 1 to 15 kHz.

As for placement, the main challenge is understanding the dispersion pattern of the amplifier's loudspeakers. Miking close to and head-on the amp produces a strong central lobe which has considerable high-frequency content within the bandwidth of the instrument itself (see 15-29a). Off-axis miking reduces high-frequency content, and backing the mic farther from the amp produces a more blended, balanced sound (see 15-29b). Also, the decrease in highs gives the impression of a heavier, bassier sound. Hanging a small microphone over the amp emphasizes a guitar's midrange and

15-29 Miking an amplifier loudspeaker. (a) Aiming a directional microphone at the loudspeaker produces a brighter sound. (b) Aiming a directional microphone at an angle to the loudspeaker produces a fuller but less bright sound.

reduces leakage. If leakage is not a problem, and even if it is, close miking with an omni works well. An omnidirectional microphone has no proximity effect—its response is uniform; it will therefore pick up various aspects of the loudspeaker dispersion pattern, and the inverse square law takes care of the leakage problem, because you are essentially force-feeding the mic from an amp that is producing a high sound-pressure level at a short mic-to-source distance. Use an omni capacitor or ribbon with fast response.

Producers also record both amp loudspeaker and direct insertion feeds simultaneously. This technique combines the drier, unreverberant but crisp sound of direct insertion with the acoustic coloring of the amplified sound. The amp and D.I. signals should be recorded on separate tracks. This provides more flexibility in the mixdown when the two sounds are combined, or if you decide not to use one of the tracks.

It should be noted that direct recording of guitars does not necessarily guarantee a leakage-free track. If a guitar pickup is near or facing a loud instrument, it will "hear" the vibrations. By turning the musician away from the direct sound waves or by putting a baffle between the instruments, leakage is reduced.

With the electric guitar, special-effects boxes are often used to add to the sonic possibilities

(see 15-30). Here, too, the various signals should be recorded on separate tracks, if possible, to allow flexibility in the mixdown.

Musicians' Amplifiers

An amp often produces annoying hum. Using a microphone with a humbuck coil can help reduce hum but not always enough. It also helps to turn up the loudness control on the guitar and turn down the volume on the amp and to use guitar cables with extra shielding. Moving the musician around the studio until a spot is located where the hum is reduced or disappears is another solution. If it is possible, convince the musician to use a smaller, lower-powered amp than is used in live concerts. There may be a problem here, however, because the change in amp produces a change in sound.

A device that avoids the variety of sound and electrical problems that often beset a miked amplifier is the *Mic Eliminator.™* The Mic Eliminator delivers the combined mic/speaker sound of a miked amp direct from an electric instrument, preamp, or speaker output, without a microphone. It has two tone color settings—brite *(sic)* and dark—providing a choice between the bright, punchy sound of a mic directly in front of a speaker's center and the warm, rounder sound achieved by placing a mic off-center at the speaker's edge.

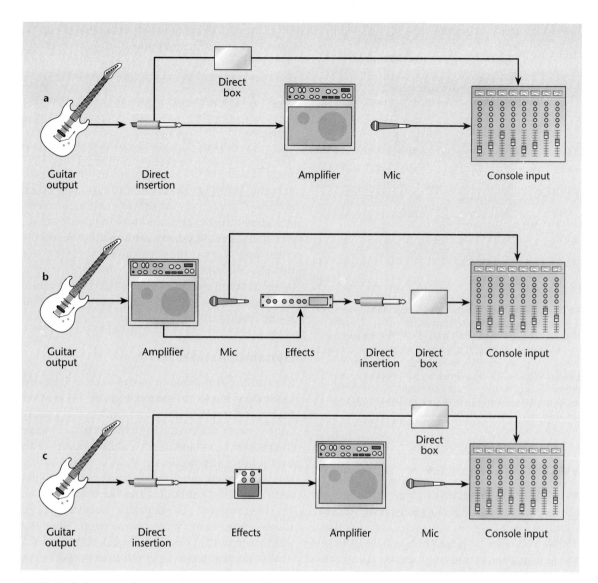

15-30 Techniques used to record direct and amplified signals simultaneously. (a) The signals are recorded on separate tracks. Special-effects boxes can be used: (b) the usual technique; (c) an alternate technique.

Leslie Loudspeaker Cabinet

The Leslie amplifier loudspeaker, most often used with an electric organ, is almost an instrument in itself (see 15-31). It is not a loudspeaker in the normal sense but is designed especially to modify sound. It contains a high-frequency loudspeaker (the tweeter) in the upper portion and a low-frequency loudspeaker (the woofer) in the lower portion. The two loudspeaker systems rotate, creating a vibrato effect. (*Vibrato* is short and repeating fluctuation in the pitch of a sound, not to be confused with *tremolo,* which is a rapid fluctuation in the amplitude of a sound.)

15-31 Miking a Leslie amplifier loudspeaker. One way is with two directional microphones, one to pick up the highs and the other to pick up the lows. The greater the mic-to-source distance, the less the chance of picking up the rotor sounds and increased tremolo and the better the sound blend. To record stereo, use either a top and bottom pair of mixed mics left and right, or just single mics panned toward the left and right. If the sound of the rotating horn is desired, place a boundary microphone inside the cabinet.

VOCALS

At its most basic level, the human voice acts like a wind instrument. The lungs expel air through the vocal cords, which vibrate and act like a double reed. The voice is then radiated through the larynx, mouth, and out into the air. Sound is modified by movement of the tongue, jaw, lips, and the rate of exhalation. Pitch is determined primarily by the vocal cords and larynx, but mouth, lip, and tongue movements change timbre. The human voice's wide-ranging and complex harmonics and overtones are a product of the mouth, nasal cavity, and chest cavity.

Although the speaking voice has a comparatively limited frequency range, the singing voice does not (see 15-32). And whereas the speaking voice is comparatively straightforward to mike and record, the singing voice can place a severe test on any microphone. The singing voice is capable of almost unlimited and subtle variations in pitch, timbre, and dynamic range. There are also plosives and sibilance—annoying popping and hissing sounds—to deal with.

Timbre

In choosing a vocal mic, the most important consideration is the singer's timbre—how edged, velvety, sharp, mellow, or resonant the voice sounds. The microphone should enhance a voice's attractive qualities and minimize the unattractive. Generally, assuming there are no serious problems with tone quality, most producers prefer to use capacitor microphones for vocals, because they can better handle the complicated pattern of harmonics and overtones in the human voice, and overall sound quality is the most natural.

Dynamic Range

Controlling the dynamic range—the quietest to loudest levels a sound source produces—is another tricky problem. Well-disciplined singers can usually control wide fluctuations in the dynamic range themselves. But many singers cannot—their voices barely move the needle on the VU meter during soft passages and pin it during loud ones. In miking these vocalists, a producer has three alternatives: (1) ride the level, (2) adjust the vocalist's microphone position, or (3) use compression. There is a fourth alternative: record the vocal on two tracks.

Riding the level works but it requires an engineer's full attention, and this may be difficult considering everything else that goes on in a recording session. Also, less-gifted singers may handle dynamic range differently each time they sing, which means that riding the level is a matter more of coping than of aiding.

The preferred methods are to use microphone technique to adjust for irregularities in a vocalist's dynamic range or to use compression, or both. In pop music, vocals are often compressed 10 to 15 dB. But to do so requires that a recordist know how to compensate after compression.

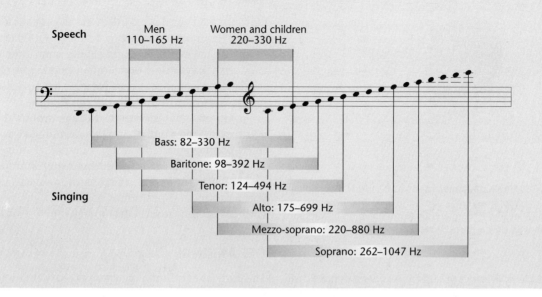

15-32 Fundamental frequency ranges for speech and singing in the human voice. Harmonics in the male singing voice extend from 1 to 12 kHz and in the female singing voice from 2 to 12 kHz.

One placement technique is to situate the singer at an average distance from the mic relative to the loudest and softest passages sung; the distance depends on the power of the singer's voice and the song. From this average distance, you can direct the singer how close to move to the mic during quiet passages and how far for the loud ones. The success of this technique depends on the vocalist's microphone technique—the ability to manage the song and the movements at the same time.

If these techniques do not work, try recording the vocal on two tracks with one track 10 dB down. If there is overload or a problem with the noise floor, the undistorted or less noisy sections of each recording can be intercut.

Breathing, Popping, and Sibilance

The closer to a microphone a performer stands, the greater the chance of picking up unwanted breathing sounds, popping sounds from *p*'s, *b*'s, *k*'s, and *t*'s, and sibilance from *s*'s. If the singer's vocal projection or the type of music permits, increasing

the mic-to-source distance significantly reduces these noises. Windscreens also help, but they tend to reduce the higher frequencies. Other ways to reduce popping and sibilance are to have the singer work slightly across mic but within the pickup pattern or to position the mic somewhat above the singer's mouth (see 15-33). If this increases nasality, position the mic at an angle from slightly below the singer's mouth. If leakage is no problem, using an omnidirectional mic permits a closer working distance because it is less susceptible to breathing, popping, and sibilant sounds. The sound may be less intimate, however, because an omnidirectional microphone picks up more indirect sound waves than does a directional mic. But the closeness of the singer should overcome the larger amount of indirect sound picked up.

Although capacitors are almost always the microphone of choice for vocals, they do tend to emphasize sibilance because of the mid- to treble-range response of many models. In such cases, and when other techniques fail to eliminate sibilance, a first-rate dynamic mic usually takes care of the

15-33 Eliminating unwanted vocal sounds. Positioning the microphone slightly above the performer's mouth is a typical miking technique used to cut down on unwanted popping, sibilance, and breathing sounds.

problem. Another reason to consider a dynamic mic for vocals is the harshness of some capacitors when used in digital recording (see "Miking Music for Digital Recording" later in this chapter).

Mic-to-Source Distance Versus Style

Generally, the style of the music sets the guidelines for mic-to-source distance. In popular music vocalists usually work close to the mic, from a few inches to a few feet, to create a tight, intimate sound. Classical and jazz vocalists work from a few feet to several feet from the mic to add room ambience, thereby opening the sound and making it airy.

When close miking, be careful of proximity effect. Rolling off the unwanted bass frequencies may be one solution, but it almost certainly will change the delicate balance of voice harmonics unless it is very carefully and knowledgeably effected. It should be emphasized that, unless a mic is specifically designed for it, positioning the mic just about touching the lips, as some vocalists are seen doing on television, and which unfortunately is imitated in the recording studio, rarely produces ideal sound. Indeed, if the microphone is not up to it, such mic technique rarely produces usable sound. If the distortion does not get you, then the oppressive "lack of air" will.

Backup Harmony Vocals

Once the lead vocal is recorded, the accompanying backup harmony vocals are overdubbed. Often this involves a few vocalists singing at the same time. If they each have their own microphone, mic-to-source distances are easier to balance, but this also means more mics to control and could require using extra tape tracks. Another technique groups the vocalists around a bidirectional or omnidirectional microphone. This reduces the number of microphones and tape tracks involved, but requires greater care in balancing and blending harmonies. Backup vocalists must be positioned to prevent any one voice or harmony from being too strong or too weak.

OFF-MIKING

The purpose of off-miking, when mixed with sound from the close mics, is to add airier, more ambient sound to the overall recording. The microphone arrays used in off-miking are often stereo arrays similar to those employed in distant miking. They are: coincident, near-coincident, and spaced.

Coincident Miking

Coincident miking, also called *X-Y miking,* employs two matched, directional microphones mounted on a vertical axis—with one mic diaphragm directly over the other—and angled apart to aim approximately toward the left and right sides of the sound source. The degree of angle, the mics' pickup pattern, and the distance from the sound source depend on the width of the stereo image you want to record (see 15-34).

A stereo pair must be matched to ensure a uniform sound, and the mics should be capacitors. Miking at a distance from the sound source, particularly with classical music, requires high-output, high-sensitivity microphones, and capacitors are the only type of microphone that meets this requirement. Moreover, the microphone preamps should be high gain, low noise.

The stereo microphone provides the same coincident pickup as the stereo pair but with two

15-34 Coincident miking technique

15-35 Near-coincident miking technique

directional microphone capsules housed in a single casing. The upper element can rotate up to 180 degrees relative to the lower element. Some stereo mics enable control of each capsule's polar pattern (see 4-13).

Coincident microphone arrays produce level (intensity) differences between channels and minimize differences in arrival time. This has the advantage of being mono-compatible because the two microphones occupy almost the same space, meaning that their signals are in phase at all frequencies.

Near-Coincident Miking

Near-coincident miking angles two directional microphones, spaced horizontally, a few inches apart (see 15-35). The few inches' difference between the near-coincident and coincident arrays adds a sense of warmth, depth, and "air" to sound compared with the coincident array. The mics are close enough to retain intensity differences between channels at low frequencies, yet far enough apart to have sufficient time delay between channels for localization at high fre-

quencies. The stereo spread can be increased or decreased with the angle or space between the mics. The time delay between channels creates a problem, however: The greater the delay, the less the chance of stereo-to-mono compatibility.

Spaced Miking

Spaced miking employs two matched microphones several feet apart, perpendicular to the sound source, and symmetrical to each other along a centerline. They reproduce a more spacious, lusher, bigger sound than any of the near-coincident arrays, but at a cost. Stereo imaging is more diffused and, therefore, less detailed. Also, because so much of the sound reaching the mics derives its directional information from time differences (in addition to intensity differences), stereo-to-mono compatibility is unreliable.

If studio acoustics and the music permit, spaced omnidirectional microphones are preferred to directional mics because they have less off-axis coloration and flatter overall response, especially in the low frequencies. Capacitors are almost always used. Spacing is determined by the width of the stereo image you desire. With omnis, of course, spacing has to be wide enough to reproduce a stereo image. If it is too wide, however, separation may be exaggerated; if spacing is too narrow, the stereo image may lack breadth.

Spaced cardioid microphones are arrayed similarly to spaced omnidirectionals, but their directionality produces a different sonic outcome. Used with an ensemble, spaced cardioids tend to emphasize the voicings that are most on-axis. They also show the effects of coloration, particularly from any studio ambience. Placement is critical to producing acceptable results with any spaced miking, but even more so with cardioids than with omnis. Spaced cardioids do provide a better chance for mono compatibility, however, because each microphone is picking up less common information, reducing the chance of phase cancellations.

Spaced nondirectional boundary microphones used for off-miking, particularly in relatively dry studios, are another possibility. Their pickup is similar to that of omnidirectionals, although around the boundary surface the polar pattern is hemispheric.

RECORDING FOR SURROUND SOUND

There are basically two ways to handle a music recording for surround sound. One is to use the miking techniques already discussed in this chapter and apply the surround-sound imaging during the mix. The other is to mic for surround sound and feed the signals directly to the surround-sound channels. This technique assumes suitable acoustics and a discrete surround-sound encoding system; that is, a system that carries three discrete front channels and stereo surrounds. (See Chapter 18 for more in-depth discussion of surround sound.) Figures 15-36 and 15-37 convey some idea of surround-sound miking.

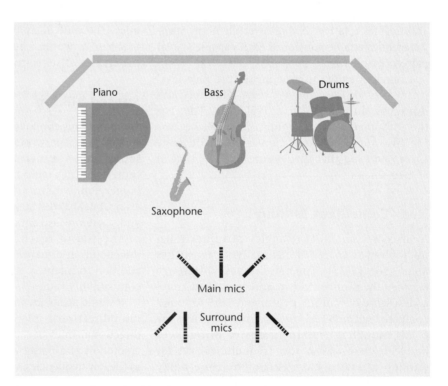

15-36 Surround-sound miking for a small ensemble. This microphone array is for a discrete surround-sound recording—front left, center, and right, and stereo surrounds.

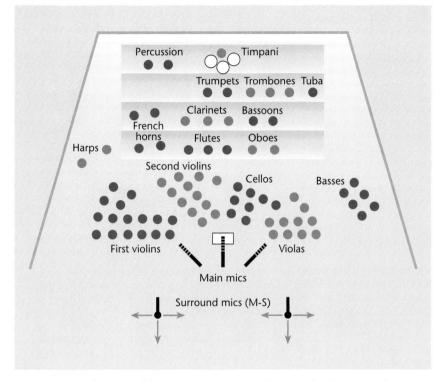

15-37 Surround-sound miking for an orchestra. In this example, the surround mics are middle-side (M-S) microphones.

MIKING STUDIO ENSEMBLES

This discussion of close miking has centered mainly on the individual instrument. There are studio situations, however, in which ensembles record as a group but are divided into smaller sections to control leakage. This requires isolating them as much as possible to avoid sonic confusion, yet blending them so that they sound cohesive. Figures 15-38 to 15-40 display a few ways to mike studio ensembles.

MIKING MUSIC FOR DIGITAL RECORDING

As clear and noise-free as digital sound can be, there are valid complaints about digital recordings: that the high end is strident, thin, and shrieky, or that there is too much unwanted noise from amplifiers, pedals, keys, bows, tongue, teeth, lips, and so on. Many of these problems can be traced to two causes: the microphones and the miking techniques that were used.

Microphones in Digital Recording

Many microphones used in analog recording are selected for their rising high-end response; these mics help deal with problems associated with analog reproduction, the most serious being the potential loss of high-frequency information during disc mastering and copying. There is little such loss in digital recording, copying, or mastering. (Uneven quality in the manufacture of CDs is, alas, another story altogether.) Therefore, using such mics for digital recording only makes the high frequencies more biting and shrill. To avoid this problem, use microphones with smooth high-end response.

15-38 Miking a jazz band when all voicings are recorded at the same time. Notice that trumpets and trombones are miked with bidirectional microphones and that the piano, acoustic bass, and drums are miked with boundary mics. Bidirectional mics are particularly useful in reducing leakage. For example, by facing the mic straight down in front of each saxophone, each mic's nulls are directed toward sound coming from the sides and rear. This is especially effective when woodwinds, or other weak instruments, are in front of brass, or other strong instruments. A high-ceilinged room is necessary for this technique to work, however.

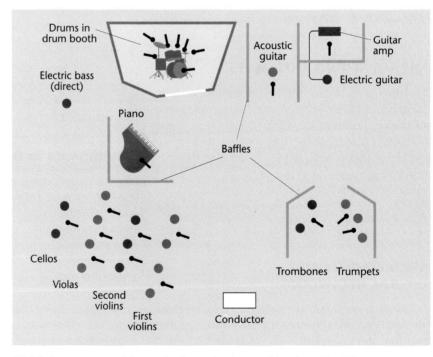

15-39 One way to position and mike a mixed ensemble when all voicings are recorded at once

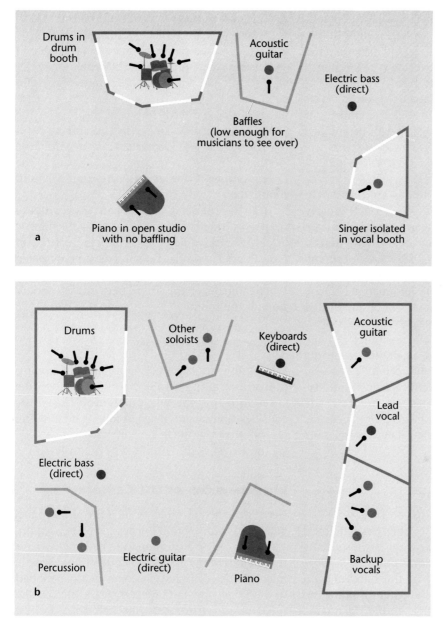

15-40 Two ways to arrange musical groups for studio recording. (a) Musicians are isolated from one another to prevent sound from one instrument from leaking into the microphone of another instrument, yet are still able to maintain visual contact. It is possible in this arrangement that the acoustic guitar sound will leak into the piano mics and vice versa. Leakage can usually be reduced, however, by supercardioid mics on both instruments rejecting sound from the sides and rear, the piano lid blocking sound coming from the front guitar baffle, and the guitarist's body blocking the piano sound coming from the back of the studio. (b) Another example of arranging a musical group in a studio to control leakage.

Recordists have returned to tube-type equipment in the signal chain—microphones, amplifiers, equalizers—to help warm the sound, offsetting the edge in digital reproduction.

Capacitor microphones have preamplifiers, which generate noise. In analog recording, this noise is usually masked. In digital recording, if preamp noise is loud enough, it will be audible. High-quality, large-diaphragm capacitors are therefore preferred, because their self-generated preamp noise is very low level.

Modern ribbon microphones are popular in digital recording. Their response is inherently nontailored, smooth, warm, and detailed, without being strident. Microphones used in digital recording should be linear—that is, output should vary in direct proportion to input. The mic should not introduce unwanted sonic information because, in digital sound, chances are it will be audible. Of course, this is the case in analog recording as well; it is just more critical in digital recording.

Furthermore, mics used in digital recording should be of the highest quality, carefully handled, and kept in clean, temperature- and humidity-controlled environments. The dust, moisture, and rough handling that may not perceptibly affect mic response in an analog recording may very well sully a digital recording.

Microphone Technique in Digital Recording

In analog recording, close miking was employed virtually pro forma, because vinyl records usually smoothed the rough spots resulting from close miking by burying some of the harshness in background surface noise. In digital recording, no such masking occurs. For example, in analog recording, when close-miking an acoustic guitar, no one is concerned about noise that might be generated by the guitarist's shirt rubbing against the instrument; in digital recording, on the other hand, the rubbing sound may be audible if the guitar is close-miked. In addition, in analog recording, noise from a musician's amplifier may

get lost in tape hiss. That will not be the case in digital recording, regardless of the mic used.

Even if mic-to-source distance is acceptable in digital recording, microphone placement may not be. For example, the upper harmonics of a violin radiate straight up in two directions. If a microphone is placed directly in one of these paths, the digital sound will be too crisp and shrieky, even though the mic is at an optimal distance from the violin. By placing the mic more in the path of the lower-frequency radiations, the digital sound should flatten.

High frequencies of brass instruments are radiated straight ahead in a relatively narrow beam. Placing a microphone directly in front of the bell produces a harsh digital recording. Placing the mic at more of an angle to the bell, to pick up a better blend of the lower frequencies, should smooth the sound.

MUSIC IN TELEVISION

Several different types of TV productions use live music, including variety, concert, and some entertainment-type talk programs. Three basic considerations are involved in miking all of them: (1) whether the musicians are seen on-camera, (2) the acoustics, and (3) the type of music.

Musicians On- or Off-Camera

Getting the best possible sound is the primary goal of every recordist. But if the musicians are seen on-camera, it can be disturbing to an audience to have them blocked by, and the picture cluttered with, microphones. Mics have become an accepted part of the TV picture, but unless they are selected and positioned with care, they can ruin a shot. Fortunately, a variety of mics that produce excellent sound are also good-looking. Even windscreens and cables now come in various colors.

If musicians are off-camera, mike them in whatever way is best, with little concern for appearance. Keep in mind that the musicians have to be able to see the conductor, if there is one.

Whether musicians are on- or off-camera, you will most likely use directional mics to cut down not only on leakage but on feedback as well. Many large studios and theaters have loudspeakers so that the audience can hear the performance better. Singers need loudspeakers on stage to hear the music blend, especially when they are not near the accompanying ensemble. With loudspeakers and microphones in the same vicinity, not only are directional mics almost a necessity to avoid feedback, but so are directional loudspeakers.

This problem is alleviated when performers use noise-canceling mics (see Chapter 4) and in-the-ear monitoring. *In-the-ear monitoring* employs small headphones to feed the music blend to the performer instead of stage monitors. A noise-canceling mic may be attached to the headset.

Acoustics

The types of studios used for large-scale TV productions, particularly with an audience present, are acoustically adequate for speech but sometimes not so for music. Therefore, most recordists use the close-miking instead of the distant-miking approach. Sound control is much better; even if the acoustics are excellent, much of today's popular music requires close miking.

Type of Music

The type of music can influence TV miking. Classical music audiences may not care to see a symphony orchestra, or string quartet for that matter, draped with microphones, but they tolerate it. They are accustomed to hearing music in excellent acoustic settings where mics are not necessary to carry the sound. Their objection is not so much that mics are in the picture but rather that mics are being used at all.

This is one reason why concert broadcasts typically originate from concert halls and not from studios. In controlled acoustic environments, the recordist can hang a few mics to achieve a natural sound blend and also keep the mics out of the picture. Even so, some of the newer concert halls have been designed with electronic enhancement built in. Loudspeakers are strategically placed either to make up for certain response deficiencies at various locations in the hall or to make frequency and loudness response uniform throughout the hall.

Popular music usually requires a mic for each sound source (or direct insertion) plus electronic enhancement. It would be impractical to use only a few mics to pick up, say, a rock band, because it would change the entire character of the sound, to say nothing of the difficulty in matching the loudness of acoustic and electric instruments.

Techniques for Miking Music in Television

For some of the common techniques used in miking music for television, see Figures 15-41 through 15-44. It is important to note that an ensemble must first be arranged to be pleasing to the eye and then miked within the constraints established by visual requirements.

MIKING MUSIC IN FILM

The microphone techniques used in recording music for film are similar to those used in conventional music recording. Ensembles are miked using either the distant- or close-miking approach. A major consideration in miking music for underscoring is that it be blended; no single voicing or group of voicings should be apparent, unless it is intended, nor should the music and the elements therein draw attention away from the picture.

If the music is being encoded in surround, another important consideration is whether the surround is matrix or discrete (see "Surround Sound" in Chapter 18). Because phase coherency is a potential problem in matrixed surround sound, close- and off-miking techniques are generally employed. With discrete surround sound, where phase coherency is less of a concern, many music producers prefer the more blended, natural, open sound that distant miking produces.

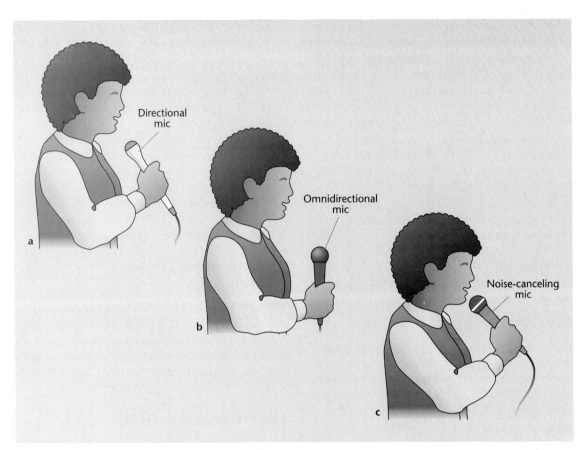

15-41 Miking vocals for TV. (a) A singer using a handheld directional microphone should hold it at about a 45-degree angle to the mouth to stay within the pickup pattern but not block the face. (b) Handheld omnidirectional mics can be held at chest level. A handheld microphone should contain a pop filter and be shock resistant, easy to hold and good-looking. (c) If the vocalist uses a noise-canceling microphone, the mic must be close to, and pointed directly at, the mouth.

15-42 Miking an instrumentalist. The customary approach in miking an instrumentalist who also sings is to use two directional mics: one to pick up the voice and the other to pick up the instrument. This technique can be obtrusive, however, when conventional mics on mic stands are employed. A better-looking approach, and one that also provides reasonably good sound, is to use a clip mount or an electric pickup on the instrument.

15-43 Miking a singer-pianist. (a) The conventional way to handle this situation has been to mount microphones on stands and mike the vocalist with a directional mic and the piano with either an omnidirectional or a cardioid mic, depending on its proximity to the sound board. This approach not only places the mics squarely in the picture, but it also runs the risk of having them jarred. Therefore, less obtrusive and safer microphone techniques have become more popular. (b) The vocalist may use a small headset microphone system or a wireless body mic. For a stereo piano, boundary or contact mics can be taped to the inside of the frame, one near the high strings, the other near the low strings (making sure that the midrange is also in the pickup). For mono, a boundary or contact mic can be taped to the piano lid over the intersection of the high and low strings, facedown. Still another technique is to place the piano mic in a clip mount and attach it to the piano frame a few feet above the sound board and equidistant between the high and low strings.

15-44 Example of a stage and microphone setup for a television variety/talk show.

The labels within the figure are as follows:

16

14

13

12 — Guest band and center-stage performing area

11

Drums
Kick: EV RE20
Snare: AKG414 with 10 dB pad
Hi-hat: Schoeps
Rack toms: MIT4 capsule
Floor toms: MDC10 10 dB pad
CMC5 preamp
Overhead Milab DC96B

10

9

8

Trumpets:
4 Milab DC96B

7 — Guests

Desk mic:
AKG 414

Trombones:
3 Milab DC96B

Bass:
Direct

Guitar:
Direct

6 — Monitor

Footlights

Piano:
2 Countryman
ISO/Max "C"

5

Boom mics:
Schoeps capsule
MDC10 –10 dB pad
CMC4 preamp

Boom 1

Bandleader trumpet:
Sanken CU41

Rhodes:
Direct

4 — Opening announce mic:
Beyer M58

Boom 2

Saxophones:
5 Milab DC96B

3 — Teleprompter desk

Monitor console
24 × 8

2

1

416   816

Sennheiser applause mics

816   416

Sennheiser applause mics

SM57   SM57

Shure
applause mics

Audience

▶ Distant miking uses two or a few microphones to record an entire ensemble.

▶ Close miking places a microphone relatively close to each sound source or group of sound sources in an ensemble.

▶ Because close miking involves miking most of the instruments in an ensemble, it means that (1) microphones should be no closer together than roughly three times the distance from any mic to its sound source to avoid phasing problems; (2) mic-to-source distances are usually close, thus reducing the interaction of music with acoustics and requiring the addition of artificial reverberation; and (3) each sound source usually requires a separate tape channel to better control the various microphone inputs.

▶ The closer a microphone is to a sound source, the more detailed, drier, and, if proximity effect is a factor, bassier is the sound. The farther a microphone is from a sound source, the more diffused, open, and reverberant is the sound.

▶ The underlying concept of distant miking is often used in-studio along with the close-miking technique to enhance a recording with a more acoustically natural, open sound. This technique is referred to as off-miking.

▶ No single close-miking technique is necessarily better than another. Microphone selection and positioning depend on many factors: the music, the musician, the quality of the instrument, the acoustics, the blend, and so on.

▶ The higher the frequency, the more directional the sound wave; the lower the frequency, the more omnidirectional the sound wave.

▶ In recording drums, tuning the drum set is critical if they are to sound good.

▶ Although the drum set consists of several different-sounding instruments, it must be miked so that they sound good individually and blend as a unit.

▶ Because most of an acoustic guitar's sound radiates from the front of the instrument, centering a microphone off the middle of the sound hole should, theoretically, provide a balanced sound. But if a mic is too close to the hole, sound is bassy or boomy. If it is moved closer to the bridge, detail is lost. If it is moved closer to the neck, presence is reduced. If it is moved farther away, intimacy is affected.

▶ Because the dynamic range of bowed string instruments is not wide, sound has to be re-inforced by using several instruments or multiple miking, or both, depending on the size of the sound required.

▶ The piano offers almost unlimited possibilities for sound shaping. Perhaps more than with many other instruments, the character of the piano sound is dependent on the quality of the piano itself.

▶ Because most woodwinds are not powerful instruments, the tendency is to close-mike them. Due to their sound radiation, however, this results in an uneven pickup. They should be miked far enough away so that the pickup sounds blended and natural.

▶ Because of their loudness and dynamic range, brass instruments require care in microphone placement and careful attention in adjusting levels at the console.

▶ Some electric instruments, such as the bass and guitar, can be recorded either by miking their amplifier loudspeaker or by direct insertion—plugging the instrument into the console—or a combination of both.

▶ Recording a vocalist is a severe test for any microphone, because the mic must be able to handle the nuances of the vocalist's timbre and dynamics as well as any breathy, popping, and sibilant sounds. Mic selection and placement depend on voice quality, style of music, and microphone presence.

- The microphone arrays used in off-miking are often stereo arrays similar to those employed in distant miking. They are: coincident, near-coincident, and spaced.

- Coincident miking, also called X-Y miking, employs two matched directional microphones mounted on a vertical axis—with one mic diaphragm directly over the other—and angled apart to aim approximately toward the left and right sides of the sound source.

- Near-coincident miking angles two directional microphones, spaced horizontally, a few inches apart.

- Spaced miking employs two matched microphones—uni- or omnidirectional—several feet apart, perpendicular to the sound source, and symmetrical to each other along a centerline.

- There are basically two ways to handle a music recording for surround sound: (1) to use conventional miking techniques during recording and apply the surround-sound imaging during the mix; and (2) to mic for surround sound during recording and feed the signals directly to the surround-sound channels.

- Because digital recording often reproduces sounds not audible in analog, the microphones used for digital recording must be of very high quality, generate very low self-noise, be carefully handled, and kept in clean, temperature- and humidity-controlled environments.

- A major consideration in miking music for underscoring is that it be blended; no single voicing or group of voicings should be apparent, unless it is intended, nor should the music and the elements therein draw attention away from the picture.

Five

Postproduction

16

Dialogue, Sound Effects, and Music in Postproduction

Most of the finished product that you *hear* in theatrical film and television is recorded in postproduction. Dialogue, frequently, is difficult to record during shooting. When it is not, directors often prefer to make refinements in post, where they have more sonic control than they do on the set, even when acceptably performed and technically usable sound is obtained during shooting. Most sound effects are more easily produced away from the set and the demands of production recording. Underscored music is often not selected or composed until production is fairly well along or completed. Moreover, music cannot be synched to picture until editing is finished.

AUTOMATED DIALOGUE REPLACEMENT

In *automated dialogue replacement (ADR)*, also known as *automatic dialogue replacement* and *looping*, dialogue is recorded or rerecorded, depending on the outcome of the production recording or the director's aesthetic preference, or both. Generally, there are two schools of thought about ADR.

Some directors believe that an original performance is preferable to a re-created one and that the background sounds that are part of the dramatic action are a natural part of the sonic environment, just as shadow is a natural part of light. They therefore prefer to use the dialogue and other sounds recorded during production, assuming that pickup is tight enough so the intelligibility of the dialogue and the sonic balances are acceptable. Other directors prefer dialogue recorded with a minimum of background sound. They want to control the ambience separately in postproduction, where they can also hone an actor's performance. Regardless of preference, however, there are times when ADR is the only way to capture dialogue, as it usually is in far-flung battle and chase scenes, for example.

Purpose and Process

Automated dialogue replacement is done in a dialogue recording studio, a relatively dry room (reverberation time is about .4 seconds for average-sized studios) with a screen, microphone, and sometimes a small audio control panel (see Figure 16-1). As the picture is projected onto the screen, the performer, wearing headphones, stands before a microphone and synchronizes the dialogue to his or her lip movements on the screen. Relatively dry rooms are necessary so that the background sound added later can be laid in with as little prerecorded ambience as possible. Too dry a studio, however, absorbs the vitality of an actor's performance and could create a claustrophobic feeling.

Not only is ambience kept to a minimum in ADR, but audio enhancements are also minimal to give the rerecording mixer the most latitude possible. Compression or a microphone pad may be applied to keep a signal from overmodulating. Sometimes spare equalization is employed to smooth intercut dialogue and transitions.

16-1 Automated dialogue recording studio and control room. The console is specially designed for ADR (and Foley recording). Among its unique features are a high number of monitor/assign channels and a low number of input channels; a room mic that solos automatically in rewind so communication is never lost; an auxiliary bus system with its own solo to enable isolating a track for the talent only and then returning them to their previous mix; Ahead/In/Past matrices for the editor, actor, studio, and control room that are time code driven; record/rehearse/playback mode selection; and spotting software.

The *automated* in automated dialogue replacement refers to the computer-controlled aspect of the procedure. The equipment is programmed to start, shuttle between cue points, and stop automatically. The computer also puts the recorder in *record* or *playback* and selects the desired playback track(s) in a multitrack recording. Cue points are designated in feet and frames or time code.

Dialogue rerecording is also referred to as *looping*, because the process once involved putting the dialogue sequences into short film loops so they could be repeated again and again without interruption. Each short section was rehearsed until the actor's dialogue was in sync with the picture and then recorded. Today, the procedure is still the same, only it is automated and the picture medium may be film or videotape.

In rerecording dialogue there are a few points worth remembering:

☑ Screen and analyze the scenes to be recorded and break them down line by line.

☑ Note such things as dialogue that is to be shouted, whispered, and so on.

☑ Get to know what the performer sounds like speaking normally so that in scenes calling for projected or quiet delivery, you have an idea of what adjustments to make in microphone placement or signal processing.

The ADR studio is a sterile setting for a performance. The acoustics are relatively dead, there is no set to help create a mood or establish a sense of environment, and there is usually no interaction among actors—they record their dialogue one at a time. (When background sound is done in ADR, involving, for example, a group of people in a restaurant, the extras record as a group.)

For all performers, but particularly for those inexperienced in ADR, listen carefully to delivery in relation to believability and how a performance will sound after background audio is added. For example, if a scene calls for an actor to talk loudly over the noise of, say, a race car, the dialogue's force and accentuation have to be convincing. Also, the dialogue may sound sufficiently loud in the

quietness of the studio, but once the race car sound is added the delivery may not be loud enough.

Adding the sound of a scene's background environment to the actor's headphone mix sometimes helps enliven performance. It may not be possible to use the precise background called for in the picture, but adding some presence helps counteract the sterility of the studio.

Recordkeeping is an often-overlooked but very important part of ADR (and of the production process in general). Keeping accurate records of track assignments and making notes about each take is not only necessary to avoid confusion but of immeasurable help to the editors and mixers, who will be working with the dialogue tracks later in postproduction. A director may choose the reading of a particular line even though the beginning of a word may not be as crisp as it should be. By noting that in the record, an editor can try to find the same sound, delivered more crisply, elsewhere in the recording and edit it in, or the mixer may be able to use equalization to add the desired amount of crispness. All with the director's approval, of course.

The goal of ADR is to make the dialogue sound as though it were recorded on location.

Dialogue Rerecording: Pros and Cons

Dialogue rerecording frees picture from sound and gives the director more flexibility and control. When there is a choice between using the original dialogue or rerecording it, directors and sound designers disagree about the benefits of looping. The question becomes, Are the added sonic control and assurance of first-rate audio quality and refined performance worth the loss of spontaneity and the unexpected?

On the one hand, regardless of the subject and style of the material, art is illusion, so there is no reason not to use whatever means necessary to produce the most polished, well-crafted product possible. Every sonic detail must be produced with the same care and precision as every visual detail. Anything less than excellent sound (and picture) quality reduces the effect of the illusion.

On the other hand, quality of performance is more important than quality of sound; "natural" is more realistic and, hence, more effective. Because actors, as a rule, do not like to re-create their performances in a rerecording studio, dialogue looping is rarely as good as the original performance recording. Even though lines sound different as a shooting day goes on, because the actor's voice changes, the difference between a production line and a looped line is always much greater than the difference between two production lines.

Actors generally prefer the natural environment and interactions on the set to the sterile environment of the ADR studio. As good as postproduction can be, many believe it cannot quite capture the dozens of tiny sounds that correspond to physical movements, such as soft exhales of anxiety, the caress of a touch, the rustling of a shirt, or an arm brushing against a tree branch. Although ADR gives directors complete control and often saves time and money, most actors agree that it is no substitute for the real thing.

SOUND EFFECTS

Generally, there are two sources of sound effects (abbreviated *SFX*): prerecorded and produced. Prerecorded sound effects are distributed on compact disc and CD-ROM. Produced SFX are obtained in four ways: They can be (1) created and synchronized to picture in postproduction in a studio often specially designed for that purpose; (2) recorded on the set during shooting; (3) collected in the field throughout production or between productions; (4) electronically generated using a synthesizer or computer. Sound effects can also be built using any one or combination of these approaches. In the interest of clarity, each approach is considered separately here.

Prerecorded Sound-Effects Libraries

Sound-effects libraries are collections of recorded sounds that can number from several hundred to many thousand, depending on the distributor. The distributor has either produced and recorded the

original sounds or collected them from other sources and obtained the rights to sell them, or both.

Advantages of Sound-Effects Libraries

A major advantage of sound-effects libraries is that for one buyout fee you get many different sounds for relatively little cost, compared with the time and expense it would take to produce them yourself (see 16-2). *Buyout* means that you own the library and have unlimited, copyright-cleared use of it.

Most broadcast stations and many production houses use libraries, because they have neither the personnel nor the budget to assign staff to produce sound effects. Think of what it would involve to produce, for example, the real sounds of a jet fly-by, a forest fire, a torpedo exploding into an aircraft carrier, or stampeding cattle.

Sound quality, or the absence thereof, was a serious problem with prerecorded sound effects before the days of the CD, when they were distributed on tape and long-playing (LP) record. The audio was analog, dynamic range was limited, tape was noisy, LPs got scratched, and too many effects sounded lifeless. Frequently, it was easy to tell that the SFX came from a recording; they

"C"		
Subject	**Category**	**Section**
Cable car bell	Bells, buzzers, whistles	4
Cafe	Backgrounds	3
Calf	Animals—barnyard	2
Camera	Hits, impacts	14
Campfire	Backgrounds	3
Canary	Birds, insects	5
Cannon	Guns, explosions	13
Cards	Sports, games	23
Carillon	Bells, buzzers, whistles	4
Carnival	Backgrounds	3
Car doors	Doors, gates, windows	10
Car horns	Horns, sirens	15
Carriage	Stagecoach, wagons	24

16-2 (a) Examples of categories and effects in a recorded sound-effects library.

Catalog Number	Subject	Description	Time
6-046	Ship's deck	Large type—anchor chain down quickly	:05
6-047	Coast Guard cutter	Operating steadily—with water sounds	:41
6-048	Water taxi	Start up—steady run—slow down	:47
6-049	Water taxi	Steady run—slow down—rev ups—with water sounds	1:25
6-050	Fishing boat	Diesel type—slow speed steady operation	:36
6-051	Tugboat	Diesel type—slow speed steady operation	:38
6-052	Tugboat	Diesel type—medium speed steady operation	:38
6-053	Outboard	Fast run-by	:32
6-054	Naval landing craft	Medium speed steady operation.	:50

16-2 *(continued)* **(b) Example of a detailed list of sound effects by category.**

sounded "canned." The sound effects on CD have greatly improved fidelity and dynamic range; that is, those effects that were digitally recorded or transferred from analog to digital with widened dynamic range and sans noise. The CD-ROM format provides the added benefits of faster access to tracks and the ability to look at sounds on-screen.

The great advantage of SFX libraries is the convenience of having thousands of digital-quality sound effects at your fingertips for relatively little cost. There are, however, disadvantages.

Disadvantages of Sound-Effects Libraries

Sound-effects libraries have three conspicuous disadvantages: (1) You give up control over the dynamics and timing of an effect; (2) ambiences vary, so in editing effects together, they may not match one another or those you require in your production; and (3) the effect may not be long enough for your needs.

Dynamics and Timing One reason why sound editors prefer to create their own effects rather than use libraries is to have control over the dynamics of a sound, particularly effects generated by humans. For example, thousands of different footstep sounds are available in effects libraries. But you might need a specific footfall that requires a certain-sized woman walking at a particular gait on a solidly packed road consisting of dirt and stone granules. Maybe no library can quite match this sound.

Timing is another reason why many sound editors prefer to create their own effects. To continue our example, if the pace of the footfall has to match action on the screen, trying to synchronize each step in the prerecorded sound effect to each step in the picture could be difficult.

Ambience Matching ambiences could present another problem with prerecorded sound effects. Suppose in a radio commercial you need footsteps walking down a hall, followed by a knock on a door that enters into that hallway. If you cut together two different sounds to achieve the overall effect, take care that the sound of the footsteps walking toward the door has the same ambience as the knock on the door. If the ambiences are different, the audience will perceive the two actions as taking place in different locales. Even if the audience could see the action, the different ambiences could be disconcerting.

To offset this problem, some sound-effects libraries provide different ambiences for specific applications: footsteps on a city street with reverb to put you in town among buildings, and without reverb to put you in a more open area; or gunshots with different qualities of ricochet to cover the various environments in which a shot may be fired. Some libraries provide collections of ambient environments, allowing you to mix the appropriate background sound with a given effect (see 16-3). In so doing, be sure that the sound

	Title	Description	Time
01	Crowd, indoor	Small crowd: small room, light conversation	3:00
02	Crowd, indoor	Small crowd: large room, general walla	3:00
03	Crowd, indoor	Medium crowd: adults and children, general walla	3:00
04	Crowd, indoor	Medium crowd: adults, heavy voice walla	3:00
05	Crowd, indoor	Medium crowd: reception area, heavy walla	3:00
06	Crowd, indoor	Medium crowd: concrete foyer, general ambience, intensity varies	3:00
07	Crowd, indoor	Medium crowd: foyer, general ambience	3:00
08	Crowd, indoor	Medium crowd: general ambience	3:00
09	Crowd, indoor	Medium crowd: general ambience, light walla	3:00
10	Crowd, indoor	Large crowd: heavy walla	3:00
11	Crowd, indoor	Large crowd: wooden hall, crowd entering seating area	3:00
12	Crowd, indoor	Large crowd: entering cathedral-style building, low crowd ambience	3:00
13	Crowd, indoor	Large crowd: large open hall, general ambience	3:00
14	Crowd, indoor	Large crowd: large concrete hall, adults and children, general ambience	3:00
15	Crowd, indoor	Large crowd: filing by, heavy footsteps, hard surface	3:00
16	Crowd, outdoor	Medium crowd: general ambience	3:00
17	Crowd, outdoor	Medium crowd: general ambience, under concrete overhang	3:00
18	Crowd, outdoor	Medium crowd: general ambience, voices, footsteps	3:00
19	Crowd, outdoor	Large crowd: adults and children, general ambience	3:00
20	Crowd, outdoor	Large crowd: general crowd ambience, busy city	3:00
21	Crowd, outdoor	Large crowd: crowd passing by, heavy walla, footsteps	3:00
22	Crowd, outdoor	Ski resort: general ambience at the bottom of a ski hill	3:00
23	Crowd, outdoor	Large crowd: street party: large celebration	3:00
24	Crowd, outdoor	Large crowd: street party: victory celebration, heavy horns, cheering	3:00

	Title	Description	Time
01	Crowd, angry	Indoor: medium crowd: parliamentary dispute	3:00
02	Crowd, concert	Indoor: large theatre: energetic crowd cheering for an encore	3:00
03	Harbor, marina	Small marina: general ambience: light boats, water lapping, loons	3:00
04	Harbor, port	Large port: general ambience: ship horns, seagulls, etc.	3:00
05	Hockey, ice	Indoor: adults: game ambience, no crowd	3:00
06	Hospital	Nurses station: general ambience, P.A. announcements	3:00
07	Hospital	Nurses station: general ambience, no announcements	3:00
08	Hospital	Intensive care room: heart monitor, ventilator, E.E.G.	3:00
09	Household, kitchen	Kitchen ambience: rinsing dishes, loading dishwasher, turning on	3:00
10	Household, dining room	Dining room: general dish noise at dinner table	3:00
11	Industry, sawmill	Indoor: general ambience	3:00
12	Industry, steelyard	Exterior: general ambience	3:00
13	Industry, winery	Bottling area: general ambience	3:00
14	Laundromat, washers	Washing area: coin slots, loading, washing	3:00
15	Laundromat, dryers	Drying area: coin slots, dryers running	3:00
16	Library	Quiet library: light voices	3:00
17	Lobby	Hotel lobby: medium crowd, voices, telephone, elevator bell	3:00
18	Lobby	Hotel lobby: medium crowd: voices, light music	3:00
19	Market	Indoor: medium crowd: general ambience	3:00
20	Market	Outdoor: medium crowd: general ambience	3:00
21	Office foyer	Large office foyer: hard surface, footsteps, light voices	3:00
22	Office foyer	Large office foyer: footsteps, voices, elevator bells	3:00
23	Parade	Various bands passing, general crowd walla	3:00
24	Parade	No music, crowd applause and cheering, various horns, sirens	3:00

16-3 Examples of ambience sound effects

effect used has very little, or no, ambient coloration of its own. Otherwise, the backgrounds will be additive or clash, or both.

Fixed Length of Sound Effects   Library SFX have fixed lengths. You need a sound to last 15 seconds, but the effect you want to use is only 7 seconds long. What to do?

If the effect is continuous, crowd sound or wind, for example, it can be looped (see "Creating Loops" later in this chapter). If it is not continuous, such as a dog barking and then growling, you are stuck unless you can find two separate effects of the same-sounding dog barking and growling. If it is possible to edit them together to meet your timing needs, be careful that the edit transition from bark to growl sounds natural.

Manipulating Library Sound Effects

Once a sound effect has been recorded, any number of things can be done to alter its sonic characteristics, thereby extending the usefulness of a library.

Altering Playing Speed   Because pitch and duration are inseparable parts of sound, it is possible to change the character of any recorded sound by varying its playing speed. This technique will not work with all sounds; some will sound obviously unnatural—either too drawn out and guttural or too fast and falsetto. But for sounds with sonic characteristics that do lend themselves to changes in pitch and duration, the effects can be remarkable.

For example, the sound effect of a low-pitched, slow, mournful wind can be changed to a ferocious howl of hurricane force by increasing its playing speed. The beeps of a car horn followed by a slight ambient reverb can be slowed to become a small ship in a small harbor and slowed still more to become a large ship in a large harbor. Hundreds of droning bees in flight can be turned into a squadron of World War II bombers by decreasing the playing speed of the effect, or turned into a horde of mosquitos by increasing playing speed.

Decreasing the playing speed of cawing jungle birds will take you from the bush to an eerie world of science fiction. A gorilla can be turned into King Kong by slowing the recording's playing speed. The possibilities are endless, and the only way to discover how flexible sounds can be is to experiment.

Playing Sound Backward   Another way to alter the characteristics of a sound is to play it backward. Many hard-disk recorders have a *reverse* command that rewrites the selected region in reverse, resulting in a backward audio effect. Some tape recorders have a *reverse play* function. On those that do not, you can play a tape backward by threading it around the capstan and pinch roller so that the tape feeds from right to left (see 16-4).

Creating Loops   Sometimes you may need a continuous effect that has to last several seconds, such as an idling car engine, a drum roll, or a steady beat. When the sound effect is shorter than the required time, it can be looped. In hard-disk systems, the *looping* command will continuously repeat the selected region. In the absence of such a system, one technique is to dub the effect to a cart

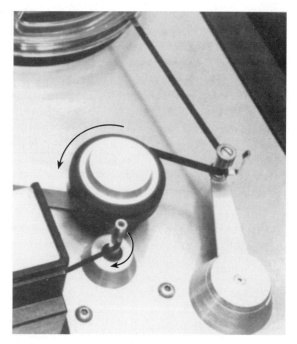

16-4 Threading technique used to play tape backward

16-5 A tape loop and one way it can be played. Longer loops can be wound around an empty feed reel or takeup reel, or both.

machine for continuous play. Many analog cart machines have a tone defeat feature. Another approach is to make tape loop.

To make a tape loop, dub a few seconds of the effect to open-reel tape, cut the tape at the beginning and end of the recording, and splice the two ends together. Be sure to follow the editing guidelines in Chapter 17 and make the edit at a point where it will not be aurally conspicuous. Figure 16-5 shows one way to play a tape loop.

In looping, make sure that the edit points are made so that the effect sounds continuous, not repetitious. That said, even well-edited loops run the risk of sounding repetitious if they play too long.

Loops can also be designed to create a sound effect. For example, taking the startup sound of a motorcycle before it cranks over and putting it into a half-second repeat can be used as the basis for the rhythmic sound of a small, enclosed machine area.

Using Signal Processing By feeding a sound effect through signal processors, such as a delay unit, flanger, or pitch shifter, it is possible to create a virtually infinite number of effects. For example, flanging a cat's meow can to turn it into an

unearthly cry; adding low frequencies to a crackling fire can make it an inferno; and chorusing a bird chirp can create a boisterous flock.

Choosing Sounds from the Titles

Titles in sound libraries are often not precise enough to be used as guides for selecting material. For example, what does "laughter," "washing machine," "window opening," or "polite applause" actually tell you about the sound effect, besides its general subject and application? Most good libraries provide short descriptions of each effect to give you an idea of its content (see 16-2). Even so, always listen before you choose, because nuance is difficult to describe.

LIVE SOUND EFFECTS

Although prerecorded sound libraries are readily available, some of which are quite good, many audio designers prefer to produce their own effects because doing so allows complete control in shaping a sound to meet a precise need. In addition, if the effect is taken from the actual source, it has the advantage of being sonically authentic. Then, too, sound designers are sometimes called on to create effects that do not already exist and they prefer to build these from live sources.

Live sound effects are collected in three ways: by creating them in a studio, by recording them on the set during shooting, and by recording them directly from the actual source, usually in the field, either during or between productions.

Foley Sound Effects

Creating sound effects in the studio goes back to the days before television, when drama was so much a part of radio programming. Surrounded by the "tools of the trade"—door frames, telephone ringers, bells, buzzers, water tubs, car fenders, cutlery, cellophane, coconut shells, virtually anything that made a sound—the effects people, usually situated in the same studio with the performers, produced many of the sounds called for in the script. (Effects that were difficult to produce in a studio were taken from recordings.) Many ingenious ways were devised to create effects in the studio. For example: The sound of a gunshot was created by closing a book smartly or slamming it on a hard, solid surface; clapping coconut shells in a box of dirt produced the sound of hoof beats; crinkling cellophane effected fire; the "vision" of a moving sailboat was generated by twisting the resined screw handle of a broom into and out of a socket and flapping a cloth lightly; and squeezing cornstarch in a gloved hand simulated walking in snow.

The term now applied to this technique is *Foley recording*, named for Jack Foley, a sound editor with Universal Pictures for many years. Given the history of radio drama and the fact that other Hollywood sound editors had been producing effects in the studio for some time, clearly Jack Foley did not invent the technique. His name became identified with it in the early fifties when he had to produce the sound of paddling a small survival raft in the ocean. Instead of going out and recording the real sound, he did it in the studio and in sync with the picture. The inventiveness and efficiency he showed in producing this and several other effects and

simultaneously recording it to picture—saving the sound editor considerable postproduction time—impressed enough people that Foley's name has since become associated with the technique. Today, the primary purposes of Foley recording are: (1) to produce sound effects that are difficult to record during production, such as far-flung action scenes or large-scale movement of people and materiel; (2) to create sounds that do not exist; and (3) to produce controlled sound effects in a regulated studio environment.

This is not to suggest that "Foleying" and sonic authenticity are mutually exclusive. A door sound cannot be any door. Does the scene call for a closet door, a bathroom door, or a front door? A closet door has little air, a bathroom door sounds more open, and a front door sounds solid, with a latch to consider.

Foley effects are produced in any acoustically dry sound studio, but, preferably, they are recorded in a specially designed facility commonly known as a *Foley stage* (see 16-6). Foley stages are acoustically dry, not only because, as with dialogue rerecording, ambiences are added later, but because reflections from loud sounds have to be kept to a minimum.

Foley effects are usually produced in sync with the visuals. The picture is shown on a screen in the studio, and when a foot falls, a door opens, a paper rustles, a floor squeaks, a man sits, a girl coughs, a punch lands, or a body splashes, a Foley person generates the effect at the precise time it occurs on the screen. Such a person is sometimes called a Foley walker, because Foley work often requires performing many different types of footsteps. In fact, many Foley artists have been dancers.

Important to successful Foleying is having a feel for the material—to become, in a sense, the actor on the screen by, among other things, recognizing body movements and the sounds they generate. John Wayne, for example, did not have a typical walk; he sort of strode and rolled. Other actors may clomp, shuffle, or glide as they walk.

Also important to creating a sound effect is studying its sonic characteristics and then finding the sound source that contains similar characteristics. Take the sound of a growing rock. There is no

16-6 A Foley studio setup. The two Foley walkers are using the various pits and equipment to perform, in sync, the sounds that should be heard with the picture.

such sound, of course. But if there were, what would it be like? Its obvious characteristics would be stretching and sharp cracking sounds. One solution is to inflate a balloon and scrape it with your fingers to create a high-pitched scraping sound. If the rock is huge and requires a throatier sound, slow down the playback speed. For the cracking sound, shellac an inflated inner tube. Once the shellac hardens, sonically isolate the valve to eliminate the sound of air escaping and let the air out of the tube. As the air escapes, the shellac will crack. Combine both sounds to get the desired effect.

There are thousands of examples of created sounds. Here are a few:

■ Using a feather duster in the spokes of a spinning bicycle wheel to create the sound of beating wings

■ Twisting stalks of celery to simulate the sound of tendons being stretched

■ Scraping a metal guitar pick or can opener over a bag of ice for the sound of ice skating

■ Scraping dry ice on metal to create the sound of a moving glacier

■ Wiping dry glass to use as the basis for a squeak from a large mouse

■ Taking the rubber ball from a computer mouse and dragging it across the face of a computer monitor to help create the sound of a bat

■ Putting a dry soil conditioner on a piece of cloth and sliding a board around to simulate the sound of skiing

■ Whipping a thin, flexible stick through the air and overdubbing it several times to create the sound of arrows whooshing through air

■ Using the slurpy, sucking sound of a bathtub drain as the basis for the sound that emphasizes a whirlpool or someone sinking into quicksand

■ Discharging compressed air in a lot of mud to create the dense bubbling sound of a molten pit

■ Pulling a fist in and out of a watermelon to produce the sound of a monster taking the heart from a living person

■ Using the venting and exhaust sounds from a cylinder of nitrogen as the basis for the sound of a freeze gun

Often it takes two, three, or more sounds plus electronic processing to come up with the appropriate sound effect:

■ The helicopter sound at the beginning of *Apocalypse Now*—the blade thwarp, the turbine whine, and the gear sound—were created by synthesizing the sounds of a real helicopter.

■ In *Back to the Future III*, the basic sound of galloping horses was created using plungers on different types of surfaces. The sound was then rerecorded and processed in various ways to match the screen action.

■ The sound of the giant boulder careening toward the frantically running Indiana Jones in *Raiders of the Lost Ark* was the processed audio of a compact car rolling down a gravel road, in neutral, with the engine off.

■ The sound of the insects coming out of the heat duct in *Arachnophobia* was produced by recording Brazilian roaches walking on aluminum. The rasping sound a tarantula makes rubbing its back legs on the bulblike back half of its body was created from the sound of grease frying mixed with high-pressure air bursts.

■ The alien voices in *Cocoon* were made up of the crystal tones of champagne glasses and a flute with all the tone gone.

■ The roar of a Los Angeles freeway recorded through a vacuum cleaner pipe served as the basis for the sound of Luke Skywalker's land speeder in *Star Wars*.

■ The sounds of the spaceship *Millennium Falcon* in *Star Wars* included tiny fan motors, a flight of World War II torpedo planes, a pair of low-frequency sine waves beating against each other, variably phased white noise with frequency nulls, a blimp, a phased atom bomb explosion, a distorted thunderclap, an F-86 jet firing afterburners, a Phantom jet idle, a 747 takeoff, an F-105 jet taxiing, and a slowed-down P-51 prop plane pass-by. Various textures were taken from each of these sounds and blended together to create the engine noises, takeoffs, and fly-bys.

■ In *Jurassic Park* the sounds of the tyrannosaurus were made up of the trumpeting sound of a baby elephant, an alligator growl, and the growls of 15 other creatures, mostly lions and tigers. The inhale of T. Rex's breathing included the sounds of lions, seals, and dolphins; the exhale included the sound of a whale's blowhole. The smashing, crashing sound of trees being cut down, particularly Sequoias, was used to create the footfalls of the larger dinosaurs. The sounds of the reptilian dinosaurs were built from the sounds of lizards, iguanas, bull snakes, a rattlesnake (flanged), and horselike snorts. A Synclavier 9600 (a highly sophisticated synthesizer and sampler) was used to process many of these sounds, including some of the dinosaur footsteps and eating sounds.

■ The spinning and moving sounds of the main character going from place to place in *The Mask* were created by twirling garden hoses and power cables to get moving-through-air sounds, layering them in a Synclavier, routing them through a loudspeaker, waving a mic in front of the loudspeaker to get a Doppler effect, then adding jets, fire *whooses,* and wind gusts.

■ The multilayered sound of the batmobile in *Batman and Robin* was made up of the sounds of an Atlas rocket engine blast, the turbocharger whine of an 800-horsepower Buick Grand National, a Ducati motorcycle, and a Porsche 917 12-cylinder racer.

Vocalizing sound effects has been done since the days of radio drama. Today they are often combined with a physical sound to create a contoured effect. It is worth noting, however, that vocalized effects work only when they do not sound like a human voice generated them.

Components and Context of a Foley Sound Effect

Being ingenious in creating a sound effect is not enough. You also have to know the components of the effect and the context in which the effect will be placed. Let us use two examples as illustrations: a car crash and footsteps.

The sound of a car crash generally has six components: (1) the skid, (2) a slight pause just before impact, (3) the impact, (4) the grinding sound of metal, (5) the shattering of glass just after impact, and (6) silence.

The sound of footsteps consists of three basic elements: (1) the impact of the heel, which is a fairly crisp sound, (2) the brush of the sole, which is a relatively soft sound, and (3) sometimes, heel or sole scrapes.

But before producing these sounds, you need to know the context in which they will be placed. For the car crash, the make, model, and year of the car will dictate the sounds of the engine, the skidding, and, after the impact, the metal and glass. The type of tires and road surface will govern the pitch and density of the riding sound; the car's speed is another factor that affects pitch. The location of the road—for example, in the city or country—will help determine the quality of the sound's ambience and reverb. If the car is swerving, tire squeals may be required. Of course, what the car crashes into will also affect the sound's design.

As for the footsteps, the height, weight, sex, and age of the person will influence the sound's density and the heaviness of the footfall. Another influence on the footfall sound is the footwear itself—shoes with leather heels and soles, pumps, spiked heels, sneakers, sandals, and so on. The choices here may relate to the hardness or softness of the footfall, and the attack of the heel sound, or lack thereof. Perhaps you would want a suction-type or squeaky-type sound with sneakers; maybe you would use a flexing sound of leather for the sandals. The gait of the walk—fast, slow, ambling, steady, or accented—will direct the tempo of the footfalls. The type of walking surface—concrete, stone, wood, linoleum,

marble, or dirt—and whether it is wet, snowy, slushy, or muddy will be sonically defined by the sound's timbre and envelope. The amount of reverberation added to the effect depends on where the footfalls occur.

Miking and Perspective in Foley Recording

The capacitor microphone is most frequently used in recording Foley effects because of its ability to "hear" subtleties and capture transients—fast bursts of sound, such as door slams, gunshots, breaking glass, and footsteps—that constitute so much of Foley work. Tube-type capacitors help smooth harsh transients and warm digitally recorded effects.

Directional capacitors—super-, hyper-, and ultracardioid—are preferred because they pick up concentrated sound with little ambience. Also, these pickup patterns provide more flexibility in changing perspectives. Moving a highly directional microphone a few inches will sound like it was moved several feet.

Factors such as dynamic range and the noise floor require a good microphone preamp. Recording loud bangs or crashes or soft nuances of paper folding or pins dropping requires the capabilities to handle both a wide variety of dynamics and considerable gain with almost no additional noise. Many standard in-console preamps are not up to the task. Limiting and compression are sometimes used in Foley recording; except for noise reduction, processing is usually done during the final stages of postproduction.

Microphone placement is critical in Foleying because the on-screen environment must be replicated as closely as possible on the Foley stage. In relation to mic-to-source distance, the closer the microphone is to a sound source, the more detailed, intimate, and drier the sound. When the microphone is farther from a sound source, the converse of that is true, but only to a certain extent on a Foley stage because the studio itself has such a short reverberation time. To help create perspective or openness, or both, in the latter instance, multiple miking is often used. Nevertheless, if a shot calls for a close environment, baffles can be used to decrease the room size. If the screen environment is more open, the object is to operate in as open a space as possible.

A critical aspect of Foley recording cannot be overstated: Make sure the effects sound integrated and do not seem to be outside, or on top of, the soundtrack. When a sound is recorded at too close a mic-to-source distance, in poor acoustics, or with the wrong equipment, it is unlikely that EQ, reverb, or other signal processing will save it.

Production Sound Effects

Some directors prefer to capture authentic sounds either as they occur on the set during production or by recording them in the field separately, or both. These directors are willing to sacrifice, within limits, the controlled environment of the Foley stage for the greater sonic realism and authenticity of the actual sound sources produced in their natural surroundings. Still, a number of factors have to be taken into consideration to obtain usable sounds.

If sounds are recorded with the dialogue as part of the action—a table being thumped, a match being struck, a toaster being popped—getting the dialogue is always more important than getting the sound effect; the microphone must be positioned for optimal pickup of the performers.

When a director wants sound recorded with dialogue, the safest course of action is to record it with a different mic than the one being used for the dialogue. If the dialogue mic is a boom, use a plant (stationary) mic for the sound effect; if the dialogue microphone is a body mic, use a boom or plant mic for the sound. This facilitates recording sound and dialogue on separate tracks and, therefore, provides flexibility in postproduction editing and mixing.

If for some reason only one mic is used, a boom would be best. Because its mic-to-source position changes with the shot, there is a better chance of capturing and maintaining perspectives with it than with a body or plant mic. Moreover, in single-camera production, a scene is shot at least a few times from different perspectives, so there is more than one opportunity to record a usable sound/dialogue relationship.

This point should be emphasized: It is standard in single-camera production to shoot and reshoot a scene. For each shot, time is taken to reposition camera, lights, and crew, to redo makeup, primp wardrobe, and so on. During this time the sound crew also should be repositioning mic(s). Take advantage of every opportunity to record audio on the set. The more takes of dialogue and sound effects you record, the greater the flexibility in editing and mixing. Even if dialogue or effects are unusable because of mediocre audio quality, it is still wise to preserve the production recording because it is often useful in dialogue rerecording and Foleying as a reference for timing, accent, or expressiveness.

You never want to mask an actor's line with a sound effect, or any other sound for that matter, or to have a sound effect call attention to itself (unless that is the intent). If sound effects are not recorded with the action but, rather, on the set before or after shooting, try to do it just before shooting. Everyone is usually in place on the set, so the acoustics will match the acoustics of the take. If an effect has to be generated by the actor, it can be. And all sounds should be generated from the sound source's location in the scene.

Also, there has to be absolute quiet; nothing else can be audible: a dog barking far in the distance, an airplane flying overhead, wind gently wafting through trees, crockery vibrating, lights buzzing, crew shuffling, actors primping. The sound effect must be recorded "in the clear" so that it carries no sonic baggage into postproduction.

This brings us back to the question: If all these added concerns go with recording sound effects on the set, why bother? Why not save time, effort, and expense and simply Foley them? There are directors who do not care for the controlled acoustics of the Foley studio or for artificially created sound. They want to capture the flavor or "air" of a particular location and preserve the unique characteristic of a sound an actor gene-rates, or fuse the authenticity of and interaction among sounds as they occur naturally.

This creates considerable challenge in moving-action scenes, such as chases, that take place over some distance. These scenes are usually covered by multiple cameras, and although multiple microphones may not be positioned with the cameras, using them will capture the sounds of far-flung action. The mics can be situated at strategic spots along the chase route with separate mixer/recorder units at each location to control the on-coming, passing, and fading sounds. In addition, if possible, a mic mounted on the means of conveyance in the chase helps greatly in postproduction editing and mixing. For example, on a getaway car, mics can be mounted to the front fender, level with the hubcaps, and aimed at a 45-degree angle toward where the rubber meets the road; or a fishpole boom can be rigged through the rear window and rested on a door for support. In a horse chase, a mic can be mounted outside the rider's clothing or fastened to the lower saddle area and pointed toward the front hooves.

Another advantage to multiple-miking sound effects is the ability to capture various perspectives of the same sound. To record an explosion, for example, positioning mics, say, 25, 50, 100, and 500 feet away provides potential for a number of sonic possibilities when editing and mixing. Another reason it is a good idea to record extremely loud sound from more than one location is that the sound can overmodulate tape to the point that much of it may not record. That is why, for example, the sound of loud weaponry is compressed—to create a more percussive sound that otherwise might be distorted or sound thinner and weaker than the actual sound.

The obvious microphone to use in many of these situations may seem to be the wireless because of its mobility. As good as wireless systems can be, however, they are still subject to interference from radio frequencies, telephone lines, and passing cars, which causes spitting and buzzing sounds. A directional capacitor microphone connected to a good mic preamp is the most dependable approach to take here. In these applications use very strong shock mounts and tough windscreens. And do not overlook the importance of wearing ear protection when you are working with loud sounds. Do not monitor these sounds directly—use your eyes and the VU (or ppm) meter instead of your ears.

Collecting Sound Effects in the Field

Live sound collected away from the set for a specific production or between productions to build effects libraries is usually collected in the field. As with most field recording, utmost care should be taken to record the effect in perspective, with no unwanted sound. It cannot be overemphasized that any recording done away from the studio also requires first-rate, circumaural headphones for reliable monitoring.

As with most sound-effects miking, the directional capacitor is preferred for reasons already noted. That said, the parabolic microphone system, using a capacitor mic, is also employed for recording sounds in the field for long-reach, highly concentrated pickup. This is particularly important when recording weaker sounds, such as insects, certain types of bird calls, or rustling leaves. Parabolics are essentially midrange instruments, so it is probably unwise to use them on sound sources with significant defining low or high frequencies. For stereo, the M-S and stereo mics are more commonly used, because they are easier to set up than coincident or spaced stereo microphones and are more accurate to aim at a sound source.

A key to collecting successful live effects in the field is making sure that the recorded effect sounds like what it is supposed to be. Placing a mic too close to a babbling brook could make it sound like boiling water or liquid bubbling in a beaker. Miking it from too far a distance, on the other hand, might destroy its liquidity. A flowing stream miked too close could sound like a river; miked too far could reduce its size and density. A recording of the inside of a submarine could sound too cavernous. Applause might sound like rain or something frying. A spraying fountain might sound like rain, applause, or something frying. Specifically, a spraying fountain often lacks the identifying liquid sound. To get the desired audio, it might be necessary to mix in a watery-type sound, such as a river or a flowing, rather than babbling, brook. A yellow jacket flying around a box could sound like a deeper, fuller-sounding bumblebee if miked too close, or a mosquito if miked too far. A gunshot recorded outdoors, in open surroundings, sounds like a firecracker; some types of revolvers sound like pop guns.

Keep three other things in mind when recording sounds in the field: Be patient, be inventive, and, if you really want authenticity, be ready to go to almost any length to obtain an effect. For example, in the film *Glory,* the sound designer wanted the effects of Civil War weaponry to be as close to authentic as possible, even to the extent of capturing the sound of real Civil War cannonballs and bullets whizzing through the air. Specially made iron cannonballs were shot from cannons forged for the film; this was recorded at 250 yards and a quarter-mile downrange. These locations were far enough from the initial explosion that it would not contaminate the sound of the projectile going by. The two distances provided a choice of whiz-by sounds and also the potential for mixing them, if necessary. Because the cannons could not be aimed very well at such distances, not one acceptable whiz-by was recorded during an entire day of taping.

For the bullet whizzes, modern rifles would not have worked, because the bullet velocity is not slow enough to produce an audible air whiz-by. Using real Civil War bullets, a recordist sat in a gully 400 yards downrange and taped the whiz-bys as the live rounds flew overhead. In the end, the cannonball whiz-bys had to be created by playing the bullet whiz-bys in reverse and slowed down.

Finally, when collecting sounds in the field, do not necessarily think literally about what it is you want to capture. Consider a sound's potential to be built into another effect. For example, the basic sound of Chewbacca the Wookiee in *Star Wars* was the growl of a real bear. Among the many different laser sounds in the film, some incorporated the buzz of inductance recorded by passing a microphone behind a television set or the guy wire twang of a transmitter tower. Other examples of transforming sound effects are cited throughout this chapter.

ELECTRONICALLY GENERATED SOUND EFFECTS

High-quality sound effects can be generated electronically with synthesizers and computers and by employing MIDI. This approach is also referred to as *electronic foley.* It is cost-efficient, convenient, and unlimited in the sounds that can be created. Electronically generated sound effects sometimes lack the "reality" directors desire, however.

Synthesized Sound Effects

A *synthesizer* is an audio instrument that uses sound generators to create waveforms. The various ways these waveforms are combined can synthesize a vast array of sonic characteristics that are similar to, but not exactly like, existing sounds and musical instruments. They can also be combined to generate a completely original sound. In other words, because the pitch, amplitude, timbre, and envelope of each synthesizer tone generator can be controlled, it is possible to build synthesized sounds from scratch.

In addition to being able to create synthesized effects, preprogrammed sound from libraries designed for specific synthesizer brands and models are available. These collections may be grouped by type of sound effect, such as punches, screams, thunder, or by instrument category, such as drum, string, brass, and keyboard sounds (see 16-7). These libraries come in various formats, such as floppy and hard disk and plug-in memory cartridge.

One complaint about synthesized sound has been its readily identifiable electronic quality. With the advent of improved synthesizer designs and software, however, this has become less of a problem. But take care to make sure that the synthesizer and sound library you use produces professional-quality sound; many do not.

The operational aspects of synthesizers and their programs are beyond the purview of this book. Even if they were not, it is extremely difficult even to begin to describe the sonic qualities of the myriad effects a synthesizer can generate. Suffice it to say,

16-7 Selected example of one synthesizer's soundfiles in the drum category

almost anything is possible. The same is true of computer-generated sound effects.

Computer-Generated Sound Effects

A principal difference between the synthesizer and the computer is that the synthesizer is a device specifically designed to create and produce sounds; the computer is not. The computer is completely software-dependent. With the appropriate software, the computer, like the synthesizer, can also store preprogrammed sounds or create them from scratch, or both. Many computer sound programs make it possible not only to call up a particular effect but to see and manipulate its waveform and, therefore, its sonic characteristics (see 17-34).

Sampling

An important sound-shaping capability of many electronic keyboards and computer software programs is *sampling*, a process whereby digital audio data representing a sonic event, acoustic or electroacoustic, is stored on disk or into a memory. The acoustic sounds can be anything a microphone can record—a shout, splash, motor sputter, song lyric, trombone solo, whatever. Electroacoustic sounds are anything electronically generated, such as those a synthesizer produces. The samples can be of any length, as brief as a drumbeat or as long as the available memory allows.

A *sampler,* which is basically a specialized digital record and playback device, may be keyboard-based, making use of musical keyboard controllers to trigger and articulate sampled audio; or it may be a rack-mountable unit, without a keyboard, which is controlled by an external keyboard or a sequencer. A *sequencer* is a device that stores messages, maintains time relationships among them, and transmits the messages when they are called for from devices connected to it. The sampler system may also be computer-based.

With most sampling systems, it is possible to produce an almost infinite variety of sound effects by shortening, lengthening, rearranging, looping, and signal-processing the stored samples. A trombone can be made to sound like a saxophone, an English horn, or a marching band of "76 trombones." One drumbeat can be processed into a thunderclap or built into a chorus of jungle drums. The crack of a baseball bat can be shaped into the rip that just precedes an explosion. Chirping birds can become a gaggle of geese. A metal trash can being hit with a hammer can provide a formidable backbeat for a rhythm track. The squeal of a pig can be transformed into a human scream.

In solid-state memory systems, such as ROM (read-only memory) or RAM (random-access memory), it is possible to access, instantly, all or part of the sample and reproduce it any number of times. The difference between ROM- and RAM-based samplers is that ROM-based samplers are factory programmed and reproduce only; RAM-based samplers allow you to both reproduce and record sound samples. The number of samples you can load into a system is limited only by the capacity of the system's storage memory.

The Samplefile

After a sample is recorded or produced, or both, it is usually saved to a storage medium, most commonly a floppy disk, hard disk, or compact disc. The stored sound data is referred to as a *samplefile*. Once stored, of course, a samplefile can be easily distributed. As a result, samplefiles of sounds are now available to production facilities in the same way that sound-effects libraries on CD are available. Other storage mediums are also used for samplefile distribution, such as CD-ROM, erasable and write-once optical discs, and tape. Samplefiles are also available on-line.

You should take two precautions before investing in a samplefile library. First, make sure that the samplefiles are in a format that is compatible with your sampler. Recently, steps have been taken to increase standardization of samplefile formats for computer-based systems. Second, make sure that the sound quality of the samples is up to professional standards; too many are not, particularly those obtained on-line.

Tips for Recording Samples

In recording samples from whatever source—acoustic or electronic—it is vital that the sound and reproduction be of good quality. Because the sample may be used many times in a variety of situations, it is disconcerting (to say the least) to hear a bad sample again and again. Moreover, if the sample has to be rerecorded, it might be difficult to reconstruct the same sonic and performance situation.

Miking

The same advice that applies to miking for digital recording (see Chapter 15) also applies to miking for sampling. Only the highest-quality microphones should be used, which usually means capacitors with high sensitivity and low noise. If percussion recorded at close mic-to-source distances requires a moving-coil mic, it should be a large-diaphragm, top-quality model.

Organizing a Sound-Effects Library

It is not unusual for an audio facility to have thousands of sound effects in its collection. Although prerecorded libraries come with an index, timing information, and, often, descriptions of the cues, and sound effects produced in-house are also catalogued, it can be time-consuming to locate and audition an effect. Database systems are available that enable you to search, locate, and audition a sound effect in seconds.

Generally, the search feature provides four ways to find a sound effect: by category, word, synonym, and catalog number. The database system can be interfaced with a multidisc CD player so that once an effect has been located, it can be auditioned from the start of the track or cued to within a split second anywhere in the track.

For example, by punching in "thunder," the user finds out that there are 56 versions of thunder available, the time of each version, and a short description of what type of thunder it is. In some systems the computer will unload the disc and play back the thunder effects called for.

MUSIC

Music for productions can be obtained in three ways: (1) by having it composed and recorded for a particular piece; (2) by choosing it from a prerecorded music library; or (3) by selecting it from a commercial CD. Because composing music for underscoring is covered in Chapter 10 and music recording is discussed in Chapter 15, the following section considers the use of prerecorded music libraries and commercial music CDs.

Prerecorded Music Libraries

Prerecorded music libraries, like prerecorded sound-effects libraries, are convenient and less expensive alternatives to commissioning the music to be composed and recorded. Music libraries are used for commercials, promos, bumpers, and drama. They provide original music composed to evoke a wide range of human emotions and information: happiness, conflict, melancholy, liveliness, danger, the future, the eighteenth century, the Far East, the bustling city, and countless others.

Music libraries provide music in a variety of styles and textures. Compositions are arranged for orchestras of various sizes, dance and military bands, rock and jazz groups, solo instruments, synthesizers—virtually any voicing or combination of voicings necessary to evoke an idea or emotion (see 16-8). Music cues are also subdivided by length and version. For example: an "industrial music" disc may have cuts of :29, :59, 1:30, and 2:30 minutes long, each with a full orchestral mix and just a rhythm track for underscoring an announcer. There are also entire music libraries recorded with reduced

OM CD 71 "**Sailing**"—Light jazz and other relaxed contemporary backgrounds characterize this new release, with a variety of uses from leisure activities and travel to cosmetics and fashion. The orchestrations are mostly acoustic and feature saxophone, guitar, and piano. This disc contains 17 full-length themes plus 22 broadcast edits.

OM CD 72 "**Hard Rock**"—From heavy metal to grunge to thrash, this disc captures the hot licks and high energy of today's contemporary rock-and-roll music. The 19 full-length themes range from Pearl Jam to Red Hot Chili Peppers. 24 broadcast edits are included.

OM CD 73 "**Zapfile 2**"—We've packed more than 150 logos, bumpers, zaps, sweepers, percussion effects, and bulletin boards into one of the single most useful discs in any music library. Seven sections include Bulletin Boards, News, Contemporary Logos, Traditional Logos, Special Effects, Percussion, and Tags and Transitions.

OM CD 74 "**New Generation**"—This disc contains 17 contemporary pop music tracks for "Generation X," ranging from quasi-rap urban funk to lush, melodic guitar ballads. The 22 broadcast edits included on the disc make it perfect for fashion, cosmetics, teen culture, or any other young subject.

OM CD 75 "**Precision**"—The pace and urgency of today's business combine with the excitement and wonder of technology in this disc, which features 17 different full-length themes and 22 broadcast edits. Applications extend to any production that deals with today's work environment.

OM CD 76 "**Da Capo**"—This disc features 18 well-known classical themes orchestrated in a variety of styles, ranging from jazz combo to rock orchestra. Tracks include the slightly serious, the cool contemporary, and outright slapstick. Famous composers include Bach, Beethoven, Mozart, and Grieg. 21 broadcast edits are also included.

OM CD 77 "**Passport**"—Ethnic music from around the world, including the Far East, Middle East, southern Europe, Mexico, South America, and Africa. This mostly contemporary disc features many authentic and exotic instruments. It's ideal for those productions that require an instant "location" identifier. 24 broadcast edits are also included.

16-8 Example of selected contents in one CD music library dynamic range for the sole purpose of music underscoring. The reduced dynamic range permits music to accompany an announcer or narrator without it calling attention to itself or overwhelming the speech.

Avoiding the "Canned" Music Sound

The problems with sound quality that used to plague analog music libraries have been eliminated for the most part with the CD. Those problems resulted in the "canned" sound—deficiencies, such as thin, raspy sound, not enough presence or brilliance, too much midrange, limited dynamic range, and so on.

Although those characteristics of canned sound have been largely eliminated in today's music libraries, you still have to be wary of another contributor to the "canned" sound: stilted and mechanical performances, and mediocre composing and arranging, which have nothing to do with the analog or digital format. Because music libraries vary in creative and sonic quality, listen to a demonstration disc before you buy. In addition to sound quality, good performance, and creative composing and arranging, also listen for true stereo imaging, realistic acoustics or ambience, and music that is not so invasive that it could draw attention away from the narrative.

Customized Music Libraries

Prerecorded music libraries have the same limitations as sound-effects libraries: fixed cues and times. Computer programs are available that customize music cues. One such program, SmartSound,® helps you assemble a jingle or a soundtrack in a number of ways: by designating openers, finales, accents, and backgrounds to times that can be specified to tenth-of-a-second accuracy. It is also possible to choose from a variety of musical styles and describe the effect you want the music to have. An editing function breaks soundfiles into moveable blocks for positioning in any order. The program makes it possible for the nonmusician to "compose" music; if assembled pieces do not fit together musically, the system conveys a warning and pro-vides functions for smoothing transitions between blocks (see 16-9).

Copyrights

By law any recorded material with a copyright may not be played over the air, copied (dubbed), or used for most nonprivate purposes without permission from the licensor—that is, the company or individual(s) holding the rights to the recorded material. Broadcasters, for example, pay fees to such major licensors as Broadcast Music, Inc. (BMI) and the American Society of Composers, Authors, and Publishers (ASCAP) for the right to play commercially recorded music on the air.

The rights to music libraries, however, usually belong to the companies that distribute them. Fees are paid to these companies. There are a variety of licensing and payment options. Some libraries are buyout-based and some charge by the region, media, length of cut, or length of use.

There are three rights to consider: mechanical, synchronization, and public performance. Mechanical rights permit rerecording the music from a purchased CD or CD-ROM. Synchronization rights allow the music to be put into a time relationship with a picture. Public performance rights authorize commercial use of the music.

Generally, when you buy a music library, you pay an annual set fee for it. (You may have the option of buying all or part of a collection, including discs added to the collection during the contract period.) Your right to use that library for profit or public performance is another matter. Depending on the distributor, you acquire usage rights for another fee determined either on the basis of *needle,* or *laser, drops*—the number of times you use music from any selection or any portion of a selection—or a fee that gives you unlimited usage rights for one or a number of years (see 16-10). (*Needle drop* was the term coined when music libraries were available on record.) Sometimes the laser-drop fee may be applied to the buyout cost. When the buyout cost has been paid in laser-drop fees, unlimited long-term usage is granted.

If you are paying on the basis of laser drops, you must fill out a clearance form listing all the laser

a

b

c

16-9 SmartSound® **(a) controller, (b) block window, and (c) sequence window.** The block window provides the source material to do the arranging and editing, which can then be dragged and dropped into the sequence window.

For those clients whose production schedule does not justify an annual blanket license, Omnimusic may be used and licensed on a laser-drop basis. The multiple laser-drop license covers the use of an unlimited number of drops within a single production.

	Non-Broadcast	Broadcast
Single Laser-Drop License	$ 50.00	$ 75.00

Multiple Laser-Drop License
(Fees based on total production length)

	Non-Broadcast	Broadcast
Production of 5 minutes or less	$ 100.00	$ 150.00
Production of 10 minutes or less	150.00	225.00
Production of 15 minutes or less	200.00	300.00
Production of 20 minutes or less	250.00	375.00
(Each additional 5 minutes)	(50.00)	(75.00)

Commercials and PSAs
(Rates are per laser drop)

	Local/Regional	National
Television or radio spot	$ 60.00	$ 100.00
Public service announcement	60.00	60.00

Duplication and Retail Sale Surcharges
(Retail sale rates include duplication)

	Duplication Only (per laser drop)	Retail Sale (per laser drop)
Up to 100 copies	no charge	no charge
Up to 1,000 copies	$ 5.00	$ 10.00
Up to 10,000 copies	10.00	25.00
Up to 50,000 copies	25.00	50.00
Up to 100,000 copies	50.00	75.00
Each additional 100,000 copies	150.00	300.00

Prices are subject to change without notice or obligation. Licenses are not valid for the use of our music in any production where the music constitutes the primary value of the production, or where the music is offered as a separate and distinct element for reuse by others, or in adult-entertainment productions.

"Broadcast" includes commercial broadcasting stations, commercial networks, and satellite and microwave networks. Productions created for company-owned networks used exclusively for non-commercial company business are considered "Non-Broadcast." "Educational" rates are available only to accredited institutions.

Multiple-use facilities, network broadcasters, cable programmers, and music wholesalers may be subject to additional license fees.

16-10 (a) Example of a laser-drop licensing rate schedule

drops used in your production. You pay whatever fee the licensor's rate card indicates. The licensor then sends you written permission to use its music, for profit, in your production. If you use any of the same music in another production, you have to pay another laser-drop fee.

Often a production contains so many laser drops that the copyright fee is prohibitively expensive. In such cases, many licensors charge a flat rate, which has become the most common way of charging usage fees.

Some organizations, such as educational institutions, small production companies, and many broadcasting stations, do not generate enough in copyright fees to make the rental of a music library worthwhile to the licensor. Therefore

The Omnimusic Broadcast Blanket

This annual synchronization license covers music use by radio and television broadcasters or producers, ad agencies, and others whose productions will be broadcast (including cable, microwave, satellite, etc.). Non-broadcast rights are included. New CD releases are included at no additional charge. $2,500.00

The Omnimusic Non-Broadcast Blanket

This annual synchronization license covers use by multimedia companies, corporate AV or video departments, film companies, and others producing corporate or educational communications not intended for broadcast. New CD releases are included at no additional charge. $2,000.00

The Omnimusic Educational Blanket

This annual synchronization license covers broadcast and non-broadcast use by accredited colleges, universities, and school districts. New CD releases are included at no additional charge. $1,500.00

Other Omnimusic Blankets

	Broadcast	Non-Broadcast	Educational
Omni Select 50 Blanket	$ 1,800.00	$ 1,500.00	$ 1,200.00
Omni Select 25 Blanket	$ 1,500.00	$ 1,200.00	$ 900.00
Omni Select 10 Blanket	$ 850.00	$ 750.00	$ 650.00

New CD releases are not included in the Select Blankets. However, upgrades are available at any time. Ask our sales representatives for details.

Multiple-year contracts for all blanket clients are available on request.

16-10 *(continued)* **(b) Example of a blanket licensing rate schedule**

many licensors rent their libraries to such organizations for a lower, flat, annual rate. This clears the music for blanket use. Such an arrangement may be renewed each year; when it terminates, most licensors require return of the library.

Using Music from Commercial CDs

Using music from commercial CDs for underscoring should be carefully considered. It carries emotional baggage and, in theatrical film and television, it is expensive.

Familiar music tends to trigger memories associated with it, which could compete with or distract from the main information. Familiar music usually does not compel the attention on the part of the listener that unfamiliar music does, which could reduce the overall impact of the communication.

Sometimes using familiar music is justified and effective, however. For example, in a story set in the 1950s, music from that era can set the appropriate tone; or in a drama about the social upheavals created by the Vietnam War, incorporating music from the late 1960s can create additional impact. But the decision to use familiar music should come only after careful consideration. It should not be used simply because it is an easier way to provide informational or emotional enhancement.

Another problem with using familiar music is that it usually comes from commercially released recordings, so obtaining copyright release could be costly. The copyright fee is definitely much more expensive than using library music and often higher than the cost of commissioning and recording original music.

Whatever the advantages and disadvantages of using prerecorded music for underscoring, directors generally prefer original to derivative music. It can be more carefully crafted to fulfill a production's cognitive or affective needs.

Using Music from Sample CDs

Sample CDs of music are available in all types of styles and instrumentations. Musical style may be hip-hop, rap, general purpose, pop rock, and so on. Samples may be of drum loops, bass and voices, funky guitar, synthesizer, keyboards, music indigenous to a particular region, and so on. A bank of samples may have several variations, such as short release, darker, and octave stacks. Rhythm samples come in a variety of *beats per minute (bpm)*.

Samples are also designed for use with particular synthesizer platforms. Accompanying manuals provide instructions for sample manipulation, which may include ways to produce alternate envelope shapes, alternate velocity curves, EQ balances, phase shifts, and stereo imaging.

Music Sampling and Copyright

The problem of sampling and copyright is a thorny issue, because a sample is so easy to produce and hide in a recording. Moreover, there are myriad samples available from sample libraries and the Internet.

Suppose that a production company leases a music library and in that library are portions of selections—accents, phrases, beat combinations—that are particularly suitable for sampling. The company redesigns them to make a new music cue. The new music cue sounds nothing like the work from which it was taken, and the samples used were only fractions of a second. Is copyright in force and, if so, who pays what to whom?

The letter of the law is straightforward: It is illegal to make derivative works of another person's copyrighted material without their express permission. In the above example, clearing usage of a sample requires the permission of the copyright owner of the original composition (the composer or publishing company) and the owner of the copyright of the master (record company, music library, or other distributor).

Other considerations in negotiating a sample clearance are: the territory of your authorized use of the sample; cost of the sample; whether there will be an ongoing royalty for as long as the sample is in use; what credits are to be given to the original copyright holder; who owns the new work; and whether new permissions must be given for other uses of the sample.

Sampling has made it possible to take any recorded sound, process it, and use it for one's own purposes. The practice has become so widespread that it has created a major controversy about royalty and copyright infringement, and millions of dollars have already been awarded for such infringement.

Using the copyrighted work of others without their permission for your own financial gain, no matter how little of that material you use, is unethical and illegal. Consider your reaction if someone took credit for and profited from material you created without sharing any of the earnings with you.

Organizing a Music Library

To better organize and more speedily retrieve the thousands of selections an audio facility may have in its music collection, database systems are available similar to those used for sound-effects collections. A user can call up a music cue by library, category, keyword, instrumentation, tempo, and version. Some computer systems allow auditioning and editing of any number of musical segments instantly.

For example, a user needs a particular music cue to last 25 seconds. The system finds, say, seven versions of that cue and plays those you wish to hear. If there are similar music cues, but in varying times of 15, 33, 45, and 66 seconds, they too can be called up, auditioned, and, with some systems, edited to conform to your timing needs.

- In automated dialogue replacement (ADR), also known as automatic dialogue replacement and looping, dialogue is recorded or rerecorded, depending on the outcome of the production recording or the director's aesthetic preference, or both.

- ADR is done in a dialogue recording studio, a relatively dry room with a screen, microphone, and sometimes a small audio control panel.

- ADR frees picture from sound and gives the director more flexibility and control. On the other hand, it involves re-creating a performance, which is not as natural or as authentic as the real thing.

- The two primary sources of sound effects (SFX) are prerecorded and produced.

- Prerecorded sound effects that can number from several dozen to several thousand are available in libraries. The major advantage of sound-effects libraries is that for relatively little cost many different, perhaps difficult-to-produce, sounds are at your fingertips. The disadvantages include the lack of control over the dynamics of the effect, possible mismatches in ambience, and the chance that the effects may sound canned.

- Sound-effects libraries can be expanded by varying a sound's playing speed, altering it through signal processing, playing it backward, and looping it.

- Producing live sound effects in the studio goes back to the days of radio drama but is commonly known as Foleying, after former film soundman Jack Foley.

- The keys to creating a sound effect are analyzing its sonic characteristics and then finding the sound source that contains similar characteristics, whatever it may be.

- The capacitor microphone is most frequently used in recording Foley effects, because of its ability to "hear" subtleties and capture transients. Tube-type capacitors help smooth transients and warm digitally recorded effects.

- A critical aspect of Foley recording is making sure that the effects sound integrated and do not seem to be outside, or on top of, the sound track.

- Some directors shun using studio-created effects, preferring to capture authentic sounds either as they occur on the set during production or by recording them in the field separately, or both.

- Sound effects can also be generated electronically with synthesizers and computers and by employing MIDI—an approach called electronic foley. A synthesizer is an audio instrument that uses sound generators to create waveforms. Computer sound effects can be generated from preprogrammed software or software that allows sounds to be produced from scratch.

- An important sound-shaping capability of many synthesizers and computer software programs is sampling, a process whereby a section of digital audio representing a sonic event, acoustic or electroacoustic, can be signal-processed into a different sound or expanded to serve as the basis for a longer sonic creation.

- In recording samples, it is important to take your time and record them with the highest fidelity; if a sample has to be rerecorded, it might be difficult to reconstruct the same sonic and performance situation.

- Sound-effects collections can be organized into databases to facilitate cataloging, locating, and auditioning them.

- Music for productions can be obtained in three ways: (1) by having it composed and recorded for a particular piece; (2) by choosing it from a prerecorded music library; or (3) by selecting it from a commercial CD.

- Prerecorded music libraries provide a relatively inexpensive way to use original music to underscore the ideas and emotions in a script.

- Most recordings are copyrighted and may not be used unless a fee is paid to the licensor. In the case of music libraries, the fee is charged on a flat-rate use or is based on the number of needle, or laser, drops in a production.

- Sampling has made it possible to take any recorded sound, including copyrighted material, process it, and use it for one's own purposes. Using any copyrighted material without permission is illegal.

- Like sound libraries, music libraries can be organized into databases to facilitate cataloging, locating, and auditioning them.

Editing

The art of editing requires the ability to see a whole and build toward it while it is still in parts. It calls for a good "ear," dexterity, coordination, and sensitivity to the aesthetics of sound. Yet with these abilities, the editor seldom gets recognition, except professionally; an effective edit does not call attention to itself. Hence the audience is usually not aware of it.

There are several reasons for editing. Program segments may need to be rearranged, shortened, or cut out altogether. Directors commonly record elements of a program out of sequence; editing makes this possible. It also makes it possible to record a segment several times and choose the best parts of each take. Editing can change the relationship of characters in a drama; redirect an entire story line; create the pace and establish timing; and eliminate mistakes, long pauses, coughing, "ahs," "ers," "ums," and other awkwardness. Parts of words can be transposed, music "recomposed," the character of a sound effect changed, and the quality of dialogue improved.

EDITING METHODS

Until the advent of digital technology, tape editing was a linear process. In *linear editing* recorded material is edited successively: One section at a time is taken from one part of a recoding and spliced to another part, or recorded material is electronically transferred from one tape to another. The material may be edited sequentially or inserted at a particular point in the tape. In either case, final assembly is sequential. It is also slow compared with nonlinear editing, which benefits from the formidable power of computer processing and data storage.

Nonlinear editing is a digital process that allows the assembly of disk-based material in or out of sequence, taken from any part of a recording, and placed in any other part of the recording almost instantly, at the touch of a few buttons. It is possible to audition the edit at any stage in the procedure and restore any change in the edited material to its original waveform at any time, quickly and seamlessly.

Although the technology is more expensive and the techniques are more involved in nonlinear editing, overall, its advantages are overwhelming compared with the linear approach. Nonlinear editing is the way most editing is done today and how almost all editing will be done in the not-too-distant future. That said, linear editing is still practiced and, therefore, warrants coverage here.

LINEAR EDITING

Two methods of linear editing are in use today: cut-and-splice tape editing and electronic editing. This entails using one tape recorder and inserting—punching in—material, or transferring material from one tape recorder to another.

Cut-and-Splice Editing of Open-Reel Analog Audiotape

The *cut-and-splice editing* method can be employed only with recordings on ¼-inch audiotape (and also film—see "Cut-and-Splice Editing of Film" later in this chapter). Multitrack tape cannot edited that way because it is not possible to edit one track without cutting into the other tracks. Videotape has never been cut-and-splice edited, except at the very beginning of its history.

Equipment

For cutting and splicing audiotape, you need the following items: metal editing block (see Figure 17-1); single-edge razor blade that should be replaced often during lengthy editing sessions so that it cannot become magnetized; indelible marker with a soft tip; *splicing tape*, made especially for audiotape, that comes in rolls for use with a dispenser; extra empty reels; a flat, clean surface; a cue sheet to keep a record of the edits made; and leader tape.

Leader tape is nonmagnetic tape used for threading, cueing, and, sometimes, timing (see 17-2). When spliced between segments of recording tape,

17-1 Cutting angles on ¼- and ½-inch editing blocks

Beginning of audiotape   End of leader

1 second at 7½ ips

17-2 Leader tape. (a) Leader tape serves as a visual reference to the beginning of a sound. Provided the sound is there, it makes cueing a tape easier and faster. (b) Plastic leader tape can also be used for timing. The arrows indicate the direction of tape travel.

Leader
tape

17-3 Light-colored leader tape visible between the tape segments

it provides an easy visual reference that facilitates spooling quickly to a desired cut (see 17-3). Leader tape is also spliced to both ends of recording tape to preserve these vulnerable points.

Leader tape is available in both plastic and paper. Paper is used mainly when extremely high sound quality is vital, because, unlike plastic leader tape, paper tape does not build up static electricity when it is wound excessively. Static electricity can affect magnetically encoded information if it builds to strong enough proportions. A problem with paper leader tape is that it tears easily.

Leader tape also comes in various colors. Studios may use a certain-colored leader tape at the head of a reel, another color at the tail of the reel, and still other colors to indicate the beginning and end of segments within a reel.

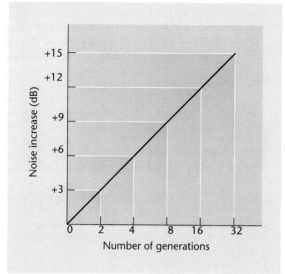

17-4 The effect that dubbing analog recordings has on sound quality

Basic Procedures

Before cutting any tape, make a duplicate—called a *dub*—of the original or master tape. Store the master, tails out, in a safe place, and use the dubbed tape for cutting and splicing. Then, if any serious mistakes are made in cutting, it is possible to make another dub from the master. Another reason for never cutting the original tape is that time code sync would be lost.

Of course, a dub is second-generation and, with analog tape, loses something in sound quality (see 17-4). But when dubbing with high-quality, well-maintained equipment, the loss in sound quality is minimal and the trade-off—a slight loss in response for the sure safety and sync preservation of the original material—is worth it.

The master tape should not be used in editing—cut-and-splice or electronic. The reason, when using the cut-and-splice method, has just been covered. Although electronic editing does not require physically cutting the tape, it may necessitate running it across the tape heads over and over again. Each pass wears the magnetic coating. The more passes a tape makes, therefore, the more the quality of sound is degraded.

Record the master tape at at least 15 ips (inches per second); if this is not possible, dub it at that speed. The faster a tape travels across the heads, the more spread out the sound is and the easier it is to edit (see 17-5). Analog sound quality is better at faster speeds, too. (Although at 30 ips, the sound on high-quality tape recorded on a high-quality recorder can be too crisp.)

Let's go through the basic procedures, step-by-step, for making a simple edit, cut, and splice. A speaker greets an audience with "Good evening [cough], ladies and gentlemen." The editing task here is to cut the cough. Once you decide what to edit, the next steps are to (1) determine exactly

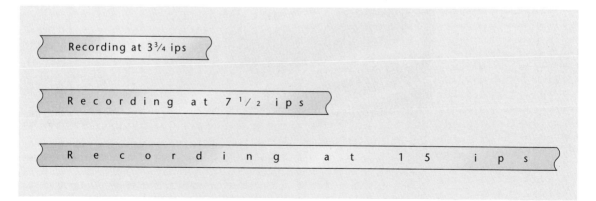

17-5 Representation of sound spread on tape at three different speeds. The faster the tape recorder speed, the more spread out the sound on the tape and the easier it is to edit.

where the edit points will be and (2) locate those points on the recording tape.

Assume that the speaker took two breaths, one after "evening" and one after the cough. For reasons that will be explained in "Techniques and Aesthetic Considerations" later in this chapter, the edit points should fall after the first breath and immediately before "ladies" (see 17-6). Once the edit points are chosen, you are ready to proceed with the cutting and splicing (see 17-7 through 17-18).

17-6 Sound to be cut and spliced with edit points indicated

17-7 Locating the first edit point. After the tape has been threaded and wound close to the edit point, put the tape recorder in *stop*. In *stop* (some machines may have a *pause*, *cue*, or *edit* button), the playback head is "live." This allows you to hear what is on the tape and manually control the tape speed as you locate the precise edit point. You are making the initial cut after the first breath. With the edit point at the playback head, put your left hand on the feed reel and your right hand on the takeup reel. Then rock the tape back and forth until you hear exactly where the first breath ends, just before the sound of the cough. Many tape recorders have a manual control to facilitate rocking the tape.

17-8 Marking the first edit point. When you locate the edit point, mark it with a marking pen or pencil. Make sure the mark is visible.

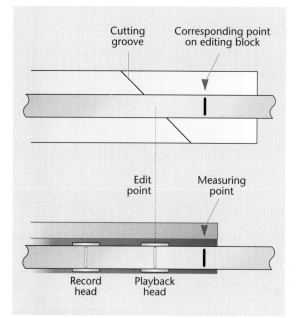

17-9 Another way to mark the edit point. You saw in Figure 17-8 one way to mark tape—at the playback head. But unless you are highly skilled, this technique could result in the head being nudged out of alignment or, worse, damaged. A safer marking procedure is to establish a measured point close to the playback head and mark the tape there.

17-10 Marking the second edit point. With the first edit marked, wind the tape to the second edit point and rock it until you locate the point just before you hear the "l" in "Ladies." After locating the second edit point, mark it. Now you are ready to cut the tape.

17-11 Using the editing block. (a) Gently lift the tape from the playback head, and (b) place it in the channel of the editing block with the first edit point on the diagonal cutting groove.

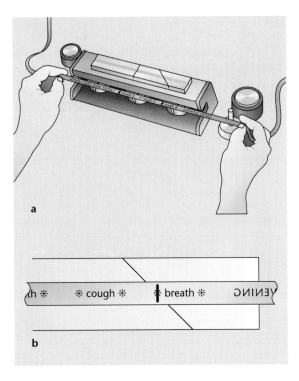

a

b

17-12 Cutting the tape. Using a razor blade, cut the tape diagonally, drawing the razor angled through the slot without bending the tape ends into the cutting groove. A diagonal cut gives the sound a split second to become established in our hearing. A vertical (90-degree) cut hits the playback head all at once, and we sometimes hear the abrupt change from one edit to another as a pop, click, or beep. Also, the diagonal cut exposes a longer tape edge than a 90-degree cut, thereby ensuring a stronger splice.

Make a diagonal cut at the first edit point

17-13 Making the second cut. Gently remove the cut tape from the channel of the editing block, find the second edit point, place the tape back in the channel over the diagonal groove, and cut on the mark.

Make another cut at the second edit point

17-14 Cuts completed. Now you are ready to splice the two edits together.

cough & breath

17-15 Marking fragments. Until you are certain that the splice has been made successfully, it is a good idea to save the deleted tape, note what is on it, and put an arrow on the tab to indicate the head end.

17-16 Joining the tape ends. Take the two tape ends and butt them together. Make sure that there is no overlap or space between them.

17-17 Splicing. Take a piece of splicing tape roughly ½ inch long and place it so that ¼ inch covers each tape end. Do not use less than ½ inch of splicing tape or the splice may break. Using your finger or a blunt instrument, press the splicing tape firmly onto the recording tape to ensure a strong splice. Make sure that no white bubbles remain on the splicing tape; they indicate that the splicing tape is not bonded firmly to the recording tape. Gently remove the tape from the editing block and play it to check the edit.

17-18 Undoing a splice. If you need to undo a splice, grasp each end of the splice point with the magnetic side of the tape facing you, form a small loop, and work the tape back and forth until one side of the splice begins to loosen. Then peel away the recording tape. Do not reuse the splicing tape.

Gap between tape ends

Mismatch in angle of cut

Overlap of tape ends

Incorrectly positioned splicing tape

17-19 Common splicing defects

Splicing tape properly is important. Figure 17-19 contains graphic examples of defective splices commonly encountered.

Cut-and-Splice Editing of Open-Reel Digital Audiotape

Cutting and splicing ¼-inch digital audiotape is possible if the stationary head ATR is designed for it. Rocking a tape back and forth across the playback head to listen for the edit point is not possible with a digital signal because the decoding system does not function at so slow a tape speed. Therefore, either an analog head or dedicated circuitry is built-in. Also, the flow of coding data is momentarily disrupted, creating a perceptible noise at the edit point. To neutralize this problem, the digital ATR effects an electronic crossfade at the edit point, interpolating the average level of the included signals to create a smooth, noiseless transition.

The angle of edit on digital tape should be 90 degrees (as opposed to the 45-degree angle recommended for analog tape) due to the high density of encoded information. Because digital ATRs use extensive error detection, tape and system irregularities resulting from a 90-degree cut are usually corrected.

Digital tape must be handled with greater care than analog tape, because it is thinner and packs high-density information that can be easily sullied. Keep handling to a minimum, and use white cotton gloves and splicers specially designed for use with digital audiotape.

Cut-and-Splice Editing of Film

Sound film is edited by cutting and splicing. The difference between cutting and splicing tape and film is that the editing of sound film must coordinate with the editing of picture film.

Equipment

Various types of equipment are used to cut and splice magnetic film. Among them are the following (see 17-20).

■ Editing table. This table must be large enough to hold all the editing equipment without the equipment being cramped; provide some storage space for film, film reels, and other materials; and be stable enough not to wobble.

■ Rewinds. These are hand-operated film winders with metal shafts that hold the film reels.

■ Viewer. A small projector that displays the film images on its screen serves as the viewer. You pull the film mounted on the rewinds through the viewer, forward or backward, at whatever speed you like.

■ Synchronizer. This device with ganged, sprocketed wheels locks in the film strips and keeps them in sync when winding and rewinding. A synchronizer has a counter that measures the film in feet and frames. Synchronization is also facilitated by edge numbers along the edge of the film at intervals of about 1 foot. There is also film that incorporates an invisible magnetic layer across the surface, and with specially equipped cameras and editors it is possible to record and display information, such as date, time, and time code, as well as edge numbers.

■ Sound reader. This audio/playback device is either contained in the viewer or attached to the synchronizer. A sound reader includes a playback

Rewind   Editing table   Viewer   Sound reader   Amplifier   Rewind

17-20 16mm film editing equipment   Cement splicer   Synchronizer head for magnetic and/or optical sound and a small amplifier-speaker.

■ Moviola.® With this device, picture and sound can be run in sync backward or forward at any speed to allow shots to be seen and heard, and individual frames can be marked for editing (see 17-21).

■ Flatbed editor. The *flatbed* or *horizontal editor* is a more flexible version of the Moviola. Basically, it uses a motor to drive multiple film reels in sync with sound for edit review and marking. Flatbeds consist of revolving discs—called plates—on which the film sits. There are separate plates for

17-21 Moviola® film-editing machine capable of magnetic or optical sound playback

the transport of sound and picture. The plates can be run independently or synchronously. In systems with two different sound transports, it is possible to hear a simple mix of two sound tracks. Flatbeds are the most commonly used film editor today (see 17-22).

■ Film splicers. These devices cut and splice film. There are two types: tape splicer and cement splicer.

Film Splicing

Tape splicing is done during rough editing to make temporary splices in picture film; (that is, when audio is not transferred to tape or disk after shooting for editing and other postproduction processing, which is now the common procedure). Splices are bound with transparent tape and can be undone without damaging the film; frame loss is minimal. The major drawback of tape-splicing picture film is that when it is projected, the splices are visible. Therefore, after final editing, the picture film must be permanently bonded with cement splices to make edits invisible. Tape is used only on work prints.

Editing Magnetic Film

Editing magnetic film is similar in technique to editing ¼-inch audiotape: You locate the edit, rock the film back and forth on the sound head to find the precise cutting point, and then mark, cut, and splice it. The main difference between editing sound film and editing audiotape is that film audio must be cut to sync with the picture.

To sync sound and picture, follow these steps:

1. Thread the picture film through the viewer, find the time code sync point or, if time code was not used, the point where the clapsticks first come together, and mark the frame with an *X*. The clapslate contains information about which scene and take it is.

2. Wind the magnetic film through the sound reader until you hear the corresponding scene and take announced. Then listen for the snap of the clapsticks coming together and mark the frame with an *X*.

3. Align the rolls of film in the synchronizer and lock them in place (see 17-23).

17-22 Horizontal or flatbed film editor. This unit holds picture and sound film reels and has a two-picture screen. This enables the editor to preview an edit before cutting the film. It is available in 16mm and 35mm or in a combination of the two formats.

Sync marks

Sound reader head

Leader preceding picture film

Magnetic film

17-23 Rolls of picture and magnetic film aligned in a synchronizer

Now in adding or cutting frames of sound, by checking the time code or frame counter and cutting or adding a like number of frames, it is possible to always maintain sync.

Magnetic film is edited only with tape, because visible splices are not a problem. Also magnetic film, like audiotape, is cut on the diagonal, not on the vertical as is picture film (see 17-24 through 17-29).

Fill Leader A recording on magnetic film, as on audiotape, is often filled with silences. Because mag film is noisier than audiotape, signal-to-noise ratio is more adversely affected when running the silent portions across the film dubber's playback head.

To counter this problem, splice *fill leader* or *spacer* into the silent portions of the mag film. Fill leader can be old picture film, not too badly

17-24 Editing magnetic film. Mark the first edit point (assume that the sound is in a head-to-tail direction) to the right of the frame line. Place the sprocket hole on the frame line directly over the diagonal cutting edge of the tape splicer.

17-25 Using the guillotine blade to cut magnetic film

17-26 Marking the second edit to the left of the frame line. Place the sprocket hole directly over the diagonal cutting edge. Then cut the film.

17-27 Butting the cut edges of the film together. Set the sprocket holes on each strip across the registration pins at the bottom of the cutting plate. The edit marks indicate that the splice point is properly aligned. Splice the film with transparent mylar splicing tape.

17-28 Trimming the splice. Press the two cutting blades in the handle of the splicer through the splicing tape.

17-29 Checking the splice. Remove the film from the splicer to check the splice for strength and to make sure the edges were trimmed cleanly.

worn or sullied. Picture film consists of an emulsion side and a base side. When using old picture film, be sure to splice it into the mag film so that the base side faces the playback heads. The emulsion side is soft and can leave residue on the heads. A more costly alternative is to use unrecorded mag film as fill leader.

Remember that when editing sound and picture film, what you pull out must have an equal number of sound and picture frames. The slightest error means that the entire film will be out of sync that number of frames from the mistake on. Beware that sometimes the magnetic film may be slightly smaller, requiring constant adjustment to ensure frame-for-frame synchronization.

Leadering and Inserting Sync Pop After arranging sound and picture in rough order during the first assembly, and making sure that sound and picture for each shot are exactly the same frame length, set up *countdown leader* in one of the gangs of the synchronizer for the picture and white leader for the sound in the gang across from the countdown leader.

Countdown leader (also called *Academy leader* and *SMPTE Universal leader*) has a sequence of descending numbers from 8 to 2. Each number lasts for 24 frames (1 second), with the exception of 2, which is a single frame. Forty-seven frames after the 2 there is an arrow with "splice here" printed underneath. The first shot is cut in here.

For the sound, set up 10 to 15 feet of white leader in the gang across from the countdown leader and mark the frame (on the white leader) that corresponds to the first picture frame. Splice into the white leader the magnetic film containing the sound for the first shot. To set up sound sync on the white leader, replace the frame corresponding to the countdown leader 2 and replace it with a *sync pop* or *sync beep*—one frame of mag film with a 1,000-Hz tone recorded on it (see 17-30).

Electronic Editing of Audiotape

Electronic editing of audiotape can be accomplished using one or two tape recorders. When it is only necessary to insert material by punching in, one tape recorder will do. **Insert editing** replaces a particular segment on a tape without altering the other recorded material and can also be accomplished using two recorders. But **assemble editing**, dubbing each program segment from a "master" to a "slave" tape in sequential order, requires two machines.

17-30 Sync pop. The sync pop is a single frame of magnetic film that provides a 1,000-Hz beep tone at the head of film reels.

Punching In

If something goes wrong during a take in a recording session and there is no extra track to try recording again, or there is not enough time, or another take would not improve the overall performance, rerecording just the subpar section is possible by an insert-editing technique called *punching in*. Because multitrack tape is usually used in a recording session, conventional cut-and-splice editing is not possible; there is no way to cut into any portion of any track without cutting in to the other tracks as well. Therefore multitrack recorders, and modern recorders in general, have electronic means of punching in—rerecording any portion of any track without affecting the rest of the recording.

Punching in is done by putting the recorded tracks into Sel Sync; playing them back to the performer(s) through headphones; and, when it is time to rerecord over the problem portion of a track, switching that track to *record*. After the appropriate section has been rerecorded, the track is taken out of record mode either by stopping the machine or by switching the track back into Sel Sync or play mode. Punching in is a clean way to edit electronically. It is quick and usually leaves no extraneous sound pulses on the tape. Although time code helps considerably in hitting the cue points precisely, unless the timing is perfect, some of the good material could also be erased. Remember, too, that levels must match between punched-in and retained material, unless the intention is otherwise.

Punching in can be used just to erase material. But if the material is brief, such as a click or pop, timing and reflexes must be precise and coordinated to avoid erasing wanted material.

Automatically Controlled Electronic Editing

With electronic editing using two or more recorders, the tape recorder you dub from—called the *master*—contains the original material; and when the recorders are synchronized, the master also controls the tape recorder(s) you are dubbing to—

Part Five: Postproduction

called the **slave(s)**. Synchronizers lock the transports of the master and slave tape recorders, allowing you to control editing functions automatically (see Chapter 11).

Although synchronizers vary in sophistication and performance features, most carry out the same basic operations. They direct (1) the operations of the master and slave machines, (2) the place where the edit points punch in and out, (3) the preroll starting point, and (4) preroll, forward, and reverse speeds. They also enable assemble and insert edits.

Synchronizers also generate edit decision lists. An **edit decision list (EDL)** is a computer-generated list of edits performed during editing. If the synchronizer does not generate an EDL, one can be handwritten.

Original protocol for stored edit decision lists conformed to the ASCII (American Standard Code for Information Interchange, pronounced "ass-key") format. It has ten fields of information:

▓ Field 1 lists the event or edit number.

▓ Field 2 lists the source recorder of the edit.

▓ Field 3 lists the edit mode—the audio track number.

▓ Field 4 lists the type of transition.

▓ Field 5 lists the duration of a transition. If the transition is a cut, field 5 is left blank because the transition is virtually instantaneous.

▓ Field 6 lists the playback recorder's start time.

▓ Field 7 lists the playback recorder's stop time.

▓ Field 8 lists the record recorder's start time.

▓ Field 9 is for convenience, because the information is not needed by the computer. It may list either the record recorder's stop time or the duration of the edit.

▓ Field 10 consists of information needed only by the computer to begin reading the next edit.

In practice, an EDL may be charted in whatever format is most functional to an editing system (see 17-31).

17-31 Example of an edit decision list

Once the edit decision list has been completed, and before final assembly can proceed, the EDL must be "cleaned." The cleaning, called "list management," is done by the computer. It checks to make sure that the information on the EDL conforms to the source recording. After the list management stage, final assembly is automatic.

The computer assembles the master tape, although some edits may be done manually if the need arises. There are two types of automatic assembly: (1) A-mode, or sequential, assembly and (2) B-mode, or checkerboard, assembly.

A-mode (sequential) assembly places edits in sequence. It starts at the first edit and continues until an event calls for a playback reel that has not been mounted. At that point the system stops until the new reel is put up. A-mode assembly is ideal for projects that require few reel changes. It is also easier to make changes using A-mode assembly. An edit decision list that has not been cleaned cannot be edited in B-mode and must use A-mode to avoid edit overlaps.

B-mode (checkerboard) assembly is faster and more efficient. It completes all of the edits that can be performed from the mounted reels. Any edit requiring an unmounted reel is skipped and a hole for it is left in the master reel, checkerboard style. B-mode assembly does require that the EDL be cleaned before editing.

NONLINEAR EDITING

Nonlinear editing allows the retrieval, assembly, and reassembly of disk-based material quickly and in any order, regardless of the material's location on the disk. The term *random-access editing* is often used synonymously with *nonlinear editing*. Of course, all editing is random access. You access a sound in one part of a recording, then you go to another sound in another part of the recording, and so on. What is usually meant by *random access* when it applies to nonlinear editing is quick access to randomly selected points in a recording. This is not to quibble with terminology but to clarify more precisely what nonlinear editing is.

Another confusion about nonlinear editing derives from the number of different digital editing systems on the market. There are stereo and multichannel systems. Most of them are hard-disk; others are optical-based. Hard-disk systems use either PC or Macintosh platforms, or their own hardware/software interface. Most hard-disk systems are dual-purpose, capable of both recording and editing in stereo or multitrack and include, at least, some types of digital effects processing and MIDI.

The following section is a distillation of the basic functions found in most hard-disk editing systems. It is intended to give you an operational overview of nonlinear editing. Although all the terms are explained, some are more common than others. In some cases, their familiarity may depend on your knowledge of a particular editing system.

Overview of Hard-Disk Nonlinear Editing

In a hard-disk editing system, audio that is encoded onto the disk takes the form of a *soundfile*. The soundfile contains information about the sound such as amplitude and duration. When the soundfile is opened, that information is displayed on the monitor, usually as a waveform. Also usually displayed is the edit screen (see 17-32).

The waveform displays the profile of a sound's amplitude over time. By being able to "see" a sound, it is easy to spot its dynamics (see 17-33). It is also possible to see greater detail in a waveform by zooming in, a feature that facilitates extremely precise editing (see 17-34). Once the soundfile is retrieved and its waveform is displayed, it can be auditioned to determine which of its sections is to be defined for editing.

As a sound is played, a play cursor, or playbar, scrolls the waveform, enabling the editor to see precisely the part and shape of the sound that is playing at any given moment. When the soundfile is longer than the screen can display, as the scroll moves to the end of the visible waveform, approaching the off-screen data, the screen is either redrawn, or *refreshed,* showing the entire updated waveform, or it continues scrolling to the end of the track.

When the editor determines what part of the sound is to be edited, the segment is highlighted in what is known as a *defined region*. Once a region is defined, the selected edit is performed only in that section of the waveform (see 17-34). The region can be cut from the waveform display, moved and/or copied to another part of the waveform or to another waveform. It can also be inverted, changed in level, envelope, frequency, and so on, up to the limits of the system.

A *marker* or *identification flag* can be placed anywhere in the waveform to facilitate jumping the play cursor at will to the desired marker points. The marker can be a graphic identifier using a number, a letter, or text (see 17-32).

At any time in the editing process, the soundfile can be auditioned in a number of ways: from

17-32 Example of an edit screen

17-33 Dynamics of a waveform

17-34 Zoom function. The section from 2.4 seconds to 3.2 seconds in the Read Only soundfile is detailed in the Modified window. The lighter sections are the *defined regions,* that is, the part of the waveforms selected for editing. The zoomed section is a "Harrumph" that interrupted a sentence in a speech.

beginning to end, from the defined region, from marker to marker, and at increased or decreased speed in either direction. This latter operation is called scrubbing.

Scrubbing is similar to rocking tape in cut-and-splice editing; it lets you move the play cursor through the defined region at any speed and listen to the section being scrubbed at the same time. Unlike rocking a tape, with scrubbing you can audibly and visibly locate the in- and out-points of a defined region.

Suppose you want to pinpoint a chord located in one section of a soundfile and use the same chord at the end of the soundfile to end the song. By moving the play cursor to an area just before the chord, you can slowly scrub the area until you find the precise location at the beginning of the first sound. This will be the first point in the defined region. Continue scrubbing until you locate the precise end point of the chord's decay and mark it as the end of the defined region. Then, as you would in word processing, copy the defined region and paste it at the proper point near the end of the scene.

Some operations in nonlinear editing are similar to those in word processing, when you delete a word entirely, or cut or copy it from one part of a sentence and paste it elsewhere in the same sentence or into another sentence. This is known as *cutting and pasting.* Once a region is defined, the *Cut* or *Delete* command removes it from its original location and copies it to the computer's memory for temporary storage. This section of computer memory is sometimes referred to as the *clipboard.* Using the *Copy* command, the defined region is added to the clipboard but is not cut from its original position. The *Paste* command copies the defined region from the clipboard and inserts it into the waveform immediately after the position of the play cursor.

There are also Shuffle and Replace commands in nonlinear editing that are similar to the Insert and Typeover operations in word processing. *Shuffle* moves the audio that originally followed the play cursor to a point immediately following the newly inserted segment. *Replace* overwrites the audio immediately following the play cursor.

It may be useful to outline the functions of the edit screen in Figure 17-32 to give you an idea of one system's approach. (See Chapter 7 for the Mix and Transport windows in the system shown in 17-32.)

Example of an Edit Screen

Mode Buttons

Shuffle Mode   In this mode the defined regions "snap" to other regions like magnets, with no gap or overlap between them.

Slip Mode   In this mode a defined region can be moved freely with spaces preceding or following it, or it can overlap a portion of another region.

Spot Mode   In this mode a defined region can be placed into a specific time code location by simply clicking it with the grabber (see "Grabber" later in this section).

Grid Mode   In this mode a defined region can be automatically lined up at a precise interval. For example, in a music recording, if the nudge/grid units selector has been set to quarter-note increments, dragging a defined region to a new location in a track will cause it to snap to the nearest quarter-note location.

Display Scale Arrows

Display scale arrows allow adjustment of the track view. The *up arrow* expands the waveform view upward, making the waveform taller. The *down*

arrow performs the opposite function. The *right arrow* expands the track to the right. The *left arrow* zooms out from the waveform, compressing the track view to show more of its duration.

Cursor Control Keys

Zoomer   This tool magnifies the portion of the track you wish to view.

Scrubber   This tool locates a precise point in the track in a manner analogous to rocking the tape reels back and forth in cut-and-splice editing.

Trimmer   This tool trims a defined region by shortening or expanding it to a desired length.

Selector   This tool selects the defined region for editing.

Grabber   This tool moves a defined region to a new track location. The grabber is used in conjunction with the four mode buttons.

Start/End/Length Buttons, Current Position Indicators, and Current Time Display

The *start box* gives the start point of the current selection. The *end box* gives the end point of the current selection. The *length box* gives the duration of the current selection. The *data indicator boxes* can be displayed in time code, minutes and seconds, bars and beats, or feet and frames.

The current time display indicates the current point of the play cursor in a track.

Nudge/Grid Units Selector

This is a pop-up menu that selects the value of the grid mode and defines the amount that a defined region can be nudged, forward or backward, into place on a track, for example, milliseconds in time code; quarter note or eighth note in bars and beats; and quarter frame or sub-frame in feet and frames.

In addition to the edit screen, there is the standard Edit menu found in word processing, except in hard-disk editing systems, of course, the Edit commands such as Cut, Copy, Paste, Delete, and so on are applied to the audio material on a track(s).

Editing Example

Let's go through a short editing procedure with a specific example, using the edit screen in 17-32. The edit example in 17-35 is guitar strums. The peaks in the waveform are where the volume goes up, and the valleys are where the volume goes down. Different types of sounds produce different types of waveforms. Vowel sounds in speech and wind sounds, for example, produce waveforms with less pronounced peaks and valleys, because they have softer attacks and longer decays.

Notice that the that first two accents in the fifth beat, which begins at roughly 00:00:02:40 (2 seconds and 40 frames), are played more strongly compared with the opening accents in the previous four beats. The challenge is to move this stronger strum from fifth beat to first so the sequence begins with more emphasis and still maintain the tempo.

Whenever possible, define a region precisely before a volume peak and end it immediately before another volume peak. In this case, that would be from the instant before the fifth beat begins, at about 00:00:02:40, to the tail end of the beat sequence at what would be roughly 00:00:03:30.

The editing procedure would be as follows: scrub the region to be edited until you are sure of the in and out edit points. If necessary, use the zoomer for a more precise look at the in and out edit points. These points can be verified using the current position indicator. Click on the selector and drag the cursor from the in to the out edit point, thereby defining the region to be edited. Once defined, clicking on the Edit menu Cut command on the removes the edit and places it on the clipboard, a temporary storage area in the computer's memory.

17-35 Editing example. Guitar strums must be edited to move fifth beat to first by (a) selecting area to edit, (b) cutting it to the clipboard, and (c) pasting it into the first position.

To replace the edited region at the beginning of the of the track, position the cursor there and click on the Edit menu Paste command. Another method of making the move is to select the shuffle mode, assuming the edit has to snap to another region, and use the grabber to actually move the defined region. If placement of the edit is critical to maintaining the beat, the grid mode may be the mode to use.

Destructive and Nondestructive Editing

Still another advantage of hard-disk editing is that the edits you make can be nondestructive. *Nondestructive editing* does not alter the original soundfile regardless of what editing or signal processing you effect. *Destructive editing*, on the other hand, permanently alters the original soundfile by overwriting it.

This raises the question: Why employ destructive editing when you can process a soundfile in any way you wish and still preserve the original? The answer is that destructive editing is necessary, for example, when memory is limited—it is easier to save a single soundfile than both the original and duplicate soundfiles—and when the edited soundfile is to be downloaded to another system.

ORGANIZING THE EDIT TRACKS

The approach to organizing edit tracks obviously depends on the number of individual sound tracks involved. If only a few tracks are to be edited, which may be the case in, say, an interview, the procedure is apparent: intercut the questions and answers so the continuity is logical. But when a number of sound tracks are involved, which is likely in drama and music recording, for example, it is necessary to devise a system whereby they are organized to facilitate editing and mixing. There is no definitive way of doing this; sound editors use various approaches. The point is: Before any editing begins, catalog all the sounds and keep a running log throughout the editing process, otherwise mixups, or worse, are inevitable. List each sound and include appropriate information, such as its content; reel location; time code address; any special instructions for editing, signal processing, or mixing; and any problems with the sound, such as noise, change in ambience, sudden dropout, a fluff in pronunciation, and so on.

In productions with dialogue, music, and sound effects, first group the sound by category (often referred to, appropriately enough, as the *DME tracks*). Then further group them in each category. For example, the dialogue tracks may be arranged by character and then divided into dialogue from the production recording and dialogue from the automated dialogue recording (ADR). Sound effects can be categorized as Foley, ambience, and cut sound effects. A *cut sound effect,* such as a splash or car ignition being turned on, requires little adjustment in editing to remain in sync with the picture.

Another way that production sound tracks are grouped is by microphone pickup. In a multicamera program, for example, the sound pickup may be from two boom, two plant, and four audience mics, each one recorded on a separate track.

In music recording, takes can be grouped by passage, for example, the first 32 measures, the final section of a movement, or a song verse. In noting each take, it saves time to indicate whether the take is worth considering for editing or should be rejected.

Once sounds have been grouped, assign them to individual tracks. In so doing, decide to the extent you can the sounds that do and do not have to overlap. This not only facilitates editing but affects a sound's placement in a track. For example, if a transition from one scene to another calls for a dissolve (gradually fading one scene out as the next scene fades in) and the accompanying music has to crossfade from one theme into another, the two different pieces of music must be placed on separate tracks. On the other hand, a cut sound effect can be placed on one track.

In editing a music selection, the best parts of several music takes are usually combined to make the composite final version, a practice called *comping*. Each take is therefore assigned to a separate track.

TECHNIQUES AND AESTHETIC CONSIDERATIONS

As the examples cited earlier suggest, editing involves more than just cutting and pasting. It helps to create correlations, juxtapositions, coherence, and pace. Therefore, beyond the operational skills it takes to edit speech, sound effects, and music, there are techniques and aesthetic considerations to bear in mind.

Differences Between Editing Sound and Editing Picture

Editing picture is one-dimensional; one shot is cut, dissolved, or faded out and in to another shot. Once the transition has been made, in terms of editing, little happens until the next transition.

Editing sound is multidimensional. Sounds are layered within each shot, so editing audio becomes more than attending to transitions. In a scene an actor may be speaking to another actor with traffic outside, a clock ticking, a bath running in another room, footsteps moving back and forth, and music underscoring the action. All these elements have to be edited so that the various sonic layers are properly matched and synchronized and the perspectives maintained.

Editing Speech

Among the considerations basic to editing speech are recognizing the sounds that make up words; cutting together similar and dissimilar sounds; handling emphasis and inflection; matching ambience (or room tone); and taking corrective action with problem tracks.

Identifying Sounds That Make Up Words

In scrubbing or rocking a sound, some sounds are easier than others to recognize. The easiest are those with striking power, such as *d, k, p,* and *t:* sounds with a pronounced attack identified sonically by a click or pop and visually by a spike in the waveform. A voiced (hard) consonant such as *v, g, z,* or *b* is formed of vocal tone as well as breath; a voiceless (soft) consonant such as *f, k, s,* or *p* is formed only

of breath. The presence or absence of vocalization creates less of a spike in the waveform but is detectable when the waveform is scrubbed at a slower speed or the tape is rocked. The vowels *a, e, i, o,* and *u* are the most difficult to identify and separate, because they lack any attack and usually blend with the other sounds in a word. When vowels begin phrases in connected speech, their sound is more readily apparent when scrubbed or rocked at a slower speed.

One way to locate vowels, or any sound that is difficult to perceive, is to listen and look for differences in pitch or look for a change, however slight, in the waveform. Suppose you had to cut between the *o* and *i* in "anoint." In pronouncing the word, the *oi* combination is usually sounded as "oy" (as in "toy" or "boy"), with the pitch going from lower to higher. Therefore, the cut can be made just before or at the pitch change.

Sometimes sounds are run together and cannot be separated in the usual way. If the word *deem* were mispronounced "dreem," you would have to delete the *r.* But scrubbed or rocked forward, the sound of the *r* runs into the sound of the *e* and is difficult to hear clearly. The waveform might show a slight rise at the *r,* but by scrubbing the sound backward, the point where the "ee" changes to the lower-pitched and more guttural "r" may be more apparent.

Editing Similar and Dissimilar Sounds

Editing dissimilar sounds in speech is easier than editing similar sounds, because they are usually distinct and flow more naturally. Consider the sentence "Sound is both challenging and creative." If we delete *both,* the edit will be made after *is* and before *challenging.* The *s* will be spliced to the *ch* and, because they are different sounds, the rhythmic transition between *is* and *challenging* is natural and distinct.

Such is not the case with speech sounds that are similar. Suppose a speaker says, "I am, as you already know, more than happy to be here," and you want to remove *as you already know.* At first glance, after the *am* and before *more* appear to be the edit points. But this could alter natural speaking rhythm, because most people do not pronounce separately adjacent words that begin and end with the same letter, such as "am more." The tendency is to slur them together so, in effect, one *m* serves both the "a" and the "ore": "amore." (Test this by saying "and Donna" or "Joe's soda.") Therefore, one of the *m*'s should be dropped to maintain the natural sound and rhythm. Probably the best place to edit is in the word *am*, just after the "a" and before the lips come together to form the "m" sound. Cutting between the *m* and *o* in *more* would be difficult and awkward.

This example assumes that the speaker enunciated the "I" and "am" distinctly. What if the two words were run together and the beginning of the "a" sound is inaudible? So long as it does not change the speaker's style, cut the *m* in "am," making the contraction "I'm" sound more natural.

You can think of this technique as *editing on, or to, the same sound.* Another way to handle similar sounds that are adjacent is to *cut within a sound.* Suppose someone says, "Nothing means more to me than my muse, or, I should say, music." Obviously, the intention was to say, "Nothing means more to me than my music." A quick look at the problem points to a cut between *my* and *muse* as the simplest edit. For the sake of illustration, let's assume "my muse" is so slurred that there is no way to cut between the words. By editing within the sound common to both words—"zi"—you can maintain the natural sound and rhythm. Cut through the *s*'s in *muse* and *music,* and splice "mus" to "sic." Clearly, the "mu" sound in both words helps make this edit possible.

Emphasis and Inflection

Another common problem for the sound editor is dealing with emphasis and inflection. Suppose the speaker says, "How are you?" with the emphasis on "you" to express concern. For some reason the "you" is garbled, and without this word it is not possible to use the phrase. If it is unimportant, there is no problem; but if it has to be kept, three alternatives are to: (1) ask the person to deliver the line again, which may be impractical if not impossible; (2) go through the recording to hear whether the person said "you" elsewhere with the

same or almost the same inflection; or (3) construct the word from similar sounds the speaker uttered.

To construct the word, you would have to listen for a "yoo" sound. Perhaps, with luck, the speaker may have said the word *unique, unusual,* or *continue.* The "yoo" sound is part of each word, and if the emphasis and audio level match, one of these "yoo's" may suffice.

As for inflection, suppose two characters exchange these lines:

Character 1: Does it have to be that way? It doesn't have to.

Character 2: I just don't know.

Character 1: Well, it shouldn't have to be that way.

The director decides that character 1 should not ask a question first but make a definite statement: "It doesn't have to be that way." Character 1 has said already, "It doesn't"; so we need a "have to be that way." Character 1 says "have to" three times. To take it from character 1's question and add "be that way" would mismatch the intended inflection and keep the statement a question—and an awkward one. To take the second "have to" would also sound unnatural because the *to* would probably be pronounced "tu." The third *to* would most likely be pronounced "tə," which is more natural. So the final edit would butt the "It doesn't" from character 1's first statement and the "have to be that way" from character 1's second statement.

Ambience

Ambience is background sound. Two other terms used synonymously are **room tone** and **presence.** Some people draw a distinction between these terms: *ambience* being any background sound that is part of a recording or has been added in postproduction; and *room tone* or *presence* being background sound recorded during actual production to provide the sound editor with the material to assemble sonically consistent backgrounds.

Editing speech recorded in different acoustic environments requires not only maintaining continuity of content but also matching the background sounds. For example, earlier in this chapter the sentence "Good evening [breath] [cough] [breath], ladies and gentlemen" was used to illustrate an edit. The cuts were made after the first breath and before "ladies." Why not cut after "evening" and before the second breath? A breath would still be there to preserve the rhythm. Does it matter which breath we use?

The difference is in the ambient sounds of the two breaths. For one thing, the cough is percussive whereas "evening" is not. Thus the reverberation after the first breath sounds different from the reverberation after the second breath. If "evening" were spliced to the breath after the cough, it would sound unnatural; the ambience does not match.

In editing two statements from the same speech when one was delivered over applause and the other over silence, or when one was delivered in a room full of people and the other was delivered after most of the audience had left, the edit will be obvious unless something is done to match the different backgrounds.

One technique used to make the transition from one statement/background to the other is by diverting the listeners' attention. In the second of the preceding examples, if the ambience during one statement was quiet when the room was filled with people, and the ambience during the second statement was reflectant when the room was almost empty, you could try to locate in the recording a cough, a murmur, someone accidentally hitting the microphone, or some other distraction. Edit the distractor between the two statements (the distractor would also contain some room background) so attention momentarily is called to it instead of to the obvious change in background sound.

Another technique used to match backgrounds is to mix one background with another to even them out. This assumes that they were recorded "in the clear" before or after the event, which, by the way, should be standard procedure.

Still another approach that works well in dialogue editing is the *backfill technique*. Assume that a scene cuts from a close-up (CU) of character 1 to a CU of character 2, then back to a CU of character 1, with a noticeable change in background sound in the second CU. Say the drone of a plane, audible in shots 1 and 3, drops out in shot 2. The in-and-out effect of the edit will draw attention to the change in sound.

To remedy this problem, you could go through the dialogue tracks until you find the same sound with no one talking. Edit it down or extend it by rerecording and editing so that it conforms to the length of shot 2. Take a modulated section of a soundfile (or unrecorded tape or magnetic film, or old picture film) and edit it to the beginning and end of the noise track for shot 2 so that the total track length equals that of the three shots. Take the original dialogue track containing the background sound and edit an unmodulated section of a track the exact length of shot 2 between shots 1 and 3. Edit a third "strip" of unmodulated track for shot 1, the dialogue without the background sound for shot 2, and blank track for shot 3. Then mix all three tracks with picture so that the same background sound is continued through the scene (see 17-36).

If there are rhythmic sounds in the background, such as a motor or a clock, take care to preserve these rhythms when editing. You may need a *chug* or a *tick* from another part of the recording to prevent any noticeable break in the background rhythm. Again, try to record the background sound separately to provide flexibility in editing.

If you are cut-and-splice editing, another way to overcome problems with backgrounds that do not cut together smoothly is to use a more diagonal cut. Cutting tape at a greater than 45-degree angle provides a split-second fade-in on a background just before a dialogue line starts.

A technique frequently used to smooth a potentially awkward transition between two ambiences is to have the sound and picture cut at slightly different places in the shot change. For example, a man and woman in two different rooms (say, a bathroom and an adjoining bedroom) are talking to each other. Cutting the audio and picture from the man to the woman at the same time would sound abrupt, if not jarring, given the obvious differences in ambience between the two rooms. To smooth the transitions, the shot of the man can begin slightly before the woman stops talking and the dialogue of the woman can begin slightly before

17-36 Backfill editing technique

17-37 Split editing smoothes the difference in ambience by cutting sound and picture at slightly different times

she is shown (see 17-37). This technique is referred to as **split editing** (see also figures 17-38 and 17-41).

Another technique used to handle background sound is *looping*. When background sound, such as crowd, wind, or room tone, is continuous, particularly through lengthy scenes, running a continuous track could be unwieldy or take up unnecessary space, or both. Selecting the automatic loop command in a hard-disk editor or making a tape loop solves this problem. But remember that to be effective a loop must sound continuous, not repetitive (see Chapter 16).

In broadcasting, field reporting is so common that the audience, to some extent, has grown used to abrupt changes in background sound and levels within the same program. Nevertheless, change should be motivated and not unnecessarily jarring. With dialogue, however, audiences are more apt to be annoyed by uneven background sound. The best thing to do during the recording is to *anticipate the editing.*

Ambience is a concern not only in editing speech; it is also an important factor when editing sound effects and music. In all three domains, ambience—background sound—is usually not effective without foreground sound. The two together bring perspective, environment, and size to a scene.

Composite Dialogue

It is not unusual for a line of dialogue to be built from different takes in the production recording or from the ADR, or both. A director may prefer three words from take 4, one word from take 7, two from take 8, and a breath from take 11.

Changing Words

Films shown on television often have dialogue changed to eliminate profanity or for legal reasons. Trying to match lip movements to the word changes is a challenge; too often it is obvious that they are not consistent with the words being heard. One technique to help remedy the problem is to look for labials, dentals, and fricatives, because within each group lip movements are interchangeable.

Labials—*m, b,* and *p*—you close your lips to say. Dentals—*c, d, s,* and *t*—you speak through the teeth. Fricatives—*f, v, s,* and *z*—are produced by forcing air through a constricted mouth and teeth.

Dialogue Processing

In dialogue processing, three problems typically occur: (1) ring-off, (2) additive ambience, and (3) defective or unusable dialogue.

Ring-off occurs when a dialogue line ends with the ambient ring of a room, and another line begins with that ring decaying under it. This can be a problem, for example, when someone is entering a room and the ring-off is decaying under the line of the entering actor. In editing, cut the ring-off and either mix it with digital reverb on a controlled basis, thereby trying to blend the ambient qualities of the two dialogue lines so that continuity is maintained underneath, or drop the ring-off and create the appropriate background values using digital reverb only. If, when cutting to the entering actor, ring-off of the old word is still perceptible under the new word, even with doctoring of the digital reverb, use a sound effect to cover the transition, with the director's concurrence, of course.

Additive ambience occurs when several actors are recorded at the same time on separate tracks of a multitrack recorder and the multiple room sounds become cumulative when the tracks are mixed. To avoid additive ambience, in the editing cut from one track to another to keep the single room sound on each track. In the case of overlapping dialogue, try to close down the room sound through digital reverb. Failing that, or if too many voices overlap, making the digital reverb processing sound too unnatural, dialogue rerecording probably would be the best alternative.

Defective or unusable dialogue occurs when, for example, actors are body-miked and stand very close to one another or hug, covering words; or when an unwanted sound, such as clothes rustling, an object being bumped, or the voice "cracking," masks a word. If there is no time to retake a scene, or if these problems go unnoticed and reediting the material is not worth the time or expense, there are alternatives. Editing in the same syllable(s) or word(s) from another part of the track is one alternative. Another is to extend the syllable(s) or word(s) so that they overlap the defect. In both cases, ambience has to be processed so that it matches the original.

To facilitate editing dialogue, *split-edit* the dialogue track into two or more separate tracks. This makes it easier to extend lines that may have been cut too short during picture editing, to overlap voices, and to carry over lines from one scene to the next. "Splitting off" dialogue also makes it easier to adjust levels in the mix (see 17-38).

17-38 Split-editing dialogue. (a) The dialogue of characters 1 and 2 as recorded during production recording. (b) Splitting off their dialogue to facilitate overlapping the lines. (c) Splitting off their dialogue to extend a line.

Editing Sound Effects

A basic consideration in editing sound effects is to match perspective. In editing the screech of tires to a car crash, the crash has to sound as though it came out of the screeching tires. It sometimes happens that the screech is heard close up and the crash far away, as if the sounds, although related, occurred in two different locations. The same thing happens in editing a police car or ambulance siren to the sounds of a screech and stop. The siren is heard in one perspective and the screech and stop are heard in another, because either the levels or the ambiences are different.

Another example is editing rain and wind, or wind, rain, and thunder, to build a storm sequence. Storms have various intensities, and the force of each component should match; violent thunder and wind hardly go with a drizzle. Here are some other guidelines that may prove helpful in editing sound effects*:

---

*Some material is based on Marvin A. Kerner, *The Art of the Sound Effects Editor.* Boston: Focal Press, 1989.

☑ Cut the effect as close to the first point of sound as possible. The effect may be preceded by low-level ambience or tape hiss, the click of a channel being opened, or some extraneous sound associated with the effect.

☑ Most sounds have a natural decay or tail. A sound may start at once but does not stop that way; even transient sounds have some trail-off. Cutting into the tail will be noticeable unless another sound comes in over it and "washes it out," or it is crossfaded with another sound, or if the cutoff occurs with a shot change to an entirely different scene.

☑ When editing in a sound effect that occurs off-screen, it is usually distracting to lay it over dialogue. Spot the effect between the lines of dialogue.

☑ When a sound effect has a definitive stop, such as a thud or an engine being turned off, if you are editing with tape, sometimes it is easier to lay in the effect by syncing it to the shot's end point and backing it into the audio track.

☑ Sometimes it is necessary to edit in an effect slightly out of sync with the picture. If you have to choose, edit it in slightly early rather than slightly late. Syncing a sound effect early is not as obvious as one out of sync late. If it is too far out of sync, of course, the point is moot.

☑ Some sounds are difficult to sync with picture, such as horse hooves. All four hooves cannot be synched. Generally, editors follow the first front leg and then establish the horse's rhythm.

☑ In the section "Editing Music to Picture" later in this chapter, it is suggested that an abrupt sound cut will not be as jarring if it is covered by an equally abrupt picture cut. Some sound effects editors prefer to avoid such a sharp change in sound by overlapping a split second or two of background on either side of the transition.

☑ In fight scenes it is not uncommon to see an actor's head-jerk occur before the attacker's fist is close enough to the face. The choice is to match the sound of the chin sock to the head-jerk or at the point where the fist is closest to the chin. Neither choice will be completely satisfactory. The sound effect should therefore be placed on the basis of where it looks best. Also, the sound of the hits should vary. A punch on the face sounds different than a punch on the head, upper body, lower body, and so on.

Editing Music

A good music editor is usually a trained musician who can read music. This is particularly helpful in working with the composer. That said, editing music is difficult to discuss in any detail, because it involves using one language—the printed word—to explain another language—the notes, chords, rhythms, and other features of abstract, temporal sound. Although there is some similarity between editing speech and music, such as consideration of space, rhythm, loudness, and inflection (intonation), there are also differences. Music contains so many simultaneous sonic elements that matching

sounds is more complex and slight mistakes in editing are more easily detected. In music editing you have to consider cutting on the right accent to maintain rhythm, tonality, relative loudness, and style. If any of these elements are aurally incompatible, the edit will be obvious.

A few guidelines and techniques may be helpful. Generally, edits that heighten intensity cut together well, such as going from quiet to loud, slow to fast, or nonrhythmic to rhythmic. A transition from a seemingly formless or meandering phrase to one that is obviously structured and definite also tends to work.

Cutting to Resolution

Perhaps one of the most useful guidelines is to cut before an accent, downbeat, or resolution. Think of the final chord in a musical phrase or song. Although it resolves the music, it is the chord before it that creates the anticipation and need for resolution; it sets up the last chord. Edit on the anticipatory note—the one requiring some resolution, however brief—so that it leads naturally to the note being joined.

Preserving Tempo

Most Western music has a *time signature*—2/4 ("two-four" not "two-fourths"), 3/4, 4/4, 3/8, 6/8, and so forth. The first numeral indicates the number of beats in each measure; the second indicates the value of the note that receives each beat. For example, in 4/4 time there are four beats to a measure and each quarter note receives a whole beat; in 3/8 time there are three beats to the measure and each eighth note receives a beat. In editing music you have to preserve the beat or else the edit will be noticeable as a jerk or stutter in the tempo. If you cannot read music or no sheet music exists, pay close attention to the waveform of the music to discern the tempo. Listen to the beat and look for the resulting spike in the waveform.

Regardless of the number of beats in a measure, some beats are strong and some are weak. When

you tap your foot to a song, it usually comes down on the strong or down beat and lifts on the weak or up beat. A song in 3/4 time, known as waltz time, is characterized by a strong beat followed by two weak beats—*one*, two, three, *one*, two, three. Beats in 2/4 time follow a *one*, two, *one*, two, strong beat/weak beat pattern. This is a rudimentary explanation of a complex subject, to be sure. The point is that when editing tempo you have to be aware of preserving the number of beats per measure as well as the accents. In a piece in 3/4 time, if you cut after the first beat in a measure, the beat you cut to should be a weak beat, and another weak beat should follow; if you cut after the third beat in a measure, you would cut to a strong beat with two weak beats to follow.

Another tape-editing technique to facilitate editing to the beat is to determine the number of beats per minute and use a ruler to measure the time in terms of tape distance. For example, if a song's tempo is 120 beats per minute and the tape is running at 15 ips, divide 120 by 60 to get the number of beats per second—two; then divide the 15 ips by 2 to get the distance of tape travel for two beats—7½ ips.

Repetitive Measures

One way to shorten or lengthen audio material through editing is to use repetitive measures in the music. These measures can be cut out to shorten material, which is obvious. To lengthen the audio using a hard-disk system is relatively straight-forward: Repetitive measures can be extended by copying and pasting them to the music track.

In tape editing, repetitive measures can be extended by dubbing them to another recorder and then cutting them back into the original recording. But if the recording is analog, the dubbed material could lose sound quality that would make perceptible the difference between the original and the copied audio. A better way would be to use digital-to-digital dubbing or to have another identical mix available and intercut the appropriate measures from it.

Of course, preserving the tempo in music editing is not an isolated consideration. There are other factors, such as key signature and musical style and texture.

Key Signature

Just as most music has a time signature to regulate its tempo, it also has a key signature—E major or B minor, for example—that determines its overall tonality. Some keys are compatible; when you change from one to the other, it sounds natural or "in tune" (see 17-39). Other keys are not, and splicing them together is jarring or sounds "out of tune," like the editing in some of the album offers on TV. Unless it is for effect, or if the picture justifies the change (discussed later in this chapter), edited music should sound consonant in order not to be noticed. Another way to cover a bad key change in an edit is with *pitch shifting*. Usually, it is easier to try bringing one of the offending keys into musical compatibility with the other key than it is to look for a sonic compromise between the two. Using an attention-grabber in the dialogue such as a cough or a distracting sound effect can also cover an unmusical edit.

Style and Texture

Each type of music and musical group has a unique style and texture. This distinguishes the style of jazz from rock, or the texture of one voice from another although both may have identical registers, or one group from another although both may play the same instruments and music.

Editing from the same piece of music usually does not present a problem in matching style and texture so long as you follow the other guidelines for editing. But if the music is from different sources, matching elements can be a problem. Normally, you would not edit different styles—a piece of classical music to rock music just because they had the same tempo, or a dance band to a military band just because they were playing the same song. The differences in sound would make the edits conspicuous and distracting.

Music in this key will segue with →	First choice	Second choice	Third choice	Fourth choice
A	A	D	E	F♯/G♭ minor
A♯ (B♭)	A♯ (B♭)	D♯ (E♭)	F	G minor
B	B	E	F♯	G♯/A♭ minor
C	C	F	G	A minor
C♯ (D♭)	C♯ (D♭)	F♯ (G)	G♯ (A♭)	A♯/B♭ minor
D	D	G	A	B minor
D♯ (E♭)	D♯ (E)	G♯ (A)	A♯ (B♭)	C minor
E	E	A	B	C♯/D♭ minor
F	F	B♭	C	D minor
F♯ (G♭)	F♯ (G♭)	B	C♯ (D♭)	D♯/E♭ minor
G	G	C	D	E minor
G♯ (A♭)	G♯ (A♭)	C♯ (D♭)	D♯ (E♭)	F minor

17-39 Compatible or consonant music keys

Editing Music to Picture

In editing music to picture, the audio has to have a purpose. Ordinarily, it is to complement what is being shown. But as pointed out in Chapter 10, it can also supplement or counterpoint the picture. The suggestion of editing loud, fast symphonic music to a soft, quiet trio is disconcerting, but if a picture cuts from a scene of violent destruction to one of desolation, the edit makes sense. In fact, it would make sense to cut from loud, jarring music to silence.

Changing from a dull tonality to a bright one, or vice versa, is not recommended generally, but if the edit is played behind a change from night to day, or day to night, the picture could justify it.

Editing two different styles, perhaps the most awkward type of change, is acceptable if the picture covers it. Cutting from Mozart to the Beatles normally offends our sensibilities, but not if the picture cuts from a shot of eighteenth-century Vienna to mid-twentieth-century London.

Another consideration in editing music to picture (or any sound for that matter) is that it not mask dialogue and sound effects (See "Mixing Versus Layering" in Chapter 18). Sometimes, however, a smooth music edit is difficult to make. In such instances a commonly used technique is to keep the music level under another sound to mask the problem in the edit.

Transitions

In editing, sequencing two sounds (or shots) involves creating a transition, which helps establish pace. In audio three techniques are used to make transitions: (1) segue (pronounced "seg-way") or cut, (2) crossfade, and (3) fade-out/fade-in.

Segue and Cut

Segue is a musical term that means "follow on." In radio it has come to refer to the playing of two or more recordings—tape or disc—with no live announcing in between or live announcing over the segue. In a broader sense, segue is analogous to the term *cut* used to describe transitions in TV and film. In this context cutting from one element to

another means establishing a picture or sound immediately after the previous picture or sound stops, and doing it at once, not gradually. In discussing the effects of this particular type of transition, we will use the broader term *cut*.

The *cut* is standard language for a small related change within the same time, place, or action, such as cutting from someone waking up, to washing, to eating breakfast; or cutting from a striking match and the eruption of a flame to an alarm sounding at a fire station. Cutting creates transitions that are sharp and well defined, picking up the rhythm of sequences and giving them a certain briskness. Cutting also tightens the pace of a production, because the change from one sound (or picture) to another is quick. Due to its aesthetic value, the cut is also used for larger transitions, such as cutting from a person walking out the door in the morning to coming back in at dinner time, or from the eruption of flames to charred remains.

The cut, in effect, butts two different sounds or groups of sounds together; in that regard it is like an edit. Like the edit, you have to give some thought to whether the effect is natural. Cutting from a fast, loud sound to one that is very slow and quiet, or vice versa, may be too abrupt; segueing two songs in keys that are incompatible may create a transition that has unwanted dissonance; or cutting from a program about folks living in poverty to a commercial for a disinfectant may raise questions of taste.

Dramas and documentaries provide more of an opportunity to make unnatural cuts, because the action or picture can cover the transition, like cutting from a furious storm to the quiet calm of its aftermath, or from a deeply moving love scene to a raucously funny bachelor party. The cut has both an informational and an aesthetic function, and either purpose justifies its use.

Crossfade

The *crossfade*—gradually fading out one sound as you fade in another—is another transition used for smaller changes in time, locale, and action, although you can vary the length of these changes somewhat by increasing or decreasing the duration of the crossfade (see 17-40). Informationally, the crossfade accomplishes the same thing as the fade-out/fade-in, but aesthetically it is softer, more fluid, and more graceful. It also maintains, rather than breaks, rhythmic continuity and pace.

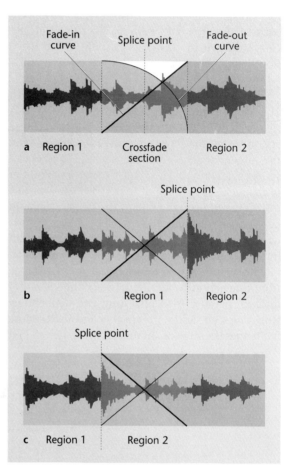

17-40 Common types of crossfades. (a) Standard, or centered, crossfade on both sides of the splice point. In this example the fade-in curve is linear and smooth, and the fade-out curve is gradual, reducing level steadily. (b) Pre-crossfade creates a crossfade before the splice point, thus maintaining the level of the beginning of region 2 instead of fading across it. Pre-crossfade is useful if there is a strong percussive downbeat or loud sound at the beginning of region 2. (c) Post-crossfade generates the crossfade after the splice point. It is useful in maintaining the level of region 1 until it ends, to keep, for example, a strong upbeat or an exclamatory sound that occurs at the end of region 1.

You can produce the crossfade in a number of ways, depending on the loudness levels of the sounds when they cross. Usually, it is more aesthetically satisfying to cross the sounds at the moment they are at full and equal loudness. This keeps audience attention "stage-center" with no loss of focus or gap in continuity, which could occur if the crossfade were made at lower levels. Crossfading at too low a level could sound like a sloppy fade-out/fade-in.

Fade-Out/Fade-In

The *fade-out/fade-in* transition is used to make a clearly defined change from one time, place, and action to another. Aesthetically, it is gentler than the cut, and it gives a stronger sense of finality to a scene that is ending and a sense of new possibilities to the scene that is beginning.

In TV and film, the rate of the fade-out/fade-in depends on the picture. Generally, the type of fade used provides not only an aesthetic effect but an informational one as well. A slow fade-out and fade-in with silence between suggests a complete break from one action to another. The change is rather marked, because it so obviously and deliberately stops one scene and starts another and also because it changes the pace or rhythm of the material. You could use this type of transition to bridge the time between a student going off to college as a freshman and his graduation, or to link a police car's hot pursuit of bank robbers and the thieves being booked at the police station. Faster fades suggest shorter lapses of time, smaller changes of location, or fewer events in a series of actions. They still provide a definite break in the presentation, but their quicker rate implies that less has happened. You should not, however, consider these guidelines as prescriptive. There are no formulas for how long transitions should be relative to the scenes they bridge, it is a matter of what "feels" right.

Audio-Leading-Video and Video-Leading-Audio

Transitions involving sound and picture often do not occur at the same time for dramatic or technical reasons. When there is a picture transition, the sound transition may not be simultaneous or vice versa; the audio or video leads or lags a portion of the previous edit (see 17-41). These are split-editing techniques known as *audio-leading-video* and *video-leading-audio*.

When the sound of the incoming scene starts before the corresponding picture appears, the audio is leading the video. For example, the picture shows

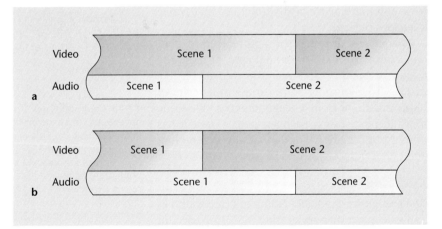

17-41 (a) Audio-leading-video split edit; (b) video-leading-audio split edit

a boy building a model airplane as the sound of a jet fighter fades in. The picture then cuts to a shot of the grown-up boy as the pilot.

When the picture of a new scene starts before the sound of the old scene has finished, the video is leading the audio. For example, the audio of a romantic song in a scene showing a couple who has just met carries into the next scene, showing the couple dancing on their honeymoon.

Listening Fatigue

Editing for long periods of time can create *listening fatigue*—reduced ability to perceive or remember the nuances of sound. In computer editing, the problem can be compounded by eyestrain. If you suffer from listening fatigue during editing, such features of sound as tempo, inflection, and tonality are continually mismatched, cuts are slightly off, and it is difficult to keep track of what should be edited to what.

One way to postpone listening fatigue is to work in a quiet acoustic environment with no predominance of midrange frequencies, because they tend to tire the listener faster. If a recording or loudspeaker system has too much midrange, equalize the monitor playback by slightly boosting the lower frequencies anywhere between 50 and 150 Hz and the frequencies above 10,000 Hz. This balances the sound and reduces its harshness and intensity. You can also attenuate the frequencies between 1,000 and 3,500 Hz, although this may reduce intelligibility. It is also important to remember to bring down playback gain after turning it up, as is often required, to hear an edit point better. Finally, take regular "ears" breaks.

MAIN POINTS

▶ Editing tape and disk permits the rearranging, shortening, or deleting of elements in a production. It allows elements to be recorded out of sequence and as often as necessary.

▶ The process of editing is either linear—the edits are made successively—or it is nonlinear—they can be made in any order.

▶ Two ways to edit sound linearly are cutting and splicing, and electronic editing—transferring information from one tape to another or punching in material.

▶ The tools used to cut and splice tape are a metal editing block, a razor blade, an indelible marker with a soft tip, and splicing and leader tape.

▶ Sound film is edited by cutting and splicing. The difference between cutting and splicing tape and film is that, for synchronization, the editing of sound film must coordinate with the editing of picture film.

▶ Various types of equipment used to cut and splice magnetic film include: editing table, rewinds, viewer, synchronizer, sound reader, Moviola or flatbed editor, and film splicer.

▶ Fill leader or spacer is spliced into silent portions of magnetic film to avoid an increase in signal-to-noise ratio.

▶ A sync pop is cut across from the Academy 2 to create an audible beep 2 seconds before the first shot.

▶ Electronic editing of audiotape can be accomplished using one or two tape recorders. One tape recorder will do when inserting material by punching in. But to assemble-edit, dubbing each program segment from a master to a slave tape in sequential order requires two machines: one to play back and one to record and play back.

- In automatic electronic editing, the master and slave tape recorders are programmed to start and stop on cue and perform the edit.

- A synchronizer locks the transports of the master and slave recorders, allowing automatic control of the editing functions.

- A synchronizer also generates an edit decision list (EDL), a computer-generated list of edits performed during editing.

- Nonlinear editing allows the retrieval, assembly, and reassembly of disk-based material quickly and in any order, regardless of the material's location on the disk.

- Audio encoded onto a hard disk takes the form of a soundfile, which is displayed in a waveform. A waveform displays the profile of a sound's amplitude over time.

- The waveform segment highlighted for editing is called the defined region.

- Scrubbing the waveform to locate an edit point precisely is similar to rocking tape in the cut-and-splice editing method.

- In nonlinear editing there are operations similar to those in word processing, such as cut, copy, paste, delete, insert, and typeover. The precise terms for these operations may differ among hard-disk editors.

- Destructive editing permanently alters the original soundfile by overwriting it. Non-destructive editing does not alter the original soundfile regardless of what editing or signal processing you effect.

- Before editing begins, organize the edit tracks by cataloging all the sounds and keep a running log throughout the editing process.

- Editing picture is one-dimensional; one shot is cut, dissolved, or faded out and in to another shot. Little happens until the next transition. Editing sound is multidimensional. Sounds are layered within each shot, so editing audio becomes more than attending to transitions.

- Among the considerations basic to editing speech are recognizing the sounds that make up words; cutting together similar and dissimilar sounds; handling emphasis and inflection; matching ambience (or room tone); and taking corrective action with problem tracks that may suffer from such things as ring-off, additive ambience, and defective or unusable dialogue.

- A fundamental consideration in editing sound effects is to match perspective.

- In editing music, attention must be paid to cutting to resolution, preserving tempo, matching keys, and matching style and texture.

- Generally, edits that heighten intensity will work, such as cutting from quiet to loud, nonrhythmic to rhythmic, slow to fast, formless to structured, or atonal to tonal.

- Mismatching of sound makes an edit obvious, unless the sound is being edited to a picture and the picture justifies the edit.

- Transitions used in audio editing include the segue or cut, the crossfade, the fade-out/fade-in, and audio-leading-video and video-leading-audio.

- It is important to avoid listening fatigue during editing; take "ears" breaks.

18 Mixing and Rerecording

Up to now, the elements that go into producing audio have been considered separately. But audiences are usually not aware of ingredients; they hear only the final product, the result of the last phases in the production process—mixing and rerecording. The procedure in getting to the final stages in production may differ among the media, but the purpose is the same: to combine the parts into a natural and integrated whole.

The term *mixing* is used in radio, television, and music recording to describe the process of combining individual audio tracks into two (stereo) or more (surround sound) master tracks. *Sweetening* is another term used to name the process in television. In theatrical film and TV, by the time the dialogue, sound effects, and music tracks reach the rerecording stage, they have been already premixed. Hence, the term **rerecording** refers to the process of combining them into their final form— stereo or surround sound.

Regardless of terminology, in addition to combining tracks into stereo or surround sound, mixing and rerecording have the same purposes:

▦ To enhance the sound quality and style of the existing audio tracks through signal processing and other means

▦ To balance levels

▦ To add special effects

▦ To create the acoustic space, artificially if necessary

- To localize the sounds within the aural frame

- To establish aural perspective

- To maintain the sonic integrity of each sound regardless of how many sounds are heard simultaneously

- To keep all essential sonic information within the frequency and dynamic ranges of the medium for which the mix (or rerecording) is being made

MIXING FOR VARIOUS MEDIA

Before proceeding with a mix, it is necessary to know on what type of delivery system it will be reproduced. It is difficult to create an optimum mix for all systems.

Radio

In doing a mix for radio, two considerations are the frequency response of the medium—AM or FM—and the wide range of receivers the listening audience uses, from the car radio to the upscale stereo component system. Although AM radio may transmit in stereo and play music from compact discs, its frequency response is mediocre—roughly 100 to 5,000 Hz. The frequency response of FM is considerably wider, from 20 to 20,000 Hz. Therefore it would seem that mixing for AM requires care to ensure that the essential sonic information is within its narrower frequency band and that in mixing for FM there is no such problem. Both statements would be true if it were not for the broad assortment of radio receivers that vary so greatly in size and sound quality, and for the variety of listening conditions under which radio is heard. There is no way to do an optimum mix, for either AM or FM, to satisfy listeners with a boom box, a portable radio the size of a hand, or car stereos that run the gamut from mediocre to excellent and are played against the sounds of the engine, road, and air conditioner.

The best approach is to mix using loudspeakers that are average in terms of frequency response, size, and cost, and to keep the essential sonic information—speech, sound effects, and music—within the

150 to 5,000 Hz band, which most radio receivers can handle. With AM radio's limited frequency response, it often helps to compress the sound to give it more power in the low end and presence in the midrange. For FM mixes, a sound check on high-quality loudspeakers is wise to make sure that the harmonics and overtones beyond 5,000 Hz are audible to the listener using a high-quality receiver.

Videotape

The frequency response of analog videotape can be as wide as 40 to 15,000 Hz; the frequency response of digital audio on videotape is even wider. Moreover, TV audio transmission goes to 15,000 Hz. But in television as in radio, mixing has to conform to the limitations of the home TV receiver.

There is also the reality that TV viewing does not usually take place in a quiet, focused environment: one parent is getting the meal together, another is talking on the phone, the kids are playing. To ensure that subtle or low-level sounds are heard, it is necessary to bring the levels above the noise floor. But TV has a comparatively narrow signal-to-noise ratio, because most television sets cannot play very loud without distortion.

Another limitation is that the sound on an edited analog master videotape may be from second-, third-, or even fourth-generation dubs. Digital sound on videotape does not appreciably degrade with dubbing. Important information (dialogue and effects as well as music) should be mixed between roughly 150 and 5,000 Hz. Boosting around 700 Hz should tighten the bass, and at around 4,000 to 5,000 Hz should enhance clarity and presence. Gentle limiting, to prevent overmodulation, and/or compressing overall sound is often a good idea, especially with digital sound, which has no headroom.

Monitor on average-type bookshelf loudspeakers most of the time. For overall referencing, occasionally switch to the big loudspeakers and small mono loudspeaker. For a TV mix, the mono loudspeaker mix is crucial, because this is what most of the audience still listens to.

Mixing for television and radio is different from mixing for compact disc (see "Compact Disc" later in this chapter). Few people listen to TV and radio on decent stereos the way they do CDs. Avoid going for a big, deep low end or for tingly, shimmery high-end sounds, because most viewers will not hear them. Make sure the essential sonic information is clear on the mono loudspeaker.

For TV and also for radio, keep the stereo mix mono-compatible by not hard-panning anything to the extreme left and right. If reverb is used, make it wetter in the mix than normal, because TV transmission diminishes reverb.

The top priority in television is what is on the screen. If there is a close-up of an actor or a lead guitarist, this is what the audience expects to hear; do not be afraid to exaggerate these or other featured elements.

Film

Dynamic range is less on an optical sound track than it is on videotape, particularly in 16mm film. Although 35mm film sound is better than 16mm, it is still not as good as sound on videotape—analog and digital. That said, the sonic improvement in theatrical films has been responsible for remarkable enhancements in 35mm sound.

In mixing music for film, it may be best to do a partial mix and let the rerecording mixer make the final adjustments when dialogue and effects are added. To this end, one of two approaches is usually taken: (1) not restricting too severely low-end and high-end roll-offs and leaving some "play" for adjustments in laboratory processing; or (2) using the "unisound" approach, which cuts out all sound below 100 to 200 Hz and above 5,000 to 6,000 Hz. This technique is preferred by some mixers, because there is not much work to do and there are fewer problems with rumble and hiss. When Dolby Stereo and surround are employed, the concern about narrow frequency response becomes less of a factor. Typical mixes for 16mm optical sound should be between 150 and 5,000 Hz with a dynamic range of 15 to 20 dB.

Compact Disc

In mixing an album for compact disc, three important factors are digital edge, distortion, and total playing time of the music. There may be other considerations as well, such as applying the Red Book and Orange Book standards (see Chapter 7).

"Digital edge" is the overly bright sonic by-product of the digital recording process that too often spoils the sound quality on a CD. Usually, it is the result of either improper miking and recording techniques (discussed in Chapter 15) or inappropriate EQ during mixing, or both. It may also be the result of poor CD mastering, but that discussion is beyond the scope of this book.

In analog sound, reasonable boosts in the upper midrange and lower treble ranges may turn out to be sonically satisfactory. But due to the clarity of digital sound, the same boosts in EQ in the same ranges may result in making these frequencies overly apparent to the point of annoyance.

Distortion can be another problem in mixing digital sound. As pointed out, there is no headroom in digital recording; levels have to be watched carefully. Once you reach zero level, you have run out of headroom—there is no place to go. In analog recording, assuming the use of high-output tape, you usually have at least 4 dBs of headroom when you reach zero level.

Trying to pack too much program material onto a music compact disc can create problems in mastering and reproduction. A CD can hold more than 70 minutes of data, and in today's marketplace discs sell on the basis of length as well as content. On a CD that has much more than 60 minutes of material, the spiral traces of the data track are pushed closer together, which makes laser tracking more difficult and can cause skipping.

Generally, a compact disc is mixed with one of three types of playback systems in mind: (1) a high-quality system with amplifier and loud-speakers capable of reproducing wide dynamic range and frequency response; (2) a medium-quality system capable of reproducing a fairly wide frequency response and dynamic range; or

(3) a low-quality system with limited dynamic range and frequency response.

For CDs being prepared for radio play, another consideration is doing a radio-friendly mix. In an album mix, most important are the integrity of the song, how the song fits within the CD, and the artist's vision. What is important in doing an alternative mix for radio is making sure the CD's dynamic range and EQ are suitable for the medium and adding compression to the overall mix to make it stand out.

Multimedia

Even though digital sound has extremely wide dynamic range and most of it is mastered in 16- or 20-bit, with 24-bit mastering becoming increasingly popular, the reproducing medium, again, is still a factor.

Multimedia usually means that the product is heard (and seen) on a computer. At this writing, many computers out there produce only 8-bit audio, which is worse than mediocre analog sound. In producing audio for multimedia, the essential information must therefore be mixed and mastered so that it can be heard within this range. Another potentially limiting factor is the data compression and expansion that is so much a part of computer signal processing.

MIXING VERSUS LAYERING

Not to quibble about semantics, but mixing suggests a blend in which the ingredients lose their uniqueness in becoming part of the whole. Although blending is important, in relation to a mix the term *layering* may be more to the point.

When sounds are combined, there are four essential objectives to keep in mind:

▉ To establish the main and supporting sounds to create focus or point of view

▉ To position the sounds to create relationships of space and distance

▉ To maintain spectral balance so that the aural space is properly weighted

▉ To maintain the definition of each sound.

These considerations come closer to the definition of layering than they do of mixing. The following discussion notwithstanding, *mixing* is the term in popular use.

Layering

Layering involves some of the most important aspects of aural communication: balance, perspective, and intelligibility. When many sounds occur at once, unless they are layered properly it could result in a loud sound drowning out a quiet sound; sounds with similar frequencies muddying one another; sounds in the same spatial position interfering with focus; and sounds that are too loud competing for attention.

Usually, when elements in a mix are muddled, it is because too many of them are sonically alike in pitch, tempo, loudness, intensity, envelope, timbre, or style. Imagine the sound track for a gothic mystery thriller. The scene: dark night, a sinister castle on a lonely mountaintop high above a black forest, silhouetted against the starless sky by flashes of lightning. You can almost hear the sound: rumbling, rolling thunder; ominous bass chords from an organ, cellos, and double basses; the low-pitched moan of the wind.

The layering seems straightforward, depending on the focus: music over wind and thunder to establish the overall scariness; wind over thunder and music to focus on the forlorn emptiness; and thunder over wind and music to center attention on the storm about to break above the haunting bleakness. But with this particular mix, setting the appropriate levels may be insufficient to communicate the effect. The sounds are so much alike—low pitched and sustained—that they may cover one another, thereby creating a combined sound that is thick and muddy, lacking clarity and definition. The frequency range, rhythm, and envelope of the sounds are too similar: low pitched, legato, weak in attack, and long in sustain.

One way to layer them more effectively is to make the wind a bit wilder, thereby sharpening its pitch. Instead of rolling thunder, start it with a sharp crack and shorten the sustain of the rumble to separate it from any similar sustain in the music. These minor changes make each sound more distinctive, with little or no loss in the overall effect on the scene.

This technique also works in complex mixes. Take a war scene: soldiers shouting, cannons booming, rifles and machine guns clattering, jet fighter planes diving to the attack, and intense orchestral music dramatically underscoring the action. Although there are six different elements, they are distinctive enough to be layered without losing their intelligibility.

The pitch of the cannons is lower than that of the rifles and machine guns; their firing rhythms and sound envelopes are also different. The rifles and machine guns are distinct because their pitch, rhythm, and envelope are not the same either. The pitch of the jets may be within the same range as that of the rifles and machine guns, but their sustained, whining type of roar is the only sound of its kind in the mix. The shouting soldiers have varied rhythms, regardless of any similarities in pitch, envelope, and intensity; and the timbres of the human voices are usually distinguishable. As for the music, its timbres, blend, and intensity are different from the other sounds. Remember, too, that the differences in loudness levels and positioning in a stereo frame will help contribute to the clarity of this mix. Appropriate signal processing can always be employed as well.

In relation to loudness and the frequency spectrum, two useful devices in maintaining intelligibility are the compressor and the equalizer. Compressing certain sounds increases flexibility in placing those sounds, because it facilitates tailoring their dynamic ranges. This is a more convenient and sonically better way to place sounds than by simply using the fader. Through modest and deft equalization, attenuating, or boosting, sounds can cut or fill holes in the aural frame, thereby also facilitating placement without affecting intelligibility.

Some scenes are so complex, however, that there are simply too many sonic elements in the SFX and music to deal with separately. In such instances try grouping them and playing no more than three or four groupings at the same time, varying levels as you go. For example, in the previous battle scene the five different elements (other than the voices) could be put into four groups: canons, guns, planes, and music. By varying levels and positioning groups in the foreground, background, and side-to-side, and moving them in, out, or through the scene, it avoids the sound track collapsing into a jumble.

Another reason not to play too many sounds at once, particularly loud sounds, is that if they stay constant the effect is lost; they lose their interest. Contrast and perspective are the keys in keeping complex scenes sonically interesting.

Still another reason why it is unwise to play too many loud sounds at the same time is annoyance. In a scene with thunderclaps, very heavy rain, a growling monster crashing through a city or countryside on the attack, kids yelling, people screaming, and cars crashing, there is no sonic relief. It is loud sound on loud sound; every moment is hard. The rerecording mix can be used to create holes in the constant loudness without diminishing intensity or fright, and can provide relief from time to time throughout the sequence. For example, the rain could be used as a buffer between two loud sounds. After a crash or scream, bring up the rain before the next loud sound hits. Or use the growl, which has low-frequency relief, to buffer two loud sounds.

Also, be wary of sounds that "eat up" certain frequencies. Water sounds in general and rain in particular are so high-frequency intense that they are difficult to blend into a mix, and the presence of other high-frequency sounds only exacerbates the problem. Deep, rumbly sounds like thunder present the same problem at the low end of the frequency spectrum. One way to handle such sounds is to look for ways to change their perspectives. With the rain, have it falling on cars, vegetation, pavement, and in puddles. With the thunder, make it louder or quieter as the perspective of the storm cloud changes in relation to the people in the scene.

Another approach to scenes with a complex sound pattern is to drop out sounds. It is opening night at the theater. There is the hubbub of gathering audience, the last-minute preparations and hysteria backstage, and the orchestra tuning up. The star is frightfully nervous, pacing the dressing room. By dropping away all the sounds except the pacing, the star's anxiety becomes greatly heightened.

In music recording, an orchestra, for example, has a variety of instruments playing at once. Their blend is important to the music's structure, but not to the extent that violins become indistinguishable from clarinets, or the trumpets and trombones drown out the French horns.

Perspective

In layering, some sounds are more important than others; the predominant one usually establishes the focus or point of view. In a commercial the announcer's voice is usually louder than any accompanying music or effects, because the main message is likely to be in the copy. In an auto racing scene, with the sounds of speeding cars, cheering crowd, and dramatic music defining the excitement, to focus on the race, have the sound of the speeding cars dominate. The crowd and the music should be in the middleground or background, with the music under to provide the dramatic support. To establish the overall dramatic excitement of the event, the music probably would convey that point of view best. Therefore, layer the speeding cars and cheering crowd under the music as supporting elements.

In music recording, it is obvious that a vocalist should stand out from the accompaniment, or that an ensemble should not overwhelm a solo instrument. When an ensemble plays all at once, there are foreground instruments—lead guitar in a rock group, violins in an orchestra, or piano in a jazz trio—and background instruments—rhythm guitar, bass, woodwinds, and drums.

Whatever the combination of effects, establishing the main and supporting sounds is fundamental to good mixing, indeed, to good dramatic tech-

nique and musical balances. But because of the psychological relationship between sound and picture, perspectives between what is heard and seen do not necessarily have to match but rather complement one another. In other words, you can "cheat" in handling perspective.

For example, take a scene in which two people are talking as they walk in the countryside and stop by a tree. The shot as they are walking is a long shot (LS), which changes to a medium close-up (MCU) at the tree. Reducing the loudness in the LS to match the visual perspective could interfere with comprehension and be annoying, because the audience would have to strain to hear and the lip movements would be difficult to see. When people speak at a distance, the difficulty in seeing lip movements and the reduced loudness inhibit comprehension. A better technique is to ride the levels at almost full loudness and roll off low-end frequencies, because the farther away the voice, the thinner the sound. Let the picture also help establish the distance and perspective. Psychologically, the picture establishes the context of the sound. This also works in reverse.

In the close-up there must be some sonic change to be consistent with the shot change. Because the close-up does not show the countryside but does show the faces better, you can establish the environment by increasing ambience in the sound track. In this case, the ambience establishes the unseen space in the picture. Furthermore, by adding the ambience, the dialogue will seem more diffused. This creates a sense of change without interfering with comprehension, because the sound is louder and the actors' lip movements are easier to see.

MIXING FOR RADIO

Many of the techniques used in mixing for radio are also applicable to TV, film, music recording, and multimedia audio, and vice versa. Some techniques may be more frequently employed in one medium than another, however.

Voice-Over Background

Z and ELIZABETH
MAUI EASTERE
Happy Holidays!

Wishing you
the brightest of holidays
and the happiest of year.

BEE ZEE COACH SERVICE

HO HO HO! HO HO! HO HO HO! HO HO HO! HO HO HO! HO HO HO! HO HO HO! HO HO HO! HO HO HO! HO HO HO! OH OH! OH OH OH

used to balance levels between an announcer and

music, or between an announcer and other sounds such as crowd noise or traffic, is to feed each sound through a limiter and set one limiter to trigger the response of the other. In the case of a voice-over-music announcement, the limiter controlling the music would be set to reduce the music level to a preset point when it is triggered by the limiter controlling the announcer's sound. As soon as the announcer speaks, the limiters' actions automatically reduce the music level. When the announcer stops speaking, the announcer's limiter triggers the music's limiter to restore the music to its preset louder level. This can also be done with a limiter and a compressor.

This technique has been used for years, but you have to be careful when setting the limit levels. If they are not precise, you will hear the limiters' annoying pumping action as they increase and decrease levels.

When an announcer or narrator is mixed with background music or sound effects, the copy is the most important element. This is why the performer's voice is in the foreground. If the music or effects become as loud as, or louder than, the performer, it forces the audience to struggle to focus attention on one of the competing elements, thereby inhibiting communication. This does not mean that the music and effects must remain in the background. During a pause in the copy, the background can be increased in level or, if it is kept under the announcer, it can be varied to help accent the message, thereby providing sonic variety to heighten interest and pace. In audio production it is worthwhile to remember that *sonic variety attracts the ear*. In fact, whether it is audio or video, the human perceptual system likes change. Shifts in focus, directed by the production, hold audience attention. This is not to suggest that confused, cluttered, frenetic production is advised. Obscuring the message with production pyrotechnics is poor communication practice.

For example, instead of using the stale donut approach to production, take time to produce the spot. It makes the station sound better and the client happier.

Backtiming and Deadpotting

Using prerecorded music to underscore or end a spot announcement, narrative, dialogue, or a program theme song may involve backtiming and deadpotting to ensure that it ends at the appropriate time. Prerecorded material has a fixed total time; it may be 3:13, 1:22.5, :11, or something else. Suppose in a commercial that the section of music used to end a spot is 18 seconds long, but only the last 11 seconds of it is needed. To get the music to end when the commercial ends, assuming a 30-second spot, the music has to start 12 seconds into the commercial. Subtracting the time of an individual element from the total time of a program or program segment is known as **backtiming**.

Deadpotting refers to starting a recording with the fader turned down all the way. To get the music to end when the spot ends, begin playing the music 12 seconds after the spot begins, just do not raise the fader. The music recording will deadpot—play with no sound feeding through—until you are ready for it. At that point, fade it in; because it started at the right time, it will also end on time. And ending music is usually a more effective close than fading it out. Of course, computers and automation can handle operations automatically once the data has been entered.

MUSIC MIXDOWN

There is a common misunderstanding about the music mixdown, namely, that it is the stage in music production when everything that went wrong in the recording session is put right. No doubt this unfortunate notion has been nurtured in recording sessions that have not met expectations when producers have glibly reassured clients, "Don't worry, we can fix it in the mixdown."

The mixdown certainly is very important to the finished product, but keep its significance in perspective. The mixdown cannot change a mediocre performance into a good one, compensate for poor microphone technique, or make a sloppy recording precise. In most instances it is the quality of the recording session that determines the overall quality of the mix.

Nevertheless, the mixdown should not be taken too lightly. A good mix cannot salvage a bad recording, but a poor mix can ruin a good one.

Procedures

There are probably as many approaches to mixing music as there are producers. But most producers generally include the following operations in proceeding with a mixdown:

1. Tape recorder heads are demagnetized and cleaned, and both the heads and the recorder are aligned.

2. Meters on the console and recorders are calibrated.

3. Inputs on the console are set to receive the signals from the multitrack recorder.

4. One master monitor channel is assigned or panned to the extreme left and another is assigned or panned to the extreme right. If the stereo mix must be mono-compatible, the monitor system also is set up for A-B (stereo/mono) referencing. A stereo display processor is often used to reference stereo-to-mono compatibility (see 18-23). For three-dimensional sound, appropriate controls—joysticks, pan pots, and so on—are positioned to locate the various voicings in the expanded aural frame.

5. The stereo master fader (or two submasters) are turned up so that the left and right signals feed to the proper tracks of the master recorder.

6. Individual channel faders are turned up.

7. Individual channels are assigned to the left, right (or both), or surround mix bus and proportioned between them using the pan pots.

8. Levels and localizing of the voicings are temporarily set.

9. The rough, unprocessed mix is auditioned for as long as it takes to decide what needs to be done in relation to equalization, reverberation, and other signal processing.

10. Individual voicings are then equalized and, at the same time, referenced to the overall mix to check blending and positioning. Usually, the rhythm tracks are done first, then the accompanying tracks, and finally the vocal tracks.

11. Other signal processing, such as compression, delay, and pitch shifting, is added where appropriate, sometimes before equalizing.

12. Reverberation is then added and equalized.

13. The mix is checked for blend, balance, definition, and spatial positioning.

14. Reference tones are recorded on the master.

15. The final mix is recorded on the master recorder.

16. The master is assembled and labeled.

17. Backup copies are made as required.

18. Premastering may be done in-studio with a recordable compact disc (CD-R).

Auditioning the Rough Mix

It is not good policy to do a mix on the same day that you finish the recording. Regardless of what you may think a recording sounds like immediately after taping, in a day or so it will sound different. It is essential to take some time between sessions to regain perspective and renew "ears." Therefore, before beginning a mix or making any final decisions about localizing, signal processing, special effects, and so on, refamiliarize yourself with the recording by auditioning it.

To do this, set the relative level and location of each voicing to achieve approximate, but satisfactory, overall loudness and positional balances. Here is one approach:

1. Set the level of the loudest or most prominent sound first, leaving plenty of headroom on the VU meter. For example, if the loudest sound is a support voicing, such as the bass drum, set the level at –10 VU; if the sound is a prominent lead voicing, such as a vocal, set the level higher, at, say, –5 VU. Leaving headroom is important because mixing almost always involves adding level during signal processing through EQ, reverb, and so on. (As discussed later in this section, too much boosting without compensating attenuation can create a number of sonic problems.)

2. Turn up the monitor level so it is comfortably loud; 85 dB-SPL is usually considered optimal. Because what is considered comfortably loud depends on personal taste, musical style, and hearing acuity, however, 85 dB-SPL is at least a good level to start with. It is critical to not set the monitor level too loud. Loud levels desensitize hearing or, in the vernacular of audio, "fry" ears, to say nothing of the potential for hearing loss. Once monitor loudness is set, try not to change it; otherwise, the reference you are using to determine sonic values and proportions will change as well.

3. Add all other tracks relative to the level of the first voicing. If you started with drums, add bass, the rest of the drum set, the other accompanying instruments, and the vocal(s). If you started with the lead or most prominent instrument, bring in the other tracks one at a time, starting with the rhythm instruments, followed by the rest of the accompaniment. Another approach is to set all instruments equally loud. Then increase levels of the lead voicings and decrease levels of the support instruments.

4. Position each instrument in the stereo, 3D, or surround space approximately where you plan to put it in the final mix.

5. Readjust fader levels to compensate for loudness changes resulting from these positional alignments.

6. If something is not working, do not force it. Maybe it is not needed. That applies, for example, to parts of a song, control settings, signal processing, and, if necessary, even to an entire instrumental track.

Once you have refamiliarized yourself with the recording and have reconfirmed its design, you are ready to do the actual mixdown. It is likely that during the mix, as various sonic alterations are made, some of the original decisions about the mix will change. This is natural. Be flexible. Do not be afraid to experiment or go with your instincts.

Signal Processing

Signal processing is so much a part of music recording that sound shaping seems impossible without it. Yet, overdependency on signal processing has created the myth that just about anything can be done with it to ensure the sonic success of a recording. These notions are misleading. Unless special effects are required or MIDI is involved, signal processing in the mixdown should be used to touch up the aural canvas, not repaint it. The greater the reliance on signal processing in the mixdown, the more likely the poorer the recording session. Nevertheless, signal processing is important, and often critical. Recordists who proudly proclaim they can do without it are foolish. The purpose of this section is only to suggest possibilities and techniques. It is not intended to imply that because signal processing offers so many options to the recordist, most of them should be used. Remember: *Less is more.*

Equalizing: How Much, Where, and When?

One question often asked of a recordist is: "What kind of a sound will I get on this instrument if I equalize so many decibels at such and such a frequency?" The question suggests that there are ways to predetermine equalization. There are not! Consider the different things that can affect sound. For example, for a guitar you might ask: "What is it made of? Is it acoustic or electric? Are the strings steel or plastic, old or new, played with

a metal or plastic pick or with the fingers? Is the guitarist heavy- or light-handed? Are there fret sounds? Is the guitar miked and, if so, with what type of microphone? How are the acoustics? What type of song is being played? What is the spatial placement of the guitar in the mix?" These influences do not even include personal taste, the most variable factor of all.

The best way to approach equalization is to (1) know the frequency ranges of the instruments involved, (2) know what each octave in the audible frequency spectrum contributes to the overall sound, (3) listen to the sound in context, and (4) have a good idea of what you want to achieve before starting the mixdown.

Also remember the following:

▦ Equalizing alters a sound's harmonic structure.

▦ Very few people, even under ideal conditions, can hear a change of 1 dB or less, and many people cannot hear changes of 2 or 3 dB.

▦ Large increases or decreases in equalizing should be avoided.

▦ Equalizing should not be used as a substitute for better microphone selection and mic placement.

▦ Only a certain number of tracks in the same frequency range should be increased or decreased. For example, on one channel you may increase by 4 dB at 5,000 Hz the sound of a snare drum to make it snappier, then on another channel you increase 2 dB at 5,000 Hz to make a cymbal sound crisper, and on a third channel you increase 3 dB at 5,000 Hz to bring out a vocal. If you consider each channel separately, there has been little equalizing at 5,000 Hz, but the cumulative boost at the same frequency, which in this example is 9 dB, could unbalance the overall blend.

▦ Equalizing often involves boosting frequencies, and that can mean more noise, among other problems. Therefore, be careful, particularly when increasing some of the unpleasant frequencies in the midrange and high end, especially with digital sound.

■ Because boosting frequencies on one track often necessitates attenuating frequencies somewhere else, consider *subtractive equalization* first. For example, if a sound is overly bright, instead of trying to mellow it by boosting the appropriate lower frequencies, reduce some of the higher frequencies responsible for the excessive brightness.

■ Frequencies above and below the range of each instrument should be filtered to reduce unwanted sound and improve definition. Be very careful not to reduce frequencies that are essential to the natural timbre of an instrument.

■ To achieve a satisfactory blend, the sounds of individual elements may have to be changed in ways that could make them unpleasant to listen to by themselves. For example, the frequencies between 1,000 and 3,500 Hz make most vocals intelligible. One way to improve the clarity of a vocal and make it stand out from its instrumental accompaniment, while maintaining the overall blend, is to boost it a few decibels in the 1,000- to 3,500-Hz range and decrease the accompaniment a few decibels in the same range. Together they should sound quite natural. Separately, however, the vocal will be somewhat harsher and thinner and the accompaniment will sound a bit dense and lifeless.

If a voice is powerful and rich with harmonics in the 5,000-Hz range, the sound is usually clear and full. Male singing voices, particularly in opera, have this sonic characteristic; female vocals usually do not.

Voices deficient in the 5,000-Hz range can be enhanced by a boost of several decibels in this area. Not only is the definition of such sounds as "t," "s," "ch," and "k" increased, but a 6-dB increase at 5,000 Hz gives an apparent increase of 3 dB to the overall mix. When mixing digital sound using these EQ values, be wary of "digital edge," that overly bright sonic by-product of the digital recording process that too often spoils sound quality on a CD.

■ Use *complementary equalization* to help define instruments and keep masking to a minimum. Many instruments have comparable frequency

18-1 Complementary EQ for bass instruments

18-2 Complementary EQ for midrange instruments

ranges, such as the bass guitar and kick drum, or the keyboard, guitar, and female vocal. Because physical law states that no two things can occupy the same space at the same time, it makes sense to equalize voicings that share frequency ranges so that they complement, rather than interfere with, one another (see Figures 18-1 and 18-2).

■ An absence of frequencies above 600 Hz adversely affects the intelligibility of consonants; an absence of frequencies below 600 Hz adversely affects the intelligibility of vowels.

■ Equal degrees of equalizing between 400 and 2,000 Hz are more noticeable than equalizing above or below that range, especially in digital sound (remember the equal loudness principle).

Most amplified instruments do not have ranges higher than 7,500 Hz; boosting above that frequency usually adds only noise.

Each sound has a naturally occurring peak at a frequency or band of frequencies that contains more energy than surrounding frequencies and by being boosted or cut enhances or mars the sound. In other words, the naturally occurring peak can become a *sweet spot* or a *sore spot*. The peaks are caused by natural harmonics and overtones or by formants. A **formant** is the resonance band in a vibrating body that mildly increases the level of specific steady-state frequencies in that band.

To find the resonance area, turn up the gain on the appropriate section of the equalizer and sweep the frequency control until the voicing sounds noticeably better or worse. Once you find the sweet or sore spot, return the equalizer's gain to zero and boost or cut the enhancing or offending frequencies to taste.

Equalization and Semantics

A major problem in equalization is describing what it sounds like. What does it mean, for example, when a producer wants "sizzle" in a cymbal sound, "fatness" in a snare sound, "brightness" in an alto saxophone sound, or "edge" to a vocal? Not only is there a problem of semantics, but you must identify the adjustments needed to achieve the desired effect. The following list should aid you in this process.

Low-frequency boost under 200 Hz adds power or weight to sound. A boost between 200 and 300 Hz can make sound woody or tubby.

Low-frequency boost below 500 Hz can make sound fat, thick, warm, or robust. It can also make sound muddy, boomy, thumpy, or barrel-like.

Flat, extended low frequencies add fullness, richness, or solidity to sound. They can also make sound rumbly.

Low-frequency roll-off thins sound. This can make it seem clean, cold, tinny, or anemic.

Mid-frequency boost between 500 Hz and 7 kHz (5 kHz area for most instruments, 1.5 to 2.5 kHz for bass instruments) can add presence, punch, edge, clarity, or definition to sound. It can also make sound muddy (hornlike), tinny (telephone-like), nasal or honky (500 Hz to 3 kHz), hard (2 to 4 kHz), strident or piercing (2 to 5 kHz), twangy (3 kHz), metallic (3 to 5 kHz), or sibilant (4 to 7 kHz).

Flat mid-frequencies sound natural or smooth. They may also lack punch or color.

Mid-frequency dip makes sound mellow. It can also hollow (500 to 1,000 Hz), muffle (5 kHz), or muddy (5 kHz) sound.

High-frequency boost above 7 kHz can enhance sound by making it bright, crisp, etched, or sizzly (cymbals). It can detract from sound by making it edgy, glassy, sibilant, or sizzly (voice).

Flat, extended high frequencies open sound, making it airy, transparent, natural, or detailed. They can also make sound too detailed or close.

High-frequency roll-off mellows, rounds, or smoothes sound. It can also dull, muffle, veil, or distance sound.*

In relation to specific instruments, the equalization values in Table 18-1 may help to refine semantics. Note that frequencies and frequency ranges listed in the table are general and intended only to provide a point of departure for more-refined sound shaping.

Compression

In Chapter 8 we discussed a number of uses of compression in sound shaping. Here are some general guidelines for applying compression to selected instruments. They should not be followed without listening and experimenting.

Drums. A long-to-medium attack time reduces the percussive effect. A short release time and wide ratio create a bigger or fuller sound.

Cymbals. Medium-to-short attack and release times and an average ratio reduce excessive ringing.

---

*Adapted from Bruce Bartlett, "Modern Recording and Music," Nov. 1982. Used by permission of *Modern Recording and Music Magazine.*

Table 18-1 Approximate equalization values for selected instruments

Instrument	Equalization values
Bass drum	Bottom ranges between 60 and 80 Hz; attenuating between 300 and 600 Hz reduces dullness, thuddiness, and cardboardlike sound; boosting between 1,600 and 5,000 Hz adds brightness, attack, and snap.
Low (floor) tom-tom	Fullness ranges between 80 and 120 Hz; brightness and attack are in the 4,000-Hz range.
High (rack) tom-tom	Fullness ranges between 220 and 240 Hz; brightness and attack are in the 5,000-Hz range.
Snare drum	Bottom ranges between 120 and 160 Hz; fatness ranges between 220 and 240 Hz; crispness ranges between 4,000 and 5,000 Hz.
Cymbals	Dullness—clank and gong—ranges between 200 and 240 Hz; brilliance, shimmer, and brightness range from 7,000 Hz up.
Bass guitar	Bottom ranges between 60 and 80 Hz; cutting around 250 Hz adds clarity; attack ranges between 700 and 1,200 Hz; string noise is around 2,500 to 3,500 Hz.
Electric guitar	Fullness ranges between 210 and 240 Hz; edge or bite ranges between 2,500 and 3,500 Hz; upper harmonic limits do not range much beyond 6,500 Hz.
Acoustic guitar	Bottom ranges between 80 and 140 Hz; fullness and body range between 220 and 240 Hz; clarity ranges between 1,600 and 5,000 Hz, with sound becoming thinner as these frequencies get higher. Steel strings are 5 to 10 dB louder than nylon strings.
Piano	Bass ranges between 80 and 120 Hz; body ranges between 65 and 130 Hz; clarity and presence range between 2,000 and 5,000 Hz, with sound becoming thinner as these frequencies get higher. The most robust sound is obtained from a concert grand; sound is less robust in a baby grand, and least robust in an upright.
Strings	Generally, sound from the bridge of a violin, viola, cello, or acoustic bass is brighter compared with sound coming from the f-holes, which is fuller. Bowing close to the bridge produces a less brilliant, gentler tone. Fullness ranges between 220 and 240 Hz; edge or scratchiness ranges between 7,000 and 10,000 Hz.

■ **Guitar.** Short attack and release times and a wide ratio increase the sustain.

■ **Keyboards.** A medium-to-long attack time, a medium-to-short release time, and a wide ratio give a fuller sound.

■ **Strings.** Short attack and release times and an average ratio add body to the sound.

■ **Vocals.** Medium-to-short attack and release times and an average ratio reduce sibilance.

Here are some specific applications of compression on selected instruments.

■ **Drums.** *Ratio:* 2:1 to 3:1 or 4:1 to 8:1; *attack time:* fast; *release time:* medium to fast; *threshold:* set to compress loudest peaks 4 to 6 dB or 6 to 8 dB. Compressing drums allows you mix them at a lower level and still retain their impact.

■ **Bass.** *Ratio:* 4:1; *attack time:* medium; *release time:* medium to fast; *threshold:* set to compress loudest peaks 2 to 4 dB. One main reason why recordists compress the bass is its low-frequency energy that tends to eat up so much of the mix's overall headroom. One cautionary note: Watch out for distortion that can be introduced by overly quick release times.

■ **Rhythm instruments** (guitar, sax, synthesizer). *Ratio:* 4:1 to 6:1; *attack time:* medium; *release time:* medium; *threshold:* set to compress loudest peaks 3 to 5 dB. Moderate compression can enrich texture and help make rhythm instruments forceful without letting them dominate the mix.

■ **Vocals.** *Ratio:* 3:1 to 4:1; *attack time:* fast to medium; *release time:* medium to fast; *threshold:* set to compress loudest peaks 3 to 6 dB. The amount of compression on a vocalist depends on the singer's technique; that is, does the singer back off slightly when hitting loud notes and lean in slightly to compensate for softer ones—which is good technique—or does the singer not compensate for dynamic range or, worse, "eat" the microphone? If the music track is dense and the vocals need to be heard, compression will have to be more aggressive. For delicate singers, use more-sensitive threshold levels and smaller ratios. For screamers, you may need to compress 6 to 8 dB to get the proper texture.

Beware that high compression levels bring out sibilance and background noise.

There are many other approaches to compression; a few other general applications are shown in Figure 18-3. The suggestions listed here are not intended to imply that all, or even most, voicings should be compressed. If you do decide to employ compression, these suggestions may prove to be good starting points.

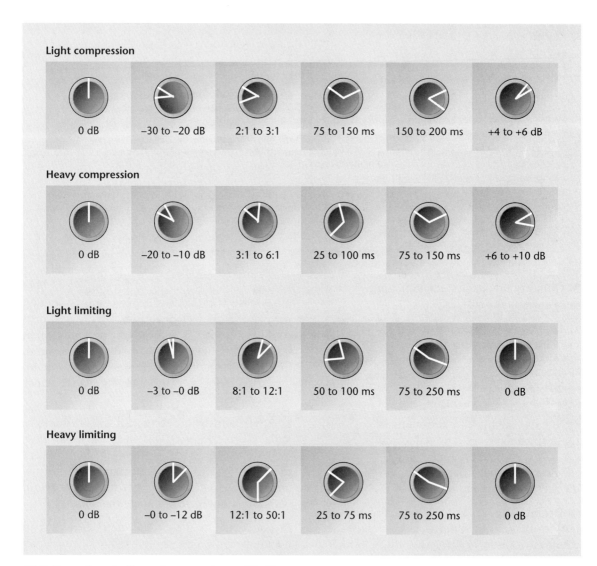

Light compression

| 0 dB | −30 to −20 dB | 2:1 to 3:1 | 75 to 150 ms | 150 to 200 ms | +4 to +6 dB |

Heavy compression

| 0 dB | −20 to −10 dB | 3:1 to 6:1 | 25 to 100 ms | 75 to 150 ms | +6 to +10 dB |

Light limiting

| 0 dB | −3 to −0 dB | 8:1 to 12:1 | 50 to 100 ms | 75 to 250 ms | 0 dB |

Heavy limiting

| 0 dB | −0 to −12 dB | 12:1 to 50:1 | 25 to 75 ms | 75 to 250 ms | 0 dB |

18-3 General applications of compression and limiting

Reverberation: Creating Acoustic Space

Due to the common practice of miking each sound component separately (for greater control) and closely (to reduce leakage), many original multitrack recordings lack a complementary acoustic environment. In such cases, the acoustics usually are added in the mixdown by artificial means using signal-processing devices such as reverb and digital delay (see Chapter 8).

If you add acoustics in the mixdown, do it after equalizing (because it is difficult to get a true sense of the effects of frequency changes in a reverberant space) and after panning (to get a better idea of how reverb affects positioning). Avoid giving widely different reverb times to various components in an ensemble, or it will sound as though they are not playing in the same space, unless it is for special effect.

The quality of the reverberation depends on the musical style. Most types of popular music work well with the sound of digital reverb or a reverb plate. Jazz usually requires a more natural-sounding acoustic environment; classical music definitely does.

In determining reverb balance, adjust it one track at a time (on the tracks to which reverb is being added). Reverb in stereo mixes should achieve a sense of depth and breadth. Reverb can be located in the mix by panning; it does not have to envelop an entire recording.

With reverberation, some equalizing may be necessary. Because plates and chambers tend to generate lower frequencies that muddy sound, attenuating the reverb between 60 and 100 Hz may be necessary to clean up the sound. If muddiness is not a problem, boosting lower frequencies gives the reverb a larger and more distant sound. Boosting higher frequencies gives the reverb a brighter, closer, more present sound.

Less expensive reverberation systems lack good treble response. By slightly boosting the high end, the reverb will sound somewhat more natural and lifelike.

If any one voicing is inevitably assigned to reverb, it is the vocal. Yet there is often the danger that the reverb's midrange will interfere with the harmonic richness of the vocal's midrange. Attenuating or notching out the reverb's competing midrange frequencies will better define the vocal and help make it stand out.

Other effects, such as *chorusing* and *accented reverb,* also can be used after reverberation. By setting the chorus for a delay between 20 and 30 ms and adding it to the reverb, sound gains a shimmering, fuller quality. Patching the reverb output into a noise gate and triggering the noise gate with selected accents from a percussive instrument such as a snare drum, piano, or tambourine can heighten as well as unify the rhythm.

Before making a final decision about the reverb you employ, do an A-B comparison. Check reverb proportions using large and small loudspeakers to make sure the reverb neither swallows sound nor is so subtle that it defies definition.

Digital Delay: Enhancing Acoustic Space

Sound reaches listeners at different times, depending on where a listener is located relative to the sound source. The closer to the sound source you are, the sooner the sound reaches you, and vice versa. Hence, a major component of reverberation is delay (see Chapter 3). To provide more-realistic reverberation, therefore, many digital reverbs include *predelay,* which sets a slight delay before reverb. If a reverb unit does not include predelay, the same effect can be generated by using a digital delay device before reverb. Predelay adds a feeling of space to the reverberation. In either case, predelay should be short; 15 to 20 ms usually suffices. (A millisecond is equivalent to about a foot in space.) On some delay devices, the longer the delay time, the poorer the signal-to-noise ratio.

Post-delay—adding delay after reverb—is another way to add dimension to sound, particularly to a vocal. In the case of the vocal, it may be necessary to boost the high end to brighten the sound or to avoid muddying it, or both.

Another handy use of delay is *stereo separation.* By feeding a mono signal through a delay to one output channel, say, the left, and the same signal directly to the right channel, you can simulate the signal as stereo. Use short delay times—15 to 20 ms—however, or the delay will be obvious and the stereo imaging may be skewed.

Synchronizing delay to tempo is yet another effect that can heighten sonic interest. This technique involves adjusting rate of delay to the music's tempo by dividing the tempo into 60,000—the dividend is the number of milliseconds per measure to which the digital delay is set.

It is also possible to create *polyrhythms*—simultaneous and sharply contrasting rhythms—by using two delays and feeding the output of one into the input of the other. Varying delay time of the second unit generates a variety of spatial effects.

In using a digital delay, there is one precaution: It should have a bandwidth of at least 12 kHz. But given the quality of sound being produced today, 15 kHz and higher is recommended.

Two features of digital delay—feedback and modulation—can be employed in various ways to help create a wide array of effects with flanging, chorusing, doubling, and slapback echo. *Feedback,* or *regeneration,* as the terms suggest, feeds a proportion of the delayed signal back into the delay line, in essence, "echoing the echo." *Modulation* is controlled by two parameters: width and speed. Width dictates how wide a range above and below the chosen delay time the modulator will be allowed to swing. You can vary the delay by any number of milliseconds above and below the designated time. Speed dictates how rapidly the time delay will oscillate.

Localizing the Musical Elements in Stereo Space

In multitrack recording, each element is recorded at an optimal level and on a separate track. If all the elements were played back in the same way, it would sound as though they were coming from precisely the same location, to say nothing about how imbalanced the voicings would be. In reality, of course, this is not the case. You therefore have to position each musical component in an aural frame by setting the levels of loudness to create front-to-back perspective, or depth, and panning to establish left-to-right stereo perspective.

In setting levels, the louder a sound, the closer it seems; and, conversely, the quieter a sound, the farther away it seems. Frequency and reverb also affect positioning. In panning stereo, there are five main areas: left, left-center, center, right-center, and right. Positioning in three-dimensional and surround sound are also considerations and are discussed later in this chapter.

There are many options in positioning various elements of an ensemble in an aural frame, but three factors enter into the decision: (1) the aural balance, (2) how the ensemble arranges itself when playing before a live audience, and (3) the type of music being played. Keep in mind that each musical style has its own values. Popular music is usually emotional and contains a strong beat. Drums and bass should therefore be well focused in the mix. Jazz and classical music are more varied and require different approaches. The mixer must have a clear idea of what the music sounds like in a natural acoustic setting before attempting a studio mix.

Sounds and where they are placed in aural space have different effects on perception. In a stereo field, these effects include the following: (1) The sound closest to the center and nearest to the listener is the most predominant; (2) a sound farther back but still in the center creates depth and a balance or a counterweight to the sound that is front and center; (3) sound placed to one side usually requires a similarly weighted sound on the opposite side or else the left-to-right aural space will seem unbalanced; and (4) the more you spread sound across the aural space, the wider the sound sources will seem.

This is not to suggest that all parts of aural space must be sonically balanced or filled at all times; that depends on the ensemble and the music. A symphony orchestra usually positions first violins to the left of the conductor, second violins to the left-center, violas to the right-center, and cellos to the right. If the music calls for just the first violins to play, it is natural for the sound to come mainly from the left. To pan the first violins left to right would establish a stereo balance, but it would be poor aesthetic judgment and would disorient the listener. To illustrate aural framing in a stereo field, see Figures 18-4 through 18-11.

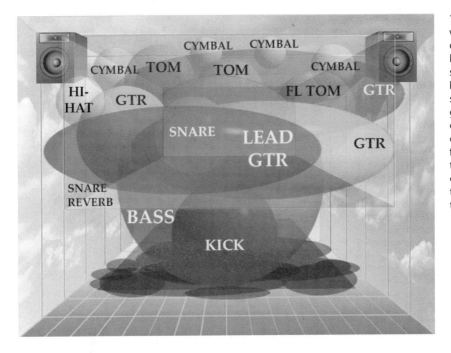

18-4 Rock mix. Quite full with lots of fattening and overlapping sounds. The lead guitar is spread in stereo with a rhythm guitar behind it and another stereo guitar in the background. The low end is clean, with a strong kick drum and bass. (In this figure and Figures 18-5 through 18-11, the size of the globes indicates the relative loudness of the voicings.)

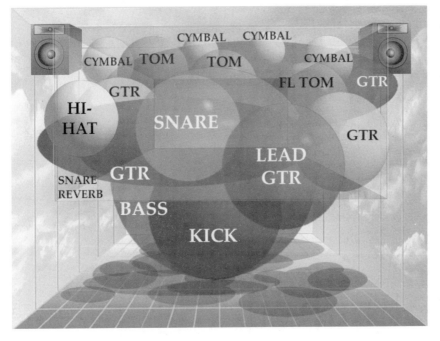

18-5 Heavy metal mix. A full, busy mix, yet with a clear low end (kick and bass). The hi-hat, snare, and lead guitar are out in front. There are multiple guitar parts with a few panned in stereo. The overall effect is a wall of sound.

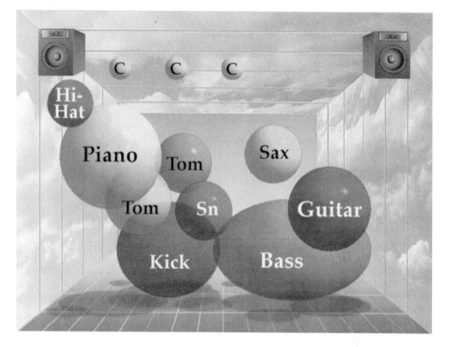

18-6 Jazz mix. Overall, a clean and clear mix with the guitar, piano, and hi-hat in front and the kick drum atypically loud for a jazz mix.

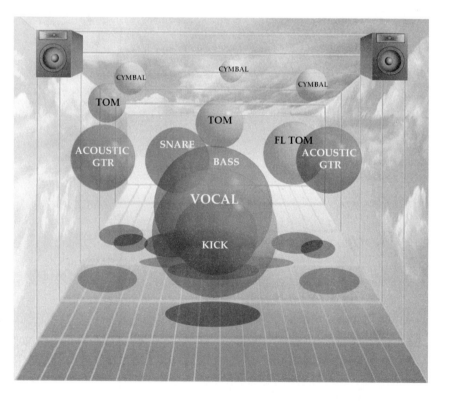

18-7 Folk music mix. A loud vocal in front of a clean, clear, spacious mix of the ensemble.

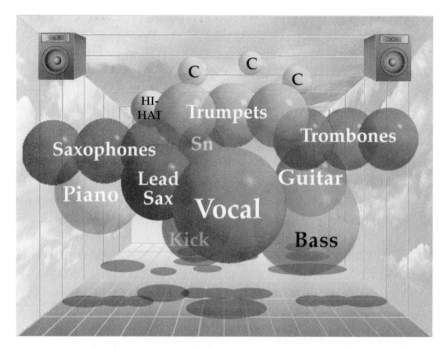

18-8 Big band mix. The vocal and horns are the prominent features of this mix.

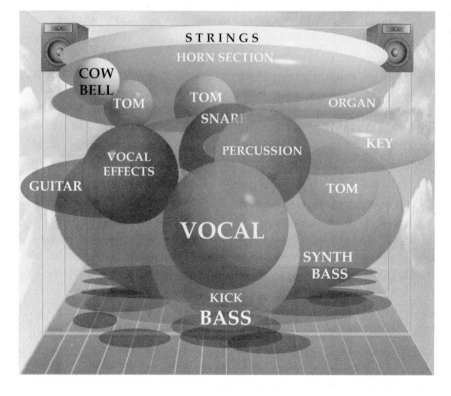

18-9 The mix on the song "Blinded Me with Science," from the album *Wireless* by Thomas Dolby

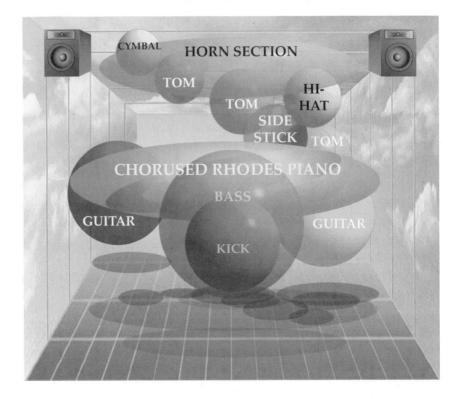

18-10 The mix on the song "Babylon Sisters," from the album *Gaucho* by Steely Dan

Three-Dimensional Sound Imaging

Almost from the beginning of recorded sound, attempts have been made to increase the dimensionality of sonic reproduction. Years before stereo became viable, recordists were experimenting with miking techniques to make sound more spacious. Binaural recording has been around for several decades, but only relatively recently have there been breakthroughs in reproduction that eliminate the need to wear headphones in order to enjoy at least a sense of the binaural experience. Several years ago the commercially failed quadraphonic sound increased the depth of sonic space by using loudspeakers to the rear as well as in front of the listener. Today a number of approaches applied during recording or mixing, or both, are being used to bring sound reproduction closer to the live listening experience (see Chapter 4). To treat three-dimensional sound imaging inclusively, that is, as it applies to music recording, film, and television, we discuss it in "Spatial Imaging of Sound" later in this chapter.

Keeping a Record

Keeping a record of settings for EQ levels, reverb send, reverb return, compression, limiting, and so on in a mixdown is essential. It may take several sessions to complete a mix, and any adjustments previously made must be reset precisely. Moreover, perceptions of a mix have a strange way of changing from one day to the next, so it is critical to be able to reference the sound to the setting.

Information in automated and computer-assisted mixdowns is stored automatically. It may be recalled for visual display or printed out in hard copy. This convenience notwithstanding, it is

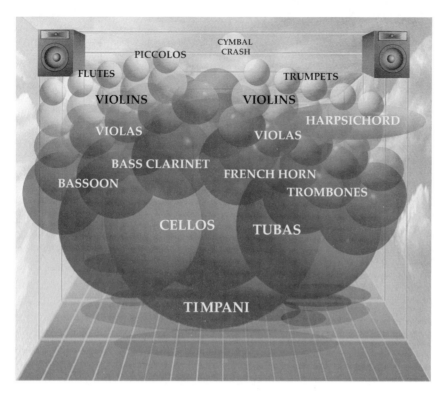

always wise to make a backup copy of all computer-encoded information.

MIXING FOR VIDEO AND FILM

Generally, the process of combining the *dialogue, music, and sound effects (DME)* tracks for video and film is accomplished during the premixing and rerecording stages. Premixing is when the various tracks are blended and smoothed into composite dialogue, sound effects, and, to some extent, music tracks in preparation for rerecording. The rerecording mix is the final stage in postproduction, when the premixed tracks are combined into stereo or surround sound. The differences in technology and release formats between television and film may account for differences in the sequence and type of operations during mixing and rerecording, but the purposes of both stages are the same for each medium: to produce a finished sound track.

Sweetening

Generally, *sweetening* is the postproduction stage in television when sound, usually dialogue and sometimes sound effects, from the edited master videotape is transferred to multitrack audiotape or hard disk. Other audio tracks, such as music and additional sound effects, are added to the multitrack tape or disk as needed. These tracks are then signal-processed, mixed, and rerecorded back to the edited master videotape or other release medium. The procedure usually occurs in four stages: (1) layover, (2) prelay, (3) premix, and (4) layback.

1. During *layover,* also called *laydown,* the audio tracks from the edited master videotape are dubbed to a multitrack audiotape or hard disk along with time code from the edited master. At the same time, a videocassette window dub of the edited master is made.

The audio from the edited master videotape is usually put on tracks 1 and 2 of the multitrack audiotape or hard disk. Time code is recorded on the last tape track with the adjacent track left blank to avoid interference from the time code track. Because this procedure requires four tracks, at least eight tracks are needed: one track each for music and effects, and one track for the overall mix, two if it is a stereo mix. Sixteen tracks or more give you added, and usually needed, leeway in sweetening. The problem of track availability is reduced considerably in hard-disk systems that provide virtual tracks in addition to the discrete tracks.

2. During **prelay** the other remaining synchronized audio elements are recorded onto separate tracks. They may be music, sound effects, or additional dialogue. Prelay also includes editing the various audio tracks to usable lengths when dubbing them to multitrack. This is to ensure that there is enough material to cover long fades, crossfades, and split-track mixing.

3. **Premixing** is the stage when all the separate tracks on the multitrack recording are smoothed, signal-processed, and mixed to two other tracks (for stereo), or more (for surround sound), of the multitrack tape or disk with the window dub being played in sync. (In film, the premix is preparatory to rerecording when dialogue, sound effects, and music receive their final mix. Therefore, dialogue, sound effects, and music are prepared for dubbing to separate reels of magnetic film instead of being combined into a stereo mix at this stage.)

4. During **layback**, the composite mix is transferred to the edited master videotape, replacing (and erasing) the old audio track(s). (see 18-12)

Premixing the Sound Track

The *premix* is the stage in film postproduction during which dialogue, sound effects, and, to some extent, music are prepared for the final rerecording mix.

Dialogue

In most situations dialogue (or any speech for that matter) must be prominent and clear, whether it is by itself or mixed with other sounds; that is, unless it is meant to serve as background **walla**. Film extras once used the nonsense word *walla* to create ambient crowd sound. Today "wallawers" actually engage in conversation for a more realistic crowd effect.

Various techniques are used to process speech, depending on the medium, voice quality, and competing sounds. Regardless of which techniques you employ, maintaining both the sonic integrity of the voice and intelligibility of the speech are most important.

Clear dialogue begins with a good master recording, whether it is the production recording or the automated dialogue recording. That means using the highest-quality microphones and recording equipment. In addition, noise reduction should be used throughout recording, premixing, and rerecording; the value of noise reduction cannot be overstated. The other techniques include the familiar signal processing of equalization, filtering, compression, limiting, and so on.

In addition to the familiar uses of equalization in dialogue premixing—to make speech intelligible and agreeable-sounding—it can be employed to smooth or match any differences between dialogue on different tracks or reels. It helps overcome anomalies in frequency response due to varying microphone techniques used during production, body microphones hidden under clothing, proximity effect, the recording system, or dubbing. Equalization also helps improve the imbalance in reverberation when the reverb time in the bass is longer than it is in the midrange and treble. Filtering helps reduce system and background noise.

Compression and limiting are commonly used to ensure that the dialogue stays within the dynamic range of the reproducing system. Remember that in recording and mixing, the important factor is how the audience will hear the sound, not the sonic capabilities of the recording or transmitting systems. Compression is also used to keep dialogue above the ambience and the noise floor

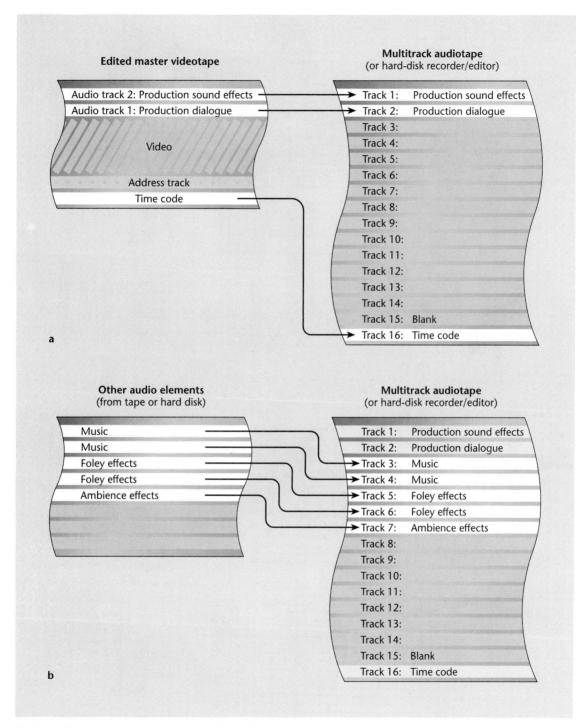

18-12 Audio sweetening (a) layover and (b) prelay. (For the sake of simplicity, these examples use videotape, audiotape, and the 4-2-4 surround sound matrix.)

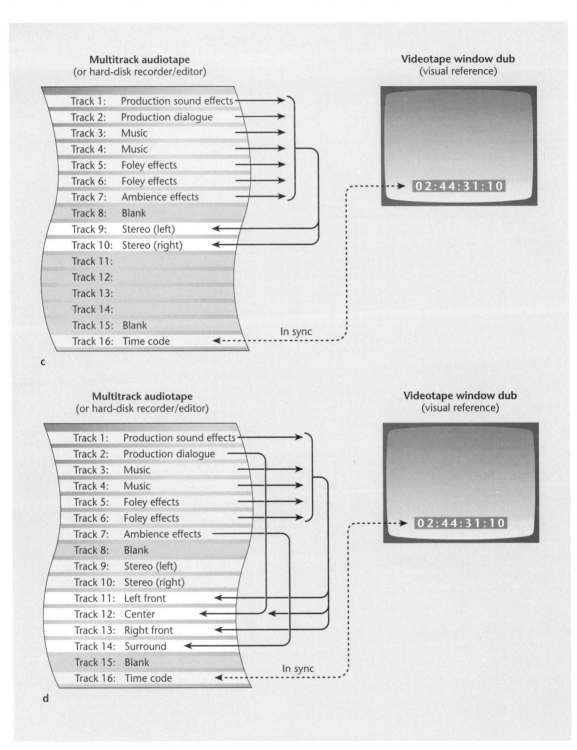

Multitrack audiotape
(or hard-disk recorder/editor)

Track 1: Production sound effects
Track 2: Production dialogue
Track 3: Music
Track 4: Music
Track 5: Foley effects
Track 6: Foley effects
Track 7: Ambience effects
Track 8: Blank
Track 9: Stereo (left)
Track 10: Stereo (right)
Track 11:
Track 12:
Track 13:
Track 14:
Track 15: Blank
Track 16: Time code

Videotape window dub
(visual reference)

02:44:31:10

In sync

c

Multitrack audiotape
(or hard-disk recorder/editor)

Track 1: Production sound effects
Track 2: Production dialogue
Track 3: Music
Track 4: Music
Track 5: Foley effects
Track 6: Foley effects
Track 7: Ambience effects
Track 8: Blank
Track 9: Stereo (left)
Track 10: Stereo (right)
Track 11: Left front
Track 12: Center
Track 13: Right front
Track 14: Surround
Track 15: Blank
Track 16: Time code

Videotape window dub
(visual reference)

02:44:31:10

In sync

d

18-12 *(continued)* **(c) Premix (stereo) and (d) premix (surround)**

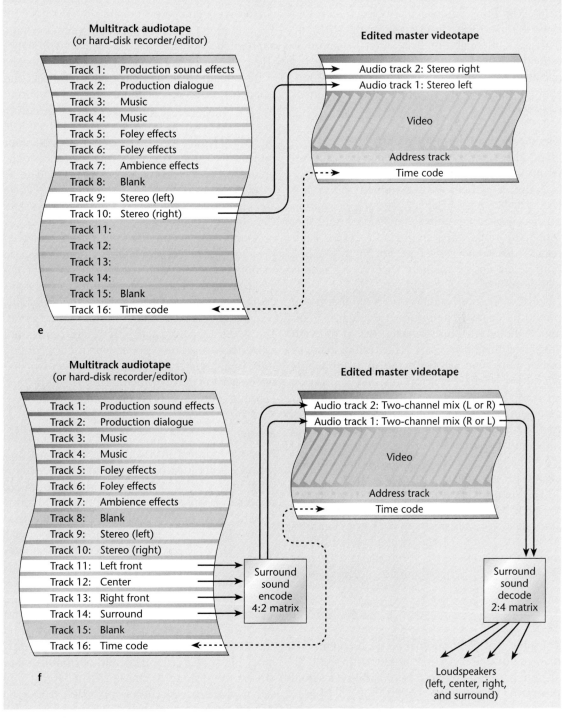

18-12 *(continued)* **(e) Layback (stereo) and (f) layback (surround)**

of the combined dialogue tracks. Compression helps keep other sonic elements, such as sound effects and music, from interfering with the dialogue's intelligibility. It is better to compress individual tracks, as opposed to compressing the overall dialogue mix, because the risk of distortion, audible pumping, and a clustered, blurred sound is considerably less.

De-essing smoothes the sibilance in speech, which can be a boon in digital recording. It also helps optical-track sound when sibilant distortion results from problems in lab processing.

Noise gates help reduce ambient noise and keep dialogue tracks relatively free of leakage from other dialogue lines and sound sources. But using too many noise gates might add, rather than reduce, noise; and if they are not top-of-the-line units or are not set properly, their gating actions will be audible.

Reverberation, in addition to its familiar use of providing acoustic definition to a space, helps match the reverberant characteristics of different ambiences that may be part of the various dialogue tracks. One type of reverberation is known as *worldizing*, whereby a microphone and loudspeaker are set up in a room in a way that is similar to their arrangement in an acoustic reverberation chamber (see Chapter 8). The room sound is recorded to add the sound of that space to a dry recording or to use it to enhance or smooth ambient backgrounds that are already part of a dialogue track.

The aural exciter can add clarity to a dialogue track and help the voice stand out at a quieter level. Short delays can add depth and apparent loudness to the voice, but be careful here; it takes only a bit more delay than necessary for the delay to become obvious and, if it is inappropriate to the narrative material, ludicrous.

Sound Effects

The same considerations that pertain to premixing dialogue also apply to premixing sound effects, although the degree and application of signal processing often differs. For example, it is more likely that sound effects will be manipulated to a greater extent than dialogue. Using a significant amount of EQ boost or cut on dialogue would change voice character dramatically, whereas with a sound effect dramatic alteration may be quite appropriate. More liberties can be taken with sound effects, because they are not as familiar to our ears as the human voice, particularly sound effects that emanate from science fiction creatures or situations. But paying attention to sonic clarity, preventing distortion, and keeping an effect within the prescribed dynamic range are no less important for sound-effect premixing than they are for dialogue premixing. This is sometimes easier said than done, because sound effects tend to be mixed "hot." There are other notable differences between dialogue and sound-effect premixing.

Sound-effect premixing usually includes effecting most, or all, of the fades. It sometimes also includes setting the relative differences in level that are to occur in the final mix. As noted later in this chapter, dialogue in film and television, generally, is centered in the stereo and surround-sound mixes, and underscored music is mixed left, center, and right. These operations are done in the rerecording mix. Sound effects are often placed in a particular screen space or moved with the action in the picture. Panning sound effects is done in the premix.

Music

Music is handled differently than dialogue and sound effects in a premix in that very little, if anything, is done at that stage to prepare it for rerecording. Musical knowledge is integral to music mixing, and not all sound people have that knowledge. Also, it is important that the music track undergo as few dubs as possible to maintain its original sonic integrity. Of the three elements in the sound track—dialogue, sound effects, and music—music is the most structurally complex and spectrally and dynamically varied. Another reason that little premixing is done with music is that by the time a music track is ready for the premix, most of what a premix would accomplish has already been done. If the music undergoes any signal processing at the premix stage, it may be some high-end boosting to compensate for high-frequency loss during subsequent processing, and compression if the music is conflicting with the dialogue that it is underscoring.

The Rerecording Mix

There is one thing about the rerecording process involving film that differs from mixing for TV and CD, and that you cannot get around: Because film is played in a large room, it is necessary to rerecord it in a large room to be sure of what you are doing. It comes down to the acoustics; things happen in a large room that do not happen in a small room.

That said, the purpose of the rerecording mix is to blend the premixed DME tracks into a seamless stereo or surround-sound recording. Depending on market level, budget, and union regulations, rerecording may be handled by the same sound people who recorded, edited, or premixed the sound, or by people who have not yet heard the track or seen the picture.

On one hand, the rerecording mix should be relatively straightforward, assuming the premix has been well produced. Gross changes should be unnecessary. On the other hand, if the rerecording mix is unsuccessful, all of the previous work goes just about for naught.

It is particularly important, therefore, that the premixed tracks are free of technical problems so that the rerecording mixer can concentrate on aesthetic points. (There may be one, two, or three rerecording mixers, depending on the scale and complexity of the material. Two mixers usually divide duties between dialogue/music and effects; three mixers handle each component separately. The dialogue mixer is usually in charge of rerecording.)

All extraneous sounds should be deleted during editing, and certainly no later than the premix. The three composite tracks should be clean at the beginning and end of each sound or sequence. Each track should be cut as close to the beginning and end of a sound as possible without cutting off soft attacks or decay.

In addition, in- and out-points of each cue must be precise—a rerecording mixer cannot be expected to pinpoint cues. A well-laid-out cue sheet is mandatory (see 18-13).

Cue Sheets

Cue sheets are essential throughout production, but they are indispensable during the premix and rerecording mix stages. The forms vary from studio to studio; they may be handwritten or computer-generated, but they must contain at least the information outlined in the following list (see 18-14, 18-15, and 18-16).

A column of time cues. This may be designated in time code, real time, or footage, depending on the medium and format. By using one column to serve all tracks, it is easy to see at a glance the relationship of cues.

What the sound is. Each cue must be identified. Identification should be both brief to avoid clutter and precise to give the mixer certainty about what the cue is.

When a sound starts. The word or words identifying a sound are written at the precise point it begins. With dialogue or narration, in-points may be indicated by a line or the first two or three words.

How a sound starts. Unless otherwise indicated, it is assumed that a sound starts clean; that is, the level has been preset before a sound's entry. If a cue is faded in, faded in slowly, crossfaded with another sound, and so on, that must be indicated on the cue sheet.

The duration of a sound. From the point at which a cue begins to the point at which it ends is its duration. The simplest way of indicating this is to draw a straight line between the two points. Avoid using different-colored markers, double and triple lines, or other graphic highlights. The cue sheet or screen should be clean and uncluttered. If the cues are handwritten, pencil is better than ink, in case changes have to be made.

When a sound ends. This can be indicated by the same word(s) used at the entry cue accompanied by the word *out* or *auto* (for automatically). This tells the mixer that the end cue is clean and has been handled in the premix.

How a sound ends. If a sound fades, crossfades, and so on, this should be indicated at the point when the sound must be out or be crossfaded. The mixer then has to decide when to begin the out cue so it has been effected by the time indicated.

Track No. DIALOGUE-1	Track No. DIALOGUE-2	Track No. EFFECTS-1	Track No. EFFECTS-2	Track No. MUSIC-1
Reel No. 1	Reel No. 2	Reel No. 3	Reel No. 4	Reel No. 5
000 DEAD SYNC	000 DEAD SYNC	000 DEAD SYNC	000 DEAD SYNC	000 DEAD SYNC
:15 SYNC POP	:15 SYNC POP	:15 SYNC POP	:15 SYNC POP	:15 SYNC POP
:30 BARB: "MORNING		:30 WIND	:30 RAIN	
:41 (LAST WORD) OKAY?"				
	:42 BEN: "ALL RIGHT			
	1:10 (LAST WORD) BYE."	1:10	1:10	1:10 LOVE THEME
		1:13	1:13	1:13
				1:18 +
1:50 BOSS: "YOU'RE				1:50 >
1:51 (LAST WORD) LATE"		1:51 DOOR CLOSE	1:51 OFFICE SOUNDS	
		1:52 FOOTSTEPS		
1:57 BEN: "HELLO	1:56			
				2:42 ⟨ ACTION THEME
	2:45 (LAST WORD) NO!"		2:45	
	2:46 AUTO			
			3:10 TIRES THRU PUDDLE	
			3:58 TIRE SCREECH	

< Fade in   > Fade out   + Raise   − Lower   ⌐ Crossfade

18-13 Rerecording cue sheet

REEL # _____ 1 _____ ¼ REEL # _____ 1 _____ PAGE # _____ 1 of 2 _____

PRODUCER _____ EDITOR _____

PRODUCTION _____

JOB # _____ PROD # _____ DATE _____

CHARACTER JOEY, SR.	FOOTAGE START STOP	MIXER NOTES	CHANNELS				DIALOGUE
			1	2	3	4	
JSR #1	187 $\frac{05}{}$ 199 $\frac{03}{}$						YOUR BEST FRIEND WROTE AND TOLD ME (BREATH)
							YOU HAD TEARDROPS IN YOUR EYES
JSR #2	201 $\frac{11}{}$						(BREATH) DADDY'S HOME (LAUGH)
	220 $\frac{03}{}$ PIX OUT						DADDY'S HOME TO (LAUGH) STAY
	USE NATURAL OUT CUE						
JSR #3	350 $\frac{11}{}$						I'M NOT A THOUSAND MILES
	360 $\frac{01}{}$						AWAY
JSR #4 (OPTIONAL)	440 $\frac{11}{}$ 444 $\frac{11}{}$	NO STREAMER					LET'S GO, LET'S GO, (LAUGH) LET'S GO
JSR #5	446 $\frac{06}{}$						THERE'S A HOUSE PARTY
	450 $\frac{10}{}$						WAY CROSS TOWN
JSR #6	450 $\frac{07}{}$ 451 $\frac{09}{}$						(LAUGH) I GUESS

18-14 Example of a cue sheet used for dialogue rerecording

SOUND EFFECTS — (Foley FX)

Triplicate: Editor   —   Mixer   —   Recordist

Production Number	Reel	Time	FX Editor	Telephone

Cue No.	Mixer Notes	Footage Start & Stop		Channels			Detailed Description and Remarks
		Start		1	2	3	
		Stop					
		Start					
		Stop					
		Start					
		Stop					
		Start					
		Stop					
		Start					
		Stop					
		Start					
		Stop					
		Start					
		Stop					
		Start					
		Stop					
		Start					
		Stop					
		Start					
		Stop					
		Start					
		Stop					
		Start					
		Stop					
		Start					
		Stop					
		Start					
		Stop					
		Start					
		Stop					

18-15 Example of a cue sheet used for recording Foley effects

PRODUCTION NO.   TITLE

DATE   COMPOSER   SHEET NO.

ACTION

DIALOGUE

EFFECTS

MUSIC

18-16 Example of a cue sheet used for music underscoring

SPATIAL IMAGING OF SOUND

Spatial imaging of sound in production today falls roughly into three formats: stereo sound, 3D (three-dimensional) sound, and surround sound. (Although much of the audience still listens to audio in mono, audio is rarely mastered that way these days. Monaural sound is one-dimensional; it reproduces only spatial depth.) Stereo sound is two-dimensional; it reproduces depth and breadth. Imaging is front-to-back and side-to-side. Three-dimensional sound creates the illusion of depth, breadth, and sometimes height in the audio field through headphones. Using the conventional two-loudspeaker stereo array in front of the listener, most 3D systems are actually two-dimensional, but improve the stereo image by effectively bringing the depth and width of the stereo frame to the outermost edges of the sound field on a plane with the listener. Surround sound reproduces the illusion of a three-dimensional sound field by positioning loudspeakers either to the front, sides, and rear of the listener or to the front and rear.

Stereo

Stereo imaging in music, television, and film is handled differently. Because stereo placement in music mixing is discussed earlier in the chapter, we'll move on to TV and film.

Natural assumptions in placing elements in a stereo mix for television and film are that dialogue and effects are positioned in relation to their on-screen locations and that music, if there is no on-screen source, fills the aural frame from the left to the right. For the most part, these assumptions are imprecise. Placement depends on the screen format, the reproduction system, and the type of material being produced.

Stereo Imaging in Television

The aesthetic demands of television and film differ, not only because of the obvious dissimilarity between the videotape and film media, but also because of the differences between their screen sizes and, hence, sonic and pictorial dimensions. Clearly, film has more space in which to place and maneuver the aural and visual elements than does television. Nevertheless, when it comes to sound, the *localization*—placement—of dialogue, sound effects, and music in the stereo frame is similar in both media.

The aesthetic challenges in mixing for stereo television are twofold. They are scale and perspective.

Scale Until the advent of stereo TV, the television loudspeaker was smaller than the screen, but, together, the scale of picture and sound images have seemed proportional. No doubt conditioning has had something to do with this perception.

With stereo TV, loudspeakers are mounted in two ways: either attached to the left and right sides of the set, or detached. Permanently attached speakers can be no farther apart than the width of the TV set. This is a limiting factor in creating a stereo image, because the aural space is so narrow. Detachable speakers can be situated an optimal distance apart; 6 feet is usually recommended to reproduce a more realistic stereo image. In fact, when sound is more spacious because of stereo, the picture seems bigger: *What we hear affects what we see.*

Perspective Despite the trend toward larger screens, television for most viewers is still a small-screen medium. It relies on close-up shots to enhance impact and to show detail that otherwise would be lost. Speech, therefore, is concentrated in the center. Trying to match sound with movement would be chaotic.

Localization of Talk and Dialogue

In television, talk and dialogue are usually kept at or near the center of the stereo frame. Unless the shot remains the same, trying to match a performer's sonic location to that person's on-screen position can disorient the audience.

For example, if in a variety show a wide shot shows (from the viewer's perspective) the host in the center, the announcer to the left, and the band leader and band to the right, and the shot does not change, the audio can come from these locations in the stereo space. If the host and announcer exchange remarks, and the shot cuts to the host on the right and the announcer to the left in a two-shot, and the shot stays that way, the host's sound can be panned toward the right and the announcer's sound can be panned toward the left. If during their interchange, however, the shots cut back and forth between one-shots of the host and the announcer, the left and right stereo imaging becomes disconcerting, because the image of either the host or the announcer is in the center of the frame when the sound is toward the left or right. When frequent shot changes occur, therefore, the best approach is to keep the overall speech toward or at the center (see 18-17).

When a performer is moving in a shot, say, from left to right, and the camera-to-source distance remains the same, the stereo image can be panned to follow the performer's movement without audience disorientation. But if the performer's camera-to-source distance changes due to cutting from wider shots to closer shots, or vice versa, or intercutting another actor into the frame, even though the first performer's momentum is clearly left to right, the dialogue has to be centered to avoid dislocation (see 18-18).

Sound Effects The handling of sound effects also should be conservative. Obvious movement should be selective and occur mostly with effects that make pronounced crossing movements. The extent of the movement has to be carefully controlled so that it is not greater than the physical dimension of the screen (unless it is surround sound).

Ambiences in stereo television certainly can be fuller than they are in mono TV. Undoubtedly,

a b c

18-17 Speech localization in a two-shot. (a) In this example, so long as the announcer and host remain positioned left and right in a medium shot (MS) and the shot does not change, their sounds can be panned toward the left and right, respectively, with no dislocation. (b) If the shot changes, say, to a medium close-up (MCU) of the announcer followed by an MCU of the host, and the stereo imaging remains the same, it will create a Ping-Pong effect. (c) If one-shots of the announcer and the host are planned, the sound in the original two-shot should be centered for both of them and carried through that way throughout the sequence. Panning the sound with the shot changes is even more sonically awkward than the Ping-Pong effect.

a b c

18-18 Sound localization in a moving shot. (a) If a subject is, say, running across the screen from left to right and the shot does not change, the stereo imaging can also move from left to right without dislocation. (b) Should the shot cut to a close-up (CU) to show perspiration on the runner's face, in which case the across-screen movement would be reflected in the moving background, the subject's sound would have to be centered. If the sound continued moving left to right in the CU, the difference between the visual and aural perspectives would be disorienting. (c) Cutting from the CU back to the wide shot, the sound once again can move across the screen with the runner without disorientation, because the perspectives match. If throughout the runner's across-screen movement there were a few cuts from the wide shot to the CU, however, the sound in the wide shots would have to be more centered to avoid the Ping-Pong effect.

the significant perceptible difference between mono and stereo TV is in the fullness and depth of the ambience.

Music Underscored music is mixed across the stereo field with the left and right sides framing the overall stereo image. Generally, in the mix of dialogue, music, and sound effects, underscored music is the one element that is usually in stereo.

Stereo Imaging in Film

The larger screen size of motion pictures allows somewhat greater flexibility in positioning stereo dialogue and sound effects, but not that much more when frequent shot changes position the actors at different camera-to-source distances. Even with the wide-screen 70mm film, stereo dislocation can occur.

Conventional stereo sound tracks in 35mm film are reproduced on three channels—left, center, and right. At least three channels are necessary because of the screen's width and the size of the audience area. Without a center channel, people sitting at the left and right would hear only the loudspeaker closest to them and receive no stereo effect.

Dialogue As a general rule, on-screen dialogue is placed in the center. If a character moves about and there are several cuts, as in television, it can become annoying to have the sound jump around, particularly if more than one character is involved. On the other hand, if characters maintain their positions in a scene, even though shots change from wide to close-up or vice versa, stereo imaging can be effected without disorienting the audience.

Sound Effects Sound effects also tend to be concentrated toward the middle. If they are stationary or move across a wide distance, they may be located and panned without distracting. But too much movement muddles the sound. Sometimes, to create the sense that an effect is positioned relative to the action, the effect is reverbed. Most of the dry effect is placed at or near screen-center, and the wet part is used to convey its placement in the frame.

Music Music is distributed across the left, center, and right channels. It is usually mixed so that it frames dialogue and effects. If there is no music (and sometimes when there is), background sounds and ambience are mixed to the left and right to create overall tone. In the 70mm large-screen format, aural perspective is somewhat more spacious and realistic.

3D Sound

Among the available 3D systems designed for application during the mix are QSound, the Roland Sound Space Processor, the Sound Retrieval System, and Spatializer.

QSound consists of eight independent parallel-processing channels, joystick controlled, each one providing sound placement outside of the physical frontal stereo loudspeaker locations. QSound is mono-compatible, as are most 3D and surround-sound systems (see "Stereo-to-Mono Compatibility" later in this chapter). QSound is also available in plug-in form for hard-disk computer recording systems, as are most spatial enhancement systems (see 18-19).

The *Roland Sound Space Processor* has three main component sections: a reverb and distance processor, to add ambience and a perception of distance to the incoming signal; a binaural signal processor; and a transaural processor that eliminates crosstalk signals from the left speaker to the right ear and from the right speaker to the left ear, thereby providing the ability for enhanced playback of binaural recordings over loudspeakers by bypassing the binaural processor. There are three operating modes: *Flying mode* allows a mono sound source to be continuously moved around the soundfield in real time; *stationary mode* allows two independent monaural sources to be statically placed anywhere within the 360-degree soundfield; *transaural mode* provides the capability to process original binaural recordings for stereo loudspeaker playback.

The *Sound Retrieval System (SRS)* is based on *head-related transfer functions (HRTF)* (see Chapter 4). It is a patented technology that creates a soundfield

18-19 (a) QSound plug-in designed for a hard disk recording/editing system and (b) its perceived auditory imaging. This 3D audio processor is intended primarily as a mixing tool. It provides independent channels of sound placement, allowing the panning of mix elements in an expanded soundfield beyond the conventional bounds of stereo.

by extracting the ambience information from the original stereo signal and modifying it using a curve for front-to-side correction and to minimize the effects of ear canal resonance. A mixing technique adds the modified signal along with additional left-plus-right information to the original left/right signals. The process creates immersion in the 3D soundfield and eliminates the "sweet spot,"

permitting the listener to move around with minimal skewing of the sonic imaging.

The *Spatializer* consists of two components: a processor that is connected into a studio's existing signal flow through the patch panel, and a portable controller unit. The system makes it possible to control each track's scale and size and near/far and front/rear positioning (see 18-20).

1 Clears all stations from solo mode into normal function mode

2 This lock-out button must be pushed in conjunction with any of the four buttons to the right

3 Places each station in calibrate or mixdown mode

4 Electronically rotates all joystick controls 90 degrees for vertical or horizontal use

5 Places entire Spatializer in Type C (for original microphone recording) or Type D/E (for mixdown)

6 Provides additional expansion energy for use with very narrow stereo sources

7 Tri-level LEDs indicate:
Yellow = signal too low
Green = signal OK
Red = signal clipping

8 TT-style input plugs provided on front panel for ease of connection to patchbay. Optional parallel-wired connectors located on rear panel

9 Stereo outputs processed in spatialization

10 Discrete (nonspatialized) outputs for left, front, right, and back signals. Front output is useful for dialogue and is isolated from the left or right outputs with joystick in front position

11 Selects spatialization types D, E_L, or E_R, or places station off-line
Type D is a directional function for use with mono sources
Type E is an expansion function used with stereo sources
E_L is for use with the left side of stereo input
E_R is for use with the right side of the same stereo input

12 Mode (L & R) LEDs
C = both amber
D = both green
E_L = left red
E_R = right red

13 Places station in solo-in-place

14 Solo/Mute (S/M LEDs)
Solo = steady green
Mute (Local) = steady red
Mute (by Solo) = flashing red

15 Writes all functions of station to MIDI

16 Places station in mute

17 Moves mono sources 350 degrees seamlessly, or scales stereo sources to any size within the soundfield

18-20 3D audio processing system. (a) Processor. (b) Controller unit.

Surround Sound

Surround sound, like 3D sound, is a psychoacoustic illusion. Most surround-sound systems encode the spatial, or positional, information from the various production tracks during final mixing or re-recording and decode that information during reproduction. Hence, they use an encoder and a decoder to handle channel matrixing which, in analog, is in a 4-2-4 format; the encoder unit is 4:2, the decoder is 2:4 (see 18-21).

There are a few different surround-sound systems. Using the Dolby process as an example, encoding takes the four sources of signals—discrete left, center, and right, and a mono surround channel—and combines the left signal with the center signal reduced by 3 dB, and the surround signal phase-shifted +90 degrees to make a combined left total (L_t) signal. The R_t signal is derived from the right signal summed with the center signal, at –3dB, and the surround signal phase-shifted by –90 degrees.

Although there is only one Dolby analog encoding format, there are two types of Dolby Surround™ analog decoders. The older version sends the L_t and R_t to the left and right loudspeakers. There is no separate center channel, so there is no center loudspeaker. The left and right front loudspeakers create a phantom center image. The S or surround signal is extracted by $L_t – R_t = S$ and delayed by 10 to 30 ms to the surround loudspeakers.

The newer Dolby decoder is called Dolby Surround Pro Logic.™ It provides a hard center channel and improves channel separation and directionality.

In digital surround formats, each signal is discrete. The Dolby system—Dolby Surround AC-3 Digital™ or Dolby Surround AC-3 Pro Logic™—uses five full-bandwidth channels and an additional low-bandwidth channel, the so-called 5.1 channel system. The *5.1 channel system* carries three front channels and stereo (left and right) surrounds plus a low-frequency channel for bass effects.

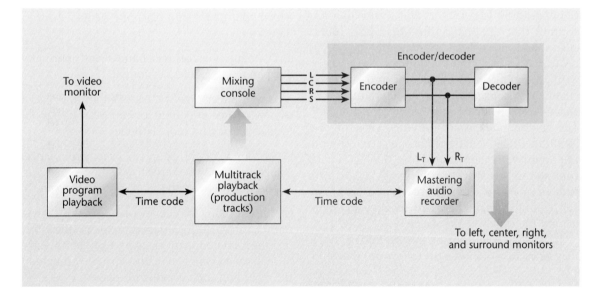

18-21 4-2-4 surround-sound matrix in a postproduction application

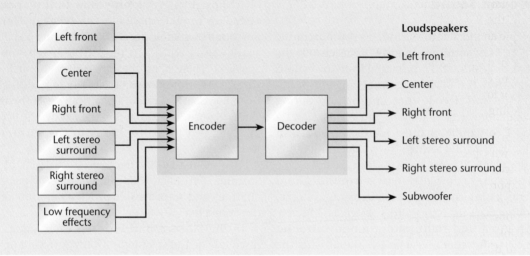

18-22 Simplified matrix of the 5.1 channel surround-sound system

The AC-3 refers to the digital compression technique used to reduce the required bandwidth (see 18-22; also see 9-13).

Mixing Surround Sound

Generally, the left, center, and right channels contain the principal audio—dialogue, sound effects, and music—and the surround channel is dedicated to background sound(s). Specifically, with the addition of the center and surround channels to conventional stereo reproduction, it creates a stable center and background imaging. The center loudspeaker provides more-precise localization, particularly of dialogue. That is more important with television sound than it is with film sound, because the TV image takes up a smaller space in the field of view. Hence, the center loudspeaker helps to localize dialogue toward the center of the screen.

In general, when mixing in surround sound, it may be useful to consider the following guidelines:

☑ The main purpose of surround sound is to provide an expanded, more realistic sense of aural space.

☑ Do not pull the audience's attention from the screen or try to overwhelm them with directional pyrotechnics in the surround-sound channels. Never try to rival what is on the screen.

☑ Mix to the visual perspective on the screen.

☑ Keep in mind the edges of the medium for which you mixing and place the elements within that frame.

☑ Dialogue goes center-channel and is usually not panned, regardless of format.

☑ Sound effects may be centered and/or placed somewhat left and right of center. Wide-screen formats allow a bit more latitude.

☑ Surround, or fill, sound is usually ambience. Sometimes it may be music to add more dimension to the front left, center, and right music spread.

☑ The matrixing format, as opposed to the discrete format, can create localization problems; therefore, mix the most dominant elements first. (In a discrete format, each channel remains separate throughout the recording and reproduction stages.)

☑ Before doing the surround mix, do the left, center, and right mixes first.

☑ When using compression or limiting on dialogue or vocals, do not process any additional ambience signal through the same compressor-limiter. This reduces the potential for the dominant sound to cause the ambience to "pump."

☑ When using signal processing, use separate processing devices for each element. Using the same processor for more than one element could, among other things, smear sonic imaging.

☑ When background sound distracts from dialogue, when a vocalist has to compete with ambience, or when crowd sound tends to drown out a sportscaster's game call, it helps to widen the voice by panning it toward the surround-sound position. If the material is recorded and it is possible to work with separate tracks, the best thing to do is change the mix.

☑ Unless it is for special effect or to be gimmicky, it is usually disconcerting to place major program elements to the side and/or behind the audience. It is one thing to position the audience in a spacious sonic environment with the action across the front and at the edges; it is another thing to put the audience in the midst of the action. To make the example another way: Most people do not listen to music sitting among the musicians, nor do they watch a battle scene from the battlefield. Reproducing that kind of listening experience has been found to be disconcerting.

That said, binaural hearing places human beings in the middle of their sonic environment all the time. Perhaps it is a matter of conditioning from years of listening to frontally imaged sound that disconcerts an audience when it is surrounded artificially by sonic action. In that case, it can be contended: Why not put the audience in the midst of the action and reorient its viewing and listening experiences? It is more realistic, after all.

All in all, the advantages of multidimensional manipulation of sound far outweigh its problems: (1) Dialogue and sound effects can be accurately localized across a wide or small screen for almost any audience position; (2) specific sound effects can be localized to the surround-sound loudspeakers; (3) ambience and environmental sounds can be designed to reach the audience from all directions; and (4) panning of sound can occur across the front sound stage and between front and surround locations.

STEREO-TO-MONO COMPATIBILITY

Although *stereo-to-mono compatibility* is not the problem it once was because stereo is the format of the day, it does warrant some attention here. In 3D and surround sound, stereo-to-mono compatibility is even less of a concern because most systems in use are mono-compatible.

Stereo discs, radio, TV, film, and multimedia notwithstanding, except for home component music systems and visits to the motion picture theater, most people still receive mediated information in mono. In virtually anything you stereo-master, therefore, its monophonic compatibility is a factor.

Stereo-to-mono compatibility must be checked and rechecked throughout a mix. What sounds good in stereo may be less than acceptable in mono. A wide and satisfactorily balanced stereo recording played in mono may be too loud. For example, a 0 VU reading at the extreme left and right in stereo is equivalent to +6 in mono. Anything assigned to the center in the stereo mix may be too loud in mono and out of context with the rest of the sound. Moreover, placing voicings extreme left or right in stereo results in a 3-dB or greater loss in their level(s) relative to the rest of the spectrum when played in mono.

So the problem of stereo-to-mono compatibility is twofold: too much sound in the center and not enough at the left and right. The reason, briefly stated, is that signals that are in phase in stereo add in mono, and signals that are out of phase in stereo cancel in mono.

Certain devices, such as the phasing analyzer or stereo display processor, are used to indicate stereo-to-mono compatibility during a mix (see 18-23). Many of today's pan pots are designed with either a 3-dB- or a 6-dB-down notch that facilitates mono compatibility.

Two other techniques are also used. One is not to put anything dead center or at the extreme left

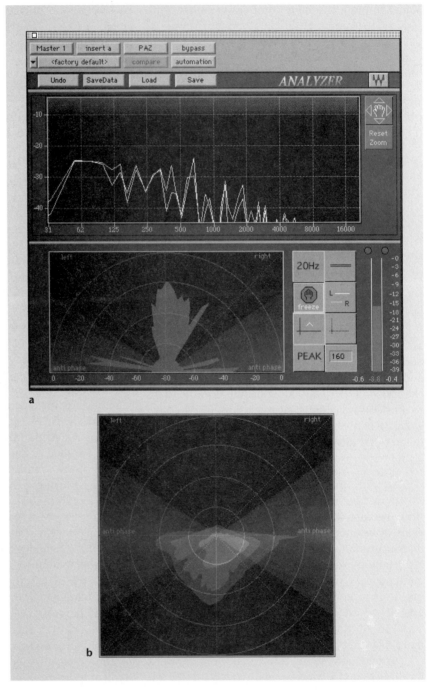

18-23 Real-time analyzer. (a) This model provides frequency analysis, a stereo position display, and loudness/peak meters. The stereo position display in this figure shows a mono-compatible stereo signal. A skewing to the left or right indicates a left-heavy or right-heavy stereo signal, respectively. (b) Stereo position display showing a badly out-of-phase stereo signal.

or right in a stereo mix. This reduces both center-channel buildup and loss of some of the left and right information when playing stereo recordings in mono. But the stereo image may not be as wide as it should be, and center imaging could be awkward.

The better technique is to be very careful of in-phase and out-of-phase signals during recording and signal processing, especially with reverb, and to constantly A-B between stereo and mono playback during a mix using both your ears and a phasing analyzer. In the A-B comparisons, always check to make sure that nothing is lost due to phase, that nothing stands out inordinately, and that the overall blend is maintained.

EVALUATING THE FINISHED PRODUCT

What makes good sound? Ask 100 audio specialists to evaluate the same sonic material and undoubtedly you will get 100 different responses. That is one of the beauties of sound: It is so personal. Who is to tell you that your taste is wrong? As a listener, if it satisfies you, that is all that matters. When sound is produced for an audience, however, professional "ears" must temper personal taste. To this end, there are generally accepted standards that audio pros agree are reasonable bases for artistic judgment.

Before discussing these standards, a word about the monitor loudspeakers is in order. Remember that the sound you evaluate is influenced by the loudspeaker reproducing it. You must therefore be thoroughly familiar with its frequency response and how it otherwise affects sonic reproduction. If a sound is overly bright or unduly dull, you have to know whether that is the result of the recording or the loudspeaker. Remember, a good way to familiarize yourself with a loudspeaker's response is to take a few test discs and well-produced commercial recordings with which you are thoroughly familiar and listen to them on the monitor system until you are confident about its response characteristics.

Intelligibility

It makes sense that if there is narration, dialogue, or song lyrics, the words must be intelligible. If not, meaning is lost. But when working with material over a long period of time, the words become so familiar that it might not be apparent that they are muffled, masked, and otherwise difficult to distinguish. In evaluating intelligibility it is therefore a good idea to do it with fresh "ears," as if you were hearing the words for the first time. If that does not give you the needed distance from the material, ask someone else if the words or lyrics are clear.

Tonal Balance

Bass, midrange, and treble frequencies should be balanced; no one octave or range of octaves should stand out. Be particularly aware of too much low end that muddies and masks sound; overly bright upper midrange and treble that brings out sibilance and noise; absence of brilliance that dulls sound; and too much midrange that causes the harshness, shrillness, or edge that annoys and fatigues.

The timbre of the voice, sound effects, and acoustic instruments should sound natural and realistic. Music and sounds generated by electric and electronic instruments do not necessarily have to sound so, unless they are supposed to.

Ensemble sound should blend as a whole. As such, solos or lead voicings should be sonically proportional in relation to the accompaniment.

Spatial Balance and Perspective

All sonic elements in aural space should be unambiguously localized; it should be clear where various sounds are coming from. Their relationships—front-to-back and side-to-side—should be in proper perspective. Dialogue spoken from the rear of a room should sound somewhat distant and reverberant; an oboe solo should be distinct yet come from its relative position in the orchestra; a vocal should not be too far in front of an ensemble or buried in it; background music should not overwhelm the announcer; crowd noise should not be more prominent than the sportscaster's voice.

Positional and loudness changes should be subtle and sound natural. They should not jar or distract by jumping out, falling back, or bouncing side-to-side (unless the change is justified in relation to the picture).

Definition

Each element should be clearly defined—identifiable, separate, and distinct—yet, if grouped, blended so that no one element stands out or crowds or masks another's sound. Each element should have its position in, and yet be a natural part of, the sound's overall spectral range and spatial arrangement.

Dynamic Range

The range of levels from softest to loudest should be as wide as the medium allows, making sure that the softest sounds are easily audible and the loudest sounds are undistorted. If compressed, sound should not seem squeezed together, nor should it surge from quiet to loud and vice versa.

Clarity

A clear recording is as noise- and distortion-free as possible. Hum, hiss, leakage, phasing, smearing, blurring from too much reverb, and harmonic, intermodulation, and loudness distortion—all muddle sound, adversely affecting clarity.

Airiness

Sound should be airy and open. It should not sound isolated, stuffy, muffled, closed-down, dead, lifeless, overwhelming, or oppressive.

Acoustical Appropriateness

Acoustics, of course, must be good, but they must also be appropriate. The space in which a character is seen and the acoustic dimension of that space must match; classical music and jazz sound most natural in an open, relatively spacious environment; acoustics for rock-and-roll can range from tight to open; a radio announcer belongs in an intimate acoustic environment.

PRODUCTION VALUES

The degree to which you are able to develop and appraise production values is what separates the mere craftsperson from the true artist. Production values relate to the material's style, interest, color, and inventiveness. It is the most difficult part of an evaluation to define or quantify, because response is qualitative and intuitive. Material with excellent production values grabs and moves you. It draws you into the production, compelling you to forget your role as objective observer; you become the audience. When this happens, it is not only the culmination of the production process, but its fulfillment.

▶ Mixing and rerecording are the phases of postproduction when the separately recorded elements are combined into a natural and integrated whole.

▶ In proceeding with a mix, it is necessary to know on what type of delivery system it will be reproduced. Radio, television, film, compact discs, and multimedia have different sonic requirements.

▶ In layering sound, it is important to: establish the main and supporting sounds to create focus or point of view; position the sounds to create relationships of space and distance; maintain spectral balance so that the aural space is properly weighted; and maintain definition of each sound.

▶ To help maintain definition, as well as intelligibility, in a mix, the various sounds should have different sonic features. These features can be varied in pitch, tempo, loudness, intensity, envelope, timbre, style, and so on.

▶ In layering sounds, it is also important to establish perspective. Some sounds are more important than others; the predominant one usually establishes the focus or point of view.

▶ One procedure in voicing-over recorded music is called a donut—fading the music after it is established and reestablishing it later at its former full level to create a hole for the announcement.

▶ When voicing-over music or sound effects, try to vary the background dynamics to help direct focus and create interest through sonic variety.

▶ Subtracting the time of an individual item from the total time of a program or program segment is known as backtiming.

▶ Playing sound with the fader off is known as deadpotting.

▶ In a music mixdown, one procedure is to evaluate the positive and negative attributes of the recording, working with one track at a time but building on the tracks already processed. When each track sounds acceptable in the context of the overall mix, blend and balance the sounds together. This may involve changing individual settings in favor of the overall mix.

▶ When equalizing, avoid large increases or decreases in EQ, do not increase or decrease too many tracks at the same frequency, and do not use equalizing as a substitute for better microphone selection and placement. Try subtractive, instead additive, equalization, and complementary EQ to keep masking to a minimum. Equalizing between 400 and 2,000 Hz is more noticeable than equalizing above and below that range. Be sure to equalize with an awareness of the frequency limits of the medium in which you are working.

▶ The quality of reverberation added to a recording in the mix depends, to a considerable extent, on musical style. Classical, jazz, and some types of folk music usually require natural-sounding acoustics; various reverberant environments may be appropriate for popular music.

▶ Do not add artificial reverberation until after signal processing and panning, because it is difficult to get a true sense of the effects of frequency and positional change in a reverberant space. Also, avoid giving widely different reverb times to the various components in an ensemble or sound track unless they are supposed to sound as though they are in different acoustic environments.

▶ Factors involved in placing musical components in the stereo frame are the aural balance, the arrangement of the ensemble when performing, and the type of music being played.

▶ Three-dimensional sound increases the depth, breadth, and height of the audio field, using the conventional, frontally positioned two-loudspeaker stereo array.

▶ Recordkeeping, whether handwritten or entered into a computer memory, is important in any type of mixing and rerecording. You never know if it will be necessary to redo a part of the mix or the entire thing.

▶ Sweetening is the four-stage postproduction procedure in television that usually involves layover (or laydown), prelay, premix, and layback.

▶ The premix is the stage in film production during which dialogue, sound effects, and, to some extent, music are prepared for the final rerecording mix.

- The purpose of the rerecording mix is to blend the premixed dialogue, sound effects, and music into a seamless stereo or surround-sound recording.

- Cue sheets are essential throughout the production process, but they are indispensable during the premix and rerecording mix stages.

- Stereo placement in film and TV usually positions dialogue and sounds in the center, and music to the left, in the center, and to the right. Large-screen film positions dialogue in the center with limited lateral movement, sound effects across a somewhat wider space but still toward the center, and music left, center, and right. The reason for such placement is to avoid disorienting the audience in relation to the on-screen sources of sound and image.

- Surround sound produces a soundfield in front of, to the sides of, and behind the listener.

- Generally, the left, center, and right channels contain the principal audio—dialogue, sound effects, and music—and are reproduced by the frontal loudspeakers. The surround-sound channel is dedicated to background sound(s) and reproduced by the side or rear loudspeakers, or both.

- In mastering stereo sound that may be reproduced on monophonic systems, the material must be mono-compatible.

- In evaluating a final product, factors that should be considered include intelligibility, tonal balance, spatial balance and perspective, definition, dynamic range, clarity, airiness, and acoustical appropriateness.

- Production values relate to the material's style, interest, color, and inventiveness.

Glossary

acoustical phase The time relationship between two or more sound waves at a given point in their cycles.

acoustics The science that deals with the behavior of sound and sound control. The properties of a room that affect the quality of sound.

active combining network (ACN) An amplifier at which the outputs of two or more signal paths are mixed together before being routed to their destination.

ADAT One of two formats used in modular digital multitrack tape recorders. It uses S-VHS videocassette tape. *ADAT* stands for Alesis Digital Audio Tape recorder. *See also* **digital tape recording system**.

additive ambience When the ambience of each track becomes cumulative in mixing a multitrack recording.

adhesion One layer of audiotape sticking to another.

ADR *See* **automated dialogue replacement**.

ADSR *See* **sound envelope**.

AES/EBU interface Internationally accepted professional digital audio interface transmitted via a balanced-line connection using XLR connectors, specified jointly by the Audio Engineering Society and the European Broadcast Union. *See also* **SPDIF**.

ambience Sounds such as reverberation, noise, and atmosphere that form a background to the main sound. Also called *room tone* and *presence,* and *atmos* in Great Britain.

amplifier A device that increases the amplitude of an electric signal.

amplitude The magnitude of a sound wave or electrical signal, measured in decibels.

amplitude processor A signal processor that affects a signal's loudness.

analog recording A method of recording in which the waveform of the recorded signal resembles the waveform of the original signal.

anechoic chamber A room that prevents all reflected sound through the dissipation or the absorption of sound waves.

assemble editing Dubbing segments from one tape or tapes to another tape in sequential order.

atmos Short for *atmosphere,* the British term for ambience. *See* **ambience**.

attack (1) The way a sound begins—that is, by plucking, bowing, striking, blowing, and so on. (2) The first part of the sound envelope.

attack time The length of time it takes a limiter or compressor to respond to the input signal.

audio-leading-video When the sound of the incoming scene starts before the corresponding picture appears. *See also* **video-leading-audio**.

automated dialogue replacement (ADR) A technique used to rerecord dialogue in synchronization with picture in postproduction. The picture is automatically replayed in short "loops" again and again so that the performers can synchronize their lip movements with the lip movements in the picture and then record the dialogue. Also known as *automatic dialog recording* and *looping. See also* **dialogue recording studio**.

azimuth Alignment of the record and playback heads so that their centerlines are parallel to each other and at right angles to the direction of the tape motion passing across the heads.

backtiming Method of subtracting the time of a program segment from the total time of a program so that the segment and the program end simultaneously.

balanced line A pair of ungrounded conductors whose voltages are opposite in polarity but equal in magnitude.

band-pass filter A filter that attenuates above and below a selected bandwidth, allowing the frequencies between to pass.

bandwidth curve The curve shaped by the number of frequencies in a bandwidth and their relative increase or decrease in level. A bandwidth of 100 to 150 Hz with 125 Hz boosted 15 dB forms a sharp, narrow bandwidth curve; a bandwidth of 100 to 6,400 Hz with a 15-dB boost at 1,200 Hz forms a more sloping, wider bandwidth curve.

bandwidth The difference between the upper and lower frequency limits of an audio component. The upper and lower frequency limits of AM radio are 535 and 1,605 kHz; therefore, the bandwidth of AM radio is 1,070 kHz.

bass The low range of the audible frequency spectrum; usually from 20 to 320 Hz.

bass roll-off Attenuating bass frequencies. The control—for example, on a microphone—used to roll off bass frequencies.

bass tip-up *See* **proximity effect**.

bias The inaudible DC or AC signal added to an audio signal to overcome nonlinearities of amplification or of the medium. In magnetic-tape recording, ultrasonic AC bias is used to linearize the tape medium, which would otherwise be highly distorted.

bias current An extremely high-frequency AC current, far beyond audibility, added during a tape recording to linearize the magnetic information.

bidirectional microphone A microphone that picks up sound to its front and back and has minimal pickup at its sides.

binaural hearing Hearing with two ears attached to and separated by the head.

binaural microphone head Two omnidirectional capacitor microphones set into the ear cavities of an artificial head, complete with pinnas. This arrangement preserves binaural localization cues during recording and reproduces sound as humans hear it, three-dimensionally. Also called *artificial head* or *dummy head stereo*.

blast filter *See* **pop filter**.

blocking Plotting performer, camera, and microphone placements and movements in a production.

board Audio mixing console.

boundary microphone A microphone whose capsule is mounted flush with or close to, but a precise distance from, a reflective surface so that there is no phase cancellation of reflected sound at audible frequencies.

bulk eraser A demagnetizer used to erase an entire roll of magnetic tape without removing it from its reel. Also known as a *degausser*.

bus A mixing network that combines the outputs of other channels.

calibration Adjusting equipment components—for example, a console and a tape recorder—according to a standard so that their measurements are similar. *See also* **electronic alignment**.

camcorder A handheld video camera with a built-in or dockable videotape recorder.

capacitor microphone A microphone that transduces acoustic energy into electric energy electrostatically.

capstan The shaft that rotates against the tape, pulling it across the heads at a constant speed.

cardioid microphone A unidirectional microphone with a heart-shaped pickup pattern.

CD-R *See* **recordable compact disc**.

CD-rewritable (CD-RW) A CD format that, as with tape, can be recorded on, erased, and used again for another recording.

CD-RW *See* **CD-rewritable**.

center frequency In peak/dip equalizing, the frequency at which maximum boost or attenuation occurs.

chorus effect Recirculating the doubling effect to make one sound source sound like several. *See also* **doubling**.

cinching Slippage between the tape layers due to loose packing. Also known as *windowing*.

clapslate A slate used in synchronizing sound and picture during filming and editing. The slate carries information such as scene and take number, production title, location of shot—e.g., indoors or outdoors—and time code. A pair of hinged boards on top of the slate—called clapsticks—clap together, producing the sound that is used to synchronize picture and sound.

clipping Audible distortion that occurs when a signal's level exceeds the limits of a particular device or circuit.

close miking Placing a microphone close to a sound source to pick up mostly direct sound and reduce ambience and leakage. *See also* **distant miking**.

coercivity The magnetic force field necessary to reduce a tape from saturation to full erasure. This value is expressed in oersteds.

coincident miking Employing two matched microphones, usually unidirectional, crossed one above the other on a vertical axis with their diaphragms. *See also* **X-Y miking**.

comb-filter effect The effect produced when a signal is time-delayed and added to itself, reinforcing some frequencies and canceling others, giving sound an unnatural, hollow coloration.

commentative sound Descriptive sound that makes a comment or interpretation. *See also* **descriptive sound** and **narrative sound**.

compander A contraction of the words *compressor* and *expander* that refers to the devices that compress an input signal and expand an output signal to reduce noise. Also known as a *noise reducer*.

complementary equalization Equalizing sounds that share similar frequency ranges so that they complement, rather than interfere with, one another.

compression (1) Reducing a signal's output level in relation to its input level to reduce dynamic range. (2) The drawing together of vibrating molecules, thus producing a high-pressure area. *See also* **rarefaction**.

compression ratio The ratio of the input and output signals in a compressor.

compression threshold The level at which a compressor acts on an input signal and the compression ratio takes effect.

compressor A signal processor with an output level that decreases as its input level increases.

condenser microphone *See* **capacitor microphone**.

console An electronic device that amplifies, processes, and combines input signals and routes them to broadcast or recording.

constructive interference When sound waves are partially out of phase and partially additive, increasing amplitude where compression and rarefaction occur at the same time.

contact microphone A microphone that attaches to a sound source and transduces the vibrations that pass through it. Also called *acoustic pickup mic*.

contextual sound Sound that emanates from and duplicates a sound source as it is. *See also* **diegetic sound**.

contrapuntal narration Juxtaposes narration and action to make a statement not carried by either element alone.

coverage angle The off-axis angle or point at which loudspeaker level is down 6 dB compared with the on-axis output level.

cps *See* **hertz**.

crossfade Fading in one sound source as another sound source fades out. At some point the sounds cross at an equal level of loudness.

crossover frequency The frequency at which the high frequencies are routed to the tweeter(s) and the low frequencies are routed to the woofer(s).

crossover network An electronic device that divides the audio spectrum into individual frequency ranges (low, high, and/or mid) before sending them to specialized loudspeakers such as the woofer(s) and tweeter(s).

crosstalk Unwanted signal leakage from one signal path to another.

crystal synchronization Synchronizing the operating speeds of a film camera and an audiotape recorder by using a crystal oscillator in both camera and recorder. The oscillator generates a sync pulse tone. *See also* **double-system recording**.

cupping Deformation of the backing of audiotape due to expansion of the magnetic coating and base.

curling Twisting of audiotape when it hangs due to a problem in the binding between the plastic and magnetic coatings.

cut (1) An instantaneous transition from one sound or picture to another. (2) To make a disc recording. (3) A decrease in level.

cut-and-splice editing Editing tape or film by physically cutting the material and joining the cut ends with splicing tape.

cycles per second (cps) *See* **hertz**.

DASH format *See* **Digital Audio Stationary Head format**.

DAT Digital audiotape.

DAW *See* **digital audio workstation**.

dB *See* **decibel**.

dBm An electrical measurement of power referenced to 1 milliwatt as dissipated across a 600-ohm load.

dB-SPL A measure of the pressure of a sound wave, expressed in decibels (dB).

dBu A unit of measurement for expressing the relationship of decibels to voltage—0.775 volt.

dBv *See* **dBu**.

dBV A measure of voltage with decibels referenced to 1 volt.

DCA *See* **digitally controlled amplifier**.

deadpotting Starting a recording with the fader turned down all the way. Also known as *dead rolling*.

decay time *See* **reverberation time**.

decibel (dB) A relative and dimensionless unit to measure the ratio of two quantities.

de-esser A compressor that reduces sibilance.

degausser *See* **bulk eraser**.

delay The time interval between a sound or signal and each of its repeats.

descriptive sound Describes sonic aspects of a scene not connected to the main action. *See also* **commentative sound** and **narrative sound**.

destructive editing Permanently alters the original sound or soundfile. *See also* **nondestructive editing**.

destructive interference When sound waves are partially out of phase and partially subtractive, decreasing amplitude where compression and rarefaction occur at different times.

dialogue recording studio A studio in which dialogue is recorded and synchronized to picture. *See also* **automated dialogue replacement**.

diaphragmatic absorber A flexible panel mounted over an air space that resonates at a frequency (or frequencies) determined by the stiffness of the panel and the size of the air space. Also called *bass trap*.

diegetic sound Sound that comes from within the story space, such as dialogue and sound effects. *See also* **nondiegetic sound**.

diffraction The spreading or bending around of sound waves as they pass an object.

diffusion The scattering of sound waves.

Digital Audio Stationary Head (DASH) format A format agreed to by Sony, Studer, and TASCAM to standardize digital recording.

digital audio workstation (DAW) A multifunctional hard-disk production system, controlled from a central location, that is integrated with and capable of being networked to other devices, such as audio, video, and MIDI sources, within or among facilities.

digital cartridge disk system An audio recorder and/or playback system that uses compact, magneto-optical disc, mini disc, floppy disk, or hard disk as the recording medium.

digital delay An electronic device designed to delay an audio signal.

digital news gathering (DNG) Reporting and gathering news from the field using digital equipment.

digital recording A method of recording in which samples of the original analog signal are encoded on tape as pulses and then decoded during playback.

digital signal processing (DSP) A software program that provides various manipulations of sound in digital format using complex algorithms.

digital tape recording system (DTRS) One of two formats used in modular digital multitrack tape recorders. It uses Hi8 videocassette tape. *See also* **ADAT**.

digital versatile disc (DVD) A compact disc providing massive data storage of digital-quality audio, video, and text.

digitally controlled amplifier (DCA) An amplifier whose gain is remotely controlled by a digital control signal.

directional microphone Any microphone that picks up sound from one direction. Also called *unidirectional microphone*.

direct narration Describes what is being seen or heard.

direct sound Sound waves that reach the listener before reflecting off any surface. *See also* **early reflections**.

distant miking Placing a microphone(s) far enough from the sound source to pick up most or all of an ensemble's blended sound including room reflections. *See also* **close miking**.

distortion The appearance of a signal in the reproduced sound that was not in the original sound. *See also* **harmonic distortion**, **intermodulation distortion**, **loudness distortion**, and **transient distortion**.

diversity reception Multiple antenna receiving system for use with wireless microphones. *See also* **nondiversity receiver**.

DNG *See* **digital news gathering**.

donut An announcement in which music is established, faded under the announcer, and reestablished after the announcer finishes reading the copy.

Doppler effect The perceived increase or decrease in frequency as a sound source moves closer to or farther from the listener.

double-system recording Filming sound and picture simultaneously but separately with a camera and a recorder. *See also* **crystal synchronization**.

doubling Mixing slightly delayed signals (15 to 35 ms) with the original signal to create a fuller, stronger, more ambient sound. *See also* **chorus effect**.

dropout (1) A sudden attenuation of sound or loss of picture due to an imperfection in the magnetic coating. (2) Sudden attenuation in a wireless microphone signal due to an obstruction or some other interference.

dry sound A sound devoid of reverberation. *See also* **wet sound**.

DSP *See* **digital signal processing**.

DTRS *See* **digital tape recording system**.

dub Transferring sound from tape or disk to another tape or disk.

DVD *See* **digital versatile disc**.

dynamic microphone A microphone that transduces energy electromagnetically. Moving-coil and ribbon microphones are dynamic.

dynamic range The range between the quietest and loudest sounds a sound source can produce without distortion.

early reflections Reflections of the original sound that reach the listener within about 40 to 50 ms of the direct sound. Also called *early sound. See also* **direct sound**.

early sound. *See* **early reflections**.

echo Sound reflections delayed by 35 ms or more that are perceived as discrete repetitions of the direct sound.

edit decision list (EDL) A list of edits, computer-generated or handwritten, used to assemble a production.

EDL *See* **edit decision list**.

EFP *See* **electronic field production**.

eigentones The resonance of sound at particular frequencies in an acoustic space. May add unwanted coloration to sound. More commonly known as *room modes*.

elasticity The capacity to return to the original shape or place after deflection or displacement.

electret microphone A capacitor microphone which, instead of requiring an external high-voltage power source, uses a permanently charged element and requires only a low-voltage power supply for the internal preamp.

electroacoustics The electrical manipulation of acoustics.

electronic alignment The adjustment of electronic and mechanical characteristics of a tape recorder to a defined standard specified by the manufacturer or by international industry bodies such as the Audio Engineering Society (AES), the National Association of Broadcasters (NAB), or the International Electrotechnical Commission (IEC). *See also* **calibration.**

electronic editing Using one tape recorder and inserting—punching in—material, or transferring material from one tape recorder (the master) to another (the slave).

electronic field production (EFP) Video production done on location, involving program materials that take some time to produce.

electronic news gathering (ENG) News production done on location, sometimes taped and sometimes live, but usually with an imminent deadline.

ENG *See* **electronic news gathering.**

enharmonic In music, two different notes that sound the same, for example, C♯ and D♭, G♯ and A♭.

EQ Equalization. *See* **equalizer.**

equalizer A signal-processing device that can boost, attenuate, or shelve frequencies in a sound source or sound system.

equal loudness principle The principle that confirms the human ear's nonlinear sensitivity to all audible frequencies: that midrange frequencies are perceived with greatest intensity and that bass and treble frequencies are perceived with lesser intensity.

erase head Electromagnetic transducer on a tape recorder that automatically demagnetizes a tape before it reaches the record head when the recorder is in the record mode.

ergonomics Designing an engineering system with human comfort and convenience in mind.

expander An amplifier in which the output signal's dynamic range is greater than that of the input signal.

fade-in Gradually increasing the loudness of a signal level from silence (or from "black" in video).

fade-out Gradually decreasing the loudness of a signal level to silence (or to "black" in video).

fade-out/fade-in A transition usually indicating a marked change in time, locale, continuity of action, and other features.

fader A device containing a resistor that is used to vary the output voltage of a circuit or component. Also known as an *attenuator,* a *gain* or *volume control,* or a *pot* or *potentiometer.*

feedback When part or all of a system's output signal is returned into its own input. Feedback can be acoustic or electronic. A commonly encountered example of acoustic feedback is the loud squeal or howl caused when the sound from a loudspeaker is picked up by a nearby microphone and reamplified. Electronic feedback is created in digital delay devices by feeding a proportion of the delayed signal back into the delay line. Also called *regeneration.*

fill leader Old picture film or unrecorded magnetic film used to fill silences on a magnetic-film recording thereby reducing the noise of recorded magnetic film. Also called *spacer.*

filter A device that removes unwanted frequencies or noise from a signal.

fixed-frequency equalizer An equalizer with several fixed frequencies usually grouped in two (high and low) or three (high, middle, and low) ranges of the frequency spectrum.

flanging Combining a direct signal and the same signal slightly delayed, and continuously varying their time relationships.

flat Frequency response in an audio system that reproduces a signal between 20 and 20,000 Hz (or between any two specified frequencies) that varies no more than ±3 dB.

flutter Frequency changes in an analog tape recording resulting from faster variations in the speed of the tape transport. *See also* **wow.**

flutter echoes Echoes between parallel walls that occur in rapid series.

FM microphone Wireless microphone.

foldback The system in a multichannel console that permits the routing of sound through a headphone monitor feed to performers in the studio.

Foley recording Producing and recording sound effects in the studio in synchronization with picture.

formant The resonance band in a vibrating body that mildly increases the level of specific steady-state frequencies in that band.

four-way system loudspeaker A loudspeaker that uses three crossover frequencies to divide the bass, midrange, and treble ranges.

frame rate The number of film frames that pass in one second of real time—frames per second (fps).

freewheel A mode in a synchronizer that allows stretches of poorly encoded time code to be passed over without altering the speed of the slave tape recorder's transport.

frequency The number of times per second that a sound source vibrates. Now expressed in hertz (Hz); formerly expressed in cycles per second (cps).

frequency response A measure of an audio system's ability to reproduce a range of frequencies with the same relative loudness; usually represented by a graph.

full coat Magnetic film in which the oxide coating covers most or all of the film width. *See also* **stripe coat.**

fundamental The lowest frequency a sound source can produce. Also called *primary frequency* and *first harmonic.*

gauss A unit of magnetic density.

graphic equalizer An equalizer with sliding controls that gives a graphic representation of the response curve chosen.

guard band The space between tracks on an audiotape recorder head to reduce crosstalk.

Haas effect *See* **precedence effect.**

hard-disk recording Using a hard-disk computer system as the recording medium, which is more versatile than tape because data storage and retrieval is random, quick, and nonlinear; storage capacity is far greater; and data is nondestructive.

hardwired Description of pieces of equipment wired to each other. *See also* **patch bay.**

harmonic distortion Nonlinear distortion caused when an audio system introduces harmonics to a signal at the output that were not present at the input.

harmonics Frequencies that are multiples of the fundamental.

headroom The amount of increase in loudness level that a tape, amplifier, or other piece of equipment can take, above working level, before overload distortion.

headset microphone A microphone attached to a pair of headphones; one headphone channel feeds the program and the other headphone channel feeds the director's cues.

headstack A multitrack tape head.

height One of the adjustments made when aligning the heads on an audiotape recorder. This adjustment aligns the height of the heads with the recording tape.

helical scanning Using one or more rotating heads that engage the tape wrapped at least partially around the head drum.

Helmholtz absorber A resonator designed to absorb specific frequencies depending on size, shape, and enclosed volume of air. The enclosed volume of air is connected to the air in the room by a narrow opening or neck. When resonant frequencies reach the neck of the enclosure, the air inside cancels those frequencies. Also called *Helmholtz resonator.*

hertz (Hz) Unit of measurement of frequency; numerically equal to cycles per second (cps).

high end The treble range of the frequency spectrum.

high-output tape High-sensitivity tape.

high-pass (low-cut) filter A filter that attenuates frequencies below a selected frequency and allows those above that point to pass.

humbuck circuit A circuit built into a microphone to reduce hum pickup.

Hz *See* **hertz.**

IEC standard The time code standard for R-DAT recording, established by the International Electrotechnical Commission.

IFB *See* **interruptible foldback system.**

IM *See* **intermodulation distortion.**

impedance The measure of the total resistance to the current flow in an AC circuit; expressed in ohms.

indirect narration Describes something other than what is being seen or heard.

indirect sound Sound waves that reflect from one or more surfaces before reaching the listener.

infrasonic The range below the frequencies audible to human hearing.

inharmonic overtones Pitches that are not exact multiples of the fundamental.

initial decay In the sound envelope, the point at which the attack begins to lose amplitude.

in-line console A console in which a channel's input, output, and monitor functions are placed in-line and located in a single input/output (I/O) module. *See also* **split-section console** and **input/output (I/O) module.**

inner ear The part of the ear that contains the auditory nerve, which transmits sound waves to the brain.

input/output (I/O) module On an in-line console, a module containing input, output, and monitor controls for a single channel.

input section On a console, the section into which signals from a sound source, such as a microphone, feed and are then routed to the output section.

insert editing In electronic editing, inserting a segment between two previously dubbed segments. Also, electronic editing segments out of sequential order.

Integrated Services Digital Network (ISDN) A public telephone service that allows inexpensive use of a flexible, wide-area, all-digital network for, among other things, recording simultaneously from various locations.

intermodulation distortion (IM) Nonlinear distortion that occurs when different frequencies pass through an amplifier at the same time and interact to create combinations of tones unrelated to the original sounds.

interruptible foldback (IFB) system A communications system that allows communication from the producer or director and selected production personnel with the on-air talent.

in-the-ear monitoring Using small headphones to feed the sound blend to on-stage performers instead of stage monitors.

in the mud Sound level so quiet that it barely "kicks" the VU meter.

in the red Sound level so loud that the VU meter "rides" over 100 percent of modulation.

inverse square law The acoustic situation in which the sound level changes in inverse proportion to the square of the distance from the sound source.

I/O module *See* **input/output module**.

ISDN *See* **Integrated Services Digital Network**.

jack Receptacle or plug connector leading to the input or output circuit of a patch bay, tape recorder, or other electronic component.

jam sync A mode in a synchronizer that produces new time code during dubbing either to match the original time code or to regenerate new address data.

lavalier microphone Microphone that used to be worn around the neck but is now worn attached to the clothing.

layback Dubbing the composite audio track from the multitrack tape to the edited master videotape, or the dialogue, sound effects, and music tracks to separate reels of magnetic film. *See also* **layover** and **prelay**.

laydown *See* **layover**.

layering When many sounds occur at once, layering involves making sure that they remain balanced, in perspective, and intelligible in the mix.

layover Dubbing the audio from the edited master videotape or audiotape, or both, to a multitrack recorder for pre-mixing. Also called *laydown*. *See also* **layback** and **prelay**.

leader tape Nonmagnetic tape spliced to the beginning and end of a tape and between segments to indicate visually when recorded material begins and ends.

limiter A compressor with an output level that does not exceed a preset ceiling regardless of the input level.

linear editing Nonrandom editing. *See also* **nonlinear editing**.

linearity Having an output that varies in direct proportion to the input.

listening fatigue A pronounced dulling of the auditory senses inhibiting perceptual judgment.

localization (1) Placement of a sound source in the stereo or surround-sound frame. (2) The direction from which a sound source seems to emanate in a stereo or surround-sound field. (3) The ability to tell the direction from which a sound is coming.

longitudinal time code (LTC) A high-frequency signal consisting of a stream of pulses produced by a time code generator used to code tape to facilitate editing and synchronization. Also known as *SMPTE time code*.

loudness distortion Distortion that occurs when the loudness of a signal is greater than the sound system can handle. Also called *overload distortion*.

low bass Frequency range between roughly 20 and 80 Hz, the lowest two octaves in the audible frequency spectrum.

low end The bass range of the frequency spectrum.

low-output tape Low-sensitivity tape.

low-pass (high-cut) filter A filter that attenuates frequencies above a selected frequency and allows those below that point to pass.

LTC *See* **longitudinal time code**.

magnetic film Sprocketed film containing sound only and no picture. See also **full coat** and **stripe coat**.

magneto-optical (MO) recording Disc-based, optical recording medium that uses tiny magnetic particles heated to extremely high temperatures.

masking The hiding of some sounds by other sounds when each is a different frequency and they are presented together.

master (1) The original recording. (2) The final tape or disc recording that is sent to the CD mastering house or to distribution.

master fader The fader that controls the combined signal level of the individual input channels on a console.

master section In a multichannel production console, the section that routes the final mix to its recording destination. It usually houses, at least, the master controls for the mixing-bus outputs, reverb send and reverb return, and master fader.

maximum sound-pressure level The level at which a microphone's output signal begins to distort, that is, produces a 3 percent total harmonic distortion (THD).

MD *See* **mini disc**.

MDM *See* **modular digital multitrack recorder**.

microphone A transducer that converts acoustic energy into electric energy. Also called *mic*.

middle ear The part of the ear that transfers sound waves from the eardrum to the inner ear.

middle-side (M-S) microphone Consists of two mic capsules housed in single casing. One capsule, usually cardioid, is the mid-position microphone. The other capsule, usually bidirectional, has each lobe oriented 90 degrees laterally.

MIDI *See* **Musical Instrument Digital Interface**.

MIDI time code (MTC) Translates SMPTE time code into MIDI messages that allow MIDI-based devices to operate on the SMPTE timing reference.

midrange The part of the frequency spectrum to which humans are most sensitive; the frequencies between 320 and 5,120 Hz.

mil One-thousandth of an inch.

milking the audience Boosting the level of an audience's sound during laughter or applause and/or reinforcing it with recorded laughter or applause.

mini disc™ (MD) Magneto-optical disc 2½ inches wide that can store more than an hour of digital-quality audio.

mini-mic Short for *miniature microphone*. Any extremely small lavalier microphone designed to be unobtrusive on-camera and which can be easily hidden in or under clothing or on a set.

mix-minus A program feed through an interruptible foldback (IFB) circuit minus the announcer's voice. *See also* **interruptible foldback system**.

mixdown The point, usually in postproduction, when all the separately recorded audio tracks are sweetened, positioned, and combined into stereo or surround sound.

mixer A small, highly portable device that mixes various elements of sound, typically coming from multiple microphones, and performs limited processing functions.

MO *See* **magneto-optical recording**.

mobile unit A car, van, or tractor-trailer equipped to produce program material on location.

modular digital multitrack (MDM) recorder An audiotape recorder that uses a videocassette transport with videocassette tape. It can record up to eight channels and, linked to multiple MDMs, can expand track capability in eight-channel increments.

monitor section The section in a console that enables the signals to be heard. The monitor section in multichannel production consoles, among other things, allows monitoring of the line or recorder input, selects various inputs to the control room and studio monitors, and controls their levels.

moving-coil loudspeaker A loudspeaker with a moving-coil element.

moving-coil microphone A microphone with a moving-coil element. The coil is connected to a diaphragm suspended in a magnetic field.

ms Milliseconds.

M-S microphone *See* **middle-side microphone**.

MTC *See* **MIDI time code**.

mult *See* **multiple**.

multidirectional microphone Microphone with more than one pickup pattern. Also called *polydirectional microphone*.

multipath In wireless microphones, when more than one radio frequency (RF) signal from the same source arrives at the receiver's front end, creating phase mismatching.

multiple (1) On a patch bay, jacks interconnected to each other and to no other circuit. They can be used to feed signals to and from sound sources. Also called *mults*. (2) An amplifier with several mic level outputs to provide individual feeds, thereby eliminating the need for many. Also called a *press bridge* or a *presidential patch*.

multiple-entry-port microphone A microphone that has more than one opening for sound waves to reach the transducer. Most of these openings are used to reject sound from the sides or back of the microphone through phase cancellation. Each port returns a different frequency range to the mic capsule out of phase with sounds reaching the front of the mic.

Musical Instrument Digital Interface (MIDI) A protocol that allows synthesizers, drum machines, sequencers, and other signal-processing devices to communicate with or control one another, or both.

narrative sound Sound effects that add more to a scene than what is apparent and so perform an informational function. *See also* **commentative sound** and **descriptive sound**.

NC *See* **noise criteria**.

near-coincident miking A stereo microphone array in which the mics are separated horizontally but the angle or space between their capsules is not more than several inches. *See also* **X-Y miking**.

near-field monitoring Monitoring with loudspeakers placed close to the operator, usually on or just behind the console's meter bridge, to reduce interference from control room acoustics at the monitoring position.

noise Any unwanted sound or signal.

noise criteria (NC) Contours of the levels of background noise that can be tolerated within an audio studio.

noise gate An expander with a threshold that can be set to reduce or eliminate unwanted low-level sounds, such as room ambience, rumble, and leakage, without affecting the wanted sounds.

noise processor A signal processor that reduces tape noise.

noise-canceling microphone A microphone designed for use close to the mouth and with excellent rejection of ambient sound.

nondestructive editing Editing that does not alter the original sound or soundfile, regardless of what editing or signal processing is effected. *See also* **destructive editing**.

nondiegetic sound Sound that is outside the story space, such as music underscoring. *See also* **diegetic sound**.

nondirectional microphone *See* **omnidirectional microphone**.

nondiversity receiver Single-antenna receiving system used with wireless microphones. *See also* **diversity reception**.

nonlinear The property of not being linear—not having an output that varies in direct proportion to the input.

nonlinear editing Instant random access to and easy rearrangement of recorded material. *See also* **linear editing**.

notch filter A filter capable of attenuating an extremely narrow bandwidth of frequencies.

octave The interval between two sounds that have a frequency ratio of 2 to 1.

oersted A unit of magnetic force.

off-mic Not being within the optimal pickup pattern of a microphone; off-axis.

off-miking Miking technique that employs microphones farther from the sound source than the close mics to add more-ambient, airier sound to the overall recording.

ohm A unit of resistance to current flow.

omnidirectional microphone Microphone that picks up sound from all directions. Also called a *nondirectional microphone*.

on-mic Being within the optimal pickup pattern of a microphone; on-axis.

open-reel audiotape recorder A tape recorder with the feed reel and takeup reel not enclosed in a cartridge, requiring that they be mounted manually.

oscillator A device that generates pure tones or sine waves.

outer ear The portion of the ear that picks up and directs sound waves through the auditory canal to the middle ear.

output section In a mixer and console, the section that routes the signals to a recorder or broadcast, or both.

overroll Recording ambience after recording narration or dialogue by letting the recorder continue to run.

overdubbing Recording new material on a separate tape track(s) while listening to the replay of a previously recorded tape track(s) in order to synchronize the old and new material.

overload Feeding a component or system more amplitude than it can handle and thereby causing overload distortion.

overload distortion *See* **loudness distortion**.

overload indicator On a console, a light-emitting diode (LED) that flashes when the input signal is approaching or has reached overload and is clipping.

overtones Harmonics that may or may not be multiples of the fundamental. Subjective response of the ear to harmonics.

pad An attenuator inserted into a component or system to reduce level.

pan pot A volume control that shifts the proportion of sound to any point from left to right between two output buses and, hence, between the two loudspeakers necessary for reproducing a stereo image. *Pan pot* is short for *panoramic potentiometer*.

parabolic microphone system A system that uses a concave dish to focus reflected sound into a microphone pointed at the center of the dish.

paragraphic equalizer An equalizer that combines the features of a parametric and a graphic equalizer.

parametric equalizer An equalizer in which the bandwidth of a selected frequency is continuously variable.

patch bay An assembly of jacks to which are wired the inputs and outputs of the audio components in a console and/or sound studio. Also called *patch panel*. *See also* **hardwired**.

patch cord A short cord or cable with a plug at each end, used to route signals in a patch bay.

peak program meter (ppm) A meter designed to indicate transient peaks in the level of a signal.

percentage of modulation The percentage of an applied signal in relation to the maximum signal a sound system can handle.

perspective miking Establishing through mic-to-source distance the audio viewpoint in relation to the performers and their environment in screen space.

phantom power Operating voltage supplied to a capacitor microphone by an external power source or mixer, thereby eliminating the need for batteries.

phase The time relationship between two or more sounds reaching a microphone or signals in a circuit. When this time relationship is coincident, the sounds or signals are in phase and their amplitudes are additive. When this time relationship is not coincident, the sounds or signals are out of phase and their amplitudes are subtractive.

phase shift A change in the phase relationship of two signals at a given time, or the phase change of one signal over an interval of time.

phasing An effect created by splitting a signal in two and time-delaying one of the signal portions.

phon A dimensionless unit of loudness level related to the ear's subjective impression of signal strength.

phone line (PL) system *See* **private line system**.

pickup pattern *See* **polar response pattern**.

pin When the needle of the VU meter hits against the peg at the right-hand corner of the red. Pinning is to be avoided because it indicates too high a loudness level and it could damage the meter.

pinch roller On a tape recorder, the spring-loaded, free-spinning rubber wheel that holds the tape against the capstan. Also called *capstan idler* and *pressure roller*.

pink noise Wideband noise that maintains constant energy per octave. *See also* **white noise**.

pitch The subjective perception of frequency.

pitch shifter A signal processor that varies the pitch of a signal.

PL system *See* **private line system.**

plant microphone A stationary mic positioned on the set to cover action that cannot easily be picked up with a boom or a body mic or to provide fill sound. Also referred to as a *fixed mic.*

playback head Electromagnetic transducer on a tape recorder that converts magnetic energy into electric energy.

polarity The relative position of two signal leads—the high (+) and the low (–)—in the same circuit.

polarity reversal The control on a console that inverts the polarity of an input signal 180 degrees. Sometimes called *phase reversal.*

polar response pattern The graph of a microphone's directional characteristics as seen from above. The graph indicates response over a 360-degree circumference in a series of concentric circles, each representing a 5-dB loss in level as the circles move inward toward the center. Also called *pickup pattern.*

polydirectional microphone *See* **multidirectional microphone.**

pop filter Foam rubber windscreen placed inside the microphone head. Particularly effective in reducing sound from plosives and blowing. Also called *blast filter.* *See also* **windscreen.**

porous absorber A sound absorber made up of porous material whose tiny air spaces are most effective at absorbing high frequencies.

pot Short for *potentiometer. See also* **fader.**

potentiometer *See* **fader.**

ppm *See* **peak program meter.**

precedence effect The tendency to perceive direct and immediate repetitions of a sound as coming from the same position or direction even if immediate repetitions coming from another direction are louder. Also known as the *Haas effect.*

prefader listen (PFL) *See* **solo.**

prelay Recording audio elements, other than those from the edit master videotape, onto a multitrack recorder. *See also* **layback** and **layover.**

premix The stage in postproduction sweetening when dialogue, sound effects, and music are prepared for final mixing.

presence Perception of a sound as being close and realistic. *See also* **ambience** and **room tone.**

press bridge *See* **multiple** (2).

print-through Unwanted transfer of a magnetic signal from one tape layer to an adjacent tape layer.

private line (PL) system An intercom system consisting of a headset with an earpiece and a small microphone used during production to connect production and technical personnel. Also called *phone line system.*

production source music Music that emanates from an on-screen singer or ensemble and is produced live during shooting or in postproduction.

proximity effect Increase in the bass response of some mics as the distance between the mic and its sound source is decreased. Also known as *bass tip-up.*

psychoacoustic processor Signal processor that adds clarity, definition, overall presence, and life, or "sizzle," to recorded sound.

psychoacoustics Study of the perception of sound stimuli.

pure tone *See* **sine wave.**

quantization Converting a waveform that is infinitely variable into a finite series of discrete levels.

radio microphone Wireless microphone.

rarefaction Temporary drawing apart of vibrating molecules, causing a partial vacuum to occur. *See also* **compression** (2).

R-DAT *See* **rotary-head digital audiotape recorder.**

read mode Mode of operation in an automated mixdown when the console controls are operated automatically by the data previously encoded in the computer. Also called *safe mode. See also* **update mode** and **write mode.**

real-time analyzer A device that shows the total energy present at all audible frequencies on an instantaneous basis.

record head Electromagnetic transducer on a tape recorder that converts electric energy into magnetic energy.

recordable compact disc (CD-R) A CD format allowing users to record one time but to play back the recorded information repeatedly.

reflected sound Reflections of the direct sound that bounce off one or more surfaces before reaching the listener.

release The time and manner in which a sound diminishes to inaudibility.

release time The length of time it takes a limiter or compressor to return to its normal level after the signal has been attenuated or withdrawn. Also known as *recovery time.*

remnance The residual magnetization from a previous recording after erasure.

remote Any broadcast done away from the studio.

rerecording The process of combining individual dialogue, sound effects, and music tracks into their final form—stereo or surround sound.

resonance Transmitting a vibration from one body to another when the frequency of the first body is exactly, or almost exactly, the natural frequency of the second body.

retentivity Measure of a tape's ability to retain magnetization after the force field has been removed. Retentivity is measured in gauss—a unit of magnetic energy.

reverberation Multiple blended, random reflections of a sound wave after the sound source has ceased vibrating. Also called *reverb* and *reverberant sound.*

reverberation time The length of time it takes a sound to die away. By definition: the time it takes a sound to decrease to one-millionth of its original intensity, or 60 dB-SPL. Also called *decay time.*

ribbon microphone A microphone with a ribbon diaphragm suspended in a magnetic field.

ride the gain Continually adjusting controls on a console or other audio equipment to maintain a more or less constant level.

ridging A bulge or depression, seen after winding, caused by deformed layer(s) of tape.

ring off When a dialogue line ends with the ambient ring of a room and another line begins with that ring decaying under it.

room modes *See* **eigentones.**

room tone Another term for *ambience.* Also called *presence.*

rotary-head digital audiotape (R-DAT) recorder Specifically, a digital cassette audiotape recorder with rotary heads. *See also* **stationary-head digital audiotape recorder.**

safe mode *See* **read mode.**

SA system *See* **studio-address system.**

S-DAT *See* **stationary-head digital audiotape recorder.**

sampler An audio device that records a short sound event—such as a note or a musical phrase—into computer memory. The samples can be played by triggering them with a MIDI signal from a MIDI controller or a MIDI sequencer.

sampling (1) Examining an analog signal at regular intervals defined by the sampling frequency (or rate). (2) A process whereby a section of digital audio representing a sonic event, acoustic or electroacoustic, is stored on disk or into a memory.

sampling frequency The frequency (or rate) at which an analog signal is sampled. Also called *sampling rate.*

scrape flutter filter A cylindrical, low-friction metal surface installed between the heads to reduce the amount of unsupported tape, thereby restricting the degree of tape movement as it passes across the heads. It reduces flutter.

scrubbing In hard-disk editing, moving the playbar cursor through the defined region at any speed to listen to a sound being readied for editing. Scrubbing is similar to rocking a tape in cut-and-splice editing.

SCSI (Small Computer Systems Interface) The standard for hardware and software command language that allows two-way communication between, primarily, hard disk and CD-ROM drives. Pronounced "scuzzy."

segue (1) Cutting from one effect to another with nothing in between. (2) Playing two recordings one after the other, with no live announcement in between.

Sel Sync™ Changing the record head into a playback head to synchronize the playback of previously recorded material with the recording of new material.

selective synchronization *See* **Sel Sync.**

self-noise The electrical noise, or hiss, an electronic device produces.

sensitivity (1) Measurement of a tape's output level capability relative to a standard reference tape. (2) Measurement of the voltage (dBV) a microphone produces, which indicates its efficiency. (3) The sound-pressure level directly in front of the loudspeaker, on-axis, at a given distance and produced by a given amount of power.

sequencer An electronic device that can be programmed to store and automatically play back a repeating series of notes on an electronic musical instrument such as a synthesizer.

shelving Maximum boost or cut at a particular frequency that remains constant at all points beyond that frequency so the response curve resembles a shelf.

shock mount A device that isolates a microphone from mechanical vibrations. It can be attached externally or built into a microphone.

shotgun microphone A highly directional microphone with a tube that resembles the barrel of a rifle.

signal-to-noise ratio (S/N) The ratio, expressed in decibels (dB), of an electronic device's nominal output to its noise floor. The wider the signal-to-noise ratio, the better.

silent film Film carrying picture only.

sine wave A pure tone or fundamental frequency with no harmonics or overtones.

single-D™ microphone *See* **single-entry-port microphone.**

single-entry-port microphone A directional microphone that uses a single port to bring sounds from the rear of the mic to the capsule. Because these sounds from the rear reach the capsule out of phase with those that reach the front of the capsule, they are canceled.

single-system recording Recording picture and sound in a film or video camera simultaneously.

slap back echo The effect created when an original signal repeats as distinct echoes that decrease in level with each repetition.

slate The part of a talkback system that feeds sound to tape. It is used to record verbal identification of the material being taped, the take number, and other information just before each recording.

slave The tape or disk to which the material on a master recording is transferred.

SMPTE time code A high-frequency signal consisting of a stream of pulses produced by a time code generator used to code tape to facilitate editing and synchronization. Also known as *longitudinal time code*.

S/N *See* **signal-to-noise ratio**.

solo A control on a multitrack console that automatically cuts off all signals feeding the monitor system except those feeding through the channel that the solo control activates. Sometimes called *prefader listen (PFL)*.

sound absorption coefficient A measure of the sound-absorbing ability of a surface. This coefficient is defined as the fraction of incident sound absorbed by a surface. Values range from 0.01 for marble to 1.00 for the materials used in an almost acoustically dead enclosure. Also known as *noise reduction coefficient (NRC)*.

sound chain The audio components that carry a signal from its sound source to its destination.

sound design The process of creating the overall sonic character of a production (usually in relation to picture).

sound designer The individual responsible for a production's overall sonic complexion.

sound envelope Changes in the loudness of a sound over time, described as occurring in four stages: attack, initial decay, sustain, and release (ADSR).

soundfile A sound stored in the memory of a hard-disk recorder/editor.

sound film Film carrying both picture and sound.

sound frequency spectrum The range of frequencies audible to human hearing: about 20 to 20,000 Hz.

sound-pressure level *See* **dB-SPL**.

sound transmission class (STC) A rating that evaluates the effectiveness of barriers in isolating sound.

source music Background music from an on-screen source, such as a stereo, radio, or juke box.

spaced miking Two, sometimes three, microphones spaced from several inches to several feet apart, depending on the width of the sound source and the acoustics, for stereo recording.

spacer *See* **fill leader**.

SPDIF (Sony/Philips Digital Interface) The consumer version of the AES/EBU interface calling for an unbalanced line using phono connectors. *See also* **AES/EBU interface**.

spectrum processor A signal processor that affects a sound's spectral range.

splicing tape A specially made adhesive tape that does not ooze, is nonmagnetic and pressure sensitive, and is used to join cut ends of audiotape and magnetic film.

split editing (1) Editing the same sound into two or more separate tracks to facilitate control of its length and in editing transitions. In dialogue, for example, this makes it easier to extend lines that may have been cut too short during picture editing, to overlap voices, and to carry over lines from one scene to the next. (2) A type of transition where the audio or video leads or lags a portion of the previous edit.

split-section console Multichannel production console in which the input, output, master, and monitor sections are separate. *See also* **in-line console**.

split-track recording Recording two separate sound sources on two separate tracks of a stereo recorder or VCR with two audio tracks.

spotting Going through a script or work print and deciding on the placement of sound effects and music.

spotting sheet Indicates the sound effect, or music, cue and whether it is synchronous or nonsynchronous, its in- and out-times, and its description.

stationary-head digital audiotape (S-DAT) recorder A fixed-head digital audiotape recorder. *See also* **rotary-head digital audiotape recorder**.

STC *See* **sound transmission class**.

stereo-to-mono compatibility Ensuring that a recording made in stereo is reproducible in mono without spatial or spectral distortion.

stereophonic microphone Two directional microphone capsules, one above the other, with separate outputs, encased in one housing.

stripe coat Magnetic film that contains two stripes of oxide coating, a wide stripe for recording single-track mono and a narrow balance stripe to ensure that the film wind on reels is smooth. *See also* **full coat**.

studio-address (SA) system An intercom system used like a public-address system to communicate with people in the studio not connected to the private-line system, such as the performers, and for general instructions to all studio personnel. Also called a *talkback*.

subtractive equalization Attenuating, rather than boosting, frequencies to achieve equalization.

sustain In the sound envelope, the period during which the sound's relative dynamics are maintained after its initial decay.

sweet spot In control room monitoring, the designated listening position that is the optimal distance away from and between the loudspeakers.

sweetening Enhancing the sound of a recording through the procedures of layover, prelay, premixing, and layback.

sync beep *See* **sync pop**.

synchronization The ability to lock two or more devices that have microprocessor intelligence so that they operate at precisely the same rate.

synchronizer (1) Device with sprocketed, ganged wheels that locks in the film reels of picture and sound so they can be wound in synchronization during editing. (2) Device that regulates the operating speeds of two or more recorders so they run in sync.

sync pop A single frame of magnetic film cut across from the Academy 2 with a 1,000-Hz tone that creates a beep. Also called *sync beep*.

sync tone The tone or pulse that synchronizes tape recorder speed and film camera speed in double-system recording.

system microphone Interchangeable microphone capsules of various directional patterns that attach to a common base. The base contains a power supply and a preamplifier.

system noise The inherent noise an electronic device or system generates.

tails out Having the end of the material on a tape or film at the head of the reel.

talkback Studio-address intercom system that permits communication from a control room microphone to a loudspeaker or headphones in the studio.

tangency One of the adjustments made when aligning the heads of an audiotape recorder. This adjustment aligns the forwardness of the heads so that the tape meets them at the correct pressure.

tape transport system The mechanical portion of the tape recorder, mounted with motors, reel spindles, heads, and controls, that carries the tape at the constant speed from the feed reel to the takeup reel.

temporal fusion When reflected sound reaches the ear within 10 to 20 ms of the original sound, the direct and reflected sound are perceived as a single sound. This effect gradually disappears as the time interval between direct and reflected sound increases from roughly 30 to 50 ms.

three-to-one rule A guideline used to reduce the phasing problems caused when a sound reaches two microphones at slightly different times. It states that no two microphones should be closer to each other than three times the distance between one of them and its sound source.

three-way system loudspeaker A loudspeaker that uses two crossover frequencies to divide the bass, midrange, and treble frequencies.

threshold of hearing The lowest sound-pressure level (SPL) at which sound becomes audible to the human ear. It is the zero reference of 0 dB-SPL.

threshold of pain The sound-pressure level at which the ear begins to feel pain, about 140 dB-SPL, although levels of around 120 dB-SPL cause discomfort.

tie line Facilitates the interconnecting of outboard devices and patch bays in a control room or between studios.

timbre The unique tone quality or color of a sound.

time code address The unique SMPTE time code number that identifies each 1/30 of a second of a recording.

time compression Altering the time of material without changing its pitch.

time processor A signal processor that affects the time interval between a signal and its repetition.

tinnitus After prolonged exposure to loud sounds, the ringing, whistling, or buzzing in the ears, even though no loud sounds are present.

TL *See* **transmission loss.**

transducer A device that converts one form of energy into another.

transient A sound that begins with a sharp attack followed by a quick decay.

transient distortion Distortion that occurs when a sound system cannot reproduce sounds that begin with sudden, explosive attacks.

transmission loss (TL) The amount of sound reduction provided by a barrier such as a wall, floor, or ceiling.

transmitter microphone Wireless microphone.

treble Frequency range between roughly 5,000 and 20,000 Hz, the highest two octaves in the audible frequency spectrum.

trim (1) To attenuate the loudness level in a component or circuit. (2) The device on a console that attenuates the loudness level at the microphone/line input.

tube microphone A capacitor microphone using a tube circuit in the preamp.

tweeter The informal name of a loudspeaker that reproduces high frequencies. *See also* **woofer.**

two-way system loudspeaker A loudspeaker that uses one crossover frequency to divide the highs from the lows.

ultrasonic Frequencies above the range of human hearing.

unbalanced line A line (or circuit) with two conductors of unequal voltage.

underscore music Nondiegetic music added to enhance the informational or emotional content of a scene.

unidirectional microphone A microphone that picks up sound from one direction. Also called *directional microphone.*

update mode Mode of operation in an automated mixdown when an encoded control can be recorded without affecting the coding of the other controls. *See also* **read mode** and **write mode.**

upper bass Frequency range between roughly 80 and 320 Hz.

upper midrange Frequency range between roughly 2,560 and 5,120 Hz.

variable-D™ microphone *See* **multiple-entry-port microphone**.

variable-speed control Device on an audiotape recorder that alters the playing speed to various rates of the recorder's set speeds.

VCA *See* **voltage-controlled amplifier**.

velocity The speed of a sound wave: 1,130 feet per second at sea level and 70 degrees Fahrenheit.

vertical interval time code (VITC) Time code that is recorded vertically on videotape and within the video signal but outside the picture area.

video-leading-audio When the picture of a new scene starts before the sound of the old scene has finished. *See also* **audio-leading-video**.

virtual track In hard-disk recording, a track that provides all the functionality of an actual track but cannot be played simultaneously with another virtual track.

VITC *See* **vertical interval time code**.

voltage-controlled amplifier (VCA) An amplifier used to decrease level. The amount of amplification is controlled by external DC voltage.

volume unit (VU) meter A meter that responds to the average voltage on the line, not true volume levels. It is calibrated in volume units and percentage of modulation.

VU *See* **volume unit meter**.

walla A nonsense word that used to be spoken by film extras to create ambient crowd sound without anything discernable actually being said.

waveform A graphical representation of a sound's characteristic shape displayed, for example, on test equipment and hard-disk editing systems.

wavelength The length of one cycle of a sound wave. Wavelength is inversely proportional to the frequency of a sound; the higher the frequency, the shorter the wavelength.

weighting network A filter used for weighting a frequency response before measurement.

wet sound A sound with reverberation or signal processing. *See also* **dry sound**.

white noise A wideband noise that contains equal energy at each frequency. *See also* **pink noise**.

windscreen Foam rubber covering specially designed to fit over the outside of a microphone head. Used to reduce plosive and blowing sounds. *See also* **pop filter**.

wireless microphone system System consisting of a transmitter that sends a microphone signal to a receiver connected to a console. Also called *radio, FM, transmitter,* or *cordless microphone*.

woofer Informal name for a loudspeaker that produces the bass frequencies. *See also* **tweeter**.

worldizing Recording room sound to add to a dry recording or to use to enhance or smooth ambient backgrounds that are already part of the dialogue track.

wow (1) Starting a recorded sound before it reaches full speed. (2) Frequency changes in an analog tape recording resulting from slower variations in the speed of the tape transport. *See also* **flutter**.

wrap One of the adjustments made when aligning the heads of an audiotape recorder. This adjustment aligns the head so that it is in full physical contact with the tape.

write mode The mode of operation in an automated mixdown during which controls are adjusted conventionally and the adjustments are encoded in the computer for retrieval in the safe mode. *See also* **read mode** and **update mode**.

XLR connector Commonly used male and female microphone plugs with a three-pin connector.

X-Y miking Coincident or near-coincident miking that places the microphones' diaphragms over or horizontal to one another. *See also* **coincident miking** and **near-coincident miking**.

zenith One of the adjustments made when aligning the heads of an audiotape recorder. This adjustment aligns the vertical angle of the heads so they are perpendicular to the tape.

Bibliography

Books

Alkin, Glyn. *Sound Recording and Reproduction,* 3rd ed. Oxford: Focal Press, 1996. Guide for newcomers to the processes involved in producing a recording, from dealing with the acoustics to producing the finished product.

Alldrin, Loren. *The Home Studio Guide to Microphones.* Emeryville, Calif.: Mix Books, 1998. Specific suggestions about products and techniques, including mic types, pickup patterns, performance, and placement.

Alten, Stanley. *Audio in Media: The Recording Studio.* Belmont, Calif.: Wadsworth Publishing, 1996. A comprehensive, nontechnical introduction to the sound theory, applied aesthetics, planning, production, and mixing techniques of in-studio music recording.

Altman, Rick, ed. *Sound Theory/Sound Practice.* New York: Routledge, 1992. Essays focusing on recent developments in film sound theory and historical perspectives. They cover such diverse topics as the motion picture industry's conversion to sound, documentary sound, voices of women in Third World cinema, and a glossary of terms for sound analysis.

Amyes, Tim. *The Technique of Audio Post-Production in Video and Film,* 2nd ed. Oxford: Focal Press, 1993. Many useful production tips. Detailed chapters on synchronization, studio and location recording, and editing.

Anderton, Craig. *The Digital Delay Handbook,* rev. ed. Woodstock, N.Y.: Beekman Publishers, 1990. Specific applications and how-to directions for applying various long, short, and multiple digital delay effects to sound shaping.

Atkinson, Don. *The Sound Production Handbook.* London: Blueprint, 1995. A primer on operational audio practices in the British broadcast industry, but with tips useful to all practitioners.

Backus, John. *The Acoustical Foundations of Music,* 2nd ed. New York: W. W. Norton, 1977. The properties, production, behavior, and reproduction of musical sound.

Ballou, Glen, ed. *Handbook for Sound Engineers: The New Audio Cyclopedia,* 2nd ed. Indianapolis: H. W. Sams, 1991. Intended successor to Howard Tremaine's classic *Audio Cyclopedia.* Mostly for the engineer but with some nontechnical material. It covers acoustics for various types of studios, electrical components for sound engineering, microphones, loudspeakers, consoles, amplifiers, signal processors, tape recorders, sound systems design, and measurement.

Bartlett, Bruce. *Stereo Microphone Techniques.* Boston: Focal Press, 1991. Practical, readable guide to stereo-miking music, news, sports, film and video sound, samples, and sound effects.

Bartlett, Bruce, and Jenny Bartlett. *Practical Recording Techniques.* Carmel, Ind.: Sams Publishing, 1992. A general guide for the nonprofessional music recordist interested in studio or location recording of popular and classical music and the spoken word. Includes guidelines for equalization, troubleshooting poor sound, recognizing high-quality sound, and evaluating the finished product.

Baskerville, David. *Music Business Handbook,* 6th ed. Denver: Sherwood, 1995. Comprehensive handbook about the music marketplace: songwriting, publishing, copyright, unions, agents, artist management, concert promotion, the record industry—including production, studios, and engineering—music in film and broadcasting, and career planning and development.

Bazelon, Irwin. *Knowing the Score: Notes on Film Music.* New York: Van Nostrand Reinhold, 1975. Includes chapters on the technique of film scoring, what film music actually does, and interviews with composers.

Bech, Soren, and O. Juhl Pedersen, eds. *Proceedings of a Symposium on Perception of Reproduced Sound,* Gammel Avernaes, Denmark, 1987. Peterborough, N.H.: Old Colony Sound Lab Books, 1987. Papers about the relationship between reproduced sound and aural perception, from the nontechnical to the esoteric.

Begault, Durand. *3-D Sound for Virtual Reality and Multimedia.* San Diego: Academic Press, 1994. The relationship between technology and perception in synthesizing auditory spatial experiences within virtual-reality and multimedia systems.

Berendt, Joachim-Ernst. *The Third Ear: On Listening to the World.* New York: Henry Holt, 1992. Sociopsychological treatise on the dominance of the ear as gatherer and processor of sensory information. Content includes comparing auditory and visual perception; thinking through the ear; sonic perceptions around the world; and what listening is.

Blauert, Jens, trans. by John S. Allen. *Spatial Hearing.* Cambridge, Mass.: MIT Press, 1983. Important book in the literature on aural perception.

Boggs, Joseph. *The Art of Watching Films,* 4th ed. Mountain View, Calif.: Mayfield Publishing, 1996. Includes chapters on sound effects and dialogue, and the musical score.

Bordwell, David, and Kristin Thompson. *Film Art: An Introduction,* 5th ed. New York: McGraw-Hill, 1995. Useful chapter about sound.

Borwick, John. *Microphones: Technology and Technique.* Oxford: Focal Press, 1990. Guide to microphone usage. First half of the book deals with a brief history of microphones, basic theory of acoustics, electricity, and magnetism. The second half is devoted to creative techniques used in miking musical instruments, voices, and ensembles for classical and popular music, and miking for television programs.

Borwick, John, ed. *Sound Recording Practice: A Handbook,* 4th ed. New York: Oxford University Press, 1995. Practical and technical articles about audio recording, on the intermediate to advanced levels, covering principles, equipment, maintenance, analog and digital sound, studio and field production, radio, television, and film, and tape and disc manufacturing.

———. *Loudspeaker and Headphone Handbook,* 2nd ed. Oxford: Focal Press, 1994. Technical reference for most aspects of loudspeakers and headphones.

Bregman, Albert. *Auditory Scene Analysis.* Cambridge, Mass.: MIT Press, 1990. A scientific treatise on the perceptual organization of sound.

Brown, Royal. *Overtones and Undertones: Reading Film Music.* Berkeley: University of California Press, 1994. Draws on film, music, and narrative theory to analyze the aesthetics of film music.

Burch, Noel. *Theory of Film Practice.* New York: Praeger, 1973. Useful chapters on music and sound effects.

Burroughs, Lou. *Microphones: Design and Application.* Plainview, N.Y.: Sagamore, 1974. Basic principles of microphone design and application. A classic reference book and still useful.

Carlin, Dan, Sr. *Music in Film and Video Productions.* Boston: Focal Press, 1991. Basic but comprehensive look at the process of composing, preparing, and producing a music score for film and TV. Content includes the roles of the various personnel involved, prescoring, recording, dubbing, editing, rerecording, tracking, and licensing.

Chion, Michael, trans. by Claudia Gorbman. *Audio-Vision: Sound on Screen.* New York: Columbia University Press, 1994. The aesthetics and functions of sound in film and television.

Copland, Aaron. *Our New Music.* New York: McGraw-Hill, 1941. Includes one of the early examinations of film music in the chapter "Music in the Films."

Dancyger, Ken. *The Technique of Film and Video Editing,* 2nd ed. Boston: Focal Press, 1997. Although devoted primarily to film and video, as the title suggests, editing sound is considered throughout the book.

DeFuria, Steve, and Joe Scacciaferro. *The Sampling Book.* Milwaukee: Hal Leonard, 1988. The technology of sampling and its creative uses including looping, splicing, multisampling, crossfading, resynthesis, sampling rates, and hands-on experiments.

DeSantis, Jayce. *How to Run a Recording Session.* Emeryville, Calif.: Mix Books, 1997. A description of the process and procedures in planning for and producing a music recording session.

Deutsch, Diana, ed. *The Psychology of Music.* Orlando: Academic Press, 1982. Advanced theoretical work dealing with ways music is processed by the listener and performer. Subject areas include acoustics, psychoacoustics, perception, and electronics.

DeVito, Albert. *Computer MIDI Desktop Publishing Dictionary.* Westbury, N.Y.: Kenyon, 1991. Features 2,500 definitions related to MIDI, computer music, and desktop publishing.

Dmytryk, Edward. *On Film Editing.* Boston: Focal Press, 1984. Includes a valuable chapter on editing dialogue.

Dowling, W. J., and D. L. Harwood. *Music Cognition.* Orlando: Academic Press, 1986. About the perception and cognition of music in relation to information processing. Includes chapters on the sense and perception of sound, emotion and meaning, and cultural contexts of musical experience. With audiocassette.

Eargle, John. *Handbook of Recording Engineering,* 3rd ed. New York: Van Nostrand Reinhold, 1996. Technical approach to the recording process, covering acoustic fundamentals, audio transmission systems, loudspeakers and monitoring, signal processing, and analog and digital recording, but with easy-to-understand techniques applied to classical and popular music recording, and music in film and video production and postproduction.

———. *Loudspeaker Handbook.* New York: Chapman & Hall, 1996. A technical reference with a practical approach.

———. *The Microphone Handbook.* Plainview, N.Y.: ELAR, 1981. Handy reference work on the basics of microphone theory and techniques for speech and classical and popular music recording in the studio and on location.

———. *Music, Sound, and Technology,* 2nd ed. New York: Van Nostrand Reinhold, 1995. The relationship to and the influence of technology on music, audio production, and perception.

Edmonds, Robert. *The Sights and Sounds of Cinema and Television.* New York: Teachers College Press, 1982. How aesthetic experience influences our feelings; with roughly one-quarter of the book devoted to sound and one-quarter devoted to the sound/picture relationship.

Eisenberg, Evan. *The Recording Angel: Explorations in Phonography.* New York: McGraw-Hill, 1987. The effects of technology on perception: how recording has changed the very nature of music and its role in our culture.

Eisler, Hanns. *Composing for Films.* New York: Oxford University Press, 1947. One of the first serious attempts to deal with the role of music in film, in general, and its relationship to picture, in particular. The aesthetics are still instructive. Also for historical interest, see *Music for Films,* by Leonid Sabaneev, trans. by S. W. Pring. London: Sir Isaac Pitman & Sons, 1935.

Essex, Jeff. *Multimedia Sound and Music Studio.* New York: Random House, 1996. Combines technical data with a how-to approach to producing sound and music on desktop platforms. With CD-ROM.

Evans, Mark. *Soundtrack: The Music of the Movies.* New York: Hopkinson & Blake, 1975. The history of film music, with chapters on the functions of the film score and the ethics and aesthetics of film music.

Everest, F. Alton. *Master Handbook of Acoustics,* 3rd ed. Blue Ridge Summit, Penn.: Tab, 1994. Basics of sound and acoustics applied to the recording studio. In addition to the customary material about the principles of sound and acoustics, coverage includes the control room, multitrack recording, and instruments for acoustic measurement.

Everest, F. Alton, and Ron Streicher. *The New Stereo Soundbook.* Blue Ridge Summit, Penn.: Tab, 1992. Stereo miking and multiple miking techniques including binaural setups.

Fletcher, Neville, and Thomas Rossing. *The Physics of Musical Instruments.* New York: Springer-Verlag, 1991. For readers with a reasonable grasp of physics, this book describes the results of acoustic investigations of most of the traditional instruments currently in use in Western music.

Ford, Ty. *Advanced Audio Production Techniques.* Boston: Focal Press, 1993. Actually, a basic book about sound production, including a chapter of insights from two audio pros.

Fraser, Douglas. *Digital Delays (and How to Use Them).* Sherman Oaks, Calif.: Alfred Publishing, 1989. Guide to the common features of digital delay, including programming and beat-conversion charts.

Gayford, Michael. *Microphone Engineering Handbook.* Oxford: Focal Press, 1994. Technical reference covering the design and use of microphones.

Giannetti, Louis. *Understanding Movies,* 7th ed. Englewood Cliffs, N.J.: Prentice-Hall, 1996. Useful chapter about sound and an analysis of *Citizen Kane* which deals with the soundtrack, in part.

Gibson, David. *The Art of Mixing.* Emeryville, Calif.: Mix Books, 1997. A unique approach to the aesthetics of mixing, using visual representation of the dynamics of sounds involved in creating a musical mix.

Gorbman, Claudia. *Unheard Melodies: Narrative Film Music.* Bloomington: Indiana University Press, 1987. Theory and analysis of the functions of music in narrative film.

Gross, Lynne, and David Reese. *Radio Production Worktext: Studio and Equipment,* 3rd ed. Boston: Focal Press, 1997. Basic audio production in a workbook approach, with self-study questions and projects. With CD.

Gross, Lynne, and Larry Ward. *Electronic Moviemaking,* 3rd ed. Belmont, Calif.: Wadsworth Publishing, 1997. Includes useful chapters about microphones and recorders, approaches to sound recording, and structuring sound.

Hagen, Earle. *Scoring for Films.* Sherman Oaks, Calif.: Alfred Publishing, 1989. The focus is on composing for motion pictures and video, the mechanics and vocabulary of scoring, the psychology and aesthetics of creating music for picture, and the responsibilities of the composer and the editor. Useful to anyone interested in the dynamics of the sound/picture relationship. With CD.

Hansen, Brad. *The Dictionary of Multimedia.* Chicago: Franklin Beedle, 1997. Covers terms and acronyms related to multimedia.

Hausman, Carl, Philip B. Benoit, and Lewis B. O'Donnell. *Modern Radio Production,* 4th ed. Belmont, Calif.: Wadsworth Publishing, 1996. The role of production in radio programming. Includes material on equipment, operating procedures, practical techniques of on-air production, editing, dubbing, using sound effects and music, and achieving dramatic effects.

Helmstetter, Anthony, and Ron Simpson. *Web Developer's Guide to Sound & Music.* Scottsdale, Ariz.: The Coriolis Group Books, 1996. Guide to interactive sound design for the Internet and the World Wide Web.

Holman, Tomlinson. *Sound for Film and Television.* Boston: Focal Press, 1997. From the developer of the THX® sound system, an introduction to sound, mainly for theatrical film, following the Hollywood audio production process. With CD.

Handel, Stephen. *Listening: An Introduction to the Perception of Auditory Events.* Cambridge, Mass.: MIT Press, 1989. Scientific approach to how we listen to and perceive sound.

Huber, David Miles. *Microphone Manual: Design and Application.* Indianapolis: H. W. Sams, 1988. Basics of microphone theory and usage applied to single and stereo microphone techniques for music recording, in-studio and on location, for speech, and video and film production.

———. *Random Access Audio.* Carmel, Ind.: Sams Publishing, 1992. Introduction to digital audio, sampling, and hard-disk recording and editing.

Huber, David, and Robert Runstein. *Modern Recording Techniques,* 4th ed. Indianapolis: H. W. Sams, 1995. Basics of multitrack audio recording for music production. In addition to the customary material on sound, microphones, consoles, and so on, the book includes discussion of synchronization, digital audio, mastering, and MIDI.

Hutchins, Carleen, et al. *The Physics of Music.* San Francisco: W. H. Freeman, 1978. Essays from *Scientific American* about the physics of music and musical instruments and the acoustics of the singing voice.

Johnson, Lincoln. *Film: Space, Time, Light, and Sound.* New York: Holt, Rinehart & Winston, 1974. Worthwhile chapter on sound.

Jones, Steve. *Rock Formation: Music, Technology, and Mass Communication.* Newbury Park, Calif.: Sage, 1992. Influence of technology on popular music, with chapters on the history of sound recording, marketing music technology, the process of sound recording, and technology and the musician.

Kalinak, Kathryn. *Settling the Score: Music and the Classical Hollywood Film.* Madison: University of Wisconsin Press, 1992. Focuses on the scores of several key Hollywood composers in "settling the score" between the cinematic visual and aural to promote music as an equal partner to the visual.

Karlin, Fred. *Listening to Movies.* New York: Schirmer Books, 1994. How music for the movies is written, performed, recorded, and mixed, and how composers work with directors in writing music for picture.

Karlin, Fred, and Rayburn Wright. *On the Track: A Guide to Contemporary Film Scoring.* New York: Schirmer Books, 1990. Mainly for the film music composer, but many useful insights into the aesthetics of composing for films. If you read music, the examples make the book all the more worthwhile. Includes a complete Click Book by Alexander Brinkman.

Keith, Michael. *The Radio Station,* 4th ed. Boston: Focal Press, 1997. With a chapter on radio production.

Kerner, Marvin A. *The Art of the Sound Effects Editor.* Boston: Focal Press, 1989. Applicable to film and television, this basic, easy-to-read book describes the responsibilities of the sound editor and the assistant sound editor, the purpose of sound effects, spotting, automated dialogue replacement, selecting sound effects, the Foley stage, dubbing, and handling foreign-language films.

Kracauer, Siegfried. *Theory of Film: The Redemption of Physical Reality.* New York: Oxford University Press, 1960. Classic, with theoretical chapters devoted to the role and effects of sound in relation to picture.

Lehrman, Paul. *Getting into Digital Recording.* Milwaukee: Hal Leonard, 1996. How digital recording works, what the jargon means, the different formats, and synchronization.

LoBrutto, Vincent. *Sound-on-Film: Interviews with Creators of Film Sound.* Westport, Conn.: Praeger Publishers, 1994. Twenty-seven prominent film sound practitioners discuss their experiences in such areas as production recording, sound effects production, ADR, and rerecording mixing.

Lockhart, Ron, and Dick Weissman. *Audio in Advertising: A Practical Guide to Producing and Recording Music, Voiceovers, and Sound Effects.* New York: Frederick Ungar, 1982. The basics.

Lyver, Des. *Basics of Video Sound.* Oxford: Focal Press, 1995. Producing sound for video.

McLeish, Robert. *Radio Production,* 3rd ed. Oxford: Focal Press, 1994. Radio broadcasting from the British perspective, with some useful audio production techniques.

Madsen, Roy Paul. *Working Cinema: Learning from the Masters.* Belmont, Calif.: Wadsworth Publishing, 1990. A fresh approach to the crafts involved in producing Hollywood feature films. The chapter "The Sound Designer" offers valuable insights by Walter Murch.

Mallinson, John. *The Foundations of Magnetic Recording.* San Diego: Academic Press, 1993. Details of magnetic recording, including formats, heads, read/write processes, computer disks, and optical recording.

Mamer, Bruce. *Film Production Technique: Creating the Accomplished Image.* Belmont, Calif.: Wadsworth Publishing, 1996. With chapters on sound, recording strategies, and editing picture and sound.

Mancini, Henry. *Sound and Scores.* Port Chester, N.Y.: Cherry Lane, 1973. How different types or combinations of ensembles, instruments, musical styles, and arrangements convey mood and meaning. With illustrations and accompanying cassette.

Manvell, Roger, and John Huntley, rev. by Richard Arnell and Peter Day. *The Technique of Film Music.* London: Focal Press, 1975. History of film music with still-worthwhile chapters on the function of music in film and the role of the music director, as well as interviews with film composers and short analyses of four film sound tracks.

Martin, George. *All You Need Is Ears.* New York: St. Martin's Press, 1979. Autobiography by the producer who "made" the Beatles, with unique and useful insights into music production, creativity, and what it means to have "ears."

Millerson, Gerald. *The Technique of Television Production,* 12th ed. Oxford: Focal Press, 1990. Worthwhile analytical and aesthetic material on sound.

Molenda, Michael, ed. *Making the Ultimate Demo.* Emeryville, Calif.: Electronic Musician Books, 1993. Insights from various perspectives.

————. *What's That Sound? The Audible Audio Dictionary.* Milwaukee: Hal Leonard, 1998. With accompanying CD, this book and disc provide written and sonic definitions of 200 popular subjective audio terms, such as *swampy, jangly, warm,* and *tinny.*

Monaco, James. *How to Read a Film: Movies, Media, and Multimedia.* New York: Oxford University Press, 1997. Includes useful material on sound.

Moore, Brian C. J. *An Introduction to the Psychology of Hearing.* San Diego: Academic Press, 1990. The scientific basics.

Mott, Robert. *Sound Effects: Radio, TV, and Film.* Boston: Focal Press, 1990. Anecdotal look at the creative uses and production of sound effects up to the 1980s.

Moylan, William. *The Art of Recording.* New York: Van Nostrand Reinhold, 1992. Unique approach to the creative, aesthetic, and perceptual considerations in music recording.

Nelson, Mico. *The Cutting Edge of Audio Production and Audio Post-Production.* White Plains, N.Y.: Knowledge Industry, 1994. Audio technology and its applications to production and postproduction in film and video.

Nisbett, Alec. *The Sound Studio,* 6th ed. Oxford: Focal Press, 1995. Latest update of the British classic, formerly titled *The Technique of the Sound Studio.*

———. *The Use of Microphones,* 4th ed. Oxford: Focal Press, 1994. A manual, with sections titled "Sound," "Microphones," "Balance," "Sound and Picture," "Music Balance," and "Control." In each section, each page of text is supported by a page of illustrations.

Olson, Harry. *Music, Physics, and Engineering.* New York: Dover, 1967. A classic. Chapters on sound waves, musical terminology and scales, resonators and radiators, musical instruments, properties of music, and acoustics are still instructive today.

Parsons, Alan, et al. *The Master Tape Book.* Reading, U.K.: APRS and the British Record Producers Guild, 1992. Procedures for putting together and preparing the master tape in analog and digital formats for final mastering.

Pasquariello, Nicholas. *Sounds of Movies: Interviews with the Creators of Feature Film Soundtracks.* San Francisco: Port Bridge Books, 1996. The experiences of 11 prominent production and postproduction mixers in film sound.

Pellman, Samuel. *An Introduction to the Creation of Electroacoustic Music.* Belmont, Calif.: Wadsworth Publishing, 1994. The theoretical principles, technology, practical applications, and aesthetic considerations of making music with modern technology.

Peterson, George, and Steve Oppenheimer. *Electronic Musician's Tech Terms.* Emeryville, Calif.: Electronic Musician Books, 1993. Dictionary of terms for audio and music production, including disk-based technology.

Pierce, John. *The Science of Musical Sound.* New York: Scientific American, 1983. Basic principles of sound in relation to music: periodicity, pitch, sound waves, resonance, the ear, hearing, power and loudness, masking, acoustics, sound reproduction, perception, illusion, and effect.

Pohlmann, Kenneth. *Principles of Digital Audio,* 3rd ed. Indianapolis: H. W. Sams, 1995. Technical reference about the fundamentals of digital sound, recording, audio interfaces, storage, reproduction, and workstations.

Prendergast, Roy. *A Neglected Art: A Critical Study of Music in Films,* 2nd ed. New York: W. W. Norton, 1992. In addition to the history of film music, this study includes the aesthetics of film music and the techniques of synchronizing music to picture and dubbing, with analyses of selections from film scores and chapters on video postproduction, digital audio, and the synthesizer.

Ratcliff, John. *Time Code: A User's Guide,* 2nd ed. Oxford: Focal Press, 1996. Reference guide to the form, standards, and control codes of the various time codes used in production today.

Ratcliff, John, and Neil Papworth. *Single Camera Stereo Sound.* Oxford: Focal Press, 1992. Stereo theory, location recording in stereo, and postproduction using the single-camera approach.

Recording Industry Sourcebook. Los Angeles: Recording Industry Sourcebook, Annual. Just about everything you need to know about the recording business from record labels to limousine services. Includes, among many things: artist management, music attorneys, performing rights societies, promotion, producers, recording and mastering studios, music programmers, and rental and supply firms.

Robeson, E. M. *The Orchestra of the Language.* New York: T. Yoseloff, 1959. The meaning and effect of spoken language as sound.

Rona, Jeff. *Synchronization: From Reel to Reel,* 2nd ed. Milwaukee: Hal Leonard, 1994. A guide for synchronization of audio, film, and video devices.

Rossing, Thomas. *The Science of Sound,* 2nd ed. Reading, Mass.: Addison-Wesley, 1990. Introduction to the various branches of acoustics and psychoacoustics. It includes physical principles, perception and measurement, musical instruments, the human voice, electrical production of sound, electronic music, room acoustics, and environmental noise.

Rumsey, Francis. *The Audio Workstation Handbook.* Oxford: Focal Press, 1996. Technical approach to digital audio and the associated technologies used in digital audio workstations.

Rumsey, Francis, and Tim McCormick. *Sound and Recording: An Introduction,* 3rd ed. Oxford: Focal Press, 1997. Survey of audio technology—analog and digital—and techniques, including MIDI and synchronization. Emphasis is on "how it works," rather than "how to work it."

Rumsey, Francis, et al. (eds.). *Acoustics and Psychoacoustics.* Oxford: Focal Press, 1996. Introductory-level book includes chapters on hearing, musical dynamics, and electronic sound processing.

Schafer, Murray. *The Tuning of the World.* New York: Alfred A. Knopf, 1977. Landmark book about the acoustic environment, or "soundscape," pre- and post-industrial; "the relationship between people and the sounds of their environment and what happens when these sounds change."

Schwartz, Tony. *The Responsive Chord.* Garden City, N.Y.: Anchor, 1974. Using his "resonance principle" as the model and advertising as the focus, the author of this classic explores how auditory communication interacts with the total communication structure in reaching and affecting specific audiences.

Siegel, Bruce. *Creative Radio Production.* Boston: Focal Press, 1992. Introduction to the hardware, but with the emphasis on the practical, operational, and creative "how to." With cassette.

Silbergleid, Michael, ed. *The Guide to Digital Television.* New York: Miller Freeman Publications, 1998. Includes a useful chapter on audio.

Skinner, Frank. *Underscore.* New York: Criterion Music, 1960. Still-useful practical and aesthetic information about scoring for motion pictures and the role of music in relation to picture.

SMPTE Made Simple: A Time Code Tutor. San Marcos, Calif.: TimeLine Vista, Inc., 1996. Booklet covering the SMPTE, VITC, and MTC time codes.

Soifer, Rosanne. *Music in Video Production.* White Plains, N.Y.: Knowledge Industry, 1991. For the video producer. About the uses and accessibility of music: aesthetics, instrumentation, a brief history of Western music and style, permissions, copyright, licensing, agencies, reuse, misappropriations, the ins and outs of commissioning original music, music libraries, and using public domain.

Sound for Picture: An Insider's Look at Audio Production in Film and Television. Editors of *Mix* magazine. Emeryville, Calif.: Mix Magazine, 1993. Compilation of articles from issues of *Mix* about how dialogue, sound effects, and music are recorded, edited, and assembled into sound tracks.

Strong, William. *The Copyright Book: A Practical Guide,* 4th ed. Cambridge, Mass.: MIT Press, 1993. Covers musical and literary works, CD-ROMs, holograms, databases, compilations, and shareware, among other categories. Not in legalese.

Talbot-Smith, Michael. *Audio Recording and Reproduction: Practical Measures for Audio Enthusiasts.* Oxford: Focal Press, 1994. Audio techniques, technical and practical, for the beginner.

———. *Broadcast Sound Technology,* 2nd ed. Oxford: Focal Press, 1995. The basics, including behavior of sound, aspects of hearing, acoustics, microphones, loudspeakers, consoles, recorders, and the principles of stereo.

———. *Sound Assistance.* Oxford: Focal Press, 1997. An operational approach to audio in radio and television studios.

———. *Sound Engineer's Pocket Book.* Oxford: Focal Press, 1995. A handy, compact source of essential data for the audio engineer.

Talbot-Smith, Michael, ed. *Audio Engineer's Reference Book.* Oxford: Focal Press, 1994. Technical reference for audio engineers.

Taub, Eric. *Gaffers, Grips, and Best Boys.* New York: St. Martin's Press, 1987. Behind-the-scenes personnel in motion pictures, including some of the sound people.

Thomas, Tony. *Film Score: Art and Craft of Movie Music.* Burbank, Calif.: Riverwood Press, 1991. Articles about Hollywood's foremost composers, with valuable insights into the techniques and aesthetics of composing for film. With film music discography and bibliography.

———. *Music for the Movies,* 2nd ed. Beverly Hills, Calif.: 1997. Useful material about film music and its informational relationship to picture.

Truax, Barry. *Acoustic Communication.* Norwood, N.J.: Ablex, 1984. Introduction to sound in an interdisciplinary framework with the aim of establishing a model for understanding acoustic and aural experience both in traditional terms and as it has been altered by technology.

Wadhams, Wayne. *Dictionary of Music Production and Engineering Technology.* New York: Schirmer, 1988. Dictionary of terminology and basic concepts in the fields of television, radio, music, and film audio production and engineering.

———. *Sound Advice: The Musician's Guide to the Record Industry.* New York: Schirmer, 1990. Covers the process from making a demo to negotiating a contract with a major label, including the important subject of artists' rights and how to protect them. Also explained are unions, music publishing, and the workings of industry organizations and associations. Many examples of different kinds of contracts.

———. *Sound Advice: The Musician's Guide to the Recording Studio.* New York: Schirmer, 1990. Basic functions and operations of a recording studio, including detailed, nontechnical discussion of recording procedures and miking techniques. With excellent companion two-disc CD set and accompanying explanatory booklets.

Watkinson, John. *The Art of Digital Audio,* 2nd ed. Oxford: Focal Press, 1994. Technical book covering digital audio theory and the various uses of digital audio in rotary- and stationary-head tape recorders, disk drives, compact disc, compact cassette (DCC), and broadcasting.

———. *Audio for Television.* Oxford: Focal Press, 1997. Includes the sound chain, loudspeakers, stereo and surround-sound systems, signal processing, and recording. Technical.

Weis, Elisabeth. *The Silent Scream.* Rutherford, N.J.: Farleigh Dickinson, 1982. Explores Alfred Hitchcock's use of the sound track in films. Included in the analyses are *Vertigo* and *Psycho.*

Weis, Elisabeth, and John Belton, eds. *Film Sound: Theory and Practice.* New York: Columbia University Press, 1985. Essays, from the highly theoretical to the practical, about the design and aesthetics of sound in relation to picture in film and television. Extensive bibliography.

White, Glenn. *The Audio Dictionary,* 2nd ed. Seattle: University of Washington Press, 1991. Dictionary of terminology and basic concepts in the fields of audio production, musical acoustics, and sound reinforcement.

White, Ira. *Audio Made Easy.* Milwaukee: Hal Leonard, 1997. Manual containing information about dealing with EQ, loudspeakers, recording techniques, and club, concert, church, and theatrical sound.

White, Paul. *Creative Recording: Effects and Processors.* Cambridgeshire, England: Music Maker Books, 1989. Book 1 in the series.

———. *Creative Recording: Microphones and Recording Techniques.* Cambridgeshire, England: Music Maker Books, 1990. Book 2 in the series.

———. *Creative Recording: Acoustics, Soundproofing, and Monitoring.* Cambridgeshire, England: Music Maker Books, 1990. Book 3 in the series.

———. *Recording Production Techniques.* Cambridgeshire, England: SOS Publications, 1993. Basic techniques aimed at the recording musician.

Whitney, John. *Digital Harmony: On the Complementarity of Music and Art.* New York: McGraw-Hill, 1982. A unique perspective on the sound/picture relationship from the experimental filmmaker discussing his hypothesis: "How the application of graphic harmony—ratio, interference, and resonance—produces the same effect that these physical facts of harmonic force have upon musical structures."

Wilkie, Godric. *The Studio Musician's Jargonbuster.* London: Musonix Publishing, 1993. Glossary of music technology and recording terms.

Winckel, Fritz. *Music, Sound, and Sensation.* New York: Dover, 1967. A study of the relationships in the laws of nature that are responsible for musical perception.

Woodward, Walt. *An Insider's Guide to Advertising Music,* rev. ed. New York: Art Direction, 1982. How and why music in advertising works, and when and how to use it.

Woram, John. *Sound Recording Handbook.* Indianapolis: H. W. Sams, 1989. Comprehensive coverage of recording technology and techniques.

Zaza, Tony. *Audio Design: Sound Recording Techniques for Film and Video.* Englewood Cliffs, N.J.: Prentice-Hall, 1991. Unique book focuses on the aesthetic and creative uses of sound in relation to picture. Provocative, sometimes highly theoretical, insights into how sound and image work together on the screen and in the mind. History of sound recording, selected films for study, many examples, and illustrations.

———. *Mechanics of Sound Recording.* Englewood Cliffs, N.J.: Prentice-Hall, 1991. Companion volume to the author's *Audio Design* that covers the technology and techniques of audio production. Many examples and illustrations.

Zettl, Herbert. *Sight, Sound, Motion: Applied Media Aesthetics,* 3rd ed. Belmont, Calif.: Wadsworth Publishing, 1999. Analysis of light, space, time, motion, and sound (two chapters) and their relationships to expression and meaning in television and film.

Periodicals

American Cinematographer Journal of film production techniques with coverage of sound from time to time. Monthly.

American Videographer Journal of video production techniques with coverage of sound from time to time. Monthly.

Audio Engineering Society (AES) Journal The journal of the Audio Engineering Society devoted mainly to research and development in audio technology. Monthly.

Audio Media Covers the audio technology scene for professional audio production engineers and broadcasters. Monthly.

BE Radio From the editors of *Broadcast Engineering,* devoted to technology in radio. Bimonthly.

Broadcast Engineering Information for engineers and equipment operators in television and radio. Monthly.

Broadcaster News about Canada's broadcasting industry, including sound production in TV and radio. Monthly.

Electronic Musician Devoted to the technology and practices that link electronics and computers with the world of music. Monthly.

EQ Covers projects in recording and sound studio techniques for the professional audio market. Monthly.

Film and Video Covers all areas of the production and postproduction process including sound. Monthly.

Home Recording Technology and techniques for the project studio recordist and musician. Monthly.

Home and Studio Recording Practical production tips, sound and music theory, and equipment for the recording musician. Monthly.

Interactivity The tools and techniques used in producing material for interactive media with regular features about audio. Monthly.

International Recording Equipment and Studio Directory Listings of studio equipment, studio equipment manufacturers, studio services, and recording studios. Annual.

Millimeter Information on the technology, craft, and use of television and film media for communication, with occasional articles about audio. Monthly.

Mix Reports and interviews on production practices, equipment, facilities, education, and trends in the major areas of professional audio—music recording, video, and film. Monthly.

Mix Annual Directory of Recording Industry Facilities and Services Comprehensive directory of recording industry facilities and services. Annual.

New Media For creators of interactive and computer materials, with regular features about audio. Monthly, except biweekly in March, June, September, and November.

One to One International news magazine for mastering, pressing, and duplicating. Bimonthly.

Post For professionals in audio, video, film, and animation, with the focus on postproduction. Monthly.

Producer For producers, directors, cinematographers, composers, and recordists. Monthly.

Professional Sound About the audio production scene in Canada. Quarterly.

Pro Audio Review Reviews cover the latest developments in audio equipment. Monthly.

Pro Sound News News magazine of developments in audio for professional recording and sound production. Monthly.

Recording For the recording musician. Monthly.

S & VC (Sound & Video Contractor) Management and engineering journal for sound and video contractors. Monthly.

SMPTE Journal The journal of the Society of Motion Picture and Television Engineers, devoted mainly to research and development in motion picture and television technology. Monthly.

Sound and Communications Covers professional audio for sound contractors and managers, with information that is often useful to the working producer. Monthly.

Sound on Sound About the European music recording scene, with a slant on technology. Monthly.

Studio Sound British publication devoted to the practical and technical aspects of audio production in broadcasting, film, and music. Monthly.

Television Broadcast News magazine covering television equipment, applications, and technology, with articles about audio. Monthly.

Variety's On Production For producers, technicians, and film enthusiasts, it covers current trends, including those in audio. Monthly.

Videography For the video production professional, with articles on sound from time to time. Monthly.

Tapes and CDs

Australian Film, Television, and Radio School. *Location Sound Recording.* Los Angeles, Calif: First Light Video Publishing, 1989. Although somewhat dated, this VHS tape still includes much useful information about microphones and on-location microphone techniques.

British Broadcasting Corporation. *Music and Sound Effects for TV.* Princeton, N.J.: Films for the Humanities, 1993. This VHS tape outlines the basic applications of sound effects and music in film and video.

British Broadcasting Corporation. *The Soundtrack.* Princeton, N.J.: Films for the Humanities, 1991. This VHS tape begins with a brief history of sound recording followed by a discussion and demonstration of location recording techniques.

Everest, F. Alton. *Critical Listening and Auditory Perception.* Emeryville, Calif.: Mix Books, 1997. Five CDs and a 200-page manual covering listening techniques, including estimating frequency, frequency band limitations, sound-level changes, components of sound quality, distortion, reverberation effects on speech and music, voice colorations, and aspects of psychoacoustics including the hearing process, complexity of delayed sounds, auditory filters, masking, and perception of pitch and timbre.

Gibson, Bill. *Killer Demos: Hot Tips & Cool Secrets.* Federal Way, Wash.: Bill and Bob's Excellent Productions, 1991. VHS with tips on making a multitrack home recording not sound like a home recording.

Gibson, Bill, and Peter Alexander. *Hit Sound Recording Course.* Newbury Park, Calif.: Katamar Entertainment Corporation, 1992. Audiocassettes and manuals for 12 units including: console operation; signal processing; recording guitars and strings, acoustic drums, drum machines, bass, vocals, keyboards, and synthesizers; panning and stereo imaging; the recording session; and the mixdown.

Hernandez, John. *Miking the Drum Set.* Claremont, Calif.: Terence Dwyer Productions, 1992. VHS tape and manual demonstrating many approaches to selecting and positioning drum microphones.

Kramer, Eddie. *Adventures in Modern Recording.* San Francisco: Premium Entertainment, 1994. Recording techniques and equipment, including basic MIDI, aimed at the project studio, on two VHS tapes.

Lubin, Tom. *Shaping Your Sound.* Los Angeles: Acrobat, 1988–1991. Six videocassettes, with manuals, covering microphones; equalizers, compressors, and noise gates; reverberation and delay; mixers and mixing; multitrack recording; and the role of the assistant sound engineer.

Moulton, Dave. *Golden Ears.* San Diego: KIQ Productions, 1993. Ear training to identify frequency problems, signal processing, reverb, delay, distortion, and so on. Eight CDs with manual.

Parsons, Mike. *Successful Sound for Video.* Princeton, N.J.: Films for the Humanities, 1997. This VHS tape includes: recording during production and postproduction; location sound; microphones; microphone techniques; multitrack recording; and mixing.

Swedien, Bruce. *Recording with Bruce Swedien,* vol. 1. San Francisco: AcuNet Corporation, 1997. Advice and techniques about music recording. VHS.

CD-ROMs

Begault, Durand. *The Sonic CD-ROM for Desktop Audio Production.* San Diego: Academic Press, 1996. Guide to producing computer audio for multimedia.

Cool School Interactus. Columbus, Ohio: Cool Breeze Systems, 1996. The basics of digital workstation operation.

Sides, Alan. *Alan Sides' Microphone Cabinet.* Emeryville, Calif.: EM Books, 1995. Lines up several professional microphones for a series of audio comparison tests on many musical instruments.

Sterling, Christopher (gen. ed.), and Stanley Alten et al. (eds.). *Focal Encyclopedia of Electronic Media.* Boston: Focal Press, 1998. Comprehensive reference directed to the applications of technology and techniques in electronic media, including extensive articles on the perception, aesthetics, and production of sound.

Reference CD-ROMs

Anechoic Orchestral Music Recording. Denon PG-6006.

Mix Reference Disc: Deluxe edition. Emeryville, Calif.: Mix Books, 1996.

The Sheffield Drum Record/The Sheffield Track Record. Sheffield Lab CD-14/20.

Sound Check. Compiled by Alan Parsons and Stephen Court.

Studio Reference Disc. Prosonus SRD.

Index

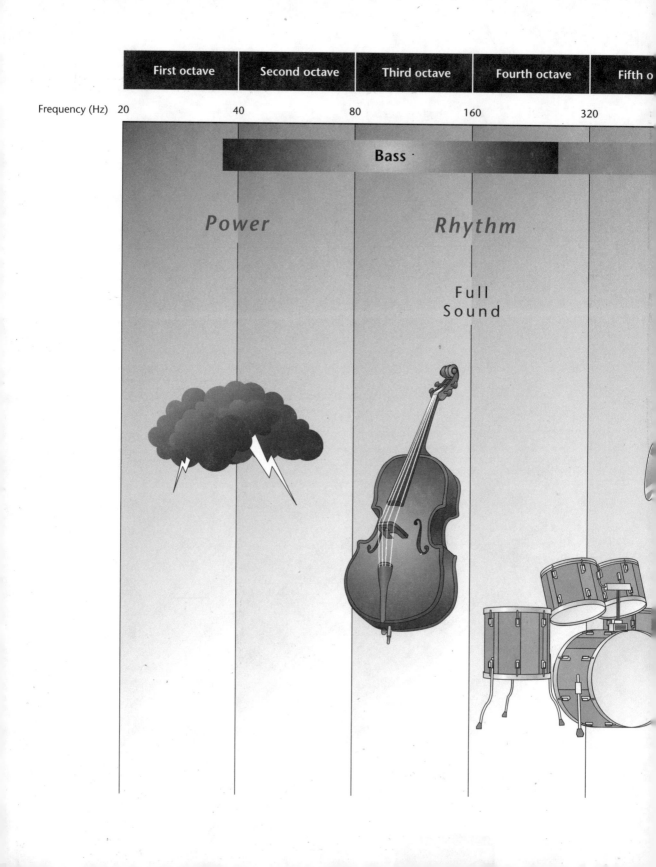

First octave	Second octave	Third octave	Fourth octave	Fifth o

Frequency (Hz) 20   40   80   160   320

Bass

Power   *Rhythm*

Full
Sound